Baltic Sea

Stralsund

Rostock

MECKLENBURG-
LOWER POMERANIA

Schwerin

MANY

BERLIN

Potsdam

Magdeburg

BRANDENBURG

SAXONY-
ANHALT

EASTERN
GERMANY

Cottbus

Halle

Leipzig

SAXONY

Dresden

rt

Jena

Chemnitz

THURINGIA

Nuremberg

ERN
ANY

Regensburg

BAVARIA

Munich

EYEWITNESS TRAVEL

GERMANY

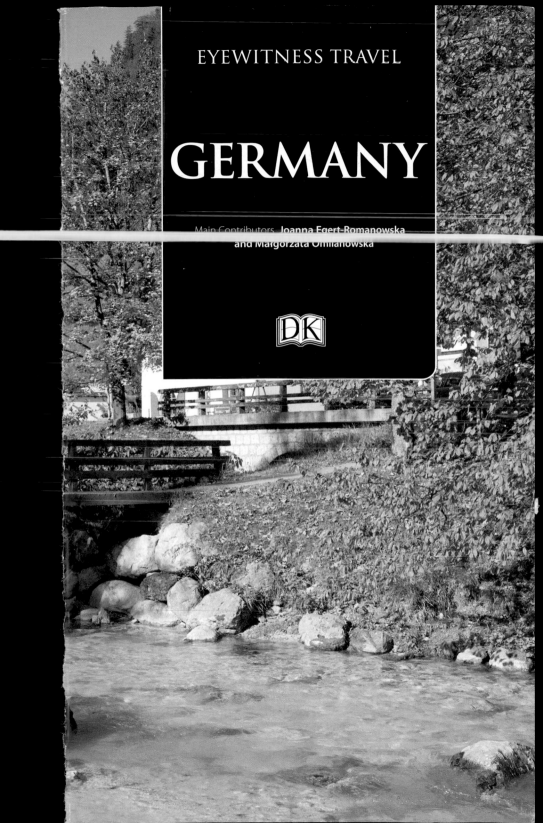

EYEWITNESS TRAVEL

GERMANY

Main Contributors **Joanna Egert-Romanowska**
and Małgorzata Omilanowska

DK

DK Penguin Random House

Produced by Wydwnictwo Wiedza i Życie, Warsaw
Contributors Małgorzata Omilanowska, Marek Stańczyk, Tomasz Torbus,
Hanna Köster, Teresa Czerniewicz–Umer
Cartographers Kartographie Huber (Munich), Magdalena Polak, Dariusz Romanowski
Photographers Adam Hajder, Dorota and Mariusz Jarymowiczowie, Wojciech Mędrzak,
Tomasz Myśluk, Paweł Wójcik
Illustrators Lena Maminajszwili, Paweł Marczak, Andrzej Wielgosz, Bohdan Wróblewski,
Magdalena Żmudzińska
DTP Designers Paweł Pasternak, Paweł Kamiński
Editors Teresa Czerniewicz-Umer, Joanna Egert-Romanowska
Production Anna Kożurno-Królikowska
Designers Ewa Roguska, Piotr Kiedrowski

Dorling Kindersley Limited

Editors Sylvia Goulding, Irene Lyford
Translators Magda Hannay, Ian Wisniewski
DTP Designers Jason Little, Conrad Van Dyk
Production Marie Ingledew, Joanna Bull

Printed and bound in Malaysia

First American Edition 2001

16 17 18 19 10 9 8 7 6 5 4 3 2 1

Published in the United States by DK Publishing,

345 Hudson Street, New York, New York 10014

**Reprinted with revisions 2003, 2004, 2005, 2006, 2007, 2008,
2010, 2012, 2014, 2016**

Copyright 2001, 2016 © Dorling Kindersley Limited, London

A Penguin Random House Company

Published in Great Britain by Dorling Kindersley Ltd

A catalog record for this book is available from the Library of Congress.

ISSN 1542-1554

ISBN 978-1-4654-4018-1

Floors are referred to throughout in accordance with European usage;
ie the "first floor" is the floor above ground level.

Front cover main image: The Church of Maria Gern set in the beautiful Untersberg,
Berchtesgadener Land, Bavaria

MIX
Paper from
responsible sources
FSC
www.fsc.org FSC™ C018179

The information in every DK Eyewitness Travel Guide is checked regularly.
Every effort has been made to ensure that this book is as up to date as possible at
the time of going to press. Some details, however, such as telephone numbers,
opening hours, prices, gallery hanging arrangements and travel information are
liable to change. The publishers cannot accept responsibility for any consequences
arising from the use of this book, nor for any material on third party websites, and
cannot guarantee that any website address in this book will be a suitable source of
travel information. We value the views and suggestions of our readers very highly.
Please write to: Publisher, DK Eyewitness Travel Guides, Dorling Kindersley, 80
Strand, London WC2R 0RL, Great Britain or email: travelguides@dk.com.

Contents

Heraldic shield over the entrance to the
Nuremberg town hall

Introducing Germany

Berlin Area by Area

Eastern Germany

◀ St Sebastian's Church in Ramsau an der Ache, with the Eisberg (Reiter Alpe) mountain in the background

Picturesque landscape in Mecklenburg

Statue of a dancing figure, Stadtmuseum in Munich *(see p218)*

Mainz Cathedral
(see pp354–5)

HOW TO USE THIS GUIDE

This guide will help you to get the most out of a visit to Germany, providing expert recommendations as well as thoroughly researched practical information. The first section, *Introducing Germany*, locates the country geographically and provides an invaluable historical and cultural context. Succeeding sections describe the main sights and attractions of the different regions and major cities. Feature spreads, with maps and photographs, focus on important sights. Information on accommodation and restaurants is provided in *Travellers' Needs*, while the *Survival Guide* has useful tips on everything you need to know from money to getting around.

Berlin

This section is divided into two parts: eastern centre and western centre. Sights outside the centre are described in the section *Further Afield*. All sights are numbered and plotted on a map of the region. Detailed information for each sight is given in numerical order to make it easy to locate within the chapter.

Sights at a Glance describes, by category, buildings in a particular area: Historic Streets and Buildings, Museums and Galleries, Churches, Parks and Gardens.

Pages marked with red refer to Berlin.

A Locator Map shows where you are in relation to the city plan.

1 **Area Map** For easy reference the sights in each area are numbered.

2 **Street-by-Street Map** gives a bird's-eye view of each sightseeing area described in the section.

Stars indicate the sights that no visitor should miss.

A suggested route for a walk is marked with a broken red line.

3 **Detailed Information** All the sights of Berlin are described individually. Addresses, telephone numbers, opening hours, admission charges and information on how to get there are given for each sight. The key to symbols is shown on the back flap.

1 Introduction The landscape, history and character of each region are described, showing how the area has changed through the ages. It also outlines the sights on offer for visitors.

Germany Area by Area

In this guide, Germany is divided into 13 areas, each of which is covered in a separate section. The most interesting cities, towns, villages and sights in the area are marked on the Area Map.

2 Regional Map This shows the main roads and the general topography of the area. All sights are numbered, and there are also details on how to get there.

Boxes contain additional information about sights.

Colour coding at the edge of every page makes it easy to find each particular region.

3 Detailed Information All major towns, places of interest and other tourist sights are listed in order and numbered according to the Regional Map. Each entry contains information on important sights.

A Visitors' Checklist for each of the main sights provides practical information to help you plan your visit.

4 Major Sights At least two pages are dedicated to each major sight. Historic buildings are dissected in order to show their interiors. Interesting towns or town centres have street maps with the main sights indicated and described.

INTRODUCING
GERMANY

DISCOVERING GERMANY

The following tours have been designed to take in as many of the country's highlights as possible, while keeping long-distance travel to a minimum. First, there are three two-day tours of Germany's most dynamic cities: Berlin, Munich and Hamburg. These itineraries can be combined to form a week-long tour; extra suggestions are supplied for those who want to extend their stay. Next come three five-day tours covering the north, centre and south of Germany. Add these tours together to create a superb two-week tour of the country. Finally, there are two themed itineraries tailored to specific interests. Pick, combine and follow your favourite tours, or simply dip in and out and be inspired.

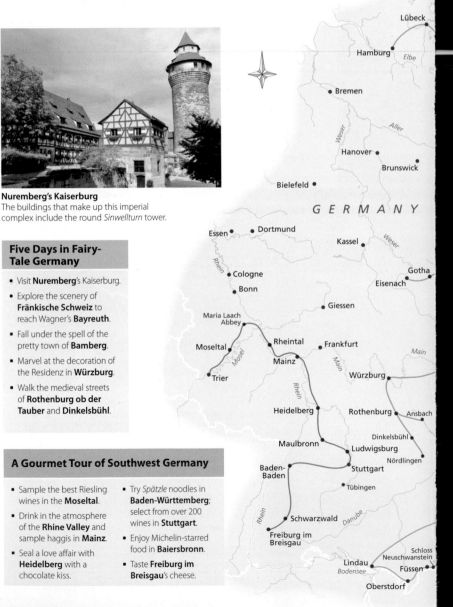

Nuremberg's Kaiserburg
The buildings that make up this imperial complex include the round *Sinwellturn* tower.

Five Days in Fairy-Tale Germany

- Visit **Nuremberg**'s Kaiserburg.
- Explore the scenery of **Fränkische Schweiz** to reach Wagner's **Bayreuth**.
- Fall under the spell of the pretty town of **Bamberg**.
- Marvel at the decoration of the Residenz in **Würzburg**.
- Walk the medieval streets of **Rothenburg ob der Tauber** and **Dinkelsbühl**.

A Gourmet Tour of Southwest Germany

- Sample the best Riesling wines in the **Moseltal**.
- Drink in the atmosphere of the **Rhine Valley** and sample haggis in **Mainz**.
- Seal a love affair with **Heidelberg** with a chocolate kiss.

- Try *Spätzle* noodles in **Baden-Württemberg**; select from over 200 wines in **Stuttgart**.
- Enjoy Michelin-starred food in **Baiersbronn**.
- Taste **Freiburg im Breisgau**'s cheese.

Lübeck
Hamburg
Elbe
Bremen
Weser
Aller
Hanover
Brunswick
Bielefeld
G E R M A N Y
Essen
Dortmund
Kassel
Weser
Rhein
Cologne
Gotha
Bonn
Eisenach
Giessen
Maria Laach
Abbey
Moseltal
Rheintal
Frankfurt
Main
Mosel
Mainz
Main
Würzburg
Trier
Rhein
Rothenburg
Ansbach
Heidelberg
Dinkelsbühl
Maulbronn
Ludwigsburg
Nördlingen
Baden-Baden
Stuttgart
Tübingen
Rhein
Schwarzwald
Danube
Freiburg im
Breisgau
Schloss
Neuschwanstein
Lindau
Füssen
Bodensee
Oberstdorf

◄ View of Sendlinger-Tor-Platz in Munich as seen during the 1950s

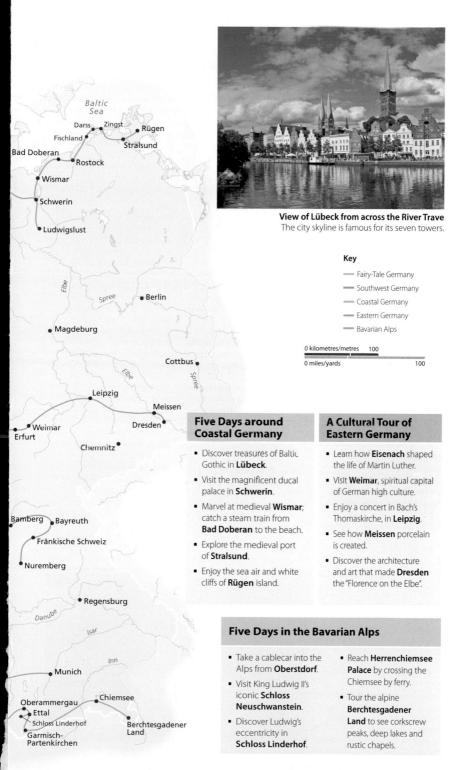

View of Lübeck from across the River Trave
The city skyline is famous for its seven towers.

Key

— Fairy-Tale Germany
— Southwest Germany
— Coastal Germany
— Eastern Germany
— Bavarian Alps

0 kilometres/metres   100

0 miles/yards   100

Five Days around Coastal Germany

- Discover treasures of Baltic Gothic in **Lübeck**.
- Visit the magnificent ducal palace in **Schwerin**.
- Marvel at medieval **Wismar**; catch a steam train from **Bad Doberan** to the beach.
- Explore the medieval port of **Stralsund**.
- Enjoy the sea air and white cliffs of **Rügen** island.

A Cultural Tour of Eastern Germany

- Learn how **Eisenach** shaped the life of Martin Luther.
- Visit **Weimar**, spiritual capital of German high culture.
- Enjoy a concert in Bach's Thomaskirche, in **Leipzig**.
- See how **Meissen** porcelain is created.
- Discover the architecture and art that made **Dresden** the "Florence on the Elbe".

Five Days in the Bavarian Alps

- Take a cablecar into the Alps from **Oberstdorf**.
- Visit King Ludwig II's iconic **Schloss Neuschwanstein**.
- Discover Ludwig's eccentricity in **Schloss Linderhof**.
- Reach **Herrenchiemsee Palace** by crossing the Chiemsee by ferry.
- Tour the alpine **Berchtesgadener Land** to see corkscrew peaks, deep lakes and rustic chapels.

Two Days in Berlin

Berlin is a rewarding city to explore, with a fascinating history and superb nightlife.

- **Arriving** Berlin has two airports. Tegel, 8 km (5 miles) from the city centre, can be reached by bus or taxi; buses also connect with the U-bahn service. Schönefeld is 20 km (12 miles) south of the city and well served by trains, S-bahn, and buses that link with the U-bahn.

Day 1
Morning Start at the icons of a reunified Germany: spiral up inside the glass dome of the **Reichstag** (*p97*), then circuit the **Brandenburger Tor** (*p73*). Beyond is **Unter den Linden** (*pp74–5*), the leafy promenade that reveals the swagger of 19th-century Prussia through monuments like the **Neue Wache** (*p75*) and nearby **St-Hedwigs-Kathedrale** (*p74*). Friedrich the Great ordered the **Französischer Dom** (*p76*) to be built on an Italianate square – this is a lovely spot for lunch.

Afternoon The handsome **Schlossbrücke** (*p76*) hints at the cultural feast to be found on **Museum Island** (*pp78–9*). The **Pergamonmuseum** (*pp80–81*), with its 170 BC altar, holds a remarkable collection of antiquities. Stop in at the **Deutscher Dom** afterwards (*p76*), then take a quiet stroll into the picturesque **Nikolaiviertel** to sense the capital's medieval roots (*p84*).

Day 2
Morning After exploring Berlin's historic core, the focus shifts to more recent history. **Checkpoint Charlie** (*p84*), the east–west border immortalized by many Cold War thrillers, is an essential stop. The darkest period in German history is chillingly laid bare in the **Jüdisches Museum** (*pp84–5*), while the wave-like **Holocaust Denkmal** (*p74*) represents the scale of the Jewish tragedy in stark sculptural form.

The imposing steel and glass dome of the Reichstag in Berlin

Afternoon Walk off lunch in the **Tiergarten** (*p91*), then pore over the Old Masters in the **Gemäldegalerie** (*pp94–5*) or crafts from the Middle Ages to the present day in the nearby **Kunstgewerbemuseum** (*p93*). For more astonishing craftsmanship, take the U-Bahn west from **Potsdamer Platz** (*p96*) to reach beautiful **Schloss Charlottenburg** (*pp102–3*). Otherwise, admire the mosaics in the shattered **Kaiser-Wilhelm-Gedächtnis-Kirche** (*p90*), the symbol of West Berlin, on the city's retail high street, **Ku'damm** (*p91*) – time, at last, for some shopping (*pp110–11*).

> **To extend your trip...**
> Wander through bohemian Berlin at **Prenzlauer Berg** (*p105*), or escape the city on the beaches of **Strandbad Wannsee** (*p108*) or the lovely **Park Sanssouci** (*pp140–41*), in **Potsdam**.

Two Days in Munich

Munich is a popular tourist destination and the gateway to Bavaria.

- **Arriving** Munich airport is served by the S-Bahn and various buses. Taxis are also available. From Munich there are good train connections with the rest of Europe.

Day 1
Morning There's no finer introduction to Munich than **Marienplatz** (*pp214–15*), boxed in by monuments of civic pride: the **Neues Rathaus** (*p219*), its façade a carnival of statues, the **Altes Rathaus** (*pp218–19*) and the **Michaelskirche** (*p216*). For a mid-morning snack of *Weisswurst*, head south to the **Viktualienmarkt** (*p218*). The icon on souvenir beer tankards is the soaring **Frauenkirche** (*p217*), unmissable because of its domed spires; however, the highlights of Munich's sacred architecture are the nearby **Bürgersaal** (*p216*) and **Asamkirche** (*p217*), the latter the most enchanting example of Bavarian Rococo you'll see.

Afternoon After the return walk via Marienplatz, stop for a beer at the **Hofbräuhaus** (*p219*), Munich's most famous beer hall and the site of Hitler's infamous Beer Hall Putsch. Suitably fortified, discover the head-spinning array of architecture, artwork and treasure on display

The entrance to Schloss Charlottenburg in Berlin

in the **Residenz** *(pp220–21)*. The former palace of Bavarian kings is so large it takes two tours just to see the half open to the public. Check if any seats are available for a night at its magical Cuvilliés-Theater.

Day 2

Morning The kings reveal their impeccable taste again through their gallery, hung in the **Alte Pinakothek** *(pp226–7)*. You can easily lose the morning among its Old Masters, with the most comprehensive lesson in German art history you'll ever receive, or among more modern works in the neighbouring **Neue Pinakothek** *(p224)* and **Pinakothek der Moderne** *(p225)* galleries. Make time to walk to nearby Königsplatz, where the Neo-Classical **Glyptothek** *(p225)* and **Propyläen** *(p225)* reveal why Munich was nicknamed "Athens on Isar". The nearby **Staatliche Antikensammlungen** *(p225)* displays Ludwig I's antiquities.

Afternoon The **Deutsches Museum** *(pp232–3)* is unbeatable for rainy days, with 20,000 exhibits spread over seven floors dedicated to science and arts. Otherwise, escape the busy city streets and head to **Schloss Nymphenburg** *(pp228–9)*, like Electress Henriette-Adelaide. Her portrait is not one of those in the Gallery of Beauties, one highlight of this Italianate garden palace. Others are the Festsaal, which tempers Rococo opulence with playful detail, and the

The awe-inspiring interior of the Michaeliskirche, Munich

The monumental organ in Hamburg's Michaeliskirche

astonishingly ornate Amalienburg hunting lodge in the gardens.

To extend your trip...

Discover **Dachau** *(p268)*, a pretty medieval town that is now synonymous with the Holocaust, or relax with a beer at **Andechs** *(p268)*.

Two Days in Hamburg

Germany's second-largest city is full of attractive parks and varied architectural styles.

- **Arriving** The airport, 8 km (5 miles) from the city, is well served by buses, the S-Bahn and trains. There are also good train and ferry services.

Day 1

Morning Decorated with statues of local heroes and the trades that made Hamburg's fortune, the vast town hall on **Rathausmarkt** *(p438)* perfectly expresses the civic pride of this city-state. On Hamburg's shopping street, Mönckeberg-strasse, **St Petrikirche** *(p438)* and **Jakobikirche** *(pp438–9)* are eloquent about past wealth; chic boutique shops on Neuer Wall and Grosse Bleichen, north of the Rathaus, reveal current prosperity. Relax with a boat trip on the **Alster lakes** *(p438)*.

Afternoon Walk around the Binnenalster lake to the **Kunsthalle** *(pp440–41)*, which features paintings by German artists such as the medieval Master Bertram, Cranach and Caspar David Friedrich. There's modern art in the adjacent Galerie der Gegenwart, and arts and crafts in the Museum für Kunst und Gewerbe, on the south side of the train station.

Day 2

Morning The port that made Hamburg's fortune is at its most evocative in **Speicherstadt** *(p439)*; merchants hoisted goods direct from its canals into the 19th-century warehouses, some converted to museums. Older wharves south are being transformed in a development known as Hafen City – the Elbephilharmonie concert hall is especially striking. Its waterside restaurants or those in the city's original merchant street, Deichstrasse, are ideal for lunch.

Afternoon Walk west along the **port** *(p442)*, perhaps stopping to explore the museum ships *Rickmer Rickmers* and *Cap San Diego*. The goal is **Landungs-brücken** *(p442)*, from where fascinating boat tours around Europe's second-largest harbour depart at regular intervals. Hamburg ships imported the tropical woods that were transformed into the Baroque fittings of the **Michaeliskirche** *(p442)*, also worth a visit for the view of the port from its observation tower. By now the nightlife will be warming up in **St Pauli** *(pp442–3)*, the former dockers' drinking quarter. Made famous by The Beatles and its red-light district, St Pauli has now been gentrified for tourist-friendly titillation.

Five Days in Fairy-Tale Germany

- **Airports** Arrive and depart from Nuremberg airport.
- **Transport** It is easy to make day trips to all destinations from Nuremberg. Trains connect the towns in an hour or so, except Frankische Schweiz. Dinkelsbühl requires a change on to a bus from Rothenburg.
- **Booking ahead** Residenz, Würzburg.

Day 1: Nuremberg
Albrecht-Dürer-Haus *(p263)*, **Sebalduskirche** *(p262)* and the wishing fountain on pretty **Hauptmarkt** *(p262)* all testify to Nuremberg's (Nürnberg) tradition for craftsmanship. For the best panoramic views, climb to the top of the 12th-century Sinwellturm, at the **Kaiserburg** *(p263)*. For lunch, snack on Nuremberg's stubby *Bratwürste*, ordered three in a bun *("Drei im Weckla")* from the food stalls located on Hauptmarkt.

Day 2: Fränkische Schweiz to Bayreuth
A driving tour in the **Fränkische Schweiz** *(p247)* reveals scenery perfectly suited to *Snow White and the Seven Dwarfs*. Forchheim has a fine medieval core, tiny Tüchersfeld could double as a Disney film set, and Pottenstein boasts the region's oldest castle. **Bayreuth** *(pp256–7)* is synonymous with Wagnerian opera; however, the **Markgräfliches Opernhaus** *(p256)* pre-dates this composer by

two centuries and is still in use even though Wagner dismissed it as too small.

Day 3: Bamberg
UNESCO-listed **Bamberg** *(pp252–5)* is immediately striking: its symphony of superb artistry, beautiful buildings and small-town charm emerged unscathed from World War II. Must-sees here are the art on Domplatz – the **Cathedral** *(pp254–5)*, plus the Neue Residenz und Staatsgalerie – and the Altes Rathaus, which leapfrogs the Regnitz river via an islet. Must-dos include having a glass of *Rauchbier* (smoked beer) at Schlenkerla.

Day 4: Würzburg
Unlike Bamberg, **Würzburg** *(pp248–51)* took a direct hit during World War II, but restoration has revived its UNESCO World Heritage Site, the prince-bishops' **Residenz** *(pp250–51)* by star architect Balthasar Neumann. Elegant and giddily opulent by turns, this 17th-century palace is fit for a ball.

Day 5: Rothenburg
Slip into a timewarp back to medieval Germany at **Rothenburg** *(pp266–7)*. A local legend says the town was spared destruction in the Thirty Years' War because its mayor downed 3.25 litres (7 pints) of wine in one gulp. In summer, tour early or at dusk (when it's pure magic) to avoid the crowds. **Dinkelsbühl** *(p258)* is another gem, while **Nördlingen** *(pp258–9)* and **Ansbach** *(p259)* are also within reach by car.

Picturesque house on a bridge in Bamberg

A Week around Coastal Germany

- **Airports** Arrive at Hamburg Airport and depart from Lübeck, Hamburg or Berlin airports.
- **Transport** Trains connect the towns in an hour or so, except the Fischland, Darß and Zingst peninsula, for which you will need a car. Boats to Hiddensee run from Stralsund from April to October.

Day 1 and 2: Hamburg
See the city itinerary on *p13*.

Day 3: Lübeck
Whether you're after culture, architecture or simply small-town charm, **Lübeck** *(pp466–9)* is the place. The Backsteingotik brick architecture of its Hanseatic heyday set the blueprint for the entire region: highlights include the Holstentor, Rathaus and soaring Marienkirche, all expressions of civic pride. While you're in town, visit the St Annen-Museum for its altar-pieces and sample delicious Lübeck marzipan from Niederegger patisserie.

Day 4: Schwerin and Ludwigslust
Encircled by lakes and well worth a diversion inland, **Schwerin** *(pp474–5)* is the capital of Mecklenburg-Lower Pomerania. Tour the fairy-tale Schloss, then discover the dukes' fine taste in art in the Staatliches Museum and the Dom. Before they built the castle here, the Mecklenburg

Panoramic view of the city of Würzburg, with the River Main flowing through it

For practical information on travelling around Germany, see pp552–9

The luxuriant gardens of Schloss Linderhof, dotted with statuary

dukes resided in **Ludwigslust** (p476). Money was tight, which is why the stucco here is actually papier-mâché.

Day 5: Wismar and Bad Doberan

Maritime flavour returns in **Wismar** (pp476–7) – the size of the Markt and merchants' Georgenkirche testifies to the wealth of this medieval port. The Nikolaikirche retains Middle Age frescoes and altarpieces. Finer still are those of the Cistercian Münster in **Bad Doberan** (p477), its interior a treasure trove. If there's time, embark for a jaunt to the beach on the "Molli" steam train.

Day 6: Rostock to Stralsund

Rostock (p480) feels gritty after the small towns before. Heavily bombed in 1942, this port town warrants a stop for its Rathaus and Marienkirche. The **Fischland, Darss and Zingst peninsula** (p480) offers a superb route west. Ahrenshoop, a former artists' village, is now a chic escape for city-slickers because of its fine beach and galleries. In UNESCO-listed **Stralsund** (p481), go to the Alter Markt and compare the architecture with Lübeck.

Day 7: Rügen

Sea, sand, spa resorts and steam trains contribute to the holiday vibe of **Rügen** (pp482–3). A popular resort since Caspar David Friedrich painted the white cliffs of the Jasmund Peninsula, today it is a national park. For a day on the beach, base yourself at Binz or slow down on Hiddensee, where transport is by bike or horse and cart.

A Week in the Bavarian Alps

- **Airports** Arrive and leave from Munich.
- **Transport** Füssen and Garmisch-Partenkirchen are accessible by train from Munich; other destinations are served by local bus. Chiemsee (Prien station) requires a return to Munich via train. Berchtesgaden requires a change at Freilassing.
- **Booking ahead** Schloss Neuschwanstein, Schloss Linderhof.

Day 1 and 2: Munich

See the city itinerary on pp12–13.

Day 3: Lindau and Oberammergau

Lindau (p288), on the Bodensee, is charming and uncomplicated. Stroll the harbour, guarded by lighthouses, gaze to the Alps on the horizon, then discover the only frescoes of Hans Holbein the Elder in the church of St Peter. For more fabulous alpine views, take a cablecar up Mount Nebelhorn, near **Oberstdorf** (p289).

Day 4: Füssen to Oberammergau

Explore the cobbled lanes of **Füssen** (p289) before a visit to Bavarian King Ludwig II's **Schloss Neuschwanstein** (pp286–7), the embodiment of fairy-tale Germany. You can't beat **Oberammergau** (p284) for postcard-pretty alpine charm. Famous for a passion

play that takes place every decade (the next one will be in 2020), it also appeals for wood carvings and colourful frescoes.

Day 5: Ettal to Garmisch-Partenkirchen

Tiny **Ettal** (p284) sits in awe of alpine peaks and a Benedictine abbey with a splendid Rococo interior. More theatrical still is the setting of **Schloss Linderhof** (p285), where eccentric King Ludwig played out his Sun King fantasies. From here it's a short drive to Germany's most celebrated alpine resort, **Garmisch-Partenkirchen** (p284), for a ride up the Zugspitze, Germany's highest mountain.

Day 6: Chiemsee

Chiemsee (pp282–3), Bavaria's largest lake, is a lovely place to while away a day. Take a boat to Herreninsel to discover the last of King Ludwig II's delusional monuments, Versailles-inspired **Herrenchiemsee Palace**, and to Fraueninsel for its Benedictine heritage. There are good walks and cycle rides on the lake shores, or spend an afternoon on the beach at Chieming.

Day 7: Berchtesgadener Land

Corkscrew peaks, deep lakes and rustic chapels create the splendid landscape of **Berchtesgadener Land** (pp280–81). Take a boat trip on the Königsee to see the pilgrimage chapel of St Bartholomä, then visit the cosy village of Ramsau an der Ache. Finally, ascend to the Eagle's Nest, Hitler's mountain retreat; dedicated buses go from Obersalzberg.

A Cultural Tour of Eastern Germany

- **Duration** 7 days – but can be extended to a 12-day tour with extra suggestions.

- **Airports** Arrive at Berlin, Leipzig-Halle or Dresden international airports and depart from Dresden International Airport.

- **Transport** Trains connect all destinations in the tour in 2 hours or less. This tour can also be done by car, but public transport will be easier. If you choose to start in Berlin, note that it's a train journey of approximately 3 hours and 30 minutes to Eisenach.

This route follows in the footsteps of giants of German culture through the sights and museums of Thuringia and Saxony. For background on Germany's cultural heroes, see *pp30–35*. If you want to extend your trip, spend a day or two in Berlin (*p12*) before heading to Eisenach.

Day 1: Eisenach
Meet three of this tour's figure-heads in **Eisenach** (*pp190–91*). Excommunicated Martin Luther translated the New Testament in the Wartburg in 1521; Lucas Cranach the Elder painted his portrait, hung in its small museum; and Johann Sebastian Bach was born in a townhouse in the old town in 1685. The story of his life as a tetchy court composer is told in a museum.

Day 2: Gotha
Marvel at the power of Thuringia's ducal dynasties as you stroll around old-town **Gotha** (*p193*), laid at the feet of the majestic Schloss Friedenstein. The dukes expressed their court's magnificence through culture, gathering superb Old Masters, antiquities and treasures in a palace museum and building one of Europe's first Baroque court theatres. Leave time to discover the palace gardens.

To extend your trip...
The Thüringerwaldbahn tram pootles through pretty countryside before arriving at Friedrichroda, in the **Thuringian Forest** (*pp194–5*).

Day 3: Erfurt
Erfurt (*pp196–7*) is a historic town with a lively university. Admire the Romanesque and medieval artworks in the Dom St Marien and St Severi-Kirche, then browse the craftshops on the Krämerbrücke. Next, visit a monastic cell in the Augustiner-kloster, where Martin Luther studied. The Angermuseum holds a collection of decorative arts and paintings.

To extend your trip...
An unknown young organist named Johann Sebastian Bach first shocked congregations with his fugal compositions in pretty **Arnstadt** (*p194*).

Day 4: Weimar
Weimar (*pp198–9*) is the birthplace of the Enlightenment and the spiritual capital of German culture. Discover its sophistication in the ducal Stadtschloss and the Herzogin-Anna-Amalia Bibliothek, then see its private face in the home of Goethe, who worked as a court adviser to Duke Carl August. Tour the houses of Schiller and Liszt, then see the last artwork by Cranach in the St Peter und St Paul church. Finally, relax with a stroll in Park an der Ilm.

The tower of Weimar's Stadtschloss

Day 5: Leipzig
The fast-paced city of **Leipzig** (*pp166–7*) has a mercantile zeal that overshadows its cultural weight as a former home of Bach, who is buried in the Thomaskirche (where he was chorister), and of Goethe, who immortalized the Auerbachs Keller restaurant in *Faust*. The Grassimuseum holds a world-class collection of decorative arts; alternatively, there's painting and sculpture in the Museum der Bildenden Künste.

Day 6: Meissen
In **Meissen** (*p171*), the tangled lanes in the old town are fun to get lost in; then, head up to the Albrechtsburg complex before visiting the porcelain factory for which the town is synonymous. The first china outside Asia was produced here in 1710. Learn how on factory tours, and see the extravagant 3.5-m (11.4-ft) high decoration that graced the dining table of Saxony Electors.

The imposing Schloss Friedenstein, in Gotha, located above the old town

Day 7: Dresden

Stroll around the Baroque buildings that earned **Dresden** *(pp172–81)* the moniker of "Florence on the Elbe": the Frauenkirche, Brühlsche Terrasse and Hofkirche. Finest of all is the **Zwinger** *(pp178–9)*. Saxony Elector Augustus the Strong held alfresco balls here; today there is an excellent gallery. For more of Augustus's glittering court, visit his Grünes Gewölbe treasury in the Residenzschloss.

The statue of Emperor Wilhelm von Rumann on Karlsplatz, Stuttgart

To extend your trip...
The bizarre landscapes of **Sächsische Schweiz** *(pp182–3)* and **Schloss Moritzburg** *(p171)* are easily accessible on day trips.

A Gourmet Tour of Southwest Germany

- **Duration** 7 days – but can be extended to a 10-day tour with extra suggestions.
- **Airports** Arrive in and depart from either Frankfurt or Stuttgart airports.
- **Transport** This tour is most easily done by car. If you choose to arrive in Frankurt Airport, you might want to spend two days in the city before hiring a car and driving to Trier.

This tour explores Rheinland-Palatinate and Baden-Württemberg, including the Schwarzwald, to uncover the food and wine of southwest Germany. If you are travelling in late summer/early autumn, look out for wine and harvest festivals in the region.

Day 1: Trier and Moseltal

The Romans left behind fine monuments in **Trier** *(pp344–7)* and a tradition of viticulture on the south-facing slopes of the **Moseltal** *(p349)*. Follow the river beneath vineyards that produce elegant Rieslings, pausing at the world's steepest vineyard, Bremmer Calmont (www.bremmer-calmont.de).

Day 2: Maria Laach and the Rheintal

Stop by the **Maria Laach** abbey *(pp362–3)* before taking a trip down the **Rhine Valley** *(pp358–9)*, famous for its castles and white wines. Relax in a *Weinstube* (bar/tavern); those in **Bacharach** *(p359)* tend to be housed in old timbered buildings, whereas in **Mainz** *(pp352–5)* they're often in smarter venues. Try the regional delicacy of *Pfälzer Saumagen* (sow's stomach stuffed with sausage, potatoes and herbs).

To extend your trip...
Frankfurt *(pp378–83)* is renowned for its *Ebbelwoi* (cider). Enjoy it in a tavern in the Sachsenhausen district.

Day 3: Heidelberg

The must-see of the university town of **Heidelberg** *(pp300–3)* is its castle. Tour its romantic shell by day, then return at night for seasonal German fare at Schlossweinstube. Inbetween, enjoy a Studentenkuss (students' kiss), a chocolate praline made in Cafe Knösel on Haspelgasse since 1830.

Dresden's magnificent Frauenkirche

Day 4: Maulbronn, Ludwigsburg and Stuttgart

Tour the UNESCO-listed monastery in **Maulbronn** *(pp306–7)* or **Ludwigsburg** *(pp310–11)*, then enjoy the local specialities *Spätzle* noodles with cheese and *Maultaschen* (large ravioli). **Stuttgart** *(pp312–17)* is as synonymous with *Weinstuben* as Munich is with beer halls – Stetter (Rosenstrasse 32) serves 200 local wines.

Day 5: Baden-Baden

You can be sure of good-quality food in **Baden-Baden** *(p305)*, the "summer capital of Europe". This is also the queen of German spa resorts. Spend an afternoon in the health-giving waters of the Friedrichs-bad, then treat yourself to a sumptuous meal.

To extend your trip...
Tübingen *(p320)* is a lovely university town and a gateway to **Schwäbische Alb** *(pp318–19)*.

Day 6: Schwarzwald

Schwarzwälder Schinken (local ham), trout and *Schwarzwälder Kirschtorte* (Black Forest gâteau laced with cherry liqueur) are the delicacies of the **Schwarz-wald** *(pp330–31)*. Stop off at **Hangloch-Wasserfall** for truly spectacular views *(p331)*.

Day 7: Freiburg im Breisgau

Kick back in the pretty town of **Freiburg im Breisgau** *(pp328–9)*. See the Münster and either buy a cheese sandwich from a stall on Münsterplatz, or join students in the cafés of its cobbled lanes.

Putting Germany on the Map

Located in the centre of Europe, between the North and Baltic Seas and the Alps, Germany covers an area of nearly 360,000 sq km (139,000 sq miles). Its neighbouring countries are Poland and the Czech Republic to the east, Austria and Switzerland to the south, France, Belgium, Luxembourg and Holland to the west, and Denmark to the north. The capital is Berlin. Its largest river is the Rhine. Germany is inhabited by over 81 million people.

Key

- National border
- Motorway
- Major road
- - - Ferry route

For map symbols see back flap

0 kilometres 100

0 miles 100

Germany: Region by Region

The Federal Republic of Germany is made up of 16 states. Bremen is the smallest state, with around 700,000 inhabitants; North Rhine-Westphalia is the most densely populated state, with 18 million inhabitants. The largest state, Bavaria, covers an area of 70,531 sq km (27,232 sq miles). Berlin, Bremen and Hamburg are self-governing city-states.

How to get there

Germany has an excellent transport system. There are 14 international airports with flights to all parts of the world; a comprehensive network of toll-free motorways that make travelling by car easy and fast; and an efficient railway system, with high-speed InterCity Express (ICE) link between major cities.

Key

▦▦▦ Motorway
▬▬▬ Major road
▦▦▦ Minor Road
▬▬▬ Minor Railway

0 km _____ 100
0 miles _____ 100

For map symbols *see back flap*

Berlin

Reinickendorf
Pankow
Weissensee
Wedding
Prenzlauer Berg
Tiergarten
Charlottenburg
Mitte
Friedrichshain
Wilmersdorf
Kreuzberg
Schöneberg
Treptow
Neukölln
Tempelhof
Steglitz

0 km   3
0 miles   3

Stralsund
Greifswald
Rostock
Wismar
Schwerin
Neubrandenburg
Neustrelitz
Pritzwalk
Wittenberge
Schwedt/Oder
Oranienburg
Stendal
Rathenow
Potsdam
BERLIN
see inset above
Magdeburg
Schönebeck
Luckenwalde
Lübbenau
Lutherstadt Wittenberg
Cottbus
Halle
Delitzsch
Hoyerswerda
Leipzig
Naumburg
Döbeln
Bautzen
Görlitz
Erfurt
Weimar
Zeitz
Dresden
Gera
Freiberg
Ilmenau
Zwickau
Chemnitz
Annaberg-Buchholz
Coburg
Hof
Cheb
Bayreuth
Erlangen
Weiden
Nuremberg
Schwandorf
Cham
Regensburg
Straubing
Deggendorf
Ingolstadt
Passau
Landshut
MUNICH
see inset left
Rosenheim

Area Colours

- Berlin

Eastern Germany

- Brandenburg
- Saxony
- Saxony-Anhalt
- Thuringia

Southern Germany

- Munich
- Bavaria
- Baden-Württemberg

Western Germany

- Rhineland-Palatinate & Saarland
- Hesse
- North Rhine-Westphalia

Northern Germany

- Hamburg, Bremen, Lower Saxony
- Schleswig-Holstein
- Mecklenburg-Lower Pomerania

A PORTRAIT OF GERMANY

Germany is a wealthy country, whose people are generally regarded as hard-working, determined and efficient. This view stems from the country's industrial might and the smooth functioning of its economy, but it overlooks other important aspects of Germany. These include its important contributions to art and culture, its breathtaking scenery and excellent tourist facilities.

Contemporary Germany is far removed from the traditional, stereotyped view of the country. In the last 60 years, it has developed into a multi-ethnic, multi-cultural melting pot. Over 7 million of Germany's inhabitants are immigrants; the majority of these are Turks, with more recent guest workers arriving from the former Yugoslavia, Italy and Greece. In the city of Stuttgart, every third inhabitant is a foreigner; in Frankfurt it is one in four. Hamburg has more mosques than any other city in Europe and, in some schools in Berlin, German children are in the minority. Almost every town has a selection of Italian, Chinese, Greek and Turkish restaurants and cafés, testifying to the multi-ethnicity of its population.

History and Romance

For many, the river Rhine epitomizes tourist Germany, particularly the romantic stretch between Mainz and Cologne. The country has far more than this to offer in the way of scenery, however. There is the ever-changing Baltic coastline, the sandy islands of the North Sea, the lakes of Mecklenburg, lonely castles perched on crags in Baden and Thuringia, mountain ranges including the Alps, the vast Bodensee lake, medieval cities and fairy-tale villages. Not all of the latter are original, as countless towns were destroyed by bombs during World War II, but many have been meticulously rebuilt to the original plans, and now it is difficult to tell the difference between the old and the new.

Verdant Alpine meadow against a backdrop of majestic, snowy peaks

◀ A wintry Bavarian scene, with Neuschwanstein Castle in the background

Procession during the Plärrer Fest, a beer festival in Augsburg

Traditions

Today's German nation has evolved over the past thousand years, mainly from various Germanic tribes, notably the Franks, Saxons, Swabians and Bavarians. Traditions and dialects have developed within regional ethnic groups that emerged as a result of historical alliances. There is no such thing as a single German tradition. Even the assumption that Germany is a country of beer-drinkers is belied by the large numbers of wine-lovers. These groups, along with consumers of stronger beverages, have given Germany a high position in the world league table for alcohol use. Nevertheless, drunks are rarely seen in Germany.

Various ethnic groups in the country are ascribed different characteristics. The people of Mecklenburg, for example, are seen as introspective, while Swabians are regarded as thrifty; the Saxons are seen as disciplined and cunning, while Bavarians are typified as a people bound by rustic traditions, quick to quarrel and fight. Indeed, one of the most popular Bavarian men's folk-dances ends with them slapping each other in the face.

A Bavarian dressed in regional costume

Bavaria, of course, is home to the traditional Oktoberfest, a beer festival that brings millions of people to Munich every year from virtually all over the world.

The people of the Rhineland have a reputation for enjoying life. Their favourite season is the Carnival period, and they spend practically the entire year preparing for this week-long event. It begins on the last Thursday before Lent, with "town soldiers", helped by the huge crowds, storming the town hall. The town councillors surrender and power passes to the masked revellers. On the Monday, the Carnival proceeds through the thronged streets of the towns on the Rhine, and the pubs are busy until the end of Shrovetide.

Carnival is rooted in ancient rituals marking the banishment of winter. This custom was most common in the south of Germany, but it also reached the Rhineland, the Palatinate and Hessen. When the German government moved back to Berlin from Bonn in the Rhineland in 1999, attempts were made to establish Carnival in the new capital, but it never really took root.

Art and Culture

Germany is a land of sagas and legends that tell of woodland spirits, beautiful princesses, magicians and sirens such as the Lorelei. These legends have had a strong influence on German art. An example is the German epic poem, the *Nibelungenlied,* which was written around 1200 on the basis of old legends. This poem was the inspiration for Richard Wagner's cycle of operas, *The Ring of the Nibelungen,* as well as for a trilogy of plays by Christian Friedrich Hebbel and a film by Fritz Lang.

Germans have won eight Nobel Prizes for Literature. The most recent prize-winner was Günter Grass, whose *Tin Drum* brought him world renown. More recently a film adaptation of the book was made by Volker Schlöndorff, which won the Golden Palm at the Cannes Film Festival. After a relatively stagnant period, the German film industry became revitalized around 1995 with a number of hits, albeit only at the national level. German cinemas are now always full and traditional cinemas are increasingly being replaced by multiplexes.

Germans read widely, even in today's age of television and the internet. Every year 70,000 new books are published in Germany and eight times that many titles are on sale. Germany is second only to the United States in the number of books published annually, while the number of bookshops per square kilometre is the highest in the world. The same applies to museums and art galleries.

Germany has over 2,000 national, provincial and local history museums, as well as numerous church museums, folk

The historical Frohnauer hammer forge near Annaberg in Saxony

museums and former royal palaces. This variety and choice owes much to the fact that, in the past, local dukes acquired collections of art in order to impress others and to demonstrate their wealth. The Bavarian dukes also built up extensive collections of machines, artisans' tools, musical instruments and minerals. As early as the 16th century, Munich was an international centre of the arts and the Grünes Gewölbe in 17th-century Dresden was one of the largest treasuries for storing fine art in Europe. Of the many art galleries to be found throughout Germany, the finest are in Cologne, Frankfurt, Stuttgart, Munich and Berlin.

Lorelei overlooking the Rhine

Music also flourishes in Germany. Most large cities have their own symphony orchestra and opera company and every year some 100 regional and local music festivals take place. Musical comedies are especially popular.

The imposing Schönburg Castle, near Oberwesel on the Rhine

Society and Politics

The scars of World War II are more evident in Eastern Germany, although they are gradually disappearing there, too. Görlitz, Bautzen, Leipzig and Weimar have now acquired a splendour that was previously hidden behind the grim façade of East Germany. The mental, social and political scars of the war and subsequent division of Germany have, however, left deeper scars. Although reunification took place on 3 October 1990, unity among the people themselves has been longer in coming. East Germans are the poor relations: the region has high unemployment rates and its people tend to regard their western counterparts as arrogant and self-assured. The latter, for their part, claim that the inhabitants of the "new states" are jealous and ungrateful despite the billions of marks and euros that have been poured into the region to equalize living standards.

The Reichstag building, where the *Bundestag* sessions are held

Germany has almost always been divided regionally into states with fluctuating borders. The present-day states were, for the most part, created after 1945 while those in East Germany were not created until forty years later. In all cases, old territorial and historical ties were taken into account. That is the reason for their evocative names, such as the "Free State of Bavaria" or the "Free State of Saxony".

There are now 16 federal states, or provinces. North Rhine-Westphalia, Baden-Württemberg and Bavaria are the largest and are like economically powerful countries. At the other end of the scale, the tiny province of Saarland has only 1.1 million inhabitants, while the Free Hanseatic City of Bremen has fewer than 700,000. The former East German states are also relatively small but all play an important role in the *Bundesrat,* or Federal Council, where they are instrumental in enacting legislation. All laws, apart from those relating to the Federation as a whole, such as defence or foreign policy, require the agreement of the *Bundesrat,* which is made up from current local governments. Depending on the number of inhabitants, each federal state has from four to six votes.

The skyline of Frankfurt am Main

A government with a majority in the *Bundestag* (parliament) cannot always count on support in the *Bundesrat,* even if it has a majority there. Each state looks after its own interests and often makes alliances with other states to achieve its own aims, without regard for party loyalty. The complex working of German federalism is based on the compromises that this system requires.

Bathers on the sandy beaches of Norddeich

Daily Life

The traditional image of German women used to be summed up in the "three Ks": *Küche, Kinder, Kirche* (kitchen, children, church). As in other Western European countries, however, this stereotype no longer holds true. Although cookery is fashionable and there are countless TV cookery programmes starring celebrity chefs, for everyday meals, ready-prepared dishes are eaten, either at the work canteen or from the super-market. The German birthrate is declining, while the anti-authoritarian model of education that was introduced in the 1960s has to some extent relieved parents of many of the more onerous duties of child-rearing. As a result, many young people show little respect for their elders. The churches, for their part, are usually empty. Although the largest churches (Catholic and Protestant) have many adherents, the vast majority are not practising believers and limit themselves to payment of church dues.

Participant in a parade celebrating the Reunification

Germans speak of themselves as a high-performance society *(Leistungsgesellschaft),* which gives the highest rewards to those who devote almost all their energies to their careers. As a result, stress is often a factor in people's lives, from schooldays onwards. In Germany today there are increasing numbers of people who live alone. Single-person households are most common in the cities and even young people regard their careers as of paramount importance. Large numbers say that they are not interested in having a family.

Nevertheless, Germans enjoy mass events such as public holidays and popular festivals. The country has the highest number of public holidays in Europe and German workers have the longest annual holidays. Its citizens are Europe's most enthusiastic travellers, each year spending more than 35 million euros on foreign holidays. When they return there is a tendency to long for the southern climes they have just visited – perhaps this explains why restaurants offering Mediterranean food are so popular.

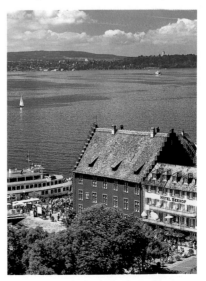

The Bodensee, a popular tourist destination

Flora and Fauna

Germany is a vast country whose varied geography has given rise to a great diversity of flora and fauna. It is famous for its forests, many of mixed deciduous trees, including oak, beech and birch. Around 31 per cent of the country is forested. The Alpine regions have a rich variety of wild flowers, with meadow species a particular feature in spring and summer. On the northern peat moors, heaths and heathers are common. Germany is home to a wide range of wildlife, including wild boar, lynx and marmots. Many valuable wildlife areas have now been placed under protection.

German Wildlife
The fauna of Germany is typical of central Europe, with a variety of woodland, wetland and Alpine birds. Of the larger mammals, visitors are most likely to see deer, squirrels and foxes. Small populations of rarer

Alpine raven species such as lynx and European beaver exist, but are threatened with extinction. Wolf and elk now pass through sparsely populated regions in the north and east.

Coastal Regions

Germany's coasts vary considerably: the North Sea coast is predominantly flat with drained land, dikes and islands; the Baltic Sea coast is hillier with sandy inlets and cliffs. Together with differences in tides and temperature, these variations determine the variety of species found along coastal regions.

Lakes

Most of Germany's lakes are grouped in the northern part of the country, mainly in the Mecklenburg region, where they are divided from the south by the mountain ranges, rifts and valleys of the Central Uplands. However, the largest lake in Germany – the Bodensee (Lake Constance) – is situated in the south, on the border with Austria and Switzerland.

Cross-leaved heath is a species of heather that is commonly found growing on the moors and peat bogs and in the damp coastal forests of northern Germany.

Sea lavender is one of the salt-tolerant species that grow along Germany's North Sea coast.

Sea holly is a beautiful thistle-like plant with an amethyst hue. It is commonly found growing in sand dunes.

Yellow floating heart grows in shallow, fertile water. Its habitats are disappearing but it still survives in the Rhine basin and on the lower Elbe.

The white water lily, with its elegant floating flowers and lush foliage, adorns lakes and reservoirs.

Yellow flag is a protected species of iris that is found amongst reeds and in damp woodlands, particularly in older, mixed species forests.

Wild boars are mammals of the pig family, living in boggy forests. They feed mainly on acorns, beechnuts and the small animals that live in the ground cover of the forest.

Deer live in leafy and mixed forests and are one of the most common mammals seen in Germany.

Marmots live on vegetation growing in the high Alpine meadows. Rodents of the squirrel family, they sleep in burrows at night and whistle loudly when anxious.

Lynx are distinguished by small tufts of hair on the tips of their ears. These mammals are becoming ever rarer.

Uplands

Upland landscapes dominate the southern part of Germany, including Bavaria. Here, the climate is mild, and forests cover nearly a third of the region. In this picturesque and popular part of the country, winter-sports centres and spa resorts are common.

Mountains

Mountain ranges in Germany vary both in age and in height above sea level. Older, not very high mountains covered with forests predominate. The Bavarian Alps are higher and more recent. Here sub-alpine plants grow, with alpine plants at higher altitudes.

Beech is one of the commonest trees found in Germany's forests of mixed deciduous species.

Holly, the symbol of Christmas with its glossy leaves and scarlet berries, is found in forests of beech or beech and fir in the west of the country.

Hepatica is a protected plant in Germany. It blooms in early spring and the seeds of the blue, star-like flowers are distributed by ants.

Gentian, with its intensely blue trumpet-like flowers, is one of the most impressive plants to be seen in the Alps. It is pollinated by bumblebees.

Edelweiss is a small flowering plant with flat, white flowers and grey-green woolly leaves. It grows high up in the Alps.

Rhododendron hirsutum is a low, dense variety of rhododendron, one of a group of plants that grow at sub-Alpine levels.

German Literature

The first known examples of written German date from the 8th century. German literature flourished in the Renaissance, although it was mainly later writers who entered the world's canon of great literature. Goethe and Schiller, who wrote many of their most famous works in the *Sturm und Drang* (Storm and Stress) era, in the late 18th century, count among the greatest. Germany also produced many dramatists, poets and novelists in the 19th and 20th centuries. German writers have won eight Nobel Prizes for literature, awarded to Nelly Sachs, Thomas Mann, Heinrich Böll and Günter Grass among others.

Gotthold Ephraim Lessing (1729–81), the most famous German writer of the Age of Enlightenment, wrote dramas such as *Nathan the Wise*, reviews of plays performed in Hamburg as well as essays on literary and cultural theory.

Erich Maria Remarque (1898–1970) emigrated from Germany in 1931. His pacifist writings, including *All Quiet on the Western Front* and *L'Arc de Triomphe*, brought him acclaim around the world.

The Brothers Grimm, Jacob Ludwig Karl (1785–1863) and Wilhelm Karl (1786–1859), were university professors and philologists, but better known as collectors and publishers of some of the world's favourite fairytales.

Friedrich Schiller (1759–1805) wrote about the concept of individual freedom in his great dramas, such as *The Robbers* and *Wallenstein*. He also wrote ballads and songs, including *Ode to Joy.*

Kiel

SCHLESWIG-HOLSTEIN

Bremerhaven   Hamburg

Bremen

LOWER SAXONY, HAMBURG AND BREMEN

Hanover

Bielefeld

Dortmund

Düsseldorf   NORTH RHINE-WESTPHALIA   Kassel

Bonn

HESSE

RHINELAND-PALATINATE AND SAARLAND

Frankfurt am Main

Saarbrücken

Stuttgart

BADEN-WÜRTTEMBERG

0 kilometres   75

0 miles   75

Thomas Mann (1875–1955) was awarded the Nobel Prize in 1929. The best-known of his novels is *Buddenbrooks*, which chronicles the life of a Lübeck family.

Gerhart Hauptmann (1862–1946), dramatist, novelist and winner of the Nobel Prize in 1912, lived and worked mainly in Silesia. *The Weavers* is his most famous drama.

Theodor Fontane (1819–98) was born in Neuruppin, and his literary activities were chiefly connected with Brandenburg. He was the author of realistic novels such as *Effi Briest*, and he wrote excellent theatre reviews.

Bertolt Brecht (1898–1956), the great dramatist, poet and director, wrote *The Threepenny Opera*, and was a co-founder of the Berliner Ensemble theatre company.

Karl May (1842–1912) was known around the world as the author of travel books but his great popularity stems from a cycle of stories featuring the Indian chief *Winnetou*, which he wrote in Radebeul.

Johann Wolfgang von Goethe (1749–1832) was the most highly acclaimed German poet and writer of the *Sturm und Drang* period. Born in Frankfurt, he spent most of his life in Weimar. His most famous work is *Faust*.

Lion Feuchtwanger (1884–1958) lived in Munich until his opposition to the National Socialists forced him to emigrate in 1933. He wrote in exile, alluding to contemporary events in his historical novels.

Map labels:
Rostock
MECKLENBURG-LOWER POMERANIA
Schwerin
Schwedt/Oder
Berlin
Potsdam
Magdeburg
BRANDENBURG
SAXONY-ANHALT
Halle
Leipzig
SAXONY
Erfurt
Gera
Dresden
Chemnitz
THURINGIA
Nuremberg
Regensburg
BAVARIA
Munich

Music in Germany

German composers have made an enormous contribution to the world's cultural heritage. Many great musical geniuses were born and worked here, including Johann Sebastian Bach and Ludwig van Beethoven. Today their work, and that of other German composers, continues to be performed to enthusiastic new generations of music-lovers in concert halls and opera houses around the world. In Germany, their work is celebrated regularly at hugely popular music festivals.

Renowned composer, Johann Sebastian Bach (1685–1750)

Early Music

During the early Middle Ages, music evolved in the courts and monasteries of Europe. The basis of sacred music was the Gregorian chant, which was introduced by Pope Gregory I in the late 6th century. An influential role in medieval court music was played by roving poets (Minnesänger), who sang love verses to a lute accompaniment. From the 14th century, German singing guilds known as Meistersinger emerged. Unlike the Minnesänger, these artistes adopted a settled lifestyle. In the succeeding centuries, both vocal and instrumental music continued to evolve, with many new forms appearing.

In the second half of the 17th century, interest in organ music developed and organ schools were established in many towns. One of the best was in Nuremberg. This was directed by Johann

Pachelbel (c.1653–1706), who worked in Vienna, Stuttgart, Erfurt and Nuremberg as a church organist. He is best known for his organ work *Canon*, a set of variations on a theme.

The first German opera, *Dafne*, was composed by Heinrich Schütz (1585–1672). Completed in 1627, the opera has unfortunately been lost.

The 18th Century

A huge flowering of musical talent took place in Germany during the 18th century, when divisions both in German politics and religion led to the development of several important artistic and cultural centres. The most renowned figure in German music in the 18th century was undoubtedly

Georg Friedrich Händel (1685–1759)

Johann Sebastian Bach who, until 1717, was associated with the Weimar court. From 1723 until his death, he was associated with Leipzig, where he was the choir master at the church of St Thomas. Bach's output as a composer is vast and embraces most of the musical forms known at that time. His Passions are today performed in many countries during Holy Week, and his Brandenburg Concertos are among his most frequently performed works. His sons – Wilhelm Friedemann, Carl Philipp Emanuel, Johann Christoph Friedrich and Johann Christian – also became acclaimed composers and made significant contributions to German classical music.

Georg Friedrich Händel was another great composer of late Baroque music. Before forging a prestigious career in England, he began as the cathedral organist in Halle, from where he transferred to the opera house in Hamburg. A friend of Händel and another important composer, Georg Philipp Telemann (1681–1767) was employed as conductor at many German courts. His work includes chamber music, operas and church music. Son of a court musician and arguably the greatest figure in classical music, Ludwig van

The Bach festival in Leipzig's Church of St Thomas

Music Festivals

Germany is a country of musical festivals, which are usually held in the summer and early autumn. Among the most popular are the festivals dedicated to the works of a single composer, such as Wagner in Bayreuth, Bach in various cities of Thuringia, Händel in Halle and Beethoven in Bonn. Apart from these specialized festivals, opera festivals with a broader repertoire are also popular. These include the outdoor opera festival in Berlin and the Sommerfestspiele in Xanten.

Beethoven (1770–1827) was born in Bonn, although he worked mainly in Vienna. Among his best-known works are his nine symphonies, as well as piano and violin concertos, two masses, various chamber works and the opera *Fidelio*.

The life of this great composer is shrouded in legend. Succeeding generations have been fascinated not just by his music, but also by the fact that he began to lose his hearing at the age of 30. During his final years, when totally deaf, he composed from memory.

Statue of Ludwig van Beethoven

The 19th Century

Romanticism brought about the flowering of opera in Germany. One of the leading creators in this tradition was the composer Ernst Theodor Amadeus Hoffmann (1776–1822), whose opera *Undine* was staged for the first time in 1816 in Berlin. Carl Maria von Weber (1786–1826) rose to prominence following the success of his opera *Der Freischütz*, which was the first opera in the German Romantic tradition. Another major figure from this time was Felix Mendelssohn-Bartholdy,

Composer Felix Mendelssohn-Bartholdy (1809–47)

whose "Wedding March" from *A Midsummer Night's Dream* accompanies wedding celebrations around the world. As well as this famous piece of music, however, Mendelssohn left a legacy that includes five symphonies, piano music, chamber music and oratorios. In 1843, Mendelssohn founded Germany's first musical conservatory, in Leipzig.

The master of chamber music was Robert Schumann (1810–56), a poet and composer whose miniature works for piano, violin sonatas and song cycles all remain popular. The Hungarian composer Franz Liszt, who worked in Weimar from 1848 to 1861, also made a significant contribution to the evolution of German music.

In the second half of the 19th century, Richard Wagner was the major influence on German opera. During his early years, he composed traditional operas such as *Tannhäuser*. He later developed his own creative synthesis, integrating lyrics with the music. This found its finest expression in his Ring cycle, which was based on medieval sagas.

Richard Wagner (1813–83)

Wagner's ideas about musical theatre, including his use of *leitmotifs* (recurring phrases), were adopted by Richard Strauss (1864–1949), who composed many operas, symphonies and songs. The first bars of his symphonic poem *Zarathustra* became a guiding musical motif in Stanley Kubrick's 1968 film *2001: A Space Odyssey*. Johannes Brahms (1833–97) composed in traditional forms

Composer and pianist Johannes Brahms (1833–97)

and was unsympathetic to the progressive ideas of Wagner and Liszt. From 1872 to 1875, Brahms was the musical director of the *Gesellschaft der Musikfreunde* (Society of Friends of Music).

The 20th Century

During the 20th century, many contemporary composers continued the traditions of the earlier masters. One renowned figure was Paul Hindemith (1895–1963), whose work includes opera, ballet and concertos. His music was banned by the Nazis in 1933 and Hindemith emigrated to the USA in 1939. Another important figure in German musical life was Carl Orff (1895–1982) whose best-known work is the oratorio *Carmina Burana*, based on 13th-century Latin and German poems found in a Benedictine monastery in Bavaria. The Austrian composer Arnold Schönberg (1874–1951) lived in Berlin during the 1920s and exerted great influence on German music.

Among the most important composers living and working in Germany today, mention should be made of Hans Werner Henze, Dieter Schnebel, Helmut Lachenmann, Moritz Eggert and Jörg Widmann.

German Painting

The diversity in German painting has its roots in the political and religious divisions that existed in the country in the past. The Old Masters working in the north, for example, were more likely to be influenced by the Netherlandish school, while artists working in the south leaned towards Italian styles. German art reached the peak of its individuality during the late-Gothic, late-Baroque and Expressionist periods – all periods when one of the chief characteristics of artistic style was strength of expression.

Emil Nolde (1867–1956), one of Germany's foremost Expressionists, painted landscapes of his native region. Pictured above is his *North Friesian Landscape*.

Master Francke (14th–15th century) was the leading representative of the North German late-Gothic style, working in Hamburg c.1410–24. He painted religious scenes and his works include *St Thomas's Altar*, of which this is a detail.

Peter von Cornelius (1783–1867) joined the Nazarenes during the anti-academic rebellion. He later became director of the academy in Düsseldorf and others. He painted the picture *The Wise and Foolish Maidens* at that time.

Adam Elsheimer (1578–1610) was born in Frankfurt am Main but spent most of his life in Rome. His poignant landscapes, such as *The Flight to Egypt* shown here, greatly influenced the development of 17th-century painting.

Kiel

SCHLESWIC HOLSTEIN

Bremerhaven   Hamburg

Bremen

LOWER SAXONY, HAMBURG AND BREMEN

Hanover

Bielefeld

Dortmund

Düsseldorf   NORTH RHINE-WESTPHALIA   Kassel

Bonn   HESSE

RHINELAND-PALATINATE AND SAARLAND   Frankfurt am Main

Saarbrücken

Stuttgart

BADEN-WÜRTTEMBERG

Freiburg

0 kilometres 80
0 miles 80

Caspar David Friedrich (1774–1840) was one of the most prominent exponents of Romanticism. He created poignant images, such as this *Traveller above the Sea of Clouds*, in which Man contemplates the power of Nature as created by God.

Max Liebermann (1847–1935) is considered one of the leading representatives of Impressionism. His *Man with Parrots* was painted during his association with the Berlin Secession.

Lionel Feininger (1871–1956) was born in the USA but spent much of his life in Germany. He lectured at the Bauhaus and painted Cubist-inspired scenes of architectural subjects, such as this *Gelmeroda IX*.

Rostock

MECKLENBURG-LOWER POMERANIA

Schwerin

Schwedt/Oder

Berlin

Potsdam

Magdeburg

BRANDENBURG

SAXONY-ANHALT

Halle

Leipzig

SAXONY

Erfurt

Gera

Dresden

THURINGIA

Chemnitz

Albrecht Dürer (1471–1528) is one of the best-known German painters. This great master of the Renaissance period was also an outstanding engraver and art-historian. His *Paumgärtners' Altar* was made for St Catherine's Church in Nuremberg.

Nuremberg

Regensburg

BAVARIA

Munich

Wilhelm Leibl (1844–1900) painted this scene of women praying in a village church in Bavaria, *Three Women in a Church*, which is regarded as one of the outstanding works of German Realism.

Castles in Germany

In a number of German regions, medieval castles are among the most characteristic features of the landscape. Some have survived only in the form of picturesque ruins, but many others, refurbished and modernized over the years, continue to be the main residence for the families for whom they were built. The most impressive grouping of great fortresses is to be found along the banks of the Mosel and the central Rhine, while, in the Münster area, you will see the most beautiful moated castles to have survived in the lowlands.

The Great Knights' Hall, where knights ate, drank and entertained, was a feature of every castle.

The 15th-century Michaels-kapelle

Marburg Castle is one of the best-preserved fortresses in Hesse. At its core is a 12th-century building, but the castle's current appearance is the result of work carried out between the 14th and 16th centuries *(see p373)*.

The Royal Room was an apartment specially designated for the use of important guests.

The Wartburg in Eisenach is one of the most important monuments in Thuringia, not only because of its excellently preserved architecture but also for its association with Martin Luther *(see pp190–91)*.

Heidelberg Castle has survived as a picturesque ruin. A Gothic-Renaissance structure of imposing proportions, it continues to captivate with its commanding position and fascinating architecture *(see pp302–3)*.

Gardens were laid out in the 19th century in an area between the castle walls and the site of the farm buildings.

Raesfeld is one of the most beautiful castles in Münsterland, a region of Westphalia that is renowned for its historic moated castles. The castle was extended in the mid-17th century for Alexandra II von Velen *(see p392)*.

19th-Century Castles

In the 19th century, many ruined castles in Germany were rebuilt in a wave of nostalgia for the Middle Ages. A number of completely new castles were built, which were modelled on medieval designs.

The Schwerin castle, originally built in the 16th century, was extensively reconstructed in 1843–57 – work inspired by French castles along the river Loire *(see p474)*.

Lichtenstein castle owes its fame to the novel *Lichtenstein* by Wilhelm Hauff and its beauty to the Romantic style of a new castle built in 1840–41 on the grounds of a pre-existing one *(see p319)*.

Evangelical Chapel

The main entrance to the castle leads through a gate house – here in the form of a tower.

Wernigerode's castle dominates the entire city. Despite later reconstruction work, it has retained a late-Gothic tower, a beautiful staircase dating from 1495 and some valuable furnishings *(see p150)*.

Burg Hohenzollern

The family seat of the Hohenzollern family, Burg Hohenzollern in Hechingen, is set on a clifftop in the Swabian Jura. The first building was established here in the 13th century and rebuilt many times over the years. The current medieval appearance is the result of work that was carried out in 1850–67 in the spirit of romantic historicism (see p318).

Burg Eltz, set high above the Mosel, is one of the most beautiful castles in Germany. Built between the 12th and 16th centuries, it has survived with very few alterations *(see p349)*.

German Scientists and Inventors

Germany is popularly regarded as a nation of practical people, so it is hardly surprising that the history books abound with the names of Germans who have made important contributions to technological progress and the development of science. They include Johann Gutenberg (c.1400–68), who invented printing with movable type, and Karl Benz (1844–1929) and Gottlieb Daimler (1834–1900) who developed the first petrol-driven car. In terms of Nobel Prize winners alone (and not counting those who received the prize for achievements in other fields), there is currently a total of 69 Germans. One of the most illustrious of these is physicist Albert Einstein (1879–1955).

1791 Alexander von Humboldt, a naturalist and geographer, discovers the presence of carbon dioxide in the air

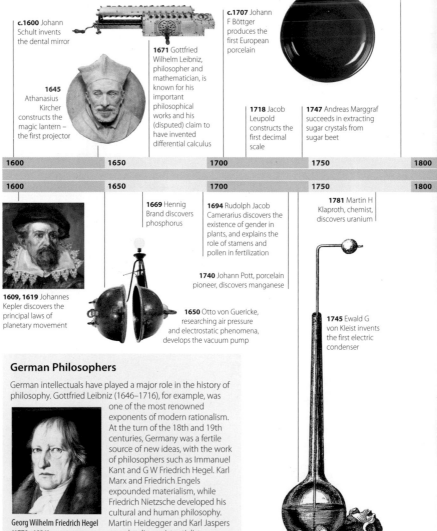

c.1600 Johann Schult invents the dental mirror

1645 Athanasius Kircher constructs the magic lantern – the first projector

1671 Gottfried Wilhelm Leibniz, philosopher and mathematician, is known for his important philosophical works and his (disputed) claim to have invented differential calculus

c.1707 Johann F Böttger produces the first European porcelain

1718 Jacob Leupold constructs the first decimal scale

1747 Andreas Marggraf succeeds in extracting sugar crystals from sugar beet

1600   1650   1700   1750   1800

1600   1650   1700   1750   1800

1669 Hennig Brand discovers phosphorus

1694 Rudolph Jacob Camerarius discovers the existence of gender in plants, and explains the role of stamens and pollen in fertilization

1781 Martin H Klaproth, chemist, discovers uranium

1740 Johann Pott, porcelain pioneer, discovers manganese

1609, 1619 Johannes Kepler discovers the principal laws of planetary movement

1650 Otto von Guericke, researching air pressure and electrostatic phenomena, develops the vacuum pump

1745 Ewald G von Kleist invents the first electric condenser

German Philosophers

German intellectuals have played a major role in the history of philosophy. Gottfried Leibniz (1646–1716), for example, was one of the most renowned exponents of modern rationalism. At the turn of the 18th and 19th centuries, Germany was a fertile source of new ideas, with the work of philosophers such as Immanuel Kant and G W Friedrich Hegel. Karl Marx and Friedrich Engels expounded materialism, while Friedrich Nietzsche developed his cultural and human philosophy. Martin Heidegger and Karl Jaspers were leading existentialists.

Georg Wilhelm Friedrich Hegel (1770–1831)

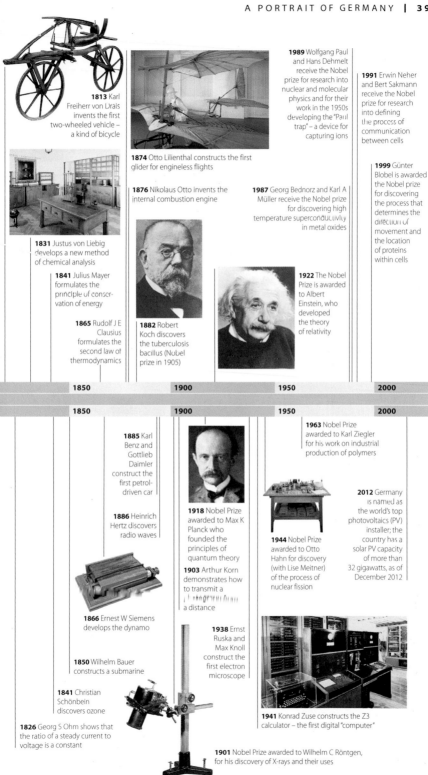

1813 Karl Freiherr von Drais invents the first two-wheeled vehicle – a kind of bicycle

1989 Wolfgang Paul and Hans Dehmelt receive the Nobel prize for research into nuclear and molecular physics and for their work in the 1950s developing the "Paul trap" – a device for capturing ions

1991 Erwin Neher and Bert Sakmann receive the Nobel prize for research into defining the process of communication between cells

1874 Otto Lilienthal constructs the first glider for engineless flights

1876 Nikolaus Otto invents the internal combustion engine

1987 Georg Bednorz and Karl A Müller receive the Nobel prize for discovering high temperature superconductivity in metal oxides

1999 Günter Blobel is awarded the Nobel prize for discovering the process that determines the direction of movement and the location of proteins within cells

1831 Justus von Liebig develops a new method of chemical analysis

1841 Julius Mayer formulates the principle of conservation of energy

1865 Rudolf J E Clausius formulates the second law of thermodynamics

1882 Robert Koch discovers the tuberculosis bacillus (Nobel prize in 1905)

1922 The Nobel Prize is awarded to Albert Einstein, who developed the theory of relativity

| 1850 | 1900 | 1950 | 2000 |

| 1850 | 1900 | 1950 | 2000 |

1885 Karl Benz and Gottlieb Daimler construct the first petrol-driven car

1963 Nobel Prize awarded to Karl Ziegler for his work on industrial production of polymers

1886 Heinrich Hertz discovers radio waves

1918 Nobel Prize awarded to Max K Planck who founded the principles of quantum theory

1903 Arthur Korn demonstrates how to transmit a photograph over a distance

1944 Nobel Prize awarded to Otto Hahn for discovery (with Lise Meitner) of the process of nuclear fission

2012 Germany is named as the world's top photovoltaics (PV) installer; the country has a solar PV capacity of more than 32 gigawatts, as of December 2012

1866 Ernest W Siemens develops the dynamo

1850 Wilhelm Bauer constructs a submarine

1938 Ernst Ruska and Max Knoll construct the first electron microscope

1841 Christian Schönbein discovers ozone

1826 Georg S Ohm shows that the ratio of a steady current to voltage is a constant

1941 Konrad Zuse constructs the Z3 calculator – the first digital "computer"

1901 Nobel Prize awarded to Wilhelm C Röntgen, for his discovery of X-rays and their uses

German Beer

Although fine wines are produced in Germany, beer is unquestionably the country's favourite alcoholic drink. Germans drink an average of 100 litres of beer annually and Bavarians lead the world in consumption, drinking an average of 215 litres each per annum. Beer is drunk on every occasion, but it tastes best in the summer when it is poured straight from a barrel at one of the numerous festivals or public holidays.

The *Mass* is a tankard that is used to serve beer in Bavaria. It holds a litre, but waitresses are used to carrying eight or nine such tankards at a time.

Historic brewing facilities in Freising *(see p269)*

German Breweries

In Germany most towns and the larger villages have a brewery. The country's oldest brewery, established in 1040, is the Weihenstephan Benedictine monastery in Freising, which is believed to be the oldest working brewery in the world. Many large breweries and consortiums produce beer that is known throughout the world, but beers produced by small operators, which are available only in a few regional pubs, are in no way inferior. When visiting Germany, do try the produce of small local breweries as well as the beer produced by the giants, such as Paulaner and Löwenbräu.

Logo of the famous Munich brewery, Paulaner

Styles of Beer

One of the most popular styles of beer is *Pils* (short for *Pilsener*) a light, bottom-fermented beer of the lager type. Of the seasonal beers, it is worth trying spring beers such as *Maibock* or *Doppelbock*, and in autumn the strong beer that is brewed especially for the Oktoberfest. In the lower Rhine valley, *Altbier* is still produced; this is a top-fermented beer, prepared by traditional methods. In the south, *Weizenbier*, a wheat beer, is also produced. The Berlin version, *Berliner Weisse* (white beer), is served with fruit juice. Dark beers, such as *Dunkel* and *Schwarzbier*, also enjoy great popularity. Breweries have their own specialities. In Bamberg, they produce *Rauchbier*, which has a light smokiness; in Kulmbach it is *Eisbock*, which gains its thicker consistency through a freezing process.

Wheat beer, Berliner Weisse

Seasonal autumn beer, Bock

The largest pub in the world, created during the Oktoberfest

Drinking Beer

In Germany, beer is served with a head. Pouring lager from a barrel is supposed to take about 10 minutes, so the head sinks to the regulation level and has a thick consistency. A small beer is normally 0.3 litre, a large one 0.5 litre. In Bavaria, however, a large beer is served in a *Mass*, a tankard holding 1 litre. When travelling in Germany, order the brew of the local brewery, ideally in a *Bierkeller* or *Bierstube* (pub) and, in summer, in a *Biergarten* (beer garden). The largest gardens are in Bavaria – Munich's *Hirschgarten* caters for 8,000 beer drinkers. The Oktoberfest, which is celebrated each year in Munich *(see p231)*, is the largest beer festival in the world.

How Beer is Brewed

The method of brewing beer that is now virtually standard dates from the 19th century, when Czech brewers first produced bottom-fermented beers at lower temperatures. The method was perfected by Gabriel Sedlmayr. Each brewery has its secrets, but the initial stages of production are the same.

A climbing plant, hops are trained to grow up special supports

Mashing vat

Barley and hops

1 The main ingredients in the production of beer are barley, hops and crystal-clear water. Other grains, including wheat and rice, can also be used – for example *Weizenbier* is made from wheat rather than barley. The first stage of brewing is malting, when the grains are soaked and left to germinate. After a few days, these are dried and then milled.

2 The milled barley is mixed with warm water and placed in a copper mashing vat. During the mashing process, the starches in the grain turn into fermentable sugars. The mash is then filtered to separate out a liquid, known as the wort, from the mash.

3 The wort is put into a copper vessel with the hops and then cooked. Depending on the amount of hops added, the beer will be more or less bitter. Traditionally the hops are added to the vessel by hand, in carefully measured proportions. Sometimes, however, they are added, as required, during the cooking process.

4 The wort is filtered again, cooled and combined with yeast. Fermentation then takes place. At temperatures above 20° C (68° F), the liquid reaches "top fermentation", which takes 3–5 days. "Bottom fermentation", where the temperature is below 12° C (54° F), takes 7–10 days.

5 The young beer produced by fermentation is left to rest in special containers that enable a higher pressure to be maintained. During this resting stage, which can last from a couple of weeks to a year or even longer, the beer matures. The effect of resting the beer is to make it stronger. Resting takes place in metal or traditional wooden barrels.

6 The mature beer, which is ready to be sold, is then transferred to bottles or cans and pasteurized. This process removes micro-organisms that threaten the quality of the beer.

Traditional wooden barrels containing resting beer

Sport in Germany

Sport has long enjoyed a significant role in German life both for active participants and spectators. The country regularly produces world champions in a variety of activities, including football, tennis and motor racing. Excellent facilities exist throughout the country for taking part in sporting activities, including sailing, swimming, climbing and skiing as well as in field- or track-based events. Southern Germany plays host to a variety of winter sports and competitions.

Robert Harting taking part in the discus competition at a Golden League meeting

Football

The largest sports organization in the country, the German Football Association has over 6 million registered members in some 25,000 clubs. The national team has won the World Cup four times – in 1954, 1974, 1990 and 2014 – and the European Cup in 1972, 1980 and 1996.

One of the outstanding figures in German football is Franz Beckenbauer, who was a member of the team that won the European Cup in 1972 and the World Cup in 1974. He trained the team that took second place in the 1986 World Cup and first place in 1990. Beckenbauer was twice named the best footballer in Europe.

The best-known club is Bayern München, which has won the German Cup a record 24 times. Matches between teams in the elite *Bundesliga* enjoy a great following. League matches are held on Friday, Saturday and Sunday afternoons while European Cup games are usually held on Wednesday evenings. The club teams include a significant number of players from abroad. The 2006 World Cup was held in Germany.

Competing in Hamburg's annual Deutsches Spring Derby

Show-Jumping and Equestrian Events

Show-jumping is another sport at which Germany excels. Since its introduction to the Olympic Games in 1912, German riders have won more than 30 gold medals and many more have been awarded silver and bronze. Major equestrian events are held in Hamburg and Aachen in June. Hamburg's Derby Week is popular with racing fans.

Lawn Tennis

The German Tennis Association is the largest in the world with over 2 million members, belonging to some 10,200 clubs. From the mid-1980s, Germany became one of the world's most successful tennis nations thanks to some outstanding players. In 1985, aged 17, Boris Becker was the youngest player to win the Wimbledon championships. He repeated his achievement in 1986 and 1989 and was runner-up to fellow-German Michael Stich in 1991. From 1987–91 Steffi Graf was ranked number one among the world's female tennis players.

Athletics

During the Cold War period, East and West German athletes competed against each other for the glory of their rival political systems as much as for the love of their sport. The extraordinary achievements of the East German athletes during that time have since been tarnished by revelations of systematic drug abuse. Since reunification, some athletes have managed to maintain their reputations, but the majority have not.

Germany's most important event, the Internationales Stadionfest (DKB-ISTAF), is held each year in Berlin, as the climax of the season.

Football match between Borussia Moenchengladbach and SC Freiburg, Moenchengladbach

Formula One

Back in the 1930s, motor-racing was dominated by the famous "Silver Arrows", made by Mercedes-Benz. Formula One has been a decidedly German discipline since its beginnings in 1950. In all the events there have always been at least three German drivers taking part. The German Formula One Grand Prix is held each July at the Hockenheim-Ring, near Heidelberg. In most years there is a second Grand Prix at the Nürburgring circuit. This is dubbed the European Grand Prix or the Luxembourg Grand Prix.

Germany's former leading Formula One driver, Michael Schumacher, won the World Championship in 1994 and 1995 and every year from 2000 to 2004. A rising talent is Sebastian Vettel, who was World Champion from 2010–2013.

The Hockenheim race track near Heidelberg

As well as in the German Alps, which have the most popular ski resorts, excellent conditions exist for downhill and cross-country skiing in the less glamorous and less expensive Black Forest in Baden-Württemberg, and the Harz Mountains in Saxony-Anhalt.

Cycling

Cycling enjoys a great following in Germany. The Tour de France is broadcast simultaneously by two television stations, and ever-increasing numbers of people are taking part in the sport, both for pleasure and competitively. Success on the cycle track has long been a German tradition, but Jan Ullrich exceeded expectations when he won gold in the long distance at the Sydney Olympics in 2000 and silver in the 2012 London Games.

Sailing

Kieler Woche is the most important regatta in the world, according to Paul Henderson, the President of the International Sailing Federation. On 1 September 1881, five officers of the Emperor's navy held a yachting race in the Bay of Kiel,

Severin Freund at a round of the FIS Ski Jumping World Cup in Willingen

Skiing

Since 1953, the last week of December and the first week of January have been dominated by the Four Ski Jumps Championship for ski jumpers. This classic event, which is held in Oberstdorf and Garmisch-Partenkirchen in Germany, as well as in Innsbruck and Bischofshofen in Austria, attracts several thousand spectators and millions of television viewers. German athletes have gained first place in this competition 16 times over the years.

as it was then called. The following year 20 yachts competed while thousands of spectators watched from the shore. The championship went on to become an international event, which gained in prestige as the Emperor took part in each race from 1894 until 1914.

Today it is traditional for the president of the German Federal Republic to formally open the regatta (in the last week of June) in which thousands of yachts from many countries take part.

Swimming

Swimming, more than any other sport in Germany, has seen a decline in success since reunification and the subsequent cessation of competition between East and West. At the 1988 Olympics in Seoul, for example, Kristin Otto won six gold medals. In 2000, the reunified German team returned from Sydney having gained only three bronze medals. Two figures who rose to the top in the past are Michael Gross, who was a member of the West German team, and Franziska van Almsick, a member of the East German team.

Franziska von Almsick during the German Swimming Championships

GERMANY THROUGH THE YEAR

Germans love to have fun and this is evident from the huge number of light-hearted events that are held throughout the year. Virtually every town has a calendar of festivals and fairs. These include folk festivals connected with local traditions – for example. celebrating the asparagus or grape harvest. Many towns preserve the tradition of an annual fair – or Jahrmarkt – known in Westphalia as *Kirmes* and in Bavaria as *Dult*. Germany is also known for its music and film festivals, which attract an international audience, as well as for organizing major international trade fairs, such as the annual Frankfurt Book Fair.

Witches participating in the Walpurgisnacht celebrations in Thale

Spring

Spring is an idyllic time to arrive in Germany. In the high mountains, conditions are still ideal for skiing, while in the valleys everything is already in bloom. In April and May the first spring fairs and festivals are held. Spring is also time for the traditional solemn observance of Easter and its associated celebrations. May Day, which is also International Labour Day, is marked both by traditional festivities and, in some cities, by demonstrations.

March

Sommergewinn *(3 weekends before Easter)* Eisenach. The largest folk festival in Thuringia, linked with a fair.
CeBIT *(beginning of March)* Hanover. International trade fairs dedicated to information technology, telecommunications and automation.
Easter During Holy Week, Passion concerts are held throughout the country and colourful church services take place, particularly in rural Catholic areas. On Easter Sunday, in cities in the Luzyce region, horse races and a gala take place.
Leipziger Buchmesse *(mid-March)* Leipzig. International book fair, with antiquarian books.

April

Thüringer Bach-Wochen *(April)*. Celebration of the life and works of Johann Sebastian Bach with concerts and lectures: held in Arnstadt, Eisenach, Erfurt, Gotha, Mühlhausen and Weimar.
Hannover Messe *(2nd half of April)* Hanover. International industrial trade fairs.

The International Dixieland Festival, held annually in Dresden in May

Hamburger Dom *(April, August and November)* Hamburg. The largest folk festival in northern Germany, held three times a year.
Walpurgisnacht *(30 April/1 May)*. On the witches' sabbath, witches gather on Brocken Mountain and in several other places in the Harz mountains.
Kurzfilmtage *(end April/ beginning of May)*. Oberhausen. The International Festival of Short Films has been held here since 1955.

May

Maibaumaufstellen *(1 May)*. In Bavarian villages, maypoles are decorated with highly ornamental wreaths.
Rhein in Flammen *(May– September)*. Festivals with firework displays, in towns in the Rhine Valley.
Hafengeburtstag *(8–10 May)* Hamburg. A huge festival with fireworks, regatta and a parade of sailing boats.
Ruhrfestspiele *(May–June)* Recklinghausen. Cultural festival with a number of concerts and performances.
International Dixieland Festival *(2nd week of May)* Dresden. A traditional jazz festival has been held here since 1971.
Blutritt *(Friday after Ascension)* Weingarten. A horseback procession carrying religious relics around the town – held here for over 450 years.
Leineweber Markt *(end of May)* Bielefeld. Street theatre, jazz and folk concerts.

Summer

In Germany the summer is a time of great open-air festivals and other outdoor events and activities. Nearly every town and village has its festival with a parade, street shows, concerts and fairs. In many places there are colourful illuminations and firework displays. Banquets and knights' tournaments are held in historic castles, while concert series are organized in palaces and castles with the tourist particularly in mind. In June, a number of classical music festivals take place, while July is a popular month for water-related festivals.

Yacht race during the annual Kieler Woche regatta in Kiel

June

Bachfest Leipzig (early June) Leipzig. International music competition dedicated to Johann Sebastian Bach.
Internationales Stadionfest (DKB-ISTAF), (2nd Sunday in June) Berlin. The largest athletics event of the season.
Luther's Wedding (second weekend in June) Wittenberg. A celebration of the marriage of Martin Luther to Katharina von Bora with music and a parade.
Spreewaldfest (June) Spreewald. Festivals are held throughout the summer in Lübben and other villages.
Fronleichnam. Observed in Catholic majority states. Processions in towns in Bavaria and in Cologne.
Christopher Street Day (mid-June). Gay and lesbian parades held in many cities, including Berlin and Cologne.

A wedding couple during the Landshuter Hochzeit festival

Kieler Woche (3rd week in June) Kiel. Huge regatta with concerts and fairs.
Open-Air-Saison (4th week in June, beginning of July) Berlin. Opera festival held on outdoor stages.
Schützenfest (June). The traditional start of the hunting season. Celebrated in many north German cities.

July

Landshuter Hochzeit (every 4th summer: next in 2017) Landshut. Re-enactment of the wedding feast of Georg, son of Duke Ludwig the Rich and Polish Princess Jadwiga. Costumed wedding

procession and medieval tournament.
Lights of Cologne (early July) Cologne. Very popular, big fireworks event.
Schwörmontag (penultimate Monday) Ulm. Folk festival with a parade by the Danube.
Kinderzeche (3rd Monday) Dinkelsbühl. Ten-day folk festival commemorating the events of the Thirty Years' War (1618–48).
Richard-Wagner-Festspiele (last week July/August) Bayreuth. Festival dedicated to the works of Richard Wagner.
Wikingerfest (even years) Schleswig. Historical festival with costumed participants, tournaments and regattas.
Maschseefest (late July) Hanover (Hannover). Summer outdoor carnival on the shores of Lake Maschsee.

August

Zissel (beginning of August) Kassel. Picturesque folk festival with parades, markets and concerts.
Mainfest. Frankfurt am Main. Feast of the river Main.
Gäubodenfest (mid-August) Straubing. Folk festival with a market and beer tasting.
Weindorf (end August) Stuttgart. Huge wine festival with wines served along with typical Swabian cuisine.

Performance of *Tannhäuser* at Richard-Wagner-Festspiele, Bayreuth

Autumn

Autumn is an extremely popular time for tourism in Germany, especially September and early October when many cities, including Berlin and Munich, organize cultural events and important festivals. The autumn is also the time when the most significant trade fairs and great sporting events take place. At this time, also, conditions in the mountains and countryside continue to be ideal for outdoor activities such as walking and cycling.

September

Berliner Festwochen, Berlin. Lasting all month, this is a major series of cultural events, opera performances, exhibitions and various literary events.
Beethovenfestival, Bonn. A musical festival celebrating the works of Beethoven in the city where he was born.
Heilbronner Herbst *(1st Saturday)* Heilbronn. Popular wine festival, which also includes parades and firework displays.
Popkomm *(mid-September)* Berlin. One of the world's biggest music industry conferences, which also features public performances by up-and-coming bands and DJs.
Berlin-Marathon *(mid-late September)* Berlin. Marathon

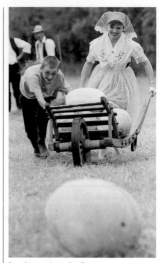

Pumpkin race during Dorffest

through the streets of the city centre, taking in several notable landmarks, with runners in various age groups and the participation of the disabled in wheelchairs.
Oktoberfest *(last two weeks of September)* Munich. World-famous beer festival held over 16 days, beginning with a parade through the city's streets. Ceremonial removal of the bung from a new barrel of beer that has been brewed for the festival.
Plärrer *(May and September)* Augsburg. Two-week festival held twice a year, considered

one of the most important in Swabia.
Dorffest im Spreewald *(end of September)* Lehde. Folk festival.
Cannstatter Wasen *(end September/beginning October)* Stuttgart. The second largest beer festival in the world.

October

Tag der Deutschen Einheit *(3 October)*. National holiday, established after re-unification. Concerts, parades and meetings.
Frankfurter Buchmesse *(2nd week in October)* Frankfurt am Main. The world's largest book fair, which attracts publishers from around the world and also features talks by authors.
Freimarkt *(mid-October)* Bremen. Two-week folk festival beginning with a procession.
Liszt-Tage Weimar. Celebration of the life and work of Franz Liszt, with concerts at which world-class musicians are invited to perform.
Colmansfest *(2nd Sunday)* Schwangau. Religious festival featuring hundreds of horses and decorated carriages.
Kasseler Musiktage *(end of October)* Kassel. One of Europe's longest-established classical music festivals.

November

Weinfest *(1st weekend in November)* Cochem. Festival celebrating the removal of the bung from the first barrel of young Mosel wine.
Martinsfest *(11 November)*. St Martin's Day is celebrated in northern Baden and the Rhineland with fairs and the essential roast goose. In the Rhine Valley, St Martin's Day signifies the beginning of the Carnival season.
Internationales Film-festival *(2nd week in November)* Mannheim-Heidelberg. Annual festival of short, documentary and educational films.

The International Book Fair in Frankfurt am Main

Berlinale – the grand festival of world cinema

Fastnacht, also known as **Fasnet, Fasching** or **Karneval** (Shrovetide). Carnival is celebrated enthusiastically in virtually every region of Germany. The most interesting events are held in the Rhine Valley, and particularly in Cologne. *Karneval am Rhein*, which marks the lasts three days of the Carnival, begins on the Thursday of the week before Ash Wednesday with a women's parade, known as *Weiberfastnacht*. On the Monday there is a superb costume parade, known as *Rosenmontagsumzug*.

Costumed revellers on the streets of Cologne during Carnival

Winter

December is synonymous with Christmas festivities. Every city has fairs where you can buy Christmas-tree decorations, delicacies and presents. In December, shops have longer opening hours and the skiing season begins in the Alps. January and February are a time for parties and balls (the Carnival season), with enjoyment reaching a peak in the last few days of the season. Then the fun continues all weekend from Thursday, reaching a height on *Rosenmontag* then diminishing on the last Tuesday of Carnival.

December

Christkindelsmarkt and **Weihnachtsmarkt**. Christmas fairs are held from the beginning

The famous Christmas market in the city of Nuremberg

of the month until Christmas Eve. The most beautiful are in Baden-Württemberg and in Bavaria, while the most renowned is held in Nuremberg.
Christmas *(25/26 December).* Traditionally celebrated throughout Germany. A Christmas tree is considered essential, together with presents and delicacies.
New Year's Eve *(31 December).* The New Year is greeted at balls, opera galas, in restaurants, clubs, private houses and in the streets and squares of city centres.

January

Four Ski Jumps Tournament *(begins 1 January).* Renowned tournament for ski-jumping held annually in Garmisch-Partenkirchen.
Sechs-Tage-Rennen *(early January)* Berlin. Spectacular cycle races with associated events, held in Berlin Velodrome.
Grüne Woche *(2nd week)* Berlin. International trade fairs dedicated to agriculture, animal breeding and the food processing industry. Producers from all over the world offer specialities from their own national cuisines.

February

Berlinale–Internationale Filmfestspiele *(2nd and 3rd weeks)* Berlin. International film festival in which major stars participate.

Public Holidays

Neujahr *New Year* (1 Jan).

Hl. Dreikönige *Three Kings* (6 Jan: Bavaria, Baden-Württemberg, Saxony-Anhalt).

Karfreitag *Good Friday.*

Ostern *Easter.*

Maifeiertag/Tag der Arbeit *Labour Day.*

Christi Himmelfahrt *Ascension.*

Pfingsten *Pentecost.*

Fronleichnam *Corpus Christi* (Bavaria, Baden-Württemberg, Hesse, North Rhine Valley-Westphalia, Rhine Valley-Palatinate and Saar).

Mariä Himmelfahrt *Assumption of the Blessed Virgin Mary* (15 Aug: Bavaria, Saar).

Nationalfeiertag *Reunification of Germany Day* (3 Oct).

Allerheiligen *All Saints* (1 Nov: Bavaria, Baden-Württemberg, North Rhine Valley-Westphalia, Rhine Valley-Palatinate).

Weihnachten *Christmas* (25/26 Dec).

The German Climate

Germany lies in a temperate climatic zone. In the north of the country, with marine influences predominating, summers tend to be quite cold and winters mild, with relatively high rainfall. In the eastern part of the country, however, the climate is more continental and this produces harsher winters and hotter summers. Germany's highest rainfall and the lowest temperatures are recorded in the Alps.

SCHLESWIG-HOLSTEIN

°C (F)	Jan	Apr	Jul	Oct
Average daily maximum temperature	2.2 (36)	10.5 (51)	20 (68)	13 (55)
Average daily minimum temperature	-2 (28)	2.2 (36) / 3 (37)	12 (54)	7 (45)
Average daily amount of sunshine	1.3 hrs	5.5 hrs	7 hrs	3 hrs
Average monthly rainfall	80 mm	55 mm	92 mm	90 mm

Average daily maximum temperature
Average daily minimum temperature
Average daily amount of sunshine
Average monthly rainfall

BREMEN, HAMBURG, LOWER SAXONY

°C (F)	Jan	Apr	Jul	Oct
	3.2 (38)	12.5 (55)	22 (72)	14 (57)
	-2 (28)	3.5 (38)	12 (54)	6 (43)
	1.3 hrs	5 hrs	6 hrs	3 hrs
	56 mm	48 mm	69 mm	55 mm

NORTH RHINE-WESTPHALIA

°C (F)	Jan	Apr	Jul	Oct
	4.5 (40)	14 (57)	23 (73)	15 (59)
	-1 (30)	3.6 (38)	12.5 (55)	6 (43)
	1.5 hrs	5 hrs	6.5 hrs	3.7 hrs
	62 mm	54 mm	84 mm	55 mm

HESSE

°C (F)	Jan	Apr	Jul	Oct
	3 (37)	14 (57)	24 (75)	14 (57)
	-2 (28)	4 (39)	13 (55)	6 (43)
	1.3 hrs	5 hrs	7.4 hrs	3.3 hrs
	44 mm	51 mm	63 mm	50 mm

RHINELAND-PALATINATE, SAARLAND

°C (F)	Jan	Apr	Jul	Oct
	3 (37)	13 (55)	23 (73)	14 (57)
	-1.5 (29)	4 (39)	12 (54)	7 (45)
	1.3 hrs	5 hrs	7 hrs	3 hrs
	60 mm	53 mm	69 mm	65 mm

BADEN-WÜRTTEMBERG

°C (F)	Jan	Apr	Jul	Oct
	4 (39)	14 (57)	23 (73)	15 (59)
	-1 (30)	5 (41)	13 (55)	7 (45)
	1.7 hrs	5 hrs	8 hrs	4 hrs
	60 mm	80 mm	95 mm	66 mm

Flensburg
Schleswig
Kiel
Hamburg
Bremen
Nienburg
Hanover
Münster
Paderborn
Dortmund
Göttingen
Düsseldorf
Kassel
Cologne
Siegen
Aachen
Bonn
Marburg
Fulda
Koblenz
Frankfurt am Main
Mainz
Trier
Würzburg
Mannheim
Saarbrücken
Heidelberg
Karlsruhe
Stuttgart
Ulm
Freiburg im Breisgau
Konstanz

0 km 100
0 miles 100

MECKLENBURG-LOWER POMERANIA

month	Jan	Apr	Jul	Oct
°C (F)			21 (70)	
		10 (50)	14 (57)	12.5 (55)
	3 (37)	4 (39)		7.5 (46)
	-2 (28)			
☀	1.5 hrs	5.5 hrs	7.5 hrs	3.5 hrs
☂	40 mm	42 mm	72 mm	50 mm

BRANDENBURG

month	Jan	Apr	Jul	Oct
°C (F)			24 (75)	
		13 (55)	13 (55)	14 (57)
	2 (36)	3.5 (38)		6 (43)
	-3 (27)			
☀	1.5 hrs	5.5 hrs	7.5 hrs	3.7 hrs
☂	44 mm	44 mm	52 mm	35 mm

BERLIN

month	Jan	Apr	Jul	Oct
°C (F)			24 (75)	
		13 (55)	13 (55)	13 (55)
	2 (36)	4 (39)		5 (41)
	-4 (25)			
☀	1.9 hrs	6.4 hrs	8.1 hrs	4.1 hrs
☂	43 mm	41 mm	70 mm	47 mm

SAXONY-ANHALT

month	Jan	Apr	Jul	Oct
°C (F)			23 (73)	
		13 (55)	12 (54)	14 (57)
	2.4 (36)	3.5 (58)		6 (43)
	-3 (27)			
☀	1.5 hrs	5 hrs	7 hrs	3.5 hrs
☂	33 mm	40 mm	48 mm	29 mm

SAXONY

month	Jan	Apr	Jul	Oct
°C (F)			22 (72)	
		12 (54)	12 (54)	13 (55)
	1.5 (35)	3 (37)		6 (43)
	-4 (39)			
☀	2 hrs	4.5 hrs	6.6 hrs	4 hrs
☂	42 mm	55 mm	76 mm	47 mm

THURINGIA

month	Jan	Apr	Jul	Oct
°C (F)			22 (72)	
		12 (54)	12 (54)	13 (55)
	1.5 (35)	3 (37)		5 (41)
	-3.5 (26)			
☀	1.7 hrs	5 hrs	7 hrs	4 hrs
☂	24.5 mm	45 mm	46 mm	33 mm

BAVARIA

month	Jan	Apr	Jul	Oct
°C (F)			23 (73)	
		14 (57)	12 (54)	13 (55)
	2 (36)	3 (37)		3 (37)
	-4 (25)			
☀	1.5 hrs	5 hrs	7.5 hrs	4 hrs
☂	46 mm	47 mm	69 mm	45 mm

MUNICH

month	Jan	Apr	Jul	Oct
°C (F)			23 (73)	
		13 (55)	12 (54)	13 (55)
	1 (34)	3 (37)		4 (39)
	-6 (43)			
☀	2.2 hrs	6 hrs	7.7 hrs	4.6 hrs
☂	59 mm	62 mm	140 mm	67 mm

Map labels: Bergen, Rostock, Wismar, Güstrow, Lübeck, Neubrandenburg, Wittenberge, Neuruppin, Stendal, Berlin, Brandenburg, Potsdam, Magdeburg, Luckenwalde, Dessau, Lutherstadt Wittenberg, Cottbus, Halle, Leipzig, Dresden, Eisenach, Altenburg, Weimar, Gotha, Chemnitz, Plauen, Hof, Bamberg, Nuremberg, Regensburg, Neuburg, Passau, Augsburg, Munich, Kempten, Garmisch-Partenkirchen

THE HISTORY OF GERMANY

Germany is a country of cultural and religious contrasts. Regional differences in culture, language and traditions arose from the historical division of the country into many small states. Such differences have been further accentuated by the recent experience of generations of Germans who, until 1990, grew up under two conflicting social systems: capitalism and communism.

Early History

In the 1st millennium BC, the basins of the Rhine, Danube and Main rivers were settled by Celts, who had been largely displaced by Germanic tribes by the 2nd century BC. In the 1st century BC the Roman legions waged wars with the Germans, and conquered the territories west of the Rhine. The settlements they founded there later developed into towns like Trier, Mainz, Cologne and Xanten. The Romans made numerous attempts to conquer the eastern regions between the Rhine and the Elbe rivers. They eventually reached the Elbe at the end of the 1st century BC, but the Germans, under the leadership of Arminius, also known as Germanus, defeated the Roman armies in the Teutoburg Forest in AD 9, and so ended their presence in this region. A system of fortifications, or *limes*, built in the 2nd century along the course of the Danube and the Rhine, divided the region into two: *Germania Romana*, the Roman province, and *Germania Libra*, free Germany. The tribes of German origin,

notably the Goths, often entered into alliances with the Romans. In the 5th century, however, they took advantage of Rome's weakness to appropriate parts of the empire for themselves.

Early Middle Ages

After the collapse of the Roman Empire, the area between the Rhine and the Elbe was ruled by the Franks, who gradually converted to Christianity from the 6th century. One of the most important figures in this process was the 8th-century missionary, St Boniface. When Charlemagne was crowned Emperor in 800, the territory of present-day Germany became part of the Frankish Empire. The Empire was partitioned by the Treaty of Verdun in 843, with the eastern part going to Ludwig the German. In the 10th century the kingdom, which was made up of numerous tribal states, passed to the house of Liudolf. Otto I, son of Heinrich I and the first king from this Saxon family, was crowned Emperor in 962 after several political and military victories, in particular his defeat of the Magyars.

			843 Treaty of Verdun and dissolution of the Frankish state	919 Coronation of the Saxon Heinrich I	962 Otto I crowned Emperor
754 Death of St Boniface	Golden Roman mask				
700		**800**		**900**	**1000**
785 Baptism of Widukind, Duke of Saxony		814 Death of Charlemagne		936 Otto I crowned King	
		800 Charlemagne crowned Emperor of the Franks		955 Otto I defeats the Magyars at the Lech River near Augsburg	8th-century reliquary

◀ *Germania Awakening*, a patriotic 19th-century work by Christian Köhler

Stained-glass window in Augsburg cathedral

Consolidating Power

With Otto being crowned emperor, the dynasty of the Saxon house of Liudolf acceded to power. It gave the country three further rulers – Otto II, Otto III and Heinrich II. In the year 925 Otto I annexed Lotharingia (present-day Lorraine). On the eastern frontier he created two "marks", the Nordmark and the Ostmark, as buffer states designed to subjugate the Slav-populated regions east of the Oder River. After Heinrich II's death, the house of the Salian Franks took the imperial throne and used their authority to limit the power of the local feudal dukes.

The Investiture Controversy

In the 11th century the empire came into conflict with the papacy. Matters came to a head in the so-called "investiture controversy". Pope Gregory VII asserted the church's right to appoint bishops. Emperor Heinrich IV, meanwhile, who had been relying on the support of the clergy he had appointed, called his bishops together and

Enamelled Romanesque medallion, dating from c.1150

asked the Pope to step down. Pope Gregory VII excommunicated Heinrich. The dukes of Saxony used the opportunity to appoint a king in opposition to Heinrich, and the Pope attempted to intervene in the dispute. Heinrich IV saw himself forced to march to Canossa in Italy, where the Pope had sought refuge, in order to stop his empire from falling apart. Doing penance in this way forced the Pope to withdraw his excommunication. However, the dispute did not end there, but continued for several years, finally ending with the Signing of the Concordat of Worms in 1122.

Hohenstaufens and Welfs

After the Salian dynasty died out in 1125 and the brief reign of Lothar III of the Saxon dynasty, another long drawn-out conflict broke out, between the houses of Hohenstaufen and Welf (known in Italian as Ghibellines and Guelphs). Imperial power went to the Hohenstaufens, while the greatest political victories were scored by Friedrich I Barbarossa (meaning "red beard"). He intended gradually to break up his subject principalities and to rule them under a feudal system. The 12th century also saw further expansion eastwards and northwards into areas inhabited by the

12th-century reliquary from the Welf family vaults

1027 Coronation of Konrad II, first Emperor of the Salians

1138 Coronation of Konrad III, first Hohenstaufen Emperor

1155 Coronation of Friedrich I Barbarossa as Emperor

1000　　　　**1050**　　　　**1100**　　　　**1150**

11th-century reliquary cross

1074 Beginning of Investiture Struggle

1077 Heinrich IV does penance at Canossa

1122 The Concordat of Worms

Portable altar from the vaults of the Welfs

northwestern Slavic tribes. From the start of the 13th century Barbarossa also conquered territories occupied by the Baltic peoples and the Estonians, which involved armed expeditions by the North German cities and orders of knights.

Friedrich II, crowned Emperor in 1220, was also King of Sicily and his Italian interests brought further conflict with the papacy. Ultimately his policies brought about the collapse of imperial power. After his death in 1250, his successor was unable to find any support, which led to the period known as the Great Interregnum.

The Interregnum

The fall of the Hohenstaufens marked the end of the old imperial system. The absence of an overall ruler led to a breakdown in law and order, and resulted in the rise of the *Raubritter* (robber-barons). To protect their common interests, the trading cities set up alliances. The collapse of imperial power, and the decline in the power of the dukes thus gradually led to an increase in the power of the German cities.

From the beginning, the imperial throne had been elective, with dukes electing the emperor from the male members of the dynasty. There was also no capital city, as the emperors moved from one city to another, thus spreading the costs of maintaining the imperial court among different

Emperor Rudolf I of Habsburg

duchies. In the 13th century a system evolved by which only seven elector-dukes had the right to elect the emperor. These were the Margrave of Brandenburg, the Elector of Palatine (or the Bavarian dukes), the Duke of Saxony, the King of Bohemia and the Archbishops of Trier, Cologne and Mainz. Starting with Rudolf I of Habsburg, who was elected king of Germany in 1273, until 1438 the kings came from the rival houses of Habsburg, Wittelsbach and Luxemburg. After 1312, the same houses also competed for the title of Emperor. The most outstanding of the 14th-century rulers of Germany was Karl IV of Luxemburg, who resided permanently in Prague. In 1338 the electors had rejected the requirement for the Pope to confirm election results. In 1356 Karl IV issued the "Golden Bull" which underlined the federal nature of the state, and clarified the rules for electing its leader.

A "Minneteppich" – part of a medieval tapestry, depicting a variety of human traits and a griffin, the mythical beast

1312 Heinrich VII crowned Emperor

1250 Beginning of the Great Interregnum

Silver coin from 1369

1200   1250   1300   1350

1273 End of the Great Interregnum and coronation of Rudolf I

1348 Prague University founded

1386 Heidelberg University founded

1356 Golden Bull issued

The Hanseatic League

The German Hanseatic League, or Hanse, was only one of many guilds of traders or cities that existed in the Middle Ages, but its important historical role made it one of the best known. Established in the 13th century, it reached its peak in the 14th century and declined again in the 16th century. Over 160 cities, primarily the trading cities of northern Germany, but also including Baltic ports as far afield as Visby, Riga and Tallinn, joined the League. It exercised total control over trade from the Baltic in the east to England in the west. The Hanseatic cities were among the wealthiest in Europe, and crafts and the arts flourished there.

Madonna of the Roses
15th-century painting by Stefan Lochner of the Cologne School.

The Wise and Foolish Maidens
The flowering of art in the Hanseatic cities brought about works such as this portal of Magdeburg Cathedral.

Hanse ships, loaded with merchandise, entering the harbour

Revenue officials awaiting the cargo

Crucifix in Lübeck Cathedral
This crucifix is one of only few painted wood-carvings made by Bernt Notke of Lübeck that have survived until today.

Round wooden cranes with swivelling arms were used to unload ships. One example still survives in Lüneburg.

Cogs
Heavy, flat-bottomed sailing ships with limited manoeuvrability, cogs were fishermen's and merchants' boats or navy vessels in the North Sea and the Baltic from the 12th to the 14th centuries.

Panoramic view of Lübeck
The vast port town of Lübeck was the largest
Hanseatic city. This 15th-century woodcut shows a
view of the city with its numerous church spires.

The Hanseatic Cities

In the major Hanseatic cities, the
most prominent buildings grew
up around the *Markt* (market
square) and along the streets
that led to the port. The market
square would contain the
Rathaus (town hall), with its
multi-functional interiors, and
the equally splendid banqueting
halls and ballrooms, such as the
Gürzenich in Cologne. The main
cathedrals in the cities were
dedicated either to St Mary or
St Nicholas. The gabled
residential houses had narrow
façades with distinctive portals.
The townscape of the port areas
was dominated by granaries,
warehouses and numerous cranes.
The cities were all enclosed and
protected by solid fortifications.

Harbour
officials in
their offices

The Leichter
was a harbour
boat used to
carry cargo from
the ships to
the warehouses.

Hamburg
merchants

**Russian
merchants**,
recognizable by
their distinctive
clothing, are
engrossed
in intense
negotiations.

The Port of Hamburg
*Hamburg, along with Bremen, Lübeck and
Gdansk, was one of the leading Hanseatic
cities. In the 14th century, it was the main
centre for trade between the North Sea and
the Baltic. This miniature, showing the port
of Hamburg, dates from the 15th century.*

The town hall in Brunswick
(Braunschweig), with its open
upper arcades and statues of the
Welfs, is one of the finest surviving
Hanseatic secular buildings.

The Kröpeliner Tor in Rostock
is one of 22 towers on the
defensive walls around the
medieval city centre.

Jan Hus being burned at the stake

The Hussite Wars and the Habsburg Dynasty

The last king and emperor of the house of Luxemburg, Sigismund, brought an end to the "Great Schism" in the Western church that had persisted since 1378. The Council of Constance, which he called in 1414, led to the election of a single, rather than two rival popes. However, new religious controversy was provoked by the death sentence for heresy passed in 1415 on Jan Hus, a religious reformer from Bohemia. The ensuing Hussite Wars ravaged the northern and western regions of Germany.

From 1482 the imperial crown went to the Habsburgs, who

Title page of the first German edition of the Bible

retained it until 1740. Attempts at political reform in the second half of the 15th century failed. The most ambitious reformer was Maximilian I. He called an Imperial Tribunal in 1495 which set about transferring part of the king's authority to the judiciary; however, it did not result in any great practical changes, although it gave slightly more power to the *Reichstag*, the imperial parliament.

The Reformation

Germany entered the 16th century as a country simmering with social conflict, gradually becoming steeped in the ideas of humanism, thanks to the writings of Erasmus of Rotterdam

Lion-shaped water jug (1540)

and others. The rise of Martin Luther, who in 1517 nailed his 95 Theses to the door of the Castle Church in Wittenberg, and who opposed the trade in indulgences conducted by the clergy, set the Reformation in motion *(see pp130–31)*. The idea of ecclesiastical reform propounded by Luther gained a growing following. His supporters included princes who hoped to profit from the secularization of church property, as well as other social classes that simply saw an opportunity to improve their lot. In 1519 Maximilian I died, and Karl V was elected to succeed him. Karl's interests were focused on Spain and the Netherlands,

1419–36 Hussite Wars

c.1450 The first printing press

Maximilian I

1540 The first stock exchanges are set up in Augsburg and Nuremberg

1517 Luther's Theses and the start of the Reformation

1400

1450

1500

1414–18 Council of Constance

1438 Coronation of Albrecht II, first Emperor of the House of Habsburg

1495 Edict banning the waging of private wars

1522 The Knights' War

1524–25 The Peasants' War

Urban life in Germany in the early 16th century, in a painting by Jörg Breu the Elder (c.1475–1537)

the religious conflicts. However, the influence of the Counter-Reformation in the early 17th century ended this stability. The Protestant Union and Catholic League were established in 1608 and 1609 respectively. Unrest in Prague, where the states with a Protestant majority opposed the election of the Catholic Ferdinand II as king of Bohemia, began the Thirty Years' War. This religious war quickly spread throughout Germany, and also drew in Denmark, Spain, Sweden and France. Much of the country and many towns were laid waste, and vast numbers of people died. Finally, in 1648, the German states, France and Sweden signed the Peace of Westphalia in Münster, resulting in major losses of territory for Germany, mainly in the north. A new political system emerged, with the German princes enjoying complete political independence, under a weakened emperor and pope. The second half of the 17th century was marked by the rebuilding of towns and the hard work of restoring the ruined economic infrastructure.

and he was unable to prevent the spread of Lutheranism. The unrest led to rebellions such as the Knights' War of 1522 and the Peasants' War of 1524, and these were followed by continuous religious conflict. In 1530 the Protestants set up the League of Schmalkalden, which was finally broken up by the Emperor in the war of 1546–7. These basically religious clashes ultimately led to the division of Germany into a northern Protestant part and a Catholic south, a situation that was sanctioned in 1555 by the Peace of Augsburg. This established the principle of *cuius regio, eius religio*, which meant that each ruler had the right to decide on the faith of the region, and the only option left for anyone of a different persuasion was to move elsewhere.

The Thirty Years' War

The second half of the 16th century was relatively stable for Germany, despite

A scene in the Thirty Years' War, in a painting by Wilhelm von Diez

Goethe in the Roman Campagna by Johann H. W. Tischbein (1787)

Absolutism and the Rise of Prussia

In the second half of the 17th century and throughout the 18th century, Germany was a loose federation of small, politically weak states in the west, and much more powerful states in the east and the south – Saxony, which was ruled by the house of Wettin, and Bavaria, ruled by the Wittelsbachs. However, the rising star was the state of Brandenburg, ruled by the house of Hohenzollern, which from 1657 also ruled Prussia. In 1701 the Elector Friedrich III crowned himself King of Prussia (as Friedrich I), and subsequently the name "Prussia" was applied to all areas ruled by the house of Hohenzollern. During the 18th century Prussia became the greatest rival to Habsburg Austria. In 1740, Friedrich II, also known as Frederick the Great, was crowned King of Prussia. Under his rule, Berlin became a major

European city and a centre of the Enlightenment. In 1740–42, in the Seven Years' War, Frederick the Great took Silesia from the Habsburgs without major losses. In 1772 he took part in the first partition of Poland.

In the second half of the 18th century Germany produced a succession of great poets and playwrights – figures such as Gotthold Ephraim Lessing, Friedrich Schiller and Johann Wolfgang von Goethe.

The Napoleonic Wars, Restoration and Revolution

From 1793 onwards the German states were involved in the Napoleonic Wars. After France's occupation of the lands west of the Rhine, a territorial reform was carried out by the Reichsdeputations Hauptschluss in 1803. This resulted in the secularization of most church property, and the total of 289 states and free cities was reduced to 112 larger states. States that gained from this supported Napoleon in his defeat of Austria in the war of 1805–7. In 1806 the Holy Roman Empire of German Nations was dissolved, and Bavaria, Saxony and Württemberg were given the status of kingdoms. Napoleon defeated Prussia at Jena and the country was occupied by France.

Portrait of Frederick the Great as successor to the throne

1701 The first king of Prussia is crowned

1702–14 Germany joins the War of Spanish Succession

1740–42 The Silesian War

Leopold Hermann von Boyen, Prussian army general

1813 Battle of the Nations at Leipzig

1700	1730	1760	1790

1710 Meissen porcelain factory opened

1700 Academy of Sciences founded in Berlin

1756–63 The Seven Years' War

1740 Frederick the Great crowned King of Prussia

1803 Territorial reform of the German states

1806 Dissolution of the Empire

1814–15 The Congress of Vienna

The tide turned for Germany at the Battle of Leipzig in 1813, when Russia, Austria and Prussia defeated the French. After Napoleon's final defeat at Waterloo in 1815, the Congress of Vienna established a German Confederation under Austrian control. Its

Victory Report at the Battle of Leipzig by Johann Peter Krafft (1839)

supreme body was the Bundestag (federal parliament), which met at Frankfurt am Main. The wars of liberation against Napoleon had led to a growth in nationalism and democratic awareness, as well as a desire for unification. In 1848 the March Revolution broke out in Berlin. Its main driving force was the urban middle class, but the revolt was finally put down by Prussian troops in 1849.

Vase with portrait of Kaiser Wilhelm II

In the 1820s and 1830s, Germany underwent rapid industrialization, and the establishment of the Zollverein (customs union) in 1834 marked the first step towards a united Germany. Uniting Germany was the main goal of the Prussian premier Otto von Bismarck. Prussia's victories over Austria in 1866 and France in 1871 resulted in the proclamation of a German Empire on 18 January 1871.

The Second Reich

The Second Reich was a federation of 25 states, and its first Chancellor was Otto von Bismarck. The unification of Germany led to a widespread confrontation between the state and the Catholic Church (known as the "Kulturkampf"). The economy, however, flourished, due to the boom in industry, in particular mining, metallurgy, electrical and chemical engineering. This led to the rise of a workers' movement, inspired by the ideas of Karl Marx. In 1875 the workers' parties united and formed the Social Democratic Party of Germany (SPD). Although the party was banned between 1878 and 1890, it rapidly gained support, and a system of social welfare for workers was gradually introduced.

At the beginning of the 20th century, Germany was a powerful state with overseas colonies. Imperialist tendencies grew, and increased tensions in European politics, particularly in the Balkans, led inevitably to war.

Fighting on the Barricades in May 1848, a fanciful picture of the revolution in Berlin by Julius Scholz

| 1834 German Customs Union (Zollverein) is established | 1848 The Communist Manifesto is published

1848–49 The March Revolution | 1871 Proclamation of the German Empire with Prussian king as Emperor Wilhelm I | 1898 Construction of the German navy begins |

| **1820** | **1850** | **1880** | **1910** |

| | 1844 Silesian weavers' uprising | 1870–71 Franco-Prussian War

1866 Prussian-Austrian War | 1890 Fall of Bismarck | |

Neo-Gothic chalice designed by K.F. Schinkel

Abandoned, bas-relief by Ernst Barlach

Bismarck's Germany

The establishment of a Reich headed by the King of Prussia on 18 January 1871 ensured Prussia's prominent role over the following decades. The Chancellor was the Prussian Prime Minister Otto von Bismarck. Thanks to large reparations paid by France and a favourable economic situation, the economy flourished throughout the Reich. This in turn fostered the development of science and culture. The cities grew rapidly, and the housing shortage led to the development of huge *Mietskasernen*, blocks of apartments for renting.

Germany in 1871
◼ The Second German Reich

Kaiser Wilhelm I
Mosaics, depicting a procession of members of the house of Hohenzollern, decorate the vestibule of the Kaiser-Wilhelm Gedächtnichskirche (memorial church) in Berlin.

The Kaiser's Family Taking a Walk in Sanssouci Park
"Happy family" portraits such as this one were often painted for propaganda purposes.

The Reichstag
The monumental Reichstag (parliament building), was built in the centre of the capital, Berlin, by the architect Paul Wallot.

Members of Parliament

Heads of the federal states

A Steel Mill in Königshütte
Germany's economic progress was achieved through a high degree of industrialization. Adolf von Menzel's painting depicts a steel mill in Königshütte, Upper Silesia.

Officer's helmet
The characteristic spiked helmet worn by German soldiers was known as a *Pickelhaube*

Ludwig II of Bavaria
The federal states, which made up the Reich, enjoyed complete autonomy. Their rulers, however, for instance King Ludwig II of Bavaria, patron of Richard Wagner and builder of "fantastic" castles and palaces, had little real political influence.

The Kaiser's wife, Augusta Victoria

Wilhelm, the heir to the throne

Mourning dress was worn by the women and black ribbons by the men as a mark of respect for the two previous Kaisers who had died in 1888 – the father and grandfather of Wilhelm II.

The Diplomatic Corps

Otto von Bismarck

Kaiser Wilhelm II

Inauguration of the Reichstag
This vast canvas by Anton von Werner (1893) shows the opening ceremony for the Reichstag after the coronation of Kaiser Wilhelm II on 25 June 1888 in the Kaiser's Palace in Berlin. The painter depicts the moment when the Kaiser delivers his speech.

Otto von Bismarck
Originating from a Pomeranian family of Junkers, the Prussian Premier and Chancellor of the Reich was one of the most prominent political figures of his time.

World War I

When Germany entered World War I in 1914, the Kaiser's generals hoped for a quick victory, but their invasion of France was halted on the Marne. The war dragged on for the next four years, devastating much of Europe, and ending in Germany's defeat. The Allied offensive in the summer of 1918 forced Germany to the negotiating table – it also led to the November revolution in Germany. Within days the state monarchs were toppled from power, Kaiser Wilhelm II abdicated, and on 9 November 1918 a republic was proclaimed. The form of government had not been decided, and at first the political advantage was held by the socialists. But the Workers' Uprising in Berlin in 1919 was defeated.

Ein Volk, ein Reich, ein Führer!

Propaganda poster for Adolf Hitler

The Weimar Republic

The Treaty of Versailles of 1919 imposed many unfavourable conditions on Germany. The country lost a great deal of her territory,

mainly to Poland, France and Lithuania, and she was obliged to pay huge reparations, undergo partial demilitarization and limit arms production.

During the Weimar Republic, Germany was riddled with instability. The economy collapsed under the heavy burden of reparation payments and the onset of hyperinflation. Constant changes of government failed to stabilize the political situation, which led to the rise both of left-wing revolutionaries and of right-wing nationalists, and to a general dissatisfaction with the country's status after the humiliating Treaty of Versailles. It is perhaps remarkable that at this time German culture flourished. However, this was not sufficient to stave off the political disaster that led to the rise of the Nazi Party (the NSDAP or National Socialist German Workers' Party).

DURCH LICHT ZUR NACHT

Cover of a Socialist magazine attacking the book-burning

The Third Reich

Adolf Hitler was appointed Chancellor by President Hindenburg on 30 January 1933 and immediately started to get rid of potential opponents. A fire that burned down the Reichstag served as a pretext for persecuting the communists, while

A Berlin synagogue burning during Kristallnacht, 1938

1914 World War I breaks out

1919 Signing of the Treaty of Versailles

1921 Adolf Hitler becomes leader of the NSDAP

1926 Germany accepted in League of Nations

1915

1920

1925

1926 Hitler Youth set up

Poster of Marlene Dietrich

BLONDE VENUS

9 Nov 1918 Declaration of the Republic

1923 Hitler's Putsch in Munich

1925 Hitler's *Mein Kampf* is published

in April 1933 a boycott of Jewish businesses began. Trade unions were banned, as were all parties apart from the Nazis. Books by "impure" authors were burned, and the work of "degenerate" artists was exhibited as a warning, marking the start of the persecution of artists and scientists, many of whom decided to emigrate. At the same time, Hitler attempted to present to the world a face of openness and success, particularly with the Berlin Olympics of 1936. Germany broke almost all the demilitarization conditions of the Versailles Treaty. The growth in arms production brought with it an improved economic situation, increasing Hitler's popularity. All his opponents who had not managed to emigrate were either killed or sent to concentration camps.

In 1935 the Nuremberg Laws were passed, which officially sanctioned the persecution of Jews. During the *Kristallnacht* (crystal night) of 9 November 1938, synagogues throughout Germany were burned and Jewish shops and homes were looted, resulting in streets littered with broken glass. Hitler's plans to conquer Europe were realized in March 1938, with the "Anschluss" (annexation) of Austria, then in 1939 German forces occupied Czechoslovakia. After obtaining peace guarantees from the USSR, Germany invaded Poland on 1 September 1939, thus starting World War II.

Pieta, sculpture by Käthe Kollwitz (1937–8)

The centre of Dresden after Allied carpet-bombing

World War II

The first two years of World War II were marked by one victory after another for the German Army, which managed to occupy half of Europe. Great Britain was the only country that succeeded in fending off Hitler. In 1941 the Wehrmacht occupied large swathes of the Soviet Union. Terror and genocide were instigated in all occupied territories. The decision to exterminate all Jews in Europe was taken at the Wannsee Conference in Berlin in January 1942. Attempts to oppose Hitler in Germany were crushed. The course of the war did not change until 1943, when on 31 January Germany suffered a major defeat in the Battle of Stalingrad.

The Allied landings in Normandy and the creation of the second front helped bring the war to an end. When Soviet forces reached Berlin in 1945 the city lay in ruins and the populace was starving. During five and a half years, 55 million people had lost their lives.

1935 Enactment of law to build up army

1938 Anschluss with Austria; occupation of Czechoslovakia

1 Sep 1939 German invasion of Poland; the beginning of World War II

30 Jan 1933 Hitler appointed Chancellor of the Reich

9/10 Nov 1938 "Kristallnacht"

The Enigma Code machine

| 0 | 1935 | 1940 | 1945 |

Poster for the Berlin Olympics in 1936

1936 Berlin Olympics

1935 November laws sanction persecution of Jews

22 Jun 1941 Germany invades USSR

20 Jan 1942 Wannsee conference

30 Apr 1945 Hitler commits suicide as Soviet troops enter Berlin

Nazi war criminals on trial at Nuremberg

The Aftermath of World War II

Germany's unconditional surrender was signed on 8 May 1945, ending the bloodiest war in human history. Peace negotiations began which were to shape the new face of Europe for decades to come. In fact, discussions on Germany's future had already taken place at the Tehran and Yalta Conferences, where the leaders of the Big Three Powers met. But it was not until the Potsdam Conference that the terms were finally agreed.

Germany lost large parts of its territory to the east, displacing the German population there. It was decided to demilitarize Germany. The four Allied powers – the USA, the USSR, Britain and France – divided Germany into zones of occupation which they would rule until democratic structures were in place. The main perpetrators of war crimes were tried in Nuremberg and sentenced to death. Unfortunately, tensions increased between the Western powers and the Soviet Union, rapidly escalating in the "Cold War", which was largely played out in occupied Germany. In 1948 the three western zones introduced a new currency, which led the Soviets to blockade the western part of Berlin. Thanks to the Berlin Airlift, which supplied the population with food and fuel,

the blockade was abandoned. On 23 May 1949 the Federal Republic (Bundesrepublik) of Germany was established in the three western zones, and on 7 October 1949 the

Germany 1949–90
- Federal Republic
- DDR

German Democratic Republic (DDR) was set up in the Soviet zone. West Berlin became an enclave inside East Germany.

Germany Divided

The German Democratic Republic was democratic only in name. It became one of the satellites of the Soviet Union, and as the westernmost outpost of the Eastern Bloc it was subject to great restrictions. Attempted protests, such as the Workers' Uprising of 17 June 1953 in Berlin, were ruthlessly suppressed. For many people the only solution was to leave the country. As the exodus of skilled workers to the West continued, on 13 August 1961 a wall with barbed wire was built to contain them. Many attempts to cross the frontier ended in death. A highly efficient

Graffiti-covered section of the Berlin Wall

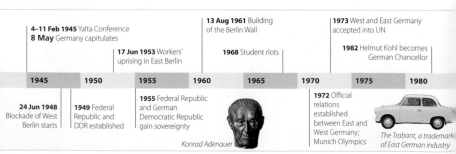

4–11 Feb 1945 Yalta Conference
8 May Germany capitulates

17 Jun 1953 Workers' uprising in East Berlin

13 Aug 1961 Building of the Berlin Wall

1968 Student riots

1973 West and East Germany accepted into UN

1982 Helmut Kohl becomes German Chancellor

1945	1950	1955	1960	1965	1970	1975	1980

24 Jun 1948 Blockade of West Berlin starts

1949 Federal Republic and DDR established

1955 Federal Republic and German Democratic Republic gain sovereignty

Konrad Adenauer

1972 Official relations established between East and West Germany; Munich Olympics

The Trabant, a trademark of East German industry

Reunification ceremony outside the Reichstag in Berlin in 1990

apparatus was set up in East Germany to watch over citizens' activities by the infamous Stasi secret police.

The first Chancellor of the Federal Republic of Germany, Konrad Adenauer, had Germany's integration into Western Europe as his main objective. Thanks to aid under the Marshall Plan, the economy rapidly recovered. Willy Brandt, first elected as Chancellor in 1969, pursued a policy of openness to the East, and recognized the German Democratic Republic.

Reunification

German reunification was made possible by a number of political events, in particular those going on in Eastern Europe. The Soviet premier Gorbachev's policy of *glasnost* led to the loosening of political constraints throughout the Eastern Bloc. Democratic changes in Poland set off a chain reaction In 1989, people started to flee the German Democratic Republic en masse via its embassy in Prague and across the Austro-Hungarian border. Then, on 9 November 1989, the Berlin Wall fell due to protests in the East, and East Germans were free to leave. When, only three weeks later, Chancellor Helmut Kohl presented a ten-point plan for German reunification, few believed

that it would happen, but the country was officially reunified on 3 October 1990. Since then, Germany has been undergoing a process of integration.

Germany Today

Since reunification Germany has increasingly shouldered responsibility in the international political and economic sphere. German troops take part in peacekeeping operations throughout the world and the country has become one of the world's strongest economic powers. With a highly regarded engineering industry producing and exporting a range of goods world-wide, including luxury cars and solar power technology, the country's financial growth continues to stand strong against the global economic downturn. Germany has also enjoyed a surge in tourism, making it one of Europe's most popular travel destinations.

Under the leadership of Federal Chancellor Angela Merkel since 2005, Germany has held a predominant position in the European Union. The country has been instrumental in helping to resolve the Euro debt crisis that continues to severely affect countries such as Greece and Spain.

Angela Merkel campaigning during the 2009 European General Elections

				2002 Floods cause havoc across Germany		2011 Germany hosts the FIFA Women's World Cup		
Helmut Kohl and Richard von Weizsäcker at the reunification ceremony **3 Oct 1990** Reunification of Germany					**2006** Germany hosts FIFA World Cup		**2013** Devastating floods in Germany and Eastern Europe are said to be the worst in over 400 years	
985	1990	1995	2000	2005	2010	2015	2020	
8 Nov 1989 Fall of the Berlin Wall	**1994** Withdrawal of last Russian military units from Berlin	**1998** Gerhard Schröder becomes Chancellor	**2000** Expo 2000 World Fair in Hanover	**2005** Ceremonial reopening of the reconstructed Frauenkirche in Dresden, a symbol of East-West efforts **2005** Angela Merkel is the first female chancellor in a "Grand Coalition" government				

BERLIN
AREA BY AREA

Berlin at a Glance

Since the reunification of Germany in 1990, Berlin has become an increasingly popular destination for visitors. The following pages provide a useful guide to places of interest both in the town centre and the outskirts, including historic monuments such as the Nikolaikirche *(see p84)*, museums, modern developments, such as the Potsdamer Platz, as well as places of recreation and amusement, such as Schlosspark *(see pp100–101)*. In the guide, we have divided central Berlin into two parts (eastern centre and western centre); these, however, do not correspond with the city's former partition into East and West Berlin.

LOCATOR MAP
See Street Finder pp118–23

The Tiergarten was once a royal hunting estate but, after 1818, it was converted into a landscaped park by Peter Joseph Lenné *(see p91)* with lakes and streams.

WESTERN CENTRE
(See pp86–97)

Spree

STRASSE DES 17 JUNI

GROSSER STERN

Landwehrkanal

KURFÜRSTENSTR

KURFÜRSTENDAMM

The Gemäldegalerie *(see pp94–5)* houses an exceptional collection of European masters, including Hans Holbein's *Portrait of George Gisze (1532).*

The Kaiser-Wilhelm-Gedächtnis-Kirche was almost totally destroyed by bombs during World War II. A new annexe was built in 1963 to a design by Egon Eiermann *(see p90).*

◄ Aerial view of Berlin

The Reichstag is a vast, Neo-Renaissance building, designed in 1884 by Paul Wallot. It now features an elliptical dome, which was designed in the 1990s by Sir Norman Foster *(see p97).*

The Pergamonmuseum owes its name to the magnificent Zeus Altar from Pergamon, which stands in the main hall. Built between 1912 and 1930, the museum houses rich collections of Greek, Roman and Asian art *(see pp80–81).*

The imposing Neo-Classical Brandenburg Gate stands at the end of Unter den Linden. It is crowned with a 6-m (20-ft) high sculpture of the Roman Quadriga driven by Victoria, the goddess of victory *(see p73).*

The Jüdisches Museum (Jewish Museum) is housed in a building designed by Daniel Libeskind. It features a symbolic projection of a broken Star of David *(see p84).*

EASTERN CENTRE

This part of Berlin is the historic centre of the city, and includes the Mitte district and parts of Kreuzberg. Its beginnings date back to the 13th century when two settlements were established on the banks of the river Spree. One was the former Cölln, situated on an island, and the other its twin settlement, Berlin. Berlin's first church, the Nikolaikirche, survives to this day.

This part of the city features most of its historic buildings, which are located mainly along Unter den Linden. It also includes the Museumsinsel, the location of the vast Berliner Dom as well as the impressive collection of museums that gives the island its name. These include the Pergamonmuseum.

During the city's partition, Mitte belonged to East Berlin while Kreuzberg was in West Berlin.

Sights at a Glance

Museums and Galleries
- ❶ Zeughaus
- ⑭ DDR Museum
- ⑯ Altes Museum
- ⑰ Neues Museum
- ⑱ Alte Nationalgalerie
- ⑲ Pergamonmuseum
- ⑳ Bode-Museum
- ㉖ Märkisches Museum
- ㉗ Checkpoint Charlie
- ㉘ Jüdisches Museum
- ㉙ Topographie des Terrors
- ㉚ Deutsches Technikmuseum Berlin

Streets and Squares
- ❸ Bebelplatz
- ❺ Unter den Linden
- ⑬ Schlossplatz
- ㉓ Alexanderplatz
- ㉕ Nikolaiviertel

Historic Buildings and Monuments
- ❶ Brandenburger Tor
- ❷ Holocaust Denkmal
- ❻ Humboldt-Universität
- ❼ Neue Wache
- ❿ Konzerthaus
- ⑫ Schlossbrücke
- ㉒ Rotes Rathaus
- ㉔ Fernsehturm

Churches
- ❹ St Hedwigs-Kathedrale
- ❾ Französischer Dom
- ⑪ Deutscher Dom
- ⑮ Berliner Dom
- ㉑ Marienkirche

0 metres 400
0 yards 400

See also Street Finder
pp118–23

◀ The Brandenburg Gate at twilight

For map symbols see back flap

Street-by-Street: Around Bebelplatz

The section of Unter den Linden between Schlossbrücke and Friedrichstrasse is one of the most attractive areas in central Berlin. As well as some magnificent Baroque and Neo-Classical buildings, many of them designed by famous architects, there are also some restored palaces that are now used as public buildings. Of particular interest is the beautiful Baroque building of the Zeughaus (the former Arsenal), which now houses the German History Museum.

❻ Humboldt University
The university courtyard teems with life all year round. Second-hand booksellers set up their stalls in front of the gate.

Equestrian statue of King Friedrich II of Prussia
This monument was erected in 1851 to mark the 111th anniversary of Friedrich II's ascension to the Prussian throne.

UNIVERSITÄTSSTRASSE

CHARLOTTENSTRASSE

0 metres 100
0 yards 100

UNTER DEN LINDEN

BEBEL-PLATZ

❺ Unter den Linden
Replanted with four rows of lime trees in 1946, this is one of the most famous streets in Berlin.

Brandenburg Gate

Altes Palais

Staatsbibliothek
Designed by Ernst von Ihne and constructed between 1903 and 1914, this impressive building houses part of the State Library collection.

Key

— Suggested route

❽ ★ Zeughaus (Deutsches Historisches Museum)
Minerva, goddess of wisdom, decorates this beautiful Baroque building, which has a wing designed by I M Pei.

Locator Map
See Street Finder maps 1, 4 & 5.

❼ ★ Neue Wache
Now serving as a memorial to all victims of war and dictatorship, this monument was designed by Karl Friedrich Schinkel.

Rotes Rathaus

HINTER DER KATH. KIRCHE

Staatsoper Unter den Linden

❹ St-Hedwigs-Kathedrale
Bas-reliefs (1837) by Theodore Wilhelm Achtermann adorn the cathedral's supports.

Kronprinzenpalais
A magnificent portal from the dismantled Bauakademie building can be found at the rear of the palace.

❶ Brandenburger Tor

Brandenburg Gate

Pariser Platz. **Map** 4 A2.
Ⓢ & Ⓤ Brandenburger Tor. 🚌 100.

The Brandenburg Gate is the quintessential symbol of Berlin. A magnificent Neo-Classical structure, modelled on the Athenian Propylaea (the entrance to the Acropolis), it was constructed between 1788 and 1791. Its sculptured decorations were completed in 1795. A pair of pavilions, once used by guards and customs officers, frames its powerful Doric colonnade and entablature. The bas-reliefs depict scenes from Greek mythology and the whole structure is crowned by Johann Gottfried Schadow's famous sculpture, *Quadriga*. In 1806, during the French occupation, the sculpture was dismantled, on Napoleon's orders, and taken to Paris. On its triumphal return in 1814, it was declared a symbol of victory, and the goddess received a staff bearing the Prussian eagle and an iron cross adorned with a laurel wreath. Throughout its history, the Brandenburg Gate has borne witness to many of Berlin's important events. Located in East Berlin, the gate was restored between 1956 and 1958, when the damaged *Quadriga* was rebuilt in West Berlin. Over the next 40 years it stood watch over the divided city, until 1989, when the first section of the Berlin Wall came down.

Frieze and sculpture, *Quadriga*, on the Brandenburg Gate

❷ Holocaust Denkmal

Map 4 A2. ⑤ & Ⓤ Brandenburger Tor. 🚌 100, 200, M85.

Germany's national Holocaust memorial was designed by American architect Peter Eisenman. Completed in 2005, it is made up of a large field with dark grey steles of various heights that symbolize the six million Jews and others murdered by the Nazis in concentration camps between 1933 and 1945.

Visitors can walk their own route, and there is an information centre underneath the memorial. There are also memorials in nearby Tiergarten to murdered homosexuals and murdered Sinti and Roma people.

The façade of St-Hedwigs-Kathedrale, with beautiful bas-relief sculptures

Relief on the façade of the Staatsoper (Opera House), Bebelplatz

❸ Bebelplatz

Map 4 C2. ⑤ & Ⓤ Friedrichstrasse. 🚌 100, 200, TXL.

Bebelplatz was intended to be the focal point of the Forum Fridericianum – an area designed to mirror the grandeur of ancient Rome. Although the plans were only partly implemented, many important buildings were eventually erected here.

In 1933, the square was the scene of the infamous book-burning act organized by the Nazis. Some 25,000 books, written by authors considered to be enemies of the Third Reich, were burned. Today, a monument in the square commemorates this dramatic event.

❹ St-Hedwigs-Kathedrale

St Hedwig's Cathedral

Bebelplatz. **Map** 4 C2. **Tel** (030) 203 48 10. ⑤ & Ⓤ Friedrichstrasse. 🚌 100, 147, 200, TXL. **Open** 10am–5pm Mon–Fri, 10am–4:30pm Sat,1pm–5pm Sun & holy days.

This huge church is the Catholic Cathedral of the Roman Archdiocese of Berlin. The initial design was similar to the Roman Pantheon. Construction began in 1747, although work continued on and off until 1887.

It was damaged during World War II and rebuilt between 1952 and 1963. The building received a reinforced concrete dome and its interior was refurbished in a modern style. The crypt contains bishops' tombs and a 16th-century Madonna.

❺ Unter den Linden

Map 1 F4, 4 A2, B2, C2, 5 D2. ⑤ & Ⓤ Brandenburger Tor. 🚌 100, 200, TXL.

One of the most famous streets in Berlin, Unter den Linden starts at Schlossplatz and runs down to Pariser Platz and the Brandenburg Gate. It was once the route to the royal hunting grounds, which were later transformed into the Tiergarten.

In the 17th century, the street was planted with lime trees, to which it owes its name. Although the original trees were removed around 1658, four rows of limes were planted in 1820.

During the 18th century, Unter den Linden became the main street of the westward-growing city and gradually came to be lined with

Wilhelm and Alexander von Humboldt

The Humboldt brothers rank among the most distinguished Berlin citizens. Wilhelm (1767–1835) was a lawyer and politician on whose initiative the Berlin University (later renamed Humboldt University) was founded in 1810. At the university, he conducted studies in comparative and historical linguistics. His brother Alexander (1769–1859), a professor at the university, researched natural science, including meteorology, oceanography and agricultural science.

Alexander von Humboldt

The 19th-century Neue Wache, now dedicated to the victims of war and dictatorship

prestigious buildings, which have been restored in the years following World War II.

Since the reunification of Germany in 1990, Unter den Linden has acquired several cafés and restaurants, as well as many smart shops. The street has also become the venue for interesting outdoor events. It is usually crowded with tourists and students browsing the bookstalls around the Humboldt Universität and the Staatsbibliothek (State Library).

❻ Humboldt Universität
Humboldt University

Unter den Linden 6. **Map** 4 C2. Ⓢ & Ⓤ Friedrichstrasse. 📟 100, 200, TXL.

The university building was constructed in 1753 for Prince Heinrich of Prussia. The overall design of the palace, with its main block and the courtyard enclosed within two wings, has been extended many times. Two marble statues by Paul Otto (1883) stand at the entrance; these represent Wilhelm and Alexander von Humboldt.

Many famous scientists have worked at the university, including physicians Rudolf Virchow and Robert Koch and physicists Max Planck and Albert Einstein. Among its graduates are Heinrich Heine, Karl Marx and Friedrich Engels.

After World War II, the university was in the Russian sector and the difficulties encountered by the students of the western zone led to the establishment in 1948 of the Freie Universität.

❼ Neue Wache

Unter den Linden 4. **Map** 4 C2. Ⓢ Hackescher Markt. 📟 100, 200, TXL. **Open** 10am–6pm daily.

Designed by Karl Friedrich Schinkel and built between 1816 and 1818, this monument is considered to be one of the finest examples of Neo-Classical architecture in Berlin. The front of the monument is dominated by a huge Doric portico with a frieze made up of bas-reliefs depicting goddesses of victory.

In 1930–31 the building was turned into a monument to soldiers killed in World War I. Following its restoration in 1960, Neue Wache became the Memorial to the Victims of Fascism and Militarism. It was rededicated in 1993 to the memory of all victims of war and dictatorship. Inside is an eternal flame and a granite slab over the ashes of an unknown soldier, a resistance fighter and a concentration camp prisoner. In the roof opening is a copy of the sculpture *Mother with her Dead Son*, by Berlin artist Käthe Kollwitz.

❽ Zeughaus

Unter den Linden 2. **Map** 5 D2. **Tel** 20 30 40. Ⓢ Hackescher Markt. 📟 100, 200, TXL. New wing: **Open** 10am–6pm daily.

This former arsenal was built in the Baroque style in 1706 under the guidance of Johann Arnold Nering, Martin Grünberg, Andreas Schlüter and Jean de Bodt. A magnificent structure, its wings surround an inner courtyard. Its exterior is decorated with Schlüter's sculptures, which include masks of dying warriors. Home to the German History Museum since 1952, it was renovated in 2005. A modern glass and steel wing, designed by architect I M Pei, now houses temporary exhibits, and there is an extensive exhibition on German history.

Part of the façade of the Zeughaus on Unter den Linden

Side elevation of the Französischer Dom, built for Huguenot refugees

❾ Französischer Dom

French Cathedral

Gendarmenmarkt 5. **Map** 4 C2. **Tel** (030) 206 49 922/3. **U** Stadtmitte or Französische Strasse. Museum: **Open** 10am–6pm Tue–Sun. Church: **Open** noon– 5pm Tue–Sun. 12:30pm Tue–Fri, 10am Sun. Viewing platform: **Open** 10:30am–7pm daily.

Although the two churches standing on opposite sides of Schauspielhaus seem identical, their only common feature is their matching front towers. The French cathedral was built for the Huguenot community, who found refuge in protestant Berlin following their expulsion from France after the revocation of the Edict of Nantes in 1598. The modest church, built between 1701 and 1705 by Louis Cayart and Abraham Quesnay, was modelled on the Huguenot church in Charenton, France, which was destroyed in 1688. The interior features a late-Baroque organ from 1754.

The structure is dominated by a massive, cylindrical tower, which is encircled by Corinthian porticos at its base. The tower and porticos were designed by Carl von Gontard and added around 1785. It houses the Huguenot Museum, which charts the history of the Huguenot community in France and Brandenburg.

A viewing platform, which is 40 m (131 ft) above the ground, is one of the city's highest historic observation platforms and offers stunning views of the skyline.

❿ Konzerthaus

Concert Hall

Gendarmenmarkt 2. **Map** 4 C2. **Tel** (030) 203 09 21 01. **U** Stadtmitte.

A late Neo-Classical jewel, this magnificent theatre building, known until recently as the Schauspielhaus, is one of the greatest achievements of Berlin's best-known architect, Karl Friedrich Schinkel. It was built between 1818 and 1821 around the ruins of Langhan's National Theatre, destroyed by fire in 1817. The portico columns were retained in the new design. Following bomb damage in World War II, it was reconstructed as a concert hall and the exterior was restored to its former glory. The Konzerthaus is now home to the Berlin Symphony Orchestra.

The whole building is decorated with sculptures alluding to drama and music. The façade, which includes a huge Ionic portico with a set of stairs, is crowned with a sculpture of Apollo riding a chariot pulled by griffins.

In front of the theatre stands a shining white marble statue of Friedrich Schiller, which was sculpted by Reinhold Begas and erected in 1869. Removed by the Nazis during the 1930s, the monument was returned to its rightful place in 1988. The statue is mounted on a high pedestal surrounded by allegorical figures representing Lyric Poetry, Drama, Philosophy and History.

⓫ Deutscher Dom

German Cathedral

Gendarmenmarkt 1. **Map** 4 C3. **Tel** (030) 227 30431. **U** Stadtmitte or Französische Strasse. Exhibition: **Open** 10am–6pm Tue–Sun (to 7pm May–Sep). in English on request.

The cathedral at the southern end of the square is an old German Protestant-Reformed church. Based on a five-petal shape, it was designed by Martin Grünberg and built in 1708 by Giovanni Simonetti. In 1785 it acquired a dome-covered tower identical to that of the French cathedral.

Burned down in 1945, it was rebuilt in 1993, with its interior adapted as exhibition space. On display is the exhibition "Milestones – Setbacks – Sidetracks". Over five floors, it traces the historical development of the parliamentary system in Germany.

Sculpture from Deutscher Dom

⓬ Schlossbrücke

Map 5 D2. Hackescher Markt. 100, 200, TXL.

This is one of the city's most beautiful bridges, connecting Schlossplatz with Unter den Linden. It was built in 1824 to a design by Karl Friedrich Schinkel. Statues were added to the top of the bridge's sparkling red-granite pillars in 1853. These figures, made of white Carrara marble, were also created by Schinkel. The statues depict tableaux from Greek mythology, such as Iris, Nike and Athena, training and looking after their favourite young warriors. The elaborate wrought-iron balustrade is decorated with intertwined sea creatures.

Interior of the Konzerthaus, formerly the Schauspielhaus

The surviving Stadtschloss portal fronting a government building

⑬ Schlossplatz

Map 5 D2. Ⓢ Hackescher Markt.
🚌 100, 147, 200, TXL.

This square was once the site of a huge residential complex known as Stadtschloss (City Castle). Built in 1451, it served as the main residence of the Brandenburg Electors. It was transformed from a castle to a palace in the mid-16th century when Elector Friedrich III (later King Friedrich I) ordered its reconstruction in the Baroque style. The main seat of the Hohenzollern family for almost 500 years until the end of the monarchy, the palace was partly burned during World War II but was provisionally restored and used as a museum.

In 1950–51, despite protests, the palace was demolished and the square was renamed Marx-Engels-Platz under the GDR.

Now all that remains is the triumphal-arch portal that once adorned the façade on the Lustgarten side. This is now incorporated into the wall of the former government building, the Staatsratgebäude, which was erected in 1964 on the square's south side. The building's decor features the remaining original sculptures, including the magnificent atlantes by the famous Dresden sculptor, Balthasar Permoser. Their inclusion was due to their propaganda value: it was from the balcony of the portal that in 1918 Karl

Liebknecht proclaimed the birth of the Socialist Republic.

In 1989 the square reverted to its original name and a former GDR government building was torn down. A palace-like building, the Humboldt-Forum, will be an international and cultural centre when complete in 2019.

⑭ DDR Museum

Karl-Liebknecht Str. 1. **Map** 5 D1.
Tel (030) 847 123 731. Ⓢ & Ⓤ
Alexanderplatz. 🚌 100, 200, TXL.
Open 10am–8pm Mon–Sun (to 10pm Sat).

This small, privately run museum provides a fascinating, interactive insight into daily life in the former East Germany. Visit a reconstructed apartment and take a simulated ride in an old Trabant car through a concrete housing estate.

⑮ Berliner Dom

Am Lustgarten. **Map** 5 D1. **Tel** (030) 20 26 91 36. Ⓢ Hackescher Markt.
🚌 100, 200, TXL **Open** Apr–Sep: 9am–8pm Mon–Sat, noon–8pm Sun; Oct–Mar: 9am–7pm Mon– Sat, noon–7pm Sun. 🎨 🚩 10am, 6pm Sun.

The original Berliner Dom was based on a modest Baroque

design by Johann Boumann. Built between 1747 and 1750, the cathedral included the original crypt of the Hohenzollern family, one of the largest of its kind in Europe. The present Neo-Baroque structure is the work of Julius Raschdorff and dates from 1894 to 1905. Following severe World War II damage, the cathedral has been restored in a simplified form. The Hohenzollern memorial chapel, which adjoined the northern walls, has been dismantled.

The Neo-Baroque interior of the Berliner Dom

Berlin's Bridges

Despite wartime damage, Berlin's bridges are still well worth seeing. The Spree river and the city's canals have some fine, exemplary architecture on their banks, while many of the bridges were designed and decorated by famous architects and sculptors. Probably the most renowned bridge is the Schlossbrücke designed by Karl Friedrich Schinkel. Further south along the Kupfergrabenkanal, the Schleusenbrücke, dating from c.1914, is decorated with reliefs of the early history of the city's bridges and sluices. The next bridge, heading south, is the Jungfernbrücke (1798), which is the last drawbridge in Berlin. The next bridge along is the Gertraudenbrücke. Another noteworthy bridge along the Spree river is the Weidendammer Brücke, built originally in 1695–7 and subsequently rebuilt in 1923, with an eagle motif adorning its balustrade. On the Spree near the Regierungsviertel is the magnificent Moltkebrücke (1886–91). The bridge is guarded by a huge griffin wielding a shield adorned with the Prussian eagle, while cherubs dressed in a military fashion hold up lamps. On the arches of the bridges are portraits of leaders, designed by Karl Begas.

Ornamental feature of a bear on the Liebknechtbrücke

Street-by-Street: Museum Island

The long island that nestles in the tributaries of the Spree river is the cradle of Berlin's history. It was here that the first settlements appeared at the beginning of the 13th century: Cölln is mentioned in documents dating back to 1237, and its twin settlement, Berlin, is mentioned a few years later, in 1244. The island's character was transformed by the construction of the Brandenburg Electors' palace, which served as their residence from 1470. Although it was razed to the ground in 1950, some interesting buildings on the north side of the island have survived, including the Berliner Dom (Berlin Cathedral) and the impressive collection of museums that give the island its name, Museumsinsel.

Locator Map
See Street Finder maps 4 & 5

㉑ Bode-Museum
A rounded corner of the building, crowned with a dome, provides a magnificent end-piece to the tip of the island.

⑲ Pergamonmuseum
Named after the Pergamon Altar housed in its main hall, this is a treasure trove of antiquities from the Near and Middle East.

⑰ ★ Neues Museum
This museum houses exhibitions on antiquities and ancient Egyptian art.

⑱ Alte Nationalgalerie
The equestrian statue of King Friedrich Wilhelm IV in front of the building is the work of Alexander Calandrelli.

⑯ ★ Altes Museum
The corners of the central building feature the figures of Castor and Pollux, heroes of Greek mythology.

0 metres 100
0 yards 100

BODESTRASSE

Lustgarten
contains a 70-ton granite bowl, the biggest in the world, which was placed in the garden in 1828.

LUSTGARTEN

Key

— Suggested route

⑯ Altes Museum

Old Museum

Am Lustgarten (Bodestrasse 1–3). **Map** 5 D1. **Tel** (030) 20 90 55 77. Ⓢ Hackescher Markt. 🚌 100, 200, TXL. **Open** 10am–6pm Mon–Wed & Fri–Sun, 10am–10pm Thu. 🖼

Designed by Karl Friedrich Schinkel, this museum building is one of the world's most beautiful Neo-Classical structures, with an impressive 87-m (285-ft) high portico supported by 18 Ionic columns. Officially opened in 1830, the museum was purpose-built to house the royal collection of art and antiquities.

Following World War II, the building was used only for temporary exhibitions. It now houses the Antikensammlung, with a magnificent collection of Greek, Roman and Etruscan antiquities.

⑰ Neues Museum

New Museum

Bodestrasse 1–3. **Map** 5 D1. Ⓢ Hackescher Markt. 🚌 100, 200, TXL. 🚊 M1, M4, M5. **Open** 10am–6pm daily (to 8pm Thu). 🖼

The Neues Museum was built on Museum Island between 1841 and 1855 to a design by Friedrich August Stüler. Until World War II, it housed a collection of antiquities, mainly ancient Egyptian art. The rooms in the museum building were decorated specifically to complement the exhibitions they contained, while wall paintings by Wilhelm von Kaulbach featured important events in world history. The building was damaged in 1945 and the museum closed. It reopened in October 2009 after reconstruction and once again houses the Egyptian Museum as well as the Museum of Prehistory and Early History.

Many sculptures, sarcophagi, murals and architectural fragments of various eras are on display, including the famous bust of Nefertiti. Most popular is the collection from 19th-century archaeological digs by Richard Lepsius and Johann Ludwig Burckhardt at Tell al-Amarna, Egypt. Tell al-Amarna was the capital founded by Pharaoh Amenhotep IV in the 14th century BC. In a break with tradition, Amenhotep and his wife, Nefertiti, are depicted in a more naturalistic manner.

⑱ Alte Nationalgalerie

Old National Gallery

Bodestrasse 1–3. **Map** 5 D1. **Tel** (030) 20 90 55 77. Ⓢ Hackescher Markt. 🚌 100, 200, TXL. 🚊 M1, M4, M5. **Open** 10am–6pm Tue–Sun, 10am–10pm Thu.

The old Nationalgalerie building, designed by Friedrich August Stüler, was erected between 1866 and 1876. It was originally intended to house the collection of modern art that had been on display in the Akademie der Künste (Art Academy). After World War II, however, the collection was split up into several sections and part of it was shown in West Berlin, where the Neue Nationalgalerie was specifically erected for this purpose *(see p92)*. This building was then renamed Alte Nationalgalerie.

Pericles' Head

Following the reunification of Germany, the modern art collections were merged again. Two new exhibition halls house historic paintings from the German Romantic era, including work by Caspar David Friedrich and Karl Friedrich Schinkel. The famous 19th-century marble sculpture of the two Prussian princesses by Johann Gottfried Schadow is also on display, as is a significant collection of works by Adolph Menzel, including his most famous painting, *The Balcony Room*.

⑲ Pergamonmuseum

The Pergamonmuseum was built between 1912 and 1930 to a design by Alfred Messels and Ludwig Hoffmann. It houses one of the most famous collections of antiquities in Europe and owes its name to the famous Pergamon Altar, which takes pride of place in the main hall (closed until 2019). Its collections are the result of intensive archaeological excavations by German expeditions to the Near and Middle East. Major renovation until after 2025 means a selection of the museum's treasures are shown in the south wing, while most of the Museum of Antiquities' pieces are displayed in the Altes Museum.

★ **Pergamon Altar** (170 BC)
This scene, featuring the goddess Athena, appears on the large frieze illustrating a battle between the gods and the giants.

Roman Mosaic
(3rd or 4th century AD) This ancient mosaic was found at Jerash, Jordan. A second part of it is in the collection of the Stark Museum of Art, Texas.

Non-exhibition rooms

Second floor

The Goddesss Athena
This enchanting Hellenistic sculpture of the goddess Athena is one of many displayed in the museum.

First floor

Ground floor

Assyrian Palace
Parts of this beautifully reconstructed palace interior, from the ancient kingdom of Assyria, date from the 12th century BC.

Façade of the Mshatta Palace (AD 744)
This fragment is from the southern façade of the Jordanian Mshatta Palace, presented to Wilhelm II by Sultan Abdul Hamid of Ottoman in 1903.

Aleppo Zimmer (c.1603)
This magnificent panelled room comes from a merchant's house in the Syrian city of Aleppo.

★ **Market Gate from Miletus** (c.120 AD)
Measuring over 16 m (52 ft) in height, this gate opened onto the southern market of Miletus, a Roman town in Asia Minor.

Key

- ⬜ Ancient Near Eastern antiquities (Vorderasiatisches Museum)
- ⬜ Islamic art (Museum für Islamische Kunst)
- ⬜ Classical antiquities
- ⬜ Non-exhibition rooms

Main entrance

Gallery Guide

The right wing houses the Museum of Near Eastern Antiquities; the first floor of the right wing houses the Museum of Islamic Art. The left wing will be closed until 2019.

★ **Ishtar Gate from Babylon**
(6th century BC) Original glazed bricks decorate both the huge Ishtar gate and the impressive Processional Way that leads up to it.

The Bode-Museum designed by Ernst von Ihne

⑳ Bode-Museum

Monbijoubrücke (Bodestrasse 1–3).
Map 1 C1. **Tel** (030) 20 90 56 01.
Hackescher Markt or Friedrichstrasse.
Open 10am–6pm daily (to 10pm Thu).
M1, M4, M5, 12.

The fourth museum building on Museumsinsel was constructed between 1897 and 1904. It was designed by Ernst von Ihne to fit the wedge-shaped northwestern end of the island. The interior was designed with the help of an art historian, Wilhelm von Bode, who was the director of the Berlin state museums at the time.

The museum displayed a rather mixed collection that included some old masters. Its original name, Kaiser Friedrich Museum, was changed after World War II. Following the reassembling of the Berlin collections, all the paintings were rehoused in the Kulturforum *(see pp88–9)*, while the Egyptian art and the papyrus collection were moved to the Ägyptisches Museum (Egyptian Museum) at the Neues Museum *(see p79)*.

Following its refurbishment, the building once again houses a collection of over 50,000 coins, plus medals and Byzantine art. It is also home to an extensive collection of sculptures, which includes the works of Tilman Riemenschneider, Donatello, Gianlorenzo Bernini and Antonio Canova. A copy of the magnificent equestrian statue of the Great Elector, Friedrich Wilhelm, by Andreas Schlüter, has also taken its place in the old hall.

㉑ Marienkirche

Karl-Liebknecht-Strasse 8. **Map** 5 E1.
Tel (030) 242 44 67. Hackescher Markt. 100, 200, TXL. **Open** Apr–Oct: 10am–9pm daily; Nov–Mar: 10am–6pm daily. 10:30am Sun.

St Mary's Church, or the Marienkirche, was first established as a parish church in the second half of the 13th century. Started around 1280, construction was completed early in the 14th century. During reconstruction works in 1380, following a fire, the church was altered slightly, but its overall shape changed only in the 15th century when it acquired the front tower. In 1790, the tower was crowned with a dome, designed by Carl Gotthard Langhans, which includes both Baroque and Neo-Gothic elements.

The Marienkirche was once hemmed in by buildings, but today it stands alone in the shadow of the Fernsehturm (Television Tower). The early

Baroque altar in the Marienkirche, designed by Andreas Krüger

Gothic hall design and the lavish decorative touches make this church one of the most interesting in Berlin. An alabaster pulpit by Andreas Schlüter, dating from 1703, is decorated with bas-reliefs of St John the Baptist and the personifications of the Virtues.

The Baroque main altar was designed by Andreas Krüger around 1762. The paintings with which it is adorned include three works by Christian Bernhard Rode.

A Gothic font, dating from 1437, is supported by three black dragons and decorated with the figures of Jesus Christ, Mary and the Apostles.

㉒ Rotes Rathaus
Red Town Hall

Rathausstrasse 15. **Map** 5 E2. &
Alexanderplatz. Klosterstrasse, TXL, 248.

This impressive structure is Berlin's main town hall. Its predecessor was a much more modest structure that, by the end of the 19th century, was inadequate to meet the needs of the growing metropolis.

The present building was designed by Hermann Friedrich Waesemann, and the construction works went on from 1861 until 1869. The architect took his main inspiration from Italian Renaissance municipal buildings, but the tower is reminiscent of Laon cathedral in France. The walls are made from red brick and it was this, rather than the political orientation of the mayors, that gave the town hall its name.

The whole building has a continuous frieze known as the "stone chronicle", which was added in 1879. The frieze features scenes and figures from the city's history and traces the development of its economy and science.

The Rotes Rathaus was severely damaged during World War II but, following its reconstruction between 1951 and 1958, it became the seat of the East Berlin authorities. The West Berlin magistrate

㉔ Fernsehturm

The television tower, called by the locals *Telespargel*, or toothpick, remains to this day the city's tallest structure at 368 m (1,207 ft). It is also the second-tallest structure in Europe. The tower was built in 1969 to a design by a team of architects including Fritz Dieter and Günter Franke, with the help of Swedish experts. However, the idea for the tower originated much earlier from Hermann Henselmann (creator of the Karl-Marx-Allee development) in the Socialist-Realist style.

View from the Tower
On a clear day the viewing platform offers a full view of Berlin. Visibility can reach up to 40 km (25 miles).

The television antenna is visible all over Berlin.

Transmitter aerial

The metal sphere is covered with steel cladding.

Tele-Café
One of the attractions of the tower is the revolving café. A full rotation takes about half an hour, so it is possible to get a bird's-eye view of the whole city while sipping a cup of coffee.

Concrete structure rising to 250 m (820 ft)

The concrete shaft contains two elevators that carry passengers to the café and viewing platform.

The monumental, red-brick town hall, known as the Rotes Rathaus

was housed in the Schöneberg town hall *(see p107)*. Following the reunification of Germany in 1990, the Rotes Rathaus became the centre of authority, housing the offices of the mayor and the Berlin cabinet.

The forecourt sculptures by Fritz Kremer, which depict Berliners helping to rebuild the city, were added in 1958.

㉓ Alexanderplatz

Map 5 E1, F1. Ⓤ & Ⓢ Alexanderplatz. 🚌 100, 200, TXL.

Alexanderplatz, or "Alex" as it is called locally, has a long history, although it would be hard now to find any visible traces of the past. Once known as Ochsenmarkt (oxen market), it was the site of a cattle and wool market. It was later renamed after Tsar Alexander I who visited Berlin in 1805. At that time, the square boasted a magnificent monumental colonnade, which was designed by Carl von Gontard.

In time, houses and shops sprang up around the square and a market hall and urban train line were built nearby. "Alex" became one of the

city's busiest spots. Its frenzied atmosphere was captured by Alfred Döblin (1878–1957) in his novel *Berlin Alexanderplatz*.

In 1929, attempts were made to develop the square, though only two office buildings were added – the Alexanderhaus and the Berolinahaus, both designed by Peter Behrens.

World War II erased most of the square's buildings and they were replaced by characterless 1960s edifices, including the Park Inn Hotel (formerly Hotel Stadt Berlin) and the Fernsehturm. However, the area has been redeveloped and is home to several shopping plazas and cinemas, as well as open-air markets during the holidays.

Riverside buildings of the Nikolaiviertel

㉕ Nikolaiviertel

Map 5 E2. **U** & **S** Alexanderplatz.
U Klosterstrasse 🚌 100, 147, 200, 248, M48.

This small area on the bank of the Spree is a favourite place for both Berliners and tourists. Some of Berlin's oldest houses stood here until they were destroyed in World War II. The redevelopment of the area, which was carried out by the GDR government between 1979 and 1987, was an interesting attempt to recreate a medieval town. Now, with the exception of one or two restored buildings, the Nikolaiviertel consists entirely of newly built replicas of historic buildings.

The **Nikolaikirche** was destroyed by bombing in 1945 and rebuilt in 1987. All that remains of the original structure, which was probably built around 1230, is the base of the two-tower façade of the present church, which dates from around 1300.

The only Baroque building in Nikolaiviertel to escape damage during World War II was the **Knoblauchhaus**, a small townhouse built in 1759 for the Knoblauch family. The current appearance of the building is the result of work carried out in 1835 when the façade was given a Neo-Classical look.

Ephraim-Palais was built in 1766 for Nathan Veitel Heinrich Ephraim, Frederick the Great's mint master and court jeweller. Parts of the original structure, which were saved from demolition, were used in the reconstruction.

㉖ Märkisches Museum

Am Köllnischen Park 5. **Map** 5 F2.
Tel (030) 30 86 62 15. **U** Märkisches Museum. **S** Jannowitzbrücke.
🚌 147, 265. **Open** 10am–6pm Tue, Thu–Sun, noon–8pm Wed. 🎫 (free 1st Wed of month). Presentation of mechanical instruments 3pm Sun.

Built between 1901 and 1908, this complex of red brick buildings was inspired by the brick-Gothic style popular in the Brandenburg region. The museum, founded in 1874, is dedicated to the cultural history of Berlin from the first settlements to today. The department "Berliner Kunst" (art), for example, presents a remarkable collection of paintings, sculpture, textiles, faiences, glass and porcelain. The main hall features the original Gothic portal from the sculpture *Quadriga*, which once crowned the Brandenburg Gate *(see p73)*. A further collection is devoted to the Berlin theatre from 1730 to 1933. One of the galleries houses some old-time mechanical musical instruments.

Surrounding the museum is the Köllnischer Park, home to three brown bears – the city mascots.

㉗ Checkpoint Charlie

Friedrichstrasse 43–45. **Map** 4 C4.
Tel (030) 253 72 50. **U** Kochstrasse.
🚌 M29. Haus am Checkpoint Charlie:
Open 9am–10pm daily. 🎫

The name of this notorious border crossing between the American and Soviet sectors comes from the word that signifies the letter C in the international phonetic alphabet: Alpha, Bravo, Charlie.

Between 1961 and 1990, Checkpoint Charlie was the only crossing for foreigners between East and West Berlin. It came to represent a symbol of both freedom and separation for the many East Germans trying to escape Soviet communism.

Today, a single watchtower is all that remains. Next to it is a museum – **Haus am Checkpoint Charlie**. Its rich collection details the years of the Cold War in Berlin.

㉘ Jüdisches Museum

Lindenstrasse 14. **Map** 4 C5. **Tel** (030) 25 99 33 00. **U** Hallesches Tor or Kochstrasse. 🚌 M29, M41, 265.
Open 10am–10pm Mon, 10am–8pm Tue–Sun.

The building housing the city's Jewish Museum is an exciting and imaginative example of 20th-century architecture. Designed by a Polish-Jewish architect based in the United States, Daniel Libeskind, the plan, shape, style and interior

The exterior of the Märkisches Museum, echoing a medieval monastery

and exterior arrangement of the building are part of a profoundly complicated philosophical programme. The museum's architecture itself is intended to convey something of the tragic history of the millions of Jews who perished in the Holocaust. For example, the zig-zag layout recalls a torn Star of David.

The interior arrangement is dominated by a gigantic empty crack, which cuts a swathe through the building. Several corridors lead to a windowless Holocaust tower.

The collection focuses on Jewish history and art. Also on display are artifacts that were once part of everyday Jewish life in Berlin.

The museum is accessible only through an underground passageway in the former Berlin-Museum building next door.

The austere, steel-clad walls of the Jüdisches Museum

㉙ Topographie des Terrors

Niederkirchnerstrasse 8. Map 4 B4. Tel (030) 25 45 09 50. ⬤ & ⓤ Potsdamer Platz, Anhalter Bahnhof. 🚌 M29. Open May–Sep: 10am–8pm daily; Oct–Apr: 10am–6pm daily.

During the Third Reich, Prinz-Albrecht-Strasse (Niederkirch-nerstrasse) was probably the most frightening address in Berlin: here, three of the most terrifying Nazi political depart-ments had their headquarters. The Neo-Classical Prinz-Albrecht

palace, which stood at Wilhelmstrasse No. 102, became the headquarters of Reinhard Heydrich and the Third Reich's security service. The school of arts and crafts at Prinz-Albrecht-Strasse No. 8 was occupied by the head of the Gestapo, Heinrich Müller, while the Hotel Prinz Albrecht at No. 9 became headquarters of the Schutzstaffel or SS.

After World War II, the bomb damaged buildings were pulled down and, in 1987, a hall was built to house an exhibition on the history of the site. The museum houses the permanent exhibition 'Topography of Terror' alongside temporary displays.

The stark exterior of the Topographie des Terrors

㉚ Deutsches Technikmuseum Berlin

Trebbiner Strasse 9. Map 4 A5. Tel (030) 90 25 40. ⓤ Gleisdreieck. 🚌 140. Open 9am–5:30pm Tue–Fri, 10am–6pm Sat & Sun. ♿ 🅿

The Technical Museum was first established in 1982 with the intention of grouping more than 100 smaller, specialized collections under one roof. The current collection is arranged on the site of the former trade hall, the size of which allows many of the museum's exhibits,

such as locomotives, water towers and storerooms, to be displayed full-size and in their original condition.

Of particular interest in the collection are the dozens of locomotives and railway carriages from different eras, as well as vintage cars. There are also exhibitions dedicated to flying, the history of paper manufacture, printing, weaving, electro-technology and computer technology. There are also two windmills, a brewery and an old forge. The section called Spectrum is especially popular with children as it allows them to try the "hands-on" experiments. One hall is dedicated to the display of aircraft and aircraft engines.

A special attraction of the Technical Museum is the Historical Brewery. The building was once used by the brewery Tucker Bräu for storing beer, but it was destroyed in World War II. Decades later, the brewery was rebuilt on four levels. Some visitors claim they can smell roasted malt.

One of dozens of locomotives displayed in the Deutsches Technikmuseum

WESTERN CENTRE

This part of Berlin includes the areas of Tiergarten, Charlottenburg and parts of Kreuzberg, as well as a small section of Mitte, which used to belong to East Berlin.

Tiergarten, which was once a royal hunting estate, became a park in the 18th century. It survives as a park to this day, although in an altered form.

To the south of Tiergarten is the Kulturforum – a large centre of museums and other cultural establishments, which was created after World War II. The neighbouring Potsdamer Platz is now an ultra-modern development, built on the wasteland that formerly divided East and West Berlin.

Although the eastern part of Charlottenburg does not feature a great number of historic buildings, it is one of the city's most attractive districts, which, after World War II, became the commercial and cultural centre of West Berlin. Kreuzberg is a lively area that is now populated by immigrants, artists and affluent young professionals.

Sights at a Glance

Museums and Galleries
- ❸ Käthe-Kollwitz-Museum
- ❼ Bauhaus-Archiv
- ❽ Bendlerblock
- ❾ Gemäldegalerie
- ❿ Kupferstichkabinett und Kunstbibliothek
- ⓫ Neue Nationalgalerie
- ⓬ Kunstgewerbemuseum
- ⓮ Musikinstrumenten-Museum
- ⓱ Regierungsviertel
- ⓲ Hamburger Bahnhof
- ⓳ Museum für Naturkunde

Streets and Squares
- ❷ Kurfürstendamm (Ku'damm)
- ❹ Zoologischer Garten
- ❺ Tiergarten
- ⓯ Potsdamer Platz

Churches
- ❶ Kaiser-Wilhelm-Gedächtniskirche

Historic Buildings and Monuments
- ❻ Siegessäule
- ⓭ Philharmonie
- ⓰ Reichstag

See also Street Finder maps pp119–122

0 metres 400
0 yards 400

Street-by-Street: Kulturforum

The idea of creating a new cultural centre in West Berlin was first mooted in 1956. The first building to go up was the Berlin Philharmonic concert hall, built from 1960 to 1963 to an innovative design by Hans Scharoun. Most other elements of the Kulturforum were realized between 1961 and 1987, and came from such famous architects as Ludwig Mies van der Rohe. The area is now a major cultural centre that attracts millions of visitors every year.

⑫ ★ **Kunstgewerbe-museum**
Among the collection at the Museum of Arts and Crafts you can see this intricately carved silver and ivory tankard, made in an Augsburg workshop around 1640.

⑩ **Kupferstichkabinett**
The large collection of prints and drawings owned by this gallery includes this portrait of Albrecht Dürer's mother.

⑨ ★ **Gemäldegalerie**
Among the most important works of the old masters exhibited in this gallery of fine art is this *Madonna in Church* by Jan van Eyck (c.1425).

Kunstbibliothek
is an Art Library that boasts a rich collection of books, graphic art and drawings.

⑪ **Neue Nationalgalerie**
Sculptures by Henry Moore and Alexander Calder stand outside this streamlined building, designed by Ludwig Mies van der Rohe.

REICHPIETSCHUFER

LANDWEHRKANAL

0 metres   50
0 yards   50

Key

— Suggested route

For hotels and restaurants in this area see pp492–3 and pp510–11

⑬ ★ Philharmonie
Its exterior covered in a layer of golden aluminium, the Berlin Philharmonic concert hall is known all over the world for its superb acoustics.

Locator Map
See Street Finder maps 1 & 3

WESTERN CENTRE

EASTERN CENTRE

SCHAROUNSTRASSE

POTSDAMER STRASSE

MATTHÄIKIRCH PLATZ

GISMUNDSTRASSE

POTSDAMER STRASSE

⑭ Musikinstrumenten-Museum
This harpsichord is part of a collection of musical instruments dating from the 16th to the 20th century.

St-Matthäus-Kirche
This 19th-century church stands out among the modern buildings of the Kulturforum.

Neue Staatsbibliothek
Hans Scharoun designed this public lending and research library built in 1978.

❶ Kaiser-Wilhelm-Gedächtnis-Kirche

This church-monument is one of Berlin's most famous landmarks. The vast Neo-Romanesque church was designed by Franz Schwechten. It was consecrated in 1895 and destroyed by bombs in 1943. After the war the ruins were removed, leaving only the front tower, at the base of which the Gedenkhalle (Memorial Hall) is situated. This hall documents the church's history and contains some original ceiling mosaics, marble reliefs and liturgical objects. In 1963, Egon Eiermann designed a new octagonal church in blue glass and a new freestanding bell tower.

VISITORS' CHECKLIST

Practical Information
Breitscheidplatz.
Map 2 B4. **Tel** (030) 218 50 23.
Open Church: 9am–7pm daily.
Gedenkhalle: 10am–6pm Mon–Sat (to 5:30pm Sat), noon–5:30pm Sun. 🕀 10am & 6pm Sun. 🖭
🖩 gedaechtniskirche-berlin.de

Transport
Ⓢ & Ⓤ Zoologischer Garten or Ⓤ Kurfürstendamm.
🚌 100, 200, X-9.

Tower Ruins
The damaged roof of the former church has become one of the best-known symbols of Berlin.

Tower Clock

★ Kaiser's Mosaic
Kaiser Heinrich I, seated on his throne, is depicted in this elaborate mosaic.

Main Altar
The massive figure of Christ on the Cross is the work of Karl Hemmeter.

Main entrance

Figure of Christ
This vast sculpture by Hermann Schaper once decorated the church altar. It survived World War II damage.

❷ Ku'damm

Map 2 A5, 2 B4. **U** Kurfürstendamm.
🚌 109, 110, X10, M19, M29, M46.

The eastern area of the Charlottenburg region, around the boulevard known as Kurfürstendamm (the Ku'damm), was developed in the 19th century. Luxurious buildings were constructed along the Ku'damm, while the areas of Breitscheidplatz and Wittenbergplatz filled up with hotels and department stores. After World War II, with the old centre (Mitte) situated in East Berlin, Charlottenburg became the centre of West Berlin. After the war the area was transformed into the heart of West Berlin, with dozens of new company headquarters and trade centres being built. It is now Berlin's main shopping street.

Mother and Child, from the Käthe-Kollwitz-Museum

❸ Käthe-Kollwitz-Museum

Fasanenstrasse 24. **Map** 2 A5. **Tel** (030) 882 52 10. **U** Uhlandstrasse or Kurfürstendamm. 🚌 109, 110, X10, M19, M29, 249. **Open** 11am–6pm daily. 🅿 📷 🌐 kaethe-kollwitz.de

This small private museum provides a unique opportunity to become acquainted with the work of Käthe Kollwitz (1867–1945). Born in Königsberg, the artist settled in Berlin where she married a doctor who worked in Prenzlauer Berg, a working-class district. Her drawings and sculptures portrayed the social

A tranquil area within the Tiergarten

problems of the poor, as well as human suffering.
This museum displays the work of Käthe Kollwitz and includes posters, drawings and sculptures as well as documents, such as letters and photographs.

❹ Zoologischer Garten
Zoological Garden

Hardenbergplatz 8 / Budapester Str. 34. **Map** 2 B3, C3, 2 B4, C4. **Tel** (030) 25 40 10. 🅂 & **U** Zoologischer Garten. 🚌 M46, X9, X10, X34, 100, 109, 149, 200, 245, 249. **Open** spring & summer: 9am–6:30pm, autumn: 9am–5:30pm, winter: 9am–4:30pm. 🅿 🌐 zoo-berlin.de

The zoological garden is actually part of the Tiergarten and dates from 1844, making this one of the oldest zoos in Germany. The main attraction is its family of polar bears. A monkey house contains a family of gorillas, and there is a specially darkened pavilion for observing nocturnal animals. A glazed wall in the hippopotamus pool enables visitors to observe these enormous animals moving through the water. The large aquarium contains sharks, piranhas and unusual animals from coral reefs. There is also a huge terrarium with an overgrown jungle that is home to a group of crocodiles. Just to the west of the zoological garden on Jebenstrasse is the **Newton-Sammlung**. This gallery houses photographs by Helmut Newton.

❺ Tiergarten

Map 2 C3, 3 D3, E3, F3.
🅂 Tiergarten or Bellevue.
🚌 100, 187, 341.

Once a forest used as the Elector's hunting reserve, the Tiergarten was transformed into a landscaped park by Peter Joseph Lenné in the 1830s. A Triumphal Avenue, lined with statues of the country's rulers and statesmen, was built in the eastern section at the end of the 19th century.
World War II inflicted huge damage, but replanting has restored the Tiergarten and its avenues are bordered with statues of figures such as Johann Wolfgang von Goethe and Richard Wagner.
Near the lake and the Landwehrkanal are memorials to Karl Liebknecht and Rosa Luxemburg, the leaders of the Spartakus movement who were assassinated in 1918.

❻ Siegessäule
Triumphal Column

Großer Stern. **Map** 3 D2. **U** Hansaplatz. 🅂 Bellevue. 🚌 100, 187, 106. **Open** Apr–Oct: 9:30am–6:30pm Mon–Fri, 9:30am–7pm Sat & Sun; Nov–Mar: 10am–5pm Mon–Fri, 10am–5:30pm Sat & Sun.

This column, based on a design by Johann Heinrich Strack, was built to commemorate victory in the Prusso-Danish war of 1864. After further Prussian victories in wars against Austria (1866) and France (1871), a gilded figure representing Victory, known as the "Goldelse", was added to the top. It originally stood in front of the Reichstag building but was moved to its present location by the Nazi government in 1938. The base is decorated with bas-reliefs commemorating battles, while higher up a mosaic frieze depicts the founding of the German Empire in 1871. An observation terrace offers magnificent views.

Siegessäule (Triumphal Column)

The captivating, streamlined buildings of the Bauhaus-Archiv

ⓐ Bauhaus-Archiv

Klingelhöferstrasse 14. **Map** 3 D4, E4.
Tel (030) 254 00 20. Ⓤ Nollendorf-
platz. 🚌 100, 187, M29. **Open** 10am–
5pm Wed–Mon. 🎨 Library: 9am–
1pm Mon–Fri. ♿ 🌐 **bauhaus.de**

The Bauhaus school of art, started
by Walter Gropius in 1919, was
one of the most influential art
institutions of the 20th century.
Originally based in Weimar, it
inspired many artists and
architects. Staff and students
included Mies van der Rohe,
Paul Klee and Wassily Kandinsky.
The school moved to Berlin in
1932 from Dessau, but was
closed by the Nazis in 1933.

After the war, the Bauhaus-
Archiv was relocated to
Darmstadt. In 1964 Walter
Gropius designed a building to
house the collection but, in 1971,
the archive was moved to Berlin
and the design was adapted to
the new site. As Gropius had died
in 1969, Alexander Cvijanovic
took over the project. Built
between 1976 and 1979 the
gleaming white building with its
glass-panelled gables houses
the archive, library and
exhibition halls.

ⓑ Bendlerblock (Gedenkstätte Deutscher Widerstand)

Stauffenbergstrasse 13–14. **Map** 3
E4, F4. **Tel** (030) 26 99 50 00.
Ⓤ Mendelssohn-Bartholdy-Park.
🚌 M29, M48. **Open** 9am–6pm Mon–
Fri (to 8pm Thu), 10am–6pm Sat &
Sun. **Closed** 1 Jan, 24, 25 & 31 Dec.

The collection of buildings
known as the Bendlerblock was

built during the Third Reich as
an extension to the German
State Naval Offices. During World
War II they were the headquarters
of the Wehrmacht (German
Army). It was here that a group
of officers planned their assassination attempt on Hitler on 20
July 1944. When the attempt led
by Claus Schenk von Stauffenberg
failed, he and his fellow
conspirators were arrested and
death sentences passed.
Stauffenberg, Friedrich Olbricht,
Werner von Haeften, and Ritter
Mertz von Quirnheim were shot
in the Bendlerblock courtyard. A
monument commemorating
this event, designed by Richard
Scheibe in 1953, stands where
the executions were carried out.

On the upper floor of the building there is an exhibition which
documents the history of the
German anti-Nazi movements.

ⓒ Gemäldegalerie

See pp94–5.

ⓓ Kupferstich-kabinett und Kunstbibliothek

Matthäikirchplatz 8. **Map** 3 F3.
Tel (030) 266 20 02. Ⓢ & Ⓤ
Potsdamer Platz or Ⓤ Mendelssohn-
Bartholdy-Park. 🚌 M48, M85, 200,
M29, M41. Kupferstichkabinett
Exhibitions: 10am–6pm Tue–Fri,
11am–6pm Sat & Sun. Studio gallery:
9am–4pm Tue–Fri. Kunstbibliothek
Exhibits: 10am–6pm Tue–Fri,
11am–6pm Sat & Sun. Library: 2–8pm
Mon, 9am–8pm Tue–Fri. 🎨 ♿ 📷

The print collections of galleries
in the former East and West

Berlin were united in 1994 in
the Kupferstichkabinett (Print
Gallery), whose collection
includes around 2,000
engraver's plates, over 520,000
prints and 80,000 drawings
and watercolours.

The **Kunstbibliothek** (Art
Library) is not only a library with
a range of publications about
the arts; it is also a museum
with an extensive collection of
posters, advertisements and
other practical forms of design.

Munch's lithograph *Girl on a Beach*,
Kupferstichkabinett

ⓚ Neue Nationalgalerie

Potsdamer Strasse 50. **Map** 3 F4.
Ⓤ & Ⓢ Potsdamer Platz or Ⓤ
Mendelssohn-Bartholdy-Park. 🚌
M48, M85, 200, M29, M41. **Closed** for a
major renovation project until 2020.
📷 ♿

After World War II, when this
magnificent collection of
modern art ended up in West
Berlin, the commission to
design a suitable building to
house it was given to Mies van
der Rohe. The result is a striking
building with a flat steel roof
over a glass hall, which is
supported only by six slender
interior struts.

The collection comprises
largely 20th-century art, but
begins with artists of the late
19th century, such as Edvard
Munch. German art is well
represented: as well as the
Bauhaus movement, the gallery
shows works by exponents of a
crass realism, such as Otto Dix.
The most celebrated artists of

Cembalo harpsichords on display at the Musikinstrumenten-Museum

other European countries are included, as are examples of post World War II art.

⑫ Kunstgewerbe-museum

Matthäikirchplatz. **Map** 3 F3. **Tel** (030) 266 42 42 42. Ⓢ Potsdamer Platz. Ⓤ Potsdamer Platz or Mendelssohn-Bartholdy-Park. 🚌 100, 123, 148, 200, M29, M41. **Open** 10am–6pm Tue–Fri 11am–6pm Sat & Sun. 🅿️ ♿ ✉️

This museum holds a rich collection embracing many genres of craft and decorative art, from the early Middle Ages to the modern day. Goldwork is especially well represented, as are metal items from the Middle Ages. Among the most valuable exhibits is a collection of medieval goldwork from the church treasures of Enger and the Guelph treasury from Brunswick. The museum also takes great pride in its collection of late Gothic and Renaissance silver from

the civic treasury in the town of Lüneberg. In addition, there are fine examples of Italian majolica, and 18th- and 19th-century German, French and Italian glass, porcelain and furniture. The collection also includes a historical fashion gallery.

⑬ Philharmonie

Philharmonic and Chamber Music Hall

Herbert-von-Karajan-Strasse 1. **Map** 3 F3. **Tel** (030) 25 48 80. Ⓢ & Ⓤ Potsdamer Platz or Ⓤ Mendelssohn-Bartholdy Park. 🚌 200, M29 M41.

Home to one of the most renowned orchestras in Europe, this unusual building is among the finest postwar architectural achievements in Europe. Built between 1960 and 1963 to a design by Hans Scharoun, the Philharmonie pioneered a new

concept for concert hall interiors, with a podium occupying the central section of the pentagonal hall, around which are galleries for the public. The exterior is reminiscent of a circus tent. The gilded exterior was added between 1978 and 1981.

Between the years 1984 to 1987 the Kammermusiksaal, which was designed by Edgar Wisniewski on the basis of sketches by Scharoun, was added to the Philharmonie. This building consolidates the aesthetics of the earlier structure by featuring a central multi-sided space covered by a fanciful tent-like roof.

⑭ Musikinstru-menten-Museum

Tiergartenstrasse 1. **Map** 1 D5. **Tel** (030) 25 48 11 78. Ⓢ & Ⓤ Potsdamer Platz. 🚌 200. **Open** 9am–5pm Tue–Fri (to 8pm Thu), 10am–5pm Sat & Sun. Wurlitzer Organ demonstration: noon Sat. 🅿️ ♿ 🖥️ **mim-berlin.de**

Behind the Philharmonie, in a small building designed by Edgar Wisniewski and Hans Scharoun between 1979 and 1984, the fascinating Museum of Musical Instruments houses a collection dating from 1888. Intriguing displays trace the development of each instrument from the 16th century to the present day. Most spectacular of all is a working Wurlitzer cinema organ dating from 1929. Saturday demonstrations of its impressive sounds attract enthusiastic crowds. There is also an archive and a library.

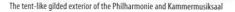

The tent-like gilded exterior of the Philharmonie and Kammermusiksaal

❾ Gemäldegalerie

The Gemäldegalerie collection is exceptional in the consistently high quality of its paintings. Unlike those in other collections, they were chosen by specialists who, from the end of the 18th century, systematically acquired pictures to represent all the major European schools. Originally displayed in the Altes Museum building *(see p79)*, the paintings achieved independent status in 1904 when they were moved to what is now the Bode-Museum *(see p82)*. After the division of Berlin in 1945, part of the collection was kept in the Bode-Museum, while the majority ended up in the Dahlem Museum *(see p108)*. Following reunification, and with the building of a new home as part of the Kulturforum development, this unique collection has finally been united again.

★ **Cupid Victorious** (1602)
Inspired by Virgil's *Omnia vincit Amor*, Caravaggio depicted a playful god trampling over the symbols of Culture, Fame, Knowledge and Power.

Madonna with Child and Angels (c.1477)
A frequent subject of Sandro Botticelli, the Madonna and Child are depicted surrounded by angels holding lilies to symbolize purity.

Circular lobby leading to the galleries

Birth of Christ (c.1480)
This beautiful religious painting is one of the few surviving paintings on wood by Martin Schongauer.

Portrait of Hieronymus Holzschuher (1526)
Albrecht Dürer painted this affectionate portrait of his friend, who was the mayor of Nuremberg.

Main entrance

The Glass of Wine
(1661/62)
Jan Vermeer's carefully composed picture of a young woman drinking wine with a young man gently hints at the relationship developing between them.

Love in the French Theatre
This picture has a companion piece called *Love in the Italian Theatre*. Both are by French painter, Jean-Antoine Watteau (1684–1721).

★ Portrait of Hendrickje Stoffels
(1656–57)
Rembrandt's portrait of his lover, Hendrickje Stoffels, is typical of his work in the way it focuses on the subject and ignores the background.

Key

- 13th–16th-century German painting
- 14th–16th-century Dutch and French painting
- 17th-century Flemish and Dutch painting
- 18th-century French, English and German painting
- 17th–18th-century Italian painting, 17th-century German, French and Spanish painting
- 13th–16th-century Italian painting
- 16th–18th-century miniatures

Gallery Guide
The main gallery contains over 900 masterpieces grouped by period and country of origin. These are complemented by around 400 works in the gallery on the lower floor.

★ Netherlandish Proverbs (1559)
Pieter Bruegel managed to illustrate more than 100 proverbs in this painting.

⑮ Potsdamer Platz

In the short space of a few years a modern financial and business district sprang up on the vast empty wasteland surrounding the Potsdamer Platz. It boasts splendid constructions designed by Renzo Piano, Arata Isozaki and Helmut Jahn. As well as office blocks, the area has many public buildings, including cinemas and a theatre, as well as a huge shopping centre – the Arkaden, plus luxury hotels, restaurants and several bars.

The Beisheim Center has a mix of exclusive apartments and international hotels.

The Sony Center

POTSDAMER PLATZ

The Sony Tower, designed by Helmut Jahn, is the most modern building in Potsdamer Platz and is curved on one side and flat on the other.

ENTLASTUNGSSTRASSE

This office building, the tallest in Potsdamer Platz, has an observation terrace and café on the 24th and 25th floors.

Arkaden, opened in autumn 1998, immediately became one of the city's favourite shopping centres.

Theater am Potsdamer Platz, designed by Italian architect Renzo Piano, hosts musicals throughout the year and is the main location for Berlinale, the annual film festival.

The Debis House, designed by Italian architect Renzo Piano.

| 0 metres | 100 |
| 0 yards | 100 |

LANDWEHRKANAL

For hotels and restaurants in this area see pp492–3 and pp510–11

The Reichstag, crowned by a dome designed by Sir Norman Foster

⓰ Reichstag

Platz der Republik. **Map** 1 E4, 4 A1, A2.
Tel (030) 22 73 21 52. Ⓤ Bundestag.
Ⓢ Brandenburger Tor. ▥ 100, M85.
Dome: **Open** by appointment only.
Assembly Hall: **Open** Apr–Oct:
9am–6pm Mon–Fri, 9am–5pm Sat–
Sun. Nov–Mar: 9am– 5pm Mon–Fri,
10am–4pm Sat & Sun.

Built to house the German
Parliament, the Reichstag was
constructed between 1884 and
1894 to a New-Renaissance
design by Paul Wallot.

In February 1933, a fire
destroyed the main hall, and
the impending world war
delayed rebuilding work for
decades. Between 1957 and
1972, the reconstructed
Reichstag was the meeting-
place for the lower house of the
German Parliament as well as a
spectacular backdrop for
festivals and rock concerts.

After German reunification in
1990, the Reichstag was the first
meeting place of a newly
elected Bundestag. The
most recent update, by Sir
Norman Foster,
transformed the
Reichstag into a
meeting hall.

⓱ Regierungs-
viertel

Government Quarter

Map 1 D3, D4 ,E3, E4; 4, 4
A1, A2. Ⓤ Bundestag.
Ⓢ Brandenburger Tor.
▥ 100, M85.

Located in the bend of the river
Spree, the new government
quarter was built between 1993

and 2003 to accomodate the
relocation of the German
government from Bonn in 1999.

Most of the buildings offer
limited access to the public,
however, several art and
political exhibitions are open
daily and art and architecture
tours run at weekends.

⓲ Hamburger
Bahnhof

Invalidenstrasse 50/51. **Map** 1 D2, B2.
Tel (030) 397 834-11. Ⓤ Zinnowitzer
strasse. Ⓢ Hauptbahnhof. ▥M41,
TXL, 120, 123, 147, 245. ▦ M6, M8,
12. **Open** 10am– 6pm Tue–Fri,
11am–8pm Sat, 11am–6pm Sun.
Closed Mon, 24 & 31 Dec. ♿ ✇ ⌖

This museum is situated in a
Neo-Renaissance building
formerly the Hamburg Railway
station, which dates from 1847.
It stood vacant after World War
II but, following refurbishment
by Josef Paul Kleihues, it was
opened to the public in 1996.
The neon installation
surrounding the
façade is the work of
Dan Flavin. The
museum houses
a magnificent
collection of
contemporary art,
including the work of
Erich Marx and, from
2004, the world-
renowned Flick
collection. The result
is one of the best
modern art
museums to be found in
Europe, which features not only
art, but also film, video, music
and design.

Jeff and Ilona (1991),
Hamburger Bahnhof

⓳ Museum für
Naturkunde

Natural History Museum

Invalidenstrasse 43. **Map** 1 E2.
Tel (030) 20 93 85 91. Ⓤ Naturkunde-
museum. ▥ 147, 245.
▦ M6, M8, 12. **Open** 9:30am–6pm
Tue–Fri, 10am–6pm Sat & Sun.
Closed 24, 25 & 31 Dec. ✇
Ⓦ naturkundemuseum-berlin.de

Occupying a purpose-built
Neo-Renaissance building
constructed between 1883 and
1889, this is one of the biggest
natural history museums in
the world, with a collection
containing over 60 million
exhibits. Although it has
undergone several periods of
extension and renovation, it
has maintained its unique
old-fashioned atmosphere.

The highlight of the museum
is the world's largest dinosaur
skeleton, which is housed in the
glass-covered courtyard. The
colossal brachiosaurus measures
23 m (75 ft) long and 12 m
(39 ft) high. It was discovered in
Tanzania, in 1909, by a German
fossil-hunting expedition.

The adjacent rooms feature
collections of shells and butter-
flies, as well as stuffed birds and
mammals. A favourite with
children is Bobby the Gorilla,
who lived in Berlin Zoo from
1928 until 1935. The museum
also has an impressive collection of minerals and meteorites.

Brachiosaurus skeleton in the
Museum für Naturkunde

FURTHER AFIELD

Berlin is a huge city with a unique character that has been shaped by the events in its history. Until 1920 the city consisted only of the districts that now comprise mainly Mitte, Tiergarten, Wedding, Prenzlauer Berg, Friedrichshain and Kreuzberg. At that time the city was surrounded by satellite towns and villages that had been evolving independently over many centuries.

In 1920, as part of great administrative reform, seven towns, 59 parishes and 27 country estates were incorporated into the city, thus creating an entirely new city covering nearly 900 sq km (350 sq miles), with a population of 3.8 million. This metropolis extended to small towns of medieval origin, such as Spandau, as well as to private manor houses and palaces, towns and smart suburban districts. Although the 20th century changed the face of many of these places, their unique characters have remained undiminished. Because of this diversity, a trip to Berlin is like exploring many different towns simultaneously.

Sights at a Glance

Museums and Galleries
1. Bröhan-Museum
2. Sammlung Berggruen
4. Langhansbau
9. Gedenkstätte Plötzensee
12. Brecht-Weigel-Gedenkstätte
13. Anne Frank Zentrum
16. Gedenkstätte Berlin-Hohenschönhausen
17. Stasi-Museum
25. Brücke-Museum

Places of Interest
7. Olympiastadion
14. Prenzlauer Berg
18. Köpenick
20. Old Flughafen Tempelhof

23. Museumszentrum Dahlem
26. Strandbad Wannsee
27. Pfaueninsel
28. Nikolskoe
29. Klein Glienicke

Streets, Squares and Parks
3. Schlosspark
15. Karl-Marx-Allee
19. Treptower Park
21. Victoriapark

Historic Buildings and Monuments
5. Schloss Charlottenburg
6. Messegelände
8. Spandau

10. Schloss Tegel
11. Neue Synagoge
22. Rathaus Schöneberg
24. Jagdschloss Grunewald

Key
- Central Berlin
- Outskirts of Berlin
- Motorway
- Main road
- Secondary road
- Railway line

0 kilometres 5
0 miles 5

Map of Greater Berlin

◄ Equestrian statue of "The Great Elector" outside Schloss Charlottenburg

For additional map symbols *see back flap*

Pablo Picasso's *Woman in a Hat* (1939), Sammlung Berggruen

❶ Bröhan-Museum

Schlossstrasse 1a. **Tel** (030) 32 69 06 00. Ⓤ Richard-Wagner-Platz & Sophie-Charlotte-Platz. Ⓢ Westend. 🚌 109, M45. **Open** 10am–6pm Tue–Sun. **Closed** 24 & 31 Dec. 🎨 (free 1st Wed).

Located in a late-Neo-Classical building is this interesting, small museum. The collection was amassed by Karl H Bröhan who, from 1966, collected works of art from the Art Nouveau (Jugendstil or Secessionist) and Art Deco styles. The paintings of artists who were particularly connected with the Berlin Secessionist movement are especially well represented. Alongside the paintings are fine examples of other media and crafts including furniture, ceramics, glassware, silverwork and textiles.

Each of the main halls features an individual artist, often employing an array of media. There is also a display of furniture by Hector Guimard, Eugène Gaillard, Henri van de Velde and Joseph Hoffmann, glasswork by Emile Gallé, and porcelain from the best European manufacturers.

❷ Sammlung Berggruen

Schlossstrasse 1. **Tel** (030) 326 95 815. Ⓤ Richard-Wagner-Platz & Sophie-Charlotte-Platz. Ⓢ Westend. 🚌 109, 309, M45. **Open** 10am–6pm Tue–Sun. 🎨 (free 4–8pm Thu.) 🅿 ♿

Heinz Berggruen assembled this tasteful collection of art dating from the late 19th and first half of the 20th century. Born and educated in Berlin, he emigrated to the US in 1936, spent most of his life in Paris, but finally entrusted his collection "Picasso and his Time" to the city of his birth. The

museum opened in what was once the west pavilion of the barracks, using the space freed up by moving the Antikensammlung to Museum Island *(see p78)*. The exhibition halls were modified according to the designs of Hilmer and Sattler, who also designed the layout of the Gemäldegalerie.

The Sammlung Berggruen is well known for its large collection of paintings, drawings and gouaches by Pablo Picasso. In addition to these, the museum displays more than 20 works by Paul Klee and paintings by other major artists – Matisse, Braque and Cézanne. The exhibition is supplemented by some excellent sculptures, particularly those of Henri Laurens and Alberto Giacometti.

❸ Schlosspark
Palace Park

Luisenplatz (Schloss Charlottenburg). Ⓤ Richard-Wagner-Platz & Sophie-Charlotte-Platz. Ⓢ Westend. 🚌 109, 309, M45. Neuer Pavillon: **Tel** (030) 32 09 14 43. Mausoleum: **Tel** (030) 32 09 14 46. **Open** Apr–Oct: 10am–6pm Tue–Sun, Nov–Mar: noon–4pm. Belvedere: **Tel** (030) 32 09 14 45. **Open** Apr–Oct: 10am–6pm Tue–Sun; Nov–Mar: noon–4pm Tue–Sun.

This extensive royal park surrounding Schloss Charlottenburg is a favourite place for Berliners to stroll. The park is largely the result of work carried out after World War II, when 18th-century prints were used to help reconstruct the layout of the original grounds. Just behind Schloss

French-style garden in the Schloss Charlottenburg park

For hotels and restaurants in this area see pp492–3 and pp510–11

Charlottenburg is a French-style Baroque garden, constructed to a strict geometrical design with a vibrant patchwork of flower beds, carefully trimmed shrubs and ornate fountains adorned with replicas of antique sculptures. Beyond the curved carp lake is a less formal English-style landscaped park, the original layout of which was created between 1819 and 1828 under the direction of the renowned royal gardener, Peter Joseph Lenné.

Designed by Karl Friedrich Schinkel and completed in 1825, the Neo-Classical **Neuer Pavillon** is a charming two-storey building with rooms ranged around a central staircase. A cast-iron balcony encircles the entire structure.

The **Mausoleum** in which Queen Luise, wife of Friedrich Wilhelm III, was laid to rest, was designed by Karl Friedrich Schinkel in the style of a Doric portico fronted temple. After the death of the king in 1840, the mausoleum was refurbished to create room for his tomb. The tombs of the king's second wife and those of Kaiser Wilhelm I and his wife were added later.

Built as a summerhouse for Friedrich Wilhelm II, with a mixture of Baroque and Neo-Classical elements, the **Belvedere** now houses the Royal Porcelain Collection, with pieces ranging from the Rococo period up to late Biedermeier.

❹ Langhansbau

Luisenplatz (Schloss Charlottenburg). **Tel** (030) 32 09 10. 🚇 Richard-Wagner-Platz. 🚌 109, 309, M45. 🕐🕐🕐 🕐🕐🕐🕐 Tue–Sun. 🔲 🔲

This Neo-Classical pavilion was designed by Carl Gotthard Langhans and added to the orangery wing of the Schloss Charlottenburg (see pp102–3) between 1787 and 1791. It was originally used as the court theatre and for many years housed a museum which documented civilizations from the Stone Age up to medieval times. The collection is now housed in the reconstructed Neues

Museum on Museum Island (see p79), and the building is used for temporary exhibitions.

❺ Schloss Charlottenburg

See pp102–3.

The Funkturm (radio tower) in Berlin's Messegelände

❻ Messegelände

Hammarskjöldplatz. 🚇 Messe Nord/ICC. 🚇 Kaiserdamm. 🚌 139, 218, X49.

The pavilions of the vast exhibition and trade halls south of Hammarskjöldplatz cover more than 160,000 sq m (1,700,000 sq ft). The original exhibition halls were built before World War I, but nothing

of these buildings remains. The oldest part is the Funkturm and the pavilions surrounding it. The building at the front (Ehrenhalle) was built in 1936 to a design by Richard Ermisch, and is one of the few surviving buildings in Berlin designed in a Fascist architectural style.

The straight motorway at the rear of the halls is the famous Avus, the first German autobahn, built in 1921. At one point adapted as a car-racing track, it now forms part of the autobahn system.

❼ Olympiastadion

Olympischer Platz. 🚉 & 🚇 Olympia-Stadion. **Tel** (030) 30 68 81 00. **Open** late Mar–May: 9am–7pm daily; Jun–mid-Sep. 9am–8pm daily; mid-Sep–Oct: 9–7pm daily; Nov–late Mar: 9am–4pm daily. 🔲 🔲 🔲 olympiastadion-berlin.de

Olympiastadion, originally known as Reichssportfeld, was built for the 1936 Olympic Games in Berlin. It was designed by Werner March in the Nazi architectural style and was inspired by the architecture of ancient Rome. To the west of the stadium lie the Maifeld and what is now called the Waldbühne. The former is an enormous assembly ground surrounded by grandstands and fronted by the Glockenturm, a 77 m (250 ft) tower, while the latter is an open-air amphi-theatre. A four-year high-tech modernization project on the stadium was completed in 2004. It now features a sweeping, illuminated roof.

The ever impressive Olympiastadion

❺ Schloss Charlottenburg

The palace in Charlottenburg was intended as a summer home for Sophie Charlotte, the wife of Elector Friedrich III. Construction began in 1695 to a design by Johann Arnold Nering. Johann Eosander Göthe enlarged the palace between 1701 and 1713, adding the orangery wing. Further extensions were undertaken between 1740 and 1746 by Frederick the Great (Friedrich II) who added the new wing.

The palace was restored to its former elegance after World War II and its richly decorated interiors are unequalled in Berlin.

First floor

Ground floor

Entrance to Langhansbau

★ Porzellankabinett
This exquisite mirrored gallery has walls lined from top to bottom with a fine display of Japanese and Chinese porcelain.

Entrance to Altes Schloss

Schlosskapelle
Only the pulpit in the court chapel is original. All the remaining furniture and fittings, including the splendid royal box, are reconstructions.

Palace Façade
The central section of the palace, decorated with Corinthian pilasters and topped with a decorative cornice, is the oldest part of the building. It is the work of Johann Arnold Nering.

Monument to the Great Elector

Fortuna
This sculpture by Richard Scheibe crowns the palace, replacing the original statue destroyed during World War II.

VISITORS' CHECKLIST

Practical Information
Spandauer Damm 20–24.
Tel (030) 32 09 10.
Altes Schloss: **Open** 10am–6pm
Tue–Sun (Nov–Mar: to 5pm).
Neuer Flügel: **Open** 10am–
6pm Wed–Mon (Nov–Mar:
to 5pm). ♿ 🚻 📷

Transport
Ⓤ Richard-Wagner-Platz &
Sophie-Charlotte-Platz.
Ⓢ Jungfernheide & Westend.
🚌 M45, 109, 309.

Key

- 🟦 Official reception rooms
- 🟦 Sophie-Charlotte's apartments
- 🟦 Neuer Flügel or Knobelsdorff-Flügel exhibition space
- 🟦 Friedrich Wilhelm II's apartments
- 🟦 Mecklenburg apartments
- 🟦 Friedrich Wilhelm IV's apartments
- 🟦 Friedrich Wilhelm II's apartments
- 🟦 Frederick the Great's apartments
- 🟦 Non-exhibition space

Friedrich Wilhelm IV's Apartments
This oval hall, decorated with mirrors and offering a delightful garden view, was the king's dining quarters and ballroom.

Weisser Saal

Goldene Galerie

Entrance to
Neuer Flügel

Frederick the Great's Apartments
Located on the upper floor of the new wing, this concert room was part of the elegant living quarters of Frederick the Great.

★ **Gersaint's Shop Sign** (1720)
An avid collector of French painting, Frederick the Great bought this and other fine canvases by Antoine Watteau for his collection.

Hohenzollern coat of arms above the main gate of Spandau's citadel

❽ Spandau

Zitadelle Spandau: Am Juliusturm 64. **Tel** (030) 354 94 40. 🚇 Zitadelle. 🚌 X33. **Open** 10am–5pm daily. 🅿 🔲 **zitadelle-spandau.de**

Spandau is one of the oldest towns within the area of greater Berlin, and it has managed to retain its own distinctive character. Although the town of Spandau was only granted a charter in 1232, evidence of the earliest settlement here dates back to the 8th century.

The area was spared the worst of the World War II bombing, so there are still some interesting sights to visit. The heart of the town is a network of medieval streets with a picturesque market square and a number of the original timber-framed houses. In the north of Spandau, sections of the town wall dating from the 15th century are still standing.

In the centre of town is the magnificent Gothic St-Nikolai-Kirche, dating from the 15th century. The church holds many valuable ecclesiastical furnishings, such as a splendid Renaissance stone altar from the end of the 16th century, a Baroque pulpit from around 1700 that came from a royal palace in Potsdam, a Gothic baptismal font and many epitaphs.

A castle was first built on the site of the Zitadelle Spandau (citadel) in the 12th century, but today only the 36 m (120 ft) Juliusturm (tower) remains. In 1560 the building of a fort was begun here, to a design by Francesco Chiaramella da Gandino. It took 30 years to complete and most of the work was supervised by architect Rochus Graf von Lynar. Although the citadel had a jail, the town's most infamous resident, Rudolf Hess, was incarcerated a short distance away in a military prison after the 1946 Nuremberg trials. In 1987, when the former deputy leader of the Nazi party died, the prison was torn down.

❾ Gedenkstätte Plötzensee

Plötzensee Memorial

Hüttigpfad 16. **Tel** (030) 26 99 50 00. 🚇 Jakob-Kaiser-Platz, then 🚌 123, 126. **Open** Mar–Oct: 9am–5pm; Nov–Feb: 9am–4pm.

A narrow street leads from Saatwinkler Damm to the site where nearly 2,500 people convicted of crimes against the

Memorial to concentration camp victims at Gedenkstätte Plötzensee

Third Reich were hanged. The Gedenkstätte Plötzensee is a simple memorial in a brick hut, which still retains the iron hooks from which the victims were suspended.

Claus Schenk von Stauffenberg and the other main figures in the assassination attempt against Hitler on 20 July 1944 were executed in the Bendlerblock *(see p92)*, but the rest of the conspirators were executed here at the Plötzensee prison.

Count Helmut James von Moltke, one of the leaders of the German resistance movement, was also killed here. He was responsible for organizing the Kreisauer Kreis – a political movement that gathered and united German opposition to Hitler.

❿ Schloss Tegel

Adelheidallee 19–21. **Tel** (030) 434 31 56. 🚇 Alt Tegel. 🚌 124, 133, 222. **Open** May–Sep: 10am, 11am, 3pm, 4pm. 🔲 compulsory.

Schloss Tegel is one of the most interesting palace complexes in Berlin. The site was occupied in the 16th century by a manor house. In the second half of the 17th century, this was rebuilt into a hunting lodge for the Elector Friedrich Wilhelm. In 1766 the ownership of the property passed to the Humboldt family and, between 1820 and 1824, Karl Friedrich Schinkel thoroughly rebuilt the palace, giving it its current style.

Decorating the elevations on the top floor of the towers are tiled bas-reliefs designed by Christian Daniel Rauch, depicting the ancient wind gods. Some of Schinkel's marvellous interiors have survived, along with several items from what was once a large collection of sculptures. The palace is still privately owned by descendants of the Humboldt family, but guided tours are offered on Mondays.

It is also worth visiting the park in which the palace stands. On the western limits of the park lies the Humboldt family tomb, also designed by

The elegant Neo-Classical façade of Schloss Tegel

Schinkel. The tomb contains a copy of a splendid sculpture by Bertel Thorwaldsen. The original piece stands inside the Schloss Tegel.

The Neue Synagoge with its splendidly reconstructed dome

⑪ Neue Synagoge
New Synagogue

Oranienburger Strasse 30. **Tel** (030) 880 28 300. ⑤ Oranienburger Strasse. 🚊 M1, M6. **Open** daily. 🚻 📷

Construction of the New Synagogue, begun in 1859 by architect Eduard Knoblauch, was completed in 1866. The design was a response to the asymmetrical shape of the plot of land, with a narrow façade flanked by a pair of towers and crowned with a dome containing a round vestibule.

With its gilded dome, this was Berlin's largest synagogue until it was partially destroyed during the infamous *Kristallnacht* in 1938. The building was damaged further by Allied bombing in 1943 and was eventually demolished in 1958. Reconstruction began in 1988

and was completed in 1995. Public exhibitions by the Centrum Judaicum are held in the front of the building.

⑫ Brecht-Weigel-Gedenkstätte
Brecht-Weigel Memorial

Chausseestrasse 125. **Tel** (030) 200 57 18 44. 🚇 Naturkunde Museum or Oranienburger Tor. 🚌 340. 🚊 M6, 12. 📷 compulsory. Every half hour (every hour on Sun). 10am–3:30pm Tue, 10am–11:30pm Wed, Fri; 10am–6:30pm Thu; 10am–3:30pm Sat, 11am–6pm Sun. **Closed** Mon, public holidays. 🚻

Playwright Bertolt Brecht was associated with Berlin from 1920, but emigrated in 1933. After the war, his left-wing views made him an attractive potential resident of the newly created German socialist state. Lured by the promise of his own theatre, he returned to Berlin in 1948 with his wife, the actress Helene Weigel.

In 1953, Brecht moved into Chausseestrasse 125 and lived there until his death in 1956. His wife founded an archive of his work, which is located on the second floor.

Bertolt Brecht's study in his former apartment

⑬ Anne Frank Zentrum

Rosenthalestrasse 39. **Tel** (030) 288 86 56 00. 🚇 Weinmeisterstraße. ⑤ Hackescher Markt. **Open** 10am–6pm Tue–Sun. 🚻 🌐 **annefrank.de**

Anne Frank's short life and her diary are at the heart of this interactive exhibition, which connects history to the present day. Visitors are encouraged to reflect on their own views through listening to young people from Berlin discussing the issues that occupied Anne Frank, such as identity, values, war and discrimination.

⑭ Prenzlauer Berg

Sammlung Industrielle Gestaltung: Kulturbrauerei entrance, Knaackstrasse 97. **Tel** (030) 473 77 79 40. 🚇 Senefelderplatz or Eberswalderstrasse. **Open** phone ahead to check.

Towards the end of the 19th century, this was one of the most impoverished, densely populated districts of Berlin, which became a centre for anti-Communist opposition.

After 1989, however, artists, professionals and students began to gather here from all parts of Germany and Europe, creating a colourful, vibrant community.

Schönhauser Allee is the main thoroughfare of Prenzlauer Berg. A former old brewery was transformed into the "Kulturbrauerei", a centre for cultural events. It also houses a museum – **Sammlung Industrielle Gestaltung** – with a collection of industrial designs from East Germany.

Heading along Sredzkistrasse you reach Husemannstrasse. This beautifully renovated street complete with shops and inns gives the impression of Berlin around the year 1900. Amid the greenery around Belforter Strasse is a water tower built in the mid-19th century. Nearby, on Schönhauser Allee, there is an old Jewish cemetery dating from 1827. Among those buried here is the renowned painter Max Liebermann.

Fragment of Socialist Realist decoration from Karl-Marx-Allee

⓯ Karl-Marx-Allee

Map 5 F1. Ⓤ Strausberger Platz or Weberwiese.

The section of Karl-Marx-Allee between Strausberger Platz and Frankfurter Tor is effectively a huge open-air museum of Socialist Realist architecture. The route to the east was named Stalinallee in 1949 and chosen as the site for the showpiece of the new German Democratic Republic. The avenue was widened to 90 m (300 ft) and, over the next ten years, huge residential tower blocks and a row of shops were built. The designers, led by Hermann Henselmann, succeeded in combining three sets of architectural guidelines. They used the Soviet wedding cake style according to the precept: "nationalistic in form but socialist in content", and linked the whole work to Berlin's own traditions. Hence there are motifs taken from famous Berlin architects Schinkel and Gontard, as well as from the renowned Meissen porcelain.

The buildings on this street, renamed Karl-Marx-Allee in 1961, are now considered historic monuments.

⓰ Gedenkstätte Berlin-Hohen-schönhausen

Genslerstrasse 66. **Tel** (030) 9860 82 30. Ⓢ Landsberger Allee, then ⨂ M5, M6. ⦿ 256. **Open** 11am–3pm Mon–Fri, 10am–4pm Sat & Sun. 🎧 English tour 2:30pm daily, public tours 2pm Sat. 📷

This museum was established in 1995 within the former Stasi detention centre. The building

was part of a huge complex built in 1938. In May 1945, the occupying Russian authorities created a special transit camp here, in which they interned war criminals and anyone under political suspicion. From 1946 the buildings were refashioned into the custody area for the KGB; in 1951, it was given over to the Stasi.

The prisoners' cells and interrogation rooms are on view, two of which have no windows and are lined with rubber. Housed in the cellars was the "submarine" – a series of cells without daylight to which the most "dangerous" suspects were brought.

⓱ Forschungs- und Gedenkstätte Normannenstrasse (Stasi-Museum)

Ruschestrasse 103 (Haus 1). **Tel** (030) 553 68 54. Ⓤ Magdalenenstrasse. **Open** 11am–6pm Mon–Fri, 2–6pm Sat–Sun. 🎧 🖥 **stasimuseum.de**

Under the German Democratic Republic, this huge complex of buildings at Ruschestrasse housed the Ministry of the Interior. It was here that the infamous Stasi (GDR secret service) had its headquarters.

The Stasi's "achievements" in infiltrating its own community were without equal in the Eastern block.

Since 1990 one of the buildings has housed a museum that displays photographs and documents depicting the activities of the Stasi. Here, you can see a model of the headquarters, and equipment that was used for bugging and spying on citizens suspected of holding unfavourable political views. You can also walk around the office of infamous Stasi chief Erich Mielke.

⓲ Köpenick

Ⓢ Spindlersfeld, then ⦿ 167 or Ⓢ Köpenick, then ⦿ 164, 167. ⨂ 27, 60, 61, 62, 68. Kunstgewerbemuseum: Schloss Köpenick, Schlossinsel. **Tel** (030) 6566 17 49. **Open** 10am–5pm Thu–Sun.

Köpenick is much older than Berlin. In the 9th century AD, this island contained a fortified settlement known as Kopanica. In about 1240 a castle was built on the island, around which a town began to evolve. Craftsmen settled here and, after 1685, a large colony of Huguenots also settled.

In the 19th century Köpenick recreated itself as an industrial town. Despite wartime devastation it has retained its historic character and, though there are no longer any 13th-century churches, it is worth strolling around the old town. By the old market square and in the neighbouring streets, modest houses have survived that recall the 18th century, alongside buildings from the end of the 19th century.

At Alt Köpenick No. 21 is a vast brick town hall built in the style of the Brandenburg Neo-Renaissance. In 1906, a famous swindle took place here and the event became the inspiration for a popular comedy by Carl Zuckmayer, *The Captain from Köpenick*. Köpenick's greatest attraction is a three-storey

Office of the infamous Stasi chief Erich Mielke at the Stasi Museum

A reconstructed drawing room from 1548 in the Kunstgewerbemuseum

Baroque palace, built between 1677 and 1681 for the heir to the throne Friedrich (later King Friedrich I), to a design by the Dutch architect Rutger van Langfield. In 2003, the **Kunstgewerbemuseum** *(see p92)* opened a suite of Renaissance and Baroque rooms to the public in the Köpenick Palace.

Gigantic wreath commemorating the Red Army in Treptower Park

⓲ Treptower Park

Archenhold-Sternwarte, Alt-Treptow. Ⓢ Treptower Park. 🚌 166, 167, 265. Archenhold-Sternwarte, **Tel** (030) 536 06 37 19. 📷 compulsory; 2–4:30pm Wed–Sun. 🖥 **sdtp.de**

The vast park in Treptow was laid out in the 1860s on the initiative and design of Johann Gustav Meyer. In 1919 it was where revolutionaries Karl Liebknecht, Wilhelm Pieck and Rosa Luxemburg assembled 150,000 striking workers.

The park is best known for the colossal monument to the Red Army. Built between 1946 and 1949, it stands on the grave of 5,000 Soviet soldiers killed in the battle for Berlin in 1945. The gateway, which leads to the mausoleum, is marked by a vast granite sculpture of a grieving Russian Motherland surrounded by statues of Red Army soldiers.

In the farthest section of the park is the astronomical observatory, **Archenhold Sternwarte**, which was built for a decorative arts exhibition in 1896. Given a permanent site in 1909, the observatory was used by Albert Einstein for a lecture on the Theory of Relativity in 1915. It is also home to the longest reflecting telescope in the world (21 m or 70 ft), and a small planetarium.

Beyond Treptower Park lies another park, Plänterwald.

⓴ Old Flughafen Tempelhof

Platz der Luftbrücke. Ⓤ Platz der Luftbrücke 🚌 104, 184

Tempelhof was once Germany's largest airport. Built in 1923, the structure is typical of Third Reich architecture. Additions to the original structure were completed in 1939.

In 1951, a monument was added in front of the airport. Designed by Edward Ludwig, it commemorates the airlifts of the Berlin Blockade. The names of those who lost their lives appear on the plinth.

After a long public debate, Tempelhof was decommissioned as a functioning airport in 2008. It has been turned into a public park and exhibition venue.

㉑ Viktoriapark

Ⓤ Platz der Luftbrücke. 🚌 104, 140.

This rambling park, with several artificial waterfalls, short trails and a small hill, was designed by Hermann Mächtig and built between 1884 and 1894. The Neo-Gothic Memorial to the Wars of Liberation at the summit of the hill is the work of Karl Friedrich Schinkel and was constructed between 1817 and 1821. The monument commemorates the Prussian victory against Napoleon's army in the Wars of Liberation. The monument's cast-iron tower is well ornamented.

In the niches of the lower section are 12 allegorical figures by Christian Daniel Rauch, Friedrich Tieck and Ludwig Wichmann. Each figure symbolizes a battle and is linked to a historic figure – either a military leader or a member of the royal family.

㉒ Rathaus Schöneberg

Schöneberg Town Hall

John-F-Kennedy-Platz. Ⓤ Rathaus Schöneberg.

The Schöneberg town hall is a gigantic building with an imposing tower, which was built between 1911 and 1914. From 1948 to 1990 it was used as the main town hall of West Berlin, and it was outside here, on 26 June 1963, that US President John F. Kennedy gave his famous speech. More than 300,000 Berliners assembled to hear the young president say *"Ich bin ein Berliner"* – "I am a Berliner", intended as an expression of solidarity from the democratic world to a city defending its right to freedom.

While Kennedy's meaning was undoubtedly clear, pedants were quick to point out that what he actually said was "I am a small doughnut".

Japanese woodcut from the Museum für Ostasiatische Kunst

㉓ Museumszentrum Dahlem

Lansstrasse 8, Dahlem. **Tel** (030) 266 42 42 42. **U** Dahlem Dorf. 🚌 M11, X83. Museum für Asiatische Kunst (Museum of Asian Art), Museum Europäischer Kulturen (Museum of European Cultures), Ethnologisches Museum (Museum of Mankind): **Open** 10am–5pm Tue–Fri, 11am–5pm Sat & Sun. 🅿 **W** smb.museum.de

Dahlem's first museums were built between 1914 and 1923, but the district was confirmed as a major cultural and education centre after World War II with the establishment of the Freie Universität and completion of the museum complex. With many of Berlin's collections fragmented, a miscellany of art and artifacts was put on display here. In the 1960s the museums were extended and the Museumszentrum was created to rival East Berlin's Museum Island.

German reunification in 1990 meant that the collections could once again be reunited and reorganized. Paintings were moved to the Kulturforum (see pp88–9), and sculptures to the Bodemuseum (see p82).

Three museums are now housed at Dahlem: the Ethnologisches Museum, which focuses on pre-industrial societies from around the world; the Museum für Asiatische Kunst, one of the largest musems of Asian art in the world and the Museum Europäischer Kulturen.

Highlights include bronzes from Benin and gold Inca jewellery at the Museum of Mankind and Japanese wood-cuts from Chinese Turkestan at the Museum of Asian Art. The Exhibition of Native North American Cultures, part of the Museum of Mankind, opened in 1999, includes a collection of 600 ceremonial objects.

㉔ Jagdschloss Grunewald

Am Grunewaldsee 29. **Tel** (030) 813 35 97. 🚌 115, X10. **Open** Apr–Oct: 10am–6pm Tue–Sun; Nov–Mar: tours only, 11am, 1pm, 3pm Sat & Sun. 🅿 **W** spsg.de

Jagdschloss Grunewald is one of the oldest surviving civic buildings in Berlin. Built for the Elector Joachim II in 1542, it was rebuilt around 1700 in a Baroque style.

In this small palace on the edge of the Grunewaldsee is Berlin's only surviving Renaissance hall, which currently houses a collection of paintings that includes a range of canvases by Rubens and van Dyck, among others.

In the east wing is the small Waldmuseum, which has a collection of illustrations depicting forest life and the history of forestry. Opposite the Jagdschloss, a hunting museum (Jagdmuseum) houses a collection of historic weapons and equipment.

㉕ Brücke-Museum

Bussardsteig 9, Dahlem. **Tel** (030) 831 20 29. 🚌 115. **Open** 11am–5pm Wed–Mon. **W** bruecke-museum.de

This elegant Functionalist building hosts a collection of German Expressionist painting linked to the Die Brücke group. It is based on almost 80 works by Schmidt-Rottluff bequeathed to the town of Dahlem in 1964. In addition to other works of art contemporary to Die Brücke, there are paintings from the later creative periods of these artists, as well as works of other closely associated artists. Nearby lie the foundation's headquarters, established in the former studio of the sculptor Bernhard Heiliger.

㉖ Strandbad Wannsee

Wannseebadweg. 🅢 Nikolassee. 🚌 112, 218.

The vast lake Wannsee, on the edge of Grunewald, is a popular destination for Berliners seeking recreation. The most developed part is the southeastern corner where there are yachting marinas and harbours. Further north is one of the largest inland beaches in Europe, Strandbad Wannsee, which was developed between 1929 and 1930 by the construction of shops, cafés and changing rooms on man-made terraces. It is also pleasant to walk around Schwanenwerder island, with its many elegant villas.

Boarding point for lake cruises on the Wannsee

The Schloss Pfaueninsel designed by Johann Brendel

㉗ Pfaueninsel

Pfaueninsel. **Tel** (030) 805 86 830.
Ⓢ Wannsee, then take 🚌 218.
🚢 Schloss Pfaueninsel. **Open** Apr–
Oct: 10am–5pm Tue–Sun. 🎫

This picturesque island, named for the peacocks that inhabit it, is now a nature reserve, reached by ferry across the Havel river. It was laid out in 1795 according to a design by Johann August Eyserbeck. Its final form, which you see today, is the work of the landscape architect Peter Joseph Lenné.

One of the most interesting sights on the island is the small romantic palace of **Schloss Pfaueninsel**. Dating from 1794, it was designed by Johann Gottlieb Brendel for Friedrich Wilhelm II and his mistress Wilhelmine Encke (the future Countess Lichtenau). The palace was built of wood, with a façade fashioned in the form of a ruined medieval castle. The cast-iron bridge that links the towers was built in 1807. The palace is open to the public in the summer months, when you can see the 18th- and 19th-century furnishings.

Other sights worth visiting include **Jakobsbrunnen** (Jacob's Well), which was built to resemble an ancient ruin. Towards the northeast corner of the island is the **Luisentempel** in the form of a Greek temple. Its sandstone portico was relocated to the island from the mausoleum in Schlosspark Charlottenburg (see pp102–3) in 1829. Nearby is a stone commemorating Johannes

Kunckel, an alchemist who lived on Pfaueninsel in the 17th century. During his quest to discover how to make gold, he discovered a method of producing ruby-coloured glass. Near the **Aviary**, home to multicoloured parrots and pheasants, is a tall fountain that was designed by Martin Friedrich Rabe in 1824.

㉘ Nikolskoe

Nikolskoer Weg. Ⓢ Wannsee, then take 🚌 316.

Across the river from Pfaueninsel (Peacock Island) is Nikolskoe. Here you'll find the Blockhaus Nikolskoe, a Russian-style *dacha* (country house) that was built in 1819 for the future Tsar Nicholas I and his wife, the daughter of King Friedrich Wilhelm III.

The house was built by the German military architect Captain Snethlage, who was responsible for

Guests on the terrace of the Blockhaus Nikolskoe in summer

the Alexandrowka estate in Potsdam (see p138). Following a fire in 1985, the *dacha* was reconstructed. It currently houses a restaurant.

Close by is the church of St Peter and Paul, which was built between 1834 and 1837, to a design by Friedrich August Stüler. The body of the church is completed by a tower crowned by an onion-shaped dome, reflecting the style of Russian Orthodox metal architecture.

㉙ Klein Glienicke

Königstr. 36. 🚌 316. **Tel** (0331) 96 94 200. **Open** Apr–Oct: 10am–6pm Tue–Sun; Nov–Mar: 10am–5pm Sat & Sun. 🎫

The palace in the palace-park of Klein Glienicke was built in 1825 according to a design by Karl Friedrich Schinkel for Prince Karl of Prussia. The charming park in which it is located was created by Peter Joseph Lenné. Beyond the Neo-Classical palace extends an irregular cluster of buildings, grouped around a courtyard, including a pergola and staff cottages. Passing by the palace, you approach the **Coach House**, also designed by Schinkel and now housing a restaurant. Nearby are an orangery and greenhouses designed by Ludwig Persius. Also by Persius is the **Klosterhof**, a mock monastery with pavilions, on whose walls are many Byzantine and Romanesque architectural elements from Italy. Towards the lake is the **Grosse Neugierde**, a circular pavilion based on the Athenian monument to Lysikrates from the 4th century BC. From here there are beautiful views across the Havel river and **Glienicker Brücke** (known under the East German regime as the bridge of unity). The border with West Berlin ran across this bridge where, during the Cold War, the exchange of spies was conducted.

Karl Friedrich Schinkel's Neo-Classical Schloss Klein Glienicke

SHOPPING IN BERLIN

With a shopping centre in every district, each selling a variety of merchandise, Berlin is a place where almost anything can be bought, so long as you know where to shop. The most popular areas are Kurfürstendamm and Friedrichstrasse, but the smaller shops in Wedding, Friedrichshain, Schöneberg and the Tiergarten are also worth a visit. Small boutiques selling flamboyant Berlin-style clothes crop up in unexpected courtyards, while the top fashion houses offer the latest in European elegance. Early on Saturday morning is often the best time to visit the city's various markets, the most popular of which – with their colourful stalls full of hats, bags and belts – can be found on Museum Island and near the Tiergarten. The Galeries Lafayette, KaDeWe and any of the city's numerous bookshops all make ideal venues for a pleasant afternoon's window shopping.

A shop-floor display in the lobby of KaDeWe

Practical Information

The majority of shops are open Monday to Saturday from 10am to 8pm. Before Christmas, many shops are open on Sundays. Some smaller stores do not accept credit cards, so be sure to have some cash.

Department Stores and Shopping Centres

The **Alexa Centre**, a large shopping mall located at Alexanderplatz, houses most of the major fashion chains. Kaufhaus Des Westens, better known as **KaDeWe** at Wittenbergplatz, is undoubtedly the biggest and the best department store in Berlin, while **Galeries Lafayette** on Friedrichstrasse is nothing less than a slice of Paris in the heart of Berlin. Perfumes, domestic accessories and clothing attract an enormous clientele.

Another very popular store is **Karstadt** on the Ku'damm.

Although the outfits sold here are less haute couture than at Galeries Lafayette, there is still an enormous choice and the top-floor restaurant offers excellent views over the city.

One of the newest shopping centres is the **Potsdamer Platz Arkaden**, which is a very popular meeting place. On a slightly smaller scale is **Das Schloss** in Steglitz, and the **Gesundbrunnencenter** is the biggest shopping passage in Berlin with stalls full of bargains. **Europa-Center** is the most visually stunning with its beautiful sculpted fountains.

Fashion

The Ku'damm and Friedrichstrasse areas play host to all the best known high street names and department stores, as well as most of the top fashion houses in Berlin. **Escada** is one of the best known of the German designers, but Berlin also has a wealth of young designers and their lines are mainly to be seen in the northern part of the Mitte area. **NIX**, for example, offers timeless clothes made from heavy, dark fabrics, while **Department Store Quartier 206** sells everything from evening dresses to casual wear and accessories. It offers only top international designer wear and many unique pieces. An exciting designer is **Antonia Goy**, who creates stunning dresses and accessories for women.

For men's fashions, once again the Ku'damm area is the place to look. **Patrick Hellmann** is certainly worth a visit with its wide choice of the best designer labels around.

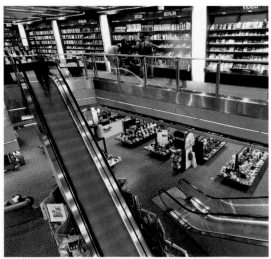

The spacious Karstadt department store on Kurfürstendamm

Store front of German fashion house Escada

Antiques

The antiques trade in Berlin is booming, and there are many markets and galleries opening all the time. Berlin's most prestigious auction house is **Galerie Bassenge**, while **ART 1900** and **Zeitlos** on Suarez-strasse offer trinkets and knick-knacks from various periods. Many Berliners spend their Saturday and Sunday mornings at flea markets browsing the stalls. In particular, the **Antik & Trödelmarkt am Ostbahnhof** is considered one of the best places to pick up bargains.

Food Products

All manner of foods and wine are available in Berlin, and they make excellent gifts and souvenirs. Kaffee und Kuchen (coffee and cakes) is a strong German tradition, so why not head to **Buchwald** and purchase one of their delicious cakes to take home. You will also find that bakeries all over the city sell traditional *Berliners* (doughnuts) along with a good value range of delicious pastries and breads.

Wine-fans will love **Viniculture**, which offers a wide range of German wines, or if you enjoy the local meats, there is a bewildering choice of organic sausages at **Fleischerei Bachhuber**.

Berlin also has several food markets. The **Winterfeldmarkt** is probably the most popular, but the **Wochenmarkt** on Wittenbergplatz also has a particularly loyal following. Additionally, the **Türkenmarkt** offers fruit and vegetables, Turkish specialities and fabrics.

Seasonal Sales

Twice a year (January and July) all the shops in Berlin empty their shelves in the end of season *Schlussverkauf*. Goods bought in a sale are officially non-returnable, though sometimes you may find you are able to negotiate with the shop assistant.

A number of shops sell "second season" items – these are new, but they were stocked for the previous season and as such are generously reduced in price and make great bargain buys.

The central "glass cone" of the Galeries Lafayette department store

DIRECTORY

Department Stores and Shopping Centres

Alexa Centre
Am Alexanderplatz
Grunerstrasse 20. **Map** 2 E3. **w** alexacentre.com

Das Schloss
Schlossstrasse 34.
Map 2 E0.

Europa-Center
Breitscheidsplatz.
Map 2 B4. **w** europa-center-berlin.de

Galeries Lafayette
Französische Strasse 23.
Map 4 C2. **Tel** (030) 20 94 80. **w** galeries-lafayette.de

Gesundbrunnen-center
Gesundbrunnen S-Bahn.

KaDeWe
Tauentzienstrasse 21.
Map 2 C5. **Tel** (030) 21 21 00. **w** kadewe-berlin.de

Karstadt
Kurfürstendamm 231.
Map 2 B4. **Tel** (030) 88 00 30. **w** karstadt.de

Potsdamer Platz Arkaden
Debis Gelände. **Map** 4 A3.
w potsdamer-platz-arkaden.de

Fashion

Antonia Goy
Brunnenstrasse 142.
Tel (030) 4465 03 86.

Department Store Quartier 206
Friedrichstr. 71. **Map** 4 C2.
Tel (030) 20 94 62 40.

Escada
Friedrichstr. 176–179. **Map** 4 C2. **Tel** (030) 238 64 04.

NIX
Oranienburger Str. 32.
Map 5 D1. **Tel** (030) 281 80 44. **w** nix-berlin.de

Patrick Hellmann
Kurfürstendamm 190–2.
Map 2 A5. **Tel** (030) 88 48 77 16.

Antiques

Antik & Trödelmarkt am Ostbahnhof
Erich-Steinfurth-Strasse.
Open Sat & Sun.

ART 1900
Kurfürstendamm 53. **Map** 2 A5. **Tel** (030) 881 56 27.

Galerie Bassenge
Erdener Strasse 5a.
Tel (030) 89 38 02 90.
Open 10am–6pm Mon–Fri.
w bassenge.com

Zeitlos
Suarezstrasse 61.
Tel (030) 405 877 91.

Food Products

Buchwald
Bartningallee 29.
Map 3 D2. **Tel** (030) 391 59 31.

Fleischerei Bachhuber
Güntzelstrasse 47.
Tel (030) 873 21 15.

Türkenmarkt
Maybachufer.
Open 11am–6:30pm Tue & Fri.

Viniculture
Grolmanstrasse 44–45.
Tel (030) 883 81 74.

Winterfeldmarkt
Wittenbergplatz.
Open 8am–1pm Wed, 8am–4pm Sat.

Wochenmarkt
Wittenbergplatz.
Open 8am–2pm Tue, 8am–4pm Fri.

ENTERTAINMENT IN BERLIN

With so much on offer, from classical drama and cabaret to variety theatre and an eclectic nightclub scene, it is possible to indulge just about any taste in Berlin. During the summer months many bars and restaurants set up outdoor tables and the areas around Unter den Linden, the Kurfürstendamm, Kreuzberg and Prenzlauer Berg in particular, seem to turn into one large social arena. The city really comes into its own at night, when its clubs, all-night cafés and cocktail bars give you the chance to dance till dawn. The city has many night-life centres, each with a slightly different character. Prenzlauer Berg is the best choice for mainstream bars, cafés and clubs, while Friedrichshain has a vibrant subculture, and Schöneberg has a lively gay scene. The Mitte district in the eastern centre offers a true mixture with its opera house and classical theatre surrounded by lively and sleek bars. On a Sunday, a quiet trip down the river or along the canals offers a pleasant way to unwind.

The Berlin Philharmonic Orchestra

Practical Information

There are so many things going on in Berlin that it can be difficult to find what you are looking for. Listings magazines like *Tip* or *Zitty* are invaluable aids and offer the widest range of suggestions. Information on festivals, sports events, cinema programmes, theatre schedules, cabarets and concerts can be found at: www.berlinonline.de and www.berlin.de.

For visitors who have not made it yet to an internet café or a kiosk, the chances are the local bar or your hotel foyer has leaflets on the wall. There are also lots of posters around town telling you what is on offer. *EXBERLINER* magazine has listings in English, and it should be available at most kiosks.

Tickets for events should generally be bought in advance, though last-minute tickets are often available from **Hekticket Theaterkassen**. The disabled, pensioners and students with the appropriate ID are often entitled to discounted tickets. All major venues will provide good wheelchair access.

Classical Music

The Berlin Philharmonic Orchestra is one of the world's finest orchestras and it performs at the beautiful **Philharmonie**, with its awe-inspiring architecture and fantastic acoustics. Chamber orchestras perform in the smaller **Kammermusiksaal** attached to the bigger hall. **Konzerthaus Berlin**, formally known as the Schauspielhaus, is another important venue for classical music, having been magnificently restored after World War II.

Opera lovers will find themselves well catered for in Berlin as there are three major opera houses. The **Staatsoper Unter den Linden's** impressive, yet conservative repertoire includes traditional German classics and Italian opera, while the **Komische Oper** is known for its broad range of lighter opera and, because its operas frequently have a long run, there are often last-minute tickets available. The **Deutsche Oper** on Bismarckstrasse is housed in a somewhat plainer building than the other opera venues, but it boasts performances ranging from Mozart to Wagner. Popular open-air concerts in summer are "Staatsoper für Alle" on Bebelplatz, which is free, and "Classic Open Air" on Gendarmenmarkt.

Music Festivals

The **Berliner Festwochen** takes place throughout the month of

Prokofiev's *The Love of Three Oranges* staged at the Komische Oper

September and top orchestras and performers come from all over the world to put on classical music concerts around the city.

Also in September, pop fans will love **Berliner Clubnacht**, which offers an opportunity to dance on 60 floors in 44 Berlin clubs.

Jazzfest Berlin takes place in July and tends to attract lovers of more traditional styles of jazz, but it also focuses on the more experimental and innovative styles of the genre in its accompanying Total Music Meeting.

Rock, Pop & Jazz

Whether it is a major event by a world-famous band or a small-scale evening of jazz improvisation, you need not look too far to find what you want. The biggest concerts tend to take place in sports halls and stadiums, like **O₂ World** and the **Olympiastadion** *(see p101)*, whilst smaller venues like **SO 36** and **Tempodrom** play host to the best new talent in popular music. In addition, a lot of the action tends to take place in the city's many bars, discos and clubs or, if you are looking for particularly atmospheric concerts, you might try those put on at the **Passionskirche**, a converted church in Kreuzberg.

Jazz clubs abound in Berlin, as the style remains very popular amongst locals. The **A-Trane** and **b-flat** are classical jazz bars where you can listen to small

Traditional jazz music at Berlin's Jazzfest

bands just about every night of the week, and **Quasimodo** is renowned for its schedule of local and touring jazz, soul and world music performers.

Apart from the typical classical jazz clubs, jazz can also be heard in many of the city's smaller bars, like **Schlot**. If it is a mixture of soul, rap and jazz you want to listen to, then head for the **Junction Bar** in Kreuzberg. The small bebop jazz club in Kreuzberg is a good choice for meeting locals, and the **Badenscher Hof Jazzclub** is always a good bet.

World Music

Berlin is home to a wide variety of world music. The Haus der Kulturen der Welt organizes all kinds of concerts at its own **Café Global** and **Kulturbrauerei** has become the main venue for world-class artists.

Latin American discos are becoming ever more popular

and **Havanna** in Schöneberg is one of the city's best.

Irish music is also well represented in Berlin's pubs – **Wild at Heart** is very popular, although it does not play Irish music all the time.

Rosa's Dance Co. at the "Tanz" dance festival, organized by the Hebbel Am Ufer (HAU)

Classical and Modern Dance

There are three major ballet groups in Berlin and they work within Berlin's opera houses. The Komische Oper has a modern repertoire, whilst the Staatsoper Unter den Linden focuses on more classical work.

The **Hebbel Am Ufer (HAU)** stages avant garde plays and welcomes troupes from all over the world and also organizes the dance festival "Tanz" every August. The seating at all three theatres is rather limited, so you need to book well in advance.

Tanzfabrik, based on Möckernstrasse in Kreuzberg, is an excellent stage for all kinds of modern dance and it also organizes dance work-shops as well as popular body-work courses.

One of the many concerts at Berlin's annual Popkomm festival

Nightlife

Among its many artistic claims, Berlin is also the techno capital of Europe, with over a million devotees celebrating the genre at a number of annual festivals.

One of the best clubs for techno lovers is **Tresor**, situated in a former power plant. The best DJs in town can be heard here.

Columbia Club is a concert venue featuring touring rock bands, so the look and style of the place changes with each performance.

If it is a good old-fashioned disco you are looking for, with happy tunes and a little less techno, the **Far Out** is the place to go.

There is also a new generation of clubs offering a sleek combination of restaurant, lounge, dance floor and event centre. Each night there is a different, often themed, party, or simply a relaxed lounge occasion. The top two locations are **40seconds**, set in an old high-rise with a great view of the night-lit city, and the exclusive **Spindler + Klatt** and **House of Weekend**. Other clubs, such as **Felix**, welcome a well-to-do clientele to contemporary pop music. By contrast, **White Trash** attracts a more alternative, hip and young urban crowd.

During the summer, you can dance to pop music in the open air at **Golgatha** in Kreuzberg's Viktoriapark.

Delicious Doughnuts is one of the best places in town for ambient, house and acid-jazz, while lovers of soul and reggae should head for the lively **Hoppetosse**. For anyone looking for something a little more intimate, the romantic atmosphere of **Sophienclub** might be worth investigating.

Those who enjoy dancing should head for **Ballhaus** in Mitte, which offers a different style each evening – either salsa, tango, swing, cha-cha or disco.

The city also has a vibrant gay and lesbian scene.

The reconstructed medieval settlement at the Museumdorf Düppel

SchwuZ, **Berghain** and **Ackerkeller** are among the best gay venues in Berlin.

Spectator Sports

As a rule, Berlin's sports teams tend to be among the country's best, and rank highly in each of their respective leagues. Hertha BSC's football matches take place in the **Olympiastadion** and Alba Berlin's basketball games are on at the O₂ Arena. For international events it is usually best to book in advance.

Lovers of horse racing have two tracks to choose from in Berlin. **Trabrennbahn** in Mariendorf is open all year and the races held here are strictly commercial. **Galopprennbahn Hoppegarten**, on the other hand, has a much more friendly, approachable feel.

Children's Activities

People of all ages are catered for in Berlin, and children are no exception. **Visit Berlin** can offer

Flamingos in the beautiful Zoologischer Garten

details of special children's discounts for many different activities. The **Zoologischer Garten** is very popular, with its playgrounds and many animal enclosures. Small children will love the **Kinderbauernhof Görlitzer Bauernhof**, which has a collection of domestic animals. In addition, Berlin's museums are well set up for children. The **Deutsches Technikmuseum** (see p85) allows children to take part in all kinds of experiments, while the **Ethnologisches Museum** prepares special exhibitions for children. A visit to the **Museumsdorf Düppel** is an excellent way to show a child life in a medieval village and the **Puppentheatermuseum** offers a chance for children to take part in minor performances.

Another option is one of the city's many lively circuses, such as **Circus Cabuwazi**, or, if it is sport that your child enjoys, it is possible to swim in many rivers, lakes and, of course, swimming pools (the **Berliner Bäder-betriebe** hotline offers useful information). Also, each district has its own ice-skating rink, but the **Eisstadion Berlin Wilmers-dorf** is by far the best, whilst **FEZ Wuhlheide** offers a special daily programme for kids.

The Story of Berlin is a fun way to experience the history of Berlin in a multi-media exhibit, and the **Berliner Gruselkabinett** (Room of Fear) is suitably scary.

The **Zeiss-Planetarium** or the **Planetarium am Insulaner** offer kids the opportunity to explore the universe in a fun, yet educational, way.

DIRECTORY

Practical Information

Hekticket Theaterkassen
Hardenbergstrasse 29d.
Map 2 B4.
Karl Liebknechtstrasse 12.
Map 5 D1. Tel 230 99 30.
w hekticket.de

Classical Music

Deutsche Oper
Bismarckstrasse 34–37.
Tel 34 38 43 43.

Komische Oper
Behrenstrasse 55–57.
Map 1 F4. Tel 47 99 74 00.

Konzerthaus Berlin
Gendarmenmarkt 2. Map 4 C2. Tel 203 09 21 01/02.

Philharmonie & Kammermusiksaal
Herbert-von-Karajan-Str. 1.
Map 3 F3. Tel 25 48 89 99.

Staatsoper Unter den Linden
Temporarily at Schiller-theater, Bismarckstrasse 110.
Tel 20 35 44 38.

Music Festivals

Berliner Clubnacht
w berlin-clubnacht.de

Berliner Festspiele
Schaperstrasse 4.
Map 2 B5. Tel 25 48 90.

Jazzfest Berlin
Schaperstrasse 24.
Tel 25 48 90.

Rock, Pop & Jazz

A-trane
Pestalozzistrasse 105.
Map 2 A3. Tel 313 25 50.

b-flat
Rosenthaler Strasse 13.
Map 5 D4.
Tel 283 31 23.

Badenscher Hof Jazzclub
Badensche Strasse 29.
Tel 861 00 80.

Junction Bar
Gneisenaustrasse 18.
Tel 694 66 02.

O₂ World
Mühlenstrasse 12–30/
O₂-Platz-1. Tel 20 60 70 80.

Olympiastadion
Olympischer Platz.
Tel 30 68 81 00.

Passionskirche
Marheineckeplatz.
Tel 69 40 12 41.

Quasimodo
Kanststr. 12a. Map 2 B4.
Tel 312 80 86.

Schlot
Chausseestrasse 18 (enter via Schlegelstrasse).
Tel 448 21 60.

SO 36
Oranienstrasse 190.
Tel 61 40 13 06.

Tempodrom
Möckernstrasse 10.
Map 4 B5.
Tel 74 73 70.

World Music

Café Global
John-Foster-Dulles-Allee 10. Map 3 F2.
Tel 39 78 71 75.

Havanna
Hauptstrasse 30.
Tel 784 8565.

Kulturbrauerei
Schönhauser Allee 36,
Prenzlauer Berg.
Tel 44 35 260.

Wild at Heart
Wiener Strasse. 20,
Kreuzberg. Tel 610 74701.

Classical and Modern Dance

Hebbel Am Ufer
Hau Eins:
Stresemannstrasse 29; Hau Zwei: Hallesches Ufer 32;
Hau Drei: Tempelhofer Ufer 10. Map 4 B5. Tel 259 00 40.

Tanzfabrik
Möckernstrasse 68.
Tel 786 58 61.

Nightlife

40seconds
Potsdamer Str. 58.
Tel 89 06 42 41.

Ackerkeller
Bergstrasse 68.
Tel 364 61356.

Ballhaus
Auguststrasse 24, Mitte.
Tel 282 92 95.

Berghain
Am Wriezener Bahnhof,
Frederichshain.
Tel 364 61356.

Columbia Club
Columbiadamm 9–11,
Kreuzberg.

Delicious Doughnuts
Rosenthaler Strasse 9.
Map 5 D1. Tel 28 09 92 74.

Far Out
Joachimstalerstrasse 15.
Map 2 B5. Tel 32 00 07 23.

Felix
Behrenstr. 72.
Map 4 A2.
Tel 301 117 152.

Golgatha
Dudenstrasse 48–64.
Tel 785 24 53.

Hoppetosse
Eichenstrasse 4.
Tel 533 203 40.

House of Weekend
Alexanderstrasse 7.
Map 5 F1.
Tel 25 89 93 66.

SchwuZ
Mehringdamm 61.
Tel 629 0880.

Sophienclub
Sophienstrasse 6.
Tel 282 45 52.

Spindler + Klatt
Köpenicker Str. 16–17.
Map 5 F3.
Tel 319 88 1860.

Tresor
Köpenicker Str. 59–73.
Tel 24 78 10111

White Trash
Schönhauser Allee 167.
Tel 50 34 86 68.

Spectator Sports

Galopprennbahn Hoppegarten
Goetheallee 1.
Tel (03342) 389 30.

Olympiastadion
Olympischer Platz.
Tel 306 88 100.

Trabrennbahn
Mariendorfer Damm 222,
Tempelhof.
Tel 740 12 12.

Children's Activities

Berliner Bäderbetriebe
Tel (01803) 10 20 20.

Berliner Grusselkabinett
Schöneberger Strasse 23a. Tel 26 55 55 46.

Circus Cabuwazi
Tel (030) 611 92 75.
w cabuwazi.de

Deutsches Technikmuseum
Trebbiner Strasse 9.
Tel 90 25 40.

Eisstadion Berlin Wilmersdorf
Fritz-Wildung-Strasse 9.
Tel 824 10 12.

Ethnologisches Museum
Lansstrasse 8.
Tel 83 01 438.

FEZ Wuhlheide
An der Wuhlheide 197,
Köpenick. Tel 53 07 10.

Kinderbauernhof Görlitzer Bauernhof
Wiener Strasse 59b.
Tel 611 74 24.

Museumsdorf Düppel
Clauertstrasse 11.
Tel 802 66 71.

Planetarium am Insulaner
Munsterdamm 90.
Tel 790 09 30.

Puppentheater-museum
Karl-Marx-Strasse 135.
Tel 687 81 32.

The Story of Berlin
Kurfürstendamm 207–208. Tel 88 72 01 00.

Visit Berlin
Tel (030) 25 00 25.
w visitberlin.de

Zeiss-Planetarium
Prenzlauer Allee 80.
Tel 42 18 45 12.

Zoologischer Garten
Hardenbergplatz 9,
Charlottenburg.
Tel 25 40 10.

Theatre and Cinema

Berlin can lay many claims to being a centre for artistic greatness, but possibly its most valid claims lie in the areas of theatre and cinema. Berlin has been the capital of German cinema since brothers Emil and Max Skladanowsky showed a series of short films to a spellbound German public in 1896. By 1918 there were already some 251 cinemas in Berlin and by 1925, the number of people involved in the film industry was nearly 50,000. At the same time, Berlin was fast becoming a landmark in European theatre thanks mainly to Reinhardt and Brecht. During the years of Nazi rule, many theatre people were killed or forced to emigrate as the stage became a propaganda machine, but after World War II a revival spread through Berlin's theatres. The popularity of theatre and cinema continues today, perpetuated by the annual Film Festival.

A Berlin International Film Festival poster from 1960

Ticket and Price Information

Tickets for both cinema and theatre are usually reasonably priced in Berlin, but there are a few tips which are useful to remember if you are planning to visit either.

Students and senior citizens do not always receive a discount at the cinema, but often Tuesday or Wednesday is declared Cinema Day, when some tickets are €1–2 cheaper. It is worth knowing that most ticket offices do not accept credit cards, so take cash.

For theatres, it is usually possible to pre-book tickets at least two weeks before a performance. You can buy them directly from the box office of the theatre, online or by telephone. Independent ticket vendors usually charge a commission of between 15 and 22 per cent.

Hekticket Theaterkassen specializes in last-minute tickets, so check with them on the day.

Major Stages

The **Deutsches Theater** and its small hall **Kammerspiele** on Schumannstrasse are top-class theatres and offer a varied repertoire of productions. At **Volksbühne** you can see performances of classical plays in modern settings and new plays by young authors.

The **Berliner Ensemble (BE)** was once managed by Bertolt Brecht and Heiner Müller. The spectacles created by these two are still performed today.

Other major venues include the **Maxim Gorki Theater**, the **Renaissance-Theater** and the **Schaubühne**.

Alternative Theatre

There are a number of alternative theatres in Berlin. The three-theatre company **Hebbel am Ufer (HAU)** is devoted to avant-garde theatre and considered the city's

best alternative stage. The smaller boulevard theatres like **Theater am Kurfürstendamm** offer different, and somewhat lighter programmes.

Other notable venues include **Bat-Studiotheater** and the **Kleines Theater**.

Musicals, Reviews and Cabarets

There are three main musical theatres in Berlin, in addition to the many small venues which fit musicals into their more general repertoire. **Friedrichstadt-Palast** and **Admiralspalast**, in the eastern part of the city, stage many of the new major shows, while the **Theater des Westens** in Charlottenburg tends to be more traditional. In addition to these is the **Theater am Potsdamer Platz**, a modern theatre that shows contemporary musical hits.

As for cabaret, there are probably as many acts in Berlin today as there were in the 1920s. **Distel**, in Friedrichstrasse, continues its success from GDR times, and **Die Stachelschweine** celebrates its popularity in western Berlin.

Other great venues for lively musicals, reviews and cabarets include **Bar jeder Vernunft**, **Chamäleon Variété**, **Scheinbar**, **Wintergarten Variété** and **Wühlmäuse**.

Open-Air Venues

Open-air venues, including cinemas, start operating as soon as the weather allows. Berlin has two open-air venues, both in the shape of ancient amphitheatres. The largest is **Waldbühne**, which seats 20,000.

The retro façade of Friedrichstadtpalast in the east of Berlin

Kindl-Bühne Wuhlheide at Wuhlheide Park in the Treptow-Köpenick area holds 17,000. Other traditional open-air venues can be found in Hasenheide and at Bethaniendamm in Kreuzberg, in Volkspark Friedrichshaln, at Potsdamer Platz or at Waldbühne, which is located near the Olympiastadion.

Big Screens and Big Films

After the fall of the Berlin Wall, many multiplex cinemas were built, the biggest being the **CinemaxX Potsdamer Platz** and the **Cinestar Sony Center**, which both screen films in the original language. In most cinemas, mainstream Anglo-American movies tend to be dubbed.

For more of an exciting experience, try the **IMAX** with its huge 3-D screen.

Studio Cinema

For those who like their movies a little less mainstream, there are plenty of small studio cinemas scattered across town that show a large number of recently released independent films. **Hackesche Höfe Kino** or **Central**, situated near Hackescher Markt, offer a pleasant break from city life and have bars of their own.

The **Arsenal**, on Potsdamer Platz, shows German film classics; if you are interested in original language films, Berlin has various options. **Cinéma Paris** in Charlottenburg is the place to go for French films, while the **Odeon** in Schöneberg specializes in English and American films.

DIRECTORY

Ticket and Price Information

Hekticket Theaterkassen
Hardenbergstrasse 29d.
Map 2 B4.
Tel 230 99 30.
W hekticket.de

Major Stages

Berliner Ensemble (BE)
Bertolt-Brecht-Platz 1.
Map 1 F3.
Tel 28 408 155.
W berliner-
ensemble.de

Deutsches Theater
Schumannstrasse 13.
Map 1 F3.
Tel 28 44 12 25.
W deutschestheater.de

Kammerspiele
Schumannstrasse 13a.
Map 1 F3.
Tel 28 44 12 22.
W deutschestheater.de

Maxim Gorki Theater
Am Festungsgraben 2.
Map 1 F1.
Tel 20 22 11 29.
W gorki.de

Renaissance-Theater
Hardenbergstrasse 6.
Map 2 A3.
Tel 312 42 02.
W renaissance-theater.
de

Schaubühne
Kurfürstendamm 153.
Tel 89 00 20.
W schaubuehne.de

Volksbühne
Rosa-Luxembourg-Platz.
Tel 240 655.

Alternative Theatre

Bat-Studiotheater
Belforter Strasse 15.
Tel 755 41 7777.
W bat-berlin.de

Kleines Theater
Südwestkorso 64.
Tel 821 20 21.
W kleines-theater-de

Hebbel am Ufer (HAU)
Hallesches Ufer 32.
Tel 25 90 04 27.

Theater am Kurfürstendamm
Kurfürstendamm 206.
Map 2 A5.
Tel 88 59 11 88.

Musicals, Reviews and Cabarets

Admiralspalast
Friedrichstrasse 101.
Map 1 F1.
Tel 47 99 74 99.
W admiralspalast.de

Bar jeder Vernunft
Schaperstrasse 24.
Map 2 B5.
Tel 883 15 82.

Chamäleon Variété
Rosenthaler Strasse
40–41. **Map** 5 D4.
Tel 4000 590.
W chamaeleon
berlin.de

Distel
Friedrichstrasse 101.
Map 1 F3.
Tel 204 47 04.

Friedrichstadt-Palast
Friedrichstrasse 107.
Map 1 F3.
Tel 23 26 23 26.
W friedrichstadt
palast.de

Scheinbar
Monumentenstrasse 9.
Tel 784 55 39.

Die Stachelschweine
Europa-Center.
Map 2 C4.
Tel 261 47 95.
W die-stachel
schweine.de

Theater am Potsdamer Platz
Marlene-Dietrich-Platz 1.
Map 4 A3.
Tel 259 244 555.
W stage-
entertainment.de

Theater des Westens
Kantstrasse 12.
Tel 260 244 555
W stage-
entertainment.de

Wintergarten Variété
Potsdamer Strasse 96.
Map 3 F4.
Tel 25 00 88 88.
W wintergarten-
variete.de

Wühlmäuse
Pommernallee 2–4.
Tel 306 73011.
W wuehlmaeuse.de

Open-Air Venues

Kindl-Bühne Wuhlheide
An der Wuhlheide 187.
Tel 30 85 75 810.
W wuhlheide.de

Waldbühne
Glockenturmstrasse 1.
Tel 74 73 75 00.

Big Screens and Big Films

CinemaxX Potsdamer Platz
Potsdamer Strasse 1–19.
Map 4 A3.
Tel (0180) 524 63 62 99.
W cinemaxx.de

Cinestar Sony Center & IMAX
Potsdamer Strasse 4.
Map 4 A3.
Tel 01805 118811.

Studio Cinema

Arsenal
Potsdamer Strasse 2.
Map 4 A3. **Tel** 26 95 51 00.

Central
Rosenthaler Strasse 39.
Map 5 D1. **Tel** 28 59 99 73.

Cinéma Paris
Kurfürstendamm 211.
Tel 881 31 19.

Hackescher Höfe Kino
Rosenthaler Strasse 40–41.
Map 5 D1. **Tel** 283 46 03.

Odeon
Hauptstrasse 115.
Tel 78 70 40 19.

BERLIN STREET FINDER

Map references given for historic buildings, hotels, restaurants, bars, shops and entertainment venues refer to the maps included in this section of the guidebook. The key map below shows the area of Berlin covered by the Street Finder. The maps include all major sightseeing areas, historic attractions, railway stations, bus stations, U-Bahn stations and the suburban stations of the S-Bahn. The names of the streets and squares on the maps are given in German. The word Straße (or STRASSE, Str) indicates a street, Allee an avenue, Platz a square, Brücke a bridge and Bahnhof a railway station.

Western Centre

Eastern Centre

Key

- Major sight
- Place of interest
- Other building
- S-Bahn station
- U-Bahn station
- Railway station
- Bus station
- Tram stop
- Hospital with emergency dept.
- Police station
- Tourist information
- Church
- Synagogue
- Railway line
- Pedestrian-only street

0 km 1
0 miles 1

Scale of Maps 1–5

0 metres 250
0 yards 250
1:15 000

EASTERN GERMANY

Eastern Germany at a Glance

The eastern region of Germany is immensely rich in tourist attractions. The imposing valley of the Elbe River, the beautiful lake district of Lower Brandenburg, attractive trails in the Harz Mountains of Saxony-Anhalt, the Thuringian Forest as well as the Erzgebirge and the Lusatian Mountains in Saxony all invite the visitor with their dramatic scenery and excellent recreational facilities.

Eastern Germany is rich in historic sights, too, ranging from the Baroque residences of Potsdam in Brandenburg to the grand architecture of Dresden and Leipzig in Saxony and the important cultural centre of Weimar in Thuringia. The most rewarding destinations in the region are featured here.

The Magdeburg Reiter, in the market square, is a gold-plated replica of a famous sandstone equestrian monument. It most likely depicts Otto the Great (see p156).

Naumburg Dom is a huge, well preserved Gothic cathedral (see pp154–5), one of Germany's greatest buildings. Splendid statues of its founders, Ekkehart and Uta, adorn the walls of the presbytery.

Erfurt Dom dominates the townscape. A massive Gothic structure, the cathedral's three towers were built on the Romanesque foundations of an earlier church.

Pritzwa
Witten
Stend
Magdeb
Schöne
Halberstadt
SAXONY-ANHALT
(See pp146–61)
Nordhausen
Halle
Mühlhausen
Naumburg
Ze
Eisenach
Weimar
Gotha
Erfurt
Jena
Ger
THURINGIA
(See pp186–201)
Suhl
Saalfeld

Weimar, with its picturesque market square (see pp198–9) and historic buildings, was an important cultural centre for many centuries. Friedrich Schiller, Johann Wolfgang von Goethe and Johann Sebastian Bach all lived here.

◀ A statue of Greek goddess Minerva in front of the main façade of Schloss Sanssouci

Sanssouci in Potsdam *(see pp140–41)*, the enchanting Baroque summer residence built for Prussia's King Frederick the Great, stands on the site of former gardens and vineyards.

LOCATOR MAP

Schloss Wörlitz is surrounded by a romantic landscaped park *(see pp160–61)* criss-crossed by a network of waterways open to pleasure boats.

The Völkerschlachtdenkmal in Leipzig *(see pp166–7)* was erected to celebrate the centenary of the battle fought by Prussia, Austria, Russia and Sweden against Napoleon's army in 1813.

The Zwinger in Dresden *(see pp178–9)*, Saxony's glorious palace and a Baroque jewel, was immaculately restored to its original glory after World War II destruction.

Wittstock

Schwedt/ Oder

Oranienburg

BERLIN

Potsdam

Frankfurt an der Oder

BRANDENBURG *(See pp132–45)*

Jüterbog

Guben

Lübbenau

Lutherstadt Wittenberg

Cottbus

Delitzsch

Hoyerswerda

Leipzig

SAXONY *(See pp162–85)*

Döbeln

Bautzen

Dresden

Zittau

Freiberg

Chemnitz

Zwickau

Annaberg-Buchholz

Meissen Porcelain

Until the early 18th century the only porcelain known in Europe was that imported from the Far East, and the Chinese jealously guarded the secrets of its production. Finally, in 1707, Johann Friedrich Böttger and Ehrenfried Walther von Tschirnhaus succeeded in developing a recipe that made it possible to produce genuine porcelain. A factory was set up in Meissen, and from 1713 it began to export its products to the entire European continent. Its first famous designers were Johann Joachim Kändler and Johann Gregor Höroldt.

The Porcelain Museum, opened in 1906, holds exhibitions and demonstrations illustrating the various stages in the manufacture of porcelain. The museum also runs courses on porcelain-making.

Böttger Stoneware

Johann Friedrich Böttger's first success in recreating Chinese ceramics came in 1707 when, with the assistance of Ehrenfried Walther von Tschirnhaus, he managed to produce stoneware almost identical to that produced in Yi Hsing. The stoneware was dark, varying in colour from red to brown.

These plates and bowls are typical examples of Böttger stoneware; its plain and simple lines were modelled on Far-Eastern designs.

The dark colour of the dishes is due to the use of red clays.

The "Yellow Lion" design, dating from c.1728, was used to decorate the first Meissen service.

Imari tree

The "Yellow Lion" was in reality a tiger.

Far-Eastern Motifs

Until the 17th century the only porcelain known in Europe came from the Far East, and the first items made from Saxon hard porcelain were initially strongly influenced by the Asian products. In Meissen, Chinese figurines and dishes were copied, adapting "European" shapes, but using Japanese or Chinese motifs for decoration. Special designs were created to adorn the services intended for the royal court. The oldest among these include the "Yellow Lion" and the "Red Dragon". New designs, inspired by European art, began to appear after 1738, and gradually replaced the Asian patterns.

Production Process

The process of porcelain production has not changed significantly over the centuries. The formula for "hard-paste" porcelain contains kaolin, quartz and feldspar. Each product is dried and fired, with glazed products being fired twice. The decoration can be applied before or after the glazing process. Hand-painted and gilded items are the most expensive.

Demonstration of the intricate art of hand-painting porcelain at the Meissen factory

Tableware

In the second half of the 18th and in the 19th centuries, porcelain manufacturers developed their own designs. This proved so popular that some remain in production to this day. The best-known Meissen designs are the "vine-leaves" and the "onion" patterns, first introduced in the 18th century. Customers can thus still replace items in the services that have graced their family tables for generations.

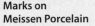

This coffee pot and cup is decorated with the cobalt "onion" pattern, depicting stylized pomegranate fruits.

Fine-Art Motifs

A new type of decoration, which became popular in the second half of the 18th century, involved the accurate copying of famous paintings or etchings onto a vase, a pot or a plate. This type of decoration proved particularly popular during the Classicist period.

Decorator copying an etching onto a vessel

Vase decorated with a miniature of a painting by Antoine Watteau

Services and Figurines

Several outstanding sculptors and painters were employed in the Meissen porcelain manufacture to design unique services and figurines for the royal courts. The most famous among them are the services designed by Johann Joachim Kändler. He also created sets of figurines to adorn dining tables, vases and censers (containers for burning incense) for decorating the home, and large religious compositions for churches.

"Swan" Service Tureen

Figurine of August III

Europa, a figure from the "Four Continents" series, designed by J. J. Kändler

Marks on Meissen Porcelain

All porcelain manufacturers mark their products with their own symbols. The symbols are generally applied under the glaze, at the bottom of the piece. The Meissen factory initially used marks that imitated Japanese or Chinese writing; later, for a short time, letters were used, and from 1724 blue trademarks in the shape of crossed swords became the standard mark. The last three symbols below identify the respective court for which each piece of porcelain was produced.

K.P.F.

Königliche Porzellan-Fabrik, trademark used in 1723

K.P.M.

Königliche Porzellan-Manufaktur, trademark used in 1723–4

X, X, X

Trademarks used from 1724

AR

Augustus Rex, the initials of King August

K.H.K

Königliche Hof-Küche

K.H.C.W.

Königliche Hof-Conditorei Warschau

Luther and the Reformation

In 1517, on the eve of All Souls' Day (31 October), Martin Luther nailed his 95 "theses" to the doors of the castle church in Wittenberg, condemning the practice of indulgences. His subsequent pronouncements, in which he criticized many aspects of the Church's teaching, made him the "father" of the Reformation movement in Germany and other countries. Luther's teaching gained the support of many of the princes, who in 1531 formed the Schmalkalden Union and started to introduce a new administration to the Church. This led to religious wars which finally ended with the Augsburg Peace Treaty, signed in 1555, which confirmed the religious division of Germany.

The Bible, translated into German by Luther, was first published in one volume in 1534. One year later an illustrated, two-volume luxury version was published in Augsburg.

The baptism of a child is performed by Philipp Melanchthon.

The Schlosskapelle in Hartenfels Castle, in Torgau *(see p168)*, was built in 1543–4 and consecrated by Martin Luther. It is generally considered to be the first church built specifically for the Lutheran community.

The Last Supper, at the centre of the altar, stresses the importance attached by Lutherans to the sacrament of communion. The figures of the Apostles are portraits of the main church reformers.

This group of faithful, listening to the sermon, includes members of Luther's family.

Martin Luther, the great theologian and religious reformer, initiator of Church reform and founder of Lutheranism, is depicted in this portrait by Lucas Cranach the Elder (1520).

Luther's Room (Lutherstube), shown here, is part of Luther's House in Wittenberg *(see p158).* The famous reformer lived here with his wife and family.

Philipp Melanchthon, an associate of Luther's and the co-founder of Lutheranism, initiated a great educational reform. He was also known as *praeceptor Germaniae,* Germany's teacher.

Reformation Altar

The main altar of St Mary's Church in Wittenberg (see pp158–9) is one of the most important works of art of the Reformation period. The central picture was painted by Lucas Cranach the Elder (c.1539), the wings by his son, Lucas Cranach the Younger, before 1547.

Cup Bearer Serving at the Table is the title of a portrait by Lucas Cranach the Younger.

Protestant confession is taken by Johannes Bugenhagen.

Sermon preached by Martin Luther, who points to the figure of the crucified Christ.

Katharina von Bora, a former nun, became Martin Luther's wife in 1525. She lies buried in the Marienkirche in Torgau *(see p168),* in a tomb which survives to this day.

BRANDENBURG

The province of Brandenburg is a lowland region criss-crossed by a dense network of rivers, canals and lakes. Quiet in part, it is also crossed by some of the main tourist routes to Berlin. Its most popular attractions are the historic sights of its capital city, Potsdam, and the Spreewald, where all day can be spent boating on the waterways of the Lusatian forests and villages.

In early medieval times, the area that was to become present-day Brandenburg was the scene of violent conflict between various Germanic tribes. The latter conquered the region, and in 1157 created the margravate of Brandenburg. Its first ruler was Albrecht der Bär (Albert the Bear), from the house of Ascan. From 1415, Brandenburg was ruled by the Hohenzollern dynasty. It was quick to embrace the Reformation, which was officially adopted here as early as 1538. In 1618, Brandenburg merged with the duchy of Prussia through personal union. The region became entangled in the Thirty Years' War and suffered devastating losses; depopulated and plundered, it took Brandenburg many years to rise from the ashes. In 1701, the Great Elector, Frederick III, crowned himself King Frederick I, and the whole region now assumed the name of Prussia.

While Berlin remained the seat of power and a strong industrial and cultural centre, 18th-century Potsdam also played an important role: it was, after all, the favourite haunt of Frederick the Great. Other towns in the region were less significant – Brandenburg was, and still is, a fairly rural region. Reunification in 1990, however, has opened up the newly created land to Berliners and tourists alike.

Travellers in Brandenburg will encounter ancient tree-lined avenues that stretch to the horizon. The Spreewald, Brandenburg's lake district, is an oasis of tranquillity, ideal for boating and cycling. Brandenburg also has grand castles in Oranienburg, Branitz just outside Cottbus and Rheinsberg, Gothic churches and monasteries in Lehnin and Chorin and the towns of Brandenburg/Havel and Potsdam.

Baroque palace in Rheinsberg, on the shores of the Grienericksee

◀ Sculptures and statues outside the Neues Palais, Potsdam

Exploring Brandenburg

Brandenburg is ideally suited for gentle exploration by bicycle or car, and its proximity to Berlin allows the visitor to make a one-day excursion to the capital. A whole day should be allocated for visiting Potsdam and the castle of Sanssouci, and another day for a boat trip in the Spreewald. A visit to Cottbus can be combined with an excursion to Frankfurt an der Oder. The best time for a visit to Chorin is the summer when concerts are held there in the ruined monastery.

Cecilienhof, the summer residence of the Hohenzollern family in Potsdam

Schloss Branitz in Cottbus

For additional map symbols *see back flap*

Key

━━━ Motorway
━━━ Major road
═══ Minor road
━╌━ Main railway
─── Minor railway
▬▬▬ International border
━━━ Regional border

Tourist boats on the Spreewald canals, near Lehde

Getting Around

There are many flights to Berlin. Brandenburg has an extensive network of motorways – the circular Berliner Ring joins with the motorways A11 from Stettin, A24 from Hamburg, Schwerin and Rostock, A2 from Hanover, A9 from Munich and Nuremberg, A12 from Frankfurt an der Oder and A13 from Cottbus and Dresden. Local roads and country lanes in Brandenburg are often narrow and twisting. The outskirts of Berlin are well served by the local train network, which provides frequent links with many small towns. There are also numerous local bus services.

0 kilometres 20

0 miles 20

Sights at a Glance

1 Elbtalaue
2 Wittstock
3 Neuruppin
4 Oranienburg
5 Brandenburg/Havel
6 Lehnin
7 *Potsdam pp138–43*
8 Chorin
9 Frankfurt an der Oder
10 Cottbus
11 Spreewald
12 Jüterbog

For hotels and restaurants in this area see pp493 and pp5112–13

❶ Elbtalaue

Road map D2. 🚉 to Wittenberge or Bad Wilsnack. 🛈 Am Markt 5, Bad Wilsnack (038791-26 20).
W bad-wilsnack.de

The Elbe valley in the western part of Prignitz is an area of gentle rolling hills and unspoiled nature. Storks, increasingly rare in Germany, still nest here. When travelling around this parkland it is worth stopping at **Pritzwalk** to admire the late-Gothic Nikolaikirche (St Nicholas church). Another place of interest is **Perleberg** with its picturesque market square featuring an original 1515 timber-frame building, a sandstone statue of the knight Roland (1546), now standing by the 1850 Town Hall, and the town's star attraction – the 15th-century Gothic Jakobskirche (church of St Jacob).

Bad Wilsnack owes its fame to the discovery of the therapeutic properties of the iron oxide-rich mud found in the surrounding marshes. Already known in medieval times, the town was an important place of pilgrimage. After a church fire, in 1384, three hosts displaying the blood of Christ were found untouched on the altar. The Gothic **Nikolaikirche** (church of St Nicholas), which survives to this day, was built soon after for the pilgrims.

Plattenburg Castle, in a scenic situation on an island, is also worth a visit. Combining late-Gothic and Renaissance architecture, it is used as a venue for concerts.

The Gothic-Renaissance Plattenburg Castle, in the Elbtalaue

Chapel of the Holy Sepulchre in Heiligengrabe, near Wittstock

❷ Wittstock

Road map E2. 🚶 13,700. 🚌
🛈 Walter-Shulz-Pl. 1, Wittstock/Dosse (03394-43 34 42). **W** wittstock.de

The small town of Wittstock was first awarded its municipal status in 1284. From the 13th century to the Reformation, Wittstock was the see of the Havelberg bishops. Although much of the town was destroyed, the original city walls remained almost completely intact, with one surviving gate – the **Gröper Tor**. All that remains of the former bishop's castle is the gate tower, which now houses a small museum. The town's star attraction is the Gothic **Marienkirche** with its late-Gothic reredos depicting the crowning of St Mary. It originated in the wood carving workshop of Claus Berg, probably after 1532. Other interesting features include the 1516 sacrarium and the late-Renaissance pulpit.

Environs
Ten km (6 miles) to the west lies **Heiligengrabe**, with its Gothic Cistercian Abbey. One of its many highlights is the 1512

Chapel of the Holy Sepulchre with an intricately sculpted gable and some charming timber-frame cloister buildings.

❸ Neuruppin

Road map E2. 🚶 27,300. 🚌
🛈 Karl-Marx-Str. 1 (03391-454 60).
W neuruppin.de.

The town of Neuruppin, in a scenic location on the shores of a large lake, the Ruppiner See, is mainly Neo-Classical in style, having been rebuilt to the design of Bernhard Matthias Brasch after the great fire of 1787. The only older buildings are the Gothic post-Dominican church and two small hospital chapels. Neuruppin is the birthplace of the architect **Karl Friedrich Schinkel** and the novelist **Theodor Fontane** (see p31).

Environs
The beautifully restored palace of **Rheinsberg**, 25 km (16 miles) to the north, was converted from 16th-century Renaissance castle in 1734–7. In 1734–40 it was the residence of the Crown Prince, who later became Frederick the Great, King of Prussia. Some 30 km (19 miles) northeast of Rheinsberg is the site of the former National Socialist concentration camp **Ravensbrück**, for women and children. It is now a place of remembrance.

Schinkel monument

❹ Oranienburg

Road map E3. 🚶 30,000. 🚉 🚌
🛈 Bernauer Str. 52 (033 01-70 48 33).
W tourismus-or.de

The star attraction of the town is **Schloss Oranienburg,** the Baroque residence built for Louisa Henrietta von Nassau-Oranien, wife of the Great Elector Friedrich Wilhelm. Designed by

Johann Gregor Memhardt and
Michael Matthias Smids, it was
built in 1651–5 and later
extended to its present H-shape.

🏛 Schloss Oranienburg
Schlossplatz 1. **Tel** (03301) 53 74 37.
Open Apr–Oct: 10am–6pm Tue–Sun;
Nov–Mar: 10am–4pm Tue–Fri,
10am–5pm Sat & Sun.

Environs
Sachsenhausen, which is
located northeast of
Oranienburg, is now a place
of remembrance and a
museum. Opened in 1936 by
the National Socialists, this
concentration camp claimed
the lives of 100,000 inmates.

🏛 Sachsenhausen
Tel (03301) 20 00. **Open** mid-Mar–
mid-Oct: 8:30am–6pm daily; mid-Oct–
mid-Mar: 8:30am–4:30pm daily.
W gedenkstaette-sachsenhausen.
de

❺ Brandenburg/ Havel

Road map E3. 👥 87,700. 🚌 🚏
ℹ Neustädtischer Markt 3 (03381-
796 360). 🎭 Havelfestspiele (Jun).
W **stadt-brandenburg.de**

Brandenburg is the oldest town
of the region. It was settled by
Slavs as early as the 6th century,
and a mission episcopate
was established here in 948.
Scenically sited on the Havel
River, it has preserved historic
centres on three islands, despite
wartime destruction. The oldest
island is the **Dominsel**, with its

Baroque palace in Caputh, north of Lehnin

Romanesque **Dom St Peter
und St Paul**. This cathedral was
constructed from 1165 to the
mid-13th century. In the 14th
century it was raised and given
new vaultings. It contains
numerous valuable Gothic
objects, including the **"Czech"
altar** (c.1375), the present main
altar (from Lehnin, 1518) and
the sacrarium of the same year.
The most valuable treasures are
on display in the **Dommuseum**.
Other sights worth visiting
are the huge, 15th-century
Katharinenkirche built
by Hinrich Brunsberg, the
Gotthardkirche, in the
Altstadt ("old town"), with its
Romanesque façade and Gothic
interior, the Gothic **Rathaus**
(Town Hall), with a statue of
Roland from 1474, and the
Stadtmuseum, a museum of
local history.

🏛 Dommuseum
Burghof 10. **Tel** (03381) 211 2221.
Open 10am–5pm daily, 12:30–5pm
Sun. 🖼 W **brandenburg-dom.de**

🏛 Stadtmuseum
Ritterstr. 96. **Tel** (03381) 58 45 01.
Open 9am–5pm Tue–Fri, 10am–5pm
Sat & Sun. 🖼

❻ Lehnin

Road map E3. 👥 3,100. 🚏
ℹ Markgrafenplatz (03382 704 480).

Visitors mainly come to see the
huge Klosterkirche (abbey)
founded for the Cistercian
order of Otto I, son of Albert
the Bear. The church was built
from the late 12th to the late
13th century, originally in
Romanesque, then in early-
Gothic style. Following the
dissolution of the monastery, in
1542, the buildings fell into
disrepair, but much of the
abbey has survived.

🏛 Klosterkirche
Klosterkirchplatz. **Tel** (03382) 76 80 10.
Open Apr–Oct: 10am–4pm Mon–Fri,
10am–5pm Sat, 1–5pm Sun; Nov–Mar:
10:30am–3:30pm Mon–Sat, 1–4pm
Sun. W **klosterkirche-lehnin.de**

Environs
Caputh, situated 23 km
(14 miles) to the north, has
an early-Baroque **Palace** built
during the second half of the
17th century, as summer
residence for the wives of the
Great Electors. The interior
has many original features.

The Gothic "Czech" altar in the Dom St Peter und St Paul in Brandenburg

❼ Potsdam

An independent city close to Berlin, Potsdam, with over 150,000 inhabitants, is also the capital of Brandenburg. The first documented reference to Potsdam dates back to AD 993; it was later granted municipal rights in 1317. The town blossomed during the times of the Great Electors and then again in the 18th century. Potsdam suffered very badly during World War II, particularly on the night of 14–15 April 1945 when Allied planes bombed the town centre.

A sculpture on display in Park Sanssouci

Sightseeing in Potsdam

Potsdam remains one of Germany's most attractive towns. Tourists flock to see the magnificent royal summer residence, Schloss Sanssouci, to stroll around Neuer Garten (new garden) with its Marmorpalais (marble palace) and Cecilienhof, to visit the old city centre and the Russian colony of Alexandrowka, to be entertained in the film studios of Babelsberg and to take a walk around the parks of Schloss Babelsberg.

🏰 Cecilienhof

Am Neuen Garten (Neuer Garten). **Tel** (0331) 969 42 44. 🚌 695. **Open** Apr–Oct: 10am–6pm Tue–Sun; Nov–Mar: 10am–5pm Tue–Sun.

The Cecilienhof residence played a brief but important role in history, when it served as the venue for the 1945 Potsdam Conference (see p143). Built between 1913 and 1917, the palace is the most recent of all Hohenzollern dynasty buildings. Designed by Paul Schultze-Naumburg in the style of an English country manor, Cecilienhof is a sprawling, asymmetrical, timber-frame building with inner courtyards and irregular breaks.

The palace remained a residence of the Hohenzollern family after they had lost the crown – the family stayed in Potsdam until February 1945. Today the palace is a hotel, where visitors interested in history are

able to relax amid green shrubs. The large, scenic park remains open to the public even when the rooms used during the Potsdam Conference are closed to visitors.

🏰 Marmorpalais

Am Neuen Garten (Neuer Garten). **Tel** (0331) 969 42 46. 🚌 695. **Open** Apr: 10am–6pm Sat & Sun; May–Oct: 10am–6pm Tue–Sun.

This small palace, situated on the edge of the lake, is a beautiful example of early Neo-Classical architecture. The palace is named after the Silesian marble used on its façade. The main part of it was built between 1787 and 1791 by Carl von Gontard to a design and under the direction of Carl Gotthard Langhans, on the initiative of King Friedrich Wilhelm II.

🚏 Alexandrowka

Russische Kolonie Allee/Puschkinallee. 🚊 92, 95. 🚌 603, 609, 638, 639.

A visit to Alexandrowka takes the visitor into the world of Pushkin's fairy tales. Wooden log cabins with intricate carvings, set in their own gardens, create a charming residential estate. They were constructed in 1826 under the direction of the German architect Snethlage, for 12 singers of a Russian choir that was established in 1812.

🚏 Holländisches Viertel

Friedrich-Ebert-Str, Kurfürstenstr., Hebbelstr., Gutenbergstr. 🚌 138, 601–604, 606–612. 🚊 92, 95.

Just as amazing as the Russian colony of Alexandrowka is the Holländisches Viertel (Dutch quarter), part of a Baroque town built in the middle of Germany.

A view of the Baroque Dutch district known as Holländisches Viertel

Dutch workers arrived in Potsdam in the early 18th century and, between 1733 and 1742, a settlement was built for them on the orders of Friedrich Wilhelm I to plans by Johann Boumann the Elder. It comprised 134 gabled houses arranged in four groups. The houses were built from small red bricks and finished with stone and plaster details.

🏛 Nikolaikirche

Alter Markt. **Tel** (0331) 270 86 02.
🚌 601, 603, 692, 694, 🚊 91, 92, 93, 95, 96, 99. **Open** Apr–Oct: 9am– 7pm daily; Nov–Mar: 9am–5pm daily.

This imposing church built in the late Neo-Classical style, is

The Nikolaikirche, with its dome resting on a colonnaded wall

indisputably the most beautiful church in Potsdam. It was built on the site of an earlier, Baroque church, which burned down in 1795. It was designed during 1828–30 by Karl Friedrich Schinkel and the building work was supervised by Ludwig Persius. The interior decoration and furnishings of the church date from the 1850s, but were mostly based on the earlier designs by Schinkel.

🚌 Marstall

Breitestr. 1a. **Tel** (0331) 271 81 12. 🚗
🚌 601, 603, 692, 694. 🚊 91, 92, 93, 95, 96, 98. **Open** 10am–6pm daily.

This long Baroque pavilion, once used as royal stables, is the only remaining building of a royal residence. It was constructed in 1714 and currently houses a film museum devoted to the history and work of the nearby Babelsberg Film Studio.

🏛 Bildergalerie

Zur Historischen Mühle. **Tel** (0331) 969 41 81. 🚌 612, 614, 695. **Open** 15 May– 15 Oct: 10am–5pm Tue–Sun. 🚗

Baroque paintings once owned by Frederick the Great, including Caravaggio's *Doubting Thomas*, Guido Reni's *Cleopatra's Death*,

as well as paintings by Rubens and van Dyck, are on show in the picture gallery situated next to Schloss Sanssouci.

Caravaggio's *Doubting Thomas*, on show in the Bildergalerie

Potsdam

① Cecilienhof
② Marmorpalais
③ Alexandrowka
④ Holländisches Viertel
⑤ Nikolaikirche
⑥ Marstall
⑦ Bildergalerie
⑧ Park Sanssouci

For additional map symbols *see back flap*

Park Sanssouci

The enormous Park Sanssouci, which occupies an area of 287 hectares (700 acres), is one of the most beautiful palace complexes in Europe. The first building to be constructed on the site was Schloss Sanssouci, built as the summer palace of Frederick the Great. It was erected in 1747, on the site of a former orchard. Over the years, Park Sanssouci was expanded considerably and other palaces and pavilions added. To enjoy the park fully, allow at least a whole day.

★ Neues Palais
Constructed between 1763 and 1769, the monumental building of the Neues Palais is crowned by a massive dome.

Römische Bäder
Shaded by pergolas overgrown with greenery, the Roman baths include a Renaissance-style villa.

KEY

① **Communs**, situated next to a pretty courtyard, has an unusually elegant character. It is now used to house palace staff.

② **Orangerie** is a large Neo-Renaissance palace. It was built in the mid-19th century to house foreign royalty and other guests.

③ **Bildergalerie**, built between 1755 and 1764, is Germany's oldest purpose-built museum building. The Baroque pavilion houses an art gallery.

Schloss Charlottenhof
This Neo-Classical palace gained its name from Charlotte von Gentzkow, the former owner of the land on which the palace was built.

For hotels and restaurants in this area see p493 and pp512–13

Lustgarten

The extensive parkland is made up of several gardens. The Lustgarten (pleasure garden) is nearest to the Orangerie.

VISITORS' CHECKLIST

Practical Information
Historic Windmill, An Der Orangerie 1 & New Palace, Am Neuen Palais 3. **Tel** (0331) 969 42 00. **Open** 8:30am–6pm Tue–Sun (Nov–Mar: to 5pm). ♿ (free access to park). 🅿 ⓦ **spsg.de**

Transport
🚌 606, 695.

Neue Kammern

Once the orangerie of the Sanssouci Palace, this Rococo pavilion was later rebuilt as a guest house.

★ Schloss Sanssouci

A beautifully terraced vineyard creates a grand approach to Schloss Sanssouci, the oldest building in the complex.

Friedenskirche

The Neo-Romanesque Church of Peace is modelled on the Basilica of San Clemente in Rome.

Chinesisches Teehaus

An exhibition of exquisite Oriental porcelain is housed in the small, Rococo-style Chinese Tea House.

0 metres	200
0 yards	200

Paintings in the music room, in Schloss Sanssouci

🏠 Schloss Sanssouci

Zur Historischen Mühle. **Tel** (0331) 969 40. **Open** Apr–Oct: 10am–6pm Tue–Sun; Nov–Mar: 10am–5pm Tue–Sun. Damenflügel: **Open** May–Oct: 10am–6pm Sat & Sun. Schlossküche: **Open** Apr–Oct: 10am–6pm Tue–Sun. 🖼

This Rococo palace was built in 1745–7 by Georg Wenzeslaus von Knobelsdorff to sketches by Frederick the Great. Knobelsdorff and Johann August Nahl designed the interior. *Sanssouci* ("carefree") was the perfect name for the enchanting castle. The Damenflügel, the castle's west wing which was added in 1840 to house ladies and gentlemen of the court, and the Schlossküche (castle kitchen) can also be visited.

🏠 Schloss Neue Kammern

Zur Historischen Mühle (Lustgarten). **Tel** (0331) 969 42 06. **Open** Apr: 10am–6pm Wed–Mon; May–Oct: 10am–6pm Tue–Sun. 📷 obligatory. 🖼

The Neue Kammern (new chambers) adjoin Schloss Sanssouci in the west, like the Bildergalerie in the east. As part of this ensemble it was originally built in 1747 as an orangery, to a design by Georg Wenzeslaus von Knobelsdorff who gave it its elegant Baroque forms. The building has an attractive roof with sloping ends and sides. In 1777 Frederick the Great ordered the building to be transformed into guest accommodation. The architect, Georg Christian Unger, left the exterior of the orangery largely untouched but converted the interior into sumptuous

suites and four elegant halls. The Rococo décor has been maintained, similar to that of other palaces and pavilions of Sanssouci.

🏛 Orangerieschloss

Maulbeerallee. (Nordischer Garten). **Tel** (0331) 969 42 80. **Open** Apr: 10am–6pm Sat & Sun; May–Oct: 10am–6pm Tue–Sun. Viewing terrace: **Open** Apr–May: 10am–5pm Sat & Sun; late May–Oct: 10am–5pm Tue–Sun.

Above the park towers the Orangerie, designed in Italian Renaissance style and crowned by a colonnade. It was built to house guests, not plants, and served as guest residence for Tsar Nicolas and his wife, King Friedrich Wilhelm IV's sister. The Orangerie was constructed in 1852–60 for the king by Friedrich August Stüler, with the final design partly based on plans by Ludwig Persius. Modelled on the Regia Hall in the Vatican, the rooms were grouped around the Raphael Hall and decorated with replicas of this great Italian master's works. The observation terrace offers a good view over Potsdam.

🏛 Chinesisches Teehaus

Ökonomieweg (Rehgarten). **Tel** (0331) 969 42 22. **Open** 15 May–15 Oct: 10am–5pm Tue–Sun.

The lustrous, gilded pavilion that can be seen glistening between the trees from a distance is the Chinese Teahouse. Chinese art was very popular during the Rococo period – people wore Chinese silk, wallpapered their rooms with Chinese designs, lacquered their furniture, drank tea from Chinese porcelain and built Chinese pavilions in their gardens. The one in Sanssouci was built in 1754–56 to a design by Johann Gottfried Büring. Circular in shape, it has a centrally located main hall surrounded by three studies. Between these are pretty *trompe l'oeil* porticos. The structure is covered with a tent roof and topped with a lantern. Gilded ornaments, columns and Chinese figures surround the pavilion. Originally a tea room and summer dining house, it houses today a collection of 18th-century porcelain.

🏛 Römische Bäder

Lenné-Str. (Park Charlottenhof). **Tel** (0331) 969 42 25. 🚌 606. 🚋 91. **Open** May–Oct: 10am–6pm Tue–Sun.

The Roman baths, situated by the edge of a lake, form a picturesque group of pavilions which served as accommodation for the king's guests. They were designed in 1829–40 by Karl Friedrich Schinkel, with the help of Ludwig Persius. The gardener's house at the front stands next to a low, asymmetrical tower, built in the style of an Italian Renaissance villa. In the background, to the left, extends the former bathing pavilion, which is currently used for temporary exhibitions. The pavilions are grouped around a garden planted with colourful shrubs and vegetables.

Figure on the roof of Chinesisches Teehaus

🏠 Schloss Charlottenhof

Geschwister-Scholl-Strasse. (Park Charlottenhof). **Tel** (0331) 969 42 02. 🚋 91. **Open** May–Oct: 10am–5pm Tue–Sun. 📷 obligatory.

This small Neo-Classical palace stands at the southern end of Park Sanssouci, known as Park Charlottenhof. Built in 1826–9 for the heir to the throne, the future King Friedrich Wilhelm IV, this small, single-storey building was designed by Karl Friedrich Schinkel in the style of a Roman villa. Some of the wall paintings, designed by Schinkel in the so-called Pompeiian style, are still in place. There is also a collection of Italian engravings. The most interesting part of the interior is the Humboldt Room. The palace is surrounded by a landscaped park designed by Peter Joseph Lenné.

🏠 Neues Palais

Am Neuen Palais. **Tel** (0331) 969 42 02. **Open** Apr–Oct: 10am–6pm Wed–Mon; Nov–Mar: 9am–5pm Wed–Mon. 🎫 📷 obligatory.

One of Germany's most beautiful palaces, this imposing Baroque structure, on the main avenue in Park Sanssouci, was built for Frederick the Great to initial plans by Georg Wenzeslaus von Knobelsdorff in 1750. Its construction, to designs by Johan Gottfried Büring, Jean Laurent Le Geay and Carl von Gontard, was delayed until 1763–9, after the Seven Years' War. The vast, three-wing structure comprises over 200 richly adorned rooms and has many

The Potsdam Conference

Towards the end of World War II, the leaders of the Allies – Winston Churchill, Franklin Roosevelt, and Joseph Stalin – met in Schloss Cecilienhof in Potsdam. The aim of this conference, which lasted from 17 July until 2 August 1945, was to resolve the problems arising at the end of the war. The main participants changed, however, before it was concluded. Churchill was replaced by newly elected Clement Attlee, and Harry S. Truman took over after President Roosevelt died. The conference set up the occupation zones, the demilitarization and monitoring of Germany, the punishment of war criminals and the reparations. It also revised the German borders. These decisions established the political balance of power in Europe, which continued for 45 years.

Attlee, Truman and Stalin in Potsdam

interesting sculptures. The south wing houses the kings' quarters.

🏠 Schloss Babelsberg

Park Babelsberg 10. **Tel** (0331) 969 42 50. **Closed** until 2016.

Built in 1833–5 for Prince Wilhelm (Kaiser Wilhelm I), by Karl Friedrich Schinkel, this extravagant castle ranks as one of his finest works. An irregular building with many towers and bay windows, built in the spirit of English Neo-Gothic, with allusions to Windsor Castle and Tudor style, it now holds the Museum of Pre-History.

🎬 Filmpark Babelsberg

Großbeerenstrasse. **Tel** (0331) 721 27 38. **Open** 15 Apr–31 Oct: 10am–6pm daily. 🎫 🌐 filmpark.de

This amazing film park was laid out on the site where Germany's first films were produced in 1912. From 1917 the studio belonged to Universum-Film-AG (UFA), which produced some of the most famous films of the silent era, including Fritz Lang's *Metropolis* and some films with Greta Garbo. The *Blue Angel*, with Marlene Dietrich, was also shot at Babelsberg, but subsequently, the studios were used to film Nazi propaganda. The studio is still operational, and the public can admire some of the old sets, the creation of special effects and stuntmen in action.

🎬 Einsteinturm

Albert-Einstein-Strasse. **Open** Oct–Mar: visits daily by arrangement with the Urania Society (0331 291 741). 🏛 604.

This tower, built in 1920–21 by Erich Mendelsohn, is one of the finest examples of German Expressionist architecture. Its fantasy forms were to demonstrate the qualities of reinforced concrete to spectacular effect. However, the cost of formwork, assembled by boat builders, limited the use of the material to the first storey, while the upper floors are plastered brickwork.

The impressive Marble Hall in the Baroque Neues Palais

❽ Chorin

Road map E2. 🚗 510. 🚉 Kloster
Chorin, Amt 11A. **Tel** (033366) 703 77.
Open Apr–Oct: 9am–6pm daily;
Nov–Mar: 9am–4pm daily. 🅿️
🎻 Choriner Musiksommer.

On the edge of the vast
Schorfheide forest, which has
been listed as a World Biosphere
Reserve by UNESCO, stands one
of Brandenburg's most beautiful
Gothic buildings – the
Cistercian **Kloster** (abbey) of
Chorin. The Cistercians arrived
here in 1258, but work on the
present Gothic abbey did not
start until 1270. The church is a
triple-nave, transeptal basilica,
with a magnificent façade.
Preserved to this day are two
wings of the monastic quarters
plus several domestic buildings.
Following the dissolution of the
monastery in 1542, the entire
complex fell into disrepair.
Today the church, deprived of
its traditional furnishings, is used
as a venue for classical concerts.
The park established by Peter
Joseph Lenné is conducive to
pleasant strolls.

Environs
For visitors to Niederfinow, the
giant **Schiffshebewerk** (barge-
lift) is a definite must. This
wonder of technology was
designed for lifting and
lowering ships from one canal
to another. Commissioned in
1934, it is 60 m (197 ft) tall and
capable of lifting barges laden
with 1,000 tonnes or more.

Portal of the St Marienkirche in Frankfurt
an der Oder

❾ Frankfurt an der Oder

Road map F3. 🚗 87,900. 🚉 🚌
🛈 Große Oderstr. 29. (0335-61 00
800). 🎻 Frankfurter Musikfesttage
(Mar); Hansefest (Jul); Kleist-Tage (Oct).

Frankfurt, on the banks of the
river Oder, was granted municipal
rights in 1253, prospered in
the 13th century and joined the
Hanseatic league in 1368. In
1945, the right bank was
ceded to Poland and is now
known as Słubice.
    Viadrina University, founded
in 1506, was reopened in 1991
and now educates both German
and Polish students. The town's
most famous son is playwright
and writer Heinrich von Kleist

(1777–1811); the Kleist-Museum,
devoted to his life and work, is in
the former garrison school. The
Gothic **Rathaus** (town hall) in the
centre escaped destruction in
World War II and now houses an
art gallery. The main church,
Marienkirche (church of St
Mary), is a vast, five-nave Gothic
hall which has stood in ruins
since 1945. Partly reconstructed,
its chancel windows feature the
"Illustrated Bible". These stained
glass paintings originate from
around 1367 and illustrate
Christ's Life and Suffering, the
Creation of the World and the
Legend of the Antichrist. Some of
the church's Gothic furnishings
were rescued and can now be
seen in **St Gertraud** (church of
St Gertrude) which dates back to
1368. The main altar from 1489
and the huge, 5m- (16ft-) tall
candelabrum from 1376 are
particularly valuable. Another
Gothic church, originally built in
1270, has been transformed into
the **C.P.E. Bach Konzerthalle**
(concert hall), named after Carl
Philipp Emmanuel Bach, son of
Johann Sebastian.

❿ Cottbus

Road map F3. 🚗 121,000.
🚉 Bahnhofstr. 🚌 🛈 Berliner Platz
6 (0355-754 20). 🎻 Karnevalsumzug
(Feb); Cottbuser Musik-Herbst (Oct).
🌐 **cottbus-tourismus.de**

Tourists rarely visit Cottbus,
despite the many attractions
offered by the town. Its

The Baroque Schloss Branitz in Cottbus

enchanting town square is surrounded by impressive Baroque buildings. The house at No. 24 is the quaint Löwen-apotheke (lion's pharmacy), which now houses a small pharmaceutical museum, the **Brandenburgisches Apothekenmuseum**, with displays of historical interiors. Nearby, the Gothic **Oberkirche St Nikolai** features an unusual original late-Gothic mesh vaulting. Another interesting Gothic structure, the **Wendenkirche** (Sorbian church), is a former Franciscan church, from the 14th–15th centuries.

Other attractions of the town include the remains of the medieval city walls with three preserved towers. Perhaps the most attractive building in Cottbus is the **Staatstheater** (state theatre) designed in Jugendstil (Art Nouveau style) by Bernhard Sehring and built in 1908.

The **Wendisches Museum** is devoted to the culture of the Sorbs which is experiencing a revival (see p185).

Schloss Branitz is a late-Baroque palace, originally built in the 18th century, at the southeastern edge of town. It became the residence of Prince Hermann von Pückler-Muskau in 1845, who had its interior redesigned by Gottfried Semper. Today, the palace houses the **Fürst-Pückler-Museum**, which exhibits paintings by Karl Blechen, a local artist from Cottbus. The star attraction of the palace is its **Park**, which was designed by Prince Pückler-Muskau himself. This vast landscaped garden includes a lake with an island on which stands a grass-covered mock-Egyptian earth pyramid containing the tomb of the extravagant and eccentric Prince.

🏛 **Schloss Branitz and Fürst-Pückler-Museum**
Kastanienallee 11. **Tel** (0355) 751 50. **Open** Apr–Oct: 10am–6pm daily; Nov–Mar: 11am–5pm Tue–Sun. 🖼

🏛 **Wendisches Museum**
Mühlenstr. 12. **Tel** (0355) 79 49 30.

Boats and canoes in the Spreewald, near Lübben

Open 10am–5pm Tue–Fri, 1–5pm Sat & Sun and bank holidays.

🏛 **Brandenburgisches Apothekenmuseum**
Altmark 24. **Tel** (0355) 239 97. **Open** visits possible with guide 11am–2pm Tue–Fri; 2pm & 3pm Sat & Sun. 🖼

⓫ Spreewald

Road map F3. 🚆 Lübben.
ℹ Raddusch, Lindenstr. 1 (035433-722 99), Lübbenau, Ehm-Welk-Str. 15 (03542-36 68). 🚆 🎭 Spreewaldfest in Lübbenau (Jul); Lübben (Sep).
🌐 **spreewald.de**

Designated as one of the World Biosphere Reserves, this marshy region, criss-crossed by hundreds of small rivers and canals, attracts large numbers of tourists each year. An all-day trip by **Kahn** (boat) or canoe, which is best started in **Lübben** or **Lübbenau**, can prove to be an unforgettable experience. The splendour of nature, numerous water birds and the endless chain of small restaurants which serve meals straight from the jetty, ensure an exciting day for the visitor. Do not miss the local speciality, pickled gherkins.

Lübben has an original Gothic church and a Baroque palace, rebuilt in the 19th century. Lübbenau features a small Baroque church and the Neo-Classical house of the von Lynar family. In **Lehde** the small open-air museum and the private collection of the **Bauernhaus-und Gurkenmuseum** – the only gherkin museum in Germany – are highly recommended.

Environs
Luckau, 18 km (11 miles) west of Lübben, has a lovely town square, surrounded by attractive Baroque houses with stucco façades, and the ornamented, 14th-century Gothic Nikolaikirche.

⓬ Jüterbog

Road map E3. 🗠 13,000. 🚆 🚌
ℹ Markt 21 (03372-46 31 13).

Jüterbog is a small, picturesque town featuring many Gothic structures including some well-preserved sections of three city walls with gates and towers, dating back to the 15th century. It also boasts a beautiful town hall with arcades and three churches. **Nikolaikirche** (church of St Nicholas), the largest of them, is a magnificent hall church, with a twin-tower façade, built in several stages. The so-called New Sacristy features a set of medieval wall paintings, while the naves contain many Gothic furnishings.

Environs
Five km (3 miles) to the north of Jüterbog stands **Kloster Zinna**, a former Cistercian Abbey with an early-Gothic stone church. It features 16th-century stained-glass windows depicting the saints Bernhard and Benedikt.

The early-Gothic ex-Cistercian Kloster Zinna, near Jüterbog

SAXONY-ANHALT

The scenic Harz mountains, a popular recreation area with fascinating rock formations and pleasant walks, are the best known attraction of Saxony-Anhalt. Yet this state also boasts a number of interesting towns, such as Lutherstadt Wittenberg and Magdeburg, steeped in history and blessed with magnificent historic remains, which range from Romanesque churches and abbeys to medieval castles.

This province consists of the areas of the former Duchy of Anhalt and the Prussian province of Saxony, that part of the Kingdom of Saxony which was incorporated into Prussia after the Congress of Vienna (1815) as punishment for supporting Napoleon.

The landscape in this region is highly varied. Its northern part, the Altmark, is a largely flat area of farmland and heath. The gentle hills of the Harz Mountains in the southwest, although not especially high (their highest peak, the Brocken, rises to only 1142 m/3747 ft), are picturesque and fairly well provided with tourist facilities. The eastern, flat part of the region is more industrialized. It also includes two very important towns: the small town of Wittenberg, where Martin Luther proclaimed his

theses in 1517, thus launching the Reformation, and Dessau, the former capital of the Duchy of Anhalt and from 1925 to 1932 the seat of the Bauhaus Art School. The southern part of the province, with its interesting and varied landscape, features one of the land's most impressive historic buildings – the gigantic Naumburg Cathedral.

After World War II Saxony-Anhalt was occupied by the Soviets, and in 1949 it was incorporated into the GDR. It underwent major industrial development, mainly due to lignite mining. The state of Saxony-Anhalt was first created in 1947, only to be abolished five years later. It was finally re-established as a federal state in 1990, with Magdeburg as its capital.

Timber-frame houses in Quedlinburg

◀ Interior of the Schlosskirche in Lutherstadt Wittenberg

Exploring Saxony–Anhalt

Touring Saxony-Anhalt can be an unforgettable experience, especially for admirers of Romanesque art, as this region abounds in churches and abbeys of that period. A visit to Wörlitz provides the opportunity to see one of Germany's most beautiful landscaped gardens. Nature lovers, hill-walkers and, in the winter, cross-country skiers should include a few days in the romantic Harz Mountains in their schedule. An added attraction here is a ride on the narrow-gauge railway drawn by a steam engine which, today as in years gone by, still links some of the most interesting places of the region.

Interior of the Gothic cathedral in Havelberg

Zoo-Park in Dessau

For additional map symbols *see back flap*

0 kilometres 15

0 miles 15

Listening to a summer water concert, in Wörlitz Park

Getting Around

The A2 motorway from Hanover to Berlin runs through
Magdeburg to the northern part of the region. Another
motorway, the A9 which links Berlin and Munich, provides easy
access to Dessau and Halle, which is also served by the recently
constructed A14 motorway from Leipzig to Magdeburg. Other
major and minor roads, well signposted, provide access to smaller
towns and villages. Larger towns are easily accessed by rail or
local bus services. In the Harz Mountains the narrow-gauge train
is an alternative form of transport.

Key

━━━ Motorway

━━━ Major road

┄┄┄ Minor road

▪ ▪ ▪ Under construction

━━━ Scenic route

━━━ Main railway

━━━ Minor railway

━━━ Regional border

△ Summit

Sights at a Glance

❶ Halberstadt
❷ Wernigerode
❹ Quedlinburg
❺ Bernburg
❻ Halle
❼ Merseburg
❽ Querfurt
❾ *Naumburg pp154–5*
❿ *Magdeburg p156*
⓫ Stendal
⓬ Havelberg
⓭ Tangermünde
⓮ Dessau
⓯ *Lutherstadt Wittenberg pp158–9*
⓰ *Wörlitz Park pp160–61*

Tours

❸ The Harz Mountain Trail

Interior of the Gothic Cathedral of Halberstadt

❶ Halberstadt

Road map D3. 🗻 42,000. 🚪 🚌
ℹ️ Hinter dem Rathause 6 (03941-55 18 15). 🌐 **halberstadt.de**

Halberstadt enjoys a picturesque location in the foothills of the Harz Mountains. Its history goes back to the 9th century, when it became a seat of a mission episcopate. Once an important town, Halberstadt had 80 per cent of its buildings destroyed during World War II. Fortunately, many of its beautiful historic buildings have been restored to their former glory.

The vast **St Stephans Dom** is the fourth successive church built on the same site. Construction began in the 13th century and the church was consecrated in 1491. The two-tower transeptial basilica ranks as one of the most beautiful pure Gothic forms in Germany. Its oldest part is the 12th-century font. Also notable are the Romanesque Crucifixion group (c.1220), set above the choir screen, and several examples of Gothic sculpture. Stained-glass windows from around 1330 have survived in the Marian Chapel, and 15th-century windows can be found along the cloisters and in the presbytery.

The adjoining chapter buildings contain one of Germany's

Romanesque Crucifixion group
in the Dom, Halberstadt

richest cathedral treasures – the **Domschatz**, with precious 12th-century tapestries, numerous sculptures and liturgical vessels.

Other interesting churches to have survived in the old town district include the Romanesque 12th-century **Liebfrauenkirche** and the Gothic **Marktkirche St Martini** with a statue of Roland, symbolizing the freedom of the city. Remaining timber-frame houses can be seen in Gröper- and Taubenstrasse.

🏛️ Domschatz
Tel 03941 24237. ◯ Apr–Oct: 10am–5:30pm daily (from 11am Sun); Nov–Mar: 10am–4pm Tue–Sun. 📷 obligatory. 🌐 **dom-und-domschatz.de**

Environs
An original 12th-century Benedictine church stands in Huysburg, 11 km (7 miles) to the northwest.

❷ Wernigerode

Road map D3. 🗻 36,000. 🚪 🚌
ℹ️ Marktplatz 10 (03943-55 37 835). 📅 Rathausfest (Jun); Schlossfestspiele (Jul & Aug). 🌐 **wernigerode.de**

Wernigerode is attractively situated at a confluence of two rivers. Timber-frame houses lean across its steep, winding streets,

and a massive castle rises above the town. The **Harzquerbahn**, a narrow-gauge railway which links the small towns and villages in the Harz Mountains, between Wernigerode and Nordhausen, provides another popular tourist attraction. The Brockenbahn runs between Wernigerode and the Brocken mountain.

Strolling around the Old Town it is well worth stepping into St John's Church, featuring a Romanesque west tower. It contains some late-Gothic features, including the font and the altar. The variety of ornaments adorning the houses in Wernigerode is truly staggering. Particularly interesting are the houses along **Breite Strasse**, the town's main shopping street which is closed to traffic.

🏰 Schloss Wernigerode
Am Schloss 1. **Tel** 03943-55 30 30. ◯ May–Oct: 10am–6pm; Nov–Apr: 10am–5pm Tue–Fri, 10am–6pm Sat & Sun. 🅿️

The fairy-tale castle, spiked with turrets, was built during the years 1861–83 on the site of an older fortress. Now a museum, it houses the Stolberg-Wernigerode family art collection. The castle ramparts afford a fantastic view of the town and the nearby Harz mountains.

Environs
The small town of **Osterwieck**, 22 km (14 miles) to the north, has over 400 timber-frame buildings, dating mainly from the 16th and 17th centuries.

The romantic façade of Schloss
Wernigerode, now a museum

❸ The Harz Mountain Trail

The tourist trail across the Harz Mountains leads through charming historic towns and villages, as well as past the other attractions of the region including some fascinating caves and unusual rock formations.

Tips for Drivers

Length: 55 km (34 miles).
Stopping places: there are many attractive restaurants all along the trail, in every town.
🖼 Walpurgisnacht, Thale: 30 Apr.

① The Rübeland Caves
Rübeland's main attractions are the Hermannshöhle and Baumannshöhle, two caves with amazing stalactites and stalagmites.

② Blankenburg
This charming mountain town is overlooked by an 18th-century castle. The Teufelsmauer, a spectacular 4-km (2-mile) long sandstone cliff, attracts many climbers.

③ Thale
Many mountain walks start in Thale, including one to the Hexentanzplatz, a platform suspended above a cliff, from where witches fly to Sabbath celebrations in the Walpurgis Night.

⑦ Harzgerode
The town has charming timber-frame houses in the Old Town, and a 16th-century castle.

⑥ Burg Falkenstein
This large castle, built in the 12th century and extended many times, is now a museum. From the castle, the visitor can enjoy a splendid view over the surrounding Harz Mountains.

④ Gernrode
The star attraction in this town is the 10th-century church of St Cyriacus. Its interior is devoid of ornaments, yet enchantingly pure in form.

⑤ Ballenstedt
The former home of the von Anhalt-Bemburg family enchants visitors to this day with its imaginative design, including the Baroque castle set in a park.

Key

■ Tour route
■ Other road
═ Scenic route

0 km   2
0 miles   2

For map symbols see back flap

The Renaissance portal of
Quedlinburg Schloss

● Quedlinburg

Road map D4. 🏔 26,000. 🚊 🚌
ℹ Markt 4 (03946-90 56 24 and 63 88
990). 🎵 Musiksommer (Jun–Sep).

The rise of the small town of
Quedlinburg was closely
connected with its convent,
established in 936 by Emperor
Otto I and his mother, St
Mathilde. On the hill above the
town stands the vast
Romanesque structure of the
Stiftskirche St Servatius
(Collegiate Church of St
Servatius), built between 1017
and 1129. Its old crypt, the
Huysburg, which belonged to
the previous church, features
Romanesque wall paintings and
contains tombs of the prioresses
and of the Emperor Henry and
his wife Mathilde. An exhibition
of treasures is shown in the
arms of the transept, including

the Romanesque reliquary of
St Servatius and the remaining
fragments of the 12th-century
Knüpfteppich (tapestry). The
Quedlinburg Schloss, a
Renaissance palace surrounded
by gardens, occupies the other
side of the hill.

Both Old and New Town of
Quedlinburg have valuable
examples of timber-frame
architecture. The buildings date
from various times – the modest
house at **Wordgasse 3**, from
around 1400, is the oldest
surviving timber-frame building
in Germany. Also noteworthy
are the numerous churches,
including the 10th-century
Norbertinenkirche, the
Wippertikirche with its early-
Romanesque crypt, and the
15th century, late-Gothic
Marktkirche St Benedicti.

● Bernburg

Road map D3. 🏔 36,000. 🚊 🚌 ℹ
Lindenplatz 9 (03471 346 9311). 🎵
Walpurgisnacht (May). 🖥 **bernberg.de**

Once the capital of one of
Anhalt's Duchies, Bernburg
enjoys a picturesque location
on the banks of the Saale River.
It has a **Bergstadt** (upper town)
and a **Talstadt** (lower town),
and its attractions include the
Gothic parish churches and
the town square with its
Baroque buildings. The most
important historic building is the
Bernburg Schloss, a castle built

on a rock. It owes its present
appearance to refurbishments
(1540–70), yet many features of
this multi-wing structure are
much older, including the
12th-century Romanesque
chapels and Gothic towers.

Burg Giebichenstein, in Halle, with the
Arts and Crafts College

● Halle

Road map D4. 🏔 232,300. 🚊 🚌
ℹ Marktplatz 13 (0345 122 99 84).
🎵 Händel-Festspiele (Jun); Hallesche
Musiktage (Nov). 🖥 **halle.de**

Halle is an old town with a rich
history in commerce and trade, its
wealth founded on the production and sale of salt. Later, the
town was turned into a centre for
the chemical industry. Halle has
preserved most of its historic
heritage. On the **Marktplatz**
(town square) stands an interesting church, **Unser Lieben Frauen**
(Our Lady), whose late-Gothic
main body (1530–54) was positioned between two pairs of
towers that had remained intact

The impressive Bernburg Schloss, built on a rock

Renaissance residence in Merseburg

from previous Romanesque churches. Nearby is the **Roter Turm** (Red Tower), an 84-m (276 ft) tall belfry, built in 1418–1506. The house at · Nikolaistrasse 5, the birthplace of Georg Friedrich Händel, now houses a small museum, the **Händel-Haus**. In Domplatz stands the early-Gothic **Dom**, built in 1280–1331 by the Dominicans and restored between 1525 and 1530 in Renaissance style.

Halle has some other medieval churches, including the late-Gothic **Moritzkirche** built in the latter part of the 14th century. It is also worth visiting the **Kunststiftung des Landes Sachsen-Anhalt**, housed in the refurbished Citadel building known as **Moritzburg** and built during 1484–1503. On the outskirts of town stands **Burg Giebichenstein**, the former castle residence of the Magdeburg bishops. The upper part of the castle remains in ruins, while the lower part houses an Arts & Crafts College.

The **Landesmuseum für Vorgeschichte** (State Museum of Prehistory) has more than 11 million exhibits. Its centrepiece is the Nebra Sky Disc, a 3,600-year-old bronze disc recognized by UNESCO as the earliest known image of the night sky.

🏛 **Kunststiftung des Landes Sachsen-Anhalt**
Friedemann-Bach-Platz 5. **Tel** (0345) 21 25 90. **Open** 10am–6pm Tue–Sun. 🎫 free last Sun of month.

🏛 **Landesmuseum für Vorgeschichte**
Richard-Wagner-Str. 9. **Tel** (0345) 52 47 30. **Open** Tue–Sun. 🎫

❼ Merseburg

Road map D4. 🚹 40,000. 🚊 🚌 ℹ Burgstr. 5 (03461-21 41 70) 🎫 Schlossfest (Jun). 🔤 **merseburg.de**

The first sight visitors see as they arrive in Merseburg is the **Domburg** – a vast complex of buildings spiked with towers, consisting of a cathedral and residences. The cathedral is not uniform in style; it includes some Romanesque elements (the eastern section and twin towers in the west) erected in the 11th and 12th centuries, and the late-Gothic triple-nave main body, which was built in 1510–17. All that remains of the older, early-Romanesque structure is the crypt, underneath the presbytery. The cathedral contains remarkable Gothic and Renaissance features, as well as numerous sarcophagi of bishops, such as that of Thilo von Troth (1470). The chapter buildings house a library with precious manuscripts, including the **Merseburg Bible** (c. 1200). Adjacent to the cathedral is a three-wing Renaissance-style **Schloss**. Magnificent portals and an attractive oriel in the castle's west wing are noteworthy.

❽ Querfurt

Road map D4. 🚹 11,000. 🚌 ℹ Markt 14 (034771-237 99) 🎫 Brunnenfest (Jun). 🔤 **querfurt.de**

The narrow streets of Querfurt are crammed with timber-frame houses, and the giant **Schloss** towers over the town square with its Renaissance town hall. The castle's present form is the result of Renaissance refurbishments, but it maintains many Romanesque features, such as the 11th-century donjon (keep), known as **Dicker Heinrich** (Fat Henry) and a 12th-century church. Also worth seeing is the burial chapel, the Baroque **Fürstenhaus** (ducal house) and a small museum, situated in the former armoury and granary.

❾ Naumburg

Road map D4. 🚹 30,500. 🚊 🚌 ℹ Markt 12 (03445-27 31 25). 🎫 Hussiten-Kirsch-Fest (Jun). 🔤 **naumburg-tourismus.de**

The town's star attraction is the **Dom** (cathedral of Saints Peter and Paul *see pp154–5*). There is a late-Gothic **Rathaus** (town hall), restored in Renaissance style, and the main square is surrounded by quaint houses. Further attractions include the **Marientor** gate (1455–6) with the puppet theatre, and the Gothic **Stadtkirche St Wenzel** (Church of St Wenceslas). The latter has two paintings by Lucas Cranach the Elder as well as the 18th-century organ that Johann Sebastian Bach played on. Friedrich Nietzsche, the philosopher, spent his childhood at No. 18 Weingarten, now a small museum.

Gothic stone retable of the main altar in Naumburg Dom

Naumburg Dom

The impressive Cathedral of Saints Peter and Paul in Naumburg is one of the finest Gothic structures in Germany. The present cathedral is the second to be built on the same site; only a section of the eastern crypt survived of the earlier Romanesque church. Construction started before 1213, with the earliest parts including the late-Romanesque east choir, the transept and the main body. The early-Gothic west choir was built in the mid-13th century, the newer Gothic east choir c.1330. The northeast towers date from the 15th century, the southwest towers from 1894.

Stained-Glass Windows in the Presbytery
The stained-glass windows depict scenes of the apostles of virtue and sin. Some sections are original 13th-century work, but two were completed in the 19th century.

★ **Founders' Statues**
The statues of Margrave Ekkehard and his wife, Uta, are true masterpieces – the artist succeeded marvellously in capturing the beauty and sensitivity of his subjects.

KEY

① West choir

② Sarcophagus of Bishop Dietrich II

③ East choir

④ **The Main Altar**, built in the mid-14th century, is a stone retable depicting the Crucifixion with the saints which was transferred from another altar.

★ **Portal of the West Reading Room**
The Gothic twin portal depicts the Crucifixion, a moving and highly expressive group sculpture by the brilliant "Naumburger Meister" whose identity remains unknown.

Pulpit
The richly ornamented pulpit basket, from 1466, and the adjoining stairs have been renovated.

★ Main Portal
The late-Romanesque, 13th-century portal is decorated on the left side with eagles. The tympanum features Christ in a mandorla (almond-shaped area) supported by angels.

East Choir Altar
This Gothic altar features the Virgin Mary with the Infant Jesus, surrounded by the figures of the saints.

St Mary's Altar
This late-Gothic triptych (c.1510) depicts the Virgin Mary with the Infant, framed by Saints Barbara and Catherine, with the apostles in the wings.

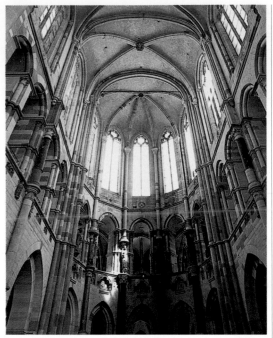

Interior of the Gothic presbytery in the Magdeburg Dom

⑩ Magdeburg

Road map D3. 🏛 235,000. 🚆 🚌
ℹ️ Ernst-Reuter-Allee 12 (0391-838 0405). 🎷 Jazzfestival (Jun), Klassik-Open Air (Jul). 🌐 **magdeburg-tourist.de**

The large-scale development of Magdeburg, today the capital of Saxony-Anhalt and a port on the river Elbe, began in the 10th century when Emperor Otto I established his main residence here. In medieval times the town became a political and cultural centre. After the abolition of the archbishopric and the destruction wrought by the Thirty Years' War, it lost its political importance. About 80 per cent was destroyed during World War II, but it is still worth a visit since many historic buildings have been reconstructed in the Old Town.

🏛 Dom St Mauritius und St Katharina
Domplatz. **Tel** (0391) 541 04 36.
Open May–Sep: 10am–6pm; Apr & Oct: 10am–5pm; Nov–Mar: 10am–4pm.
The vast Magdeburg cathedral is one of the most important Gothic churches in Germany. Its

construction, which started in 1209 on the site of an earlier Romanesque church, was completed in 1520, although much of it was built by the mid-14th century. The result is a lofty, aisled basilica with transept, cloisters, a ring of chapels surrounding the presbytery and a vast twin-tower façade. The cathedral has several magnificent, original sculptures. Other notable features include the tomb of Emperor Otto I, as well as the 12th-century bronze tomb plaques of archbishops Friedrich von Wettin and Wichmann.

The memorial for the dead of World War I is the work of Ernst Barlach, dating from 1929. Visitors to the cathedral may notice several elements that were preserved from ancient structures and have been incorporated into the walls or used as ornaments inside the building.

🏛 Kulturhistorisches Museum
Otto-von-Guericke-Str. 68–73.
Tel (0391) 540 35 01. **Open** 10am–5pm Tue–Sun. 🖼
This museum contains works of art, archaeological finds and historic documents of the town. Its most valuable exhibit is the Magdeburger Reiter (Magdeburg Rider), a sculpture dating from around 1240 of an unknown ruler on a horse (probably Otto I).

🏛 Kloster Unser Lieben Frauen
Regierungsstr. 4–6. Kunstmuseum **Tel** (0391) 56 50 20. **Open** 10am–5pm Tue–Sun. 🖼
This austere Romanesque church, Magdeburg's oldest building, was built for the Norbertine order during the second half of the 11th and the early 12th centuries. Stripped of all its ornaments, it now serves as a concert hall. The adjacent Romanesque abbey is a museum with medieval and modern sculptures (Barlach, Rodin).

🏛 Halle an der Buttergasse
Alter Markt. Weinkeller Buttergasse.
The basement of a late-Romanesque market hall from c.1200 was rediscovered in 1948, and is used today as a wine cellar.

🏛 Rathaus
Alter Markt.
The present Baroque town hall, built in 1691–8 on the site of an earlier, late-Romanesque town hall, was restored after World War II.

🏛 Pfarrkirche St Johannis
Am Johannisberg 1.
Viewing tower:
Tel (0391) 59 34 50.
Open Mar–Oct: 10am–6pm Tue–Sun; Nov–Feb: 10–5pm. 🖼
Near the market square is the Gothic church of St John, destroyed during World War II and later rebuilt. In 1524 Martin Luther preached here. Today it is used as a concert hall.

Kloster Unser Lieben Frauen in Magdeburg

For hotels and restaurants in this area see pp493–4 and pp513–14

⑪ Stendal

Road map D3. 🖼 39,600. 🚌 🚆
ℹ️ Kornmarkt 8 (03931-65 11 90).
🎪 Rolandfest (early Jul).
🆆 stendal.de

In medieval times Stendal was one of the richest towns of the Brandenburg margravate, and its most valuable historical remains date from that period. The late-Gothic **St Nikolai** cathedral was built in 1423–67, on the foundations of a Romanesque Augustinian church. Its star attractions are 15th-century stained-glass windows in the presbytery and the transept.

The late-Gothic, 15th-century church **St Marien** (St Mary) has some original Gothic elements, and the oldest parts of the **Rathaus** (town hall) date back to the 14th century. Other attractions include the remains of the town walls, with a beautiful tower, **Uenglinger Torturm**.

Gothic traceries of the cloisters in the Dom, Havelberg

⑫ Havelberg

Road map D3. 🖼 7,000. 🚆
ℹ️ Uferstr 1 (039387-79 091).
🆆 havelberg.de

Havelberg played an important role in the Christianization of this region, with a mission episcopate established here as early as the mid-10th century. The present cathedral – **Dom St Marien** – was built in 1150–70, and although redesigned in the early 14th century, it nevertheless maintained its Romanesque character. Its most interesting features include

Back of the Gothic Rathaus in the market square in Tangermünde

huge stone candelabra taken from the former reading room, dating back to around 1300, and the present reading room, which is decorated with reliefs carved in the workshop of the Parler family, in Prague, between 1396 and 1411.

⑬ Tangermünde

Road map D3. 🖼 10,000. 🚌 🚆
ℹ️ Markt 2 (039322-223 93).
🆆 tourismus-tangermuende.de

Situated at the confluence of the Tanger and Elbe rivers, this town grew rapidly during medieval times. For centuries it remained the seat of the Brandenburg margraves, and King Charles IV chose it as his second residence. The town joined the Hanseatic League, and grew in status thanks to its trade links.

The **Rathaus** (town hall) has timber-frame architecture and houses the municipal museum.

The only remains of the old castle are its main tower and the **Kanzlei** (chancellery) dating to 1377. King Charles IV brought the Augustinian monks to town and had the **St Stephanskirche** (church of St Stephen) built for them. Construction continued until the end of the 15th century. This magnificent, late-Gothic hall church with transept and cloister contains interesting features: a 1624 organ made in

the Hamburg workshop of Hans Scherer the Younger, the 1619 pulpit created by Christopher Dehne and a font dating from 1508, the work of Heinrich Mente.

The east wing of the beautiful Gothic **Rathaus** (town hall) dates back to 1430 and is the work of Heinrich Brunsberg, its richly ornamented spire being typical of his work. The west wing with its arcades was added around 1480, and the external stairs date from the 19th century.

Tangermünde has retained some remains of the city walls, dating from around 1300 and including a magnificent late-Gothic gate, the **Neustädter Tor**, whose tall, cylindrical tower has intricate, lacy ceramic ornaments.

🏛 **Rathaus (Stadtgeschichtliches Museum)**
Am Markt. **Tel** (039322) 42 153.
Open 10am–5pm Tue–Sun.

Environs
A Romanesque **Klosterkirche** (abbey) in Jerichow, 10 km (6 miles) north of Tangermünde, is the earliest brick structure of the region. It was built in the 1150s, for Norbertine monks. The west towers were completed during the 15th century. Its austere, triple-nave vaulted interior is impressive. There are also many remains of the former abbey.

Interior of the former Norbertinenkirche, in Jerichow, north of Tangermünde

⑭ Dessau

Road map E3. 🗻 84,400. 🚗 🚌
ℹ️ Zerbster Str. 2c (0340-204 14 42).
🎭 Kurt-Weill-Fest (late Feb–Mar),
Elbmusikfest (Jun). 🆆 **dessau.de**

Dessau, once a magnificent city
and the capital of the duchy of
Anhalt-Dessau, is less attractive
today, yet it has some excellent
historic sights. In the town
centre are some interesting
Baroque churches and the
Johannbau, the remains of a
Renaissance ducal residence.

Dessau is also known for the
Bauhaus complex. Built in 1925
to a design by Walter Gropius, it
is the home of the famous art
school, which moved here from
Weimar. The **Bauhausmuseum**
is housed in one of its wings.
Nearby, in Friedrich-Ebert-
Allee, five of the so-called
Meisterhäuser – master houses
for the Art College professors –
have survived World War II. The
houses of Lyonel Feininger and
Paul Klee are open to the public.
Wassily Kandinsky was also a
former resident. The **Kornhaus**,
on Elballee, restored in 1996,
contains a restaurant, café
and dance hall.

Many splendid residences set
in landscaped gardens were
built in 18th- and 19th-century
Dessau. In the town centre
stands a Neo-Classical palace,
Schloss Georgium, built in 1780
to a design by Friedrich Wilhelm
von Erdmannsdorff. Today it
houses a collection of old
masters, including works by
Rubens, Hals and Cranach.

🏛️ **Bauhausmuseum**
Gropiusallee 38. **Tel** (0340) 65 080.
Open 10am–6pm daily. 🎟️
🆆 **bauhaus-dessau.de**

🏠 **Schloss Georgium**
Puschkinallee 100. **Tel** (0340) 61 38 74.
Open 10am–5pm Tue–Sun. 🎟️

Environs
Haldeburg, which is situated
on the outskirts of Dessau, has a
Neo-Gothic hunting lodge built
in 1782–3, and Mosigkau boasts
Schloss Mosigkau, Princess
Anna Wilhelmina's Baroque
residence, designed by Christian
Friedrich Damm. It contains
some excellent examples of
17th-century painting.

In **Oranienbaum**, 12 km
(7 miles) east of Dessau, stands
a late-17th-century, early-
Baroque palace that was built
for Princess Henrietta Katharine
of Orange by the Dutch
architect Cornelius Ryckwaert.

🏠 **Schloss Mosigkau**
Knobelsdorffallee 2. **Tel** (0340) 50 255
721. **Open** Apr, Oct: 10am–5pm Sat &
Sun; May–Sep: 10am–6pm Tue–Sun.
Closed Dec–Mar. 📷 🎟️

⑮ Lutherstadt Wittenberg

Road map E3. 🗻 55,000. 🚗 🚌
ℹ️ Schlossplatz 2 (03491-41 48 48).
🎭 Wittenberger Stadtfest & Luthers
Hochzeit (Jun). 🆆 **wittenberg.de**

This small town, named after its
most famous resident, Martin
Luther, enjoys a scenic position
on the banks of the Elbe River.

Its main development took
place during the 16th century,
under the Great Elector,
Frederick the Wise. Wittenberg
became the capital of the
Reformation thanks to the work
of Martin Luther and Philipp
Melanchthon, and as such it
attracts many visitors. Another
famous resident of that period
was the painter Lucas Cranach
the Elder.

🏠 **Schloss Wittenberg**
Schlossplatz. Museum für Naturkunde
und Völkerkunde (Museum of
Natural History and Ethnography):
Tel (03491) 43 34 920. **Open** 9am–
5pm Tue–Sun. 🎟️

Built for Frederick the Wise in
1489–1525, the castle was greatly
altered during reconstruction
following fire and wartime
damage. A museum is housed
in the west wing.

The tomb of Frederick the Wise,
in Schlosskirche

🏠 **Schlosskirche**
Schlossplatz. **Tel** (03491) 40 25 85.
Open May–Oct: 10am–6pm Mon–Sat,
11:30–6pm Sun; Nov–Apr:10am–4pm
Mon–Sat, 11:30am–4pm Sun.

Built after 1497, this church was
made famous by Martin Luther,
who allegedly posted his theses
on its door in 1517. The original
door no longer exists, but
the church contains many
interesting tombs, including
that of Frederick the Wise,
created in 1527 in the workshop
of Hans Vischer, as well as
modest tombs of Martin Luther
and Melanchthon.

Schloss Georgium in Dessau

⊞ Cranachhaus

Markt 4. **Tel** (03491) 420 19 11.
Open 10am–5pm Mon–Sat (from
1pm Sun). **Closed** Nov–Apr: Mon.

This beautiful, early
16th-century Renaissance
house once belonged to
Lucas Cranach the Elder and
was the birthplace of his son,
Lucas Cranach the Younger.
His studio was located at
No. 1 Schlossstrasse.

⊞ Rathaus

Markt 26. **Open** 10am–5pm Tue–Sun.
The Renaissance town hall
was built in 1523–35, and later
twice extended in the 16th
century. In its forecourt are two
19th-century monuments: to
Martin Luther by Gottfried
Schadow and to Philipp Melanchthon by Friedrich Drake.

⛪ Marienkirche

Kirchplatz. **Tel** (03491) 40 44 15.
Open Easter–Oct: 10am–6pm daily
(Sun from 11:30am); Nov–Easter:
10am–5pm daily (Sun from 11.30am).

The Gothic church of St Mary
with its twin-tower façade
was built between the 13th
and 15th centuries. Luther

The market square with Baroque fountain, in Lutherstadt Wittenberg

was married to Katharina von
Bora in this church where
he also preached, and six of
their children were baptised.
Inside there is a magnificent
Reformation altar (constructed
in 1547), the work of father
and son Cranach, as well as
interesting tombs and epitaphs.

⊞ Melanchthonhaus

Collegienstr. 60. **Tel** (03491) 40 32 79.
Open Apr–Oct: 10am–6pm daily;
Nov–Mar: 10am–5pm Tue–Sun. ♿

This museum is devoted to
Luther's closest ally, Philipp

Schwarzerd, generally known
as Melanchthon.

⊞ Lutherhaus

Collegienstr. 54.
Tel (03491) 42 030. **Open** same as
Melanchthonhaus. ♿

The museum, which is in
the former residence of Martin
Luther and his family, also
chronicles the work of Lucas
Cranach the Elder. It has a
large number of documents
relating to the Reformation
and Luther's translation
of the Bible.

Lutherstadt Wittenberg Town Centre

① Schloss Wittenberg
② Schlosskirche
③ Cranachhaus
④ Rathaus
⑤ Marienkirche
⑥ Melanchthonhaus
⑦ Lutherhaus

For keys to symbols *see back flap*

⑯ Wörlitz Park

Wörlitz is a charming, English-style landscaped garden, the first of its kind in continental Europe. It was established in stages, commencing in 1764, for Prince Leopold III, Frederick Franz of Anhalt-Dessau. Many famous gardeners worked in Wörlitz, including Johann Christian Neumark and Johann Leopold Ludwig Schoch, as well as the architect Friedrich Wilhelm von Erdmannsdorff. The country house (1769–1773), the first building in the Classical style in Germany, houses a valuable collection of sculpture, furniture and paintings. Another interesting collection, including Swiss glass pictures, can be admired in the Gotisches Haus.

Floratempel
Modelled on an ancient temple with columns, this Neo-Classical temple served as a music pavilion.

★ **Gotisches Haus**
This house, built in stages, is one of the earliest examples of German Neo-Gothic style. On display inside is a unique collection of Swiss glass pictures.

SCHOCHS GARTEN

Kleines Walloch

Floratempel

Palmenbaus

SCHOCHS GARTEN

Gotisches Haus

Nympbäum

Wörlitzer See

② *Rosen-Insel*

① *Rousseau-Insel*

Schloss

SCHLOSS-GARTEN

Kirche

Gre Ha

Ga

NEUMARKS-GARTEN

Marstall

Propstei

Friedericken-brücke

KEY

① **Rousseau-Insel**, lined with poplars, was modelled on Ermenonville, the island where the French philosopher was first buried.

② **Rosen-Insel**, or rose island, was created as one of several artificial islands in the part of the garden designed by Johann Christian Neumark.

③ **The Pantheon**, built in 1795–6, houses a collection of antique sculptures.

④ **Stein** (Rock Island) is a working artificial volcano modelled on Mount Vesuvius in Italy.

Gondolas on the Lake
Romantic gondolas wait by the jetties to take tourists across the lake.

VISITORS' CHECKLIST

Practical Information
 Förstergasse 26 (034905 310
09). W **woerlitz-information.de**
Schloss: **Open** Apr & Oct:
11am–5pm Tue–Fri; 10am–5pm
Sat & Sun.

Transport

Lake Concert
Classical concerts are held on Wörlitz Lake in the evening
during the summer season. The audience is all afloat in boats.

Amalien-Insel
In keeping with the fashion of the
day, this artificial island, on Großes
Walloch lake, has a grotto, which
provides a cool resting place.

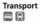
③
Pantheon

WEIDEN-
HEGER

Herderinsel Großes
Walloch

*Amalien-
Insel*

ugoge

NEUE
ANLAGEN

④
Stein

Wörlitzer See
The largest of
the three lakes,
which are all
joined by
canals, this is
prettiest when
the water lilies
are in bloom.

★ **Synagogue**
Built in 1790 and modelled on the
Vesta Temple in Rome, the
synagogue was gutted by the
National Socialists in 1938 and now
shows a Jewish history exhibit.

0 metres   500
0 yards   500

SAXONY

Saxony has a long history and is rich in historic sites. Its capital city, Dresden, ranks among the most beautiful and interesting towns in Germany, despite the devastation it suffered during World War II. The region also boasts the enchanting Erzgebirge Mountains and the glorious scenery of "Saxon Switzerland", where the mighty Elbe river runs amid fantastic rock formations.

In the 10th century, Emperor Otto I created an eastern border province (margravate) in the area presently known as Saxony. It quickly grew in size as it expanded into neighbouring territories inhabited by the Polabian Slavs. It was divided and part became the Meissen margravate, ruled by the powerful house of Wettin from 1089. This dynasty's political power increased when it acquired the Saxon Electorate in 1423; subsequently the entire region under their rule became known as "Saxony".

From 1697 until 1763 Saxony was united with Poland, and the Saxon Great Electors, Frederick Augustus the Strong and his son Frederick Augustus II, were also kings of Poland. During this period Saxony flourished, and Dresden became a major centre of the arts and culture until the Seven Years' War (1756–63) put an end to the region's prosperity. In 1806, Saxony declared itself on the side of Napoleon, and the Great Elector acquired the title of King. But Saxony paid a heavy price for supporting Napoleon – following the Congress of Vienna (1815), the kingdom lost the northern half of its territory to Prussia, and in 1871 it was incorporated into the German Empire.

At the end of World War II Saxony was in the Soviet-occupied zone and became part of the GDR in 1949. Since 1990 it has been a state in the Federal Republic of Germany. Saxony is densely populated and in some parts heavily industrialized, but it also has many interesting and unspoiled towns.

The scenic Bastei rocks in Saxon Switzerland

◀ Night-time view of Dresden's Brühlsche Terrace

Exploring Saxony

When travelling in Saxony, a visit to Dresden is a must. Visitors should set aside several days to explore its historic sights and magnificent museums. Dresden is also a convenient base for excursions to the attractive landscapes of the Sächsische Schweiz ("Saxon Switzerland") and further afield – to Bautzen, Görlitz and Zittau, or to the Erzgebirge Mountains, towards Freiberg and Chemnitz. Another town worth visiting, at least for a day, is Leipzig with its historic sights, cultural events, trade fairs and exhibitions.

The Old Town of Bautzen, situated high above the banks of the Spree River

Sights at a Glance

1 *Leipzig pp166–7*
2 Torgau
3 Mulde Valley
4 Zwickau
5 Chemnitz
6 Augustusburg
8 Freiberg
9 Meissen
10 Moritzburg
11 *Dresden pp172–81*
12 Pirna
14 Kamenz
15 Bautzen
16 Bad Muskau
17 Görlitz
18 Zittau

Tours

7 Sächsische Silberstrasse
13 Sächsische Schweiz

For additional map symbols *see back flap*

Lutherstadt Wittenberg
Bad Düben
Delitzsch
Halle
Rackwitz
Eilenburg
Wurzen
LEIPZIG 1
Markkleeberg
Oscha
Zwenkau
Leisnig
Colditz
Rochlitz
Burg Kriebste
Wechselburg
Rochsburg 3
Mittweida
Hainichi
Meerane
AUGUSTUSBU
Erfurt
Glauchau
CHEMNITZ 5
Neukirchen
ZWICKAU 4
Reichenbach
Schneeberg
Annaberg Buchholz
Plauen
Auerbach
Auersberg 1019m △
Oberwiesenthal
Fichtelberg 1214m △
Oelsnitz
Nuremberg
Vogtland
TORGAU 2
MULDE VALLEY
SÄCHSISCHE SILBERSTRA
87
107
6
186
95
175
A72
93
A4
173
92
93
A72
95
92

Key

━━━ Motorway
━━ Major road
┈┈┈ Minor road
━━ Scenic route
━━ Main railway
── Minor railway
━━ Country border
━━ International border
△ Summit

The giant castle and cathedral complex in Meissen

Getting Around

Leipzig and Dresden both have airports, as well as excellent train and road connections with the rest of Germany. The A6 motorway runs west from Görlitz, through Dresden and Chemnitz; the A13 links Dresden with Berlin, and the A14 with Leipzig. Other roads, national and regional, are clearly signposted, and all the towns described in this guide can also be reached by local buses.

Saddle horses grazing on paddocks near Kamenz

Young musicians in the Barockgarten, in Großsedlitz, near Dresden

❶ Leipzig

Granted town status in 1165, Leipzig is not only one of Germany's leading commercial towns, but also a centre of culture and learning, with a university founded in 1409. An important centre for the German publishing and book trade, it is the home of the Deutsche Bücherei, the German national library established in 1912. During the various trade fairs, such as the Book Fair in spring, it receives a great number of visitors, and it has much to offer in terms of entertainment, including concerts by the renowned Gewandhaus symphony orchestra and the Thomanerchor boys' choir, which boasts Johann Sebastian Bach as a past choirmaster.

Impressively lofty interior of the Neo-Classical Nikolaikirche

Exploring Leipzig

Most of the interesting sights can be found in the old town encircled by the ring road, which includes Europe's biggest railway station, the **Hauptbahnhof**, built in 1902–15 to a design by William Lossow and Max Hans Kühne. The heart of musical Leipzig beats in the eastern part of the old town, around Augustusplatz. Here stands the **Neues Gewandhaus** (built 1977– 81) and the **Opernhaus** (built 1959– 60). The University Tower nearby is being redesigned.

In Nikolaikirchhof stands the **Nikolaikirche** (church of St Nicholas). The present church was built during the 16th century, although the lower sections of its north tower date from the 12th century. It has Neo-Classical furnishings. The **Alte Handelsbörse** (old stock exchange) in Naschmarkt is an early-Baroque building,

designed by Johann Georg Starcke. Built in 1678–87 and reconstructed almost from the ground after World War II, it is now a concert hall. In front of the building stands a monument (1903) to Goethe showing him as a student.

In the market square, near the beautiful Renaissance town hall, is the **Alte Waage**, the old municipal weigh-house, a Renaissance work by Hieronymus Lotter. It was built in 1555 and reconstructed in 1964 following damage in World War II.

The area to the south of the town square is taken up by a block of trade fair buildings. The most interesting are the beautifully restored **Specks Hof** (Reichestrasse/Nikolaistrasse), the oldest arcade in Leipzig with three enclosed courts built between 1908 and 1929, and **Mädlerpassage**, built in 1912–14, a Modernist commercial building with a passageway connecting Grimmaische Strasse and Naschmarkt. Beneath it is the **Auerbachs Keller**, magnificent, 16th-century vaults, immortalized by Goethe in *Faust* and featuring a room that bears his name. The **Commerzbank** (Klostergasse/Thomasgasse) and the **Riquet Café**, a fine Viennese-style coffee house, are attractive Art Nouveau buildings.

Lovers of Johann Sebastian Bach's music will wish to visit the **Thomaskirche**, the magnificent late-Gothic church of St Thomas, built in 1482–96, where Bach was the choirmaster from 1723. It now contains the composer's

tomb. Worth noting are the beautiful Renaissance galleries built by Hieronymus Lotter, in 1570. The famous Thomanerchor choir still sings at services on Friday evenings and Saturday afternoons, and organ concerts are held in the churches of St Thomas and St Nicholas during the summer months. Bach is also commemorated with a monument in front of the church (1908). Nearby, the **Bosehaus**, a Baroque 17th-century building, is the home of the Bachmuseum, devoted to the composer.

🏛 Grassimuseum

Johannisplatz 5–11. Museum für Völkerkunde: **Tel** (0341) 97 31 900. Museum für Angewandte Kunst: **Tel** (0341) 22 29 100. Museum für Musikinstrumente: **Tel** (0341) 97 30 750. **Open** Library and museum shop with workshops and lectures. Exhibitions: 10am–6pm Tue–Sun. 🔳 grassimuseum.de

The Grassimuseum is one of Germany's greatest museum complexes, housing three fascinating collections: the Museum für Völkerkunde (ethnography) with exhibits from around the world; the Museum für Musikinstrumente (musical instruments) with a magnificent collection, including the world's oldest surviving clavichord, and the Museum für Angewandte Kunst (decorative arts) with its stunning gold and ivory ornaments, as well as the valuable town treasury.

🏛 Deutsches Buch- und Schriftmuseum

Deutscher Platz 1. **Tel** (0341) 227 13 24. **Open** 9am–4pm Mon–Sat.

The early-Baroque pavilion of the Alte Handelsbörse, the old stock exchange

The Russische Kirche, a pastiche of the churches in Novgorod

This museum is devoted to the history of German literature. It contains rare manuscripts and old prints.

Museum der Bildenden Künste

Katharinenstr. 10 (Sachsenplatz). **Tel** (0341) 216 999 20. **Open** 10am–6pm Tue & Thu–Sun, noon–8pm Wed.

This museum has an excellent collection of German masters, including Lucas Cranach the Elder, Martin Schongauer and Caspar David Friedrich, as well as other magnificent European paintings. There are canvases by Jan van Eyck, Rubens, Frans Hals, Tintoretto and sculptures by Balthasar Permoser, Antonio Canova and Auguste Rodin.

Russische Kirche

Philipp-Rosenthal-Str. 51a. **Tel** (0341) 878 14 53. **Open** 10am–5pm daily (to 4pm in winter).

The Russian Orthodox Church of St Alexius was built in 1912–13 to commemorate the 22,000 Russian soldiers who died in 1813, in the Battle of the Nations. The architect, Vladimir Pokrowski, based his design on the churches of Novgorod in Russia.

Völkerschlachtdenkmal

Strasse des 18 Oktober 100. **Tel** (0341) 241 68 70. **Open** Apr–Oct: 10am–6pm daily, Nov–Mar: 10am–4pm daily.

This giant, Teutonic-style monument is the work of architect Bruno Schmitz. Completed for the centenary of the 1813 Battle of the Nations, which pitched the combined Prussian, Austrian and Russian armies against Napoleon, it now houses a small museum.

Altes Rathaus

Markt 1. **Tel** (0341) 261 77 60. Museum für Geschichte der Stadt Leipzig: **Open** 10am–6pm Tue–Sun.

VISITORS' CHECKLIST

Practical Information
Road map E4.
Tel (0341) 710 42 60.
Katharinenstrasse 8 (0341-710 42 60). Leipziger Buchmesse (Mar); Leipziger Orgelsommer (Jul–Aug); Internationaler Johann-Sebastian-Bach Wettbewerb (Jul); Leipziger Jazztage (Oct).
leipzig.travel.de

Transport
Flughafen Leipzig–Halle.
Willy-Brandt-Platz.

The grand Renaissance town hall, built in 1556 to a design by Hieronymus Lotter, is now the home of the municipal museum. One room is devoted to Felix Mendelssohn-Bartholdy, who conducted the symphony orchestra from 1835 until his death in 1847.

Bacharchive und Bachmuseum

Thomaskirchhof 15–16. **Tel** (0341) 913 72 202. **Open** 10am–6pm daily.

This museum houses archives and documents relating to the life and works of the composer J. S. Bach.

Leipzig City Centre

1. Opernhaus
2. Gewandhaus
3. Nikolaikirche
4. Alte Handelsbörse
5. Alte Waage
6. Altes Rathaus
7. Mädlerpassage
8. Thomaskirche

Doorway of Schloss Hartenfels, with its coat of arms, in Torgau

❷ Torgau

Road map E4. 🏛 23,000. 🚇 🚌 🅸
Markt 1 (03421-70 140). 🎭 Torgauer
Auszugsfest (May). **W** torgau.eu

This small town, with its scenic
location on the Elbe, was once
the favourite residence of the
Saxon Electors. Its main square
is surrounded by attractive
houses of various styles, in
particular Renaissance. The
Renaissance **Rathaus** (town
hall), built in 1561–77, has a
lovely semicircular oriel. Other
old town attractions include the
Marienkirche, a late-Gothic
church with an extended
Romanesque west section. The
interior has many original
features, including a painting by
Lucas Cranach the Elder, *The
Fourteen Helpers*, and the tomb
of Luther's wife, Katharina von
Bora, who died in Torgau.

The main historic building in
Torgau is the Renaissance
Schloss Hartenfels, built on the
site of a 10th-century castle. Its
courtyard is surrounded by
clusters of residential wings,
including the late-Gothic
Albrechtspalast built in 1470–85,
the Johann-Friedrich-Bau
(1533–6) with its beautiful
external spiral staircase and
the early-Baroque west wing
(1616–23). The **Schlosskapelle**
(castle chapel), which was
consecrated by Martin Luther
in 1544, is considered to be
one of the oldest churches built
for Protestants.

❸ Mulde Valley

Road map E4.

Several magnificent old castles
nestle in the scenic hills at the
confluence of two rivers –
the Zwickauer Mulde and the
Freiberger Mulde. In the
small town of **Colditz**, with its
timber-frame houses, lovely
Renaissance town hall and
Gothic church of St Egidien,
stands a huge Gothic castle
built in 1578–91 on the site of
an 11th-century castle. During
World War II it was a famous
prisoner-of-war camp known as
Oflag IVC.

In **Rochlitz**, 11 km (7 miles)
south of Colditz, stands another
large castle, built in stages from
the 12th to the 16th centuries.
Travelling further south you will
encounter other castles: the
Wechselburg, a reconstructed
Baroque castle featuring a late-
Romanesque collegiate church,
as well as the Renaissance castle in
Rochsburg. In the neighbouring
Zschopau valley stands the
magnificent, oval **Burg
Kriebstein**, built in stages and
completed in the late 14th
century. This fortress houses
a small museum and
concert hall, and
medieval music
concerts are
held here during
the summer.

❹ Zwickau

Road map E4.
🏛 120,000. 🚇 🚌
🅸 Hauptstr. 6 (0375-
27 13 240). 🎭 Robert-
Schumann-Tage (Jun);
TrabiTreffen (Jun).
W zwickau.de

An old commercial
town, Zwickau
flourished in the 15th
and 16th centuries.
Today it is known for
the Trabant cars that
were produced here
during the GDR era.
Almost all the town's
attractions can be
found in the old
town, on the banks
of the Zwickauer

Mulde river. The most important
historic building in the town is
the **Dom St Marien** (cathedral
of St Mary), a magnificent late-
Gothic hall-church built 1453–
1537. Preserved to this day
are its original main altar
dating from 1479, the work of
Michael Wolgemut, the grand
architectural Holy Tomb of
Michael Heuffner, dating from
1507, as well as a Renaissance
font and a pulpit of 1538, both
by Paul Speck.

Also worth visiting in the old
town are the **Old Pharmacy**, the
Schumann-Haus, the composer's
birthplace (1810), and the
Renaissance **Gewandhaus**
(cloth house), once the seat of
the Drapers' Guild and now a
theatre and museum.

❺ Chemnitz

Road map E4. 🏛 260,000.
🚇 Georgstr. 🚌 Markt. 🅸 Markt 1
(0371-690 680/ 0371-19 433).
W chemnitz-tourismus.de

After World War II, when 90 per
cent of its buildings had been
reduced to rubble, the town
was rebuilt in the Socialist-

Gate of the Renaissance pulpit in the Dom St Marien,
in Zwickau

Lew Kerbel's monument to Karl Marx at the Stadthalle in Chemnitz

Realist style and renamed Karl-Marx-Stadt. Only a handful of historic buildings escaped destruction. The most interesting is the **Schlosskirche**, the former Benedictine abbey church St Maria, built at the turn of the 15th and 16th centuries.

Sights in the town centre include the reconstructed **Altes Rathaus** (old town hall), the Gothic **Roter Turm** (red tower) and remains of fortifications. In the main square is the reconstructed Baroque **Siegertsches Haus**, originally built in 1737–41 to a design by Johann Christoph Naumann. The new town centre is dominated by the vast **Stadthalle** (city hall) with Lew Kerbel's 1971 monument to Karl Marx. The **König-Albert-Kunstsammlungen** has a museum of natural history and a fine arts collection, including works by Karl Schmidt-Rottluff.

Kunstsammlungen Chemnitz
Theaterplatz 1. **Tel** (0371) 488 44 24.
Open 11am–6pm Tue–Sun.
Bibliothek. 1–6pm Wed.

❻ Augustusburg

Road map E4. 5,000.
Marienberger Str. 24 (037291-395 50). Schloss: **Open** Apr–Oct: 9:30am–6pm daily; Nov–Mar: 10am–5pm daily.
W augustusburg.de

The small town is insignificant compared with the vast palace complex bearing the same name. The best way to get there is by cable car, from Erdmannsdorf. This Renaissance hunting palace was built for the Great Elector, Augustus, in 1567–72, on the site of the former Schloss Schellenberg, which had been destroyed by fire. Constructed under Hieronymus Lotter and Erhard van der Meer, it is a symmetrical, square building with towered pavilions at each corner, joined by galleries, gates and a chapel to the east, with an altar by Lucas Cranach the Younger. Today the palace houses several museums devoted to motor-cycles, coaches and hunting.

❼ Sächsische Silberstrasse

See pp170–71.

❽ Freiberg

Road map E4. 45,000.
Burgstr. 1 (03731-27 36 64).
Bergstadtfest (Jun), Silbermann-Tage (Sep). **W** freiberg-service.de

Development of this mining town was due to the discovery of silver deposits, and Freiberg was granted town status in 1186. It escaped World War II with remarkably little damage.

Today its attractions include the reconstructed old town and many historic buildings, the gem among them being the **Dom St Marien** (cathedral). This late-Gothic hall-church, erected at the end of the 15th century, features a stunning main portal, the Goldene Pforte, dating from 1225–30. Inside are many original items, such as a tulip-shaped pulpit (1505) and two Baroque organs by Gottfried Silbermann. Organ recitals take place on Thursdays at 8pm, May through to October.

When visiting nearby Untermarkt, it is worth going to the **Stadt- und Bergbaumuseum** (municipal and mining museum) which explains the history of mining in the area, as well as the collection of minerals at the **Mineralien- und Lagerstätten sammlung der Bergakademie**.
A stroll along the winding streets will take the visitor to **Obermarkt**, where the 15th-century Gothic town hall, a fountain with the statue of the town's founder and attractive houses can be seen.

Otto of Meissen, founder of Freiberg

Dom St Marien
Untermarkt 1. Goldene Pforte:
Tel (03731) 225 98. May–Oct: 10am–noon, 2–5pm daily; Nov–Apr: 11am–noon, 2–4pm daily. With organ presentation: 11:30am Sun.

Stadt- und Bergbaumuseum
Am Dom 1. **Tel** (03731) 202 50.
Open 10am–5pm Tue–Sun.

Mineralien- und Lagerstättensammlung der Bergakademie
Brennhausgasse 14. **Tel** (03731) 39 22 64. **Open** 9am–noon & 1–4pm Wed–Fri, 9am–4pm Sat.

Façade of the Renaissance Schloss Augustusburg

⑦ Sächsische Silberstrasse

The Saxon silver route, through the Erzgebirge (mineral ore mountains), takes the visitor to some of the most interesting and scenic places of the region. Silver was mined here from the 12th century, and mining traditions have been preserved to this day. Small towns entice visitors with their interesting parish churches, former mining settlements, museums and disused mines.

① **Schneeberg** A small mining town, which to this day cultivates its art and crafts traditions, Schneeberg is also famous for the St Wolfgangkirche, with an altar masterpiece by Lucas Cranach the Elder.

② **Oberwiesenthal** This important wintersports resort, close to the Czech border and at the foot of the Fichtelberg, offers a ski-jump, downhill ski runs and toboggan runs.

③ **Annaberg-Buchholz** Although the town enjoyed only a brief spell of prosperity in the 16th century, its church from that period, St Annen, ranks among the most beautiful examples of late-Gothic architecture in Saxony.

0 km 5
0 miles 5

Wolkenstein
Ehrenfrie-dersdorf
Obernhau
Aue
Lauter
Schwarzenberg
174
171
174
101
95
⑥
⑤
④
③
①
②

⑥ **Marienberg** This small town, with its wonderful Renaissance town hall, is known mainly for the production of furniture.

Key

■ Suggested route
= Other road
▬ Scenic route
—· State boundary
❈ Viewpoint

⑤ **Greifensteine** Fantastic, craggy rock formations in the north of the region, shaped like an amphitheatre, attract rock-climbers and hill-walkers.

④ **Frohnau** The biggest attraction of this town is its old forge, featuring the Frohnauer Hammer, a huge original hammer that remained in use until 1904.

Tips for Drivers

Length of the route: 55 km (34 miles).
Stopping points: inns and restaurants in every town.

❾ Meissen

Road map 4E. 🚶 36,000. 🚌 🚍 ℹ️
Markt 3 (03521-419 40). 🎉 Stadt- und
Weinfest (Sep). 🌐 **stadt-meissen.de**

Meissen is famous for its
porcelain manufacture *(see
pp128–9)*. Its history began in
929, when Henry I made it the
bridgehead for his expansion to
the east, into Slav territories. In
966 Meissen became the capital
of the newly established
Meissen margravate, and in
968 a bishopric.

This town has retained much
of its charm. In the town square
is the late-Gothic **Rathaus**
(town hall), built in 1472–8,
some beautiful Renaissance
houses and the **Frauenkirche**,
a late-Gothic, 15th-century
church boasting the world's
oldest porcelain carillon, which
was hung here in 1929. It is also
worth taking a stroll to St Afra's
church, built in the 13th century
for the Augustian monks.

🏰 Albrechtsburg

Domplatz 1. **Tel** (03521) 47 070.
Open Mar–Oct: 10am–6pm daily;
Nov–Feb: 10am–5pm daily.
Closed 24, 25, 31. Dec. 📷

The Albrechtsburg is a vast,
fortified hilltop complex with
a cathedral and an Elector's
palace. The latter was built in
1471–89 for the Wettin brothers,
Ernst and Albrecht. Designed by
Arnold von Westfalen, its special
feature is the magnificent
external spiral staircase. From
1710 the palace was used as a
porcelain factory. It was restored
to its former glory in 1864. Huge
wall paintings of this period,

showing historical scenes, are
the work of Wilhelm Römann.
The cathedral church of St John
the Evangelist and St Donat,
built from the mid-13th century
to the early 15th century, has
some splendid early-Gothic
sculptures, an altar by Lucas
Cranach the Elder in the
Georgskapelle and ducal tombs
in the Fürstenkapelle.

🏛 Staatliche Porzellan-Manufaktur

Talstrasse 9. **Tel** (03521) 46 87 00.
Open May–Oct: 9am–6pm daily;
Nov–Apr: 9am–5pm daily.
🌐 **meissen.com**

The first porcelain factory in
Europe was set up in 1710 in
the castle and moved to its
present premises in 1865.
Documents relating to the
history of the factory and many
interesting examples of its
products are on display in
the exhibition rooms. Guided
tours and demonstrations
take the visitor through all
the stages of the porcelain
manufacturing process.

The Baroque hunting lodge in Moritzburg

❿ Moritzburg

Road map 4E. 🚌 ℹ️ Schlossallee
3b (035207-85 40). 🎉 Kammer-
musikfestival (Aug); Fischzug (Oct).

The first hunting lodge in
this marshy region was built
in the mid-16th century, for
Moritz of Saxony. The present
Schloss Moritzburg is the result
of extensive alterations ordered
by Augustus the Strong,
directed by Matthäus Daniel
Pöppelmann, and carried out
in 1723–26. The result is a
square building, with four
cylindrical corner towers. Much
of the interior has survived,
including period furnishings
and hunting trophies.

Also open to visitors is the
17th-century castle chapel
decorated with splendid stucco
ornaments. Augustus the
Strong ordered the marshes
to be drained, and the newly
available land to be transformed
into landscaped gardens and
lakes. The **Fasanenschlösschen**
(little pheasant castle) in the
eastern part of the gardens
features several interesting
Rococo interiors, and also
houses a zoological exhibition.

It was in Moritzburg that
the German artist Käthe Kollwitz
spent the last years of her life in
Moritzburg. The house in which
she lived and worked is now the
Käthe-Kollwitz-Gedenkstätte.

🏰 Schloss Moritzburg

Tel (035207) 8730. **Open** Feb–Mar:
10am–4pm Sat & Sun; Apr–Oct:
10am–5:30pm daily; Nov–Dec:
10am–4pm Tue–Sun. 📷

🏰 Fasanenschlösschen

Open as above. 🎧 compulsory.

The late-Gothic Rathaus in Meissen

⑪ Dresden

One of Germany's most beautiful cities, Dresden first gained its pre-eminence in the year 1485, when the Albertine Wettins decided to establish their residence here. The town blossomed during the 18th century when it became a cultural centre and acquired many magnificent buildings. Almost all of these, however, were completely destroyed during the night of 13/14 February 1945, when British and American air forces mounted a vast carpet-bombing raid on the city. Today, meticulous restoration work is in progress to return the historic city centre to its former glory, now with renewed effort because of the damage caused by flooding in 2002.

Roof top view of Frauenkirche's dome

One of Dresden's foremost landmarks, the monumental Hofkirche, in winter

🎭 Sächsische Staatsoper

Theaterplatz 2. **Tel** (0351) 49 110. **Tours Tel** (0351) 79 66 305.

The imposing, Neo-Renaissance building of the Saxon state opera is one of Dresden's landmarks. It is also known as Semperoper after its creator, the famous architect Gottfried Semper, who designed it twice: the first building, erected in 1838–41, burned down in 1869, the second one was completed in 1878. Reconstruction after World War II dragged on until 1985. The opera house was the venue for many world premieres, including *Tannhäuser* and *The Flying Dutchman* by Richard Wagner, as well as many works by Richard Strauss.

In front of the opera, in Theaterplatz, is a monument to the Saxon King Johann, by Johannes Schilling.

🎭 Schinkelwache

Theaterplatz. **Tel** (0351) 49 11 705 (box office). **Open** 10am– 6pm Mon–Fri, 10am–1pm Sat & Sun.

This small Neo-Classical building, with its sophisticated lines and its immaculate proportions, is the work of the famous Berlin architect, Karl Friedrich Schinkel. It was built between 1830 and 1832.

⛪ Hofkirche

Theaterplatz. (Entrance on Schlossplatz). **Open** daily.

This monumental Baroque royal church has served as the Catholic Dom (cathedral church) of the Dresden-Meissen Diocese since 1980. The presence of this Catholic church in staunchly Protestant Saxony was dictated by political necessity: in his struggle for the Polish crown, the Elector, Augustus the Strong, was forced to convert to Catholicism. The church was designed by an Italian architect, Gaetano Chiaveri, and built in 1738–51.

The church's interior has two-tier passageways which run from the main nave to the side naves. Rebuilt after World War II, it features a magnificent Rococo pulpit by Balthasar Permoser, a painting by Anton Raphael Mengus entitled *Assumption* in the main altar, and the vast organ – the last work of Gottfried Silbermann.

⛪ Frauenkirche

An der Frauenkirche. **Tel** (0351) 65 60 656. **Open** 10am–noon, 1pm–6pm daily.

This giant church, designed by Georg Bähr and built in 1726–43, has been restored to its former glory. Once again, the shining, giant dome dominates the city's skyline. Completely destroyed in 1945 by Allied bombing, its shell survived intact, only to collapse later. Reconstruction began in 1993 and is now complete. Notable features include an elegant cupola and, inside, a colourful dome.

🎭 Residenzschloss

Taschenberg 2. **Grünes Gewölbe Tel** (0351) 49 142 000. **Open** 10am–6pm Wed–Mon. **Hausmannsturm Open** 10am–6pm Wed–Mon.

Façade of a wing of the Residenzschloss, with *sgraffito* decoration

This former residence of the Wettin family was built in stages from the late 15th to the 17th centuries. It houses some of the most beautiful art collections in East Germany, including the world famous Grünes Gewölbe (Green Vaults), a vast collection of royal jewels, gems and table decorations. Book in advance for the ground-floor "vault". The Hausmannsturm, which is a tall tower, affords a great view of the Dresden skyline.

🏛 Fürstenzug
Augustusstrasse

Langer Gang (long walk) is a long building, erected in 1586–91, which connects the castle with the Johanneum. The elegant

façade facing the courtyard is decorated with *sgraffito* and has shady arcades supported by slim columns. It provided an excellent backdrop for tournaments and parades. The wall facing the street features the so-called Fürstenzug (procession of dukes) – a magnificent, 102 m (111 yd)-long frieze depicting the procession of many Saxon rulers. The frieze was originally created by Wilhelm Walther in 1872–6 using the *sgraffito* technique, but it was replaced in 1907 by 24,000 Meissen porcelain tiles.

🏛 Verkehrsmuseum (Johanneum)
Augustusstr. 1. **Tel** (0351) 86 440. **Open** 10am–5pm Tue–Sun.

This late 16th-century Renaissance building, originally designed as royal stables by Paul Buchner, was refurbished in the mid-18th century and housed first a gallery of paintings, later an armoury and a porcelain collection. Since 1956 it has been a museum of transport, with old trams, locomotives, a collection of vintage cars and models of famous German ships.

Fragment of the Fürstenzug, outside Langer Gang

Dresden City Centre

0 metres   100
0 yards   100

For map symbols *see back flap*

⊞ Brühlsche Terrasse

Brühlsche Terrasse.

Once part of the town's fortifications, this attractive terrace subsequently lost its military importance and was transformed into magnificent gardens by the diplomat and patron of arts Heinrich von Brühl, after whom it is named. Offering splendid views over the River Elbe, it was known as "the balcony of Europe". There are several great buildings on the terraces – the first one, seen from Schlossplatz, is the Neo-Renaissance **Landtag** (parliament building); next to it is a small Neo-Baroque building, the **Secundogenitur** library built for the second generation of Brühls, now a popular café; this is followed by the **Kunstakademie** (art academy), known as Zitronenpresse (lemon squeezer) because of its ribbed glass dome. Among the statues and monuments on the terrace are works by the sculptor Ernst Rietschel, the architect Gottfried Semper and the painter Caspar David Friedrich.

⊞ Albertinum

Brühlsche Terrasse. **Tel** (0351) 491 45 90. Galerie Neue Meister. **Open** 10am–6pm Tue–Sun. **W** skd.museum

Originally a royal arsenal, the Albertinum was rebuilt in its current Neo-Renaissance style in the 1880s by Carl Adolf Canzler. Forty years earlier, Bernhard von Lindenau had donated his considerable fortune to the city to set up a collection of contemporary art, which was then displayed in the Albertinum. Today, the building houses two magnificent collections. That of the **Galerie Neue Meister**, which was established in the mid-19th

Two Women on Tahiti, Paul Gauguin, 1892, in the Albertinum

century, contains paintings from the 19th and 20th centuries, including works by the German Impressionists Lovis Corinth and Max Liebermann, landscapes by Caspar David Friedrich, canvases by the Nazarine group of painters and works by European masters such as Edgar Degas, Paul Gauguin, Vincent van Gogh, Édouard Manet and Claude Monet.

The Albertinum's other collection, the **Skulpturensammlung**, is a small collection of sculptures, including remarkable late Baroque and early Rococo works by Balthasar Permoser.

⊡ Kreuzkirche

An der Kreuzkirche 6. **Tel** (0351) 439 39 20. **Open** Summer: 10am–6pm Mon–Fri; winter: 10am–4pm Mon–Fri. Tower: 10am–5pm daily.

The present Baroque/Neo-Classical church was built in 1764–92 to a design by Johann Georg Schmidt. To commemorate the shelling in World War II, the interior has not been fully restored. The Cross of Nails from the ruins of Coventry Cathedral in England creates a powerful symbolic link between the two countries.

⊞ Goldener Reiter

Neustädter Markt.

The **Neustadt** (new town), on the right bank of the Elbe, lost much of its former glory through destruction in World War II. Visitors may therefore be surprised to come across this glistening, gilded equestrian statue of Augustus the Strong in the middle of a square, at the end of the plane tree-lined Hauptstrasse. The monument, which was erected in 1736, is the work of Jean Joseph Vinache, court sculptor to Augustus.

The Goldener Reiter in the new town

⊞ Neues Rathaus

Dr-Külz-Ring.

The giant Neo-Renaissance new town hall, in the southwest of the old town, was erected in 1905–1910. Its round tower (70 m/230 ft), crowned with a gilded statue of Hercules, offers a good view of the old city centre. In the foyer is a large model of the city as planned for 2015.

⊞ Museum für Sächsische Volkskunst (Jägerhof)

Köpckestr. 1. **Tel** (0351) 49 14 20 00. **Open** 10am–6pm Tue–Sun.

This Renaissance hunting lodge on the north bank of the Elbe was built between 1568 and 1613. Its west wing – the only part that escaped destruction – now houses a museum of ethnography with collections

Secundogenitur library on Brühlsche Terrasse

◄ Moritzburg Castle and its reflected façade, Saxony

of Saxon culture and traditions, especially from the Erzgebirge Mountains.

🏛 Japanisches Palais
Palaisplatz ll. **Tel** (0351) 81 44 08 41. Museum für Völkerkunde (Museum of Ethnography): **Open** 10am–6pm Tue–Sun. Landesmuseum für Vorgeschichte (State Museum of Prehistory): **Open** 10am–6pm Tue–Sun. Senckenberg Naturhistorische Sammlungen: **Open** 10am–6pm Tue–Sun.

The Baroque Schloss Pillnitz, Augustus the Strong's summer residence

Originally the Dutch Palais, this three-wing structure was built in 1715. It was extended in 1729–31, by Zacharias Longuelune, for Augustus the Strong's Japanese porcelain collection, at which time the palace changed its name. For years the palace served as a library; today it holds spectacular exhibitions run by the above-mentioned museums.

🏛 Pfunds Molkerei
Bautzner Str. 79. **Tel** (0351) 80 80 80. **Open** 10am–6pm Mon–Sat, 10am–3pm Sun. 🌐 **pfunds.de**
In the 19th-century part of the Neustadt, with its many bars, galleries, pubs and fringe theatres, stands this old dairy founded by Paul Pfund. Its interior is lined with dazzling, multi-coloured tiles, showing Neo-Renaissance motifs relating to the dairy's products. Today there is a shop which offers hundreds of dairy products, as well as a small bar, where visitors can sample the specialities.

🏛 Kraszewski-Museum
Nordstr. 28. **Tel** (0351) 804 44 50. **Open** 1–6pm Wed–Sun.
This small museum is devoted to the life of the Polish writer Józef Ignaz v Kraszewski who, having escaped arrest in Warsaw, settled in Dresden in 1853. Inspired by the town's history, several of his novels (for example *Hrabina*

Cosel, Brühl) are set during the time of Augustus the Strong.

🌳 Großer Garten
City centre.
The history of this great garden goes back to the 17th century, although it has been redesigned several times since. At the park's centre stands an early Baroque palace built in 1678–83 to a design by Johann Georg Starcke. A miniature railway takes visitors to Carolasee, a boating lake. It also stops at the botanical gardens in the northwest section of the park, and at the zoo. The Mosaik-brunnen (mosaic fountain) nearby was designed by Hans Poelzig and built in 1926.

🏛 Blaues Wunder
Loschwitz/Blasewitzer Brücke.
The suspension bridge which spans the River Elbe in the eastern part of the town is painted blue and nicknamed "blue wonder". Built in 1891–3, its main span is 141.5 m (464 ft) long. The bridge leads to Loschwitz, a neighbourhood in a picturesque location amidst hills, which has many attractive villas and small palaces built in the 19th century.

🏛 Schloss Pillnitz
Tel (0351) 261 30. Kunstgewerbemuseum Bergpalais: **Open** May–Oct: 10am–6pm Tue–Sun.

Wasserpalais: **Open** May–Oct: 10am–6pm Wed–Mon.

This charming summer residence, on the banks of the Elbe, was built in 1720–23 by Augustus the Strong and designed by Matthäus Daniel Pöppelmann. There are two parallel palaces: the Berg-palais (mountain palace) and the Wasserpalais (water palace); the latter can be reached by stairs directly from the river jetty. Between 1818 and 1826 the two palaces were joined by a third one, the Neues Palais. Today the Bergpalais houses a fascinating museum of decorative art. The main attraction, however, is the park, laid out in English and Chinese styles, with an orangery and pavilions.

🏛 Karl-May-Museum
Radebeul, Karl-May-Str. 5. **Tel** (0351) 837 30 10. **Open** Mar–Oct: 9am–6pm; Nov–Feb: 10am–4pm Tue –Sun. **Closed** 1 Jan, 24, 25, 31 Dec.

Radebeul, 5 km (3 miles) northwest of Dresden, is much visited by the fans of Winnteou, a fictional Indian chief, and his friend Old Shatterhand. A museum is devoted to the life and work of the author, Karl May, who lived and died in Radebeul. It also displays May's large collection of Native American costumes and other items.

The suspension bridge across the Elbe River, nicknamed "Blaues Wunder"

For hotels and restaurants in this area see p494 and pp514–16

The Zwinger

The most famous building in Dresden is the Zwinger, a beautiful Baroque structure. Its name means "intermural", and it was built in the space between the former town fortifications. Commissioned by Augustus the Strong, it was constructed in 1709–32 to a design by Matthäus Daniel Pöppelmann, with the help of the sculptor Balthasar Permoser. Its spacious courtyard, once used to stage tournaments, festivals and firework displays, is completely surrounded by galleries into which are set pavilions and gates. Today it houses several art collections.

Mathematisch-Physikalischer Salon
A valuable collection of scientific instruments, clocks, sextants and globes, including a 13th-century Arabic globe of the sky.

Kronentor
This gate owes its name (crown gate) to the crown positioned on top of its dome.

Main entrance

KEY

① **Glockenspielpavillon** was formerly known as Stadtpavillon (town pavilion). However, the name was changed to carillon pavilion when it acquired a carillon with Meissen porcelain bells, in 1924–36.

② **Allegorical figures** crown the balustrades.

③ **Courtyard**

★ **Porzellansammlung**
The porcelain collection holds Japanese and Chinese pieces but its centrepiece is a collection of Meissen porcelain, including parts of the stunning Swan Service made for Heinrich Brühl, to a design by Joachim Kaendler.

Wallpavillon
A stunning marriage of architecture and sculpture, this Baroque masterpiece is crowned by a statue of Hercules, symbolizing the Elector, Augustus the Strong.

Galerie Alte Meister
This gallery of old masters occupies the wing which was added by Gottfried Semper (*see pp180–81*).

★ Nymphenbad
This fountain features tritons and nymphs, sculptures, and grottoes, which were popular in the Baroque era.

Gemäldegalerie Alte Meister

The Dresden gallery of old masters contains what is considered
to be one of Europe's finest art collections. Its core consists of
the canvases collected by the Wettin family from the 16th
century, but the majority of exhibits were purchased at the
order of King Augustus II the Strong and his son Augustus III.
It was during that time that the gallery was moved to its own
premises – first to the Johanneum and later to its present
home in the Zwinger, built by Gottfried Semper in 1847–55.

Gallery Guide

*Until 2017, during an overhaul of the gallery building, there will
be an interim presentation of about 400 paintings in the
eastern wing of the building. The areas shown in the key below
are not relevant during the restoration, but all of the paintings
are on display in the eastern wing.*

2nd floor

1st floor

Dresden
landscapes and
portraits

Ground
floor

Portrait of a Man (c.1633)
This highly expressive portrait, by
Diego Rodríguez de Silva y Velázquez,
remained unfinished, yet it still
captivates with its powerful imagery.

Key

- ⬜ 15th–17th-century Italian painting
- ⬜ 15th–16th-century German painting
- ⬜ Canaletto and scenes of Dresden
- ⬜ 17th-century Dutch and
  Flemish painting
- ⬜ 17th-century French painting
- ⬜ Spanish painting
- ⬜ 18th-century Italian and
  French painting
- ⬜ German, Czech, Austrian, English
  and Swiss painting
- ⬜ Non-exhibition space

★ **Self-Portrait with Saskia**
(c.1635) This magnificent painting depicting
Rembrandt with his wife, Saskia, is
considered by some to be a representation
of the Prodigal Son of the Bible.

Main entrance

Girl Reading a Letter
(c.1659) This exquisite painting, of a lone woman by the window reading a letter, is among the finest works by Jan Vermeer van Delft.

VISITORS' CHECKLIST

Practical Information
Theaterplatz 1. **Tel** (0351) 491 46679. **Open** 10am–6pm Tue–Sun; limited access during works. 🅿️
🏛️ 🎫 ♿ ✉️ 🌐 skd.museum

Feast of Love (c.1717)
The so-called *fête galante* is one of many splendid paintings by Antoine Watteau, depicting a flirtatious group in a park.

Tribute Money (c.1516)
Titian depicts the theme of this popular New Testament parable in an unusual way, zooming in on the figures of Christ and a Pharisee who shows him a coin.

Miniatures

Madonna and Infant Triptych (1437)
This superb small triptych depicting the Virgin Mary with the Holy Infant, St Catherine and the Archangel St Michael, is one of very few works signed by its creator, Jan van Eyck.

Tapestry room

★ Sistine Madonna (1512/13)
This enchanting picture of the Madonna and Child by Raphael owes its name to St Sixtus's church in Piacenza, for which Pope Julius II had commissioned it.

Sleeping Venus (c.1508–10)
This famous nude was probably painted by Giorgione, but when he died of the plague in 1510, his friend, Titian, completed the work.

Underground vaults

Market square with Renaissance Rathaus (town hall) in Pirna

⑫ Pirna

Road map F4. ⚒ 38,000. 🚃 🚌
ℹ Am Markt 7 (03501-55 64 47).
🎭 Stadtfest (Jun). 🌐 **pirna.de**

In the old town, on the banks of the River Elbe, Pirna has preserved an amazingly regular, chequerboard pattern of streets. Time has been kind to the many historic buildings in this town. Its greatest attraction is the **Marienkirche**, a late-Gothic hall-church with fanciful vaulting designed by Peter Ulrich von Pirna and painted by Jobst Dorndorff, in 1545–6. Inside, an original late-Gothic font and a Renaissance main altar can be seen.

Other interesting buildings are the mid-16th century **Rathaus** (town hall) with its Gothic portals, the beautiful houses in the town square and the ex-Dominican, Gothic church of St Heinrich. **Schloss Sonnenstein**, extended during the 17th and 18th centuries, towers above the old town.

Environs
10 km (6 miles) southwest of Pirna is the picturesque **Schloss Weesenstein**, much altered from its Gothic origins until the 19th century. It houses a small museum with an interesting collection of wallpapers.

🏛 **Museum Schloss Weesenstein**
Müglitztal, Am Schlossberg 1.
Tel (035027) 6260. **Open** Apr–Oct: 9am–6pm; Nov–Mar: 10am–5pm Tue–Sun.

⑬ Sächsische Schweiz

Saxon Switzerland, the wonderfully wild region around the gorge cut into the Lusatian mountains by the River Elbe, features stunningly bizarre rock formations and several formidable castles. The best way to explore the area is on foot as many places are inaccessible to cars. Alternatively you can admire the spectacular scenery from a boat, on the Elbe.

① **Großsedlitz** This vast Baroque park, established after 1719 to a design by Johann Christoph Knöffel, continues to delight visitors to this day with its flower beds and numerous sculptures.

⑦ **Stolpen** The 35-year-old Countess Cosel, one of Augustus II the Strong's mistresses, was imprisoned in this castle, built on rock.

⑥ **Bastei** The "bastion" comprises so-called inselbergs – bizarre, tall rock formations that rise abruptly. Connected by foot-bridges, they offer splendid views.

[Map labels: 6, Weissig, Heidenau, Pirna, Elba, Gottleuba, Teplice]

② **Festung Königstein**
This powerful fortress was built in the second half of the 16th century on the site of a medieval castle, and altered in subsequent centuries. Spectacular views have made it a popular tourist destination.

③ **Lilienstein**
This tall rock, which has to be climbed on foot, rewards the visitor with splendid views of Festung Königstein.

④ **Burg Hohnstein**
The castle, which holds within its walls a medieval building, is now a museum and one of Germany's largest youth hostels.

⑤ **Bad Schandau** A small spa that is popular as a base for walking tours into the surrounding mountains. A small railway, the Kirnitzschtalbahn, takes visitors to a scenic waterfall, the Lichtenhainer Wasserfall

Key

▬ Tour route

═ Road

▬ Scenic route

0 km ———— 4

0 miles ———— 4

Tips for Visitors

Length of tour: 41 km (25 miles).
Stopping places: inns and restaurants in every town.
Suggestions: walk from the railway at the Lichtenhainer Waterfalls to the Kuhstall (cow stable) and Barbarine needle rocks.

Gothic altar from 1513 in St Annen church, in Kamenz

ⓔ Kamenz

Road map F4. 🏔 16,800. 🚃 🚌
ℹ️ Schulplatz 5 (03578 379 205). 🎭
Hutbergfest (May). 🌐 kamenz.de

The best time for a visit to Kamenz is the end of May or June, when the rhododendrons that cover the Hutberg (294 m/965 ft high) are in flower. The poet, Gotthold Ephraim Lessing, was born in Kamenz in 1729. Although his house no longer exists, the **Lessingmuseum**, founded in 1929, is devoted to his work.

A great fire destroyed much of the town in 1842, but it spared the late-Gothic **St Marien** church, a four-nave 15th-century structure with Gothic altars and other interesting features. Equally noteworthy for their furnishings are the Gothic ex-Franciscan **St Annen** church and the unusual hall-church **Katechismuskirche**. Originally part of the town's fortification system, it has a row of loopholes on its upper storey. The old cemetery and the Gothic funereal church **Begräbniskirche St Just** are also worth a visit. As is the **Museum der Westlausitz**, a museum of the local region.

🏛 **Lessingmuseum**
Lessingplatz 1–3. **Tel** (03578) 380 50. **Open** 9am–5pm Tue–Fri, 1pm–5pm Sat & Sun.

ⓕ Bautzen

Road map F4. 🏔 44,000. 🚃 🚌
ℹ️ Hauptmarkt 1 (03591-4 20 16). 🎭
Vogelhochzeit (Jan); Lausitzer Fischwochen (Oct). 🌐 bautzen.de

This town is scenically situated on a high rock overhanging the Spree River valley. Known mainly for its top-security jail for political prisoners during the GDR era, today it enchants visitors with its beautifully reconstructed old town. Many signs are bilingual, German and Sorbian, reflecting the fact that Bautzen is the cultural capital of the Sorbs. The winding streets with their original houses, the city walls, the curiously crooked **Reichenturm** tower and the Baroque town hall in the town square form a very attractive complex. It is also worth

Impressive Baroque entrance to the Domstift in Bautzen

climbing the 15th-century **Alte Wasserkunst**, a tower that pumped Spree water up to the town. It is the symbol of Bautzen and offers splendid views.

The cathedral **Dom St Peter** is now used jointly by Catholics (choir) and Protestants (nave). The late-Gothic **Schloss Ortenburg** houses the **Sorbisches Museum**, devoted to Sorbian history and culture.

🏛 **Sorbisches Museum**
Ortenburg 3. **Tel** (03591) 42 403. **Open** Apr–Oct: 10am–5pm Tue–Sun; Nov–Mar: 10am–4pm Tue–Sun.

Doorway of the Neo-Renaissance palace in Bad Muskau

ⓖ Bad Muskau

Road map F4. 🏔 4,170. 🚌
ℹ️ Schlossstr. 6 (035771-504 92).
🌐 badmuskau.de

Bad Muskau, a small town and spa, boasts one of Saxony's most beautiful parks, which has been included in the UNESCO Cultural Heritage list. It was created in 1815–45 by the writer Prince Hermann von Pückler-Muskau. The Neo-Renaissance palace at its centre was destroyed in World War II and reopened after reconstruction in 2008. The English-style landscaped park surrounding it, a nature reserve since 1952, is well worth visiting. Its main part, on the northern shores of the Lusatian Neisse River, is in Poland. A joint Polish-German programme has opened the entire area to visitors from both sides of the border.

Baroque Neptune fountain in Untermarkt, in Görlitz

⑰ Görlitz

Road map F4. 🏔 66,000. 🚊 🚌
ℹ️ Obermarkt 32 (03581-475 70).
🎭 Kultursommer (May Sep);
Sommertheater (Jul); Strassentheater-
festival (Aug). 🌐 **goerlitz.de**

This border town, whose eastern part, Zgorzelec, has belonged to Poland since 1945, boasts a long history. Its oldest records date back to 1071. Founded in 1210–20, the town flourished in the 15th and 16th centuries. In 1990 an extensive restoration plan was begun, and now visitors can see its historic buildings in their former glory.

The charming houses in **Obermarkt** (upper market), the Renaissance portals and decorations on houses in Brüderstrasse and the fascinating **Untermarkt** (lower market), with its vast town hall complex, enchant everyone. The older wing of the town hall, the work of Wendel Roskopf, has an amazing external staircase with Renaissance ornaments, and winds around the statue of Justice.

One of the most remarkable churches is the imposing five-nave, 15th-century **Haupt-stadtpfarrkirche St Peter und St Paul** whose Baroque furnishings are among the finest in Saxony. Also noteworthy is the **Oberkirche**, with an original Gothic main altar and 15th-century wall paintings in the side nave. One of Görlitz's curiosities is the **Heiliges Grab** (Holy tomb), built in 1481–1504, a group of three chapels that are replicas of churches in Jerusalem. Görlitz still has remains of its medieval town fortifications with original towers and gates, including the **Kaisertrutz**, a 15th-century barbican, extended in the 19th century and now home to the town's art collection.

Environs
The small town of **Ostritz**, 16 km (10 miles) to the south, has a charming original Cistercian abbey, St Marienthal (1230). Its red-and-white buildings are to this day inhabited by nuns, who show visitors around and serve food and home-brewed beer.

⑱ Zittau

Road map F4. 🏔 28,000. 🚊 🚌
ℹ️ Markt 1 (03583-75 22 00).
🎭 Klosterfest (Ascension) (May); Fest am Dreiländereck (Jun); Stadtfest (Jul).
🌐 **zittau.eu**

Zittau is an excellent starting point for excursions into the Zittau Mountains, a paradise for rock-climbers, walkers and nature lovers. The town itself is splendidly preserved, with many historic buildings, such as the beautiful, Baroque **Noacksches Haus** (Markt 2). The Neo-Renaissance **Rathaus** (town hall) was built in 1840–45, to a design by Carl Augustus Schramm. The **Johanniskirche**, by Karl Friedrich Schinkel, combines elements of Neo-Classical and Neo-Gothic styles and is an excellent example of Historicist architecture.

Environs
The charming spa town of **Oybin**, 9 km (6 miles) south of Zittau, can be reached by narrow-gauge railway. Its attractions include the hilltop ruins of a Gothic abbey, immortalized by Caspar David Friedrich. It is worth timing your visit for a Saturday evening in summer, when you can witness the procession of torch-bearing monks or listen to a concert.

Fountain with a statue of Roland, the French knight, in Zittau

The Sorbs

The Sorbs, also known as the Lusatians or Wends, are an indigenous Slav minority who live in the eastern regions of Saxony and Brandenburg. Their ancestors, the Lusatian Slavs, were conquered by Germans in the 10th century. Although condemned to extermination by the National Socialists, today they enjoy complete cultural autonomy. The revival of their language and traditions is apparent in the bilingual signs in towns.

THURINGIA

Thuringia is a beautiful state, with much to entice the visitor. The Thuringian Forest, in the south, is a highland area densely covered with spruce, beech and oak forests, inviting visitors to ramble along its enchanted trails, while the area's medieval abbeys, castles and charming small towns are popular destinations with those who are interested in art and history.

The Kingdom of Thuring, as it was known in the 5th century, was conquered by the Franks, in the following century. The demise of the Thuringian landgraves, who had ruled here for hundreds of years, resulted in the outbreak of the Thuringian War of Secession. It ended in 1264, with most of Thuringia falling into the hands of the Wettin dynasty.

Split into several smaller principalities, the region lost its political might, but driven by the ambitions of many of its rulers, magnificent castles, churches and abbeys were built everywhere. Thanks to enlightened royal sponsors many towns became important cultural centres, such as 18th-century Weimar, whose residents at one time included Johann Wolfgang von Goethe, Friedrich Schiller, Johann Gottfried Herder and Christoph Martin Wieland.

After World War II, Thuringia was initially occupied by the US Army, but it soon passed into the Soviet sphere of influence, and in 1949 it became part of the GDR. In 1952 Thuringia lost its status as a federal state, but this was later restored in the reunited Federal Republic of Germany, in 1990.

The majority of tourist attractions can be found in the southern part of the state. The Thuringian Forest has many popular health resorts and wintersport centres, such as Oberhof. This highland area, cut with deep river gullies, is littered with medieval castles built on steep crags. Many of these are now no more than picturesque ruins, but others, such as the Wartburg, have been completely restored to their former glory, and today delight visitors with their magnificent interiors.

Schloss Belvedere, the royal summer residence in Weimar

◀ A stream running through the beautiful Thüringer Wald (Thuringian Forest)

Exploring Thuringia

A visit to Thuringia is most enjoyable in late summer, when the magnificent forests of the Thuringian Mountains are set ablaze with all the hues of red and yellow as the leaves turn colour, or in spring when verdant green cloaks the trees. Allow at least one day to explore Erfurt, the state's capital city, with a further two days in Weimar. Eisenach, with its magnificent Wartburg castle, is also a must.

Street vendor selling hand-painted Easter eggs in Erfurt

Sights at a Glance

1. Eisenach-Wartburg pp190–91
2. Heiligenstadt
3. Mühlhausen
4. Sondershausen
5. Kyffhäuser Mountains
6. Gotha
8. Erfurt pp196–7
9. Weimar pp198–9

10. Jena
11. Rudolstadt
12. Saalfeld
13. Gera
14. Altenburg

Walks

7. Thüringer Wald
   (Thuringian Forest)

Petersburg fortress in Erfurt

For additional map symbols *see back flap*

The fields near Meiningen, in the Thuringian Forest

Key

━━━ Motorway
━━━ Major road
━━━ Minor road
┄┄┄ Main railway
─── Minor railway
━━━ Regional border

Getting Around

Erfurt has an airport. The A4 motorway running through Thuringia links Gera with Jena, Weimar, Erfurt, Gotha and Eisenach. Other towns can be reached by local roads, which are clearly signposted. When touring the Thuringian Forest it is well worth following one of the marked tourist routes, such as Klassikerstrasse (the route of the classics) or Porzellanstrasse (porcelain street).

The Renaissance town hall in Gotha

❶ Eisenach – Wartburg

The mighty fortress towering above the town is the legendary castle which was probably founded by Ludwig the Jumper, in the late 11th century. Reputedly, it was the setting for the singing contest immortalized by Wagner in his opera *Tannhäuser*. Between 1211 and 1228 the castle was the home of Saint Elizabeth of Thuringia, and from 4 May 1521 until March 1522 Martin Luther found refuge here while he translated the New Testament into German. Major reconstruction in the 19th century gave the castle its old-time romantic character.

Festsaal
The impressive and ornate Festival Hall extends over the entire length and width of the Romanesque Palas. Today, it is the venue for a number of events.

★ Elisabethkemenate
The mosaics adorning the walls of St Elizabeth's rooms illustrate the story of the saint's life. They were designed by August Oetken and placed in 1902–06.

KEY

① **Neue Kemenate**, the "new chambers", were added during the mid-19th century. Today they house an art collection with beautiful sculptures from Tilman Riemenschneider's workshop.

② **Bergfried** is a vast, square tower crowned with a cross, beautifully restored in the 19th-century.

Landgrafenzimmer
In 1854 the landgraves' chambers in the oldest part of the castle, the Palas, were decorated with paintings depicting the castle's history, by Moritz von Schwind.

For hotels and restaurants in this area see pp494–5 and pp516–17

Vogtei

In 1872 this building acquired an original oriel window (c.1475), brought here from the Harsdörffersches House in Nuremberg.

★ **Lutherstube**

The room where Martin Luther lived and worked for ten months is very plainly furnished and has simple wood-panelling on the walls.

Entrance gate

Exploring Eisenach

The town, at the foot of the castle hill, was founded in the middle of the 12th century and played an important political role in medieval times. There are interesting remains of fortifications, dating from the late 12th century, which include a Romanesque gate, the Nikolaitor. The Nikolaikirche nearby, also Romanesque in style, once belonged to the Benedictine Sisters. In the market square is a 16th-century town hall, and in Lutherplatz stands the house where Martin Luther once lived; it is now a small museum of his work.

🏛 **Predigerkirche**
Predigerplatz 4. **Tel** (03691) 78 46 78. **Open** 11am–5pm Tue–Sun. 📷
This church, built in honour of Elisabeth von Thüringen shortly after she had been canonized, is part of the Thüringer Museum and has been used for changing exhibitions since 1899. It also houses a permanent exhibition, "Medieval Art in Thuringia".

🏛 **Automobile Welt Eisenach**
F. Naumanstr. 10. **Tel** (03691) 77 21 2. **Open** 11am–5pm Tue–Sun.
This car museum celebrates the local car manufacturing industry in Eisenach. Its collection includes old BMWs and Wartburgs.

🏛 **Bachhaus**
Frauenplan 21. **Tel** (03691) 7 93 40. **Open** 10am–6pm daily. 📷
w bachhaus.de
Johann Sebastian Bach was born in Eisenach in 1685. His birthplace is now demolished, but this small museum nearby is devoted to his life and work.

The Bachhaus and museum, surrounded by a garden

➋ Heiligenstadt

Road map C4. 🗺 17,500. 🚍 🚌
ℹ️ Wilhelmstr. 50 (03606-67 71 41).
🌐 heilbad-heiligenstadt.de

This pleasant spa and health resort, well placed for visiting the gardens of Eichsfeld, is worth an extended stop. Heiligenstadt is the birthplace of Tilman Riemenschneider, an outstanding sculptor of the Gothic era; it is also the place where the poet and writer Heinrich Heine was baptized in 1825, at the age of 28.

Heiligenstadt has several churches worth visiting, including the Gothic **Pfarrkirche St Marien** with its original wall paintings dating from around 1500. Not far from the church stands the **Friedhofskapelle St Annen**, an octagonal Gothic cemetery chapel. The town's most interesting church, however, is the **Stiftskirche St Martin**, dating back to the 14th–15th centuries. It has a well-preserved Romanesque crypt and an amusing Gothic pulpit, made in the shape of a book-holding chorister.

➌ Mühlhausen

Road map D4. 🗺 38,000. 🚍 🚌
ℹ️ Ratsstr. 20 (03601-40 47 70).
🎭 Mühlhauser Stadtkirmes (Aug).
🌐 muehlhausen.de

Mühlhausen is one of Thuringia's older towns, with its earliest records dating back to AD 967. In medieval times it enjoyed the status of an imperial free town, which could explain why it became the centre of political activities during the 1525 Peasants' War, led by Thomas Müntzer, a local clergyman. In

Part of the well-preserved town walls surrounding Mühlhausen

1975, on the 450th anniversary of the revolt, the town underwent restoration, and it delights visitors to this day with its beautifully preserved old town surrounded by **city walls**, including gates and towers, which have survived almost intact.

Mühlhausen's streets are lined with charming timber-frame houses. It is also worth stepping into one of the six Gothic churches in this area. The **Pfarrkirche Divi Blasii**, built for the Teutonic Knights, has 14th-century stained-glass windows in the presbytery. The ex-Franciscan **Barfüßerklosterkirche** (on the Kornmarkt) houses a museum devoted to the Peasants' War. The huge five-nave 14th-century **Marienkirche**, a hall-church, is one of Thuringia's largest sacral buildings. It has a magnificent main portal and late-Gothic altars. Another interesting historic structure is the **Rathaus** (town hall), in a narrow street between the old and the new town. This vast complex was enlarged several times, from medieval times until the 18th century.

➍ Sondershausen

Road map D4. 🗺 23,000. 🚌
ℹ️ Markt 9 (03632-78 81 11).
🎭 Residenzfest (Jun), Schlossfest-spiele (Jul). 🌐 sondershausen.de

Sondershausen was the capital city of the small principality of Schwarzburg-Sondershausen. The town's main attraction is the **Schloss** (ducal palace), a sprawling building built in stages from the 16th to the 19th century. The palace features some interesting original interiors. Particularly noteworthy are the **Am Wendelstein** rooms, decorated with 17th-century stucco ornaments, as well as the Neo-Classical Liebhabertheater (connoisseurs' theatre, c.1835) and the Baroque Riesensaal (giants' hall), a ballroom with 16 enormous statues of ancient gods. When strolling around the palace gardens it is worth looking at the **Karussell**, an octagonal building dating from 1700.

The most interesting Neo-Classical building complex in town can be found around **Marktplatz** (market square).

Environs
In the **Hainleite** hills, 4.5 km (3 miles) south of Sonders-hausen, stands the Jagdschloss Zum Possen, once an 18th-century hunting lodge, now an inn. The timber-frame observation tower nearby, dating from 1781, affords beautiful views of the district. **Nordhausen**, situated 20 km (12 miles) to the north, is worth visiting for its attractive timber-frame houses and its 14th-century cathedral, Dom zum Heiligen Kreuz, with a Romanesque crypt.

The extensive façade of the ducal palace in Sondershausen

Monument to Wilhelm I in the Kyffhäuser Mountains

❺ Kyffhäuser Mountains

Road map D4. 🛈 Bad Frankenhausen, Anger 14 (034671-71 717).

This small mountain range along the border between Thuringia and Saxony-Anhalt is not only picturesque but is also shrouded in legends and associated with important historic events.

According to one legend, the Emperor Frederick I Barbarossa found his final resting place in one of the caves. Allegedly, he did not drown during the Crusades, as historic records would have us believe, but is waiting here, in the company of six knights. As soon as his beard is long enough to wind three times around the table, it is said, he will return to save Germany from oppression. On the site of the former imperial palace now stands a giant monument with a figure of Barbarossa and an equestrian statue of Emperor Wilhelm I, the work of Bruno Schmitz, erected in 1891–6.

A small health resort, **Bad Frankenhausen**, nestles at the foot of the mountains. It has a number of Gothic churches, including Oberkirche, famed for its leaning tower, and a Renaissance palace, now home to a small museum. Nearby, on the **Schlachtberg** (slaughter mountain), the decisive battle in the Peasants' War took place. The **Pavilion Museum** there holds a vast panoramic picture of the battle, painted in 1971–5.

❻ Gotha

Road map D4. 🛈 48,000. 🚖 🚌 🛈 Hauptmarkt 33 (03621-50 78 57 12). 🎭 Gothardusfest (May). 🌐 **gotha.de**

From 1640 the old commercial town of Gotha was the capital of Saxe-Gotha and later of Saxe-Coburg-Gotha Duchy, the dynasty from which Prince Albert, Queen Victoria's husband, descended. The vast ducal palace, **Schloss Friedenstein**, built in 1643–55, towers above the city. This mighty rectangular structure was the first Baroque building in Thuringia.

Particularly noteworthy are the ballroom, the palace chapel with the ducal sarcophagi in the crypt and the court theatre, built in 1683. The palace museum houses an art collection including works by famous artists such as Peter Paul Rubens, Anton van Dyck, Frans Hals and Jan van Goyen. The palace garden is also worth a visit. To the south of the palace

stands a Neo-Renaissance building, which was purpose-built for the ducal art collection. Now it houses the **Museum der Natur**, a natural history museum. The Renaissance town hall (1567–77) in the old town is surrounded by a number of interesting houses.

Gotha played an important role in the German workers' movement: the Socialist Workers' Party (today's SPD), was founded here in 1875. The conference hall has been reconstructed and houses the **Gedenkstätte der Deutschen Arbeiterbewegung** (memorial to the German workers' movement).

🏠 Schloss Friedenstein
Tel 03621-8234 51. **Open** May–Oct: 10am–5pm Tue–Sun; Nov–Apr: 10am–4pm Tue–Sun.

🏛 Gedenkstätte der Deutschen Arbeiterbewegung
Am Tivoli 3. **Tel** (03621) 70 41 27. **Open** only by prior arrangement.

Doorway of the Renaissance town hall on the Hauptmarkt, in Gotha

❼ Thüringer Wald (Thuringian Forest)

Narrow, winding roads lead through the mountains, which are densely covered with spruce forests. Small towns, charming spas and wintersports resorts nestle in the valleys, while the ruins of once fearsome castles occupy the hilltops. This is prime walking country, and Gotha is the best starting point for a walking holiday. For a longer hike, stop in Ilmenau, and from there follow the upward trail marked G, to a hunters' shelter and a foresters' lodge.

① Friedrichroda

The Neo-Gothic Reinhardsbrunn castle in Friedrichroda was the place where Queen Victoria met her fiancé, Prince Albert von Sachsen-Coburg-Gotha, in 1840.

⑨ Drei Gleichen

This name, meaning "three of the same", refers to three castles – Mühlburg and Burg Gleichen have stood in ruins for centuries, but the third castle, Wachsenburg, has survived and now serves as a hotel.

⑧ Arnstadt

This picturesque town, once the home of Johann Sebastian Bach, features a town hall in the Mannerist style, dating from the late 16th century. Other places of interest are an early-Gothic church and a Baroque palace that is now home to a wax museum.

Tips for Walkers

Length: 150 km (90 miles).
Stopping places: inns and restaurants in every town.
Suggestions: walk along the Goethe-Wanderweg trail, from Ilmenau. Train journey by the Thüringerwaldbahn, from Gotha via Friedrichroda to Tabarz.

*Map labels:* E40 · Eisenach · Gotha · 247 · ① · 62 · ② · Bad Salzingen · Werra · ③ · THÜRINGER · ④ · Zella-Mehlis · ⑤ · Meiningen · Werra · 89 · Hildburghausen

② Trusetal
The magnificent waterfall in Trusetal, the work of human hands, was built in the mid-19th century. Another site worth visiting is the nearby Marienglashöhle in Friedrichroda, an unusual crystal grotto.

③ Schmalkalden
This charming little town, packed with timber-frame houses, attracts visitors to the Wilhelmsburg, its Renaissance palace, and to Neue Hütte, an interesting old smelting plant dating from 1835.

④ Oberhof
This is a popular wintersports resort, with excellent ski-jumps. In the summer it is worth visiting the Rennsteiggarten, the town's botanical gardens with a vast collection of alpine plants.

⑤ Suhl
Famous from the 16th century as a centre of arms manufacture, Suhl's history can today be gleaned in the local Waffenmuseum (armaments museum).

0 km   10
0 miles   10

Erfurt   Weimar

E40

Gera

8

4

85

7

6   Rudolstadt

Bad Blankenburg

Schwarza

281

Elsfeld

⑥ Ilmenau
This small university town, teeming with life, is the starting point of the so-called Goethe Wanderweg, a walking trail leading to all the places where the famous poet once stayed.

⑦ Paulinzelle
The 12th-century Romanesque abbey, now in ruins, was once a home for Benedictine monks, but it was later abandoned during the Reformation.

Key
━━━ Suggested route
■■■ Other road
═══ Scenic route

❽ Erfurt

The Thuringian capital, Erfurt, is also the oldest town in the region – its earliest historic records date from AD729, and in AD742 a bishopric was founded here. As an important trading post between east and west, the town grew quickly. Erfurt University was founded in 1392; it became a stronghold for radical thought, and Martin Luther was one of its pupils. Until the 17th century, Erfurt was famous for its red dyes extracted from the madder root; in the 18th century the town became a horticultural centre, and to this day it hosts an impressive garden show in one of Germany's largest parks.

Picturesque half-timbered houses, lining the Krämerbrücke

Exploring Erfurt

The town, on the banks of the river Gera, is dominated by two hills. On the higher one, **Petersberg**, stands a huge fortress surrounding a Romanesque church, while the lower **Domberg** has two churches, the **Dom St Marien** and the **St Severikirche**. From the Domplatz, at the foot of the hill, a row of narrow streets leads to Fischmarkt. If you cross the river here, you will get to Erfurt's old commercial district and its market square, the Anger.

🏛 Dom St Marien

Domberg. **Tel** (0361) 646 12 65.
Open Apr–Oct: 9am–6pm Mon–Sat, 1–6pm Sun; Nov–Mar: 10am–5pm Mon–Sat, 1–5pm Sun. 🎧

The wide stairs leading from Domplatz to the main entrance of the cathedral provide a good view over the 14th-century Gothic presbytery, which is supported by a massive vaulted substructure, known as the Kavaten. The main body of the cathedral dates from the 15th century, but its huge towers are the remains of an earlier Romanesque building. **Maria**

Gloriosa, a huge bell 2.5 m (8 ft) in diameter, hangs in the centre tower. Cast by Gerhard Wou in 1497, it is one of the largest bells in the world. The church interior has well preserved Gothic decorations and rich furnishings. Particularly valuable are the 14th- and 15th-century stained-glass windows, the Gothic stalls (c.1370) and Wolfram, a Romanesque

Rich furnishings in the Gothic interior of Dom St Marien

bronze candelabra, (c.1160), shaped like a man.

🏛 St Severi-Kirche

Domberg. **Tel** (0361) 57 69 60.
Open Apr–Oct: 9am–6pm Mon–Sat, 1–6pm Sun; Nov–Mar: 10am–5pm Mon–Sat, 1–5pm Sun.

This five-nave Gothic hall-church, next to the cathedral, dates from the late 13th and early 14th century. Inside it has the Gothic sarcophagus of St Severus, from about 1365, a huge font of 1467 and interesting Gothic altars.

▦ Fischmarkt

This small market square, with its Neo-Gothic town hall (1870–74), is surrounded by houses dating from various periods, including the 16th-century Renaissance buildings **Zum Breiten Herd** (No. 13, To the Wide Hearth) and **Zum Roten Ochsen** (No. 7, To the Red Ox). On the streets off the market square are three Gothic churches: Michaeliskirche, opposite the ruins of the late-Gothic university buildings, the twin-nave llerheiligenkirche (late 13th to early 14th century), and the ex-Dominican Predigerkirche.

▦ Krämerbrücke

The "merchant bridge" which spans the River Gera is one of Erfurt's most interesting structures. The present stone bridge was built around 1325. It is lined by 32 houses with shops, dating mainly from the 17th to 19th centuries, which replaced its 60 original medieval houses. On its eastern viaduct stands Ägidienkirche, a 14th-century Gothic church.

🏛 Augustinerkloster–Augustinerkirche

Augustinerstr. 10. **Tel** (0361) 576 60 10.
📷 10am–4pm daily. 🎧

This early Gothic church was built for Augustinian monks at the end of the 13th century. Particularly noteworthy are its original Gothic stained-glass windows. In the neighbouring monastery, the reconstructed cell where Martin Luther lived as a monk can be admired.

Fischmarkt, surrounded by houses from various periods

🏛 Stadtmuseum

Johannesstr. 169. **Tel** (0361) 655 56 51. **Open** 10am–6pm Tue–Sun.

Erfurt's history museum is housed in a beautiful, late-Renaissance building called **Zum Stockfisch** (To the Dried Cod), built in 1607.

🎪 Anger

Now pedestrianized, this is a market square and Erfurt's main shopping street, lined with attractive 19th-century mansions and commercial premises. There are two Gothic churches: **Kaufmanns-kirche** and **Reglerkirche**, with a huge Gothic altar dating from around 1470. At Nos. 37 and 38 there is the **Dacherödensches Haus**, a complex of beautiful Renaissance buildings.

🏛 Angermuseum

Anger 18. **Tel** (0361) 55 45 615. **Open** 10am–6pm Tue–Sun. Barfüßerkirche: Barfüßerstr. 20. **Tel** (0361) 55 45 615. **Open** Mar–Nov: 10am–6pm Tue–Sun. 🌐

The museum, housed in a Baroque building, has a collection of decorative and sacred arts including paintings by Lucas Cranach the Elder, and 19th- and 20th-century German works. One of its rooms is decorated with Expressionist murals (1923–4) by Erich Heckel. The medieval section is in the presbytery of the **Barfüßerkirche**, a former Franciscan church that was destroyed during World War II.

VISITORS' CHECKLIST

Practical Information
Road map D4. 🏘 200,000. ℹ Benediktplatz 1 (0361-66400). 🎭 Krämerbrückenfest (Jun), Weinfest (Aug), Petersbergfest (Sep), Christmas market (Dec). 🌐 **erfurt-tourismus.de**

Transport
✈ Flughafenstrasse 4 (0361-65 60). 🚌 Am Bahnhofsplatz. 🚐 Bürgermeister-Wagner-Strasse.

🏛 EGA and Gartenbaumuseum

Cyriaksburg, Gothaer Str. 38. **Tel** (0361) 223 22 0. **Open** 10am–4pm daily (to 8pm May–Oct). Museum: **Tel** (0361) 22 39 90. **Open** 10am–6pm Tue–Sun. **Closed** Jan & Feb. 🌐

On the hill around Erfurt's ruined castle (c.1480) are the grounds of the International Garden Show (Erfurter Gartenausstellung). As well as exhibition halls, show gardens and a butterfly house, there is a museum of horticulture and beekeeping.

Environs

Molsdorf, 10 km (6 miles) to the southeast, has a lovely 16th-century Baroque palace set in landscaped parkland, with a museum.

Erfurt City Centre

① Dom St Marien
② St Severi-Kirche
③ Fischmarkt
④ Krämerbrücke
⑤ Augustinerkirche
⑥ Stadtmuseum
⑦ Anger
⑧ Angermuseum

| 0 metres | 300 |
| 0 yards | 300 |

For additional map symbols see back flap

⑨ Weimar

Had it not been for the enlightened sponsorship of its rulers, Weimar would have become just another residential town in Thuringia. The town flourished, particularly under Duke Carl Augustus and his wife Anna Amalia, when Goethe, Schiller and Herder lived here. Famous 19th- and 20th-century residents included Franz Liszt, Richard Strauss, Friedrich Nietzsche and many distinguished writers and artists associated with the Bauhaus School, which was founded here in 1919. It also gave its name to the Weimar Republic, the democratic German State, lasting from World War I to 1933.

Exploring Weimar

Weimar is relatively small and most of its tourist attractions are near the town centre, on the left bank of the Ilm River. In the north of the centre are the Neues Museum and the Stadtmuseum (municipal museum). Many interesting buildings can be found around Theaterplatz, from where you proceed towards the Markt to visit the ducal palace. In the south of the centre are the former homes of Goethe and Liszt.

⊞ Neues Museum

Weimarplatz 5. **Tel** (03643) 545 400. **Open** Apr–Oct: 11am–6pm Tue–Sun; Nov–Mar: 11am–4pm Tue–Sun.

This Neo-Renaissance building, once the Landesmuseum (regional museum), was transformed into a gallery in 1999. It displays changing exhibits of modern art, with an emphasis on colour.

⊞ Stadtmuseum

Karl-Liebknecht-Str. 5–9. **Tel** (03643) 826 00. **Open** 11am–5pm Tue–Sun.

This museum is devoted to the history of Weimar, but it also holds an interesting natural history collection. It is housed in a Neo-Classical house, which was built in the late 18th century for the publisher Justin Bertuch.

St Peter und St Paul, also known as the Herderkirche

🎭 Deutsches Nationaltheater

Theaterplatz 2. **Tel** (03643) 75 50.

The present Neo-Classical building, built in 1906–7 to a design by Heilmann & Littmann, is the third theatre to stand on this site. Famous conductors who worked here include Franz Liszt and Richard Strauss, and it was also the venue for the world premiere of Wagner's *Lohengrin*. In 1919 the National Congress sat in the Nationaltheater and passed the new constitution for the Weimar Republic. In front of the theatre is a monument to Goethe (who founded the theatre) and Schiller, by the sculptor Ernst Rietschel (1857).

⊞ Bauhaus-Museum

Theaterplatz. **Tel** (03643) 545 400. **Open** 10am–6pm daily.

This museum is devoted to the famous art school, which was founded in Weimar in 1919, moved to Dessau in 1925 *(see p158)* and later, in 1933, to Berlin *(see p92)*.

⊞ Wittumspalais

Theaterplatz. **Tel** (03643) 545 401. **Open** Apr–Oct: 10am–6pm Wed–Mon; Nov–Mar: 10am–4pm Wed–Mon.

The Dowager Duchess Anna Amalia lived in this Baroque palace, designed by Johann Gottfried Schlegel and built in 1767–9. Visitors can admire fine interiors and mementos of the Enlightenment figure Christoph-Martin Wieland.

⊞ Schillerhaus

Schillerstr. 12. **Tel** (03643) 545 401. **Open** Apr–Sep: 9am–6pm Tue–Fri & Sun (to 7pm Sat); Oct: 9am–6pm Tue–Sun; Nov–Mar: 9am–4pm Tue–Sun.

The museum is in the house where Friedrich Schiller wrote *Wilhelm Tell* (1804) and spent the last years of his life.

⛪ St Peter und St Paul

Herderplatz. **Tel** (03643) 85 15 18. **Open** Apr–Oct: 10am–6pm Mon–Fri, 10am–noon & 2–4pm Sat; Nov–Mar: 11am–noon & 2–4pm daily.

This late-Gothic hall-church has Baroque furnishings and an original altar painted by the Cranachs. It is also known as the Herderkirche, after the poet who preached here.

⊞ Kirms-Krackow-Haus

Jakobstr. 10. **Tel** (03643) 545 401. **Open** Apr–Oct: 10am–6pm Tue–Sun. **Closed** Nov–Apr.

This Renaissance house, which was extended in the late 18th century, illustrates how people lived in Goethe's time.

🏰 Stadtschloss

Burgplatz 4. Schlossmuseum: **Tel** (03643) 54 59 60. **Open** Apr–Oct: 10am–6pm Tue–Sun; Nov–Mar: 10am–4pm Tue–Sun.

This vast ducal castle was rebuilt in the Neo-Classical style for Duke Carl August. It has original interiors and fine paintings from the Weimar Art School, and a gallery devoted to Lucas Cranach.

The Stadtschloss in Burgplatz, with its tall Renaissance tower

For hotels and restaurants in this area see pp494–5 and pp516–17

Picturesque Baroque summer residence known as Schloss Belvedere

🏛 Herzogin-Anna-Amalia Bibliothek

Platz der Demokratie 4. **Tel** (03643) 54 52 00. **Open** 9.30am–2.30pm Tue–Sun.

This former Mannerist palace, also known as Grünes Schloss (green castle), became the duchess' library in 1761–6. Its oval Rococo interior is one of the finest of its type in Europe.

🏛 Schloss Belvedere

Tel (03643) 545 400. **Open** Apr–Oct: 10am–6pm Tue–Sun.

This ducal summer residence, which was built between 1724 and 1732 in Belvedere Park, has a fine collection of decorative art from the Rococo period and a wonderful park.

🏛 Goethes Wohnhaus and National Museum

Frauenplan 1. **Tel** (03643) 54 53 00.

Open Apr–Oct: 9am–6pm, Nov–Mar: 9am–4pm. **Closed** Mon.

This house was presented to Goethe by the Duke Carl Augustus. Here the writer wrote his most famous work, *Faust*. Today the museum shows items associated with Goethe and other Enlightenment poets from Weimar.

🏠 Goethes Gartenhaus

Park an der Ilm. **Open** Apr–Oct: 10am–6pm Wed–Mon; Nov–Mar: 10am–4pm Wed–Mon.

Goethe's first home in Weimar, this small villa is in the pleasant park alongside the River Ilm which Goethe helped design.

🏛 Liszt Museum

Marienstr. 17. **Tel** (03643) 54 54 01. **Open** Apr–Dec: 10am–6pm Tue–Sun. **Closed** Jan–Mar.

Franz Liszt lived here in 1869–86, while he composed the *Hungarian Rhapsody*. His apartment and the room in which he worked have been preserved to this day.

Environs

Buchenwald, 8 km (5 miles) north of Weimar, was the site of a concentration camp set up by the Nazis. During the period 1937 to 1945, over 54,000 people were killed here. It is now a place of remembrance, a museum and a documentation centre.

🏛 Buchenwald

Tel (03643) 430 100. **Open** Apr–Oct: 10am–6pm Tue–Sun; Nov–Mar: 10am–4pm Tue–Sun.

Weimar City Centre

1. Stadtmuseum
2. Deutsches Nationaltheater
3. Bauhaus-Museum
4. Wittumspalais
5. Schillerhaus
6. St Peter und St Paul
7. Krims-Krackow-Haus
8. Stadtschloss
9. Grünes Schloss
10. Goethe-Museum

0 metres 300
0 yards 300

Key to Symbols *see back flap*

The modest Gothic town hall on Marktplatz, in Jena

⑩ Jena

Road map D4. 🚐 100,000. 🚌 🚍
ℹ Markt 16 (03641-49 80 50).
🎪 Altstadtfest (Sep).
🌐 jenatourismus.de

Jena is famous for the world-renowned Carl-Zeiss–Jena Optical Works and its university, founded in 1558. One of the most important schools in Germany, its former tutors included Schiller, Fichte and Hegel. The oldest university building is the **Collegium Jenense**. The main building was built by Theodor Fischer in 1905–8. The complex includes a 120-m (394-ft) cylindrical tower block, completed in 1972 and known as the "phallus Jenensis".

In the town's main square, Marktplatz, stands the late-Gothic **Rathaus** (town hall), dating from the early 15th century. Once every hour, a figure known as the Schnapphans tries to catch a ball, a symbol of the human soul. The Gothic church of **St Michael** nearby was built in the 15th and the 16th centuries. The **Stadtmusem Alte Göhre** has an interesting collection of regional history. In Unterer Markt the **Romantikerhaus** is worth a visit; formerly the home of Johann Gottlieb Fichte, it now houses a museum devoted to the Romantic period.

Also worth visiting are the **Optisches Museum** on the history of the Carl Zeiss Works and the **Zeiss-Planetarium**, the world's oldest of its type. In the north, the **Goethe-Gedenkstätte**

is a museum devoted to Goethe's work as poet, politician and scientist.

🏛 **Stadtmuseum Göhre**
Markt 7. **Tel** (03641) 498 261. **Open** 10am–5pm Tue–Sun, 3–10pm Thu.

🏛 **Romantikerhaus**
Unterer Markt 12A. **Tel** (03641) 49 82 49. **Open** 10am–5pm Tue–Sun.

🏛 **Optisches Museum**
Carl-Zeiss-Platz 12. **Tel** (03641) 44 31 65. **Open** 10am–4:30pm Tue–Fri, 11am–5pm Sat.

Historical Zeiss-Workshop
🕰 11:30am Sat.

Environs
Dornburg, 12 km (8 miles) to the northeast, has three palaces: the Altes Schloss, a Gothic castle transformed in the Renaissance; the Renaissanceschloss (1539–47) and the charming Rokokoschloss (1736–41).

⑪ Rudolstadt

Road map D4. 🚐 28,000. 🚌 🚍
ℹ Marktstr. 5 (03672-48 64 40).
🎪 Tanz-und Folk Fest (Jul).
🌐 rudolstadt.de

Although Rudolstadt has the Gothic-Renaissance St Andreas church, a fascinating 16th-century town hall and some historic houses, tourists come here mainly to see majestic **Schloss Heidecksburg**, a vast palace perched on a hill. Its present form is mainly the result of reconstruction work carried out in the mid-18th century by Johann Christoph Knöffel and Gottfried Heinrich Krone. Inside

Baroque Schloss Heidecksburg towering over Rudolstadt

are some beautifully arranged Rococo state rooms. The museum also has a splendid porcelain collection, a gallery of paintings and the so-called Schiller's Room. From the castle there are fantastic views of the Schwarza valley.

🏰 **Schloss Heidecksburg**
Schlossbezirk 1. **Tel** (03672) 42 900. **Open** Apr–Oct: 10am–6pm Tue–Sun; Nov–Mar: 10am–5pm Tue–Sun.

Entrance gate to the 11th-century Schloss Ranis, near Saalfeld

⑫ Saalfeld

Road map D4. 🚐 34,000. 🚌
🚍 ℹ Am Markt 6 (03671-339 50).
🎪 Zunftmarkt (Jun).

Saalfeld flourished in the 14th–16th centuries. From 1680 it was the seat of the Duchy of Sachsen–Saalfeld, and the magnificent Baroque **Schloss**, built between 1676 and 1720, dates from this period. The former palace chapel, now used as a concert hall, is particularly noteworthy. Also worth visiting is the **Johanniskirche**, a late-Gothic hall-church with interesting furnishings, a valuable Gothic Holy Tomb and the sculpted life-size figure of John the Baptist, carved by Hans Gottwalt, a student of Tilman Riemenschneider.

Another interesting building in Saalfeld is the early-Renaissance **Rathaus** (town hall), built in 1529–37. The town also has well preserved medieval town fortifications with gates and towers. In the southern part of the town stands the **Hoher Schwarm**, ruins of a 13th-century Gothic castle. In Garnsdorf, on the outskirts of Saalfeld, are the **Feengrotten**, grottoes created by both natural and human activity. From the mid-16th century until 1846 alum slate was mined in this cave, called "Jeremiasglück" (Jeremiah's good fortune). It was finally closed due to humidity, but the dripping water has created some astonishingly colourful stalagmites and stalactites.

⊡ Feengrotten Grottoneum
Feengrottenweg 2. **Tel** (03671) 550 40.
Open May–Oct: 9.30am–5pm daily,
Nov–Apr: 10:30am–3:30pm daily.

Environs

From Saalfeld it is worth taking a trip to the Hohenwarte-Talsperre, an artificial lake and paradise for watersports enthusiasts. **Burg Ranis**, a scenic hill-top castle, was probably built in the 11th century for an emperor. Later it became the seat of the Thuringian landgraves, Meissen margraves and the counts of Schwarzburg. Now it houses a museum of the region's natural history.

⑬ Gera

Road map D4. 🚇 121,000. 🚌 🚍
🛈 Heinrich Str. 35 (0365-830 44 80).
🎭 International Open Air Theatre
Festival (Jun), Geraer Höhlerfest (Sep).

The second largest town in Thuringia, Gera is not impressive at first sight, but it has many attractions, including a picturesque **Rathaus** (town hall) whose oldest, Renaissance part dates from 1573–6. The Geraer Elleblon, on the right-hand side of the entrance, is a unit of measurement equal to 57 cm (22 in). A short distance from the market square, in Nikolaiberg, you will find the **Salvatorkirche**. This Baroque church got its Secession-style interior in 1903, after a fire. The theatre (1900–02) was designed in the same style, by Heinrich Seeling. The Küchengarten

Picturesque Altenburg Castle complex

(kitchen garden) surrounds the ruins of **Schloss Osterstein** of which only the Baroque orangerie remains. It now houses the **Kunstsammlung**, with paintings by Lucas Cranach the Elder, Max Liebermann and others.

Otto Dix, a leading artist of the *Neue Sachlichkeit*, was born in Gera, and his birthplace has been turned into the **Otto-Dix-Haus**.

⊡ Kunstsammlung
Küchengartenallee 4. **Tel** (0365) 838
42 50. **Open** 11am–6pm Tue–Sun.

▥ Otto-Dix-Haus
Mohrenplatz 4. **Tel** (0365) 832 49 27.
Open 11am–6pm Tue–Sun.

The multi-coloured Renaissance doorway of the Rathaus in Gera

⑭ Altenburg

Road map E4. 🚇 45,000. 🚌 🚍
🛈 Markt 17 (03447-51 28 00).
🎭 Prinzenraubfest (Jul); Altstadtfest
(Aug). 🌐 altenburg-tourismus.de

In Germany, Altenburg is known as "Skatstadt", the town of skat, a traditional and very popular card game. Altenburg also has some fascinating historic remains. The **Schloss** (ducal castle), which towers over the old town, has a 10th-century tower, reconstructed mainly in the Baroque style. Today the castle houses the **Spielkartenmuseum** (museum of playing cards). The late-Gothic castle church is also worth seeing. It has rich Baroque furnishings and an organ that was played by the composer Bach. Next to the castle gardens is the **Lindenau-Museum**, with Augustus von Lindenau's collection of 16th–20th century paintings and sculptures, including works by Simone Martini, Fra Angelico, Auguste Rodin, Ernst Barlach and Max Liebermann. The old town, at the foot of the hill, has a beautiful Renaissance town hall with an enormous octagonal turret. In Brühl is the fountain and the figures of skat players, as well as the Baroque **Seckendorffsche Palais** and the Renaissance chancellery.

▥ Schloss und Spielkartenmuseum
Schloss 2–4. **Tel** (03447) 51 27 12.
Open 10am–5pm Tue–Sun.

▥ Lindenau-Museum
Gabelentzstrasse 5. **Tel** (03447) 895 53.
Open noon–6pm Tue–Fri, 10am–6pm
Sat, Sun.

SOUTHERN GERMANY

Southern Germany at a Glance

The southern regions of Germany, with their wealth of natural beauty, historic sights and folk culture, are particularly attractive to tourists. This part of the country includes two *Länder*: Bavaria, famous for its Alps, beer and the fairytale castle of Ludwig II at Neuschwanstein, and Baden-Württemberg, whose highlights include the Bodensee lake, Heidelberg and taking a trip on the scenic Schwarzwaldbahn railway line between Offenburg and Villingen.

Locator Map

Aschaffenburg

Würz

Mannheim

Heidelberg

Karlsruhe

Heilbronn

Baden-Baden   Pforzheim   Stuttgart   Aalen

Offenburg   Reutlingen   Ulm

BADEN-
WÜRTTEMBERG
(See pp292–331)

Biberach

Freiburg
in Breisgau   Tuttlingen

Schaffhausen   Kempte

Konstanz

Würzburg Residenz
Set in a magnificent park on the eastern outskirts of the town, this imposing bishop's palace was built between 1720 and 1744, to a design by Balthasar Neumann. The palace is constructed in a U-shape, with a central pavilion flanked by four two-storey courts.

Heidelberg Castle is one of Germany's finest examples of a Gothic-Renaissance fortress. Its origins go back to the 13th century, but new buildings sprang up around the inner courtyard during the 16th century as the castle gained importance as a royal residence.

Maulbronn Abbey,
founded in the heart of the Stromberg region in 1147, is one of the best-preserved abbeys in Europe. It was established by Cistercian monks with the bequest of a knight named Walter von Lomersheim and provides a graphic account of the austere life led by the monks.

◄ Neuschwanstein Castle, near Füssen

Vierzehnheiligen Church, built in 1743–72 to a design by Balthasar Neumann, is one of the most famous examples of South German Rococo. The monumental "Altar of Mercy" (Gnadenaltar) includes statues of the Fourteen Saints of the Intercession, to whom the church is dedicated.

Nördlingen Town Hall was built in the 14th century, but its present form dates from the early 17th century. Prisoners used to be held in a space beneath the external stone stairway. By the wooden entrance is a wall carving of a medieval fool bearing a German inscription that translates as "Now there are two of us."

Coburg

Hof

Bamberg

Bayreuth

Erlangen

Weiden

Nuremberg

Schwandorf

nsbach

Cham

Regensburg

BAVARIA
(See pp242–91)

Ingolstadt

Straubing

Deggendorf

Passau

Landshut

Augsburg

Altötting

Munich

Landsberg
am Lech

Rosenheim

Kaufbeuren

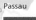

0 kilometres   50

0 miles   50

Neuschwanstein Castle is one of the three castles built for the Bavarian King Ludwig II (1845–86), involving enormous effort and expenditure. Standing on a high rock, overlooking a lake, the castle was the fulfilment of the King's vision, which was greatly inspired by the operas of Wagner.

The Frauenkirche in Munich was completed in 1488 and features two 99-m (325-ft) high towers crowned with copper domes. The church is one of the largest in southern Germany.

The Baroque in Southern Germany

Because of religious conflicts and the Thirty Years' War (1618–48), the Baroque style did not flourish in Germany until the 18th century. Then it did so most lavishly in the southern, Catholic regions of the country. Here, influenced by Italian architecture, the Baroque reached new heights of flamboyance: the impressive spaciousness of religious buildings provided the setting for dynamic compositions in sculpture, fine stuccowork and vividly coloured *trompe l'oeil* paintings. Southern Germany's major artists of the 18th century included Balthasar Neumann, François de Cuvilliés and the Asam brothers.

The main altar in Rohr, which was created by Egid Quirin Asam in 1723, is in the form of a proscenium (stage) with wings. The sculptural group depicts the Assumption of the Virgin Mary into Heaven.

Ceiling frescoes were a basic element of the Baroque interior. This example by Johann Baptist Zimmermann in the Wieskirche in Steingaden, presents a glowing vision of the afterlife.

Galleries with curved balustrades add vitality to the interior.

Figures of saints clad in flowing, dynamic robes and standing in curving, asymmetrical poses, complement the rich iconography and complex composition of the altars.

Light plays a vital role in enlivening the interior decoration.

18th-century monasteries in southern Germany, like this one in Ottobeuren with its imposing stairway, are reminiscent of royal residences.

Late Baroque church façades, such as that of the Theatinerkirche in Munich, have a "rippled" design that creates an unusual effect of light and shadow.

Vaults with fine painting and exquisite stuccowork round off the architectural elements.

The pulpit and other furnishings are designed to blend harmoniously with the decoration.

The Monstrance in Passau is a fine example of the art of 18th-century goldsmiths, who created these receptacles for the consecrated Host.

Baroque Interiors

Although they may seem over-elaborate, the late Baroque interiors of southern German churches are carefully planned compositions intended to have a powerful effect. Their magnificent combination of architecture, sculpture and painting, and often organ music, resulted in "Gesamtkunstwerk" – a homogenous work that combines all the arts.

Stuccowork fills every interior space that is not decorated with paintings. Sometimes gilded, sometimes white, it may depict complex scenes or, in some cases, be adorned with ornamental designs.

Baroque Residences

South German Baroque was not limited solely to religious architecture. As well as the magnificent monasteries and pilgrimage churches, it was also the inspiration for the impressive residences that were built by abbots, as well as by bishops. As in the rest of Europe, these were modelled on the French royal palace in Versailles with its imposing grandeur, striking interiors and breathtaking gardens.

The Baroque vestibule in the Neues Schloss in Schleißheim (see pp268–9) is decorated with exquisite stuccowork and frescoes.

Schloss Nymphenburg was a summer residence of the rulers of Bavaria. It has a grand driveway and a park (see pp228–9).

Schloss Favorite is a small palace that forms part of a huge Baroque-style residence in Ludwigsburg (see pp310–11).

The German Alps

Part of Germany extends into a fairly moderate section of the Alps, Western Europe's highest mountain range. They stretch from the Bodensee (Lake Constance) to Berchtesgaden. A section of the northern calcareous Alps belonging to the Eastern Alps of Allgäu, Bavaria and Salzburg falls within Germany. The mountains are a holidaymaker's paradise all year round. In the summer mountain walks can be enjoyed, with well-marked trails, as well as climbing, hang-gliding and paragliding; in the winter skiing is possible in superbly equipped resorts.

Alpine meadows are rich pasture lands, providing premium quality hay. They are also home to a rich variety of wildflowers.

Mountain streams have, over the years, cut a path through the rocks to create picturesque ravines. One of the most beautiful is this one at Wimbachklamm.

Mountain peaks with their breathtaking jagged rocks.

Local architecture blends happily into the landscape.

The Alpine Lakes

A melting glacier created many lakes in Bavaria. Their clear, unpolluted waters attract all kinds of watersports enthusiasts, while the picturesque surroundings are equally popular with other recreational users.

The Königssee, with its crystal-clear waters, is located high in the Berchtesgaden National Park.

The Watzmann is Germany's second-highest peak.

Schwarzeck

Steinplatte

Reit im Winkl

Oberaudorf

Schliersee

The **Zugspitze**, at 2,962m (9,700 ft), is the highest peak in all of Germany.

Alpine Flora and Fauna

Alpine vegetation varies according to height above sea level. On the lower slopes are mixed deciduous forests. Higher up are Alpine forests, generally coniferous. Above the tree line, dwarf mountain pine grow and higher still are stretches of high-altitude meadows. Beyond this is bare rock. Wild goats are found above the tree line and chamois in the foothills.

The Alpine ibex lives only in the Italian and Swiss Alps. This wild goat with long, backward-curving horns is a rare sight.

The mouflon is a wild sheep with large horns. It is also found in Corsica and Sardinia.

Alpine rock jasmine forms carpets of colour on the mountain slopes.

The Alpine pasqueflower is a white variant of the species that tolerates the harsh soil and climatic conditions of its Alpine habitat.

The peacock butterfly is a common Eurasian species that has adapted successfully to the harsh Alpine environment.

Alpine thrift, with its round heads of pink and purple flowers, is a delightful sight.

Tegernsee

Walchensee is overlooked by one of the largest hydroelectric power stations in Germany.

Garmisch-Partenkirchen is one of the venues of the annual Four Ski Jumps competition.

Kochelsee

Alpspitze

The Zugspitze is the highest peak in Germany.

MUNICH

The capital of Bavaria, Munich (München) is sometimes called "Germany's secret capital". Lying right at the heart of Europe, the city rapidly overshadowed once powerful neighbours, such as Ingolstadt, Augsburg and Nuremberg, to become southern Germany's main metropolis. With its vibrant cosmopolitan atmosphere, fine buildings, museums and shops, it is one of the country's most popular tourist destinations.

The citizens of Munich have been known for centuries for their love of the arts. The masterpieces that were created here during the Baroque and Rococo periods were equal to Italian and French works.

In the 19th century, the town's development continued along Neo-Classical lines, gaining for it the name of "Athens on Isar". Just how appropriate the name is can be seen when strolling along Ludwigstrasse or Königsplatz or visiting the Glyptothek, which houses Ludwig I's collection of Greek and Roman sculptures.

In the late 19th century the Munich Academy of Fine Arts was amongst Europe's best art schools. Not many cities have as great a choice of world-class theatres, operas and museums as can be found here in Munich.

But it is not only art that gives Munich its unique charm. The country's biggest folk festival, the Oktoberfest, is held each year in Theresienwiese, where visitors to the town can join in the revelries or just sit and watch, ordering a plate of sauerkraut with sausages and washing it down with some of the excellent Bavarian beer.

When planning a shopping trip to Munich visitors can be sure that its shops are equal to those of Paris and Milan, not only in the breadth of their range but also in terms of their prices.

The town is also one of Germany's main centres of high-tech and media industries. Many TV stations and film studios, as well as over 300 book and newspaper publishers, have their main offices in Munich.

The Neo-Gothic Rathaus in Marienplatz, Munich's central square

◀ Interior and ceiling of the Antiquarium Hall in the Residenz Museum

Exploring Munich

Munich, or München locally, the capital of Bavaria, is exceptionally rich in interesting museums, churches and historic sights. This urban conurbation of about 1.4 million inhabitants increasingly swallows up the neighbouring areas. Many tourist attractions are located outside the town centre but, thanks to excellent public transport, it is easy to visit them. It is worth taking a trip to Nymphenburg to visit the famous palace and gardens there. Another interesting excursion is a stroll along Leopoldstrasse or Theresienwiese, where the huge, annual Oktoberfest is held.

The distinctive towers of Munich's skyline

Sights at a Glance

Churches

❶ Bürgersaal
❷ Michaelskirche
❸ Dreifaltigkeitskirche
❹ Frauenkirche
❻ Asamkirche
⓰ Theatinerkirche (St Cajetan)
⓴ Ludwigskirche

Buildings

❿ Altes Rathaus
⓫ Neues Rathaus
⓮ Residenz (pp220–21)
⓯ Feldherrnhalle
㉑ Bayerische Staatsbibliothek
㉚ Propyläen
㉜ Schloss Nymphenburg (pp228–9)
㊱ Villa Stuck

Museums and Galleries

❺ Deutsches Jagd- und Fischereimuseum
❼ Stadtmuseum
❽ Jüdisches Zentrum Jakobsplatz
⓬ Museum Fünf Kontinente
⓱ Haus der Kunst
⓲ Bayerisches Nationalmuseum
⓳ Schack-Galerie
⓴ Archäologische Staatssammlung
㉓ Museum Brandhorst
㉔ Neue Pinakothek
㉕ Alte Pinakothek (pp226–7)
㉖ Pinakothek der Moderne
㉗ NS-Dokumentationszentrum
㉘ Glyptothek
㉙ Staatliche Antikensammlungen
㉛ Lenbachhaus
㉟ Deutsches Museum (pp232–3)

Other Attractions

❾ Viktualienmarkt
⓭ Hofbräuhaus
㉝ Olympiapark
㉞ Englischer Garten
㊲ Bavaria-Filmstadt
㊳ Theresienwiese

Getting There

Munich is an important railway junction and has its own international airport. It also has motorway connections with all the major towns and cities in Germany.

0 metres 400
0 yards 400

ENGLISCHER GARTEN

LEHEL

ALTSTADT

Marienplatz

Isartor

Universität

Odeonsplatz

Lehel

HOFGARTEN

Television Tower in Olympiapark

Greater Munich

Schwabing

Bogenhausen

Pasing

Laim

Berg am Laim

Hadern

Sendling

Fürstenried

Giesing

Perlach

0 kilometres 3
0 miles 3

Street-by-Street: Around Marienplatz

In medieval times, Marienplatz was Munich's salt- and corn-market. The origins of Munich itself lie with a handful of monks who built their abbey here, giving the place its name (from the word for 'monks') and its heraldic arms. In 1175 town status was officially bestowed on Munich and in 1180 the town was allocated to the Wittelsbachs, who soon established a residence here. During the Reformation, Munich became a bastion of Catholicism and an important centre of the Counter-Reformation. Its magnificent churches, the Altes Rathaus (old town hall) and the Residenz all bear witness to that era.

KARLSPLATZ

HERZOG-MAX-STR

KAPELLEN

NEUHAUSER STRASSE

DAMENSTIFTSTR

Karlstor
Known as the Karl's Gate, the west entrance to the old town was part of the medieval fortifications. It was given its present name in 1791, in honour of Elector Karl Theodore.

Augustinerbräu
The oldest and most celebrated brewery in Munich was founded by Augustinian monks in 1328. It currently occupies two 19th-century houses with picturesque façades.

0 metres		50
0 yards		50

❶ ★ Bürgersaal
Bürgersaal was built in 1709–10 for a Marian congregation (followers of the Virgin Mary), as a place of meeting and worship. It includes an upper and lower church. Rupert Mayer, an opponent of Nazism, is buried in the crypt. He was beatified in 1987.

❷ Michaelskirche
The interior of St Michael's Church is surprisingly large. The massive barrel vaulting over the nave is the second largest after St Peter's Basilica in Rome.

Key

— Suggested route

❺ Deutsches Jagd- und Fischereimuseum
A huge collection of hunting and fishing exhibits is housed in the Augustinerkirche. The deconsecrated church, which has an ornate Rococo interior, once belonged to the Augustinian order.

Locator Map
See Street Finder maps pp238–41.

❹ ★ Frauenkirche
Heavily damaged in 1944–45, this imposing church, with its landmark dome-topped towers, has been rebuilt along Gothic lines.

❿ ★ Neues Rathaus
The ornate façade of the new town hall includes figures from Bavarian legend and history. The bronze statue at the top is the "Münchner Kindl" – a character that features in the city's heraldic arms.

St Mary's Column

ETTSTRASSE

RABEN

KAUFINGERSTRASSE

ROSENSTRASSE

RINDERMARKT

MARIEN-PLATZ

DIENERSTR

Isartor

Viktualienmarkt

❾ ★ Altes Rathaus
The old town hall was remodelled in its original 15th-century style in the late 19th century. It was rebuilt again after World War II. It now houses a collection of historic toys.

Interior of the Bürgersaal, featuring original 19th-century frescoes

❶ Bürgersaal

Neuhauser Strasse 14. **Map** 2 A4.
Tel (089) 219 97 20. Ⓤ or Ⓢ Karlsplatz.
🚊 18, 19, 20, 21, 27. Lower church
hall: **Open** 8:30am–7pm daily. Upper
church hall: **Open** 10:30am–noon daily.

This church belonging to the
Marian congregation was
designed by Giovanni Antonio
Viscardi and built by Johann
Georg Ettenhofer in 1709–10.
(The Marian congregation,
founded in 1563, is linked to the
Jesuit order.)
    The church was damaged
during World War II, but still
features original frescoes. In
the oratory is a figure of the
Guardian Angel by Ignaz
Günther (1770), a fine example
of south-Bavarian Rococo.
Rupert Mayer, parish priest
during World War II and
Munich's leading opponent of
Nazism, is buried in the crypt.

❷ Michaelskirche

St Michael's Church

Neuhauser Strasse 6. **Map** 2 A4.
Ⓤ or Ⓢ Karlsplatz. 🚊 18, 19, 20,
21, 27. **Open** 10am–7pm Mon & Fri,
8am–8:15pm Tue, 8am–7pm Wed,
Thu & Sat, 7am–10:15pm Sun.

The monumental St Michael's
Church was built by Duke
Wilhelm V for the Jesuits who

arrived here in 1559. The foundation stone was laid in 1585
and initial building work on the
first church, which was smaller
than the present one,
commenced in 1588. However,
the tower in front of the presbytery collapsed, demolishing
a large part of the building.
A transept and new presbytery
were added to the remaining part
of the building and the church
– which was the first Jesuit
church in northern Europe –
was consecrated in 1597. The

Statue of St Michael at the entrance
to Michaelskirche

interior of Michaelskirche is
awe-inspiring, with its wide, well-
proportioned nave, three pairs
of shallow chapels on either side,
a short transept and an elongated
presbytery. It is not certain who
was the architect of the project,
but it is believed that Wolfgang
Müller created the main body of
the church and Wendel Dietrich
the Mannerist façade. Later
extensions are thought to be
the work of a Dutch architect,
Friedrich Sustris.
    In the church crypt, which is
open to the public, are the
tombs of many members of the
Wittelsbach dynasty, including
King Ludwig II.

❸ Dreifaltigkeits-kirche

Holy Trinity Church

Pacellistrasse 6. **Map** 2 A3. 🚊 19.
Open 7:30am–7pm daily.

The Baroque church of the
Holy Trinity is one of the few
historic buildings in the city
that avoided bomb damage in
World War II. The church was
built as a votive gift from the
city's aristocracy and clergy
in the hope of averting the
dangers threatened by the
War of the Spanish Succession
(1702–14). The foundation
stone was laid in 1711 and

the church was consecrated seven years later. The royal architect, Giovanni Antonio Viscardi, assisted by Enrico Zucalli and Georg Ettenhofer, created a building that is one of the most beautiful examples of Italian Baroque in Munich. The church's original features include the dome fresco by Cosmas Damian Asam, *The Adoration of the Trinity*.

❹ Frauenkirche

Frauenplatz 1. **Map** 2 B4. **Tel** (089) 290 08 20 [U] or [S] Karlsplatz & Marienplatz. 🚋 19. Church: **Open** 7am–7pm Sat–Wed, 7am–8:30pm Thu, 7am–6pm Fri. Tower: **Open** 7am–7pm Sat–Wed, 7am–8:30pm Thu, 7am–6pm Fri.

The site of the Frauenkirche was originally occupied by a Marian chapel, built in the 13th century. Some two hundred years later, Prince Sigismund ordered a new, much bigger church to be built on the site. Its architects were Jörg von Halspach and Lukas Rottaler. The Frauenkirche was completed in 1488, though the distinctive copper onion domes were not added to its towers until 1525. The church is one of southern Germany's biggest Gothic structures, which can accommodate a congregation of about 2,000.

A triple-nave hall with no transept features rows of side chapels, a gallery surrounding the choir and a monumental western tower. The whole huge structure measures over 100 m (330 ft) in length and almost 40 m (130 ft) wide.

The church treasures that escaped destruction during World War II include a Marian painting, dating from around 1500, by Jan Polak; the altar of St Andrew in St Sebastian's chapel, with statues by Meister von Rabenden and paintings by Jan Polak, dating from 1510; and the monumental tomb of Emperor Ludwig IV of Bavaria, the work of Hans Krumpper (1619–22).

Carving on main Frauenkirche portal

❺ Deutsches Jagd- und Fischereimuseum

German Museum of Hunting and Fishing

Neuhauser Strasse 2. **Map** 2 A4. **Tel** (089) 22 05 22. [U] or [S] Marienplatz. 🚋 18, 19, 20, 21, 27. **Open** 9:30am–5pm Mon–Wed, Fri–Sun, 9:30am–9pm Thu. 📷

Immediately adjacent to St Michael's Church is the Augustinerkloster, the former Augustinian church, which now houses the Museum of Hunting and Fishing. The original building dates from around 1300 (the first Augustinian monks arrived here in 1294). It was rebuilt in the mid-15th century and then remodelled in the Baroque style in 1620–21. The church was deconsecrated in 1803.

Since 1966, the building's ornate Rococo interior has housed a very interesting museum, with a collection of weapons dating from the Renaissance, Baroque and Rococo periods, as well as hunting trophies and related paintings, prints and dioramas. Artists

Pulpit in the Rococo-style Asamkirche

represented in the museum's collection include several great names such as Rubens, Snyders and Antonio Pisanello.

❻ Asamkirche

Asams' Church

Sendlinger Strasse 32. **Map** 2 A5. [U] Sendlinger Tor. 🚋 16, 17, 18, 27. 🚌 52, 152. **Open** 8am–7:30pm daily. ✝ 5pm Tue, Thu, Fri; 10am Sun. 📷 noon Sat (May–Sep).

Officially known as St Johann-Nepomuk, this gem of Rococo architecture stands in Sendlingerstrasse and is part of a complex built by the Asam brothers in the mid-18th century. In 1729–30, the sculptor and stuccoist Egid Quirin Asam acquired two properties that he intended to convert into a family home. He subsequently acquired a plot adjacent to these properties, where he wished to build a church devoted to the newly canonized St Nepomuk, a Bohemian monk who had drowned in the Vltava river in Prague. Above the entrance to the church is a statue of the saint.

At the same time, Cosmas Damian, the brother of Egid Quirin Asam, bought a plot on which he built the presbytery. The church building adjoins the residential house of Egid Quirin. The two buildings were joined by a corridor and from one of his bedroom windows the artist could see the main altar.

In this small but unique church, the Asam brothers achieved a rare and striking unity of style. In the dimly lit interior, with its dynamically shaped single nave, no surface is left unembellished. The eye is drawn to the altar, which features a sculpted group of the Holy Trinity.

A Wilhelm von Kaulbach painting (1847) in the Stadtmuseum

❼ Stadtmuseum
Town Museum

St Jakobsplatz 1. **Map** 2 A5. **Tel** (089) 23 32 23 70. Ⓤ or Ⓢ Marienplatz. Ⓤ Sendlinger Tor. **Open** 10am–6pm Tue–Sun. 🅿 💻 🆆 **muenchner-stadtmuseum.de**

A few steps away from the Viktualienmarkt, on St Jakobsplatz, stands the Town Museum. Its rich collection has been housed since 1880 in the former arsenal building, which was built in 1491–93 by Lucas Rottaler. It is one of Munich's most fascinating museums, with exhibits such as *Typisch München!* (Typical Munich!) illustrating the everyday lives of the city's citizens from the Middle Ages to the present day.

Its greatest treasures are the famous ten dancing Moors by Erasmus Grasser (1480), carved in lime wood and originally numbering 18. Also on the ground floor, in the Waffenhalle, is a splendid collection of arms. Other displays include furniture (in styles ranging from Baroque to Art Deco), photographs, film, brewing equipment and musical instruments. There is also a large doll collection, which includes original puppets, and a collection of paintings and prints.

The museum regularly stages special exhibitions. A cinema, the *Filmmuseum*, puts on nightly showings of English-language films.

❽ Jüdisches Zentrum Jakobsplatz
Jewish Centre Jakobsplatz

St Jakobsplatz 16. **Map** 2 A5. Ⓤ or Ⓢ Marienplatz. **Tel** (089) 23 39 60 96. Jewish Museum: **Open** 10am–6pm Tue–Sun. 🅿 🆆 **juedisches-museum-muenchen.de**

The Jewish Museum, the Jewish Community Centre of Munich and Upper Bavaria, and the main synagogue, Ohel Jakob, together constitute a prestigious modern centre for Munich's Jewish community.

The museum is housed in a cube-shaped building. Three floors of exhibitions, plus a library and a learning centre, all provide extensive information on Jewish culture and history and highlight important aspects of contemporary Jewish life.

The synagogue is crowned by a light-flooded roof. The community centre contains the administrative department, the rabbinate, conference rooms, a kindergarten, a public full-time school, a youth and arts centre and a kosher restaurant.

❾ Viktualienmarkt

Peterplatz-Frauenstrasse. **Map** 2 B5. Ⓤ or Ⓢ Marienplatz. 🚌 52.

Right at the heart of the city is the Viktualienmarkt, a large square that has been the city's main marketplace for over 200 years. Apart from stalls selling vegetables and fruit brought in daily from suburban orchards or village gardens, the local beer

Colourfully laden market stalls in Munich's Viktualienmarkt

garden provides a welcome retreat for a beer or snack.

One of the features of the square is a statue of famous Munich actor and comedian Karl Valentin (1882–1948), also commemorated in the nearby Valentin Karlstadt Musäum.

An impressive view over the market can be enjoyed from the tower of Peterskirche (St Peter's Church), alongside the square.

Signs of the Zodiac adorning the clock face on the Altes Rathaus

❿ Altes Rathaus
Old Town Hall

Marienplatz 15. **Map** 2 B4. Ⓤ or Ⓢ Marienplatz. **Closed** to visitors. Spielzeugmuseum: **Tel** (089) 29 40 01. **Open** 10am–5:30pm daily. 🅿 🆆 **spielzeugmuseum-muenchen.de**

Munich's old town hall stands in the eastern part of Marienplatz, immediately next to the new town hall. The original building, which has been remodelled several times, was built in 1470–75 by Jörg von Halspach, who also designed the Marian church.

The building's present Neo-Gothic look is the result of remodelling work carried out between 1877 and 1934, when the nearby dual carriageway ring road was being built.

The interior of the building, which was restored following World War II bomb damage, features the Dance Hall with a wooden cradle vault. It is adorned with an old frieze featuring 87 (originally 99) heraldic arms painted by Ulrich Füetrer in 1478, and a further seven carved by Erasmus Grasser in 1477. The figures standing by the walls are copies of the famous dancing Moors, whose originals by Erasmus

Grasser (1480) are kept in the Town Museum (Stadtmuseum).

The lofty tower rising above the old city gate (Talbrucktor) was remade in 1975 based on pictures dating from 1493. Since 1983, the tower has housed the toy collection of the Spielzeugmuseum.

⓫ Neues Rathaus
New Town Hall

Marienplatz 8. **Map** 2 B4. **Tel** (089) 233 00. 🇺 or 🇸 Marienplatz.
Open Town Hall and Tower: May–Oct: 10am–7pm daily; Nov–Apr: 10am–5pm Mon–Fri. 🚫 🖵 Carillons: Mar–Oct: 11am, noon, 5pm daily; Nov–Feb: 11am, noon daily.

The Neo-Gothic new town hall standing in Marienplatz was built by Georg Hauberrisser in 1867–1909. Its 100-m (330-ft) high façade features a fascinating set of statues depicting Bavarian dukes, kings and electors, saints, mythical and allegorical figures as well as a variety of gargoyles inspired by medieval bestiaries. The central façade features an 80-m (260-ft) high clock tower, known as Glockenspiele.

Each day, at 11am and 5pm, the bells ring out a carillon, while mechanical knights fight a tournament and a crowd dances. The latter is a reenactment of the first coopers' dance, which was held in 1517 to boost the morale of citizens when they were beset by the plague. Other mechanical figures appear in the windows on the seventh floor in the evenings (9:30pm in summer, 7:30pm in winter). These are flanked by figures of the town guardsman carrying a lantern and the Guardian Angel blessing a Munich child, the *"Münchner Kindl"*.

Richly decorated entrance to the Museum Fünf Kontinente

Statue on façade of Neues Rathaus

⓬ Museum Fünf Kontinente
Five Continents Museum

Maximilianstrasse 42. **Map** 3 D4. **Tel** (089) 210 136 100. 🚉 19. **Open** 9:30am–5:30pm, Tue–Sun. 🚫 🖵

On the opposite side of the ring road from the Maximilianeum (the Upper Bavaria Government building) is the Bavarian museum of ethnography. Built in 1858–65, to a design by E Riedel, its façade is decorated with eight figures personifying the virtues of the Bavarian people: patriotism, diligence, magnanimity, piety, loyalty, justice, courage and wisdom. Originally intended to house the Bavarian National Museum (now in Prinzregentenstrasse), the building has been home to the ethnography museum since 1925. It is the second largest (after Berlin) ethnographic museum in Germany.

The origins of the museum's collection go back to 1702, when curios taken from the treasures of various Bavarian rulers were exhibited in a gallery in the gardens of the residence. Attention began to focus on ethnography after expansion of the collection in 1868. The museum currently houses some 300,000 exhibits depicting the art and culture of non-European nations, with a particular emphasis on the Far East (China and Japan), South America and Eastern and Central Africa. The collection is presented in a series of changing exhibitions.

⓭ Hofbräuhaus

Platzl 9. **Map** 2 C4. **Tel** (089) 290 136 100. 🇺 or 🇸 Marienplatz. **Open** 9am–11:30pm daily. 🌐 hofbraeuhaus.de

The Hofbräuhaus is the most popular beer hall in Munich and a great tourist attraction. Established as a court brewery in 1589 by Wilhelm V, it was originally housed in Alter Hof, but moved to Platzl in 1654. In 1830 permission was granted to build an inn where beer could be sold to the public.

The Neo-Renaissance form of the building dates from 1896. The Schwemme, on the ground floor, is a large hall with painted ceiling and room for about 1,000 guests. The Festsaal, on the first floor, has a barrel-shaped vault and can accommodate 1,300 guests.

In a courtyard, surrounded by chestnut trees, is the beer garden, which is always very popular during the summer.

Guests enjoying a drink in the beer garden of the Hofbräuhaus

⑭ Residenz

This former residence of Bavarian kings has housed a museum since 1920. Over the years, the original Wittelsbachs' castle, which had stood on the site since the 14th century, was gradually extended. Major work in the 17th century included new surroundings for the Brunnenhof and the construction of buildings around the imperial courtyard, Hofkapelle and Reiche Kapelle. Königsbau and Festsaalbau were added in the first half of the 19th century. The Renaissance façade includes two magnificent portals and features a statue of the Holy Virgin as Patroness of Bavaria (Patrona Boiariae).

Hofkapelle
This imposing chapel, dating from the early 17th century, was modelled on St Michael's Church. Vault decorations date from 1614.

Reiche Kapelle
This was the private chapel of Maximilian I. Though smaller than the Residenz's other chapel, it is richly furnished.

Grottenhof
In the eastern section of this courtyard is this grotto lined with crystal, coloured shells and tufa.

Antiquarium
The lavish Antiquarium banqueting hall was completed in 1571, and is the oldest part of the Residenz. The vaults above the windows have frescoes depicting 102 Bavarian towns and scenes.

★ Cuvilliés-Theater
Opened in 1753, this masterpiece of theatre architecture was designed by François de Cuvilliés, and is considered to be Europe's finest surviving Rococo theatre. The world premiere of Mozart's *Idomeneo* was staged in the theatre on 29 January 1781.

★ Schatzkammer V
Room V's collection includes items such as the Bavarian crown insignia and a sword belonging to Duke Christoph of Bavaria.

Entrance

Nationaltheater

Schatzkammer
Besides royal insignia, liturgical vessels and various everyday objects, the treasure house contains some unusual gold and jewellery items. The star attraction of Room III is this small equestrian statue of St George, the work (1586–97) of Friedrich Sustris.

⑮ Feldherrnhalle

Odeonsplatz. **Map** 2 B3.
🅤 Odeonsplatz. 🚊 19. 🚌 100.
Open daily.

Until 1816, the site of this monumental building was occupied by a Gothic town gate – Schwabinger Tor. In the early 19th century, however, when Kings Maximilian I Joseph and Ludwig I decided to expand Munich northwards and westwards, their chief architect, Leo von Klenze, ordered the gate to be pulled down, as it stood in the way of the prestigious thoroughfare (Ludwigstrasse) that he intended to build.

Built in 1841–44, the Feldherrnhalle was designed by Friedrich von Gärtner, who modelled it on the Loggia dei Lanzi in Florence. Intended as a monument to the heroes of Bavaria, the interior contains statues of two great military leaders, Johann Tilly and Karl Philipp von Wrede by Ludwig Schwanthaler.

The central carved composition devoted to the heroes of the 1870–71 Franco-Prussian War is much newer, dating from 1882. It was designed by Ferdinand von Miller.

The Feldherrnhalle was the scene of Hitler's unsuccessful "Beer-hall Putsch", after which he was arrested. This resulted in the loggia acquiring a certain cult status in Nazi propaganda.

Hitler and the Feldherrnhalle

On the evening of 8 November 1923, Adolf Hitler announced the start of the "people's revolution" in the Bürgerbräukeller and ordered the takeover of the central districts of Munich. On 9 November a march of some 2,000 people acting on his orders was stopped by a police cordon outside the Feldherrnhalle in Residenzstrasse. Four policemen and 16 of Hitler's supporters were shot. The marchers were dispersed, and Hitler fled to Uffing am Starnberger See, but was arrested and imprisoned. When Hitler finally came to power in 1933, he turned what became known as the Hitler-Putsch into a central element of the Nazi cult.

The accused in the trial against the participants in the Hitler-Putsch of 1923

⑯ St Kajetan

St Cajetan's Church

Salvatorplatz 2a. **Map** 2 B3. 🅤 or Ⓢ Marienplatz. 🚊 19. **Open** 7am–8pm daily. 🆆 **theatinerkirche.de**

In Odeonsplatz, next to Feldherrnhalle, stands one of the most magnificent churches in Munich, St Cajetan's Church. When Henrietta Adelaide of Savoy presented the Elector Ferdinand with his long-awaited heir, Maximilian, the happy parents vowed to build an abbey in commemoration. The project was given to an Italian architect, Agostino Baralli, who based his design on St Andrea della Valle, in Rome.

Although construction work on the church ended in 1690, the façade – designed by François de Cuvilliés – was not completed until 1765–68. The interior of the church is adorned with stuccos by Giovanni Antonio Viscardi and furnished in rich Baroque style. Its twin towers and copper dome are dominant features on the Munich skyline.

⑰ Haus der Kunst

Arts House

Prinzregentenstrasse 1. **Map** 3 D2.
Tel (089) 21 12 71 13. 🚌 100.
Open 10am–8pm daily (to10pm Thu).
🅿 🆆 **hausderkunst.de**

Built between 1933 and 1937, the Neo-Classical building is the work of a Nazi architect, Paul Ludwig Trost. It opened its doors in 1937 with a display of propaganda art, which was proclaimed by the Nazis as "truly German".

Since 1945 the building has become a dynamic centre of modern art that is famous for its temporary exhibitions.

Its central hall, the former Ehrenhalle (Hall of Honour), which was subdivided into smaller spaces, was reopened in stages, each stage accompanied by a special exhibition. In 2006 the hall once again became the centre of the building and is used as a space for events and temporary installations. In the

Pediment on the gable of Theatinerkirche, with copper dome behind foyer is a permanent exhibition documenting the history of the building. Oddly, the building also houses P1, one of Munich's most prestigious clubs.

From 2016, the museum will close while renovations by architect David Chipperfield are carried out.

⑱ Bayerisches Nationalmuseum
Bavarian National Museum

Prinzregentenstrasse 3. **Map** 3 E3. **Tel** (089) 211 24 01. 🚊 17. 🚌 100. **Open** 10am–5pm Tue–Wed, Fri–Sun, 10am–8pm Thu. 🅦 **bayerisches-nationalmuseum.de**

The Bavarian National Museum was founded in 1855 by King Maximilian II. Between 1894 and 1900 it acquired a new building in Prinzregentenstrasse, designed by Gabriel von Seidel; this building alone is worth a closer look. The complex structure consists of wings representing various architectural styles, while the ground floor features halls that are built in styles that are appropriate to their exhibits. This means that the visitor can see Romanesque and Gothic art in Neo-Romanesque and Neo-Gothic rooms, Renaissance art in Neo-Renaissance rooms and Baroque in Neo-Baroque rooms. The individual rooms have been arranged in subject groups, with paintings and sculptures supplemented by superb collections of decorative art and everyday objects, including furniture. The exhibits include a beautiful sculpture of the Madonna by Tilman Riemenschneider.

The first-floor collections are arranged thematically and include German porcelain, clocks, glass paintings, ivory

Conrad Meit's *Judith* (1515), Bavarian National Museum

carvings, textiles and gold items. Particularly interesting is a collection of small oil sketches, painted by artists when designing some large-scale compositions, such as an altar or a ceiling painting.

A special annexe houses the Bollert Collection, which contains sculptures from the late-Gothic period.

Poster advertising an exhibition at the Schack-Galerie

⑲ Schack-Galerie

Prinzregentenstrasse 9. **Map** 3 E3. **Tel** (089) 23 80 52 24. **Open** 10am–6pm Wed–Sun (1st & 3rd Wed of month. to 8pm). 🚌 100. 🚊 17. 🅦 **pinakothek.de**

The magnificent collection of German paintings on display in this gallery come from the private collection of Adolf Friedrich von Schack. They are housed in this elegant building built in 1907 by Max Littmann for use by the Prussian Legation.

As Schack's main interest was in 19th-century painting, the gallery features works that represent the Romantic period, including Leo von Klenze and Carl Spitzweg, as well as witty, fairy-tale works by Moritz von Schwind. Particularly notable are his *Morning, In the Woods* and *Rübezahl* – in which the mythical Guardian of the

Riesengebirge Mountains wanders through an enchanted forest. Late 19th-century painters are represented by Franz von Lenbach, Anselm Feuerbach and, above all, by Arnold Böcklin. Böcklin's Romantic works, which are full of symbolism, include *Villa on the Coast* and *Man Scaring a Deer*. The gallery has a large collection of landscapes, including Italian scenes by German masters, as well as a valuable collection of paintings devoted to historic themes.

⑳ Archäologische Staatssammlung
Prehistory Museum

Lerchenfeldstrasse 2. **Map** 3 E2. **Tel** (089) 211 24 02. 🚊 17. 🚌 100. **Open** 9:30am–5pm Tue–Sun. 🅦 **archaeologie-bayern.de**

Immediately adjacent to the Bavarian National Museum is the Prehistory Museum, which was founded in 1885 by King Ludwig II. Since 1976, this spacious building has housed a rich collection of artifacts from various parts of Bavaria. The oldest items in the collection date from the Palaeolithic era while later exhibits illustrate the region's early history. The collection includes Bronze Age, Roman and early medieval treasures.

A 3rd-century mosaic floor from a Roman villa, on display in the Prehistory Museum

㉑ Bayerische Staatsbibliothek
Bavarian National Library

Ludwigstrasse 16. **Map** 2 C1, C2.
Tel (089) 286 38 23 22. Ⓤ Odeonsplatz, Universität. **Open** times vary.
🚹 (telephone bookings required).
🌐 **bsb-muenchen.de**

The monumental Bavarian national library was designed by Friedrich von Gärtner, who took over, in 1827, from Leo von Klenze as the main architect on the prestigious Ludwigstrasse project – commissioned by King Ludwig I. Gärtner was also responsible for the Feldherrnhalle, Siegestor, St Ludwig's Church, and the university building.

This massive structure, in a style reminiscent of the Italian Renaissance, was erected between 1832 and 1843. Its external staircase is adorned with the seated figures of Thucydides, Hippocrates, Homer and Aristotle, by Ludwig von Schwanthaler.

Equally impressive are the stairs leading to the main rooms, which are modelled on the Scala dei Gianti of the Doge Palace in Venice. With its collection of 5 million volumes, the library is on a par with the Berlin Staatsbibliothek *(see p72)* as the biggest in Germany.

The imposing twin-tower façade of Munich's Ludwigskirche

㉒ Ludwigskirche
St Ludwig's Church

Ludwigstrasse 20. **Map** 2 C1.
Ⓤ Universität. **Open** 8am–8pm daily (to 8:45pm Tue; 7pm Sat).

Inspired by the Romanesque churches of Lombardy, Friedrich von Gärtner built this monumental basilica between 1829 and 1844.

The vast interior features magnificent frescoes designed by the main exponent of the Nazarene style, Peter von Cornelius, and painted by his associates. Von Cornelius himself painted the massive choir fresco, *The Last Judgement*, which rivals in size Michelangelo's *Last Judgement*.

㉓ Museum Brandhorst

Theresienstr. 35a. **Map** 2 B1. **Tel** (089) 238 05 22 86. Ⓤ Köningsplatz.
🚌 100, 154. 🚊 27. **Open** 10am–6pm Tue–Sun, 10am–8pm Thu. 🅿️
🌐 **museum-brandhorst.de**

Museum Brandhorst features the modern and contemporary art of the Udo and Anette Brandhorst collection. It comprises over 700 works, including more than 60 works by Cy Twombly, and an impressively large collection of Andy Warhol's works. Other artists represented include Joseph Beuys, Damien Hirst, Jean-Michel Basquiat, Sigmar Polke and Mike Kelley.

Original editions of over a hundred books illustrated by Picasso are also on display.

㉔ Neue Pinakothek
The New Pinakothek

Barer Strasse 27. **Map** 2 A1. **Tel** (089) 23 80 51 95. Ⓤ Theresienstrasse.
🚊 2. 🚊 27. **Open** 10am–6pm Thu–Mon, 10am–8pm Wed. 🅿️
🌐 **neue-pinakothek.de**

This building, designed by architect Alexander von Branca from 1975–1981, features a representative collection of German works. This includes Neo-Classicism through Romanticism, the "Nazarenes",

German and Austrian Biedermeier, Realism, Historicism, Impressionism, Pointillism and Secession paintings.

It also includes works by renowned French Realists, Impressionists, Post-Impressionists and Symbolists, purchased in 1909–11, when the gallery's director was the art historian Hugo von Tschudi.

The space between the Old and New Pinakothek is a sculpture park that features a work by Henry Moore.

Goya's *Marquesa de Caballero* in the Neue Pinakothek

㉕ Alte Pinakothek
The Old Pinakothek

See pp226–7.

㉖ Pinakothek der Moderne

Barer Strasse 40. **Map** 2 A2. **Tel** (089) 23 80 53 60. Ⓤ Königsplatz. 🚌 53.
🚊 27. **Open** 10am–6pm Tue–Wed & Fri–Sun, 10am–8pm Thu. 🅿️🚹📷
🌐 **pinakothek-der-moderne.de**

Designed by German architect Stephan Braunfels, this gallery complements the collections in the Alte and Neue Pinakoteks, bringing together the worlds of art, design, graphics, jewellery and architecture under one roof.

Highlights include Cubist works by Picasso and Georges Braque, and paintings by Matisse, Giorgio De Chirico and Max Beckmann. Pop Art, Minimal

Façade of the Glyptothek, with its central column portico

Art and photorealism are also represented. The international design collection is outstanding.

㉗ NS-Dokumenta-tionszentrum

NS-Documentation Centre for the History of National Socialism

Brienner Strasse 34. **Map** 1 F2. **Tel** (089) 23 36 70 00. Ⓤ Königsplatz. **Open** 10am–7pm Tue–Sun. 🖼 Ⓦ **ns-dokumentationszentrum-muenchen.de**

This documentation centre in a six-storey white cube is a prominent reminder of Munich's role in the rise of Nazi ideology. Built on the site of the so-called Braunes Haus ("brown house"), the former party headquarters of the Nazi Party, the centre has excellent permanent and temporary exhibitions, a learning centre and an educational programme.

㉘ Glyptothek

Glyptotheca

Königsplatz 3. **Map** 1 F2. **Tel** (089) 28 61 00. Ⓤ Königsplatz. **Open** 10am–5pm Tue–Sun, 10am–8pm Thu.

The Königsplatz complex, including Glyptothek and Propylaeum, was the work of Leo von Klenze. It was built in 1816–34 to house Ludwig I's collection of Greek and Roman sculptures and was the first public museum to be devoted to a single art discipline.

The most famous pieces in the museum's collection are the ancient statue of a young man, *Apollo of Terentia* (560 BC), the tomb stele of Mnesareta (380 BC) and sculptures from the front of the Aphaia temple of Aegina.

㉙ Staatliche Antiken-sammlungen

The National Collection of Antiquities

Königsplatz 1. **Map** 1 F2. **Tel** (089) 59 98 88 30. Ⓤ Königsplatz. **Open** 10am–5pm Tue–Sun, 10am–8pm Wed. 🖼

Built in 1838–48 by Georg Friedrich Ziebland, this building is on the south side of the Königsplatz. Since 1967, it has housed one of the world's finest collections of antique vases from the 5th and 6th centuries BC. There are also many other masterpieces of Greek, Roman and Etruscan ornamental art, jewellery and small statues. Among the famous exhibits is a golden Greek necklace from the 4th century BC.

㉚ Propyläen

Königsplatz. **Map** 1 F2. Ⓤ Königsplatz.

Derived from the Propylaea to the Athenian Acropolis, this magnificent Neo-Classical structure stands at the end of Brienner Strasse and is visible from as far as Karolinenplatz. Built by Leo von Klenze in 1846–62, its austere form, featuring three portals provides an excellent final touch to the composition of Königsplatz by linking together the National Collection of Antiquities and the Glyptotheca.

The Propyläen is also a symbolic gateway to the new parts of the city. It was funded by the private foundation of King Ludwig I, although built after his abdication.

The carved decorations depict scenes from the Greek War of Liberation against Turkey (1821–29), led by King Otto I, son of Ludwig I.

㉛ Lenbachhaus

Luisenstrasse 33. **Map** 1 F2. **Tel** (089) 23 33 20 00. Ⓤ Königsplatz. Kunstbau: **Open** 10am–9pm Tue, 10am–6pm Wed–Sun. Ⓦ **lenbachhaus.de**

This Italian-style villa was built between 1887 and 1891 by Gabriel von Seidl for painter Franz von Lenbach.

Since 1929, it has housed the Municipal Art Gallery. As well as masterpieces such as *Portrait of a Man* by Jan Polak (c.1500), it also has the world's biggest collection of works by the *Blaue Reiter* (The Blue Rider) artists. Kandinsky was a leading proponent of this movement.

The Kunstbau, part of Lenbachhaus, is in a subway station under Königsplatz. It features temporary exhibitions.

Fountain in the beautiful front garden of the Lenbachhaus

㉕ Alte Pinakothek

Construction work on the Alte Pinakothek began in 1826 and was completed 10 years later. Leo von Klenze designed the Italian Renaissance-style building. During the Renaissance period, Wilhelm IV the Steadfast (ruled 1508–50) decided to adorn his residence with historic paintings. By the 18th century, an outstanding collection of 14th- to 18th-century paintings had been amassed. While a major renovation project to improve the lighting and make the building energy-efficient is carried out the museum remains open, but admission may be reduced.

St Luke Painting the Madonna (c.1484)
This is one of the most frequently copied masterpieces by the Dutch painter Roger van der Weyden.

★ Four Apostles (1526)
These two panels were painted by Albrecht Dürer, a founding figure of the German school of art. They were acquired in 1627 by Maximilian I from the town of Nuremberg.

Emperor Charles V (1548)
This portrait was painted by the Venetian artist Titian during the Emperor's visit to the Reich's Parliament in Augsburg.

Main entrance

Key

- ☐ Flemish and Dutch paintings
- ☐ German paintings
- ☐ Italian paintings
- ☐ French paintings
- ☐ Spanish paintings
- ☐ Temporary exhibitions
- ☐ Non-exhibition space

Adoration of the Magi (1504)
The depiction of the adoration is just one small part of the most important altarpiece by Hans Holbein the Elder.

Rape of the Daughters of Leukippos (1618)
A highlight of the museum is the Rubens collection, which includes his depiction of the abduction of Hilaeria and Phoibe by Castor and Pollux.

VISITORS' CHECKLIST

Practical Information
Barer Strasse 27. **Map** 2 A1.
Tel (089) 23 80 52 16.
Open 10am–6pm Wed–Sun, 10am–8pm Tue. (admission free to under 18s.)
w alte-pinakothek.de

Transport
100. 27. **U** Königsplatz.

Gallery Guide

The ground-floor rooms of the gallery are devoted to the works of German old masters dating from the 16th and 17th centuries. On the first floor are works by Dutch, Flemish, French, German, Italian and Spanish artists.

First floor

★ **Descent from the Cross** (1633)
Rembrandt's dramatic vision of the Saviour's sacrifice emotively depicts Christ's passion.

Disrobing of Christ (c.1583–84)
The gallery's small but interesting collection of Spanish paintings includes this work by El Greco, one of his three most important compositions.

Ground floor

★ **Land of Cockaigne** (1567)
In this vividly detailed painting by Pieter Bruegel the Elder, the Flemish artist depicts the mythical land of plenty. The work is an ironic condemnation of gluttony and laziness, themes that are depicted in its many humorous scenes.

❷ Schloss Nymphenburg

One of Europe's most beautiful palaces, Schloss Nymphenburg grew up around an Italianate villa built in 1663–64 for the Electress Henriette-Adelaide to a design by Agostino Barelli. The palace was dedicated to the pastoral goddess Flora and her nymphs, hence the name. Several additions were made over the years, including four pavilions. These were designed by Joseph Effner and Enrico Zuccalli who directed works from 1715. Built to the side of the original villa, these were connected by arcaded passageways.

★ Gallery of Beauties
Portraits of royal favourites include this one of Helene Sedlmayr, a 17-year-old girl from Munich.

Entrance to Schloss Nymphenburg
Seen in this view are the original Italianate villa and two of the side pavilions that were added later.

Marstallmuseum
The former stables house a collection of carriages that once belonged to Bavarian rulers. They include the magnificent carriages of Ludwig II.

Porcelain Factory
Established in 1747 by Franz Anton Bustelli and transferred to Nymphenburg in 1761, this is one of the oldest porcelain factories in Europe.

Key

— Suggested route

KEY

① **Museum Mensch und Natur** is devoted to the research of geology and human biology.

★ Amalienburg
The interior of this hunting lodge in the Schlosspark is a superb example of Rococo style by François de Cuvilliés.

Magdalenenklause
After a lifetime of revels, Maximilian Emanuel commissioned a hermitage where he could pray and meditate. It was completed in 1725.

Badenburg

Pagodenburg

Lackkabinett
This small 17th-century cabinet owes its name to its panels of black and red Chinese lacquer.

Botanical Garden
A collection of botanical specimens, including many rare plants, is featured in this fascinating garden.

★ Festsaal (Steinernen Saal)
Featuring decorations devoted to the goddess Flora, this vast Rococo ballroom is the work of father and son Johann Baptist and Franz Zimmermann.

Impressive panorama from the platform of the television tower in Olympiapark

③ Olympiapark

Tel (089) 30 670. Ⓤ Olympiazentrum.
⊞ 20, 21. 🚌 173. Television tower:
Open 9am–midnight daily. ♿
ⓦ **olympiapark.de**

Built for the 1972 Olympic
Games, this vast sports stadium
can be spotted from almost anywhere in Munich, as it is the site
of a 290-m (950-ft) high television
tower, the Olympiaturm. At the
top of the tower there is a
viewing platform that affords
amazing views, and a restaurant.
   The stadium has three main
facilities: the Olympic Stadium,
which seats 62,000 spectators,
the Olympic Hall and the Swimming Hall. In what is one of the
most original constructions of
20th-century German architecture, all three are covered by a
vast transparent canopy,
stretched between a series of tall
masts to form an irregular tent.
   The stadium includes many
other facilities, such as an
indoor skating rink, a cycle
racing track and tennis courts.

The sports complex is located
beside the park's artificial lake.
   Apart from sporting events,
the Olympiapark hosts many
popular events, including
fireworks displays and regular
open-air rock and pop concerts
in the summer months.
   Next to the park are the BMW
Museum and BMW Welt,
featuring the world's largest
permanent BMW collection.

③ Englischer Garten

Ⓤ Giselastrasse. 🚌 54. **Map** 3 E1

The idea of creating this garden,
which would be open to all the
inhabitants of Munich and not
only to its aristocracy, came
from Count von Rumford, an
American-born chemist and
physicist who lived in Bavaria
from 1784. As the region's
Minister of War, he was
responsible for reorganizing the
Bavarian army. His idea of
creating a garden of this size –
the garden covers an area of
5 sq km (1,235 acres) –
right in the centre of a
large city, was quite
unique in Germany. In
1789, taking advantage
of his influential
position, he persuaded
Karl Theodor to put his
plans into action.
   The project leader
was Friedrich Ludwig
von Sckell. He was
brought to Munich from
Schwetzingen by the
Elector to create the
garden on an area of
former marshland.
Opened in 1808, the

Karl-Theodor-Park is today
known simply as the Englischer
Garten (English Garden). It is a
popular place for long walks,
jogging or just lying on the
grass in the cool shade of a
spreading old tree.
   There are some interesting
old buildings in the park, such
as the Monopteros, a Neo-
Classical temple by Leo von
Klenze (1837), and the Chinese
Tower (1789–90), which is
similar to the pagoda in
London's Kew Gardens. The
Tower stands in one of the
park's beer gardens.
   It is also worth dropping in
to the Japanese Teahouse,
where the gentle art of tea
brewing is demonstrated.

③ Deutsches Museum

See pp232–3.

Franz von Stuck's *Die Sünde*, on display in
the Villa Stuck

③ Villa Stuck

Prinzregentenstrasse 60. **Tel** (089) 45
55 51 0. ⊞ 18. 🚌 100. **Open** 11am–
6pm Tue–Sun. ♿

This villa was the home of the
famous painter Franz von Stuck,
the co-founder of the Munich
Secession school of painting.
As well as numerous portraits,
nudes and sculptures, Von
Stuck was the creator of many
mythological and allegorical
scenes, all painted in dark
colours and full of eroticism.

Chinese Tower in the Englischer Garten

Submarine used in the film *Das Boot*, displayed in Bavaria-Filmstadt

These include eight variations (1893) on the theme of sin. His *Amazon* (1897) stands in front of the villa.

Franz von Stuck built the villa in 1897–98, to his own design, decorating it with his own paintings and sculptures. Since 1968, it has housed a museum. A permanent exhibition of Stuck's work is displayed in the magnificent music room on the ground floor, while the second-floor rooms are used for temporary exhibitions devoted mainly to early 20th-century art.

➌ Bavaria-Filmstadt

Bavariafilmplatz 7. **Tel** (089) 64 99 20 00. 🚋 25. **Open** Apr–Oct: 9am–6pm daily; Nov–Mar: 10am–5pm daily. 📷 only; in English at 1pm daily. 📷
📹 **filmstadt.de**

Commonly known as Holly-wood on Isar, this vast site in the southern suburb of Geiselgasteig covers an area of over 3.5 sq km (865 acres).

Since 1919 the world's greatest cinema stars have worked here, including Orson Welles and Billy Wilder. The British film director Alfred Hitchcock made his first films here (*The Pleasure Garden*, 1925 and *The Mountain Eagle*, 1926). Elizabeth Taylor, Gina Lollobrigida and Romy Schneider have all stood in front of the cameras here.

Strolling visitors to the site will often come across some well-known characters who have appeared in films such as *E.T.* or *The Neverending Story*, which were filmed here. The sets of other films made here, including *Enemy Mine* and

Cabaret, can also be seen. You can also peep into the submarine that was reconstructed for Wolfgang Petersen's classic film *Das Boot* (1981) – the film follows the voyage of a submarine during World War II. The Bullyversum (named after "Bully" Herbig, a German comedian, actor and director) is an interactive 3-D adventure.

VIP tours of the Filmstadt include fascinating demonstrations of many technical film-making tricks and techniques. A special attraction is the cinema called Showscan, whose seats move according to the story on the screen, giving visitors the sensation of a trip through the universe or of flying through the tunnels of an old silver mine.

Oktoberfest

Munich's Oktoberfest is one of the biggest folk fairs in Europe. In 1810 the site on which it is held was the venue for a horse race, held to celebrate the marriage of Ludwig (later King of Bavaria) and Thérèse von Saxe-Hildburghausen. A few years later it became the venue for an autumn fair that has grown into an enormous event over the years. Chief amongst the attractions is beer, drunk in vast quantities, in marquees erected by the breweries. The festival starts in late September with a huge procession through the town

➌ Theresienwiese

Theresienhöhe. 🚇 Theresienwiese.
🎡 Oktoberfest (Sep–Oct).

For most of the year this is simply a vast oval meadow encircled by the Bavariaring. Theresienwiese comes into its own once a year, however, during the Oktoberfest. Then it turns into a gigantic, boisterous beer-drinking venue, with stalls, marquees, funfair and loud music.

Towering above the meadow is a monumental 18-m (59-ft) high statue, symbol of the state of Bavaria. Made in 1844–50, the statue is the work of Ludwig Schwanthaler. It incorporates an internal staircase leading to the figure's head, where there is a viewing platform.

Just behind the statue is the Ruhmeshalle, a Neo-Classical building surrounded by a colonnade. Designed by Leo von Klenze and built in 1843–53, the building contains numerous busts of eminent Bavarians.

Bavaria statue in Theresienwiese

Revellers at the annual Oktoberfest in Theresienwiese

and the ceremonial opening of the first barrel of beer. It finishes, 16 days later, on the first Sunday of October.

㉟ Deutsches Museum

The Deutsches Museum, one of the oldest and largest museums of technology and engineering in the world, draws over 1.4 million visitors each year. It was founded in 1903 by Oskar von Miller, an engineer. The building in which it is housed, located on the Museum Island, was designed by Gabriel von Seidl in 1925. The collections cover most aspects of technology, from its history to its greatest achievements. The museum also houses one of the world's largest libraries of technology.

Exterior of the Museum
The building combines Neo-Baroque, Neo-Classical and modern elements.

Decorative Arts
This plate with the portrait of a lady from Ludwig I's "gallery of beauty" is an example of reproduction techniques applied to porcelain. The ceramics section illustrates the development of faience, stoneware and porcelain.

Second floor

★ Physics
Galileo's workshop features a large collection of the scientific equipment used by the famous astronomer and physicist to establish the basic laws of mechanics.

First floor

★ Pharmaceutics
Among the exhibits in this section is a model of a human cell magnified 350,000 times and graphically illustrating how it functions.

Museum Guide

The museum's 20,000 exhibits are displayed over seven floors. While those on the lower floors include heavy vehicles and sections on chemistry, physics, scientific instruments and aeronautics, those on the middle floors relate to the decorative arts. The upper floors are devoted to astronomy, computers and microelectronics.

Main entrance

Ground floor

Sixth floor

Fifth floor

Fourth floor

Third floor

Telecommunications
The Philips camera of 1967 was one of the first colour television cameras in the world.

Key to Floorplan

- 🟦 Design and Technology
- 🟦 Centre for New Technology
- 🟦 Kids' Kingdom
- 🟦 Physics and Chemistry
- 🟦 Musical Instruments
- 🟦 Decorative Arts
- 🟦 Time, Weights and Measures
- 🟦 Automation, Microelectronics and Telecommunications
- 🟦 Astronomy
- 🟦 Agriculture and Geodesy
- 🟦 Aviation
- 🟦 Miscellaneous

★ Musical Instruments
The keyboard instruments room contains the earliest southern German organ and a 17th-century inlaid harpsichord.

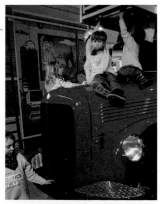

Kids' Kingdom
This is an area where children between the ages of 3 and 8 can learn about science and technology in a fun and imaginative way. There are many exciting exhibits, including a giant guitar, a fire engine and an electric light cinema.

SHOPPING IN MUNICH

Munich often claims to be Germany's richest and most sophisticated city, and so when it comes to shopping you are sure not to be disappointed. The key shopping areas are dotted around the centre of the city. You can conveniently walk around the pedestrianized central area, with numerous options for taking a break for lunch or a coffee. Not to be missed is the visual and gourmet treat of the Viktualienmarkt food market, the classic department store Ludwig Beck and some of the smaller speciality stores tucked away in side streets. In the less commercial shopping streets, stores tend to open late morning or in the afternoon only.

Main Shopping Areas

Munich's key luxury shopping street is Maximilianstrasse along with those streets connected to it, namely Theatinerstrasse, Brienerstrasse and Residenzstrasse. Here you will find all the top international brands and jewellery stores. For more affordable and high street shops head to the central pedestrianized area between Kaufingerstrasse, Neuhauserstrasse and Marienplatz. Here you will find family stores, large chains, mid-market fashion, souvenirs and department stores. For less conventional areas with small specialist boutiques and local designers seek out the Glockenbachviertel around Hans-Sachs Strasse, or streets radiating out from Gärtnerplatz, home to the Art Nouveau State Theatre and relaxed cafés. Schwabing is the young Bohemian area with a variety of casualwear and jeanswear stores, plus fashion boutiques and plenty of laid-back bistros and coffee bars.

Department Stores and Shopping Centres

The most famous department store in Munich is **Ludwig Beck**, which has a particularly impressive Christmas decorations department in December. **Galeria Kaufhof** is another large national department store chain offering several floors of goods. Shopping Centres *(Einkaufspassagen)* are also aplenty. **Fünf Höfe** ("the five courtyards") is central and upmarket. It sits between Theatiner, Maffei, Kardinal-Faulhaber and Salvator streets and mixes shopping, art and culture with cafés including a great restaurant/café attached to the Kunsthalle art museum. Munich has three other large shopping malls. **Olympia-Einkaufszentrum** (OEZ) is vast with over 140 stores on two levels. **Perlacher Einkaufs-passage (PEP)** shopping mall (PEP) has over 110 stores. The **Riem Arcaden** is home to the largest branch of H&M, a huge Lego store, C&A and Ludwig Beck Fashion.

Pedestrianized shopping area in central Munich

Fashion

Munich has a wide variety of shops for clothes and accessories. Try the following boutiques to find Munich-style chic. **Theresa** has the best choice of designer fashion and accessories, while **Trachten Angermaier** sells Bavarian folk costumes, including dirndls, and **Off & Co** in Schwabing has fashion items for men and women. Hohenzollernstrasse in Schwabing is a good place to shop for youthful street fashion and trainers. For traditional Bavarian Loden costumes take a look in **Lodenfrey**.

Children's Shops

Munich is a stylish and expensive city and parents love to dress their children accordingly. This means there are some good shopping opportunities for kids' clothing and toys, mainly in the department stores and C&A. A large central store for mother, baby and toys is **Schlichting**, as well as

The exclusive shopping centre, Fünf Höfe

One of the city's regularly held flea markets

Phelinchen for fashionable clothing for children up to 8 years old. **Obletter Spielwaren** is the largest and best toy shop in town. **Die Puppenstube** is also good for old-fashioned toys and gifts.

Flea Markets

Flea markets are popular, especially at the weekends. Most take place on Saturday, some every two weeks and most only from spring to late autumn. The key ones around Munich are **Zenith Flohmarkt** and **Antik Palast** flea market at Lilienthalallee, every weekend, and **Flohmarkt**

Riem, the largest flea market in Bavaria, at the trade show grounds.

Food Shopping

Viktualienmarkt *(see p218)* is a huge produce market, selling fruit, vegetables, spices, meat, poultry, fish, preserves and flowers. It is a feast for all the senses and a permanent fixture – open daily. *Bio* is the German word for organic and Germans have always been enthusiastic about organic produce. **Basic Bio** is a good organic supermarket in the city centre. For a selection of gourmet treats head to **Dallmayr** or **Käfer**, the city's top

delicatessens, while butchers' shops sell the famous Bavarian white sausages.

Christmas Market

Munich holds a traditional Christmas market *(Christkindlmarkt)* from the first week of Advent until Christmas Eve. The market is a great tourist attraction and special trips are organized from all over Europe. Wooden stalls sell a huge variety of handcrafted decorations, in particular wooden mangers and tree decorations, all delicately carved, in addition to candles, ornaments, food and mulled wine.

Christkindlmarkt, Munich's Christmas market

DIRECTORY

Department Stores and Shopping Centres

Fünf Höfe
Theatinerstrasse.
Map 2 B4.
🔲 fuenfhoefe.de

Galeria Kaufhof
Kaufingerstrasse 1–5.
Map 2 B4.
Tel (089) 231851.
🔲 galeria-kaufhof.de

Ludwig Beck
Marienplatz 11.
Map 2 B4.
Tel (089) 236910.
🔲 ludwigbeck.de

Olympia-Einkaufszentrum
Hanauer Strasse 68.
🔲 olympia-einkaufszentrum.de

Perlacher Einkaufspassage (PEP)
Ollenhauerstrasse 6.
🔲 einkaufscenter-neuperlach.de

Riem Arcaden
Willy-Brandt-Platz 5.
🔲 riem-arcaden.de

Fashion

Lodenfrey
Maffeistrasse 7. **Map** 2 B4.
🔲 lodenfrey.com

Off & Co
Promenadeplatz 1.
🔲 offandco.com

Theresa
Maffeistrasse 3. **Map** 2 B4.
🔲 mytheresa.com

Trachten Angermaier
Rosental 11 and Landsberger Str. 101–103.
🔲 trachten-angermaier.de

Children's Shops

Die Puppenstube
Luisenstrasse 68.
Tel (089) 2723267.

Obletter Spielwaren
Karlsplatz 11.
🔲 obletter.de

Phelinchen
Croissant-Rust-Strasse 1.
🔲 phelinchen.de

Schlichting
Maximilianstrasse 35.
Map 2 B4.
🔲 schlichting.de

Flea Markets

Antik Palast
Lilienthalallee 29.
🔲 antikpalast muenchen.de

Flohmarkt Riem
Am Messeturm.
Tel (089) 960 51632.
🔲 flohmarkt-riem.com

Zenith Flohmarkt
Lilienthalallee.
Tel 0176 6287 6374.
🔲 flohmarkt-freimann.de

Food Shopping

Basic Bio
Westenriederstrasse 11
Map 2 C5.
Tel (089) 242 0890.
🔲 basic-ag.de

Dallmayr
Dienerstrasse 14–15.
Map 2 B4.
🔲 dallmayr.de

Käfer
Prinzregentenstrasse 73.
🔲 feinkost-kaefer.de

Viktualienmarkt
Petersplatz-Frauenstrasse.
Map 2 B5.

ENTERTAINMENT IN MUNICH

Munich is best known for the Oktoberfest, the Olympic grounds and Hofbräuhaus, but it also has an international reputation as a city of culture. There are 56 theatres, three large orchestras and one opera house. Munich has the rich and the powerful of its past to thank for creating and preserving its many splendid venues. This cultured metropolis on the Isar caters to all tastes, from traditional to modern, whether in theatre, music or film. There are several festivals during the year, as well as various sporting events, when the city comes alive, attracting visitors from all over the world.

Entertainment Guides and Tickets

Munich Found is the best events magazine and the **Munich Tourist Board** has comprehensive listings of events happening all over Munich. Also, check the Thursday edition of *Süddeutsche Zeitung* and the daily *Münchner Merkur*.

You can book tickets direct from box offices by phone or in person. There are also two **Zentraler Kartenverkauf** ticket kiosks in Marienplatz underground concourse, or use the **Abendzeitung Schalterhalle** (kiosk).

Theatre, Opera and Classical Music

State theatres are subsidized and so tickets are very reasonably priced. The Bavarian State Orchestra, Opera and Ballet all perform at the **Nationaltheater**. The **Deutsches Theater** offers musicals and shows, while the **Prinzregententheater** has the Bavarian State Opera and a concert hall. The Art Nouveau **Staatstheater am Gärtnerplatz** presents opera, ballet, operetta, musicals and the Symphony Orchestra. **Gasteig Culture Center** is a world-class concert hall, home to the Munich Philharmonic Orchestra. In July the city also hosts an opera festival that has been running since 1875.

Music and Dance

The **Pasinger Fabrik** offers a good programme of jazz, chansons and café theatre. There are numerous dance events and dance clubs. Big name artists, such as James Blunt, Massive Attack and the Rolling Stones, tend to perform at the **Circus Krone Bau**, **Zenith Kulturhalle**, Gasteig Culture Center, **Olympiahalle** and the **Olympic Stadium**.

Film

As the centre of the German film industry Munich offers 76 cinemas, the **Bavaria Film Studios** and a college for film and television. Try the English tour of the studios daily at 1pm.

Munich's world-famous Oktoberfest

The **Munich Film Festival** in July boasts over 200 films on 15 screens, almost all of them German, European or world premieres.

Festivals

Munich's most famous festival is the **Oktoberfest**. From late September to mid-October it takes over a dedicated fairground, Theresienwiese, with beer tents, traditional Bavarian brass bands, people dressed in traditional Bavarian costume (*Trachten*), fairground rides and the famous iced gingerbread hearts, *Lebkuchen*. There is also the **Tollwood Festival** in July and December, which has music, food, a circus, performances in tents, family fun and a craft fair. Munich also celebrates the *Dult* on three occasions throughout the year. *Dult* is the old word for street fair or market and there are traditional stalls and merry-go-rounds. Carnival or *Fasching* is celebrated throughout Munich with parties, processions and dressing up, but it is not as important here as in other cities.

Sport

Most Münchners love the outdoors. Many make regular

The imposing Nationaltheater on Max-Joseph-Platz

Munich's ultra-modern Allianz Arena

trips to the not too distant Alps. Running, skiing, rollerblading, cycling, Nordic walking and football are all very popular. The English Garden in the city centre is a huge park where people rollerblade, cycle, run or just meet up with friends.

Munich has two football teams: FC Bayern and TSV 1860 München, also known as "the Lions" because they are sponsored by the Löwenbräu Munich brewery with a lion as its coat of arms. The **Allianz Arena** is the fantastic stadium built for the 2006 World Cup. It is an architectural marvel which lights up in various colours.

For Bayern Munich merchandise head to the **FC Bayern Shop** in the Arena. The shop website gives details of other stores located at Central Station and the Hofbräuhaus.

Other key sporting events are the Bavarian International Tennis Championships (ATP tournament), the BMW International Golf Open and Munich Blade Night, Monday evenings from April to September, when rollerbladers take over the streets. Runners will enjoy the Media Marathon and also the Münchner Stadtlauf (city run). A sport unique to Munich is surfing on the River Isar at the weirs.

Kids' Entertainment

Children will love Kids Kingdom – **Kinderreich** – in the Deutsches Museum. The area is designated for children and has giant interactive games and water games, plus a real fire engine. Adults can only enter with their kids. Several playgrounds can be found along the River Isar in the city centre, but the best is **Westpark Spielzone Ost**, which can be reached by the underground. The **Sea Life Olympiapark** centre also provides an excellent outing, as does the zoo at **Tierpark Hellabrunn**.

Sea life exhibit at Olympiapark, Munich

DIRECTORY

MUNICH STREET FINDER

Map references given in this chapter for sights (and in the Munich hotel and restaurant listings at the back of the book) refer to the maps here. The key map below shows the area of Munich covered by the *Street Finder*. The maps include the major sightseeing areas, historic attractions, railway stations, bus stations, U-Bahn and S-Bahn stations and train stations. The word Straße (Str.) indicates a street, Platz a square, Brücke a bridge and Bahnhof a railway station.

Key to the Munich Street Finder

- ⬛ Major sight
- ⬛ Place of interest
- ⬜ Other building
- Ⓢ S-Bahn station
- Ⓤ U-Bahn station
- 🚉 Railway station
- 𝒊 Tourist information
- ✚ Hospital with casualty unit
- Police station
- ✝ Church
- ═ Railway line
- Pedestrianized street

Scale of Maps 1–3

| 0 metres | 200 |
| 0 yards | 200 |

BAVARIA

Bavaria is the biggest federal state in the Federal Republic of Germany. It is made up of regions that, in the past, were either independent secular territories or bishoprics. It includes former free towns of the Holy Roman Empire, such as Nördlingen, Rothenburg ob der Tauber, Dinkelsbühl, Nuremberg and Augsburg, which lost their independence to Bavaria only in the early 19th century.

The area that is now known as Bavaria was inhabited in early times by Celts and Romans. The German Baiovarii, who the territory was named after, arrived here during the 5th and 6th centuries. In the second half of the 6th century, the area was conquered by the Franks then, from 1180 until 1918, Bavaria was ruled by the Wittelsbach dynasty. During medieval times, this split into the Upper Bavarian line (Straubing, Ingolstadt and Munich) and the Lower Bavarian line (Landshut). In 1505, separate provinces were once again combined into a single country. During the 16th and 17th centuries the duchy of Bavaria was the bulwark of Roman Catholicism within the Holy Roman Empire and during the reign of Maximilian I, Bavaria fought against the Protestant

Union in the Thirty Years' War. For his loyalty to Rome, Maximilian I was rewarded in 1623 with the title of Elector, which meant that he could vote in elections for the Emperor. Following the fall of the Holy Roman Empire, Bavaria became a kingdom and remained as such until 1918.

Bavaria's turbulent history has left behind a rich architectural and cultural heritage. In addition to Roman antiquities, Baroque fortresses and fairy-tale castles, the region also has more than its share of glorious Alpine scenery, beer halls and colourful festivals, all of which make this one of the most popular parts of Germany for tourists. The capital, Munich, is a lively cosmopolitan city of wide boulevards and leafy squares with a wide choice of shops, restaurants, cinemas and theatres.

Girls dressed in national costume celebrating St Leonard's Festival

◀ Clock face of the brick Gothic Frauenkirche, or Church of Our Lady, in Nuremberg

Exploring Bavaria

Bavaria is a paradise for tourists. Its beautiful lakes attract lovers of water sports, while the mountainous regions of the Bavarian Forest offer the unspoiled charms of nature. The Alps, with their charming mountain hostels and numerous ski-lifts, provide endless possibilities for enjoyment. Towns and villages feature magnificent historic sights and the capital, Munich, combines the advantages of a lively metropolis with a peaceful atmosphere that is not often found in large cities.

The façade and central rotunda of Bayreuth's Eremitage

Sights at a Glance

0 kilometres 30

0 miles 30

The beautiful riverside town of Passau

Key

- Motorway
- Major road
- Minor road
- Main railway
- Minor railway
- International border
- Regional border
- △ Summit

Leipzig ↑

Chemnitz →

OBURG

ichtenfels

VIERZEHN-
HEILIGEN

Hollfeld

ÄNKISCHE SCHWEIZ

rmannstadt

5

Pottenstein

Forchheim

angen

NÜRNBERG
(NUREMBERG)

vabach

Neumarkt in
der Oberpfalz

B A Y E R N

ERCHING **9**

14 EICHSTÄTT

OLSTADT **23**

EUBURG AN
ER DONAU **24**

Schrobenhausen

DACHAU **20**

rmering

NDECHS **18**

NDERHOF
ETTAL
GARMISCH-PARTENKIRCHEN

Hof

Kulmbach

Entenbühl
936m

Weiden in
der Oberpfalz

Prague ↗

Wernberg-
Köblitz

10 AMBERG

Schwandorf

Roding

REGENSBURG **28** **15** DONAUSTAUF

Aufhausen

DINGOLFING

25 LANDSHUT

Moosburg

FREISING

Erding

21 SCHLEISSHEIM

München
(Munich)

Wasserburg
am Inn

Wolfratshausen

Rosenheim

8 BAYREUTH

Signalberg
886m

Schwarzach

Cham

Großer Arber
1456m

Zwiesel

Oberaltteich

27 STRAUBING

Deggendorf

Landau
an der Isar

26

Arnstorf

Pfarrkirchen

ALTÖTTING

29

12 BURGHAUSEN **30**

12 Inn

20

CHIEMSEE

34

Chieming

Bad Reichenhall

33

BERCHTESGADENER
LAND

Großer Rachel
1453m

Finsterau

Grafenau

Freyung

12

32 PASSAU

Bad Füssing

Pocking

Salzburg

Innsbruck ↓

Getting Around

Munich, Nuremberg and Augsburg are all served by
international airports, while fast train services operate
throughout the region. The main motorways are the A93
linking Saxony with Ratisbon, the A9 between Thuringia
and Munich, the A3 between Frankfurt and Passau and
the A8, which runs between Stuttgart and Salzburg.

Nuremberg's imposing Kaiserburg,
overlooking the city

For additional map symbols *see back flap*

Red sandstone exterior of Schloss Johannisburg, Aschaffenburg

❶ Aschaffenburg

Road map C5. 🏛 41,000. 🚃
ℹ️ Schlossplatz 1 (06021-39 58 00).

Situated in Lower Franconia, Aschaffenburg enjoys a scenic position on the hilly right bank of the river Main. The town became the second seat of the Mainz bishops in the 13th century, the first being Mainz.

The northwest part of the old town features a majestic, red sandstone riverside castle, **Schloss Johannisburg**, which was once occupied by the Mainz bishops-electors.

The castle gallery holds a fine collection of European paintings, dating from the 15th to the 18th century. It includes works by Hans Baldung Grien and the most important collection of Lucas Cranach canvases in Europe. In the castle library are valuable medieval codices, such as the 10th-century *Book of Gospel Readings (Evangelarium)* from Fulda.

Occupying a scenic position above a vineyard a short distance to the northwest of the castle is Pompejanum. The Bavarian king Ludwig I was so fascinated with the discovery of Pompeii that he ordered a replica of the Castor and Pollux villa *(Casa di Castore e Polluce)* to be built. This he filled with his rich collection of antiquities.

After undergoing restoration work to repair war damage, the museum opened its doors to the public again in 1994.

🏠 **Schloss Johannisburg**
Schlossplatz 4. **Tel** (06021) 38 65 70.
⏰ Apr–Sep: 9am–6pm Tue–Sun; Oct–Mar: 10am–4pm Tue–Sun. 📷

❷ Pommersfelden

Road map D5. ℹ️ Hauptstrasse 11 (09548-922 00).

On the edge of the Steigerwald – a popular hiking area – is the small village of Pommersfelden, which is dominated by its magnificent Baroque palace, **Schloss Weißenstein**. The palace was commissioned by the Mainz Archbishop and Elector and the Prince-Bishop of Bamberg, Lothar Franz von Schönborn. It was built, in only five years (1711–16), to a design by the famous architect, Johann Dientzenhofer.

This masterpiece of secular Baroque architecture is worth visiting for several reasons. Particularly interesting is the three-storey-high ornamental ceiling by Johann Rudolf Byss. The most spectacular room is the Marble Hall, which features paintings by Michael Rottmayr. The well-preserved interior of the palace houses a gallery, a library, and a valuable collection of furniture. After visiting the palace, you can take a stroll around its gardens, which were created by Maximilian

von Welsch in 1715, in what was the then fashionable, geometric French style. It is now laid out in English-garden style.

🏠 **Schloss Weißenstein**
Tel (09548) 98180. **Open** Apr–Oct: 10am–5pm daily. 📷 every hour. 🏛
🌐 schoenborn.de

❸ Coburg

Road map D5. 🏛 41,000. 🚃
ℹ️ Herrngasse 4 (09561-89 8000).

Former residence of the Wettin family, Coburg is situated on the bank of the river Itz. It is dominated by a massive fortress, the **Veste Coburg**, which is one of the largest in Germany. Coburg's origins go back to the 11th century, but its present-day appearance is mainly the result of remodelling that was carried out in the 16th and the 17th centuries.

The fortress consists of a number of buildings clustered around several courtyards and surrounded by a triple line of walls. The complex is now a museum, housing various collections, including prints and drawings, arms and armour.

In 1530, the fortress provided refuge to Martin Luther who, as an outlaw, hid here from April until October. The room in which he hid is furnished with antique furniture and features a portrait of Luther,

Ornate entrance to Coburg's Stadthaus

painted by Lucas Cranach the Younger.

Among the most important buildings in the old town are the late-Gothic church of St Maurice and a beautiful Renaissance college building that was founded by Prince Johann Casimir in 1605. On the opposite side of the market square is the town hall, originally built in 1577–79 and remodelled in the 18th century.

Further along is the town castle, **Schloss Ehrenburg**, which was built in the 16th century on the site of a dissolved Franciscan monastery. The castle burned down in 1693 and was subsequently rebuilt. The façade facing the square was remodelled by Karl Friedrich Schinkel in Neo-Gothic style.

The castle has some fine interiors, including the Baroque Riesensaal and Weisser Saal and a chapel with rich stucco decorations.

🏠 **Veste Coburg**
Tel (09561) 87 90. **Open** Apr–Oct: 9:30am–5pm daily; Nov–Mar: 1–4pm Tue–Sun. 🅿 🆆 **kunstsamm lungen-coburg.de**

🏠 **Schloss Ehrenburg**
Schlossplatz 1. **Tel** (09561) 808 832. **Open** Apr–Sep: 9am–5pm Tue–Sun; Oct–Mar: 10am–3pm Tue–Sun. 🎫 every hour. 🅿

❹ Vierzehnheiligen

Bad Staffelstein. **Road map** D5. **Tel** (09571) 950 80. **Open** Apr–Oct: 6:30am–8pm; Nov–Mar: 7:30am–5pm. 🚐 🆆 **vierzehnheiligen.de**

High above the river Main is Banz Abbey, a Benedictine monastery built in 1695 by Johann Leonhard and Leonhard Dientzenhofer. Opposite is the pilgrimage church of the Fourteen Saints of Intercession. The first two chapels, built in the 15th and 16th centuries, became too small to accommodate the growing numbers of pilgrims so, in 1741,

Interior of the monumental, Baroque Vierzehnheiligen church

the foundation stone was laid for the monumental new church, designed by Balthasar Neumann. Built in 1743–72, this is one of the most famous masterpieces of South German Baroque, with magnificent Rococo furnishings. The building is a cross-shaped basilica, with a monumental twin-tower façade.

The interior has an exceptionally dynamic style, achieved by combining the longitudinal and central planes: the three ovals laid along the main axis join with the two circles of the transept. The centrepiece of the nave is the "Altar of Mercy", which stands at the spot where, according to a 1446 legend, a shepherd had visions of the infant Christ with the fourteen Saints of Intercession. The altar features statues of the fourteen saints, and are the work of J M and F X Feuchtmayr (1763). The rich stucco decorations and frescoes were crafted by Giuseppe Appiani.

Madonna from Marienkapelle in Ebermannstadt

❺ Fränkische Schweiz

Road map D5. 🛈 Oberes Tor 1, Ebermannstadt (09191-86 1054).

The area popularly known as Franconian Switzerland (*Fränkische Schweiz*) covers the area between Nuremberg, Bamberg and Bayreuth. One of Germany's most beautiful tourist regions, it offers green meadows, magnificent highlands covered with cornfields, imposing castles perched on top of high rocks, fabulous dolomite rocks and deep caves with stalactites. Its towns and villages, with their charming inns and timber-frame houses, look like a setting for *Snow White and Seven Dwarfs*.

The main routes across the area run alongside its rivers – the Wiesent, Leinleiter, Püttlach and Trubach. The Wiesent, which is ideal for canoeing, cuts across the region from east to west, joining the river Regnitz near the town of Forchheim. The town features many timber-frame houses, including the old town hall dating from the 14th to the 16th century. Near Forchheim, in **Ebermannstadt**, is a Marian church with a fine Madonna. The federal route B470 leads to the picturesque village of Tüchersfeld, which is built into the rocks. A good base for exploring this area is the village of Pottenstein. St Elizabeth of Thuringia is said to have stayed here in 1227. To the east of the castle is a cave with impressive stalactites.

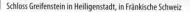
Schloss Greifenstein in Heiligenstadt, in Fränkische Schweiz

⑥ Würzburg

The bombing raid on Würzburg on 16 March 1945 lasted for about 20 minutes and destroyed over 80 per cent of the town's buildings. It seemed that Würzburg, which occupies a picturesque position on the banks of the river Main, had been erased from the face of the earth. Like Dresden, however, the town rose from the ashes and once again it enchants visitors with its rich heritage of historic sights. As well as being a popular tourist destination, Würzburg is also an important commercial and cultural centre for Lower Franconia and home of the excellent Franconian wine.

View over Würzburg, with Dom St Kilian in the foreground

🏛 Residenz
See pp250–51.

🏛 Dom St Kilian
Domplatz. **Tel** (0931) 38 66 29 00. **Open** 10am–5pm Mon– Sat, 1–6pm Sun and holidays.

Next to the great cathedral churches of Mainz, Speyer and Worms, this is Germany's fourth largest Romanesque church. It was built in 1045–1188, its patron saint an Irish monk who came to Würzburg in AD 686.

The church is a three-nave basilica with a transept and a twin-tower façade. Inside, the Romanesque main nave with its flat roof contrasts sharply with the Baroque stucco embellishments of the choir.

In the north nave is an interesting group of bishops' tombs, including two that are the work of Tilman Riemenschneider. At the end of the north transept is a chapel, which was built by Balthasar Neumann for the bishops of the House of Schönborn.

🏛 Neumünster
St-Kilians-Platz.

Just north of the cathedral, the Neumünster church was built in the 11th century at the burial site of St Kilian and his fellow Irish martyrs, St Kolonat and St Totnan.

The church's imposing Baroque dome and its red sandstone façade date from the 18th century. Featured in the interior are numerous works of art, including a late 15th-century Madonna and the *Man of Sorrow* by the 15th-century

The beautiful red sandstone façade of Neumünster-Kirche

German sculptor Tilman Riemenschneider. The north door leads to a lovely small courtyard; the remains of the cloister date from the Hohenstauf period. Under a lime tree is the resting place of a famous medieval minstrel Walther von der Vogelweide.

A procession is held each year on St Kilian's day (8 July) when theological students carry the skulls of the martyrs, contained in a transparent box, from the west crypt to the cathedral where they are put on public display.

🏛 Bürgerspital
Theaterstrasse.

The Bürgerspital was founded in 1319 by Johann von Steren. Hospitals like this originally provided charitable care for the old as well as the infirm, and today this institution provides care for over one hundred elderly residents of Würzburg. It operates as a self-financing foundation, its main source of income being from vine-growing. Residents are given a quarter of a litre (½ pint) of an excellent home-produced wine each day, with double the ration on Sundays. Visitors can also sample various vintages.

🏛 Juliusspital
Juliuspromenade. **Tel** (0931) 393 14 00. **Open** Apr–mid-Dec: guided tours by appointment. **W** juliusspital.de

Founded in 1576 by Julius Echter, Juliusspital was remodelled in the 17th and the 18th centuries. The Rococo pharmacy (1760–65) in the hospital arcades has survived intact and is well worth a visit.

🏛 Rathaus
Rueckermainstrasse.

Würzburg's picturesque town hall was built in several stages. Begun in the 13th century, it was subsequently extended in the 15th and 16th centuries. Particularly noteworthy are the beautiful 16th-century paintings on the façade and the late-Renaissance tower, Roter Turm, which dates from around 1660.

🏛 Alte Mainbrücke
Connecting the old town and Festung Marienberg, this

For hotels and restaurants in this area see pp496–7 and pp519–22

An old crane near Alte Mainbrücke over the river Main

beautiful bridge was built in 1473–1543. It is the oldest bridge over the Main.

🏰 Festung Marienberg

Fürstenbau-Museum: **Tel** (0931) 355 170. **Open** 16 Mar–Oct: 9am–6pm Tue–Sun. **Close**: Nov–Mar. 🚗 **W** schloesser.bayern.de
Mainfränkisches Museum: **Tel** (0931) 205 940. **Open** Apr–Oct: 10am–5pm Tue–Sun; Nov–Mar: 10am–4pm Tue–Sun. 🚗 Castle tours: ⏱ 16 Mar–Oct: 11am, 2pm, 3pm, 4pm Tue–Fri; 10am, 11am, 1pm, 2pm, 3pm (in English), 4pm Sat & Sun.

Built on the site of an old Celtic stronghold, the Marienberg Fortress towers above the town.

In AD 707 a church was built here and, in 1201, work began on a fortress that served as the residence of the prince-bishops until 1719. Within its fortifications stands the first original donjon church dating from the 13th century, and the Renaissance-Baroque palace. The museum exhibits illustrate the 1,200-year history of the town. The former arsenal now houses the Franconian Museum with its valuable collection of sculptures by Tilman Riemenschneider.

🏛 Kappele

Mergentheimer Strasse.
Standing at the top of a hill at the southwestern end of the

VISITORS' CHECKLIST

Practical Information
Road map C5. 🚉 128,000.
ℹ Falkenhaus, Marktplatz 9 (0931-372398). 🎭 Afrikafestival (May), Würzburger Weindorf (May/Jun), Mozartfest (Jun), Kilianifest (Jul), Bachtage (Nov–Dec).

Transport
✈ Frankfurt, 120 km (75 miles) west. 🚉 Hauptbahnhof.

city, this twin-towered Baroque chapel is the work of Balthasar Neumann (1747–50). Its interior is lavishly decorated with beautiful wall paintings by Matthias Günther.

Festung Marienberg, built on a hill overlooking the river Main

Würzburg City Centre

① Residenz
② Dom St Kilian
③ Neumünster
④ Bürgerspital
⑤ Juliusspital
⑥ Rathaus
⑦ Alte Mainbrücke
⑧ Festung Marienberg

Residenz in Würzburg

This vast complex was commissioned by two prince-bishops, the brothers Johann Philipp Franz and Friedrich Karl von Schönborn. Its construction between 1720 and 1744 was supervised by several architects, including Johann Lukas von Hildebrandt and Maximilian von Welsch. However, the Residenz (which is on UNESCO's World Heritage list) is mainly associated with the architect Balthasar Neumann, who was responsible for the overall design.

Main entrance

Martin-von-Wagner-Museum entrance

★ Treppenhaus
The work of the Venetian artist Giovanni Battista Tiepolo, the largest fresco in the world adorns the vault of the staircase.

Frankonia-Brunnen
This fountain, designed by Ferdinand von Miller, was constructed in the parade square in front of the Residenz. It was funded by donations from the inhabitants of Würzburg.

KEY

① Napoleon's bedroom

The Coat of Arms of the Patron
The richly carved coat of arms are by Johann Wolfgang von der Auwery and are the personal arms of Friedrich Karl von Schönborn, Prince-Bishop of Bamberg and Würzburg.

⋏ Kaisersaal
The centrepiece of the palace, the sumptuous emperor's chamber, testifies to the close relationship between Würzburg and the Holy Roman Empire. There are Tiepolo frescoes here too.

Garden Hall
This vast, low hall has Rococo stucco works by Antonio Bossi, dating from 1749. There is also a painting on the vaulting by Johan Zick dating from 1750, depicting *The Feast of the Gods* and *Diana Resting*.

Venetian Room
This room is named after three tapestries depicting the Venetian carnival. Further ornaments include decorative panels with paintings by Johann Thalhofer, a pupil of Rudolph Byss.

★ Hofkirche
The church interior is richly decorated with paintings, sculptures and stucco ornaments. The side altars were designed by Johann Lukas von Hildebrandt and feature paintings by Giovanni Battista Tiepolo.

❼ Bamberg

Situated on seven hills like ancient Rome, Bamberg features a splendidly preserved old town, encircled by the branches of the river Regnitz. The town is famous not only for its exceptional artistic heritage but also for its excellent beer, produced by one of the nine breweries that operate here. Its long history goes back to AD 902, when the Babenberg family established their residence here. The town grew and prospered in the wake of the Thirty Years' War. In 1993, Bamberg became a UNESCO World Heritage Site.

Beautiful rose garden at the rear of the Neue Residenz

Exploring Bamberg

A good place to start sightseeing is the Domplatz, one of Germany's loveliest squares, with its magnificent cathedral church and the old bishop's palace. After visiting the Neue Residenz you can go down to the river, where you will find the water palace, Concordia. The old town is reached by crossing one of two bridges – Untere or Obere Brücke.

🏛 Dom
See pp254–5.

🏛 Alte Hofhaltung Historisches Museum
Domplatz 7. **Tel** (0951) 871 142. **Open** May–Oct: 9am–5pm Tue–Sun. 🅿 🚇 **schloesser-bayern.de**

On the west side of Domplatz stands a magnificent portal, with statues of the imperial couple Heinrich II and Kunigunde. This is the gate to the former bishop's residence, built at the turn of the 15th and 16th centuries in place of an old fortress of Heinrich II. Within the building's wings is a pleasant courtyard. Inside is a museum that focuses on the history of the region.

🏛 Neue Residenz und Staatsgalerie
Domplatz 8. **Tel** (0951) 519 390. **Open** Apr–Sep: 9am–6pm daily; Oct–Mar: 10–4pm daily. 🚇 **schloesser-bayern.de**

The Neue Residenz, with its richly decorated apartments and the Emperor's Room, was built in 1695–1704 and is the work of Johann Leonhard Dientzenhofer. Its walls are adorned with magnificent frescoes painted by the Tyrolean artist Melchior Steidl. The walls and pillars feature the Habsburg family tree, while 16 statues represent Emperors of the Holy Roman Empire. The Neue Residenz houses a collection of old German masters, including *The Flood* by Hans Baldung Grien and three canvases by Lucas Cranach the Elder.

🏛 Karmelitenkloster
Karmelitenplatz 1. **Open** 9–11.30am, 2:30–5:30pm daily.

The hospital-abbey complex of St Theodore was founded in the late 12th century by Bishop Eberhard. Since 1589 the church and abbey have belonged to the Carmelite order. The south tower and Romanesque portal are the remains of the massive 12th-century basilica. The interior of the church was redesigned in the late 17th and early 18th centuries so the altar is now situated at its western end, while the entrance is on the site of the previous presbytery. The layout of the cloisters on the south side of the church is typical of Cistercian designs.

🏛 Wasserschloss Concordia
Concordiastrasse. **Closed** to the public. This magnificent Baroque palace, which enjoys a scenic position on the water's edge, was built for Counsellor Böttinger between 1716 and 1722, to a design by Johann Dientzenhofer. The building now houses a science institute.

The Baroque palace Concordia on the bank of the river Regnitz

Picturesque fishermen's cottages in Klein-Venedig

🏛 Altes Rathaus

The Baroque lower bridge, Untere Brücke, provides a magnificent view over the upper bridge, Obere Brücke, with its fabulous town hall. This originally Gothic seat of the municipal authorities was remodelled in 1744–56 by Jakob Michael Küchel. The half-timbered structure of the Rottmeisterhaus, which seems to be gliding over the waves of the river Regnitz, was added in 1688.

🏛 Klein-Venedig

"Little Venice" is a district of fishermen's cottages, their picturesque façades adorned with pots of geraniums. Visitors come here for a glass of Rauchbier – a local beer with a smoky flavour – while they enjoy the view.

🏛 Grüner Markt

With its historic houses and adjacent Maximilianplatz, Grüner Markt lies at the heart of the old town. It features the magnificent Baroque St Martin's Church, built in 1686–91 by the Dientzenhofer brothers. Also notable is the late-Baroque St Catherine Hospital and Seminary, built by Balthasar Neumann, which now serves as the town hall.

🏛 Kloster Michelsberg

Michelsberg. **Fränkisches Brauereimuseum: Open:** Closed for extensive renovation. 🖾
🆆 **brauereimuseum.de**

The Benedictine abbey that stood on this site was founded in 1015. The surviving church was built after 1121 and later remodelled in the 16th and 17th centuries. On the ceiling of the church are paintings depicting almost 600 species of medicinal plants. The abbey's Baroque buildings date from the 17th and 18th centuries and are the work of Johann Dientzenhofer and Balthasar Neumann. The abbey's brewery now houses a museum. The church interior is closed for ongoing renovations.

🏛 Schloss Seehof

Memmelsdorf. **Tel** (0951) 409 571.
Open Apr–Oct: 9am–6pm Tue–Sun.
🖾 🖾 🆆 **schloesser-bayern.de**

Built and designed by Antonio Petrini in 1686, this was originally the summer residence of the prince-bishops of Bamberg. The nine magnificent state rooms have been beautifully restored.

Façade of Schloss Seehof in Memmelsdorf

Bamberg City Centre

① Dom
② Alte Hofhaltung
③ Neue Residenz und Staatsgalerie
④ Karmeliterkloster
⑤ Wasserschloss Concordia
⑥ Altes Rathaus
⑦ Klein-Venedig
⑧ Kloster Michelsberg

0 metres   300
0 yards   300

Bamberg Cathedral

Bamberg's skyline is dominated by the cathedral of St Peter and St George, which combines the late Romanesque and early French-Gothic styles. It was founded in 1004 and consecrated in 1012, and again in 1237 after being demolished by fire and then rebuilt. This is a triple-nave basilica with two choirs, whose apses are flanked by two pairs of towers. The cloisters were built between 1399 and 1457, while the monumental sculptures adorning the portals date from the 13th century. The western choir holds the only papal grave in Germany, that of Pope Clement II, who had been the local bishop.

Interior
The illuminated main nave features a graceful, early Gothic, cross-ribbed vault.

★ Bamberger Reiter
By the northwestern pillar of the eastern choir stands the famous equestrian statue of the "Bamberg Rider", dating from about 1230. Many scholars have puzzled over the identity of the rider, but the riddle remains unsolved.

★ Tomb of Heinrich II and Kunigunde
This beautiful sarcophagus of the imperial couple is the work of Tilman Riemenschneider, completed in 1513.

KEY

① Marienpforte
② St George's Choir
③ St Peter's Choir

Emperor's Cloak
The Diocesan Museum houses an exhibition of sacral art. It also features a collection of imperial vestments, including Heinrich II's blue cloak of stars.

Marienpforte
This magnificent stonework adorns the main entrance. The tympanum features reliefs depicting scenes from the Last Judgement.

Hochaltar des Peterschores
The main altar of the west choir is adorned with sculptures depicting the Crucifixion (1648–49) by Justus Glesker.

★ Marian Altar by Veit Stoß
Veit Stoß was commissioned to create this altar by his son, Andrew Stoß, who was a Carmelite prior in Nuremberg at the time. After the victory of the Reformation in Nuremberg, however, he moved to Bamberg in 1543.

❽ Bayreuth

Lovers of German music associate this town with the composer Richard Wagner (1813–83), who took up residence here in 1872. Established in 1231, Bayreuth originally belonged to the family of Count von Andechs-Meran; in 1248 it passed to the margraves of Nuremberg (von Zollern) and, since 1806, Franconian Bayreuth has belonged to Bavaria. The town flourished during the 17th and 18th centuries when it was the residence of the margraves, particularly during the time of Margravine Wilhelmine, sister of the Prussian King Frederick the Great and wife of Margrave Frederick.

Extraordinary Baroque interior of the Markgräfliches Opernhaus

🎭 Markgräfliches Opernhaus

Opernstrasse 14. **Tel** (0921) 759 69 22. **Open** Apr–Sep: 9am–6pm daily; Oct–Mar: 10am–4pm daily (information centre and part of auditorium only as rest closed for renovation to 2017).

One of the finest theatres in Europe, the Markgräfliches Opera House was built in the 1740s by Joseph Saint-Pierre. Its ornate Baroque interior was designed by Giuseppe Galli Bibiena and his son Carlo, who came from a famous Bolognese family of theatre architects.

🏰 Neues Schloss

Ludwigstrasse 21. **Tel** (0921) 759 69 21. **Open** Apr–Sep: 9am–6pm daily; Oct–Mar: 10am–4pm daily.

The Neues Schloss (New Castle) was commissioned by Margravine Wilhelmine and built by Joseph Saint-Pierre. The elongated, three-storey structure combines classical lines with a rustic ground floor. The Italian wing was added in 1759. Nearly all the rooms have retained their original Baroque and Rococo decor. The park is arranged in a typically English style.

🏛 Villa Wahnfried

Richard-Wagner-Museum: Richard-Wagner-Strasse 48. **Tel** (0921) 75 72 80. **Closed** for renovations; expected to reopen in 2016. 🅦 **wagnermuseum.de**

On the northeast side of the castle garden is Villa Wahnfried. Built for Wagner by Carl Wölfel, the villa was destroyed during World War II but was restored in the 1970s. In the garden is Wagner's tomb and that of his wife Cosima, the daughter of Franz Liszt.

🏛 Franz-Liszt-Museum

Wahnfriedstrasse 9. **Tel** (0921) 516 64 88. **Open** Sep–Jun: 10am–noon, 2–5pm daily; Jul–Aug: 10am–5pm daily.

A short distance from Villa Wahnfried, at the junction of Wahnfriedstrasse and Lisztstrasse, stands the house in which Hungarian composer Franz Liszt died in 1886. It is now a museum dedicated to the composer.

🏛 Eremitage

4 km (2.5 miles) northeast of town. **Tel** (0921) 759 69 37. Castle: **Open** Apr–Sep: 9am–6pm daily; 1 Oct–15 Oct: 10am–4pm. **Closed** 16 Oct–Mar. Park: **Open** daily.

In 1715–18, following the example of the French king Louis XIV and the fashion among the nobility for playing at ascetism, Margrave Georg Wilhelm ordered the building of the Eremitage complex as a retreat. With its horseshoe-shaped orangery, the hermitage (or Altes Schloss) was given to Margravine Wilhelmine as a birthday present. She then set about transforming it into a pleasure palace.

Richard Wagner (1813–1883)

The German composer is inseparably linked with Bayreuth, where he enjoyed his greatest artistic triumphs. His career, which did not run smoothly in early days, began in Magdeburg, Königsberg and Riga. From there he had to flee, via London to Paris, from his pursuing creditors. His reputation was firmly established by successful performances of his romantic operas *The Flying Dutchman* (1843) and *Tannhäuser* (1845) in Dresden. Wagner's long-time sponsor was the eccentric Bavarian king, Ludwig II. From 1872 Wagner lived in Bayreuth, where the Festspielhaus was built specifically for the operas.

Bust of Wagner by Arno Breker (1939)

Tomb of Wagner and his wife in the garden of Villa Wahnfried

Festspielhaus, specially designed venue for the annual Wagner Festival

Festspielhaus
Festspielhügel. **Tel** (0921) 787 80.
Sep–Oct: 10am, 11am, 2pm,
3pm daily; Nov: 2pm Sat; Dec–Apr
10am, 2pm daily.

Each July and August, Wagner
festivals are held in this theatre,
built between 1872–75 to a
design by Gottfried Semper. The
world premiere of *The Ring of
the Nibelung* played here in 1876.

Environs
Approximately 20 km (12 miles)
to the northwest of Bayreuth is
the town of **Kulmbach**. Famous
for its countless breweries, the
town hosts a big beer festival
each year, in July and August. Its
town hall has a beautiful, Rococo
façade dating from 1752. From
here you can walk to the castle
hill to visit the Plassenburg
Fortress, which has belonged to
the Hohenzollern family since
1340. Until 1604, this was the
seat of the von Brandenburg-
Kulmbach margraves. This vast
structure was built in 1560–70.
The gem in its crown is the
Renaissance courtyard with
arcades (Schöner Hof). The castle
houses a vast collection of tin
figurines, with some 30,000
items. In **Ködnitz**, to the
southeast of Kulmbach, is the
Upper Franconian Village School
Museum. Based on the original
school furnishings and various
old photographs, the exhibition
illustrates the teaching methods
that were used in this region
more than a hundred years ago.
Some 25 km (16 miles) from
Bayreuth, in Sanspareil Park near
Hollfeld, is the **Felsentheater** –
an unusual 80-seat theatre set
in a natural grotto.

Felsentheater, in a natural grotto in
Sanspareil Park near Bayreuth

Bayreuth City Centre
① Markgräfliches Opernhaus
② Neues Schloss
③ Villa Wahnfried
④ Franz-Liszt-Museum

0 metres 200
0 yards 200

For additional map symbols *see back flap*

❾ Berching

Map D6. 🚹 7,500. ℹ Petten-koferplatz 12 (08462-205 13).

This charming little town, situated in the valley of the river Sulz, boasts a history that stretches back to the 9th century. To this day it retains the complete enclosure of its medieval city walls, including towers and gates with old oak doors. The most beautiful of the towers is the *Chinesische Turm* (the Chinese Tower).

The regional museum is well worth visiting, as are some of the local churches. These include an early Gothic church, Mariä Himmelfahrt, remodelled after 1756 by M Seybold and featuring some beautiful Rococo stucco ornaments. The Baroque St Lorenz, with its 13th century tower and original late-Gothic altar, is also noteworthy.

❿ Amberg

Map D5. 🚹 43,000. ℹ Hallplatz 2 (09621-102 39).

Situated at the edge of the Franconian Jura, on the banks of the river Vils, Amberg owes its development to local iron ore deposits and the steel industry. The well-preserved, oval-shaped old town is still encircled by medieval walls. At the centre is an enchanting market square with the vast 15th-century late-Gothic hall-church, Pfarrkirche St Martin, and Gothic town hall (1356), both still with their original interiors.

Amberg was once the residential town of the Rhine palatines, whose Renaissance palace and chancellery have survived to the present day.

The symbol of Amberg is the Stadtbrille, the bridge spanning the river Vils, whose arches reflected in the river resemble a pair of spectacles – hence its nickname "the town's spectacles".

The late-Gothic main altar in St George's Church, Dinkelsbühl

⓫ Dinkelsbühl

Map D6. 🚹 11,000. 🚃 ℹ Altrathausplatz 14, (09851-902 440). 🎭 Kinderzeche (mid-Jul).

This old Franconian town is one of the best-preserved medieval urban complexes in Germany. The walls surrounding the city include four towers – Wörnitzer, Nördlinger, Seringer and Rothenburger Tor – which are all almost intact. The residential district of the town consists mainly of timber-framed houses.

The finest example of these is the Deutsches Haus, which stands opposite St George's Church. Dating from the late 15th to the early 16th century, the house once belonged to the Drechsel-Deufstetten family and is now a hotel-restaurant.

The late-Gothic Church of St George is a triple-nave hall-church with no transept. Together with the presbytery, it forms one large interior crowned with magnificent network vaults. The most valuable items of the interior furnishings include the pulpit, the font – which dates from around 1500 – and the Crucifixion in the main altar, which is attributed to Michael Wolgemut. A fine view of the town can be obtained from the church tower.

In Turmgasse stands the Baroque palace of the Teutonic Order, built in 1760–64 by Mathias Binder.

⓬ Nördlingen

Map D6. 🚹 20,000. 🚃 ℹ Marktplatz 2 (09081-841 16). 🎭 Stabenfest (May), Nördlinger Pfingstmesse Scharlachrennen (Jun), Sommerfestspiele (Jul), Historisches Stadtmauerfest (every third year in Sep; next in 2016 and 2019).

The town is situated in the Ries Basin, which is an immense and well-preserved crater that was formed millions of years ago by a meteor strike.

During the Middle Ages Nördlingen was a free town of the Holy Roman Empire and an important trade centre. The fortification walls that surround the city include five gates and 12 towers (dating from the 14th to the 15th centuries) that have survived intact to this day.

The late-Gothic church of St George was built by Nikolaus Eseler, who also built the St George Church in Dinkelsbühl. The church is a triple-nave hall-church with round pillars and network vaults. Its imposing west tower, known as the Daniel Tower, offers a magnificent panoramic view of the town and its environs.

The symbol of Amberg is the bridge named "the town spectacles"

The St Salvator's Church features original Gothic altars and a portal that has the scene of the *Last Judgement* in the tympanum. The former hospital of the Holy Spirit is now home to an interesting **Stadtmuseum**. The 14th-century town hall features a striking external stone stairway (1618).

Statue from the Tanzhaus façade

iii Stadtmuseum
Vordere Gerbergasse 1. **Tel** (09081) 848 10. **Open** mid Mar–Oct: 1:30–4:30pm Tue–Sun. Nov–mid-Mar: open only to guided tours (book in advance by telephone).

⓭ Ansbach

Map D6. 40,000. Johann-Sebastian-Bach-Platz 1 (0981-512 43). Ansbacher Frühlingsfest (May), Bach-Woche (every two years in Jul: the next one is in 2017), Ansbacher Rokokospiele (Jul), Heimatfest (Jul).

The town situated west of Nuremberg, began its history in AD 748 with the foundation of a Benedictine Abbey by a man named Gumbert. A settlement called Onoldsbach, which sprang up nearby, is now called Ansbach. From 1460 until 1791 Ansbach was the home of the von Brandenburg-Ansbach margraves and in 1791 it was incorporated into Prussia; after 1806 it passed into Bavaria. The Markgräfliche

residence is situated in the northeastern part of the Old Town. Remodelled several times it is now a Baroque Neo-Classical structure. Its 27 original state apartments include the Mirror Room, Mirror Gallery, Dining Room and Audience Room. It now houses the Museum of Faience and Porcelain. The nearby Hofgarten has a 102-m (335-ft) long Orangery. It also houses a Kaspar Hauser Collection.

iii Markgrafenmuseum
Kaspar-Hauser-Platz 1. **Tel** (0981) 977 50 56. **Open** 10am–5pm daily. **Closed** Mon (Oct–Apr).

iii Markgräfliche Residenz "Ansbacher Fayence und Porzellan"
Promenade 27. **Tel** (0981) 953 83 90. **Open** Apr–Sep: 9am–6pm Tue–Sun; Oct–Mar: 10am–4pm Tue–Sun.

⓮ Eichstätt

Map D6. 15,000. Domplatz 8 (08421-600 1400).

Willibald, a close companion and compatriot of the Anglo-Saxon missionary Boniface, established a missionary-abbey (Eihstat) here. Soon afterwards Eichstätt became an episcopal town. In 1634 a fire ripped through the town, destroying four-fifths of its houses and four churches; after this the town was rebuilt in Baroque style.

Eichstätt is home to the country's only Catholic university, established in 1980. On the outskirts of town, on a hill overlooking the River

Majestic Walhalla near Donaustauf

Altmühl, stands the picturesque Willibald Castle, which until the 18th century was the residence of prince-bishops. Now it houses an interesting museum of artifacts from the Jurassic era, where visitors can see a very well preserved skeleton of *archaeopteryx*.

A new bishop's residence was built nearby from 1702 until 1768. Its west wing features a magnificent staircase and the Mirror Room, in which the works of Mauritio Pedetti, Johann Jakob Berg and Michael Franz are displayed.

⓯ Donaustauf

Walhalla. **Tel** (09403) 96 16 80. **Open** Apr–Sep: 9am–5:45pm; Oct: 9am–4:45pm; Nov–Mar: 10am–11:45am & 1–3:45pm.

In 1830–42 Leo von Klenze built the Walhalla *(see above)*. This monument to the national glory occupies a scenic location on the River Danube. The building stands on a raised terrace and has the form of a Neo-Classical columned temple (similar to the Parthenon in Athens). It is adorned with 121 marble busts of artists and scientists.

Orangery of the Markgräfliche residence, in Ansbach

⑯ Nürnberg (Nuremberg)

Situated on the river Pegnitz, Nuremberg is not only a paradise for lovers of its famous gingerbread and sausages but is also the symbol of Germany's history. The earliest records of the town, the second largest in Bavaria, date from 1050 when it was a trading settlement. From 1219 Nuremberg, a free town of the Holy Roman Empire, was an important centre of craft and commerce. Its most rapid development took place in the 15th and 16th centuries, when many prominent artists, craftsmen and intellectuals worked here, making Nuremberg one of the cultural centres of Europe.

Picturesque alley near Frauentor

Exploring Lorenzer Alstadt

The southern part of the old town, known as Lorenzer Alstadt, is separated from the northern part by the river Pegnitz and encircled to the south by the city walls. Many of the area's historic treasures were carefully reconstructed following severe bomb damage during World War II.

🏛 Frauentor

Frauentorgraben.
Frauentor is one of the most attractive gates into the old town. It is installed in the massive city walls that were

constructed during the 15th and 16th centuries. The vast tower, Dicker Turm, was erected nearby in the 15th century. Königstor, a magnificent gate that once stood to the right of Dicker Turm, was dismantled in the 19th century. Beyond Frauentor are a number of alleys with half-timbered houses, shops and cafés, built after the war.

🏛 Marthakirche

Königstrasse 74–78.
Dating from the 14th century, the small hospital church of St Martha is tucked between the surrounding houses. Though its interior is virtually devoid of furnishing, it features some magnificent Gothic stained-glass windows, which date from around 1390.

🏛 Mauthalle

Hallplatz 2.
The massive structure that dominates Königstrasse is a Gothic granary built in 1498–1502 by Hans Beheim the Elder.

Sights at a Glance

① Frauentor
② Marthakirche
③ Mauthalle
④ Germanisches Nationalmuseum
⑤ St Lorenz-Kirche
⑥ Lorenzer Platz
⑦ Heilig-Geist-Spital
⑧ Hauptmarkt
⑨ Frauenkirche
⑩ Rathaus
⑪ Spielzeugmuseum
⑫ Sebalduskirche
⑬ Egidienkirche
⑭ Kaiserburg
⑮ Albrecht-Dürer-Haus

It originally housed the town's municipal scales and the customs office. In the 19th century, the building was converted into a department store and continues in that role today, following post-war reconstruction.

🏛 Germanisches Nationalmuseum

See pp264–5.

🏛 St Lorenz-Kirche

Lorenzer Platz.
One of the most important buildings in Nuremberg is the

Panoramic view over the rooftops of Nuremberg

For hotels and restaurants in this area see pp496–7 and pp519–22

Impressive Mauthalle dominating Königstrasse

crucifix within the main altar and the magnificent statue of the Archangel Michael standing by the second pillar of the main nave. There are also several Gothic altars and some magnificent 15th-century stained-glass windows (1493–95). The pillars of the nave are adorned with a number of fascinating statues of

Gothic original. Diagonally across the square is the Nassauer Haus, a Gothic mansion whose lower storeys were built in the 13th century. The upper floors were added in the 15th century.

A short distance from the square, in Karolinenstrasse, is a fine sculpture by Henry Moore.

✚ Heilig-Geist-Spital

In the centre of town, on the banks of the river Pegnitz, stands the Hospital of the Holy Spirit. Founded in 1332, this is one of the largest hospitals built in the Middle Ages and features a lovely inner courtyard with wooden galleries. The wing that spans the river was built during extension works in 1488–1527. Lepers were kept at some distance from the other patients, in a separate half-timbered building that was specially erected for the purpose. From 1424 until 1796, the insignia of the Holy Roman Empire were kept here rather than in the castle.

The Heilig-Geist-Spital now houses a retirement home and a restaurant. The entrance to the building is on the northern side of the river.

Gothic church of St Lorenz, whose basilic disposition largely was built around 1270–1350. The vast hall presbytery was added much later, in 1439–77. On entering the church it is worth taking a look at the magnificent main portal, which is adorned with sculptures. In the main nave of the church, suspended from the ceiling above the altar, is a superb group sculpture, *Annunciation*, the work of Veit Stoß (1519). He was also the creator of the

the Apostles, dating from the late 14th century.

🏛 Lorenzer Platz

Overlooked by the church of St Lorenz, Lorenzer Platz is a popular meeting place for the citizens of Nuremberg and visitors alike. Outside the church is the Fountain of the Virtues, *Tugendbrunnen* (1589), with water cascading from the breasts of its seven Virtues. Nearby is a statue of St Lorenz, which is a copy of the 1350

Heilig-Geist-Spital reflected in the waters of the river Pegnitz

Exploring Nürnberg (Nuremberg)

Nuremberg was once an important publishing centre. Schedel's *Liber Chronicarum* was published here in 1493 and, in 1543 – following the town's official adoption of the Reformation in 1525 – *The Revolutions of the Celestial Spheres* by Copernicus was published. The Thirty Years' War ended the town's development but, during the 19th century, it became the focus for the Pan-German movement. In 1945–49 the town was the scene of the trials for war crimes of Nazi leaders.

Detail of *Schöner Brunnen*, in Hauptmarkt

🏛 Hauptmarkt

Each year the Hauptmarkt provides a picturesque setting for the town's famous Christkindlesmarkt, which goes on throughout Advent. At this famous market you can buy gingerbread, enjoy the taste of German sausages, warm yourself with a glass of mulled wine spiced with cloves and buy locally made souvenirs.

Nuremberg's star attraction is the Gothic *Schöner Brunnen* (Beautiful Fountain), which was probably erected around 1385 but replaced in the early 20th century with a replica. It consists of a

19-metre (62-ft) high, finely carved spire standing at the centre of an octagonal pool. The pool is surrounded by a Renaissance grille that includes the famous golden ring: the local tradition is that if you turn the ring three times, your wishes will come true. The pool is adorned with the statues of philosophers, evangelists and church fathers, while the spire is decorated with the statues of Electors and of Jewish and Christian heroes. Features and details of the original fountain are kept in the **Germanisches National-museum** (see pp264–5).

🏛 Frauenkirche

Hauptmarkt. **Open** daily.

Commissioned by Emperor Charles IV, this Gothic hall-church dates from 1352–58. Over its richly decorated vestibule is the oriel of the west choir. Its gable contains a clock from Männleinlaufen, installed in 1509. Each day at noon the clock displays a procession of Electors paying homage to the Emperor. Also noteworthy is the Gothic altar *(Tucher Altar)*, which dates from 1445.

🏛 Rathaus

Rathausplatz.

The present town hall consists of several sections. Facing the Rathausplatz is the oldest, Gothic part, built in 1332–40 and remodelled in the early 15th century. Behind, facing Hauptmarkt, is the Renaissance part, built in 1616–22 by Jakob Wolff. Its magnificent portals are decorated with heraldic motifs. The courtyard features a fountain dating from 1557.

🏛 Spielzeugmuseum

Karlstrasse 13–15. **Tel** (0911) 231 31 64. **Open** 10am–5pm Tue–Fri, 10am–6pm Sat & Sun. **Closed** Good Friday, 24, 25, 26, 31 Dec. 🅿

This enchanting toy museum, established in 1971, houses a magnificent collection of tin soldiers and a huge collection of dolls and puppets. Its greatest attraction, however, is a collection of antique dolls' houses, filled with miniature furniture and equipment.

🏛 Sebalduskirche

Winklerstrasse 26. **Open** Jan–Mar: 9:30am–4pm daily; Apr–May & mid-Sep–Dec: 9:30am–6pm daily; Jun–mid-Sep: 9:30am–8pm daily.

The oldest of Nuremberg's churches, Sebalduskirche was built in 1230–73 as a Romanesque, two-choir basilica. During remodelling in the 14th century, it was given two side naves and a soaring western hall-choir. The Gothic towers were completed in the late 15th century. At the centre of the presbytery is the magnificent tomb of St Sebald. This cast bronze structure was made by Peter Vischer the Elder. It houses a silver coffin (1397) containing relics of the saint. The church features some splendid carvings by Veit Stoß, including a magnificent statue of St Andrew (1505), which stands in the ambulatory around the presbytery, the Volckamersche Passion (1499) and the Crucifixion scene in the main altar (1520). Also noteworthy is the magnificent Gothic font and the Tucher family epitaph by Hans von Kulmbach (1513).

Heraldic arms adorning the tympanum of the town hall portal

For hotels and restaurants in this area see pp496–7 and pp519–22

The timber-frame building of the Albrecht-Dürer-Haus

🔢 Egidienkirche

Egidienplatz.

Egidienkirche is the only surviving Baroque church in Nuremberg. Its façade, built after the fire of 1696, hides a building containing elements of the previous Romanesque-Gothic Benedictine church. The older chapels, including the Euchariuskapelle, Tetzelkapellethe and Wolfgang-kapelle, survive to this day.

🔢 Kaiserburg

Kaiserburg-Museum: Innerer Burghof. **Tel** (0911) 244 65 90. **Open** Apr–Sep: 9am–6pm daily; Oct–Mar: 10am–4pm daily. 🔷 🚾 **kaiserburg-nuernberg.de**

The three castles that tower over Nuremberg include the central burgraves' castle, with the Free Reich's buildings to the east, and the Imperial castle (whose origins go back to the 12th century) to the west. When climbing up the Burgstrasse you will first reach the Fünfeckturm (Pentagonal Tower), which dates from 1040. The oldest building in town, it is an architectural relic of the von Zollern burgraves' castle.

At its foot are the Kaiserstallung (Emperor's stables), which now houses a youth hostel. A continued climb will bring you to the courtyard of the imperial palace, which features a round tower (*Sinwellturm*) dating from the 12th century, and a deep well – the *Tiefe Brunnen*. Passing through the inner gate of the castle you will finally reach its heart, the residential building.

🏛 Albrecht-Dürer-Haus

Albrecht-Dürer-Strasse 39. **Tel** (0911) 231 25 68. **Open** 10am–5pm Tue–Fri (to 8pm Thu), 10am–6pm Sat & Sun; Jul–Sep & during Christkindlesmarkt: also open 10am–5pm Mon. 🔷 🎴 🚾 **museen.nuernberg.de**

Spending much of his childhood in a house on the corner of Burgstrasse and Obere Schmiedgasse, the renowned artist and engraver Albrecht Dürer lived in this house from 1509 until his death in 1528. On the 300th anniversary of his death, the building was bought by the town and many rooms have since been reconstructed. The third-floor room now contains a printing press dating from Dürer's time.

Copies of his pictures provide a useful insight into the work of this famous Nuremberg citizen.

🏛 St-Johannis-Friedhof

Am Johannisfriedhof.

The St John's Cemetery is one of the best preserved and most important in Europe. Established in 1518, it has provided a resting place for many famous people, including Albrecht Dürer (No. 649), the sculptor Veit Stoß (No. 268), the goldsmith Wenzel Jamnitzer (No. 664) and the painter Anselm Feuerbach (No. 715). The cemetery also contains a rich array of tombs from the 16th, 17th and 18th centuries.

🏛 Dokumentationszentrum Reichsparteitagsgelände

Bayernstrasse. 110. **Tel** (0911) 231 56 66. **Open** 9am–6pm Mon–Fri, 10am–6pm Sat & Sun. 🔷

This vast, unfinished building complex in the southern part of town dates from the Nazi era, built for National Party gatherings. The building now houses a historical exhibition and archive, reminding and educating visitors of its horrifying past.

The buildings of the Kaiserburg, towering over the town

Nuremberg: Germanisches Nationalmuseum

This museum, which was officially opened in 1852, was founded by a Franconian aristocrat named Hans von Aufsess. It houses a unique collection of antiquities from the German-speaking world. In 1945, towards the end of World War II, the buildings that had originally housed the museum were bombed. The architecture of the modern building, which was completed in 1993, cleverly incorporates the remaining fragments of a former Carthusian abbey. Among the most valuable items in the museum's collection are works by Tilman Riemenschneider, Konrad Witz, Lucas Cranach the Elder, Albrecht Altdorfer, Albrecht Dürer and Hans Baldung Grien.

Madonna with Child Crowned by Angels
This picture was painted by Hans Holbein the Elder (c.1465–1524) who created many festive altarpieces using warm colours.

★ Archangel (1516)
This enchanting wood-carving of the archangel Raphaël is one of many works produced by Veit Stoss after his return from Cracow.

Cloisters

Former Carthusian church

Ground floor

Entrance to study collections and library

Brooch from Domagnano
This Ostrogothic buckle from the 5th century AD, shaped like an eagle, was discovered in the late 19th century in Domagnano, in San Marino. It probably belonged to a rich Ostrogothic aristocrat.

★ Cover of the Codex Aureus
The richly ornamented cover of the *Codex Aureus*, also known as the Golden Gospel Book of Echternach, was produced in Trier in the 10th century.

Gallery Guide

The exhibits have been arranged in sections, ranging from prehistory to the Middle Ages, and are located on the ground and first floors. Twentieth-century art is on the second floor and the toy collection is housed separately.

First floor

Library

VISITORS' CHECKLIST

Practical Information
Kartäusergasse 1. **Tel** (0911) 133 10. **Open** 10am–6pm Tue–Sun (to 9pm Wed). **Closed** Shrove Tue, 24, 25, 31 Dec.
W **gnm.de**

Torquetum
Johannes Praetorius from Nuremberg produced this engraved copper device in 1568, designed to measure the positions of the stars.

★ **Portrait of Michael Wolgemut** (1516)
Albrecht Dürer painted this portrait of his predecessor and master, Wolgemut, 30 years after commencing work at his studio.

★ **Schlüsselfeld Vessel**
This beautiful silver-gold sailing ship, supported by a two-tailed mermaid, is an ornamental table vessel made in 1503 by an unidentified goldsmith from Nuremberg.

Key to Floorplan

- ☐ Textiles and folk art
- ☐ Pre-1800 decorative arts
- ☐ Child Museum guide
- ■ Scientific instruments and pharmaceutical history
- ☐ Musical instruments and applied arts
- ■ Pre-1700 everyday culture
- ☐ Middle Ages
- ☐ Arms and armour, garden sculpture
- ☐ Prehistory and early history
- ■ Archive, prints and drawings, coins and medals
- ☐ Renaissance, Baroque, Enlightenment
- ☐ Non-exhibition space

⑰ Street-by-Street: Rothenburg ob der Tauber

If you want to sample the atmosphere of the Middle Ages, visit Rothenburg on the river Tauber, whose origins go back to the 12th century. Rothenburg was granted the status of a free town within the Holy Roman Empire in 1274 but its major growth took place in the 15th century. During the Thirty Years' War (1618–48) the town, which fought on the Protestant side, was captured by the Emperor's army. Little has changed since that time and the city walls still surround Gothic cathedrals and an array of gabled houses.

Reichsstadtmuseum
The former Dominican abbey now houses a museum devoted to the town's history. The abbey kitchen – the oldest surviving kitchen in Germany – is also open to visitors.

Franziskanerkirche
In this Gothic church is a retable depicting *The Stigmatization of St Francis*, believed to be an early work by Tilman Riemenschneider.

★ St Jakobs Kirche
In the Gothic church of St Jakob (built between 1311 and 1485) is the superb Zwölfbotenaltar by Friedrich Herlin.

★ Mittelalterliches Kriminalmuseum
Many blood-curdling exhibits are on display at this museum, which houses a collection of instruments of torture and punishment.

HERRNGASSE

MARKT–PLATZ

HAFENGASSE

OBERE SCHMIEDGASSE

View from Burggarten
The castle garden (Burggarten) is reached through Burgtor, the tallest of the town's gates. The garden, which during the Middle Ages was the site of the Hohenstaufen family castle, provides a magnificent view over the town and the river valley.

Galgentor
Galgentor, an old execution place, is also known as Würzburger Tor, since it is the gate leading to Würzburg.

Rödertor
The best preserved segments of the old city walls are around the Rödertor gate, which dates from the late 14th century.

★ Rathaus
The town hall consists of the surviving Gothic section with a tower, and the later Renaissance structure with Baroque arcades.

Key

— Suggested route

⓲ Andechs

Road map D7. *i* Andechser Strasse 16 (08152-932 50).

The village of Andechs, at the summit of the 700-m (2,300-ft) high Holy Mountain of the same name, is not only the destination of pilgrimages to the local church, but also of many less spiritual trips to the *Bräustüberl*, where visitors can refresh themselves with a glass or two of the excellent beer brewed by local monks.

The present triple-nave Gothic hall-church was built in 1420–25. Its Rococo interior dates from 1755. The lower tier of the main altar contains the famous *Miraculous Statue of the Mother of God* (1468), while the upper tier features the *Immaculata* by Hans Degler (1609). On selected feast days, holy relics are displayed on the altar gallery.

Ammersee near the Holy Mountain of Andechs

⓳ Landsberg am Lech

Road map D7. ⚠ 24,000. 🚉 *i* Hauptplatz 152 (08191-12 82 46).

The history of Landsberg goes back to 1160 when Henry the Lion built his castle here, on the right bank of the river Lech. During the 13th century, the surrounding settlement grew into a town, which soon became a major trading centre. Religious conflicts, culminating in the Thirty Years'War, put an end to the town's development but, in the late 17th century, the town once again became

an important commercial and cultural centre. Adolf Hitler wrote *Mein Kampf* here, while serving a prison term for his unsuccessful coup attempt in Munich.

At the heart of Landsberg is the Hauptplatz with its Baroque town hall and the intricately carved 14th-century tower, Schmalztor.

In Ludwigstrasse is the late-Gothic parish church, Stadtpfarrkirche Maria Himmelfahrt, whose Baroque-style interior features a statue of the *Madonna and Child* by Hans Multscher. Bayertor, the original town gate, is in the eastern part of the old town.

The town's **Neues Stadt-museum** is a useful source of information on local history.

iii Neues Stadtmuseum
Von-Helfenstein-Gasse 426. **Tel** (08191) 12 83 60. **Open** 2–5pm Tue–Sun, 11am–5pm Sat & Sun. 🅿

⓴ Dachau

Road map D6. ⚠ 35,000. 🚉 *i* Konrad-Adenauer-Strasse 1 (08131-75286 or 75287).

For most people the name Dachau is inextricably linked with the concentration camp that was built here by the Nazis in 1933. Since 1965, the whole site has been designated as a memorial, **KZ-Gedenkstätte Dachau**, to over 40,000 prisoners who died there, with a permanent exhibition in the former domestic quarters of the camp.

Dachau is a beautiful town with many historic buildings. On the southwestern edge of the old town stands **Schloss Dachau**, summer residence of the Wittelsbachs. The palace that stands here today was created in the 18th century from the western wing of an earlier castle, the work of Joseph Effner.

In the early 19th century the area surrounding the castle housed a colony of artists who

Relief from the church façade in Landsberg

had tired of city life. They were known as *Malschule Neu-Dachau*. Even earlier, however, the beauty of the surrounding countryside had been discovered by the impressionist painter Max Liebermann (1847–1935). The **Dachauer Gemäldegalerie** contains works of art inspired by local scenery, including one by Liebermann.

iii Dachauer Gemäldegalerie
Konrad-Adenauer-Strasse 3. **Tel** (08131) 56 750. **Open** 11am–5pm Tue–Fri, 1–5pm Sat & Sun. 🅿

🏰 Schloss Dachau
Schlossstrasse 2. **Tel** (08131) 879 23. **Open** Apr–Sep: 9am–6pm Tue–Sun; Oct–Mar: 10am–4pm Tue–Sun. **Closed** 1 Jan; Shrove Tue; 24, 25 & 31 Dec. 🅿

🏛 KZ-Gedenkstätte Dachau
Alte Römerstrasse 75. **Tel** (08131) 66 99 70. **Open** 9am–5pm daily. **Closed** 24 Dec.

㉑ Schleißheim

Road map D6. Oberschleißheim.

Schleißheim is situated barely 14 km (9 miles) from Munich, making it within easy reach for an afternoon visit to its Baroque palace and park.

Surrounded by canals and now somewhat neglected, the park was established in the 17th and 18th centuries and includes

Baroque façade of the Wittelsbach palace, Schloss Dachau

three palaces. The modest **Altes Schloss** was built in 1623 for Prince Wilhelm V. Now it houses an exhibition of religious folk art.

Schloss Lustheim is a small, Baroque, hermitage-type palace, built in 1684–87 by Enrico Zucalli for the Elector Max Emanuel. As well as its beautiful interiors and stunning frescoes, it boasts a magnificent collection of Meissen porcelain, which is displayed in the **Museum Meißener Porzellan**.

The newest building is the **Neues Schloss**, designed by Enrico Zucalli. Work begun in 1701 but was not completed until the second half of the 18th century. Despite wartime damage, it retains many original features. It now houses exhibits belonging to the Bavarian State Museum.

The imposing bulk of the Neues Schloss in Ingolstadt

🏠 **Altes Schloss**
Tel (089) 315 87 20. **Open** as Neues Schloss. ♿

🏠 **Neues Schloss**
Tel (089) 315 87 20. **Open** Apr–Sep: 9am–6pm Tue–Sun; Oct–Mar: 10am–4pm Tue–Sun. **Closed** Mon. ♿

🏠 **Schloss Lustheim**
Tel (089) 315 87 20. **Open** Apr–Sep: 9am–6pm Tue–Sun; Oct–Mar: 10am–4pm Tue–Sun. ♿

Museum Meißener Porzellan
Tel (089) 315 87 242. **Open** Apr–Sep: 9am–6pm Tue–Sun; Oct–Mar: 10am–4pm Tue–Sun.

㉒ Freising

Road map D6. 🚗 40,000. 🚉
ℹ️ Marienplatz 7 (08161-544 41 11).

Situated on the banks of the river Isar, just 20 minutes by train from Munich, is the old town of Freising. Its history is closely connected with St Korbinian, who founded the bishopric here in the early 8th century. Korbinian died around AD 725 and his remains still lie in the crypt of the Dom – the Cathedral Church of the Birth of the Virgin Mary and St Korbinian (1159–1205). This is a five-nave basilica, without transept, with an elongated choir and a massive twin-tower western façade. Its interior was remodelled in Baroque style by

the Asam brothers, in 1724–25. The four-nave Romanesque crypt features a famous column, which is decorated with carvings of fantastic animals *(Bestiensäule)*. Nearby is the **Diözesanmuseum,** whose vast ecclesiastical collection includes two paintings by Rubens.

At the southwestern end of the old town is a former monastery, Weihenstephan, home to the world's longest-established brewery and a botanical garden.

🏛️ **Diözesanmuseum**
Domberg 21. **Tel** (08161) 487 90. **Closed** due to reopen 2016–17. ♿

㉓ Ingolstadt

Road map D6. 🚗 130, 000. 🚉
ℹ️ Rathausplatz 2 (0841-305 30 30).

Lying on the river Danube, this former seat of the Wittelsbach family features many important historic buildings dating from the Middle Ages and the Renaissance and Baroque periods. Among the

most outstanding is the Church of the Virgin Mary, a triple-nave hall structure with circular pillars, chapels and choir with an ambulatory. Inside is the original Gothic-Renaissance main altar dating from 1572.

Another notable building is the Neues Schloss, built between the 15th and 18th centuries, with its stately rooms and Gothic chapel. It now houses the **Bayerisches Armeemuseum**.

A true gem of Bavarian architecture is the **Church of St Maria Victoria**, the work of Cosmas Damian Asam.

The **Deutsches Medizinhistorisches Museum** exhibits medical instruments and has a garden with medicinal plants.

🏛️ **Bayerisches Armeemuseum**
Neues Schloss, Paradeplatz 4. **Tel** (0841) 937 70. **Open** 9am–5:30pm Tue–Fri, 10am–5:30pm Sat & Sun. ♿

🏛️ **Deutsches Medizin historisches Museum**
Anatomiestrasse 18–20. **Tel** (0841) 305 28 60. **Open** 10am–5pm Tue–Sun. ♿

Striking Baroque interior of the Church of St Maria Victoria, Ingolstadt

Arcaded courtyard of Neuburg Castle

❷ Neuburg an der Donau

Road map D6. 🏛 25,000. 🚂 ℹ️
Ottheinrichplatz 118 (08431-552 40).

Perched on a promontory overlooking the river Danube, Neuburg is one of Bavaria's loveliest towns. During the Middle Ages, it changed hands frequently but was eventually ruled by Ottheinrich the Magnanimous, under whom the town grew and prospered on an unprecedented scale. He was the founder of the castle, built between 1534 and 1665, whose massive round towers still dominate the town. Its earliest part is the east wing. The courtyard, which is surrounded by arcades, features beautiful frescoes by Hans Schroer. In the tower is a staircase adorned with paintings. The castle chapel, completed in 1543, is one of the oldest, purpose-built Protestant churches in Germany.

In Amalienstrasse, leading down towards the town, stands the former Jesuits' College and the Court Church (Hofkirche). Work on the church began in the late 16th century and was completed in 1627. It was intended to be a Protestant church, but the ruling family converted back to Catholicism during its construction and it was taken over by the Jesuits who turned it into a counter-reformation Marian church.

The triple-nave hall-structure has an exquisite interior decorated in gold, white and grey.

Among many old buildings that survive in the town centre are the Graf-Veri-Haus and the Baron-von-Hartman-Haus in Herrenstrasse. To the east of town stands the Grünau Castle (Jagdschloss), built for Ottheinrich in 1530–55.

Heraldic crest on Neuberg Castle

Environs
18 km (11 miles) to the south, Schrobenhausen is the birthplace of the painter Franz von Lenbach, who was born in 1836. A museum in Ulrich-Peisser-Gasse is devoted to his life and work. While there, it is worth visiting St Jacob's Church, to see the fine 15th-century wall painting there.

🏛 **Schlossmuseum Neuburg**
Residenzstrasse 2. **Tel** (08431) 88 97.
Open Apr–Sep: 9am–6pm Tue–Sun; Oct–Mar: 10am–4pm Tue–Sun. ♿
🆆 **schloesser.bayern.de**

❷ Landshut

Road map E6. 🏛 57,000. 🚂
ℹ️ Altstadt 315 (0871-92 20 50).
🎭 Fürstenhochzeit (every 4 years, next in 2017), Hofmusiktage (every 2 years, next in 2016), Frühjahrsdult (Apr–May), Bartlmädult (Aug), Haferlmarkt (Sep).

The earliest records of Landshut date from 1150. One hundred years later this was already a town and the main centre of power of the Dukes of Lower

Bavaria. In 1475 the town was the scene of a lavish medieval wedding, when Duke Georg of the House of Wittelsbach married the Polish Princess Jadwiga. Since 1903 the town has held regular re-enactments of the wedding feast (Landshuter Fürstenhochzeit).

Landshut has preserved its medieval urban layout, with two wide parallel streets, Altstadt and Neustadt, with clusters of historic 15th–16th century buildings. Opposite the town hall in Alstadt is the **Stadtresidenz**, a town house modelled on the Palazzo del Tè in Mantua. Sometimes known as the "Italian House", this was the first Renaissance palace to be built in Germany.

The vast brick church of St Martin (1385–1500) is a triple-nave, narrow hall-church featuring a presbytery, network vaults (1459) and the tallest church tower in Bavaria.

Landshut is dominated by the fortified 13th–16th century **Burg Trausnitz**, featuring a medieval tower, a Renaissance palace (1568–78) and the **Kunst- und Wunderkammer** ("room of arts and wonder"), a branch of the Bayerisches Nationalmuseum (*see p223*).

Environs
From Landshut, it is worth taking a trip to Moosburg, situated 14 km (9 miles) to the

Stained-glass window in Landshut depicting Duke Georg and Jadwiga

west. Its early 13th-century Church of St Castulus features a 14-m (46-ft) high Marian altar by Hans Leinberger (1514).

🏠 Burg Trausnitz & Kunst-und Wunderkammer
Tel (0871) 92 41 10. **Open** Apr–Sep: 9am–6pm daily; Oct–Mar: 10am–4pm.
🏠 🔲 burg-trausnitz.de

🏠 Stadtresidenz
Altstadt 79. **Tel** (0871) 92 41 10. **Open** Apr–Sep: 9am–6pm Tue–Sun; Oct–Mar: 10am–4pm Tue–Sun.
🔲 obligatory. 🏞

Interior of St George's Chapel in Burg Trausnitz

㉖ Dingolfing

Road map E6. 🏔 15,400. 🛈 Im Bruckstadel, Fischerei 9 (08731) 32 71 00.

The main tourist attraction in this small town on the banks of the river Isar is its Gothic castle. Built in the 15th century by the Bavarian dukes, this vast edifice now houses the Regional Museum. It is also worth taking a stroll to see Pfarrkirche St Johannes, a late-Gothic brick building dating from the late 15th century. Although what remains of its furnishings are merely the poor remnants of its former glory, nevertheless the church is still considered one of the most beautiful Gothic buildings in Bavaria.

Environs
In Landau an der Isar, situated 13 km (8 miles) to the east of Dingolfing, stands the picturesque Baroque church of Mariä Himmelfahrt, dating from the first half of the 18th century. There is also an interesting small church, the Steinfelskirche (c.1700) inside a natural rock cave. In Arnstorf, 30 km (19 miles) to the east, is one of the few remaining Bavarian castles on water. Known as the Oberes Schloß, the castle was probably built in the 15th century and remodelled during the 17th and 18th centuries.

㉗ Straubing

Road map E6. 🏔 45,000. 🚌
🛈 Theresienplatz 2 (09421-94 43 07).
🎭 Agnes-Bernauer-Festspiel (Jul, every four years, next in 2019), Gäubodenvolksfest (Aug).

This market town enjoys a picturesque setting on the river Danube. The 600-m (1,970-ft) long market square is arranged into two sections, Theresienplatz and Ludwigplatz, and is part of the former trade route that led to Prague. The area is lined with historic buildings in Baroque, Neo-Classical and Secession styles.

At the centre of the market square stands the landmark 14th-century municipal tower, which offers a splendid view over the towns of the Bavarian Forest. At Ludwigplatz 23 is the "Lion's Pharmacy", where the famous Biedermeier painter Karl Spitzweg worked as an apprentice in 1828–30.

Turning from Theresienplatz into Seminargasse or Jakobsgasse, you will reach the monumental brick structure of the parish church of St Jakob (1400–1590). This triple-nave hall-church, crowned with a network vault, retains many original features, including stained-glass windows in the chapels of Maria-Hilf-Kapelle (1420) and St Bartholomew. The so-called Moses' Window in the Chapel of St Joseph was made in 1490 in Nuremberg, based on a sketch provided by Wilhelm Playdenwurff. In the Cobbler's Chapel (Schusterkapelle) hangs a painting of *Madonna and Child*, by Hans Holbein (c.1500). Overlooking the Danube is a 14th–15th-century castle, formerly a ducal residence. The Agnes-Bernauer Festival, held every four years, takes place in the courtyard of the castle. The Gäuboden-volksfest is the second largest folk festival in Bavaria after the Munich Oktoberfest. The **Gäuboden-museum** has a magnificent collection of Roman artifacts.

Environs
In the tiny village of Aufhausen, 21 km (12 miles) to the west, is the beautiful late-Baroque pilgrimage church of Maria Schnee. Built by Johann Michael Fischer in 1736–51, it includes magnificent wall paintings by the Asam brothers and a statue of the Madonna. Commissioned by Duke Wilhelm V of Bavaria, the Gnadenmadonna is believed to pardon sins.

In Oberalteich, some 10 km (6 miles) to the east, is the beautiful church of St Peter and St Paul built in the early 17th century for the Benedictine order. Inside, an unusual hanging staircase leads to the galleries, while the vestibule is decorated with stucco ornaments, depicting bird motifs.

In Windberg, 22 km (14 miles) east of Oberalteich, is a Romanesque Marian church whose main portal (c.1220) features an image of the Madonna in the tympanum.

🏛 Gäubodenmuseum
Fraunhoferstrasse. **Tel** (09421) 974 110. **Open** 10am–4pm Tue–Sun. 🏞

Main altar in Ursulinenkirche, Straubing

㉘ Regensburg (Ratisbon)

Regensburg was once a Celtic settlement and later a campsite of the Roman legions. The outline of the Roman camp is still visible around St Peter's Cathedral. In the early 6th century, Regensburg was the seat of the Agilolfa ruling family, and in AD 739, a monk named Boniface established a bishopric here. From AD 843, Regensburg was the seat of the Eastern Frankish ruler, Ludwig the German. From 1245 it was a free town of the Holy Roman Empire and throughout the Middle Ages remained South Germany's fastest growing commercial and cultural centre. The city centre is a UNESCO World Heritage Site.

Picturesque Steinere Brücke leading to the old town of Regensburg

🏛 Steinerne Brücke
An outstanding example of medieval engineering, this 310-m (1,000-ft) long bridge over the Danube was built in 1135–46. It provides the best panoramic view of Regensburg. Near the bridge gate, Brückentor, stands an enormous salt ware-house topped with a vast five-storey roof.

🏛 Wurstküche (Wurstkuchle)
Thundorferstrasse 3. **Tel** (0941) 46 62 10. **Open** 8am–7pm daily.

Immediately behind the salt warehouse is the famous *Wurstküche* (sausage kitchen), which has probably occupied this site since as early as the 12th century and may have served as a canteen for the builders of the bridge. Its Regensburger sausages are definitely worth trying.

🏛 Altes Rathaus
Rathausplatz. 📷 Mon–Sat. Reichstagsmuseum. **Tel** (0941) 507 34 40. 📷 Jan & Feb: 10am, 11:30am, 1:30pm, 3pm daily ; Mar, Nov, Dec: 10am, 11:30am, 1:30pm, 2pm (in English), 3pm, 3:30pm daily; (every 30 mins) Apr–Oct: 9:30am–noon, 1:30–4pm daily (English tours 3pm). 📷

In Rathausplatz stands an old 15th-century town hall with a 13th-century tower. It contains a splendid, richly decorated hall – *Reichssaal* – where the Perpetual Imperial Diet (the first parliament of the Holy Roman Empire) sat between 1663 and 1806. Benches in the chamber were coloured to indicate who could sit where: for example, red benches for Electors. The adjoining new

Late-Gothic oriel on the side elevation of the Altes Rathaus

town hall dates from the late 17th–early 18th century.

🏛 Dom St Peter
Domschatzmuseum
Krauterermarkt 3. **Tel** (0941) 57 645. **Open** Apr–Oct: 11am–5pm Tue–Sat, noon–5pm Sun; Dec–6 Jan: 10am–4pm Sun; 7 Jan–Mar: 10am–4pm Fri & Sat, noon–4pm Sun. **Closed** Nov. 📷

Towering above the city, on the site of the former Roman military camp, is the massive brick structure of St Peter's Cathedral. Built between 1250 and 1525, its imposing western towers were added only in 1859–69. The master architect, Ludwig, modelled his design for the building on French examples (the Rayonnant style). The stained-glass windows of the choir date from the early 14th century. The **Domschatz-museum** has a collection of ecclesiastical vestments.

[Map of Regensburg old town showing streets including BADSTRASSE, KEPLERSTRASSE, WEISSGERBERGRABEN, LUDWIGSTRASSE, GESANDTENSTR, SCHOTTENSTRASSE, WAFFNERGASSE, HELENENSTRASSE, and landmarks: Eiserner Steg, Keple Gedächtnishau, Thon-Dittr Palais, Haus zum Goldenen Kreuz, ARNULFS-PLATZ, ⑦ St Jakob Kirche, BISMARCK-PLATZ, Dreieinigkeitski, Dominikaner-kloster, EMMERA-PLATZ, St Emr, Schloss und Taxi]

| 0 metres | | 300 |
| 0 yards | | 300 |

19th-century spires on the Gothic St Peter's Cathedral

Sights at a Glance

① Steinerne Brücke
② Wurstküche
③ Altes Rathaus
④ Dom St Peter
⑤ Alte Kapelle
⑥ Schloss Thurn und Taxis
⑦ St Jakob Kirche

🏛 Alte Kapelle
Alter Kornmarkt.

The Old Chapel is really a Marian collegiate church. It stands on the foundations of an older, early Romanesque chapel dating from the Carolingian period. The building has been remodelled several times and contains some beautiful Rococo stuccoes by Anton Landes.

🏰 Schloss Thurn und Taxis
Emmeramsplatz 5. **Tel** (0941) 504 82 42. **Open** daily. **Closed** 1–12 Jan. ⏰ Mar–Oct: 10:30am–4:30pm (hourly) daily; Nov–Mar: 10:30am– 3:30pm (hourly exc 12:30pm) daily. 🎫

In the south end of the town you will find the buildings and churches of the former St Emmeram Abbey, which have been tastefully incorporated into the palace complex of the ducal family von Thurn und Taxis. These include a Gothic cloister dating from the 12th–14th centuries, a library

VISITORS' CHECKLIST

Practical Information
Road map D6. 🚃 142,000. ℹ Altes Rathaus (0941 507 44 10). 🎭 Frühjahrsdult (Whitsun), Bach-Woche (Jun), Bayerisches Jazz-Weekend (Jul), Herbstdult (Aug–Sep), Christkindlmarkt & Domspatzen concerts (Dec). 🌐 **regensburg.de**

Enchanting Rococo interior of Alte Kapelle

with magnificent frescoes by Cosmas Damian Asam and the burial chapel. In 1998, the Bavarian State Museum opened a branch here, the Schatzkammer, which has valuable collections of decorative art.

🏛 Baumburger Turm
Watmarkt.

Regensburg has many unique ancestral palaces dating from the 14th–15th centuries, with high towers modelled on Northern Italian architecture. Some 20 of the original 60 towers have survived. One of the most beautiful is the residential tower, Baumburger Turm. Nearby, at Watmarkt 5, stands the equally beautiful Goliathhaus, where Oskar Schindler lived for a time in 1945. A commemorative plaque has been placed at the rear of the building.

Gothic portals of St Emmeram Abbey in Schloss Thurn und Taxis

Winter view of Gnadenkapelle complex, from Altötting

❷ Altötting

Road map D7. ▲ 11,000.
🅸 Kapellplatz 2a (08671-50 62 19).
🅿 🎫 pilgrimages to Altötting
(Whitsun). 🆆 altoetting.de

Altötting is renowned as the earliest destination of pilgrimages to the "Miraculous Statue" of the Virgin Mary (1330). The statue stands in the Wallfahrtskapelle St Maria, which consists of two parts. The central, octagonal chapel, **Gnadenkapelle** (c.AD 750) was once the baptistery. The external chapel was built in 1494 and the ambulatory in 1517. It also houses the so-called "Silver Prince", representing the miraculously cured son of the Prince-Elector, Karl Albrecht. Many Bavarian royals wished to be buried here.

Nearby is the interesting Romanesque-Gothic church of St Philip and St Jacob (1228–30 and 1499–1520). Its Neo-Classical interior contains many tombstones, while a separate chapel, Tillykapelle, is the burial place of Johann Tserclaes von Tilly, a hero of the Thirty Years' War and the Emperor's general.

The **Schatzkammer** (Treasury) was housed in the former sacristy, but after Pope Benedict XVI turned it into a chapel in 2006 a new Schatzkammer and Wallfahrtsmuseum (Pilgrimage Museum) were built. The collection includes an exquisite example of French enamel and gold artwork, the *Goldenes Rössl* (Golden Steed), which dates from around 1400. Despite its name, the theme of this work is the Adoration of the Magi. It was commissioned by Isobel of Bavaria as a New Year gift for her husband, Charles VI of France.

🏛 Neue Schatzkammer and Wallfahrtsmuseum
Kapellplatz 4. **Tel** (08671) 924 2015.
Open Feb–Mar: Mon–Sat; Apr–Oct: daily. **Closed** Nov–mid-Mar.

Walkway around Gnadenkapelle, in Altötting, filled with offerings

❸ Burghausen

Road map E6. ▲ 19,500. 🅸
Stadtplatz 112 (08677-887 140). 🅿

The very picturesque town of Burghausen is situated on the river Salzach. Towering over the town, the river and the lake is **Burghausen Castle**, the world's longest castle, built on a high ridge stretching for 1,050 m

(1,150 yds). Work on the castle started in 1253, but most of the buildings were erected during the reign of King George the Rich and therefore have magnificent, late-Gothic forms. The king's wife, Jadwiga Jagiellon, whom he married in grand style in Landshut *(see p270)*, was later rejected by him and she spent her final days in the fortress of Burghausen.

The castle consists of two main parts: the main castle, with tower, the residential quarters, the courtyard and domestic buildings; and the castle approach (Vorburg). The residential building has some fine 15th- and 16th-century paintings. A special door links the Prince's quarters with the "internal" Chapel of St Elizabeth. Next to the chapel is the mid-13th-century Dürnitz, which served originally as a ballroom and banqueting hall.

The castle approach consists of five courtyards (Vorhof). In the fourth courtyard is the "external" Chapel of St Jadwiga (Aussere Burgkapelle St Hedwig) – the work of Wolfgang Wiesinger, a native of Salzburg (1489). This has numerous original buildings, including the town hall, which was created by combining three burgher houses dating from the 14th–15th centuries The parish church of St Jakob (1353–1513) in Burghausen is a three-nave basilica.

🏰 Burghausen Castle
Tel (08677) 887 140.

🏛 Museum
Open Apr–Sep: 9am–6pm daily; Oct–Mar: 10am–4pm daily. 🖼

Panoramic view of Burghausen, with its vast castle complex on the hill

㉑ Bayerischer Wald

The Bavarian forest stretches north to the Danube, between Regensburg and Passau. It is part of Central Europe's largest woodland and provides idyllic grounds for a variety of outdoor pursuits. The local rocks contain large quantities of quartz, which contributed to the early development of the glass industry here. To this day, the region produces some fine, blown-glass artifacts. The region also hosts a number of popular festivals throughout the year.

① Zwiesel
In the old glassworks, which survive to this day, you can watch workers using blow irons to produce vases, jugs and other objects made of glass.

② Frauenau
Along with Zwiesel, this is the oldest centre of glass production in the area. The local museum illustrates the town's history.

③ Spiegelau
Spiegelau is one of the most popular starting points for tourists planning hiking trips into the mountains.

④ Grafenau
The main attractions of this small town are its snuff and furniture museums and the old town hall.

NATIONALPARK BAYERISCHER WALD

Cham · Regen

Deggendorf

0 km — 8
0 miles — 8

Strakonitz

Passau

⑤ Freyung
The main attraction of the town is the Schloss (Castle) Wolfstein, which now houses a museum of hunting and fishing.

⑥ Finsterau
Situated close to a vast artificial lake, Finsterau has an interesting open-air museum that displays examples of the local building trade.

Key
▪ Suggested route
— Other road
▪ Scenic route
☀ Viewpoint

Tips For Walkers

Starting point: Zwiesel.
Distance: 82 km (51 miles).
Getting there: train to Frauenau, on the Zwiesel-Granau line; or Bodenmais, terminus of another branch line from Zwiesel.

⚫ Street-by-Street: Passau

Passau, whose long history goes back to Roman times, lies on a peninsula between the rivers Danube and Inn, near the Austrian border. During the second half of the 5th century, St Severinus established a monastery in Passau as well as several more nearby. In 739, an Irish monk called Boniface, known as "Germany's Apostle", founded a bishopric here and for many years this was the largest diocese of the Holy Roman Empire. Large parts of the town were destroyed by fires in 1662 and 1680. Reconstruction was carried out by Italian artists, who gave the town its Baroque, Rococo and Neo-Classical façades. However, Passau retains a medieval feel in its narrow alleys and archways.

Passauer Glasmuseum
Opposite the old town hall is the beautiful patrician Hotel Wilder Mann, which now houses the Glasmuseum. The museum's vast collection includes valuable examples of Bohemian, Austrian and Bavarian glasswork.

★ Dom St Stephan
St Stephan's Cathedral is a true masterpiece of Italian Baroque, built by Italian architect Carlo Lurago to replace the original Gothic structure, which was largely destroyed by fire in the 17th century.

★ Altes Rathaus
Dating from the 14th–15th century, the old town hall was created by combining eight patrician houses. The structure features a Neo-Gothic tower.

Neue Bischofsresidenz
Built by Domenico d'Angeli and Antonio Beduzzi in 1713–30, the Neue Residenz has a pilaster façade with protruding balconies and roof balustrade.

Map labels: Deggendorf · ANGER STRA · GROSSE MESSERGASSE · SCHROT GASSE · Passau-Hauptbahnhof · DOMPLATZ · University · INNKAI · MARIEN-BRÜCKE

◀ The entrance to the harbour Lindau on Lake Constance

★ **Veste Oberhaus**
This former castle of the prince-bishops now houses the Oberhaus-Museum, with displays on local and regional history and the work of local artists.

Schaiblingsturm
On the bank of the river Inn are the remains of Passau's Gothic town walls. They include this tower, built in 1250.

PRINZREGENT
LUITPOLD BRÜCKE

O R T

| 0 metres | 100 |
| 0 yards | 100 |

★ **Wallfahrtskirche Mariahilf**
High above the banks of the river Inn stands this early-Baroque abbey complex dating from 1627–30. It includes a pretty twin-towered pilgrimage church.

Key
— Suggested route

❸ Berchtesgadener Land

Berchtesgadener Land is one of the most beautiful regions, not just in Germany, but in the whole of Europe. It occupies the area of the Berchtesgadener Alps whose boundaries are defined by the river Saalach to the west, the river Salzach to the east, the "Stony Sea" *(Steinernes Meer)* to the south and, to the north, Untersberg, which is 1,972 m (7,500 ft) above sea level. To the south of Berchtesgaden village lies the National Park (Nationalpark Berchtesgaden).

★ **Ramsau an der Ache**
Set in an enchanting location in the Ramsau Valley, this village is a popular base for visitors to the area. Spectacular views of the mountains can be enjoyed from the small parish church.

Hintersee
This scenic lake has given its name to a picturesque hamlet nearby. A walk around the lake takes about one hour.

LATTEN GEBIRG

REITER ALPE

HINTERSEE

Ramsau

Wimbachklam

NATIONAL- PARK BERCHTESGADEN

Kehlsteinhaus

Standing on the summit of Kehlstein, this stone building resembling a mountain shelter is known as the Adlerhorst (Eagle's Nest). It was given to Hitler as a birthday present in 1939 by one of his closest allies, Martin Bormann, and it became one of the Führer's favourite residences. The approach to the building is a true engineering masterpiece: the initial section, the Kehlsteinstrasse, is a scenic mountain road, which passes through five tunnels and offers some breathtaking views. The final ascent is via a lift. The whole project took 13 months to complete. After the war, the

Eagle's Nest fell into the hands of the Americans, then, in 1960, it passed into private hands. The building now houses a restaurant that is very popular with tourists, not only because of its history but also for the spectacular views that it provides over part of the Alps.

KEY

① **Nationalpark Berchtesgaden**, is home to many rare species of plants and animals. You can visit this magnificent national park by joining organized tours between May and October.

Berchtesgaden
The capital of the region features many historic buildings. The Schloss, originally an Augustinian priory, now houses the art treasures collected by Crown Prince Ruprecht. The local salt mine has been a source of wealth since the 16th century.

Wallfahrtskirche Maria Gern
One of the loveliest Baroque buildings in the region, the pilgrimage church of Maria Gern was built in 1709 in this idyllic location.

Key
- Major road
- Minor road
- River
- Viewpoint

UNTERS-BERG

Winkl
Maria Gern
Bischofs-wiesen
Hallein
Berchtes-gaden
Schönau am Königssee
Königssee
KÖNIGSSEE
OBERSEE

0 km 5
0 miles 5

★ Königssee
Germany's highest lake, Königssee is the focal point of Berchtesgadener Land. Lying 600 m (2,000 ft) above sea level, it covers an area of 5.5 sq km (1,360 acres) and reaches a depth of 188 m (616 ft).

㉞ Touring Chiemsee

Bavaria's largest lake, Chiemsee is a real paradise for watersports enthusiasts, with sailors, water-skiers, swimmers and divers all enjoying the opportunities it offers. The lake is set amidst magnificent Alpine scenery in the region known as the Chiemgau, which stretches eastwards from Rosenheim to the border with Austria along the river Salzach. Chiemsee is surrounded by numerous small towns and villages and dotted with islands, some of which feature fascinating historic buildings. Excellent land, water and rail transport facilities ensure trouble-free travel to all destinations in the area.

Fraueninsel
Like its neighbour Herreninsel, this island is rich in art treasures. Its abbey (Klosterkirche) was founded in 766 and taken over by Benedictine nuns in the mid-9th century.

Stock
The harbour town of Stock is connected by narrow-gauge steam railway to the Chiemsee's main resort of Prien. The railway, the Chiemseebahn, is over one hundred years old.

Obing

Hinzing

Halfing

HARTSEE Eggstätt

Bad Endorf

LANGBÜRGNER SEE

SIMSSEE

Stock

Prien

Harras

Urschalling

Bernau

Urschalling
The 12th-century church of St Jakobus features magnificent wall paintings dating from the 13th and 14th centuries.

Herrenchiemsee Palace
In 1873, King Ludwig II bought Herreninsel, with the intention of building a replica of the Palace of Versailles here. Funds ran out and the project was not completed, but the magnificent central section and park are well worth visiting.

Key

▬ Motorway
▬ Major road
═ Minor road
═ River
✥ Viewpoint

Seeon Abbey

This post-Benedictine abbey, surrounded by the waters of Klostersee, was built in stages during the 11th and 12th centuries. It was remodelled in 1428–33 by Konrad Pürkel, a master-builder from Burghausen.

Castle in the Rock

One of the most interesting curiosities of this region is the "Höhlenburg" – a castle carved into a rock on the bank of the river Traun, some 30 m (98 ft) above water level. Visits are allowed only with a guide.

Chieming

Chieming lies on the eastern shore of the lake. Its 6-km (4-mile) long beach is an ideal place for sunbathing and swimming in the waters of the lake.

0 km   4

0 miles   4

Chiemsee

Lying at an altitude of 518 m (1,700 ft), the lake covers an area of 80 sq km (20,000 acres) with a depth of 70 m (230 ft). Its size makes it popular with sailing enthusiasts.

Colourful Alpine inn, dating from 1612, in Oberammergau

㉟ Garmisch-Partenkirchen

Road map D7. 27,000. 🚉 ℹ️
Richard Strauss-Platz 2 (08821 18 07
00). 🎿 Neujahrs-Springen (1 Jan);
Hornschlitten-Rennen (6 Jan); Ski
World Cup Races; Richard-Strauss-
Tage (Jun). 🆆 gapa.de

Lying in the valley of the river
Loisach, Garmisch-Parten-
kirchen is the best-known resort
in the Bavarian Alps. To say that
it offers ideal skiing conditions
would be to state the
obvious. In 1936, it
hosted the Winter
Olympic Games and,
in 1978, the World
Skiing Championships.
From Garmisch-
Partenkirchen,
Germany's highest
peak, Zugspitze
(2964 m/9,720 ft),
can be reached by
taking the narrow-
gauge railway to
Zugspitzblatt and
from there a cable
car, which reaches
the summit in a few
minutes. Garmisch
Partenkirchen's parish church of
St Martin (Alte Pfarrkirche St
Martin) is worth a visit. It was built
in the 13th century and extended
in the 15th century and features
some well-preserved Gothic
wall paintings and net vaulting.
The **Werdenfels Museum**
shows how people in this
region lived in the past, with a
collection of furniture, clothing
and room reconstructions.

🏛 **Werdenfels Museum**
Ludwigstrasse 47. **Tel** (08821) 751 710.
Open 10am–5pm Tue–Sun. 🎴
🆆 werdenfels-museum.de

Oriel window in
Garmisch-Partenkirchen

㊱ Oberammergau

Road map D7. 🏔 5,200. ℹ️ Eugen-
Papst-Strasse 9A (08822-922 740).
🎿 König-Ludwig-Lauf (Feb);
Oberammergauer Passionsspiele (May–
Oct, every ten years: 2020); König-
Ludwig-Feuer (24 Aug).
🆆 ammergauer-alpen.de

Situated some 20 km (12 miles)
north of Garmisch-Partenkirchen,
and standing on the site of a
9th-century Welfs' fort,
Oberammergau is world famous
for its folk art and passion
plays. The Thirty Years'
War (1618–48) and
the plague of 1632
came close to
wiping out the entire
population of the
village. Its surviving
inhabitants pledged
that if they were
saved from extinction
they would stage for
ever more a play
about Christ's
Passion. No further
deaths occurred and,
to this day, the
villagers have kept
their pledge. Every ten years
(the next is in 2020), some 2,500
people take part in the six-hour-
long spectacle, in which they

transform themselves from
Bavarians into Jews and Romans
from the time of Christ. About
one hundred performances
are staged between mid-May
and mid-October in the
huge Passionsspielhaus.

Among the buildings worth
seeing in Oberammergau are
the Rococo church of Saint
Peter and Saint Paul (1735–40)
and the famous *Pilatushaus*,
with its illusionist painting of
Christ before Pilate on the
façade. The **Oberammergau
Museum** has a notable
collection of wooden cribs.

🏛 **Oberammergau Museum**
Dorfstrasse 8. **Tel** (08822) 941 36.
Open 10am–5pm Tue–Sun.
Closed Feb, Mar, Nov. 🎴

㊲ Ettal

Road map D7. 🏔 974.

About 4 km (2.5 miles) from
Oberammergau is the tiny resort
of Ettal, which is best known for
its Benedictine abbey, founded
by Emperor Ludwig IV of Bavaria.
The abbey's foundation stone
was laid in 1330, while the Church
of the Virgin Mary and the
convent were consecrated in
1370. The church building is a
Gothic structure but, in 1710–52,
Josef Enrico Zuccalli and Franz
Schmuzer carried out major
remodelling work in the
Baroque style. The church
interior is decorated with rich
Rococo stuccowork by Johann
Baptist and Johann Georg
Ubelhör, and wall paintings
by Martin Knoller.

The monastery produces fine
fruit, hay and honey liqueurs,
flavoured brandies and beer.

The Baroque Benedictine abbey in Ettal

❸ Linderhof

In the early 1850s, Linderhof was bought by the Bavarian King Maximilian II. This remote mountain district had great appeal to the young heir to the throne, Ludwig, later to become the eccentric King Ludwig II. In 1874, work started on remodelling the existing *Königshäuschen* (royal cottage) in the Neo-Rococo style. The palace is surrounded by a delightful garden, which is dotted with romantic little buildings, including *Schwanenweiher* (Swan Lake), *Venusgrotte* (Venus grotto) and the *Marokkanisches Haus* (Moroccan house).

VISITORS' CHECKLIST

Practical Information
Road map D7. Schloss Linderhof.
Tel (08822) 920 30. **Open** Apr–15 Oct: 9am–6pm daily; 16 Oct–Mar: 10am–4pm daily.
W schlosslinderhof.de

Tapestry Room
The walls of this room are painted in a style that is reminiscent of tapestry work, with depictions of pastoral scenes.

Reception Room
Although the palace was intended as a private residence, King Ludwig II insisted on the provision of a suitably ornate and regal reception room.

Dining Room
Designed by Christian Jank, the dining room was completed in 1872. It features gilded panelling by Phillip Perron and stuccowork by Theobald Behler.

Mirror Hall
The design of Linderhof's Mirror Hall was based on the Mirror Room of the royal residence in Munich *(see pp220–21).*

Terraces
Terraces in front of the palace are adorned with sculptures and include a pool with a fountain.

⑲ Schloss Neuschwanstein

Set amidst magnificent mountain scenery high above Forggensee, Alpsee and Schwansee, this fairy-tale castle was built in 1869–86 for the eccentric Bavarian King Ludwig II, to a design by the theatre designer Christian Jank. When deciding to build this imposing residence, the king was undoubtedly inspired by Wartburg Castle in Thuringia *(see pp190–91)*, which he visited in 1867. The pale grey limestone castle, which draws on a variety of historical styles, is a steep 30-minute walk from the nearby village of Hohenschwangau and offers spectacular views of the surrounding scenery.

★ **Singers' Hall**
The Sängersaal was modelled on the singing room of the Wartburg castle in Eisenach.

Vestibule
The walls of the vestibule and of other rooms in the castle are lavishly covered with paintings depicting scenes from old German myths and legends.

★ **Throne Room**
The gilded interior of the throne room reminds one of Byzantine temples and the palace church of All Saints (Hofkirche) in the Residenz *(see pp220–21)* in Munich.

KEY

① **Study**

② **Two-storey arcades** surround the castle courtyard.

③ **Gatehouse** provided the king with temporary accommodation during the castle's construction, completed in 1872.

Dining Room
Like other rooms in the palace, the dining room includes fabulous pictures, intricately carved panels and beautifully decorated furniture, all bearing witness to the skill and artistry of the 19th-century craftsmen.

★ Castle Building
Schloss Neuschwanstein is the archetypal fairy-tale castle and has provided the inspiration for countless toy models, book illustrations and film sets.

Courtyard
The heart of the castle was supposed to have been a mighty 90-m (295-ft) high tower with a Gothic castle church. It was never built, but in 1988 its planned position was marked in white stone.

②

③

Main entrance

⑩ Hohenschwangau

Road map D7. 🚐 Schwangau 3,818. 🛈 Schwangau, Münchenerstr. 2 (08362-819 80). Ticket service: Hohenschwangau Alpseestr. 12 (08362 930 830).

The skyline of Schwangau is dominated by two castles, Schloss Neuschwanstein (left) and the majestic **Schloss Hohenschwangau**. The fortified castle that occupied this site in the Middle Ages was remodelled in 1538–47 and, in 1567, it passed into the hands of the Wittelsbach family. It was destroyed during the Tyrolean War but in 1832 the heir to the throne (later Maximilian II) ordered the ruins to be rebuilt in Neo-Gothic style. The plans were prepared by the painter Domenico Quaglio; after his death, work on the castle was continued by the architects Georg Friedrich Ziebland and Joseph Daniel Ohlmüller.

This four-storey building, standing on medieval foundations, is flanked by angular towers. The wall paintings that decorate the rooms of the castle date from 1835–36. Their iconographic content, which is based on old Germanic sagas, is the work of Moritz von Schwind. A walk around the castle provides an excellent opportunity to study the Wittelsbach family history and to see the mid-19th century furnishings. There are magnificent views of the surroundings from the castle's lovely terraced gardens.

🏠 **Schloss Hohenschwangau**
Tel (08362) 930 830. **Open** Apr–mid-Oct: 9am–6pm daily; mid-Oct–Mar: 10am–4pm daily. **Closed** 24 Dec. 🔳
🌐 hohenschwangau.de

Neo-Gothic castle of Maximilian II in Hohenschwangau

The Rococo Throne Room in the Kempten Residenz

⓫ Kempten

Road map C7. 🅰 65,000. 🚉
ℹ Rathausplatz 22 (0831-252 52 37).
🎭 Allgäuer Festwochen (Aug).
🌐 kempten.de

Kempten lies at the centre of one of Germany's most attractive tourist regions, the Allgäu, which stretches from Bodensee (Lake Constance) to the west and the river Lech to the east. The town, which boasts a history of over 2,000 years, was first mentioned by the Greek geographer and historian Strabon as a Celtic settlement, Kambodunon. Later, the Romans established Cambodunum on the right bank of the river Iller. Along with Augusta Vinde-licorum (Augsburg) and Castra Regina (Regensburg), this was one of the most important towns in the Roman province of Raetia.

Medieval Kempten grew around a Benedictine Abbey, founded in 752. In the north-western part of town is the church of St Lorenz.

A triple nave, galleried basilica with an octagonal cupola and a twin-tower façade, this is the work of Michael Beer and Johann Serro. The town's parish church of St Mang dates from the 15th century and in the Rathausplatz is an attractive town hall dating from 1474. The **Kempten Residenz** is a historic property in beautiful grounds. On the right bank of the river Iller is the **Archäologischer Park**, with excavated remains of Roman Cambodunum. The 13th-century Erasmuskapelle chapel is also worth visiting.

🏛 **Kempten Residenz**
Residenzplatz 4–6. **Tel** (0831) 256 251.
Open Apr–Sep: 9am–4pm Tue–Sun; Oct: 10am–4pm Tue–Sun; Nov & Jan–Mar: 10am–4pm Sat; Dec: 12.15–4pm daily. 🅿 📷 📹 🌐 schloesser.bayern.de

🏛 **Archäologischer Park Cambodunum**
Cambodunumweg 3. **Tel** (0831) 252 369. **Open** May–Oct: 10am–5pm Tue–Sun; Nov–Apr: 10am–4:30pm Tue–Sun. **Closed** Dec–Mar.

⓬ Lindau

Road map C7. 🅰 24,000. 🚉
ℹ Alfred-Nobel-Platz 1 (08382-26 00 30). 🎭 Lindauer Kinderfest (Jul).

In Roman times Lindau was a fishing settlement, which used to lie over three islands. The first historic records of the town date from 882. On the south side of the old-town island lies the harbour with its 13th-century lighthouse (Mangturm). The new light-house (Neuer Leuchtturm), built in 1856, stands on the neighbouring pier and offers a splendid view over the lake and the Alps. The marble Lion of Bavaria opposite is the symbol of Lindau.

The old town features many historic buildings, such as the Gothic-Renaissance town hall in Reichsplatz, which was built in 1422–36 and later remodelled in 1578. The picturesque Maximilianstrasse is lined with the houses of rich patricians; their shady arcades (Brodlauben) are typical of Lindau architecture.

In Schrannenplatz, in the northwest area of the town, stands the church of St Peter. Since 1928 this has been the war memorial chapel for World War I victims. Its eastern section dates from the mid-12th century while the bigger, western section was built between 1425 and 1480. The interior contains many wall paintings, including some by Hans Holbein the Elder dating from 1485–90. Nearby stands the Diebsturm (Thief's Tower) of 1380. The **Stadtmuseum** (town museum) is housed in Haus zum Cavazzen (1729) in Marktplatz, which also features a lovely Neptune fountain.

On the south side of the Market Square stands the Protestant Church of St Stephen, which dates from the 12th century and was remodelled in Baroque style in 1782. The Catholic Church of St Mary, built in 1748–52, has a lovely Rococo interior.

🏛 **Stadtmuseum Lindau**
Marktplatz 6. **Tel** (08382) 94 40 73.
Open Apr–Oct: 10am–6pm daily.

Epitaph of the family of Andreas Bertsch, in the Stadtmuseum Lindau

For hotels and restaurants in this area see pp496–7 and pp519–22

㊼ Oberstdorf

Road map C7. 🚠 10,000. 🚉
ℹ️ Prinzregenten-Platz 1 (08322-70 00).

Oberstdorf lies in the valley of the River Iller. The ideal skiing conditions and the mild all-year-round climate make this one of the most popular health resorts and winter sports centres in Germany. Nearby is the skiing stadium (Schattenberg-Skistadion) with its famous ski-jump, where the annual "four ski-jump" tournament starts each year.

Although the fire of 1865 destroyed large sections of the settlement here, some of the most important historic buildings escaped. These include Seelenkapelle, whose façade is decorated with a 16th-century wall painting typical of the region, and two chapels, Lorettokapelle and Joseph-skapelle, which were joined together in 1707. Just to the east of Oberstdorf is the 2,224-m (7,300-ft) Mount Nebelhorn, whose summit can be reached in a few minutes by cable car. This offers a spectacular view over the majestic Allgäuer Alps as well as providing an excellent starting point for mountain hiking.

㊺ Füssen

Road map D7. 🚠 16,000. 🚉
ℹ️ Kaiser-Maximilian-Platz 1 (08362-938 50).

Situated conveniently on an important trade route, Füssen experienced its most rapid growth in the late Middle Ages, as witnessed by many of the buildings in Reichenstrasse and the remains of the town fortifications, which include Sebastiantor and sections of the walls with five turrets.

Madonna in the Church of St Mang, in Füssen

Perched on a rock, high above the town, stands the palace of the Augsburg prince-bishops. Started in 1291 by the Bavarian Prince Ludwig II the Severe, construction was continued in 1490–1503 by the Augsburg bishops. The residential buildings of the palace range around a courtyard whose walls are decorated with *trompe l'oeil* door and window frames.

At the foot of the castle stands the former Benedictine Abbey (Kloster St Mang), which was erected in the 9th century at the burial site of St Magnus, the "Apostle of the Allgäu". The only surviving part of the abbey is the late 10th-century crypt with the remains of wall paintings.

Late-Baroque interior of the Abbey Library, in Ottobeuren

㊻ Ottobeuren

Road map C7. 🚠 8,000.
ℹ️ Marktplatz 14 (08332-92 19 50).

Situated 13 km (8 miles) from Memmingen, the small health resort of Ottobeuren is the site of one of Germany's most famous Benedictine abbeys. Founded in 764, the abbey is still a place of prayer and work for the monks who live here, having withstood even the radical secularization of 1803. In the 18th century the abbey was remodelled by the Abbot Rupert II. The foundation stone for the building complex was laid in 1717 and work began under the direction of Simpert Kraemer. The new buildings were completed in 1731. The richly decorated interiors, with stuccoes by Andrea Maini, still survive. A new abbey church was built between 1737 and 1766 with construction supervised initially by Simpert Kramer. In 1748, this was taken over by Johann Michael Fischer, who was responsible for its final appearance.

The interior of the church has a magnificent unity of style: Rococo stuccoes by Johann Michael Feuchtmayr are in perfect harmony with the vault frescoes by Johann Jakob Zeiller as well as the splendid altars and stalls by Martin Hörmann and Johann Zeiller's brother Franz Anton Zeiller. The abbey's three organs, which are particularly beautiful, can be heard at regularly held recitals.

Ski-jump complex in Oberstdorf

⑯ Augsburg

Situated at the confluence of the Lech and Wertach rivers, Augsburg is the third largest town in Bavaria and one of the oldest in Germany. As early as 15 BC this was the site of a Roman camp, which later became a town known as Augusta Vindelicorum. Until the end of the 13th century, the town was ruled by powerful bishops. From 1316, as a Free Imperial City of the Holy Roman Empire, Augsburg grew to become one of the richest and most powerful cities in Germany. The Thirty Years' War (1618–48), however, put an end to the town's prosperity.

Augustusbrunnen
Incorporating a statue of the Emperor Augustus, the fountain was created in the workshop of Dutchman Hubert Gerhard in 1594.

Dom

PHIL.-WELSER-STRASSE

Church of St Anna
The star attraction of this unassuming ex-Carmelite church is the Renaissance memorial chapel endowed by the brothers Ulrich and Jacob Fugger in 1509.

ANNASTRASSE

BGM.-FISCHER-STRASSE

Maximilianmuseum
Set in a Renaissance patrician mansion, the museum has a splendid collection of work by local gold- and silversmiths.

WALLSTRASSE

KÖNIGS-PLATZ

Zeughaus
A bronze group by Hans Reichle, *St Michael Overcoming Satan* (1607), adorns the façade of the former arsenal building by Elias Holl, the most important early Baroque architect.

View of the monumental Gothic Dom of the Holy Virgin

Practical Information

Road Map D6. 🚗 265,000.
ℹ️ Rathausplatz 1 (0821-50 20 70). 🎭 Frühjahrsplärrer (week following Easter), Mozartsommer (Jul), Friedenfest (8 Aug), Herbstplärrer (Aug/Sep).
w augsburg-tourismus.de

Transport
✈️ Munich, 90 km (55 miles) east.
🚌

★ Rathaus

The town hall, built by Elias Holl in 1615–20, is widely considered the most significant secular Renaissance building north of the Alps.

★ Maximilianstrasse

Augsburg's main thoroughfare is the most beautiful street in southern Germany, with notable fountains by Adrian de Vries.

★ Fuggerhäuser

Commissioned by Jacob II Fugger (1459–1525) for himself and his family, this Italian-style building, with two arcaded courtyards, was built in 1512–15.

St Ulrich-
und-Afra

Key

— Suggested route

St Moritz Kirche

🔺 Dom of the Holy Virgin (Dom Unserer Lieben Frau)

Frauentorstr. 1. **Open** 7am–6pm.
Originally a Romanesque twin-choir, pillared basilica with crypt, western transept and two towers, dating from 994–1065, the structure was remodelled between 1331 and 1431 along Gothic lines. The church was given two further side aisles, a choir with an ambulatory and a French-style ring of chapels. Original features include the richly carved portals and the famous Romanesque bronze door with 35 panels depicting allegorical figures. There are some unique stained-glass windows, dating from 1140.

🏠 Fuggerei

Fuggerei-Museum, Mittlere Gasse14.
Tel (0821) 319 88 10. **Open** Apr–Oct: 8am–8pm daily; Nov–Mar: 9am–6pm daily. 🚻

The Fuggerei, in Augsburg's Jakobervorstadt (Jacob's Suburb), is Europe's oldest social housing estate. It was founded in 1516 by Jacob Fugger, a member of what was then the richest family in Europe. The intention was to provide homes for the town's poorest citizens, particularly families with children. Today, however, it has evolved into a home for retired citizens.

The 52 houses in Fuggerei were built in 1516–25 and line six streets. They are surrounded by gardens. One of the buildings houses the **Fuggerei-Museum**, which is devoted to the history of the estate and has a fascinating shop, the Himmlisches Fuggereilädle.

BADEN-WÜRTTEMBERG

This German state, which includes territories of the former Grand Duchy of Baden, is one of the country's most popular tourist destinations. Its charming old university towns, such as Tübingen and Heidelberg, historic castles, luxurious resorts and the magnificent recreation areas of the Schwarzwald (Black Forest) and Bodensee (Lake Constance) guarantee enjoyable and memorable holidays.

This region's turbulent history, which has been ruled over the years by Palatinate electors, counts and finally kings of Württemberg, as well as by margraves and Grand Dukes of Baden, has given the province its cultural and religious diversity.

This southwestern area of Germany was the cradle of two great dynasties that played a significant part in German and European history and culture. The Hohenstaufen family – which originated from Swabia – produced kings and emperors who ruled during the most magnificent period of the German Middle Ages (1138–1254). These included Frederick I Barbarossa and Frederick II. The Hohenzollern family, also from Swabia, produced Brandenburg dukes, Prussian kings including Frederick the Great and German emperors from 1871–1918.

In Heidelberg the enlightened elector Ruprecht I founded the first university in Germany in 1386 and shortly after this epoch-making event, further universities were established in Tübingen and Freiburg im Breisgau. Many towns and villages in the region can boast a history going back to Roman times. The Romans used to grow vines in the area of Baden-Württemberg and now wines from the region are renowned worldwide for their high quality.

Baden-Württemberg, however, does not only represent an illustrious past, but also an impressive present. Unemployment figures for the region are the lowest in Germany, and many companies that are known and respected throughout the world – such as Bosch, Daimler, Porsche and the software company SAP – have their production plants here.

Magnificent French-style garden in front of the palace in Ludwigsburg

◄ Ornate façade within the walls of Heidelberg Castle

Baden-Württemberg

With its magnificent castles, luxurious resorts and the beautiful recreation areas of the Schwarzwald (Black Forest), Baden-Württemberg is one of Germany's most popular tourist destinations. In addition, the region's long and turbulent history has given it a rich cultural and religious diversity. The southwest region of Germany was the cradle of two dynasties that played important roles in German and European history and culture – the Hohenstaufen and Hohenzollern families. The great number of urban centres in the state is due to the influence of these two families. Baden-Württemberg also has more universities than any other state in Germany, the oldest being located at Heidelberg, Tübingen and Freiburg im Breisgau.

The picturesque castle in Sigmaringen, in the region of Schwäbische Alb

Key

- ▬▬ Motorway
- ▬ Major road
- ⋯⋯ Minor road
- ⋯⋯ Main railway
- ── Minor railway
- ▬ International border
- ▬ Regional border
- △ Summit

The Gothic town hall in Ulm

For additional map symbols see back flap

0 kilometres   20

0 miles   20

Getting Around

The main communication centres of the area are Stuttgart, which has an international airport, and Mannheim. Main motorways include the A5 from Frankfurt to Basel, via Heidelberg, Karlsruhe, Baden-Baden and Freiburg; the A81 from Würzburg to Constance, via Tauberbischofsheim, Heilbronn, Stuttgart and Schwäbische Alb; the A6 from Mannheim to Ansbach, via Heilbronn and Crailsheim; and the A8 from Karlsruhe to Ulm, via Stuttgart.

Sights at a Glance

1. Wertheim
2. Tauberbischofsheim
3. Bad Mergentheim
4. Weikersheim
5. Creglingen
6. Mannheim
7. Schwetzingen
8. Bruchsal
9. *Heidelberg pp300–3*
10. Karlsruhe
11. Baden-Baden
12. *Maulbronn pp306–7*
13. Heilbronn
14. Schwäbisch Hall
15. Schwäbisch Gmünd
16. Bad Wimpfen
17. Marbach
18. Esslingen
19. *Ludwigsburg pp310–11*
20. *Stuttgart pp312–17*
21. Schwäbische Alb
22. Tübingen
23. Rottweil
24. Ulm
25. Ravensburg
26. Weingarten
27. Salem
28. *Bodensee pp324–25*
29. *Freiburg im Breisgau pp328–9*
30. *Schwarzwald (Black Forest) pp330–31*

Palace façade in Bruchsal

❶ Wertheim

Road map C5. 🗺 24,500. 🚉
ℹ Gerbergasse 16 (09342-935 090).
🎪 Altstadtfest (Jul), Burgweinfest (Aug).

The rivers Tauber and Main meet at Wertheim, whose historic records date from 1183. A gun-powder explosion in 1619 plus the destruction caused by the Thirty Years' War turned the **Wertheimer Burg** into a romantic ruin. Its tall watch-tower offers great views.

Not far from Wertheim's market square is a Baroque Protestant church, dating from the 15th–18th centuries. It is home to tombs of the von Wertheim family and the most spectacular is the tomb of Count Ludwig II von Löwenstein-Wertheim and his wife. Also worth visiting are the **Glasmuseum** (exhibits range from jewellery to scientific instruments), **Grafschaftsmuseum Wertheim** (local fairy tales feature in the collection) and **Museum Schlösschen im Hofgarten** (the "castle in the courtyard" houses paintings and Parisian porcelain).

🏛 **Glasmuseum**
Mühlenstrasse 24. **Tel** (09342) 68 66. **Open** Apr–Oct & Dec–6 Jan: 10am–5pm Tue–Thu, 1–6pm Fri–Sun & hols. 🎟

🏛 **Grafschaftsmuseum Wertheim**
Rathausgasse 6–10. **Tel** (09342) 30 15 11. **Open** 10am–noon, 2:30–4:30pm Tue–Sat (Sat: pm only), 2–5pm Sun. 🎟

🏛 **Museum Schlösschen im Hofgarten**
Würzburger Strasse 30. **Tel** (09342) 301 511. **Open** Apr–Oct: 2–5pm Wed–Sat, noon–6pm Sun & hols.

Half-timbered houses and tower, Tauberbischofsheim

❷ Tauberbischofsheim

Road map C5. 🗺 13,000. 🚉
ℹ Marktplatz 8 (09341-803 33).

Boniface, the Anglo-Saxon missionary to the German tribes, established Germany's first nunnery in AD 735. Its first prioress, Lioba, who was related to Boni-face, gave her name to the Baroque church that stands in Tauberbischofs-heim's market square.

The town, which enjoys a picturesque location in the valley of the river Tauber, still has a group of original half-timbered houses. On the market square is the Baroque Rehhof (1702) and the old "Star Pharmacy" in a house once occupied by Georg Michael Franck, grandfather of the Romantic poets Clemens and Bettina Brentano.

In the eastern section of Hauptstrasse stands Haus Mackert – a Baroque mansion built in 1744 for a wealthy wine merchant. In Schlossplatz is the Kurmainzisches Schloss, an imposing edifice built in the 15th–16th centuries, that now houses the **Landschaftsmuseum**.

🏛 **Landschaftsmuseum Kurmainzisches Schloss**
Tel (09341) 37 60. **Open** Palm Sunday–Oct: 2–4:30pm Tue–Sat, 10am–noon & 2–4:30pm Sun. 🎟

❸ Bad Mergentheim

Road map C5. 🗺 25,000. 🚉
ℹ Marktplatz 1 (07931-574 815).
🎪 Markelsheimer Weinfest (after Whitsun).

Heraldic crest from the castle in Bad Mergentheim

Lying in a charming spot on the river Tauber, Bad Mergentheim was, from 1525 until 1809, the seat of the Grand Masters of the religious order of the "House of the Hospitallers of Saint Mary of the Teutons in Jerusalem", more commonly known as the Teutonic Knights. When three Hohenlohe brothers entered the Order in 1220, they contributed to it their share of their father's estate. This laid the foundations for one of the most powerful Teutonic commands at the heart of the Holy Roman Empire. From 1244 until 1250 Heinrich von Hohenlohe held the office of Grand Master.

The former Hohenlohe's castle, built in the 12th–13th centuries, was remodelled in Renaissance style in 1565–74 by Michael Bronner and Blasius Berwart. They gave the castle its winding stairs and the opulent decor of the staircase. The Baroque-Rococo Schlosskirche dominates the complex. Its interior was designed by François

Scenic castle ruins in Wertheim

de Cuvilliés, while the ceiling fresco (The Victorious Cross) is the work of Nicolaus Stuber. The castle is now the home of a very interesting museum, the **Deutschordensmuseum**.

Many of the town's historic buildings survive to this day, including the 13th-century Church of the Knights of St John of Jerusalem and the Dominican church containing the epitaph of the Grand Master Walther von Cronberg. The **Pfarrkirche** (Parish church) in the Stuppach district contains a masterpiece by Grünewald (1519), known as the *Madonna of Stuppach*.

⌂ Pfarrkirche in Stuppach
Grünewald Str. 45. **Tel** (07931) 26 05. **Open** May–Oct: 8:30am–6:30pm daily; Mar, Apr & Nov: 11am–4pm. ♿

▥ Deutschordensmuseum
Schloss. **Tel** (07931) 522 12. **Open** Apr–Oct: 10:30am–5pm Tue–Sun; Nov–Mar: 2–5pm Tue–Sat, 10:30am–5pm Sun. ♿

❹ Weikersheim

Road map C5. ▨ 8,000. **ℹ** Am Marktplatz 7 (07934-102 55).

Eleven kilometres (7 miles) east of Bad Mergentheim is the picturesque little town of Weikersheim. A Rococo fountain from 1768 is at the centre of the market square while the late-Gothic parish church is on the north side. The latter is a triple-nave hall-church with a single-tower western façade and two towers by the choir. Inside are many tombs of the von Hohenlohe family. Also on the market square stands the **Tauberländer Dorfmuseum**, which charts the history of rural life in Franconia. In the western part of town stands the very well preserved **Schloss Weikersheim**, the palace complex of the Counts von Hohenlohe, which

Figure of drummer in Weikersheim's Hofgarten

dates from the 16th–18th centuries. Its highlight is undoubtedly the vast Rittersaal, a sumptuous banqueting hall that measures 35 m (115 ft) long x 12 m (39 ft) wide x 9 m (29 ft) high. The counts and their aristocratic guests used to enter this room on horseback. Its very rare, original furnishings include paintings and reliefs depicting hunting scenes.

A true rarity is the original Baroque Hofgarten (palace garden), designed by Daniel Matthieu and built in 1709.

⌂ Schloss Weikersheim
Tel (07934) 992 950. **Open** Apr–Oct: 9am–6pm daily; Nov–Mar: 10am–noon & 1:30–5pm daily. ♿ ▢

▥ Tauberländer Dorfmuseum
Marktplatz. **Tel** (07934) 12 09. **Open** Apr–Oct: 1.30–5pm Fri–Sun. ♿

❺ Creglingen

Road map C5. ▨ 5,000. ▭ **ℹ** Bad Mergentheimer Str. (07933-6 31).

Upstream from Weikersheim, on the Bavarian border, is the small town of Creglingen. Here, sometime in the distant past, a ploughman found a luminous holy wafer in a clod of earth and within a few years, the **Herrgottskirche** was built, where the host was put on display for visiting pilgrims. Between 1502 and 1506 Tilman Riemenschneider carved an

Altar by Tilman Riemenschneider, in Creglingen's Herrgottskirche

altar for the church. The main theme of the polyptych is the *Assumption of the Virgin Mary*, considered to be the artist's masterpiece.

The town is also home to the famous **Fingerhutmuseum** (Thimble Museum).

⌂ Herrgottskirche
Schirmbacher Strasse 16. **Tel** (07933) 338 or 508. **Open** Feb–Nov–Dec: 1–4pm Tue–Sun; Apr–Oct: 9.15am–6pm daily. ♿

▥ Fingerhutmuseum
Kohlersmühle 6. **Tel** (07933) 370. **Open** Apr–Oct: 10am–12:30pm & 2–5pm Tue–Sun; Nov–Mar: 1–4pm Tue–Sun. **Closed** Jan & Feb. ♿

Teutonic Order

The Order of the Hospital of St Mary of the German House in Jerusalem was officially founded in Acre (Akkon) in 1190. Its aim was to care for sick pilgrims or Crusaders wounded in fights with the Saracens. In 1231–83, the Teutonic Knights took over all of Prussia and in 1308–09 all Eastern Pomerania around Danzig, and they moved their headquarters from Venice to Marienburg on the river Nogat. In 1525 the Grand Master, Albrecht von Hohenzollern-Ansbach, converted to Lutheranism and secularized Teutonic Prussia. However, the Order remained in existence in the Holy Roman Empire: its German Master, Walter von Cronberg, who had his residence in Mergentheim, became *de facto* Grand Master. Napoleon abolished the Order in 1809, but it still exists today, with its headquarters based in Vienna since 1848.

The Wasserturm (Water Tower) in Friedrichsplatz, Mannheim

❻ Mannheim

Road map B5. 🏙 326,000. 🚆
🛈 Willy-Brandt-Platz 3 (0621-29 38 700). 🎬 Mannheim-Heidelberger Filmfestival (mid-Oct). 🅦 **tourist-mannheim.de**

Mannheim existed as a fishing hamlet as far back as 766. In 1606, Elector Frederick IV the Righteous ordered a fortress to be built on the site, at the junction of the rivers Rhine and Neckar. A trading settlement sprang up nearby and was soon granted town status. Having been repeatedly destroyed through the years, the town was finally rebuilt in Baroque style during the reign of the Elector Johann Wilhelm.

The town-centre layout follows the regular Baroque pattern of the early 18th century, when the town was divided into 136 regular squares. In 1720, when Elector Charles III Philip decided to move his residence from Heidelberg to Mannheim, the foundation stone for a Baroque palace was laid in the grounds of a former citadel.

Statue of Elector Karl Theodor in Mannheim's Jesuitenkirche

With over 400 rooms, this became one of the largest and most opulent of all German palaces. Like the residences of many European rulers at that time, it was modelled on Versailles. The main palace has a horseshoe layout, and its symmetry is emphasized by a central projecting entrance. Building work was done by Johann Clemens Froimont, Alessandro Galli da Bibiena, Nicolas de Pigage and Guillaume d'Hauberat.

The second largest town of the region, Mannheim boasts many other historic buildings, including the post-Jesuit Church of St Ignatius and St Francis Xavier, designed by Alessandro Galli da Bibiena and built in 1733–60. Original wall-paintings by Egid Quirin Asam no longer exist, but the altars have survived to this day. These include JI Saler's *Silver Madonna in Radiant Glory* (1747). Also worth visiting are the Baroque Altes Rathaus (1701–23) and Secessionist buildings in Friedrichsplatz such as the Kunsthalle and Wasserturm – the symbol of Mannheim.

The town has several interesting museums: the **Kunsthalle Mannheim** has a large collection of 19th- and 20th-century art, including Francis Bacon's *Study After Velasquez's Portrait of Pope Innocent X*. The museum is renowned for its major temporary exhibitions. The **Reiss-Engelhorn-Museen** has a fine collection of 18th-century Dutch paintings and sections devoted to early history and ethnography. Another big attraction in Mannheim is the **TECHNOSEUM** (Museum of Technology and Labour). Opened in 1990, this houses a

collection of historic machinery. Mannheim saw the first official demonstration of many inventions that have now become part of everyday life. In 1817, Baron Karl Friedrich von Sauerbronn demonstrated his first bicycle in the town and, in 1886, Carl Friedrich Benz unveiled his first automobile, produced at the nearby factory.

🏛 **Kunsthalle Mannheim**
Friedrichsplatz 4. **Tel** (0621) 293 64 52. **Open** 11am–6pm Tue–Sun (to 8pm Wed). **Closed** Carnival, 1 May, 24, 31 Dec. 🅦

🏛 **TECHNOSEUM**
Museumsstrasse 1. **Tel** (0621) 429 09. **Open** 9am–5pm daily. **Closed** Good Friday, 24, 31 Dec. 🅦

🏛 **Reiss-Engelhorn-Museen**
Quadrat D5 and C5. **Tel** (0621) 293 31 50. **Open** 11am–6pm Tue–Sun. 🅦
🅦 **rem-mannheim.de**

Paul Cézanne's *Pipe Smoker* (c.1890), in the Städtische Kunsthalle, Mannheim

❼ Schwetzingen

Road map C6. 🏙 21,500.
🛈 Dreikönigstr. 3 (06202-94 58 75). 🎭 Schwetzinger Festspiele (May), Mozartkonzerte (Sep).

Schwetzingen's Baroque-Renaissance palace was built during the reign of the Electors Johann Wilhelm, Charles II Philip and Karl Theodor as their summer residence. Erected on the site of a medieval castle that was later converted into a hunting lodge, it is one of the best known palace complexes of 18th-century Europe. The

Baroque Schwetzingen Palace, set amid beautiful gardens

conversion of the 16th-century hunting lodge was carried out by J A Breuning and the side wings were built by Alessandro Galli da Bibiena. The magnificent Rococo theatre, designed by Nicolas de Pigage, was built in 1752, while the palace garden is the work of Johann Ludwig Petri, who designed it in the French style. The garden includes a mosque with two minarets and a bathhouse. In 1776 Friedrich Ludwig von Sckell converted it into an English-style garden.

Heraldic insignia from Bruchsal Palace

palace to be built for himself and his court. The foundation stone of **Schloss Bruchsal** was laid in 1722 and the building works were carried out by Maximilian von Welsch, who was responsible for the right wing, and Michael Rohrer, who built the left wing between 1723 and 1728. The main body, preceded by a ceremonial courtyard, was designed by Baron Anselm von Grünstein. The central part of the palace is occupied by a magnificent staircase built by the great

Balthasar Neumann, with stuccowork by Johann Michael Feuchtmayer and paintings by Johann and Januarius Zick. The palace suffered severe bomb damage in 1945, but its major part was reconstructed between 1964 and 1975.

St Peter's church was built in 1740–49 by Johann Georg to Balthasar Neumann's 1736 design. The church features magnificent Baroque tombs of Schönborn and his successor Cardinal Franz Christoph von Hutten. The palace garden was designed in the French style by Johann Scheer.

This former residence of prince-bishops now houses a section of the Karlsruhe Museum, which features Germany's largest collection of Flemish and French tapestries. It is also home to the **Deutsches Musikautomaten Museum**, which includes 500 mechanical musical instruments. Short demonstrations are given on these throughout the day.

🏛 Schloss Bruchsal
Schönbornstrasse 2. **Tel** (07251) 74 26 61. **Open** 10am–5pm Tue–Sun & hols. 📷 hourly. **Closed** 24, 25, 31 Dec. ♿ Deutsches Musikautomaten Museum: **Open** 10am–5pm Tue–Sun. 📷 11am, 3pm. **Closed** Shrove Tuesday, 24, 25, 31 Dec. ♿ 🖵 schloss-bruchsal.de

🏛 Schloss Schwetzingen
Tel (06202) 12 88 28. Schloss: **Open** Apr–Oct: 11am–4pm Tue–Sun; Nov–Mar: 2pm Fri, 11am, 2pm, 3pm Sat & Sun. 📷 obligatory. Garden: **Tel** (06202) 65 88 80. **Open** Apr–Oct: 9am–8pm daily; Nov–Mar: 9am–5pm daily. 🖵 schloss-schwetzingen.de

❽ Bruchsal

Road map: C6. 🚊 43,000. 🚉 🛈 Am Alten Schloss 2 (07251-505 94 61).

Bruchsal belonged to the Bishops of Speyer from 1056 until 1803, since when it has been part of Baden. The town rose to prominence in the 17th century, when the Prince-Bishop of Speyer, Damian Hugo von Schönborn moved his residence from Speyer to Bruchsal. He not only initiated the town's development but, most importantly, ordered a

Central façade of the Baroque Schloss Bruchsal

❾ Street-by-Street: Heidelberg

Situated on the banks of the river Neckar, Heidelberg is one of Germany's most beautiful towns. For centuries it was a centre of political power, with a lively and influential cultural life. In 1386, Germany's first university was established here by the Elector Ruprecht I. Building of the palace began during his reign, continuing until the mid-17th century. However, in the late 17th century, French incursions totally destroyed medieval Heidelberg, including the castle. The town was subsequently rebuilt in the early 18th century in Baroque style.

Marktplatz
Now adorned with the Neptune Fountain, the market square was, in the past, the site of executions and the burning of witches and heretics.

★ Heiliggeistkirche
Built in 1400–41 on the site of a late-Romanesque basilica, the Church of the Holy Spirit is the town's oldest sanctuary.

HAUPTSTRASSE

HEILIGGEISTSTRASSE

FISCHMA

OBERE NECKARSTRASSE

STEINGASSE

LAUERSTRASSE

NECKARSTADEN

| 0 metres | 60 |
| 0 yards | 60 |

Philosophenweg
Built in 1817 on the slopes of Heiligenberg, at an altitude of 200 m (650 ft), the "Philosophers' Walk" offers magnificent views of Heidelberg and its castle.

★ Alte Brücke
This imposing, nine-span bridge over the river Neckar was built in 1786–88 by Mathias Maier. In the background is the Heidelberger Schloss.

★ Haus zum Ritter
Built in 1592 for the family of a rich cloth merchant, the Haus zum Ritter is a fine example of German Mannerist style. It now houses a luxury hotel and restaurant.

Hexenturm
The tower was once part of the 13th-century medieval town fortifications.

VISITORS' CHECKLIST

Practical Information
Road map: C6. 🚶 139,000.
ℹ️ Willy-Brandt-Platz 1 (Hauptbahnhof) (06221-584 44 44).
🎬 Mannheim-Heidelberger Filmfestival (mid-Oct), Schlossfestspiele (Jul & Aug), Weindorf (Sep), Heidelberger Herbst (Sep), Schlossbeleuchtung (Jun, Jul, Sep).

Transport
🚇

M E R I A N S T R A S S E

H E U G A S S E

UNIVERSITÄTS-PLATZ

Universitätsbibliothek

H A U P T S T R A S S E

U N T E R E   S T R A S S E

Alte Universität
The old university building, designed by local architect Johann Adam Breuning, was built in 1712–35.

F U S S E M E R G A S S E

L A U E R S T R A S S E

Jesuitenkirche
This church was built in 1712–51 for the Jesuits, who arrived in Heidelberg in 1698. The ornaments on the monumental façade were carved by Paul Egell.

Key

— Suggested route

Heidelberg Castle

Towering over the town, the majestic castle is really a vast residential complex that was built and repeatedly extended between the 13th and 17th centuries. Originally a supremely well-fortified Gothic castle, but now mostly in ruins, this was the seat of the House of Wittelsbach palatines. After remodelling in the 16th century, the castle became one of Germany's most beautiful Renaissance residences. However, its splendour was extinguished by the Thirty Years' War and the 1689 war with France, during which most of the structure was destroyed.

★ **Ottheinrichsbau**
The Deutsches Apothekenmuseum is housed within the shell of this Renaissance building. It features Baroque and Rococo workshops and a travelling pharmacy.

★ **Friedrichsbau**
One of the latest parts of the castle is Friedrich's Palace, which dates from 1601–07. On the façade are statues of the Wittelsbach dynasty, including Charles the Great.

Englischer Bau
These imposing ruins in the castle complex are the remains of a 17th-century building that Friedrich V built for his wife Elizabeth Stuart.

KEY

① **Castle moat**

② **The bell tower**, which was erected in the early 15th century, was remodelled frequently in subsequent years.

③ **Brunnenhalle** is a Gothic loggia that features early-Romanesque columns taken from the palace of Charles the Great in Ingelheim.

④ **Torturm**

VISITORS' CHECKLIST

Practical Information
Schlossberg. **Tel** (06221) 53 84 31.
Open 8am–6pm daily. 🎫 Großes
Fass: **Open** 8am–5:30pm daily.
🅿 **w** **schloss-heidelberg.de**
Deutsches Apothekenmuseum:
Tel (06221) 258 80. **Open** 10am–
5pm (to 6pm Apr–Oct). **Closed** 1
Jan, 31 Dec. **w** **deutsches-**
apotheken-museum.de

Pulverturm
Built during the reign of the
Elector Ruprecht, this
14th-century tower once formed
part of the castle defences.

Main entrance

④

③

★ Ruprechtsbau
Built around 1400 by a master
builder from Frankfurt, this is the
oldest surviving part of the castle.

🏛 Alte Universität
Grabengasse 1. **Tel** (06221) 54 21 52.
Universitätsmuseum: **Open** Apr–Sep:
10am–6pm Tue–Sun; Oct: 10am–4pm
Tue–Sun; Nov–Mar: 10am–4pm Tue–
Sat. 🅿 **w** **uni-heidelberg.de**

Designed by Mainz architect
Johann Adam Breuning, the
university was built in 1712–35.
On the north wall and ceiling
are allegorical paintings by
Ferdinand Keller. In front of the
building is a fountain crowned
by a sculpture in the form of the
heraldic Palatinate lion.

🏛 Universitätsbibliothek
Plöck 107–109. **Tel** (06221) 54 23 80.
Ausstellungsraum: **Open** 10am–6pm
Mon–Sat.

The monumental building of
the university library, designed
by Joseph Durm of Karlsruhe,
was erected in 1901–05 near
the church of St Peter. The
Heidelberg library, with over
2 million volumes, is one of the
largest in Germany. The
exhibition rooms hold many
precious manuscripts and old
prints, including the famous
Codex Manesse, illustrated with
137 beautiful miniatures.

🏛 Kurpfälzisches Museum
Hauptstrasse 97. **Tel** (06221) 58 34
020. **Open** 10am–6pm Tue–Sun. 🅿
The French Count Charles de
Graimberg spent the bulk of his
considerable fortune on building
up an extensive collection of
fine drawings, paintings, arms
and various curios associated
with the history of the Palatinate
and the castle of Heidelberg. In
1879, his collection became the
property of the town and forms
the core of this very interesting
museum, which also includes a
fascinating archaeology section.

🏛 Heiliggeistkirche
Hauptstrasse.
This collegiate church, whose
Baroque dome is a city landmark, was built in 1400–41. The
canons of the college were also
university scholars and therefore
the church aisle features special
galleries for the extensive collections of library books – *Bibliotheca
Palatina*. The choir features a
tombstone of Ruprecht III and his
wife, Elisabeth von Hohenzollern.

⑩ Karlsruhe

Road map B6. 🚗 269,000. 🚆
ℹ️ Bahnhofsplatz 6 (0721 3720 5383).
🌐 **karlsruhe-tourismus.de**
🎭 Internationales Trachten-und-Folklorefest (Jun).

Karlsruhe, which is one of the "youngest" towns in Germany, flourished during the 19th century as a centre for science and art. In 1945, it lost its status as a regional capital, but is now the seat of the Bundesverfass-ungsgericht – the highest courts of the Federal Republic.

The town originated in 1715 when the margrave of Baden, Karl Wilhelm von Baden-Durlach, ordered a lodge to be built in the middle of his favourite hunting grounds. Karl liked the area and the lodge so much that he decided to move his residence here and live the remainder of his days in peace – hence the town's name, meaning "Karl's rest". The original Baroque-style design was expanded during the reign of his successor, Karl Friedrich.

The palace, which forms the hub of 32 streets, was designed by Leopoldo Retti, Mauritio Pedetti, Balthasar Neumann, Philippe de la Guépière and others, and built in 1749–81. The town is based on a fan-like plan, spreading from a base formed by the open-sided wings of the palace. The rest of the circle, whose centre is marked by the octagonal palace tower (1715), is filled with green areas, inclu-ding the palace garden. In the early 19th century, the town was remodelled along Neo-Classical lines. The main architect

A pyramid containing the tomb of Karl Wilhelm von Baden-Durlach in Karlsruhe

of this large-scale project was Friedrich Weinbrenner, who created this masterpiece of urban design. The equilateral market square is positioned along the palace axis. It is filled with similar but not identical buildings and features a central pyramid containing Karl Wilhelm's tomb. South of Marktplatz is the circular Rondellplatz. Wein-brenner's other works include the monumental town hall (1811–25), the Protestant town church and the Catholic parish church of St Stephen.

Karlsruhe has some very interesting museums. The Badisches Landesmuseum in the castle features a large collec-tion of antiquities, decorative arts, sculpture, porcelain and furniture, from the Middle Ages to the present day. In a Neo-Renaissance building (1843–46) is the **Staatliche Kunsthalle**, with

its large collection of mainly German and Dutch paintings from the 16th–19th centuries. These include the famous *Crucifixion* by Grünewald (1523).

Entirely different in character are the collections of the Zentrum für Kunst und Medientech-nologie (ZKM) – an establishment that has combined the role of art college and museum since 1997. It occupies a former ammunitions factory in the western part of the town. Its core is the **Museum für Neue Kunst**, featuring installations, computer art and videos and other work by contemporary artists. The **Stadtmuseum im Prinz-Max-Palais**, based in a mansion named after the last chancellor of the Kaiserreich, contains the local history museum.

🏛️ Staatliche Kunsthalle
Hans-Thoma-Strasse 2–6.
Tel (0721) 9 26 33 59. **Open** 10am–6pm Tue–Sun. 🎫 🌐 **kunsthalle-karlsruhe.de**

🏛️ Museum für Neue Kunst
Lorenzstrasse 19. **Tel** (0721) 8100 1325.
Open 10am–6pm Wed–Fri, 11am–6pm Sat & Sun. 🎫

🏛️ Stadtmuseum im Prinz-Max-Palais
Karlstrasse 10. **Tel** (0721) 1 33 42 31.
Open 10am–6pm Tue & Fri, 10am–7pm Thu, 2–6pm Sat, 11am–6pm Sun.

The Baroque residence of the Dukes of Baden in Karlsruhe

⓫ Baden–Baden

Road map B6. ⚊ 50,000. ✈ Baden
Airport (5 km/3 miles northwest of
town). ☐ ☐ Schwarzwaldstrasse 52
& "i-Punkt" in der Trinkhalle (07221-275
23). ☑ **baden-baden.de**

Known as the "summer capital
of Europe", this elegant spa
resort is one of the oldest towns
in Germany and was once the
favourite destination of
European aristocracy from
Russia to Portugal. Even before
the Romans built their camp
here around AD 80, the site was
occupied by a Celtic settlement
of the Latenian period.

In the early years of the modern
era, *Civitas Aurelia Aquensis* –
known simply as Aquae – was
already known in Italy for the
therapeutic properties of its
waters. In the 3rd century AD,
Aquae was conquered by the
Germanic tribe of Alamains and
in the 6th century AD by the
Francs, who built a fortress in
the town. The Margrave
Hermann II, known as "Marchio
de Baduon", was the first
important ruler of Baden.

During the horrific Black Death,
the qualities of the local waters
were once again recognized as
beneficial to health. During the
Palatinate War of Succession,
Baden-Baden was almost
totally destroyed but, by the
end of the 18th century, it had
become one of Europe's most
fashionable resorts.

The old town of
Baden-Baden lies at the
foot of the Schlossberg
(castle hill). The oldest
surviving building in
the town is the Gothic
collegiate church, built
during the 13th–15th
centuries and then
remodelled in the
18th century. It contains
several valuable
epitaphs. To the south
of the church is the
bathing hall –
Friedrichsbad – which
was built in Neo-
Renaissance style in
1877. Nearby stands
the magnificent New
Palace, which was the
residence of margraves

Baden-Baden's casino, set in the elegant Kurhaus

from the 15th century onwards.
It was remodelled along German
Renaissance lines in the 16th
century by Kaspar Weinhart. The
interiors are decorated with
paintings by Tobias Stimmer.

Most of the spa buildings are
the work of Friedrich Wein-
brenner. His elegant Kurhaus in
Werderstrasse has been used as
a casino since 1838. The most
famous gamester at the casino
was Fyodor Dostoevsky, who
was not always lucky at roulette.
His novel *The Gambler* (1866) is
supposedly set in Baden-Baden.
Nearby is the Trinkhalle (pump
room), with its mineral water
fountains. Built in 1839–42, it is
decorated with wall paintings
illustrating Schwarzwald (Black
Forest) legends.

Rising behind the spa area
is the last project completed
by Leo von Klenze before his
death – the Orthodox burial
chapel of a Romanian

aristocratic family, the Stourdza
Mausoleum. In Schillerstrasse is
the villa built in 1867 for the
Russian writer, Ivan Turgenev,
who lived here until 1872.

🏛 Brahmshaus

Maximilianstrasse 85. **Tel** (07221)
99872. **Open** 3–5pm Mon, Wed, Fri,
10am–1pm Sun (10am–4pm daily
during Brahmstage). 🖼

The exhibition displayed in
this house is devoted to the
life and works of the German
composer Johannes Brahms
who lived here from 1865
until 1874.

⛪ Kloster Lichtenthal

Hauptstrasse 40. **Tel** (07221) 50 49 10.
Open 3pm Wed, Sat, Sun. 📷 Group
tours (minimum 7 persons), advance
telephone booking required. 🖼

This Cistercian nuns' abbey,
situated on the outskirts of
town, has a church dating
from the 14th–15th centuries.
Its ducal chapel contains
many epitaphs of the Baden
margraves. The abbey also has
an interesting museum.

🏛 Staatliche Kunsthalle Baden-Baden

Lichtentaler Allee 8a. **Tel** (07221) 300
7600. **Open** 11am–6pm Tue–Sun.
☑ **kunsthalle-baden-baden.de**

The Staatliche Kunsthalle
Baden-Baden is an exhibition
venue that specializes in
modern and contemporary art.

🏛 Stadtmuseum

Lichtentaler Allee 10. **Tel** (07221) 93 22
72. **Open** 11am–6pm Tue–Sun.

The Stadtmuseum includes
sections on glass, porcelain and
paintings, as well as some old
gambling equipment.

The Neo-Renaissance Trinkhalle (pump room)
in Baden-Baden

⑫ Maulbronn

Situated on the edge of the Stromberg region, Maulbronn grew up around a Cistercian monastery, which was founded in 1147 in the valley of the river Salzach by monks who came here from Alsace. The church, built in 1147–78, is an elongated, triple-nave basilica with a transept and a chancel. The early Gothic porch in front of the church was added in 1220. Outside the enclosure are domestic buildings, such as a former mill, a forge, a bakery and a guest house. Defence walls with turrets and a gate tower encircle the entire complex, which was designated a UNESCO World Heritage Site in 1993.

Cloisters
In the Middle Ages, monks meditated as they walked around the cloisters, which gave them protection from bad weather. Talking was strictly forbidden.

★ Brunnenkapelle
Built opposite the entrance to the refectory, the Well Chapel, with its intricate Gothic forms, is where the monks used to wash their hands before meals.

Inner Courtyard
Once a garden, the monastery's inner courtyard is surrounded by cloisters. It is a place that inspires contemplation.

KEY

① **Cloisters**

The Porch
The porch, also known as "Paradise", was built onto the church façade in the early 13th century.

★ Chapter House
The monks assembled in this Gothic hall to discuss affairs affecting the monastery. The hall has two naves, which are supported by three pillars.

VISITORS' CHECKLIST

Practical Information
Road map: C6. 🚗 6,400.
ℹ️ Stadtverwaltung Maulbronn, Klosterhof 31 (07043-10 30).
Ⓦ **kloster-maulbronn.de**
Infozentrum: Klosterhof 5. **Tel** (07043) 92 66 10. **Open** Mar–Oct: 9am–5:30pm (Nov–Feb: closed Mon). 🕚 11:15am, 3pm. ♿

Church Interior
Originally the church had a wooden ceiling. In 1424 it was replaced with a network vault, which stands in stark contrast to the plain walls.

★ Mourning
This Gothic relief, made in around 1390 in the Parler family workshop, was part of an altar, which no longer exists. Today, it can be seen on the chancel in the monastery's choir.

★ Stalls
Richly decorated with carved ornaments, the late-Gothic stalls date from around 1450.

⑬ Heilbronn

Road map C6. 👥 119,000. 🚉
ℹ️ Kaiserstrasse 17 (07131-56 22 70).
🎭 Pferdemarkt (Feb), Neckarfest (Jun).

Heilbronn's earliest records date from the 8th century, when the town was known as "Helibrunna". By the late 19th century, Heilbronn had become Württemberg's main industrial centre, with a large port on the river Neckar. Having suffered major destruction during World War II, the town's surviving buildings include the church of St Kilian, a Gothic basilica from the second half of the 13th century, with a triple-nave hall-choir flanked by two towers. The western tower was built in 1508–29. The magnificent altarpiece is an original late-Gothic polyptych, the work of Hans Seyffer (1498). Near the 15th–16th-century Rathaus (town hall) is a house reputed to have been the home of Käthchen, a character in Heinrich von Kleist's play *Das Käthchen von Heilbronn*. Near the rebuilt church of St Peter and St Paul (originally the church of the Teutonic Order) stands the former Teutonic convent – the Deutschhof.

Heilbronn is also one of Germany's largest wine-producing towns.

Isaak Habrecht's astronomical clock on Heilbronn town hall

Half-timbered houses on the bank of the river Kocher, in Schwäbisch Hall

⑭ Schwäbisch Hall

Road map C6. 👥 35,000. 🚉
ℹ️ Am Markt 9 (0791-75 12 46).
🎭 Kuchen-und Brunnenfest der Haller Salzsieder (Whitsun).

Archaeological excavations in 1939 proved the existence of a Celtic settlement on this site as early as 500 BC. The town features a great number of historic buildings from various periods, including many half-timbered 15th–16th-century houses, Baroque town houses, and a Rococo town hall and town palace (Keckenburg). The most interesting building is the hall-church of St Michael, whose Gothic main body was built in 1427–56. The Romanesque tower on the western façade, however, dates from the 12th century. The late-Gothic hall-choir (1495–1527) is famous for its decorative network vaults. Original furnishings include the main altar, the stalls and the Holy Sepulchre.

⑮ Schwäbisch Gmünd

Road map C6. 👥 63,400. 🚉
ℹ️ Marktplatz 37/1 (07171-60 34 250). 🎭 Internationales Schatten-theater Festival (Jun), European Church Music (Jul).

This town – the birthplace of the architect Peter Parler and painters Hans Baldung Grien and Jörg Ratgeb – was

Madonna with Child, in Marktplatz, Schwäbisch Gmünd

once renowned throughout Europe for the magnificent goods produced by its goldsmiths. It has many great historic buildings, mainly churches, such as the late-Romanesque church of St John, which dates from around 1220, but was subsequently remodelled. The church of St Cross is famous not only for being the first Gothic hall-church in southern Germany, but also the first major work of the famous family of architects – the Parlers. This triple-nave hall with a hall-choir, featuring an ambulatory and a ring of side chapels, was built in several stages, between 1320 and 1521. Its western façade has a high triangular top with blind windows. Inside the church are many valuable historic relics, such as the Holy Sepulchre (1400), the stalls, which date from around 1550, and the organ gallery (1688). Other interesting structures in the town include the town fortifications and several half-timbered houses.

⑯ Bad Wimpfen

Road map C6. 👥 6,676. 🚉
ℹ️ Hauptstrasse 45 (07063-9 72 00).
🎭 Talmarkt (Jun/Jul), Zunftmarkt (Aug), Weihnachtsmarkt (Dec).
🌐 badwimpfen.de

The town of Bad Wimpfen was created out of two settlements, Bad Wimpfen am Berg and Bad Wimpfen im Tal, which remain distinct to this day. The settlement on top of the hill grew around the Hohenstauf family palace, whose chapel and well-preserved arcade windows, resting on pairs of decorated columns, can still be seen. Built at the order of Frederick I Barbarossa in 1165 75, this was the main and the biggest imperial palace (Kaiserpfalz) of the Holy Roman Empire. One of the surviving towers offers a spectacular view over the Neckar valley.

Set in a picturesque location, Bad Wimpfen features many half-timbered houses dating from the 16th–18th centuries.

Bad Wimpfen im Tal is built around the former collegiate church of St Peter and St Paul. This is a triple-nave basilica with transept, two eastern towers and cloister, dating from the 13th–15th centuries. The south façade of the transept and the portal are richly decorated with carvings, which are probably the work of Erwin von Steinbach, one of the builders of Strasbourg Cathedral. The church interior features many original carved statues and stalls.

⑰ Marbach

Road map C6. 🖼1,450. 🚊
ℹ️ Marktstrasse 23 (07144-10 20).

This small town would probably never merit an entry in any guidebook were it not for the fact that the great writer Friedrich Schiller was born here in 1759. The modest, half timbered house, in which the famous poet spent his childhood, has survived to this day and is now a small museum – the **Schiller-Geburtshaus**. The town also possesses a vast museum of literature (**Schiller-Nationalmuseum**), which is housed in a Neo-Baroque palace. Its collection is not limited to the life and work of Schiller, but also includes many documents relating to German literature.

Other attractions in Marbach include some of the original half-timbered houses and the remains of the town walls and town gates in the old town. The late-Gothic Alexanderkirche is also worth a visit. Built in the second half of the 12th century by Aberlin Jörg, it features interesting network vaulting covered with ornamental paintings.

🎭 **Schiller-Geburtshaus**
Niklastorstrasse 31.
Tel (07144) 175 67.
Open 9am–5pm daily.
Closed 24, 25, 26, 31 Dec. 🔲

🏛️ **Schiller-Nationalmuseum**
Schillerhöhe 8–10. **Tel** (07144) 84 80.
Open 10am–6pm Tue–Sun.
Closed 24, 25, 26, 31 Dec. 🔲

⑱ Esslingen

Road map C6. 🖼92,000.
ℹ️ Marktplatz 2 (0711-39 69 39 69).

Set among vineyards on the banks of the river Neckar, the beautiful town of Esslingen is famous for its sparkling wines. The town's historic buildings were fortunate in surviving intact the ravages of World War II. A walk through the winding streets and narrow alleys of the old centre will yield many interesting sights, while a climb to the top of the hill affords a splendid view of the town and the Neckar valley, as well as the amazing **Innere Brücke**, a 14th-century bridge. From there visitors can descend towards the market square, stopping on the way to visit Frauenkirche, a Gothic hall-church dating from the 14th century. Its front tower, the work of Ulrich and Matthäus von Ensingen, was added later. In the market square is the Stadtkirche St Dionysius, the oldest church in town, built in the 13th century on the site of an earlier, 8th-century building. Inside are magnificent early-Gothic stained-glass windows and late-15th-century Gothic furnishings, including the choir partition, the sacrarium and the font. The nearby church of St Paul, built in the mid-13th century for the Dominicans, is the oldest surviving Dominican church in Germany. In neighbouring Rathausplatz stands the half-timbered old town hall. Altes Rathaus, with its beautiful Renaissance façade, and the Baroque new town hall. Designed as a palace for Gottlieb von Palm by Gottlieb David Kandlers, the Neues Rathaus was built between 1748 and 1751.

Friedrich Schiller statue in Marbach

The picturesque houses and chapel of Esslingen's 14th-century Innere Brücke

⑲ Ludwigsburg

Situated near Stuttgart and known as the "Versailles of Swabia", Ludwigsburg was founded in 1704 on the initiative of Eberhard Ludwig, Duke of Württemberg. At the heart of the town is the vast palace complex, which the Duke ordered to be built for his mistress, Countess Wilhelmine von Grävenitz. The construction of the palace, which was carried out between 1704 and 1733, involved many outstanding architects and interior decorators, including Philipp Jenisch, Johann Nette, Donato Frisoni and Diego Carlone.

Northern Garden
This magnificent Baroque park is the venue for a flower show ("Blooming Baroque") that is held here during the summer.

★ **Western Gallery**
The gallery features opulent stucco ornaments by Ricardo Retti and Diego Carlone (1712–15).

★ **Marble Hall**
This vast hall in the new wing of the palace was remodelled in 1816, but still retains some of its Baroque interior decor.

★ **Queen's Library**
The library is housed in the east wing of the palace, in the apartments arranged for Queen Charlotte Mathilde.

★ **Schloss Favorite**
The "Favorite" hunting lodge was built between 1716 and 1723, but its interior has been remodelled in Neo-Classical style.

VISITORS' CHECKLIST

Practical Information
Road map: C6. 80,000.
Eberhardstrasse 1 (07141-910 22 52). Residenzschloss: Schlosstrasse 30. **Tel** (07141) 18 20 04. 10am–5pm (every 30 mins). In English: mid-Mar–mid-Nov: 1:30pm Mon–Fri, 11am, 1:30pm, 3:15pm Sat & Sun; mid-Nov–mid-Mar: 1:30pm. Mode-, Keramik-museums, Barockgalerie: **Open** 10am–5pm daily.

Transport

Märchengarten
The landscaped section of the park includes the "Fairy-tale Garden", which contains figures and models from German fairy-tales.

Emichsburg
This romantic castle, built in 1798–1802, was named after the founder of the Württemberg dynasty.

KEY

① **The new wing** of the palace houses a museum devoted to court art of the Neo-Classical period.

② **The old wing** contains the palace's oldest apartments.

③ **The upper fruit garden** attracts visitors with its picturesque paths, which are lined with apple trees and grapevines.

④ **Restaurant and café**

⑳ Stuttgart

The capital of Baden-Württemberg, Stuttgart is one of the largest and most important towns of the Federal Republic. It grew from a 10th-century stud farm, known as Stutengarten, to become the ducal (1321) and later the royal (1806) capital of Württemberg. Beautifully situated among picturesque hills, the town is a major industrial centre with many important manufacturing plants. It is also a well-known publishing and cultural centre, with a world-famous ballet company, chamber orchestra and splendid art collections.

Exploring Stuttgart

Start your tour of Stuttgart at Schlossplatz, continuing along Königstrasse towards the Palace Gardens, with their many interesting buildings, and stopping to pay a visit to the Staatsgalerie, whose extension was designed by the British architect James Stirling. From there you can return via Konrad-Adenauer-Strasse, heading towards Karlsplatz, then to Schillerplatz and Marktplatz with its magnificent town hall, finally ending the walk at Hegelhaus museum.

🏛 Schlossplatz

At the centre of the square stands the **Jubiläumssäule** – a column erected in 1842–46 to celebrate the 25-year reign of Wilhelm I. The square also features sculptures by many famous artists, including Alexander Calder and Alfred Hrdlicka. The east side of the square features a huge palace complex, **Neues Schloss**, built in 1746–1807, while on the opposite side stands **Königsbau**, a Neo-Classical structure erected in 1856–60.

Neo-Classical façade of Stuttgart's Staatstheater

🏛 Kunstmuseum Stuttgart

Kleiner Schlossplatz 1. **Tel** (0711) 216 196 00. **Open** 10am–6pm Tue–Sun (to 9pm Fri). 🏛 🖉 📷
W **kunstmuseum-stuttgart.de**

The spectacular glass cube of the Kunstmuseum Stuttgart was designed by the Berlin architects Hascher & Jehle. It houses the Municipal Art Collection, which includes works by such artists as Adolf Hölzel, Joseph Kosuth, Dieter Krieg, Dieter Roth, the Swabian Impressionists and has an outstanding collection of Otto Dix's work.

🔲 Schlossgarten

The magnificent gardens stretching north of the Neues Schloss were established in the early 19th century. They have maintained, to this day, much of their original charm, with neat avenues and interesting sculptures. The attractions include the **Carl-Zeiss-Planetarium**, which runs an excellent science programme, using equipment made by the famous optics company.

On the edge of the park stands a vast Neo-Classical theatre building, the **Württembergisches Staatstheater**, built in 1909–12 by Max Littmann. In 1982–3 it was given a new, dome-covered wing, the Theaterpavilion, designed by Gottfried Böhm.

🏛 Staatsgalerie

See pp316–17.

🏰 Altes Schloss

Landesmuseum Württemberg
Schillerplatz 6. **Tel** (0 711) 895 3511.
Open 10am–5pm Tue–Sun. 🏰
W **landesmuseum-stuttgart.de**

When Württemberg castle burned down in 1311, it was decided to move the family seat to Stuttgart. In 1325, the existing small castle was extended, creating Dütnitzbau. This wing has survived and can be seen from Karlsplatz. A large-scale Renaissance remodelling project, designed by Aberlin Tresch and carried out in 1553–78, gave the castle its square layout, with three-storey arcaded cloisters encircling the inner courtyard. The southwestern wing contains the Schlosskapelle (chapel), the first sacral building in Stuttgart built especially for the Protestants. The castle now houses the **Landesmuseum**

The façade of Stuttgart's Neues Schloss, combining Baroque and Neo-Classical elements

Cloistered courtyard of the Renaissance Altes Schloss

Württemberg, which includes vast collections of decorative art, including those displaying the ducal and royal insignia of Württemberg. The prehistory section includes jewellery from the Frankish period and the preserved tomb of a Celtic nobleman from Hochdorf.

🎦 Schillerplatz

This is undoubtedly one of Stuttgart's most beautiful areas. It is here that the stud farm that gave Stuttgart its name is said to have stood. Today, a pensive statue of Friedrich Schiller, the work of the Danish sculptor Bertel Thorwaldsen (1839), occupies the centre of the square.

Schillerplatz is surrounded by historic buildings: the **Old Chancellery**, built in 1542–44 and extended upwards in 1566,

now houses a restaurant, the Prinzenbau (1605–78), and the Stiftsfruchtkasten, an attractive gabled granary (1578), now home to a museum of musical instruments.

⛪ Stiftskirche (Hl. Kreuz)

Stiftstrasse 12.
From the south side of Schillerplatz there is a view of the presbytery of the collegiate church of the Holy Cross. This Gothic church, the work of Hänslin and Aberlin Jörg, was built in the 15th century and incorporated the walls of the previous, early-Gothic church. Despite World War II damage, this renovated church still has the original stone gallery of the dukes of Württemberg, built in 1576–84 by Simon Schlör to a design by Johann Steiner, as well as Gothic furnishings.

VISITORS' CHECKLIST

Road map C6. ⚠ 586,000.
ℹ Königstrasse 1A (0711-22 280). 🎆 Frühlingsfest (Apr/May), Stuttgarter Weindorf (Aug/Sep, Oct/Nov), Fellbacher Herbst (Oct), Weihnachtsmarkt (Dec).
🅦 **stuttgart-tourist.de**

Transport
✈ South of town. 🚉

🏛 Hegel-Haus

Eberhardstrasse 53. **Tel** (0/11) 216 964 10. **Open** 10am–5:30pm Mon–Fri, 10am–6:30pm Thu, 10am–4pm Sat.
Georg Wilhelm Friedrich Hegel – the creator of one of the most important modern philosophical systems – was born in this house on 27 August 1770.
The house is now a museum, which houses an exhibition devoted to the life and work of the famous philosopher.

Figures of saints adorning the façade of the Stiftskirche

Stuttgart City Centre

① Schlossplatz
② Kunstmuseum Stuttgart
③ Schlossgarten
④ Staatsgalerie
⑤ Altes Schloss
⑥ Schillerplatz
⑦ Stiftskirche Hl. Kreuz
⑧ Hegel-Haus

Weißenhofsiedlung, Porsche-Museum
Hauptbahnhof
BAD CANNSTATT, WAIBLINGEN
Planetarium
Linden-Museum
KRIEGSBERGSTRASSE
Schloss Solitude
Hauptbahnhof (Arnulf-Klett-Platz)
Staatsgalerie
SCHILLERSTRASSE
Mercedes-Benz Museum
Keplerstr. (Friedrichsbau)
Schlossgarten
③
Staatstheater
④ Staatsgalerie
Liederhalle
Königstrasse
Kunstmuseum
SCHLOSS-PLATZ ①
Neues Schloss
Wilhelms-palais
Hospitalkirche
Fruchtkasten
Schlossplatz
Charlotten-platz
Hohe Strasse
Stadtmitte
SCHILLER-PLATZ ⑥
⑤ Altes Schloss
⑦
Stiftskirche Hl. Kreuz
Markt-halle
MARKT-PLATZ
Stadtmitte (Rotebühlplatz)
Hegel-Haus ⑧
Flughafen 7 km (4 miles)
Fernsehturm
SINDELFINGEN
Leonards-kirche
Rathaus

0 metres 300
0 yards 300

For additional map symbols see back flap

🏛 Linden-Museum/ Staatl. Museum für Völkerkunde

Hegelplatz 1. **Tel** (0711) 2 02 23.
Open 10am–5pm Tue–Sat, 10am–6pm Sun. 🅿 📶 **lindenmuseum.de**

The Linden Museum is one of Germany's finest ethnology museums. It was founded by Count Karl von Linden, who was also its director from 1889 until 1910. The museum contains many fascinating exhibits from all over the world, including figures from the Indonesian theatre of shadows, a Tibetan sand mandala, a 6th–8th-century mask from Peru in South America and a full-size reproduction of an Islamic bazaar.

Peruvian mask in the Linden-Museum

🏛 Weißenhofsiedlung

Weissenhofmuseum im Haus Le Corbusier, Am Weißenhof 20.
Tel (0711) 2 57 91 87. **Open** 11am–6pm Tue–Fri, 10am–6pm Sat & Sun.
Architektur-Galerie: **Tel** (0711) 257 14 34. **Open** 2–6pm Tue–Sat, noon–5pm Sun. 📶 **weissenhof.de**

A building exhibition held in 1927 in Stuttgart had housing as its main theme. It left behind an estate that still exists today, although it was badly bombed during World War II. Most of the houses represent functionalism, which was being promoted at the time by the Bauhaus. The estate, which was to serve as an example to others, has some interesting houses, including

works by Mies van der Rohe (Am Weißenhof 14–29), Le Corbusier (Rathenaustrasse 1–3), Peter Behrens (Hölzelweg 3–5) and Hans Scharoun (Hölzelweg 1).

🏛 Liederhalle

Berliner Platz 1.

A must for all lovers of modern architecture, Liederhalle, in the centre of Stuttgart, is a successful synthesis of tradition and modernism. Built in 1955–56 by Adolf Abel and Rolf Gutbrod, this fine cultural and congress centre, with three concert halls clustered around an irregular hall, is still impressive today.

🏛 Mercedes-Benz Museum

Mercedesstrasse 100. **Tel** (0711) 173 00 00. **Open** 9am–6pm Tue–Sun.
Closed public holidays.

To the east of the town centre, in the Obertürkheim district, is the famous Mercedes-Benz Museum. Its splendid collection illustrates the development of motorcar production, from the earliest models to today's state-of-the-art, computerized products. Set up to celebrate the centenary of their inventions, the museum features over 70 historic vehicles, all in immaculate condition. The collection includes the world's two oldest automobiles, Gottlieb Daimler's horseless carriage and Carl

Some of the models on display in the Mercedes-Benz Museum

Benz's three-wheeled automobile from 1886. Also on display is a hand-made limousine that was built in the 1930s for the Emperor of Japan and the first "Popemobile", which was built for Pope Paul VI.

Another interesting exhibit is the famous 1950s racing car, *Silberpfeil* (Silver Arrow), as well as models that were built for attempts on world speed records. Also on display are scores of the latest models that have been produced by the company. The visitor can also learn the history of Daimler-Benz AG, which was created by the merger in 1926 of Daimler-Motoren-Gesellschaft and Benz & Cie., Rhein. The company's subsequent 1999 merger with Chrysler created one of the world's largest car manufacturing concerns, Daimler-Chrysler.

🏛 Fernsehturm

Closed due to reopen late 2015.
Built between 1954 and 1956 this television tower was the world's first to be built entirely from ferro-concrete. It is 217 m (712 ft) high and stands on top of a wooded hill, Hoher Bopser. Its observation platform provides splendid views over Schwäbische Alb, Schwarzwald and, on a clear day, even the Alps.

🏛 Porsche-Museum

Porscheplatz 1. **Tel** (01805) 356 911.
Open 9am–6pm Tue–Sun.

The Porsche museum was revamped and reopened in 2009. The exhibition area is made up of a steel structure resting on

House designed by Le Corbusier in Weißenhofsiedlung

For hotels and restaurants in this area see pp497–8 and pp522–4

just three concrete cores, giving it the appearance of hovering in space. More than 80 cars are on display, ranging from the Lohner-Porsche, the world's first hybrid automobile built in 1900, to the latest generation of the Porsche 911. There are also historical archives, an open workshop, a restaurant and café.

🏛 Markthalle
Dorotheenstrasse 4. **Open** 7:30am–6:30pm Mon–Fri, 7am–5pm Sat.

Stuttgart's market hall, built in 1912–14 in Art Nouveau style on the site of an earlier vegetable market, is one of the finest in Europe. Built as a food exchange, it has magnificent frescoes. Today it still sells fresh fruit and vegetables to the general public, and also houses a small restaurant and café.

🏛 Schloss Solitude
Solitude 1. **Tel** (0711) 69 66 99. **Open** Apr–Oct: 10am–noon, 1:30–5pm Tue–Sat, 10am–5pm Sun; Nov–Mar: 1:30–4pm Tue–Sat, 10am–4pm Sun. 🎟 obligatory. 🌳 garden free.

This exquisite small palace, standing on the slopes of a hill, was built for Prince Karl Eugene in 1763–67. The Prince not only commissioned the residence, but also took an active part in its design, which is the work of Pierre Louis Philippe de la Guêpière, who introduced the Louis XVI-style to Germany. Many consider this palace to be his masterpiece.

Following its full restoration in 1990, and the provision of 45 residential studio apartments, the palace now serves art students on scholarships from all over the world. A 15-km (9-mile) long, straight road connects Schloss Solitude with Ludwigsburg.

🏛 Bad Cannstatt
Once an independent health resort, Bad Cannstatt is now a district of Stuttgart. Set in a beautiful park, it has a late-Gothic parish hall-church, a Neo-Classical town hall and a Kursaal (spa-house), built in 1825–42. One of its attractions is the Neo-Classical Schloss Rosenstein, built in 1824–29 at the request of King Wilhelm I, based on amended designs by John Papworth. The King was also the initiator of the beautiful "Wilhelm's complex". This includes a Moorish-style villa located in a symmetrically laid-out park, with many Oriental-style pavilions and other decorative elements. Completed in the 1840s, its main designer was Karl Ludwig Wilhelm von Zanth. The park has now been transformed into a botanical-zoological garden.

Environs
Stuttgart provides a convenient base for exploring the surroundings. In **Sindelfingen**, 15 km (9 miles) southwest, it is worth visiting the Romanesque Church of St Martin Canons, which was founded in 1083. While you are there, take a stroll along Lange Strasse to the old town hall, which dates from 1478 and is joined with the Salt House (1592). The two buildings, both half-timbered in their upper sections, now house the town museum.

A little further to the west, **Weil der Stadt** is the birthplace of the astronomer Johannes Kepler and the reformer Johannes Brenz. The town's late-Gothic church of St Peter and St Paul was completed in 1492 by Aberlin Jörg. Inside is a beautiful Renaissance sacrarium, dating from 1611. The Marktplatz, with a statue of Kepler at its centre, has a Renaissance town hall (1582). Nearby, at Keplergasse 2, stands the house in which the famous astronomer was born and which now houses a small museum, the Kepler-Museum.

Another place worthy of a visit is **Waiblingen**, 10 km (6 miles) to the northeast of Stuttgart. It features a Romanesque church, the vaults of which are decorated with some splendid wall paintings dating from 1515.

The façade of the Schloss Solitude, in the hills to the west of Stuttgart's centre

Staatsgalerie

The Staatsgalerie grew from the museum of fine arts founded in 1843 by King Wilhelm I and containing the king's private collection. Now it ranks among the finest of German galleries. As well as its own magnificent collection of old masters and modern artists, the gallery has an extensive collection of graphics. In 1984 the art gallery acquired an extension designed by James Stirling.

★ Iphigenie
(1871)
Anselm Feuerbach's painting was inspired by a play by Goethe, *Iphigenie auf Tauris*.

Entrance to Alte Staatsgalerie

Crossing of the Rhine near Rhenen (1642)
The Dutch painter Jan van Goyen became famous for his evocative landscapes, which were often executed in uniform tones of lead-grey or brown-green.

★ St Paul in Prison (1627)
In this, one of his earliest works, Rembrandt depicted the Apostle Paul awaiting death in a humble cell.

Entrance to Neue Staatsgalerie

Bathsheba at her Toilet
(c.1485)
In this painting, which is a fragment of a lost triptych illustrating Justice, Hans Memling uses the Old Testament story of Bathsheba to exemplify the abuse of power, intervention by God and the reformation of a sinner.

Key

- ☐ 14th–19th-century art
- ☐ 19th-century art
- ☐ 20th-century art
- ☐ Contemporary art
- ☐ Temporary exhibitions
- ☐ Non-exhibition rooms

Spring Fields (1887)
One of the leading members of the French Impressionist movement, Claude Monet was unsurpassed in his rendition of iridescent light.

VISITORS' CHECKLIST

Konrad-Adenauer-Strasse 30–32.
Tel (0711) 47 04 00.
Open 10am–6pm Tue, Wed, Fri–Sun, 10am–8pm Thu.
W **staatsgalerie.de**

Mother and Child (1905)
This painting by Pablo Picasso represents his "pink period", which preceded the famous Cubist experiments of this great Spanish artist.

Female Nude Reclining on a White Pillow (1917)
Amadeo Modigliani became famous for his idiosyncratic portraits and female nudes.

First floor

The Mourning of Christ (c.1490)
This subtle depiction of Christ is the work of the Venetian artist Giovanni Bellini.

Ground floor

Gallery Guide
Permanent exhibitions are located over the first floor of the two buildings. In the Alte Staatsgalerie are works by the old masters and from the 19th-century. The Neue Staatsgalerie holds 20th-century art.

㉑ Schwäbische Alb

The mountain range of Schwäbische Alb (the Swabian Jura) extends like an arc, 220 km (137 miles) long and 40 km (25 miles) wide, from the area around Tuttlingen and Sigmaringen, in southwest Germany, to Nördlinger Ries, at the border between the federal counties of Baden-Württemberg and Bavaria. The highest peak in the range is Lemberg (1,015 m/ 3,330 ft). Beech woods and scented juniper shrubs dominate the mellow landscape, whose whole system of interconnected stalagmitic caves was carved from the sedimentary limestone rocks.

Hechingen
On the outskirts of Hechingen, the remains of a 1st–3rd-century AD Roman villa are open to the public.

Haigerloch
In the vaults of this castle Is a vast bunker that was used as an atomic research laboratory towards the end of World War II.

★ Burg Hohenzollern
The ancestral seat of the Hohenzollern family was remodelled in 1850–67. Only the 15th-century St Michaelkapelle survives from the original fortress.

★ Beuron
Beuron's magnificent Benedictine Abbey was founded in the 11th century. Its subsequent remodelling resulted in a Baroque structure, which survives to this day.

Key

▰ Motorway
═ Main road
═ Secondary road
─ River
☀ Viewpoint

Swabian Jura Landscape
The gentle hills and enchanting villages attract hikers and tourists from all over the world.

Hohenneuffen
A massive castle dominates the tiny town of Neuffen. It is the most impressive ruin in the Swabian Jura.

Burg Lichtenstein
This romantic castle was immortalized in a novel by Wilhelm Hauff.

★ **Sigmaringen**
The town's skyline is dominated by the castle, which was reconstructed following a fire in 1893. Only the towers of the medieval fortress remain.

0 km   5
0 miles   5

㉒ Tübingen

Road map C6. 85,000.
i An der Neckarbrücke 1 (07071-913 60). Mon, Wed, Fri.
w tuebingen.info.de

Along with Heidelberg and Freiburg im Breisgau, Tübingen is the home of one of southern Germany's three most famous universities. It was founded in 1477 by Count Eberhard the Bearded.

The first records of the fortress that later gave rise to a settlement on this site date from 1078. By around 1231, the settlement had become a town. In 1342, Tübingen passed to the counts of Württemberg, having previously belonged to the counts Palatinate.

Schloss Hohentübingen, which towers over the town, has a magnificent gateway (Unteres Tor). Built in 1606, it is richly adorned with the coat of arms of the House of Württemberg. The walled castle complex, with its central courtyard and long approach, was built in stages during 1507–15, 1534–42 and 1606.

A walk along the Burgsteige takes you to the picturesque old town. Here, at the centre of Marktplatz, is the Neptune Fountain, the work of Heinrich Schickhard, dating from 1617. In the western corner of the square is a lovely Renaissance

Tübingen's Gothic-Renaissance town hall

town hall, built in 1435 and extended in the 16th century. It features an astronomical clock, which dates from 1511. *Sgraffiti* on the western façade dates from 1876; those on the elevations facing Haaggasse date from the 16th century.

The collegiate church of St George (**Stiftskirche St Georg**), built in 1440–1529, is a triple-nave hall with rows of side chapels, galleries and a single tower. Of particular note are the ducal tombs, the late-Gothic reading-room and the stained-glass windows of the choir, dating from 1475. Magnificent stalls, adorned with carved figures of the Prophets, date from the late 15th century.

The bookstore in Holzmarkt *(Buchhandlung Heckenhauer)*

is where Hermann Hesse once served as an apprentice bookseller. On the banks of the Neckar stands the **Hölderlinturm**, in which the German poet Hölderlin lived from 1807 until his death. Not far from here stands the large building of the Alte Burse, which was built in 1478–80 and later remodelled in 1803–1805. The building was once used to accommodate students and as a lecture hall. Martin Luther's close associate, Philipp Melanchthon, lectured here between 1514 and 1518.

The Protestant seminary in Neckarhalde was founded by Prince Ulrich in 1536. Its graduates include the poets Hölderlin, Mörike and Schiller and the philosophers Hegel and Schelling.

The **Kunsthalle** is famous throughout Germany not only for its temporary exhibitions, but also for its fine collection of modern art. Other popular attractions in Tübingen include the **Stadtmuseum**, which is devoted to the town's history, and the **Auto- und Spielzeugmuseum**, which combines cars and toys.

Museum Schloss Hohentübingen
Burgsteige 11. **Tel** (07071) 297 73 84. **Open** 10am–5pm Wed–Sun (to 7pm Thu).

Stiftskirche St Georg
Tel (07071) 525 83. **Open** 9am–4pm daily.

Hölderlinturm
Bursagasse 6. **Tel** (07071) 254 245. **Open** 10am–noon, 3–5pm Tue–Fri, 2– 5pm Sat, Sun & public hols.

Kunsthalle
Philosophenweg 76. **Tel** (07071) 969 10. **Closed** for renovations; due to reopen early 2017. **w** kunsthalle-tuebingen.de

Statdtmuseum
Kornhausstrasse 10. **Tel** (07071) 204 17 11 or 94 54 60. **Open** 11am–5pm Tue–Sun.

Auto-und Spielzeugmuseum
Brunnenstrasse 18. **Tel** (07071) 92 90 90. **Open** 10am–noon, 2–5pm Wed–Fri, 10am–5pm Sat, Sun & public hols. **Closed** 22–24 & 31 Dec, 12 & 13 Jan.
w boxenstop-tuebingen.de

Unteres Tor leading to Schloss Hohentübingen

㉓ Rottweil

Road map C7. ⚑ 24,000. ⚑
ℹ Hauptstrasse 21 (0741-49 42 80).
🎭 Fasnet (last Mon of Carnival),
Jazzfest (May), Klassikfestival (Jun),
Ferienzauber (Aug). **W** rottweil.de

Situated on the banks of the
river Neckar, Rottweil is one
of the oldest towns in Baden-
Württemberg. It grew from a
Roman settlement that was
established on a hilltop here in
AD 73. In 1234 Rottweil was
granted town status and, by
1401, it had become a free
town of the Holy Roman
Empire. Between 1463 and
1802 it belonged to the Swiss
Confederation, which was
founded in 1291 by the cantons
of Uri, Schwyz and Unterwalden.
In 1802, the town passed
into the rule of the dukes
of Württemberg.

Rottweil has many historic
remains, including sections of
the fortified city walls, with
several well-preserved turrets.

The parish church of St Cross
(Heilig-Kreuz-Münster), built in
1230–1534, has a triple-nave
basilica with stellar and network
vaults. Late-Gothic altars, including St Bartholomew's, by
Michael Wolgemut and a crucifix
attributed to Veit Stoss, are
among its features.

To the south of the church
stands the late-Gothic town
hall (1521). On the opposite side
of the street, at Hauptstrasse 20,
the **Stadtmuseum** has an outstanding collection of

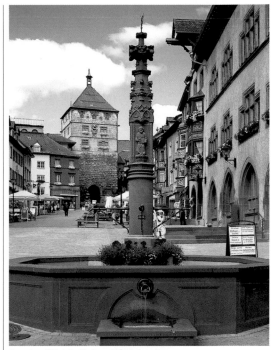

Fountain and "Black Gate" in Rottweil's main street, Hauptstrasse

prehistoric remains. The
Dominikanermuseum has
an interesting exhibition of
Roman relics. These include the
famous Orpheus mosaic,
dating from the 2nd century
AD, and an outstanding
collection of late-Gothic
sculpture, including the
statue of St Barbara by
Multscher (c.1450).

The Hauptstrasse is lined
with burghers' houses,
displaying characteristic
oriel windows. One of the
most beautiful historic
buildings in Rottweil is
the Kapellenkirche, built in
1330–1478. Its 70-metre (230-ft)
tower and three portals are
adorned with carved
ornaments reminiscent of the
French Gothic style. The
Baroque interior features
frescoes by Josef Fiertmayer,
who was a pupil of renowned
painter and architect Cosmas
Damian Asam. The Gothic
Dominican church, built in
1266–82 and remodelled in the
18th century, has some frescoes
by Joseph Wannenmacher

Kapellenturm,
Rottweil

(1755). Roman baths dating
from the 2nd century AD have
been excavated at the corner
of what is now the cemetery.

Rottweil is famous for
its carnival processions
(Fasnet), a tradition that
goes back to the Middle
Ages. A collection of
carnival costumes can be
seen in the Stadtmuseum.
The **Puppen- und
Spielzeugmuseum** is
home to a fine collection
of historic dolls and
toys which is perfect
for keeping the
children entertained.

🏛 **Stadtmuseum**
Hauptstraße 20. **Tel** (0741) 494
330. **Open** 2–4pm Tue–Sun. 🈵

🏛 **Dominikanermuseum**
Kriegsdamm 4. **Tel** (0741) 7662.
Open 10am–5pm Tue–Sun.
Closed public holidays. 🈵

🏛 **Puppen- und
Spielzeugmuseum**
Hauptstraße 49. **Tel** (0741) 942 21 77.
Open 10am–12:30pm, 2pm–5:30pm
Wed–Fri, 10am–12:30pm Sat, 2–5pm
Sun. 🈵

Crucifixion attributed to Veit Stoss in
Heilig-Kreuz-Münster, Rottweil

㉔ Ulm

Road map C6. 🚗 115,000. 🚉
ℹ️ Münsterplatz 50 (0731-161 28 30.
🎣 Fischerstechen (every 4th year in
Jul, next is 2017), Schwörmontag (3rd
Mon in Jul), Stadtfest (Jun).
🌐 tourismus.ulm.de

Lying on the river Danube, Ulm dates back to 854. It became a town in 1165 then, in 1274, a free town of the Holy Roman Empire. During the 15th century Ulm was one of the richest towns in Europe but the Thirty Years' War put an end to its rapid development. In 1810 Ulm came under the rule of the Württemberg kings. The town is renowned as the birthplace of Albert Einstein. During World War II, most of the old town was destroyed during bombing raids.

The Münster is a true masterpiece of European Gothic architecture. A vast, five-nave basilica, its 161-m (530-ft) high west tower is the highest church tower in the world. The cathedral's

Gothic font in Ulm Cathedral

construction, from 1377 until 1545, was overseen by the greatest builders of the German Gothic – Heinrich and Michael Parler, Urlich von Ensingen, Hans Kun and Matthäus Böblinger. The unfinished cathedral was extended in 1844–90, based on the original medieval design. The interior contains many outstanding features, including the altar by

Astronomical clock on Ulm's Gothic-Renaissance town hall

Hans Multscher (1443), the famous stalls with figures of philosophers, poets, prophets and apostles carved by Jörg Syrlin the Elder, 15th-century stained-glass windows, and the font, by Jörg Syrlin the Younger.

The town has many fine historic buildings, including the Gothic-Renaissance town hall, which is decorated with brightly coloured frescoes and features an astronomical clock. Other features of Marktplatz include the Gothic fountain *Fischkasten* (Fish Crate), dating from 1482, and the Reichenauer Hof, which dates from 1370–1535.

The **Ulmer Museum**, which is housed in a number of historic 16th- and 17th-century buildings, has a collection of art spanning a period from the Middle Ages up to the present day. The collection includes the work of local artists, such as Hans Multscher. The **Museum der Brotkultur** specializes in artifacts related to bread and bread-making, including items depicting bread in art and graphic designs.

🏛️ **Ulmer Museum**
Marktplatz 9. **Tel** (0731) 161 43 30.
Open 11am–5pm Tue–Sun, 11am–8pm Thu (during exhibitions). 🖼️

🏛️ **Museum der Brotkultur**
Salzstadelgasse 10. **Tel** (0731) 699 55.
Open 10am–5pm daily. 🖼️
🌐 museum-brotkultur.de

㉕ Ravensburg

Road map: C7. 🚗 45,000. 🚉
ℹ️ Kirchstrasse 16 (0751-828 00).
🎭 Fasnet (Feb), Rutenfest (Jul).
🌐 ravensburg.de

The first historic records of the "Ravespurc" fortress date from 1088, when it was one of the seats of the Welf family. It is believed to be the birthplace of

Main altar by Hans Multscher in Ravensburg's Liebfrauenkirche

Henry the Lion, the powerful Duke of Saxony and Bavaria, born in 1129. The settlement that sprang up at the foot of the castle became a free imperial city in 1276. From 1395, paper was produced here and, during the 15th century, the town became one of the richest in Germany from its involvement in the linen trade.

Standing in Kirchstrasse is the 14th-century parish church of Liebfrauenkirche, which retains original 15th-century features, including the main altar and some fine stained-glass windows.

In Marienplatz stands the late-Gothic town hall (14th–15th century), with its lovely Renaissance bay window. Also in Marienplatz is the Waaghaus (1498), which housed the weigh-house and mint on the ground floor, with a trading hall upstairs, when Ravensburg was engaged in coin production. The watchtower (*Blaserturm*) is crowned by a Renaissance octagon that has become the symbol of the town. Another attractive building here is the Lederhaus, which dates from 1513–14. Near the town hall is the old 14th–15th century granary (*Kornhaus*).

Marktstrasse features many old burgher houses. No. 59, the oldest house in town, dates from 1179. The neighbouring house was built in 1446. The tall white cylindrical tower that can be seen from here is known as the "sack of flour" (*Mehlsack*). It was erected in the 16th century. A magnificent view of the town can be obtained from Veitsburg, which occupies the site of the original Welf castle.

For hotels and restaurants in this area see pp497–8 and pp522–4

Former Cistercian abbey complex in Salem, now a secular building

㉖ Weingarten

Road map: C7. 🏔 24,500. 🚌
ℹ️ Münsterplatz 1 (0751-40 52 32).
🎭 Blutritt (day after Ascension)

The House of Welf founded
a Benedictine abbey in
Weingarten in 1056. During the
Romanesque period, around
1190, the monks of the abbey
produced a chronicle of the
House of Welfs, known as
the *Welfenchronik*.

Ambitious plans, drawn up in
the 18th century at the initiative
of Abbot Sebastian Hyller,
provided for an extension of
the abbey and the construction
of another vast complex of
buildings. Two side courtyards
and four external courtyards,
encircled with curved galleries
with smaller pavilions, were
planned to be grouped around
the church. These were designed
by Casper Moosbrugger, Franz
Beer, Donato Giuseppe Frisoni
and others, and built in 1715–24.

The church is reminiscent of
the Basilica of St Peter's in
Rome. Although it is half the
size of the latter, it is never
theless an immense structure.
Inside are some magnificent
ceiling frescoes by Cosmas
Damian Asam, while the
carved and inlaid choir stalls
are the work of Joseph Anton
Feuchtmayer. Also of note is the
organ by Josef Gabler. In an
ingenious design, the organ
pipes are concealed within a
series of towers to avoid
obscuring the windows of the
façade. The **Alamannenmuseum**
has a fascinating exhibition

of relicts that have been found
in graves dating from the
Merovingian period.

🏛 Alamannenmuseum
Karlstr. 28. **Tel** (0751) 40 52 55.
Open 2–5pm Tue–Sun. 🔲

㉗ Salem

Road map: C7. 🏔 8,500.
ℹ️ Schloss Salem (07553-91 77 15).

The first Cistercian monks
arrived in Salmansweiler (now
known as Salem) in 1134.
Between 1299 and 1414 they
built a church according to
the rules of their order, which
espoused poverty and banned
any decoration of the buildings.

The abbey is a triple-nave
basilica with transept and
straight-end choir. Its austere
façade is relieved by blind
windows, some of which have
attractive traceries. In later years
the restraints of poverty were

relaxed to the extent that the
abbey now has an interesting
tabernacle (1500), stalls (1594)
and early-Renaissance altars
(dating from the 18th century).

The new abbey buildings
were built between 1700 and
1710 and constitute **Schloss
Salem**. The buildings include
some richly decorated abbot's
apartments and the extremely
impressive Emperor's room
(*Kaisersaal*), which was built
between 1708 and 1710.

Since its secularization in
1802, the abbey has been the
private property of the Baden
margraves who keep some of
their art collection here. The
west wing houses a private
boarding school founded by
Kurt Hahn, who also founded
Gordonstoun in Scotland.

🏠 Schloss Salem
Tel (07553) 916 53. **Open** Apr–Oct:
9:30am–6pm Mon–Sat, 10:30am–6pm
Sun. 🔲

Ceiling fresco in Weingarten's abbey

❷⑧ Bodensee

Sometimes known as Lake Constance, the Bodensee lies on the border of Germany, Switzerland and Austria. The area surrounding the lake is one of the most attractive in Germany, in terms of both natural beauty and cultural heritage. Towns and villages around the shores feature countless reminders of past times and cultures. The best time for a visit is summer, when local fishermen stage colourful fairs and water sports are possible.

Bodensee
The lake is 15 km (9 miles) across at its widest point and 63 km (39 miles) long. It lies at an altitude of 395 m (1,295 ft) and reaches 252 m (826 ft) in depth.

Reichenau
The greatest attraction of this island is the Benedictine abbey, which was famed during the era of Otto the Great (10th century) for its illuminated manuscripts. It has a beautiful Romanesque-Gothic church and an intoxicating herb garden.

Stockach

Ludwigshafen

Überlin

ÜBERLINGER SEE

Singen

Radolfzell

Gottmadingen

ZELLERSEE

Reichenau

Ma

Konstan

UNTERSEE

Kreuzlingen

★ Mainau
Mainau is known as the "Island of Flowers". The most beautiful displays are in the park surrounding the Baroque palace, which was built in 1739–46. It is currently owned by the Lennart Bernadotte family.

KEY

① **Friedrichshafen** is best known for its Zeppelin-Museum. The first Zeppelin airships were tested here in 1900.

② **Langenargen** has an enchanting, small Moorish-style palace named Montfort.

★ **Konstanz** (Constance)
The largest town in the region, its main attraction is the magnificent 11th-century Romanesque cathedral. The vaults over the central aisle were built between 1679 and 1683.

For hotels and restaurants in this area see pp497–8 and pp522–4

Meersburg

The exquisite Baroque town of Meersburg has two residences – the Baroque Neues Schloss and the Altes Schloss. The latter is a 16th-century structure built on top of a hill. It contains within its walls an old Carolingian palace.

VISITORS' CHECKLIST

Practical Information
Road map 7 C. *i* Bahnhofplatz 43, Konstanz (07531-13 30 30).
w konstanz-tourismus.de
Sea Life Centre: Hafenstr. 9, Konstanz. **Tel** (07531)-12 82 70. **Open** Sep–Jun: 10am–5pm daily; Jul & Aug: 10am–6pm daily.
w visitsealife.com Museum Reichenau: Ergat 1–3. **Tel** (07534) 99 93 21. **Open** Apr–Oct: 10:30am–4:30pm daily (Jul & Aug: to 5:30pm); Nov–Mar: 2–5pm Sat, Sun & hols.

★ Wasserburg

This charming church, with a tower crowned with an onion-shaped dome, is one of the most frequently photographed sights in this region.

Lindau

This island town has so many historic buildings that the whole area has been listed as a historic monument *(see p288)*.

Meersburg

GERMANY

BODENSEE

Romanshorn

Wasserburg

SWITZERLAND

Lindau

• Arbon

AUSTRIA

• Bregenz

• Rorschach

Key

- Motorway
- Major road
- Minor road
- River
- Ferry or catamaran route
- International border

0 km   5

0 miles   5

㉙ Freiburg im Breisgau

The dukes of Zähringen first established Freiburg in 1120. The town, which later belonged to the counts von Urach, became so rich over the years that, in 1368, it bought its freedom and voluntarily placed itself under the protection of the Habsburgs. Marshal Vauban fortified the town in the 17th century, when Freiburg briefly belonged to France. Since 1805 it has been part of Baden. Situated between Kaiserstuhl and Feldberg, it is a natural gateway to the southern Schwarzwald (Black Forest).

Freiburg University
Freiburg University occupies a Baroque post-Jesuit complex. In the main entrance stands this statue of the pensive Aristotle.

This former Jesuit church belongs to the university complex.

0 metres 50
0 yards 50

Railway station

Tourist information

RATHAUS-PLATZ

RATHAUSGASSE

BERTOLDSTRASSE

Fischerau
Fischerau and, parallel to it, Gerberau are picturesque streets in the old town, running along the Gewerbebach stream.

Key
— Suggested route

Bertoldsbrunnen
(Bertold's fountain) stands at the intersection of Bertholdstrasse and Kaiser-Joseph-Strasse, known as "Kaj(

Martinstor
St Martin's Gate was part of the 13th-century town fortifications. Its present appearance is the result of work carried out in 1900.

◄ An example of the beautiful stained glass windows in Freiburg im Breisgau's Münster

Haus zum Walfisch
The façade of the Whale House in Franziskanergasse, with its lovely bay window, is a magnificent example of late-Gothic style.

Münsterplatz
The picturesque square at the foot of the cathedral, lined by houses of various periods, from Gothic to Rococo, is still used for markets.

VISITORS' CHECKLIST

Practical Information
Road map B7. 197,000.
Rathausplatz 2–4 (0761-388 18 80). Fasnet (end of carnival), Frühlingsmesse (May), Internationales Zeltmusikfest (Jun), Weintage (Jun), Weinkost (Jun), Herbstmesse (Oct), Umwelt-Film-Festival (Oct).
w freiburg.de

Transport

KAISER-JOSEPH-STRASSE

SCHUSTERSTRASSE

SALZSTRASSE

MÜNSTERPLATZ

Augustiner Museum

★ Bächle
From the Middle Ages, fast-flowing canals have been running along the streets, draining excess surface waters, and providing the water needed to extinguish the frequent fires.

★ Münster – the Main Altar
The cathedral, which started in c.1200 as a Romanesque basilica, was completed by 1513 in the French Gothic style. Inside is the original main altar by Hans Baldung Grien.

★ Kaufhaus
Completed in 1520, with ground-floor arcades and richly adorned gables, the Kaufhaus (literally buying house) was used by local merchants for meetings, conferences and lively festivities.

⑩ Schwarzwald (Black Forest)

Covered with tall fir trees and spruces, the Schwarzwald is one of Germany's most picturesque regions. The area is famous not just for its cuckoo clocks, *Kirschwasser* (schnaps) and *Schwarzwälder Kirschtorte* (Black Forest Gâteau); in the past, Celts and later the Romans came to appreciate the therapeutic qualities of the local spring waters. (The sources of the rivers Donau and Neckar are here.) The area is also a paradise for skiers, climbers, ramblers, hang-glider pilots and sailors.

★ Staufen im Breisgau
The town is also known as Fauststadt: Dr Faustus, who had resided here, died in 1539 – he is variously reputed to have blown himself up, to have been strangled or to have had his neck broken.

Todtnau
Todtnau is not only a sports centre and a base for hikers and cyclists: it also has a fanstastic annual festival devoted entirely to *Schwarzwälder Kirschtorte* (Black Forest Gateau).

Friesenheim
Lahr
Herbolzheim
Rhein
Emmendin
Dreisam
Teningen
Denzlingen
Freiburg im Breisg
Bad Krozingen
Staufen im Breisgau
Müllheim
SCHWARZWALD
Todtmo
Kandern
Wiese
Wehr
Lörrach
Rheinfelden
Basel

Todtmoos
The heart of this resort is the Baroque pilgrimage church, which dates from the 17th–18th centuries. Popular dog-sleigh races are held annually in the town.

VISITORS' CHECKLIST

Practical Information
Road map B7. **i** Wehratalstr. 19,
Todtmoos (07674-906 00.
W todtmoos.de
Offenburger Weinmarkt,
Weihnachtsmarkt. Dog-sleigh
races in Todtmoos (Jan) and
Bernau (Feb), Schlosskonzerte
in Rastatt (Jul).

Gutach

In the open-air museum near the
small town of Gutach visitors can
see the Schwarzwald's oldest house
– the Vogtsbauernhof – which
dates from the 16th century.

★ Furtwangen

The main attraction of Furtwangen is its clock museum
(Uhrenmuseum), which houses a collection of more than
8,000 varied chronometers.

Hangloch-Wasserfall

This magnificent mountain
waterfall near Todtnau is one of the
most beautiful in the Black Forest.

★ St Blasien

In the beautiful health resort of
St Blasien is a Benedictine Abbey,
founded in the 9th century. Crowned
with a vast dome, its church (1783)
is an excellent example of early
Neo-Classical style.

0 km   10
0 miles   10

Key

Motorway

Main road

Secondary road

River

Viewpoint

WESTERN GERMANY

Western Germany at a Glance

Famed for its excellent wines and the festivities of Cologne's annual carnival, Western Germany is the country's wealthiest and most heavily industrialized region. The Ruhr district still harbours enormous industrial potential, while Frankfurt am Main is Germany's largest financial centre. The region is also rich in tourist attractions – visitors are drawn to the romantic castles which line the Rhine and Mosel valleys, to Cologne with its majestic twin-towered cathedral, the spa town of Aachen, the museums of Frankfurt and Kassel and the imposing Romanesque cathedrals of Speyer, Worms and Mainz.

Locator Map

Rheine

Gronau

Münster

Coesfeld

Kleve

NORTH RHINE-WESTPHALIA
(See pp386–419)

Hamm

Dortm

Essen

Hage

Duisburg

Düsseldorf

Wuppertal

Solingen

Aachen

Cologne

Hennef

Bonn

Koble

Prüm

Wittlich

Bac
Kreuznach

Trier

RHINELAND-PALATINATE & SAARLAND
(See pp340–63)

Kaiserslautern

Saarbrücken

Pirmasen

Cologne Cathedral *(see pp406–7)*, which was not completed until the 19th century, is generally considered one of the most outstanding Gothic buildings in Germany.

| 0 kilometres | 100 |
| 0 miles | 100 |

Maria Laach *(see pp362–3)* is a charming, beautifully preserved Romanesque abbey in a tranquil, isolated setting on the shores of the Laacher See.

◄ The Saar river bend, near Mettlach, Saarland

Detmold is best known for its magnificent castle *(see p419)* – one of the most beautiful examples of the "Weser Renaissance" style of architecture.

The Museum Fridericianum in Kassel *(see pp368–9)*, originally built to house Friederich II's art collection, has hosted the *documenta*, an exhibition of contemporary art that has achieved international acclaim, every four to five years since 1955.

Minden

Bielefeld

Detmold

Wiedenbrück

Paderborn

Warburg

Meschede   Kassel

HESSE
(See pp364–85)

gen

Marburg   Bad Hersfeld

Alsfeld

Wetzlar   Giessen   Fulda

Frankfurt
am Main

esbaden

Mainz

Darmstadt

ms

Ludwigshafen

eyer

ndau

Fulda Cathedral *(see p372)* is one of the finest Baroque churches in Hesse. It was built on the site of the previous Romanesque church and follows the original layout.

The old town in Frankfurt am Main *(see p379)* is centred around the Römerberg – a square surrounded by attractive half-timbered houses, with the Fountain of Justice as a focal point.

Wine in Western Germany

Of the great European vineyards, Germany's are the farthest north. There are 13 wine-growing regions in Germany, but the most famous German vineyards are those in the western part of the country, especially the Rheingau, Pfalz, Rheinhessen and Mosel regions. The most widely drunk alcoholic beverage in Germany is beer – unlike in France, Italy or Spain – and therefore the wines produced here are mainly high-quality wines of named vineyards, with a relatively low production of table wine.

The Mosel region produces superb white wines from the Riesling grape. The highest quality wines are those labelled Prädikatswein.

Vineyards in Edenkoben, in the southern part of the Weinstraße *(see p351)*, in the Palatinate

NORTH RHINE-WESTPHALIA

Coesfeld
Duisburg
Essen
Dortmund
Hagen
Düsseldorf
Wuppertal
Aachen
Cologne
Bonn
Koblenz
Wittlich
Trier

RHINELAND-PALATINATE & SAARLAND

Saarbrücken

Important Facts About German Wine

Region and climate
Gentle, rocky hills stretching along the river bends – perfect for Rieslings – are typical of the Mosel and Rheingau regions. Clay and limestone soil, appropriate for the Müller-Thurgau variety, are found in Hesse on the Rhine. The German climate is considerably more severe than that of southern countries, which gives the wines a slightly sharp, refreshing taste.

Typical grape varieties
The most popular red variety is the Spätburgunder, known in France as Pinot Noir, which produces a heavy wine with a strong flavour. White grapes are much more popular, especially the famous Rieslings, from which the best white wines are produced, the Müller-Thurgau, which gives a light wine with a fruity bouquet, the Grauburgunder (Pinot Grigio) and the Weißburgunder (Pinot Blanc). Less well-known are: Silvaner, Gewürztraminer and Gutedel. Rosé wines are produced from the Portugieser variety, cultivated in the Rhineland–Palatinate (Pfalz) and Rheinhessen.

Famous wine producers
Mosel-Saar-Ruwer: Fritz Haag, Heymann-Löwenstein, Karthäuserhof, Dr Loosen, Egon Müller, J.J. Prüm, C. von Schubert, Willi Schaefer; Rheingau: Georg Breuer, Robert Weil; Rheinhessen: Gunderloch, Keller; Pfalz: Müller-Catoir, Georg Mosbacher, Dr Bürklin-Wolf, Reichsrat von Buhl.

The Nahe is famous for its white wines, produced from Silvaner as well as Riesling and Müller-Thurgau grapes.

The Rheingau, where the "Rhine" wines are made, is well known for its Rieslings, particularly the Johannisberger Riesling. A famous vineyard is Prinz von Hessen.

The fountain of the "Wine Witch" in the small town of Winningen, in the Mosel region

Wine Regions

Two well-known wine regions are the Mosel and the Rheingau. Exceptional Rieslings are produced here as well as smaller amounts of other wines. The Rheingau produces a full-bodied red wine in addition to the dominant Rieslings. Rheinhessen produces not only several types of white and red wines, but also a rose, as does the Palatinate.

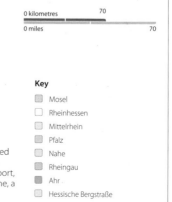

Wine cellars in the former Cistercian monastery at Eberbach in the Rheingau region

0 kilometres	70
0 miles	70

Liebfraumilch has been produced in the Rheinhessen region for over 40 years. Originally designed for export, it is a sweetish, medium-class of wine, a blend of several grape varieties.

Key

- ▢ Mosel
- ▢ Rheinhessen
- ▢ Mittelrhein
- ▢ Pfalz
- ▢ Nahe
- ▢ Rheingau
- ▢ Ahr
- ▢ Hessische Bergstraße

Romanesque Architecture

Western Germany boasts some of the most interesting examples of Romanesque architecture in the whole of Europe. Charlemagne's famous chapel in Aachen was erected as early as the Carolingian period. The cathedral in Trier and the church of St Maria im Kapitol in Cologne are among the most outstanding creations of early-Romanesque architecture of the Frankish dynasty. In the 12th century, the most important German centres of art were Cologne and the towns of the central Rhineland, with three magnificent cathedrals in Speyer, Mainz and Worms, and the monastery in Maria Laach, preserved to this day.

Aachen Cathedral is one of a complex of buildings built under the rule of Charlemagne in about 800 AD, It inspired Romanesque architecture across Europe.

The front elevation of the St Gotthard-Kapelle in Mainz has upper galleries with arcades decorated with friezes. This is a common feature of Romanesque architecture.

Twin western towers

Gallery above the vestibule

The northern portal of the Dom in Worms is framed by an offset architrave and flanked by pairs of columns, as are the portals of many other Romanesque cathedrals.

Lavishly decorated main portal

The monastery in Maria Laach has many capitals with intricate decorations, such as these carvings with human faces.

Cross-vaulting (or cross-ribbed vaulting)

Tower at the intersection of the nave and transept

The portal of the Dom in Trier has a magnificent tympanum, depicting Christ with the Virgin Mary and St Peter.

Romanesque Cathedrals

Cathedrals of the type shown here were built with a basilica-type internal arrangement, including a transept and presbytery, and a double choir usually ending in a semicircular apse. The Dom in Speyer has a massive twin-towered west front, as shown here. The other pair of towers rises above the presbytery, and the intersection of the nave and transept has a lower, broad fifth tower.

The system of vaults also acts as support.

Twin eastern towers

Romanesque Capitals

Romanesque churches in the Rhine Valley feature exquisite stone sculptures. The capitals, with their extraordinary variety of form, ranging from simple blocks to fine figurative or animal-decorated compositions, are of particular interest.

Water leaf capital of a bonded column

Simplified Corinthian capital

The St Gotthard-Kapelle in Mainz, next to the Dom, was the archbishop's personal chapel for private prayer. It is comparable to similar private buildings in secular palaces.

Cushion (or block or cube) capital

Zoömorphic (animal-decorated) capital

RHINELAND–PALATINATE AND SAARLAND

The Rhineland-Palatinate is one of Germany's most romantic regions, attracting visitors with its vineyards, gentle hills and fairy-tale castles along the Rhine and Mosel valleys. Several towns, such as Trier, have kept reminders of their Roman heritage.

These two states, which border France in the west, did not emerge in their present form until after World War II. The Rhineland-Palatinate was created from the previously independent Bavarian Palatinate and the southern part of the Central Rhineland, making it a true jigsaw-puzzle of territories without a coherent history. The Saarland was under French rule until 1956. Today, it forms a bridge between France and Germany, the two driving forces of European unity.

The turbulent history of the region has left many traces. The picturesque Mosel Valley is lined with grand medieval fortresses, such as Burg Eltz, while Worms on the Rhine is the setting for most of the Nibelungen legend as well as the residence of the mythical king of Burgundy, Gunther. The Nibelung treasure is still said to lie at the bottom of the Rhine. The impressive cathedral in Worms, along with the Romanesque cathedrals of Speyer and Mainz, is a fascinating example of medieval sacral architecture.

The "Deutsches Eck" in Koblenz is the strategic spot where the Mosel flows into the Rhine, and Koblenz also marks the beginning of the romantic Rhine Valley. A boat trip upriver, justifiably popular with visitors, will pass some spectacular rocky scenery, including the famous Lorelei Rock and countless castles set among vineyards on either side of the gorge.

The famous ironworks complex in Völklingen is a reminder of a bygone era, when most of the Saarland's inhabitants were active in mining, steelworks and other heavy industries.

Panorama of Saarbrücken, with the Saar river in the foreground

◀ The majestic ceiling in the Hall of Banners, in Burg Eltz

Exploring Rhineland-Palatinate and Saarland

White wine enthusiasts come here, attracted by the beautiful, picturesque valleys of the Rhine and Mosel rivers, with their medieval castles and small towns. Travelling along the Deutsche Weinstrasse (German wine route), Germany's oldest tourist route, visitors can see fascinating historic buildings and taste the different types of wine made by the numerous small vineyards scattered throughout the entire region. Speyer and Mainz have monumental Romanesque cathedrals, while Trier boasts many interesting Roman relics. The huge ironworks in Völklingen is a surprising sight, transporting visitors back to a time when heavy industry ruled much of the region.

The imposing red-sandstone building of the Dom in Mainz

0 kilometres   20

0 miles   20

The proud complex of Schloss Stolzenfels near Koblenz, designed by Karl Friedrich Schinkel

For additional map symbols *see back flap*

The interior of the Dom in Trier

Sights at a Glance

① *Trier pp344–7*
② *Saarland p348*
④ *Speyer*
⑤ *Worms*
⑦ *Mainz pp352–5*
⑨ *Koblenz pp360–61*
⑩ *Maria Laach pp362–3*

Suggested routes

③ *Moseltal*
⑥ *Deutsche Weinstrasse*
⑧ *Rheintal*

Key

━━━ Motorway
┄┄┄ Under construction
━━━ Major road
═══ Minor road
━━━ Scenic route
━━━ Main railway
──── Minor railway
▬▬▬ International border
▬▬▬ Regional border
△ Summit

Getting Around

The A65 motorway links Karlsruhe with Ludwigshafen, and continues from there towards Luxembourg or Lorraine, via Homburg and Saarbrücken. The A32, and later the A4, leads from Saarbrücken to Metz or Strasbourg. The A1 runs northwards from Friedrichsthal to Trier and the Mosel Valley. Intercity trains offer a frequent and convenient service; Hahn, Frankfurt am Main and Cologne/Bonn (Konrad-Adenauer-Flughafen) have international airports.

❶ Trier

One of Germany's oldest towns, Trier was founded in 17 BC as *Augusta Treverorum*, supposedly by the Emperor Augustus himself. In the 3rd and 4th centuries it was an imperial seat and the capital of the *Belgica prima* province. In the 5th century the town, which now numbered 70,000 inhabitants, was conquered and destroyed by Germanic tribes. Trier never returned to its former importance – in the 17th century it had a mere 3,600 inhabitants, and 100 years later they still numbered fewer than 4,000. The town, which is also the birthplace of Karl Marx, has a rich architectural heritage.

🏛 Porta Nigra

Tel (0651) 97 80 80 (tourist office).
Open Mar & Oct: 9am–5pm daily;
Apr–Sep: 9am–6pm daily; Nov–Feb:
9am–4pm daily. 🅿

This town gate, named *Porta Nigra* (black gate) in the Middle Ages because of the colour of its weathered stone, was erected in the 2nd century (a similar gate would have stood at the town's southern entrance). The oldest German defensive structure, it still impresses with its colossal size: 36 m (118 ft) long, 21.5 m (70.5 ft) wide and 30 m (27 ft) high. Two gateways lead onto a small inner courtyard, and there are two tiers of defence galleries with large open windows. It is flanked by the four-storey western tower and the three-storey unfinished eastern tower.
In the 12th century, the building was transformed into the two-storey church of St Simeon and served as such until the early 19th century. Porta Nigra is a UNESCO World Heritage Site.

Petrusbrunnen (fountain of St Peter) in Hauptmarkt

🏛 Hauptmarkt

Trier's main market square, one of the most attractive in Germany, dates back to the 10th century. The Marktkreuz (market cross) erected around the same time symbolized the town's right to hold markets. Today a copy of the original cross is mounted on a granite Roman column, with a relief of the Lamb of God. On the southeastern side of the square is the Petrusbrunnen (St Peter's fountain), from 1595, with sculptures of St Peter and the Four Virtues. On the southwestern side stands the 15th-century Steipe, with a steep gabled roof. Originally it was used by the town councillors as a guesthouse and banqueting hall. The Baroque Rotes Haus (red house) next door dates from 1683. Löwen-apotheke, in a 17th-century building on the southeastern side of the square, is Germany's oldest pharmacy, its records dating back to the 13th century.

🏛 Museum am Dom Trier

Bischof-Stein-Platz 1. **Tel** (0651) 710 52 55. **Open** 9am–5pm Tue–Sat; 1–5pm Sun. **Closed** 1 Jan, 24–26, 31 Dec & public hols. 🅿

A 19th-century former Prussian prison near the cathedral now houses the art collection of the Diocese, including early Christian works of art. Its most prized possession is a 3rd-century ceiling painting from the imperial palace that once stood on the site of the cathedral. Rediscovered in 1945, the fresco painstakingly reassembled over the following decades. Another exhibit is the reconstructed crypt of the Benedictine church of St Maximin, which has 9th-century Carolingian wall paintings.

⛪ Dom St Peter

Tel (0651) 979 07 90. **Open** Apr–Oct: 6:30am–6pm daily; Nov–Mar: 6:30am–5:30pm). 🅿 🆆 **trierer-dom.de**
The present cathedral, a UNESCO World Heritage Site, incorporates the remains of an older 4th-century church. The oldest cathedral in Germany, it was constructed in stages – in the early 11th century, late 12th century, mid-13th century and 14th century. It is a triple-nave, two-choir basilica with transept and six towers, and its furnishings include several outstanding objects, such as the tomb of the papal envoy Ivo (1144).

⛪ Liebfrauenkirche

Liebfrauenstr. **Tel** (0651) 979 07 90. **Open** daily but times vary; check website. 🅿 🆆 **liebfrauen-trierer.de**
Adjoining the cathedral is the Liebfrauenkirche (Church of Our Dear Lady), built in 1235–60 and also a UNESCO World Heritage Site. Along with the cathedral

The magnificent *Porta Nigra*, gigantic Roman gateway into Trier

For hotels and restaurants in this area see p499 and pp524–5

Aula Palatina (Konstantin-Basilika)

Konstantinplatz. **Tel** (0651) 42 570. **Open** Apr–Oct: 10am–6pm Mon–Sat, 1–4pm Sun; Nov–Mar: 10am–noon & 2–4pm Mon–Sat, 1–4pm Sun.

Another UNESCO World Heritage Site, the *Aula Palatina* (Palatinate hall) dates from AD 310. An elongated, rectangular brick building 67 m (220 ft) long, 27.5 m (90 ft) wide and 30 m (98 ft) high with a vast semicircular apse, it served as the throne hall of the Roman emperor or his representative. Following the town's sacking by Germanic tribes, the building was reduced to rubble. In the 12th century the apse was converted into a tower, to accommodate the archbishop. In the 17th century,

VISITORS' CHECKLIST

Road map A5. 99,000. An der Porta Nigra (0651-97 80 80). trier-info.de

Transport

the *Aula Palatina* was integrated into the newly built palace and its eastern wall partly demolished. During Napoleonic and Prussian times, the hall served as army barracks. The Prussian king Friedrich Wilhelm IV eventually ordered its reconstruction. From 1856 it has served as the Protestant church of St Saviour. Restored after bombing in 1944, its giant size still seems remarkable.

The Liebfrauenkirche – one of the country's earliest Gothic churches

in Marburg, this is one of the earliest examples of German Gothic architecture. Its ground plan is based on the Greek cross, and the tower above the dome accentuates the intersection of the naves. Its western portal is richly decorated with carved ornaments and iconographic symbols. The interior features many outstanding relics, including 15th-century wall paintings on 12 columns, which symbolize the apostles. Important tombs include that of a local nobleman, Karl von Metternich (1636).

The monumental, austere exterior of the Aula Palatina

Trier City Centre

0 metres 400
0 yards 400

Portal of the Kurfürstliches Palais

🏠 Kurfürstliches Palais

Konstantinplatz. **Open** only by appointment; occasional tours and concerts (ask at tourist information).

The Kurfürstliches Palais is considered to be one of the most beautiful Rococo palaces in the world. It has undergone several transformations over the centuries and remains of the earlier buildings can still be seen. The present building was designed by Johannes Seiz and built in 1756–62 for Archbishop Johann Philipp von Walderdorff. The sculptures were created by Ferdinand Tietz. The central tympanum shows Pomona, Venus, Apollo and a group of angels. The stairs, which lead from the garden to the inner staircase, were designed in the 18th century, but not built until 1981. They have beautiful hand-rails with typical Rococo motifs. The gardens are equally beautiful and include a miniature garden, a landscape garden and a mother-and-child area.

🏛 Rheinisches Landesmuseum

Weimarer Allee 1. **Tel** (0651) 977 40. **Open** 10am–5pm Tue–Sun. **Closed** 1 Jan, 24, 25 & 26 Dec. 🅿

Only a few steps separate the electoral palace from the Rhine regional museum founded in 1877. Its collections are grouped into four sections: prehistoric, Roman, Franconian-Merovingian, and medieval to contemporary.

The largest space is devoted to Roman relics. Among the star exhibits are a magnificent mosaic depicting Bacchus, from the dining room of a Roman villa, and the lovely statuette of a nymph, undoubtedly the work of a major artist. Also on display is the largest treasure of gold coins from the Roman imperial age. Equally impressive is a stone carving showing a ship loaded with four giant barrels, sailing on the Mosel River. Dating from AD 220, the carving decorated the tomb of a local wine-merchant.

📖 Stadtbibliothek

Weberbach 25.

The municipal library contains a number of important collections that were assembled here in the early 19th century, when many monastic libraries closed down. Among its treasures the library holds 74 full-page miniatures of the famous Trier Apocalypse (c.800), as well as one of the few surviving copies of the first Bible printed by Gutenberg.

🏠 Kaiserthermen

Weimarer Allee/Kaiserstr. **Tel** (0651) 442 62. **Open** Apr–Sep: 9am–6pm; Oct & Mar: 9am–5pm; Nov–Feb: 9am–4pm daily. 🅿

Not far from the Rheinisches Landesmuseum are the remains of the vast imperial baths. Built in the early 4th century, during

the reign of Constantine, they were the third largest bathing complex in the Roman world. The remaining sections of the walls and foundations indicate the former layout. Best preserved are the walls of the *caldarium*, the room with the hot water pool. Next to it is the round *tepidarium*, the warm baths. The spacious *frigidarium* was used for cold baths. Considerable room was given to the *palaestra*, an outdoor exercise area.

🏠 Viehmarktthermen

Viehmarktplatz. **Tel** (0651) 994 10 57. **Open** 9am–5pm Tue–Sun.

Following excavations completed in 1994, the remains of these Roman baths, along with those of medieval refuse pits and the cellars of a Capucin monastery, are now on display to the pubic under a large glass canopy.

📖 Jesuitenkirche

Jesuitenstr. 13. **Open** 8:30am–5pm daily.

The Gothic Church of the Holy Trinity was built for Franciscan friars, who settled in Trier before 1238. The surviving church, from the late 13th century, went to the Jesuits in 1570. The college (1610–14) was transferred to the university following the dissolution of the Jesuit Order. It now houses a theological seminary. In the church, the tomb of Friedrich von Spee (1591–1635) is worth a visit.

Nymph in Rheinisches Landesmuseum

Vast complex of the Kaiserthermen (imperial baths)

Amphitheater

Petrisberg. **Tel** (0651) 730 10. **Open**
Apr–Sep: 9am–6pm; Oct & Mar: 9am–
5pm; Nov–Feb: 9am–4pm daily.

Near the imperial baths are
the ruins of the Roman amphitheatre, dating from the 1st
century AD. This was the scene
of gladiatorial fights and animal
contests. The entire structure,
consisting of an elliptical arena
and a stepped auditorium, was
surrounded by a high wall,
divided into individual storeys
by colonnaded arcades. The
complex was designed to seat
up to 20,000 people. In the 5th
century the inhabitants of Trier
used the amphitheatre as a
place of refuge from the
increasingly frequent raids by
Germanic tribes.

Heiligkreuzkapelle

Arnulfstrasse/Rotbachstrasse.
The Chapel of the Holy Cross,
in a secluded spot, is one of
Trier's more interesting historic
buildings. Built in the Romanesque style in the second half
of the 11th century, at the
initiative of the parson of Arnulfa
Cathedral, it is a small building
with a ground plan in the shape
of the Greek cross and an octagonal tower set within the cross.
Although it suffered serious
damage during World War II, it
was meticulously restored to its
original state in the years 1957–8.

Basilika St Matthias

Matthiasstrasse 85. **Tel** (0651) 170 90.
Open 8am–7pm daily.
This church's history dates back
to the 5th century, when it
became the burial place of
St Eucharius, the first bishop of
Trier. From the 8th century, the
church was run by Benedictine
monks. In the 10th–11th
centuries a new church was
erected as burial site of the
relics of the apostle, St Matthew.
It was twice remodelled at the
turn of the 15th to 16th centuries, when it acquired its rich
Gothic vaults. The present
abbey dates from the 16th
century. The shrine holding the
apostle's relics ensured that
the church became one of the
most important destinations
for pilgrims in the region.

The ruins of Barbaratherme, ancient Roman baths

Barbaratherme

Südallee. **Closed** until further notice
(dilapidated) but visible from street.
Not far from the Roman bridge
across the Mosel River are
the ruins of the Barbara baths,
dating from the 2nd century
AD. Although above ground
not much has been preserved,
the extensive system of underground heating channels, the
hypocaustum, clearly demonstrates the original size of this
public bath complex. In the
Middle Ages, Patrician and
aristocratic families transformed
the baths into their residences.
In the 17th century Jesuit monks
dismantled the remaining
structures, and used the
recovered building materials to
construct their own college.

St Maximin-Kirche

Maximinstrasse. **Tel** (0651) 979 07 90.
obligatory.
In the Middle Ages there were
as many as four abbeys in Trier.
St Maximin Abbey was founded
on the burial site of its patron
saint, who died in AD 325. The
surviving church was built in
the 13th century, on the foundations of the previous buildings.
Its Romanesque–Gothic forms
were partly obscured by the
remodelling work carried out in
1580–1698. Now deconsecrated,
the church is used as a music
venue. It is possible to book
guided tours of the atmospheric
crypt. The Carolingian wall
paintings that originally adorned
the crypt are now in the Museum
am Dom Trier *(see p344)*.

St Paulin-Kirche

Thebäerstrasse. **Tel** (0651) 270 850.
Open Mar–Sep: 9am–6pm Mon, Wed–
Sat, 11am–6pm Tue, 10am–6pm Sun;
Oct–Feb: 9am–5pm Mon, Wed–Sat,
11am–5pm Tue, 10am–7:30pm Sun.

This church was built in the
12th century, on the foundations of an older Christian
chapel. In 1674 it was blown up
by the French army. St Paulin, its
patron saint and bishop in Trier,
was one of the few to voice his
opposition to the Aryan credo
of Emperor Constantine II, in
which he rejected the divinity of
Christ and proclaimed himself
alone to be made in God's
image. Paulin did not meet with
a martyr's death, but was exiled
to Phrygia (now Turkey), where
he died in 358. The present
church, a true gem of Rococo
architecture, was designed by
Balthasar Neumann, who also
created the main altar.

Baroque ceiling paintings in the Rococo
St Paulin-Kirche

❷ Saarland

This German state, bordered by Luxembourg and France, was long disputed between France and Germany, but has now been firmly integrated into the Federal Republic. Almost forgotten are its coal and steel industries, which declined in the 1960s and 70s. The region has seen a turbulent history – it was ruled in turn by Celts, Romans and Franks. In the 17th century, on the order of Louis XIV, Vauban built the town-fortress of Saarlouis. Saarbrücken, an 18th-century town, is famous for its Baroque architecture, mostly created by Friedrich Joachim Stengel.

Von Nassau-Saarbrücken family tombs in Saarbrücken

Saarbrücken

Road map B6. 🚊 190,000. 🚆
ℹ️ Rathaus St Johann, Rathausplatz 1 (0681-95 90 92 00). 🎬 Max Ophüls-Preis (Jan), Perspectives du Théâtre (May), Saar Spektakel (Aug). 🌐 saarbruecken.de

The capital of Saarland, Saarbrücken was first built as the Franconian fortress of *Sarabrucca*. The town, on the Saar River, flourished in the 17th and 18th century, under the rule of Duke Wilhelm Heinrich von Nassau-Saarbrücken.

The churches and other prestigious buildings are largely the work of Friedrich Joachim Stengel, court architect to the von Nassau-Saarbrücken family. He designed the Catholic **Basilika St Johann** (1754–8) in the market square, as well as the monumental **Schloss**, the palace on the opposite bank of the Saar (1739–48). Its original, modern façade, created in 1989 after damage in World War II, is the work of the architect Gottfried Böhm.

Opposite the Schloss stands the **Altes Rathaus** (old town hall), dating from 1748–50, which today houses an interesting museum of ethnography. The Protestant **Ludwigskirche**

(1762–75) is one of the last works completed by Stengel. A true architectural gem, it is laid out in the shape of a Greek cross. The **Stiftskirche St Arnual**, in the southwestern part of the town, contains the splendid Gothic and Renaissance tombs of the von Nassau-Saarbrücken family. Since 1960 it has also featured a "German–French Garden". One of the garden's entrances leads to Gulliver-Miniwelt (miniature world of Gulliver), where small versions of the world's most famous buildings are exhibited.

Völklinger Hütte, the historic steelworks in Völklingen

Völklingen

Road map B6. 🚊 43,500.
ℹ️ Neuen Bahnhof, Rathausstr. 55 (06898-132 800).

About 10 km (6 miles) west of Saarbrücken lies the small industrial town of Völklingen, which was granted town status in 1937. In 1881, Carl Röchling, a native of Saarbrücken, bought a small steel mill, the **Völklinger Hütte**, which he soon developed as the heart of his family's industrial empire. The steel mill still exists, and in 1994 it became a UNESCO World Heritage Site, listed as a historical object of international importance. Another attraction is an early 20th-century housing estate.

Homburg

Road map B6. 🚊 42,000. ℹ️ Rathaus, Am Forum 5 (06 841-10 11 66).

This town grew up around the Hohenburg castle, which now is just a picturesque ruin. In the Schlossberg nearby were unearthed the remains of a fortress, which was built in 1680–92 by Sébastien Le Preste Vauban on the orders of the French King Louis XIV. The greatest attraction of Homburg, however, is its Schlossberg caves, the largest man-made caves in Europe, cut into the red sandstone.

Ottweiler

Road map B5. 🚊 16,000.
ℹ️ Schlosshof 5 (06 824-35 11).

The small picturesque town of Ottweiler has a beautifully preserved old town. The Alter Turm (old tower), which in the 15th century formed part of the town's fortifications, now serves as a belfry to the parish church, whose origins go back to the 15th century. Its present Baroque form was the work of Friedrich Joachim Stengel from 1756–7.

Rathausplatz is a beautifully proportioned complex of historic houses, mostly the homes of wealthy citizens, dating from the 17th and 18th centuries. Many have half-timbered upper halves. The Altes Rathaus (old town hall, 1714) combines two different building methods – the base is stone, the top half-timbered. In Schlossplatz is the Renaissance Hesse Haus (c.1590).

For hotels and restaurants in this area see p499 and pp524–5

❸ Moseltal

The Mosel river, 545 km (338 miles) long, is one of the longest tributaries of the Rhine. The Mosel valley between Trier and Koblenz, where the Mosel flows into the Rhine, is one of the most beautiful parts of Germany. On both sides of the river, romantic castles tower over endless vineyards, where excellent white grapes are grown – both are typical features of the charming landscape.

② **Burg Thurant** Near the town of Alken stands Thurant castle, which was built in the 13th century. It is the only twin-towered castle along the Mosel.

⑥ **Cochem** The castle in Cochem, originally built in the 11th century, was completely destroyed by French soldiers in 1689. The present castle was rebuilt in the 19th century.

① **Matthias-Kapelle** This late-Romanesque chapel was once used to house the remains of the Apostle Matthew. These were later transferred to the Matthiaskirche in Trier.

⑤ **Burg Pyrmont** Pyrmont's grim 13th-century medieval castle was remodelled and extended several times during the Baroque era.

④ **Burg Eltz** The von Eltz family castle, whose history goes back to the 16th century, remains in private hands to this day, but it is open to visitors.

③ **Ehrenburg** The first fortress, rising to 235 m (771 ft) above sea level, was built in 1120. It was frequently remodelled in later years.

Tips for Drivers

Length of the route: about 75 km (46 miles).
Stopping-off points: there are numerous restaurants and cafés in Cochem; small pubs can be found along the entire route.
Additional attractions: a boat trip on the Mosel River, from Koblenz to Cochem or Trier.

⑦ **Burg Arras** This fortress was built around 900–950 as part of the fortifications against frequent pillaging raids by Normans.

Key

■■ Suggested route

▬ Scenic route

— Other road

∷∷ River, lake

❋ Viewpoint

0 km   5

0 miles   5

Altar in the Dreifaltigkeitskirche, in Speyer

❹ Speyer

Road map B6. 🏠 47,000. 🚉
ℹ️ Maximilianstrasse 13 (06232-14 23 92). 🎭 Brezelfest (Jul), Kaisertafel (Aug), Altstadtfest (Sep), Bauernmarkt (Sep).

In the 7th century, Speyer was the seat of a diocese. As a free city of the Holy Roman Empire from 1294 until 1779, 50 sessions of the imperial parliament took place here. The most famous session was in 1529, when the Protestant states of the Holy Roman Empire lodged a protest (hence "Protestant") against the decisions of the Catholic majority.

The most important historic building in Speyer is the Romanesque **Kaiserdom** (St Maria und St Stephan), a World Heritage Site. For a time, before being superseded by the gigantic abbey of Cluny in Burgundy, this was the largest monumental Romanesque building in Europe. The Dom, built in 1025–61 on the initiative of Conrad II, is a triple-nave, cross-vaulted basilica with transept, vestibule, choir, apse and several towers. Its magnificent triple-nave crypt, the burial place of Salian emperors, has stunning stone carvings, some worked by Lombard stonemasons. **St Afra's**, dating from around 1100, has some interesting sculptures, including *Christ Bearing His Cross* and *Annunciation* (c.1470). The Domnapf, a vast stone bowl seen at the forecourt of the cathedral, dates from 1490. It was used during enthroning ceremonies,

when the newly anointed bishop would order it to be filled with wine right to the brim in order to win the hearts of his flock.

Another 11th-century interesting building is the **Mikwe** in Judenbadgasse, a ritual Jewish bath for women, and the remains of a synagogue nearby. To the west of the Dom stand the remains of the medieval fortifications including the **Altpörtel**, a 14th- to 16th-century town gate. The late-Baroque **Dreifaltigkeitskirche** (church of the Holy Trinity), built in 1701–17, is an architectural masterpiece with marvellous interiors

❺ Worms

Road map B5. 🏠 83,000. 🚉
ℹ️ Neumarkt 14 (06241-250 45).

Worms is one of the oldest towns in Germany. In the Middle Ages it was the home of the Reich's Parliament, hosting more than 100 sessions. The **Dom St Peter** is one of the largest late-Romanesque cathedrals in Germany, along with the cathedrals in Mainz and Speyer. It was built in 1171–1230 as a two-choir basilica, with eastern transept, four towers and two domes. Its northern nave includes five beautiful sandstone reliefs from a Gothic cloister, which no longer exists. The interior furnishings date mainly from modern times. Particularly noteworthy is the high altar designed in the 18th century by Balthasar

A relief from 1488, in the Dom in Worms

Tombstones in the Heiliger Sand Jewish cemetery in Worms

Neumann, and the stalls dating from 1760. A short distance from the cathedral is the Marktplatz (market square), with the interesting **Dreifaltigkeitskirche** church of the Holy Trinity (1709–25). Northeast of the square stands the **Stiftskirche St Paul** (church of St Paul), built in the 11th–12th centuries and completed in the 18th century, with original 13th century wall paintings. Nearby is the only surviving Renaissance residential building in Worms, the **Rotes Haus** (red house).

In the western part of the old town is the **Heiliger Sand** (holy sands), the oldest Jewish cemetery in Europe; the earliest tombstones date from the 11th and 12th centuries. Also worth a visit is the 14th-century **Liebfrauenkirche** (Church of Our Dear Lady). The most noteworthy feature of the **Magnuskirche** (11th–12th centuries) is its crypt, from around AD 800, while the **Stiftskirche St Martin** (late 11th century) has some interesting portals.

The vast Romanesque Dom St Peter in Worms

Deutsche Weinstrasse

The "German Wine Route" starts in Bockenheim and ends in Schweigen, near the Alsatian town of Weißenburg. The tour suggested here includes the most interesting sections of this route. This is one of the most beautiful parts of Germany, where visitors will encounter aspects of German and European historical and cultural heritage at every step, set among the picturesque scenery of the endless vineyards covering the sun-drenched slopes of the Pfälzer Wald.

⑧ Bad Dürkheim
This famous resort is best known for its annual Wurstmarkt, held in September. Despite its name, it celebrates the wine harvest, and sausages take second place.

① St Martin
Not much remains of the Romanesque church of St Martin, but the 16–18th-century buildings surviving in the town continue to enchant visitors.

⑦ Hambacher Schloss
The castle's fame is based on the Hambacher Fest when, on 27 May 1832, students protested against the fragmentation of Germany. It was restored and is now a national monument and museum.

NATURPARK PFÄLZER WALD

⑤ Landau
This little town has the remains of the fortress built by Vauban, and an extraordinarily beautiful post-Augustinian church.

④ Trifels
This grim, ruined castle once served as a prison for many important people, including the King of England, Richard the Lionheart.

③ Leinsweiler
Hilltop Hof Neukastel was once the home of the German impressionist artist Max Slevogt, and to this day, wall paintings by the artist can be seen here.

② Bad Bergzabern
This town has some interesting Renaissance remains, including the Gasthaus zum Engel (Angel's Inn) and a royal castle.

Kingbeach

Tips for Drivers

Length: 83 km (51 miles).
Stopping-off points: Landau has many cafés and restaurants. The spa town of Bad Dürkheim, with its cafés and wine bars, is also a good place to stop.
Signs: Look for signposts showing a bunch of grapes or a wine jug.

① Dörrenbach
The star attractions in this small town are the half-timbered town hall and the Gothic church surrounded by fortifications.

0 km   5
0 miles   5

Key

■■■ Suggested route
■■■ Scenic route
═══ Other road
═══ River, lake
⚘ Viewpoint

❼ Mainz

The town, which grew out of the Roman military camp *Moguntiacum* established in 39 BC, is today the capital of the Rhineland-Palatinate. Mainz is the home of an important German television station (ZDF). It is also the main centre of trade for the popular Rhine wines. Its splendid late-Romanesque cathedral symbolizes the power of the Kurfürsten, the prince-electors, who used to crown German kings. Indisputably the town's most famous son is Johannes Gutenberg – the inventor of printing.

🏛 Kurfürstliches Schloss

Peter-Altmeier-Allee.
Römisch-Germanisches
Zentralmuseum.
Tel (06131) 91 240.
Open 10am–6pm
Tue–Sun.

Statue of Gutenberg
in Gutenbergplatz

Construction of the Baroque electoral palace, which began in 1627 during the rule of Archbishop Georg von Greifenclau, was completed more than a century later, in 1775–6, under Johann Friedrich Carl Joseph von Erthal. Today the palace houses the fascinating museum of Roman and Germanic history.

🏛 Gutenberg-Museum

Liebfrauenplatz 5. **Tel** (06131) 12 26 40. **Open** 9am–5pm Tue–Sat, 11am–5pm Sun. **Closed** public holidays. 🅿

Johannes Gensfleisch zum Gutenberg became famous as the inventor of the printing process using movable metal type. The letters were cast in a special apparatus and set in columns. Gutenberg himself prepared the Bible for printing and publication In 1454–5. From the original 200 copies, only 46 have survived to this day.

The museum, which opened in 1900, shows a reconstruction of the master's workshop from 1450. The collection comprises priceless early books, including the Gutenberg Bible and the Psalter published in 1457 by Fust & Schöffer, Gutenberg's erstwhile partners and latterday creditors. The Psalter was the first work to be printed using three different colours of inks.

🏛 Mainzer Dom

See pp354–5.

🏛 Gutenbergplatz

A short distance from the Protestant parish church of St John is Gutenbergplatz, a pleasant square with a statue of the inventor. Set in its paving stones is a line marking the 50th parallel. The Staatstheater (state theatre) in the square is a late Neo-Classical building (1829–33).

Historic half-timbered houses in Kirschgarten

🏛 Kirschgarten

Near the Baroque hospital of St Roch, built in 1721 and now an old people's home, runs a street called Kirschgarten (cherry orchard). This is one of the loveliest parts of old Mainz, which suffered serious damage in World War II. The well-preserved complex of historic half-timbered houses, dating from the 16th–18th centuries, makes this district worth visiting and a pleasant place for a stroll.

⛪ St Stephan-Kirche

Kleine Weißgasse 12. **Tel** (06131) 23 16 40. **Open** Mar–Oct: 10am–5pm Mon–Sat, noon–4:30pm Sun; Nov–Feb: 10am–4:30pm Mon–Sat, noon–5pm Sun.

This Gothic parish church was built in stages on the site of an edifice dating from the 10th century. Construction began in the mid-13th century and continued until the end of the 15th century. The resulting church is a triple-nave hall with eastern transept and a single-nave choir. The adjacent late 15th-century cloisters are a true gem of late-Gothic design. The original stained-glass windows in the presbytery, destroyed in World War II, were replaced by six new ones in 1978–81, designed and partly made by Marc Chagall. Set against a

The Baroque Kurfürstliches Schloss and museum

Landing stage for boats on the Rhine

beautiful blue background,
they depict biblical scenes,
including Abraham with the
three travellers, the Patriarch
pleading to God to spare the
righteous in Sodom and
Gomorrah, Jacob's dream, and
Moses with the Tablets of the
Ten Commandments.

The church interior contains
many other interesting original
features. The four large brass
candelabra were cast in Mainz
in 1509. The small polyptych
depicting the Crucifixion dates
from around 1400, while its
movable wings were made

some 100 years later. The niche
below the tower contains the
Holy Tomb (c.1450).

Römersteine
Southeast of the University
campus are the impressive
remains of the Roman aqueduct,
dating from the 1st century AD.
The Zahlbach valley was a
vantage point for the
southwestern flank of the Roman
camp, *Castrum Moguntiacum*,
but it presented a major
technical problem of supplying
the camp with drinking water.
The aqueduct was built by

Roman engineers. Although
some of its pillars were 23 m
(75 ft) high, the present remains
only reach up to 10 m (32 ft).

Environs
The pride of **Oppenheim**, a
centre of the wine trade 20 km
(12 miles) to the south, is its
Gothic Katharinenkirche, a
church built of red sandstone
in the 13th–14th centuries.
The neighbouring hill and the
ruins of Landskron castle
provide the most spectacular
view over the Rhine valley. The
Weinbaumuseum, museum of
viticulture, is also worth visiting.

Mainz City Centre

① Kurfürstliches Schloss
② Gutenberg Museum
③ Mainzer Dom
④ Gutenbergplatz
⑤ Kirschgarten
⑥ St Stephan-Kirche

0 metres 250
0 yards 250

For key to symbols *see back flap*

Mainzer Dom

The greatest attraction of Mainz is its superb St Martin cathedral, gleaming red in the sunshine. Together with those of Speyer and Worms it is one of the only three Romanesque imperial cathedrals to have survived almost intact to this day. Its basic framework was laid out in 1081–1137 and 1183–1239, but its oldest parts date from the early 11th century, with the Gothic side chapels added during the 13th and 14th centuries. Although neither the Gothic altars nor the magnificent choir screen have survived to this day, it is still possible to see the large group of bishops' monuments from the 13th to the 19th century.

Portal of the "Memorie" Burial Chapel
The late-Gothic portal, leading to the Romanesque burial chapel of the cathedral canons, was made by Madern Gerthener, after 1425.

Pulpit
This Neo-Gothic pulpit was made in 1834 by Joseph Scholl.

St Stephen's Choir
The Romanesque eastern choir, one of the first parts to be built, is simpler in style than other parts of the cathedral.

KEY

① **Round staircase towers** are from the previous building, built in the early 11th century.

② **Two large and two small towers** are symmetrically positioned on the ends of the cathedral.

★ **Monument of Heinrich Ferdinand von der Leyen**
This Baroque monument of the Dom rector, the work of Johann Mauritz Gröninger, was erected during his lifetime, in 1706.

VISITORS' CHECKLIST

Practical Information
Dom: Markt 10. **Tel** (06131) 25 34 12. **Open** Mar–Oct: 9am–6.30pm Mon–Fri, 9am–4pm Sat, 12.45–3pm, 4–6.30pm Sun; Nov–Feb: 9am–5pm Mon–Fri, 9am–4pm Sat, 12.45–3pm, 4–5pm Sun. Bischöfliches Dom- und Diözesanmuseum: Domstr. 3. **Tel** (06131) 25 33 44. **Open** 10am–5pm Tue–Fri, 11am–6pm Sat & Sun.

St Martin's Choir
The late-Romanesque western choir with its trefoil closing is an early 13th-century addition.

★ **Stalls**
These superb Rococo oak stalls encircle almost the entire presbytery. They were created by Franz Anton Hermann, who completed them in 1767.

Main entrance

Tomb of Jakob von Liebenstein
The late-Gothic tomb of the archbishop von Liebenstein, who died in 1508, is the work of an unknown artist. It depicts the deceased in draped robes, lying under an ornate canopy.

⑥ Rhine Valley (Rheintal)

The Celts called it *Renos*, the Romans *Rhenus*, while to Germanic tribes it was the Rhein, or *Vater Rhein* ("Father Rhine"), as it is known today. The source of this mighty, 1320-km (825-mile) long river is in Switzerland, from where it flows through or past Liechtenstein, Germany, France and the Netherlands, yet the Germans regard it as "their" river. The Rhine is steeped in many legends – it was into this river that Hagen von Tronje, faithful follower of King Gunther and slayer of Siegfried, threw the treasure of the Nibelungs, and Lohengrin's swan is said to appear near the town of Kleve *(see p393)* to this day.

Bonn
Bendorf
Rhein
Siegen
Koble
Trier
Saarbrücken

① **Stolzenfels** The existing castle complex has little in common with the original 13th-century fortress, which burned down in 1688. In the early 19th century, the ruins were bought by the future king Friedrich Wilhelm IV. The castle, designed by the famous Prussian architect Karl Friedrich Schinkel, was built in 1833–45.

0 kilometres   5

0 miles   5

Saarbrücken

② **Boppard** Boppard's most famous sights are the remains of the Roman military camp of Bodobrica, the church of St Severus (12th–13th centuries), famous for its wall paintings, and the medieval market square, built on the site of Roman hot baths. Michael Thonet, the creator of famous chairs made from bent wood, was born here in 1796.

Tips for Walkers

Length of the route: about 125 km (78 miles).
Stopping-off points: the best places to stop are Boppard or Bacharach, offering the widest choice of bars and restaurants.
Further attractions: a boat trip on the Rhine river, from Koblenz to Mainz.

③ **Burg Rheinfels** This castle ruin was begun in 1245 by Count Diether V of Katzenelnbogen, and was partially destroyed by French Revolutionary army troops in 1797. Some of the outer buildings are a luxury hotel, wellness centre and restaurant.

◀ The River Mosel near Trittenheim, Rheinland-Palatinate

⑧ **Marksburg** From 1117 this castle, which towers over the Rhine and the small town of Braubach, has been owned at different times by the von Braubachs and the powerful Epstein family. The Marksburg is the only castle along this stretch of the Rhine which has never been damaged.

⑦ **Loreley** The Loreley Rock, onto which many boats have been smashed by the strong currents, has been a source of inspiration for many poets. A 19th-century legend tells of a beautiful blonde siren combing her hair and luring unlucky sailors to their deaths with her song.

④ **Pfalzgrafenstein** In the middle of the Rhine River stands the proud and mighty fortress of Pfalzgrafenstein – one of the most beautifully situated castles in the Rhineland. Its origins date back to 1326, but its present shape is the result of Baroque refurbishments in the 17th–18th centuries.

⑤ **Bacharach** The town has a unique complex of historic buildings, with fortified town walls, the church of St Peter, the ruins of the Gothic chapel of St Werner, and Burg Stahleck – the castle towering over the town which today houses a youth hostel.

⑥ **Burg Sooneck** In the 13th century, Sooneck castle was the home of various robber knights. The fortress fell into ruin in the late 17th century, due to frequent raids by the French. In the 19th century it was bought by the Hohenzollerns, who rebuilt the castle in its original form.

Limburg

Rüdesheim

Bingen

Lorch

Kaub

Werwesel

Kaiserslautern

Mannheim

Ems

Ems

Key

Motorway
Suggested route
Scenic route
River
Viewpoint

⑨ Koblenz

The name which the Romans gave to their camp in 9 BC – *castellum apud confluentes,* meaning the "camp at the confluence" – reflects the town's strategic importance, for it is here that the Mosel flows into the Rhine. From the Middle Ages until the 19th century, Koblenz was the seat of the powerful archbishop-electors of Trier. It was also the birthplace of Prince von Metternich, the 19th-century Austrian statesman. Today it is a modern metropolis which attracts many visitors, and is the main centre of the region's cultural life.

Romanesque twin-tower façade of the Basilika St Kastor

⊞ Deutsches Eck

Ludwig-Museum im Deutschherren-haus: Danziger Freiheit 1. **Tel** (0261) 30 40 40. **Open** 9am–6pm daily.

The "German corner" is the place where the Mosel flows into the Rhine. Here stands the enormous equestrian statue of Emperor Wilhelm I. Designed by Bruno Schmitz, it was erected in 1897, destroyed in World War II and replaced with a copy in 1993. The name refers to the complex of buildings known as Deutsch-herrenhaus belonging to the Order of Teutonic Knights. Only part of the three-wing residence of the Order's Commander, built in the early 14th century, has survived to this day. The building now houses the Ludwig-Museum, with a collection of modern art.

⑪ Basilika St Kastor

Kastorstrasse 7. **Open** 9am–6pm daily.

The collegial church of St Kastor was built in 817–36 on the initi-ative of the archbishop of Trier, on a site previously occupied by an early Christian church. The treaty of Verdun, which divided the Carolingian Empire between the three sons of Ludwig I the Pious, was signed here in 843. The present appearance of the church is the result of extensions from the 11th–13th centuries. Inside are beautiful wall epitaphs of the Trier archbishops Kuno von Falkenstein (1388) and Werner von Königstein (1418).

⊞ Florinsmarkt

This square takes its name from the Romanesque-Gothic church of St Florin, which dates from the 12th and 14th centuries. The historic Kaufhaus, found on the square, dates from 1419–25. The image of a horse-rider shows the robber baron Johann von Kobem, beheaded for his crimes in 1536, who now sticks his tongue out every half hour. To its right stands the late-Gothic Schöffenhaus, and to its left is the Baroque Bürresheimer Hof, from 1659–60.

⊞ Mittelrhein-Museum

Zentralplatz 1. **Tel** (0261) 129 25 20. **Open** 10am–6pm Tue–Sun.
Ⓦ **mittelrhein-museum.de**

The modern Forum Confluentes building near the river houses the Mittelrhein-Museum, which covers 2,000 years of Central Rhine region. It houses an impressive collection of archaeology and medieval art. One remarkable exhibit is the original head of the Emperor Wilhelm I statue, at the river's confluence.

The Renaissance Alte Burg, now housing archives and a library

⑪ Alte Burg

Burgstrasse 1.

In the Middle Ages, the powerful von Arken family had a fortified residence built for themselves in the northwestern section of the Roman fortifications. In 1277 the building was taken over by Heinrich von Finstingen, the archbishop of Trier, who ordered its extension. The fortress was to protect him from the citizens of Koblenz who were striving for independence. Successive archbishops continued with the conversion of the building, which acquired its final shape in the 17th century. The eastern Renaissance façade of the complex is particularly attractive. Today it houses the municipal archives and parts of the library.

The spur between the Mosel and the Rhine, called Deutsches Eck

For hotels and restaurants in this area see p499 and pp524–5

⛪ Liebfrauenkirche

An der Liebfrauenkirche 1.
Tel (0261) 315 50.
Open Apr–Oct: 8:15am–
7pm daily; Nov–Mar:
8:15am–6pm Mon–Sat,
9am–5pm Sun.

At the highest point in
the old town stands the
Romanesque church of
Our Dear Lady. Its history
dates back to early
Christian times, but its
present form is the
result of remodelling
work carried out in
1182–1250. A triple

Statue of
the Madonna
in Liebfrauenkirche

nave basilica with galleries, it has
a twin-tower western façade.
The beautiful, elongated Gothic
choir was added in 1404–30.

🏰 Kurfürstliches Schloss

Neustadt. **Closed** to the public.

Not far from the bridge across
the Rhine stands the electoral
palace, an example of the
Rhineland's early Neo-Classical
architecture. It was built, and for a
short time occupied, by Clemens
Wenzeslaus von Sachsen, the last
of Trier's electors. Construction of
the castle began in 1777,
designed by Michael d'Ixnard,
and continued until 1786,
overseen by Antoine François
Peyère the Younger.

🏰 Festung Ehrenbreitstein

Fortress **Open** Apr–Oct:
10am–6pm daily; Nov–Mar:
10am–5pm daily.
Landesmuseum Koblenz
Tel (0261) 66750. **Open**
Apr–Oct: 10am–6pm daily;
Nov–Mar: 10am–5pm
daily.

On the opposite side of
the Rhine stands the
mighty fortress of
Ehrenbreitstein, one of
the largest in the world
and barely changed
since Prussian days.
A smaller fortress was erected on
this site in 1000, and extended in
subsequent years by the
archbishops and electors of Trier,
who lived in it from 1648 to
1786. Trier's holiest relic, the Rock
Christi (vestments of Christ) was
kept here. The fortress offers

splendid views over Koblenz, the
Rhine and the Mosel. Today, it is
home to the **Landesmuseum
Koblenz** (regional museum)
with an interesting collection on
the development of technology,
and to the **Rhein-Museum** with
hydrological collections.

VISITORS' CHECKLIST

Practical Information
Road map: B5. 109,300.
ℹ Bahnhofplatz 17 (0261-
19433). Internationale
Musiktage (Mar/Apr), Altstadtfest
mit dem Fest der Stadtteile (Jun/
Jul), Koblenzer Gauklerfest (Jun),
Rhein in Flammen (Aug),
Schängelmarkt (Sep), Koblenzer
Mendelssohn-Tage (autumn).
w koblenz-touristik.de

Transport

The Classical façade of the Kurfürstliches Schloss

Koblenz City Centre

① Deutsches Eck
② Basilika St Kastor
③ Florinsmarkt
④ Mittelrhein-Museum
⑤ Alte Burg
⑥ Liebfrauenkirche
⑦ Kurfürstliches Schloss
⑧ Festung Ehrenbreitstein

0 metres 250
0 yards 250

⑩ Maria Laach

A true masterpiece of German and European Romanesque architecture, the Maria Laach Abbey stands next to the Laacher See, a lake formed in the crater of an extinct volcano. Its construction started in 1093 at the behest of Heinrich II, who also lies buried here. Building continued from 1093 until 1220. Until secularization in 1802, the Abbey was the home of the Benedictines. Since 1892 the church has once again been resounding with Gregorian chants, which are sung here several times a day.

View from the West
The monumental western façade of the abbey consists of a semicircular apse, a massive, square 43-m (141-ft) tall central tower, and two slim 35-m (115-ft) tall flanking towers.

★ Tomb of Heinrich II
The tomb of the Count Palatine Heinrich II, who died in 1095, dates from about 1280. His effigy has been reproduced in a magnificent walnut wood block, which to this day has kept its original colours.

Löwenbrunnen
The lion fountain, which adorns the atrium, was made in 1928. It was modelled on the famous Alhambra fountain in Granada, Spain.

Detail from a Column Capital
The western entrance is surrounded by columns with interesting capitals. Carved figures can be seen, including that of a devil recording the sins of each entrant and others which are pulling each other's hair out.

Main entrance

Church entrance

Mosaics

The interior is decorated with paintings and mosaics created over centuries by artists of the Beuronese School. In the main eastern apse is a mosaic of Christ the Ruler dating from 1911.

Stained-glass Windows
Three vast stained-glass windows in the main eastern apse were made by a contemporary artist, W. Rupprecht, in 1956.

★ **High Altar**
Among the most precious works preserved in the church is the late-Romanesque canopy of 1220–50, rising above the high altar.

★ **Crypt**
The vaults of the exquisite early-Romanesque crypt are supported by austere square capitals. This is also the resting-place of Gilbert, the first abbot at Maria Laach.

KEY

① **The "Paradise"**, the courtyard, is meant to symbolize the Garden of Eden.

② **The church towers** have arcaded galleries, typical of Romanesque style.

HESSE

Hesse lies in the very heart of present-day Germany. Scattered over the region are reminders of its former glory: Roman camps, Carolingian buildings, Romanesque churches and Gothic cathedrals with lofty spires. Territorial partitions, so typical of the former German Reich, brought about the blossoming of art and architecture during the Renaissance and the Baroque eras.

A post-World War II creation, the borders of this federal state roughly approximate those of its 13th-century forerunner. For most of its history, Hesse was divided between Hesse-Darmstadt and Hesse-Kassel.

Today, when admiring the distinctive panorama of Frankfurt am Main – its towering banks and skyscrapers more reminiscent of New York's Manhattan than of a European metropolis – it is hard to believe that this was the birthplace of Goethe. The importance of this city extends far beyond Hesse: it is the financial centre of the European Union, and its annual Book Fair is the largest event of its kind in the world.

Darmstadt became famous as a centre for Jugendstil (Art Nouveau) early in the 20th century. Wiesbaden is the seat of Hesse's state government, and Marburg is one of the best-known university towns. In the 16th century, at the times of fierce religious feuds, the first Protestant university was built here. The Church of St Elizabeth is one of the earliest examples of Gothic architecture in the region. Lovers of modern art will know of Kassel – every five years it hosts the *documenta*, an exciting exhibition of artistic developments.

Hesse has much more to offer. The Waldecker Land, near Kassel, boasts the Eder lake and attractive health resorts. Eberbach in the picturesque Rheingau, the wine-growing area around Eltville, has a well-preserved former Cistercian abbey, which has been used as a film setting.

Park and Baroque Orangery of the palace complex in Fulda

◀ The dramatic juxtaposition of old and new buildings in Frankfurt am Main

Exploring Hesse

Eltville, situated in the Rheingau, one of Germany's most important wine-producing regions, is famous for its Riesling wine. Frankfurt am Main, known around the world as a great financial and commercial centre, also has fantastic museums, drawing visitors with their outstanding art collections, while the International Book Fair is a true paradise for readers and bookworms. In the 19th century, wealthy socialites chose Bad Homburg as their favourite spa, while the romantic town of Marburg still has the lively atmosphere of a university town.

The Dom in Limburg, overlooking the Lahn river

The giant Niederwalddenkmal near Rüdesheim

Sights at a Glance

For additional map symbols *see back flap*

Warburg

Arolsen

Göttingen

KASSEL

Kaufungen

Meißner
754m

FRITZLAR

Melsungen

Bad
Wildungen

Borken

Rotenburg

Bebra

Eisenach

Bad Hersfeld

Itallendorf

ALSFELD

Altenburg

Hünfeld

Lauterbach

Taufstein
772m

FULDA

Wasserkuppe
950m

Neuhof

Schlüchtern

Schweinfurt

zburg

The Messeturm in the Frankfurt fairgrounds,
designed by Helmut Jahn

Getting Around

The A7 motorway, cutting across Hesse in
a north–south direction, provides a fast
transport link. Starting from Hanover, it
runs through Göttingen, Kassel and Fulda
to Würzburg in Bavaria. The A4 runs from
Dresden, via Weimar, to Bad Hersfeld. From
there visitors can take the A7 or the A5,
towards Gießen, Bad Homburg, Frankfurt
am Main and onwards to Darmstadt and
Heidelberg. The fast ICE railway connects
Kassel and Frankfurt am Main with Basel
(in Switzerland), Stuttgart, Berlin and
Munich. Frankfurt am Main has one of
Europe's largest airports, and there are also
international flights from Kassel.

0 kilometres 20

0 miles 20

Key

━━ Motorway

= = Motorway under construction

━ Major road

⋯⋯ Minor road

⋯ Main railway

━ Minor railway

▬ Regional border

△ Summit

Statue of the Brothers Grimm in Hanau

❶ Kassel

The cultural, scientific and commercial centre of northern Hesse, Kassel suffered severe damage during World War II due to the armaments industries based here, and much of the town has been rebuilt in functional 1950s style. Today, Kassel has become synonymous with one of the most important shows of contemporary art – *documenta* – held here every five years (the 13th documenta is scheduled for 2017). The town is equally famous for its outstanding collection of European art, housed in the splendid Schloss Wilhelmshöhe, as well as for its parks and gardens, especially the large forest-park adjoining the castle.

17th-century cameo-decorated tureen in the Landesmuseum

�� Hessisches Landesmuseum

Brüder-Grimm-Platz 5. **Tel** (0561) 316 800. **Closed** until late 2015/early 2016. **W** museum-kassel.de

Outstanding items in the Neo-Baroque Hesse Regional Museum, built in 1910–13, are the astronomical instruments, originally installed in 1560 in a landgrave's castle, which no longer exists. The ethnographic section has displays of Hessian folk costumes and regional craft items.

The Landesmuseum also houses the Tapetenmuseum (wallpaper museum). Established in 1923, the museum presents the history of wallpaper and the

Wallpaper (1670–80), in the Tapetenmuseum

methods of its production around the world. The collection includes examples of leather wall coverings (cordovans) and wallpapers representing Secession and Art-Deco styles. *Vues de Suisse* (views of Switzerland), dating from 1802, is one of the earliest examples of scenic wallpaper. It was printed using 95 different inks and 1,024 wooden blocks. Equally famous is the panoramic *Rénaud et Armide*, from the workshop of Joseph Dufours, printed in 1828 using 2,386 wooden blocks.

⊞ Neue Galerie

Schöne Aussicht 1. **Tel** (0561) 316 80 400. **Open** 10am–5pm Tue–Sun (to 8pm Thu). **W** museum-kassel.de

The New Gallery, founded in 1976 and devoted to 19th- and 20th-century art, occupies a Neo-Classicist building from 1871–74. The gallery's collection includes a number of canvases by artists such as Carl Schuch, Max Slevogt and Lovis Corinth. The splendid collection of 20th-century paintings focuses on German Expressionism. An entire room is also devoted to the installations of the controversial sculptor and performance artist Joseph Beuys.

⊞ Brüder-Grimm-Museum

Weinbergstrasse 21. **Tel** (0561) 787 41 24 . **Open** 10am–6pm Tue–Sun. **Closed** 1 Jan. 🛇 🖾 🖾 **W** grimmwelt.de

Although brothers Jacob and Wilhelm Grimm were born in Hanau, they lived in Kassel from 1798 until 1830, and this museum presents the lives and works of the famous fairy-tale tellers and philologers using five themes, and many original first editions. Art installations, films and hands-on activities will interest visitors of all ages. The rooftop terrace has excellent views over Kassel.

An illustration for Cinderella, one of the Grimm fairy-tales

⊞ Kunsthalle Fridericianum

Friedrichsplatz 18. **Tel** (0561) 707 27 20. **Open** 11am–6pm Tue–Sun. 🛇 **W** fridericianum.org

Königsplatz and Friedrichsplatz were designed by the court architect, Simon Louis du Ry. The northwestern side of the latter is occupied by the Neo-Classical Fridericianum, built by du Ry in 1769–76. Its founder, Landgrave Friedrich II, had always intended it to be a museum, and it became the second public museum (after the British Museum in London) to be built in Europe, and the first one on the European mainland. Since 1955, the Fridricianum has been the main venue for Kassel's multi-media contemporary art show – the *documenta*, which every five years takes over the entire city. An additional exhibition hall, the Documentahalle, was opened in 1992, in the nearby Staatstheater.

⊞ Ottoneum

Steinweg 2. Naturkundemuseum **Tel** (0561) 787 40 66. **Open** 10am–5pm Tue–Sun (to 8pm Wed, 6pm Sun). 🛇

The Ottoneum, home of the first permanent theatre in Germany

The Ottoneum (1604–5), built for Landgrave Maurice the Learned, was Germany's first permanent theatre. Designed by Wilhelm Vernukken and remodelled in the late 17th century by Paul du Ry, it was converted into a natural history museum in 1885.

🔲 Orangerie

An der Karlsaue 20c. **Tel** (0561) 316 80 500. Astronomisch-Physikalisches Kabinett and Planetarium: **Open** 10am–5pm Tue–Sun (until 8pm Thu). **Closed** 24, 25, 31 Dec. Zeiss-Planetarium: 📷 2pm Tue, Sat, 3pm Wed, Fri, Sun, 2 & 7pm Thu. 🔁 (free Fri.) **W museum-kassel.de**

The southern part of Kassel is home to Karlsaue, a vast palace and garden complex named after its founder, Landgrave Karl.

The site was earlier occupied by a small Renaissance Schloss (1568), surrounded by a garden. In 1702–10 Pierre-Etienne Monnot built the large Orangery, which now houses a fascinating museum of astronomy and technology. Monnot is also the creator of Marmorbad, a bath pavilion from 1722, while the kitchen pavilion was designed by Simon Louis du Ry in 1765.

🔲 Wilhelmshöhe

Gemäldegalerie Alter Meister. Schloss Wilhelmshöhe. **Tel** (0561) 31 68 00. **Open** 10am–5pm Tue–Sun (until 8pm Thu). **Closed** 1 May, 24, 25, 31 Dec. 🔁 (admission to park is free).

At the top of Wilhelmshöher Allee, designed in 1781, stands Wilhelmshöhe, a magnificent palace and large, attractive park. The palace is situated along the axis of the avenue that runs up the hill, through a long forest glade. An incredible series of cascades runs down the hillside above the palace. At the top of the hill is the Octogon, crowned with the statue of Hercules, the symbol of the town. The palace was designed by Simon Louis du Ry and Heinrich Christoph Jussow and built in 1793–1801 for the Elector

Wilhelm. Now it houses the Gemäldegalerie Alte Meister with its outstanding collection of European masters including paintings by Rubens, Titian, Rembrandt, Dürer and Poussin.

Cascades, with Octogon and Hercules statue, in Wilhelmshöhe

Kassel City Centre

① Hessisches Landesmuseum and Deutsches Tapetenmuseum
② Neue Galerie
③ Brüder-Grimm-Museum
④ Fridericianum
⑤ Ottoneum
⑥ Orangerie

0 metres 300
0 yards 300

For keys to symbols *see back flap*

❷ Fritzlar

Road map C4. 🏚 15,500. 🚉 🚌
🛈 Rathaus, Zwischen den Krämen 5
(05622-98 86 43). 🎪 Pferdemarkt
(Jul), Stadtfest (Aug).

The beautiful town of Fritzlar has preserved its original, nearly complete ring of medieval walls with watch-towers, bastions and over 450 half-timbered houses from various periods. In the early 8th century, St Boniface, the apostle of Germany, had the holy oak of the Germanic god Donar, which grew here, cut down to build a Christian chapel. In 724 he founded the Benedictine **Dom** (abbey of St Peter). In 1118 the original church was replaced by a cruciform, vaulted basilica with a triple-nave crypt, and this was remodelled in the 13th and 14th centuries. Adjacent to the church is a lovely 14th-century ambulatory. The church interior is rich in historic treasures. The east wall of the transept is decorated with wall paintings from c.1320, and the south nave includes a Pietà (1300). The 14th-century **parish church** of the Franciscan Order nearby has a lovely painting of the Madonna, on the northern wall of the choir.

In Fritzlar's picturesque old town stands the **Rathaus** (town hall), whose lower floors date from the 12th century, while the upper ones were added in the 15th century. The exquisite **Hochzeitshaus** (wedding house), in the street of the same name, is a Renaissance half-timbered house, built in 1580–90, which now houses a museum. Another interesting sight is the **Alte Brücke**, a 13th-century stone bridge spanning the Eder River.

Relief of St Martin, on the walls of the Rathaus in Fritzlar

❸ Waldecker Land

The Waldecker Land, situated west of Kassel, was once an independent county and later, until 1929, a free state within the German Reich. Today this region, with its Eder-Stausee (reservoir), is one of the most attractive tourist regions in Germany. The wooded hills provide a perfect setting for long rambles, the roads and tracks are ideally suited for cycling tours and the rivers and lakes permit visitors to practise a wide variety of watersports.

② **Korbach**
Korbach is a beautiful old town with many half-timbered houses. Worth seeing are the Gothic church of St Kilian with its interesting 14th-century pulpit, and the church of St Nicholas, with the Baroque tomb of Georg Friedrich von Waldeck (1692).

Paderb

⑤ **Frankenberg**
This small town is brimming with half-timbered houses. The town hall (1509), also half-timbered, has humorous polychrome wood-carvings. The Gothic Marienkirche with its 15th-century wall paintings is also worth visiting.

Key

▬ Motorway
▬ Suggested route
▬ Scenic road
═ Other road
═ River, lake
🔆 Viewpoint

| 0 kilometres | 10 |
| 0 miles | 10 |

① **Bad Arolsen**
Both the sculptor Christian Daniel Rauch and the painter Wilhelm von Kaulbach were born in this spa town, and they are commemorated in two museums. The star attraction, however, is the Baroque castle (1713–28) of the von Waldeck family, designed by Julius Ludwig Rothweil.

③ **Waldeck**
The old fortress of Waldeck is now a hotel. It offers superb views over the Eder-Stausee reservoir and the small town of Waldeck with its 18th-century half-timbered houses. The Gothic town church has a high altar (c.1500), devoted to the Virgin Mary.

④ **Bad Wildungen**
This popular spa town has many charming half-timbered houses. The church has a priceless altar painted with scenes of the Passion by Konrad von Soest (1403).

Tips for Visitors

Length of route: 110 km (68 miles).
Stopping-off points: There are many good cafés and restaurants in every town along the route.
Further attractions: Cruises and ferries run on the Edersee. A viewing platform on top of the Peterskopf hill, near Hemfurth, can be reached by electric train.

Höxter

Warburg

Twiste

Diemelstadt

Warmebach

Twiste

Wolfhagen

Eder-Stausee

Eder

Fritzlar

Bad Hersfeld

Wohra

burg

Projecting gate of the Baroque Stadtschloss in Fulda

❹ Fulda

Road map C5. 🚊 65,000. 🚉
ℹ️ Bonifatiusplatz 1 (0661-102 18 14).

Fulda's history began in March 744, when Sturmius, a pupil of St Boniface, laid the foundation stone for the Benedictine abbey. Ten years later the body of St Boniface, who had been killed by Frisian pagans, was laid to rest here. The town, which grew around the abbey, experienced its heyday during the Baroque period, and a new Baroque building, designed by Johann Dientzenhofer, was built in 1704–12 on the foundations of the old abbey. The **Dom St Salvator und Bonifatius** is a triple-nave basilica with a dome above the nave intersection, a monumental eastern façade and a shrine with the saint's relics under the high altar, in the western section.

Opposite the cathedral stands the **Stadtschloss** (former episcopal palace), a shoe-shaped edifice, built by Johann Dientzenhofer and Andreas Gallasini, with richly decorated Baroque and Rococo interiors. Particularly noteworthy are the Kaisersaal (imperial hall) on the ground floor, the magnificent Fürstensaal (hall of princes) and the charming Rococo-style Spiegelsaal (chamber of mirrors) on the first floor. Today, some of the palace chambers hold an impressive collection of porcelain. The palace complex includes a large landscaped garden. To the north of the Dom stands the round **Michaels-kirche**, a Carolingian chapel dating from 822, one of the

oldest church buildings in Germany. Inside the church has a ring of eight columns and a crypt supported by a single column. The circular gallery, the long side nave and the western tower are 11th-century additions.

Other interesting sights in Fulda are the Baroque **Heilig-Geist-Kirche** (church of the Holy Spirit; closed to the public), built in 1729–33 by Andreas Gallasini, and the late 18th-century parish church of St Blasius. In the 8th century, five abbeys were established on the four hills surrounding the town. On Petersberg stands the former Benedictine **Propsteikirche St Peter (Liobakirche)**, from the 9th–15th centuries, with a Carolingian crypt. Inside the church is one of Germany's oldest wall paintings, dating from 836–47.

The Brothers Grimm

The two brothers are known around the world as collectors of German folk-tales, which were first published in 1812 and subsequently translated into most languages. Fairy-tales such as *Hänsel and Gretel, Cinderella* and *Little Red Riding Hood* have been favourites for generations of children. Above all, however, the brothers were scholars. In his *German Grammar*, published in 1819, Jacob Grimm proved that all German dialects sprang from a common origin, and thus laid the foundations of German philology. The Grimm Brothers also initiated the publication of the *Dictionary of the German Language*.

❺ Alsfeld

Road map C4. 🚊 18,000. 🚉
ℹ️ Markt 3 (06631-18 21 65).
🎭 Pfingstfest (Whitsun), Historischer Markt (Jun), Fairy-Tale Day (Jun), Stadt- und Heimatfest (Aug), Historischer Markt (Sep). 🌐 alsfeld.de

The first historic records of Alsfeld date from the late 9th century. Today the town attracts visitors with its pretty old town with numerous 16th–17th century half-timbered houses. On the eastern side of the town square stands a grand late-Gothic **Rathaus** (town hall), built in 1512–16, and one of the finest examples of half-timbered structures anywhere in Germany. Other interesting features in the market square are the stone **Weinhaus**, with its distinctive stepped gable (1538), and the Renaissance **Hochzeitshaus** (wedding

Half-timbered houses in Alsfeld

house), dating from 1565. Opposite the town hall stands the **Stumpfhaus** (1609), its façade beautifully decorated with wood carvings and paintings. From the town hall runs the picturesque Fulder Gasse, with the Gothic parish church **Walpurgiskirche** (13th–15th centuries), which has 15th-century wall paintings. In Rossmarkt stands the former Augustian **Dreifaltigkeits-kirche** (church of the Holy Trinity), from the 13th–15th centuries. It was from here that in 1522 the monk Tilemann Schnabel began to spread the Reformation in Alsfeld.

The **Märchenhaus** (Fairy-Tale House) on Markt has several rooms devoted to the tales of the Brothers Grimm and a collection of puppets. The 18th-century **castle** in Altenburg, 2 km (1 mile) from Alsfeld, enjoys a hilltop position.

Detail on the Rathaus, in Marburg

❻ Marburg

Road map C4. 👥 80,000. 🚆
ℹ️ Pilgrimstein 26 (06421-991 20).
🎭 Maieinsingen (30 Apr), 3-Tage Marburg (Jul), Elisabethmarkt (Oct), Weihnachtsmarkt (Dec).
🌐 **marburg.de**

When in 1248 the county of Hesse broke away from Thuringia, Marburg became one of the most important seats of the landgraves. The first landgrave, Heinrich II, lived in the castle that towers over the town. The town's history is inseparably linked with the 13th-century figure of Elisabeth of Thuringia, wife of Ludwig IV, who devoted her life to the poor and the sick here. In 1527, Philipp the Magnanimous founded the first Protestant university in the Reich at Marburg. He also instigated the first Marburg Colloquy in 1529, to unify the Protestant faith. The "articles" presented by Martin Luther to Melanchthon and Zwingli later formed the basis for the Augsburg Creed. Today, Marburg is a picturesque university town. A tour of the

town should start from the **Elisabethkirche**, at the bottom of the hill. Built in 1235–83, it is (after Trier) Germany's second purely Gothic church. There is a large set of Gothic altars from the early 16th century, including the altars of St Elisabeth (1513) and of the Holy Family (1511). Next to the north choir entrance stands the statue of St Elisabeth with a model of the church (1480). The choir contains the tomb of the Saint, positioned under the baldachin (c 1280). The vestry houses the greatest treasure, the reliquary of St Elisabeth (1235–49). In the south choir is an interesting group of monuments to the Hessian landgraves, from the 13th–16th centuries.

The **Kunstmuseum Marburg** holds a collection of paintings produced after 1500, with a predominance of 19th- and 20th-century German artists. Around the market square stands a group of historic, half-timbered houses from the 14th–17th centuries. Particularly pretty are the Sonne (sun, No. 14), the Stiefel (boot, No. 17) and the house at No. 19. The Steinernes Haus (stone house, No. 18), built in 1318, is the oldest in Marburg, along with that at No. 13 Hirschgasse. At No. 16 Markt is the Renaissance Künstlerhaus (artists' house). High above the town towers

The Gothic portal of the Elisabethkirche in Marburg

the **Landgrafenschloss**, the landgraves' castle dating from the 10th–16th centuries. The two-storey Fürstenbau (dukes' building) has a large ducal chamber, dating from 1330. The Wilhelmsbau was built in 1492–8. It houses a museum of sacral art with mementos of the debate between Luther, Zwingli and Melanchthon.

🏛️ **Elisabethkirche**
Elisabethstrasse. **Tel** (06421) 655 73.
Open Apr–Oct: 9am–5pm Mon–Sat, 11am–5pm Sun; Nov–Mar: 10am–4pm Mon–Sat, 11am–4pm Sun.

🏛️ **Kunstmuseum Marburg**
Biegenstrasse 11. **Tel** (06421) 282 23 55. **Open** 11am–1pm & 2–5pm Tue–Sun. 🅰️

🏛️ **Landgrafenschloss und Museum für Kulturgeschichte**
Schloss 1. **Tel** (06421) 282 58 71.
Open 10am–6pm Tue–Sun (Nov–Mar: to 4pm). 🅰️

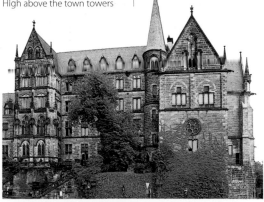

The Alte Universität (old university) in Marburg

⑦ Gießen

Road map C4. 🏛 72,000. 🚉
ℹ️ Berliner Platz 2 (0641-306 18 90).

Giessen was granted town status in 1248, and in 1607 it acquired its university. In Brandplatz stands the partially reconstructed **Altes Schloss** (old palace), dating from the 14th–15th centuries. Now the home of the Oberhessisches Museum, it holds a large collection of art dating from the Gothic period to today.

The **Botanischer Garten** is one of Germany's oldest botanical gardens, established in 1609 for the purposes of scientific research. To the north of it stands the **Neues Schloss** (new palace), built in 1533–9 for Landgrave Philipp the Magnanimous. It miraculously escaped damage when the town was bombed in 1944. The Wallenfelssches Haus nearby houses interesting ethnological collections. The only remaining part of the Gothic **Pfarrkirche St Pankratius**, which was almost completely destroyed in 1944, is its tower, dating from 1500.

At No. 2 Georg-Schlosser-Strasse is the **Burgmannen-haus**, an attractive half-timbered mansion dating from the 14th century.

Portal of the Altes Schloss in Gießen

Along with the old stable block in Dammstrasse, it is the only half-timbered building that has survived to this day.

⑧ Wetzlar

Road map C5. 🏛 52,000. 🚉
ℹ️ Domplatz 8 (06441-997 755).
🌐 wetzlar.de

Occupying a picturesque spot on the banks of the Lahn river, Wetzlar is overlooked by the ruins of the 12th-century **Kalsmunt** fortress. It was built for the Emperor Friedrich I Barbarossa (1122–90). Only parts of the tower remain intact. The **Dom** (Collegiate Church of St Mary) was begun in 897 but by the late 15th century had only been partly completed. The splendid western double portal has remained unusable for the last 500 years – although the iconography of the tympanum was finished, the stairs leading to the entrance were never built. If they had been built, they would have led not to the church's nave, but to a courtyard. Wetzlar's Dom is a rare, perhaps even unique surviving example of the typical appearance of most European churches in the mid-15th century. Inside are several interesting historic artifacts, including the statue of the *Madonna on the Moon Crescent* (mid-15th century) and a late-Renaissance *Crucifixion*.

In 1772, the young Johann Wolfgang Goethe spent three months in Wetzlar working as an apprentice at the court of appeal. During this time he fell in love with Charlotte Buff, called Lotte, who was engaged to one of Goethe's friends. The **Lottehaus**, her former home, has a collection of items relating to Goethe and Lotte. It was the suicide of a friend, Karl Wilhelm Jerusalem, who lived in the 18th-century **Jerusalemhaus** at No. 5 Schillerplatz, that

inspired Goethe to write his tragic novel, *The Sorrows of Young Werther* (1774). Jerusalem had suffered unrequited love, just like Goethe. The novel, which was published two years later, made Goethe famous around Europe, but it also unwittingly led many young men to commit suicide.

The Gothic south tower of the Dom in Wetzlar

⑨ Weilburg

Road map B5. 🏛 13,500. 🚉
ℹ️ Mauerstraße 6 (06471-314 67).

Weilburg enjoys a particularly scenic location in a bend of the Lahn River. The town is dominated by the Renaissance–Baroque **Schloss** of the Nassau-Weilburg family. The monumental castle complex was created in stages. Its main section dates from the Renaissance era; the east wing was built in 1533–9; the south and west wings in 1540–48 and the west tower in 1567. The northern part of the palace was completed in 1570–73. In the late-17th century, various Baroque additions were made, mainly to the interior of the castle. The 16th-century furnishings show the rich ornamentation typical of the German Renaissance. The **Obere Orangerie** (upper orangery), built in 1703–5 and today used for temporary exhibitions, and the **Hofkirche** (castle church), dating from 1707–13, are the work of Ludwig Rothweil. Terraces lead from the castle to the Lahn river, which is crossed by an 18th-century stone bridge. In Frankfurtstrasse stands the **Heiliggrabkapelle** (Chapel of the Holy Sepulchre), dating from 1505.

⑩ Limburg

Road map B5. 🗻 31,000. 🚃
ℹ️ Bahnhofsplatz 2 (06431-61 66).

Limburg's history dates back to the 8th century. In 1821, the town became the see of a newly created diocese.

The **Dom** (collegiate cathedral church of St George) towers high above the Lahn river. This monumental building, whose style combines late-Romanesque and early French-Gothic, was erected in 1190–1250. Its well-proportioned interior contains a rich variety of historic artifacts, including some 13th-century wall paintings in the presbytery and the transept, a font dating from the same period and the tombstone of Konrad Kurzbold, who founded the first church on this site.

To the south of the Dom stands the **Burg** (castle), an irregular structure built in the 13th–16th centuries. It houses the interesting **Diözesan-museum** (Diocese museum).

Limburg has many original examples of beautiful half-timbered buildings. The houses at No. 1 Römerstrasse, No. 6 Kolpingstrasse, No. 4 Kleine Rütsche and No. 11 Kornmarkt date from the last decade of

Romanesque–Gothic wall painting in the Dom in Limburg

the 13th century. Near the 14th-century **Alte Lahnbrücke** (old Lahn bridge), with its defensive towers, stands a mansion belonging to the Cistercians of Eberbach. The post-Franciscan Sebastiankirche (church of St Sebastian) dates from the 14th and 18th centuries.

⑪ Bad Homburg

Road map C5. 🗻 52,000. 🚃
ℹ️ Kurhaus, Louisenstrasse 58 (06172-178 37 10). 🎵 Fugato Organ Festival (Sep every two years – next in 2016, 2018), Laternenfest (Sep yearly).

Bad Homburg grew up around a fortress whose earliest records date back to 1180. Friedrich II von Hessen-Homburg initiated the conversion of the medieval castle into the **Schloss**, a

Baroque palace built in 1678–86. It features a magnificent Festsaal (ballroom) and Spiegelkabinett (hall of mirrors). The only part of the former complex remaining today is the 14th-century Weißer Turm (white tower). Following the annexation of Hesse-Homburg by Prussia in 1866, the palace became the favourite summer residence of the royal then (from 1871) imperial family.

Along with Baden-Baden and Wiesbaden, Homburg was one of Germany's most fashionable spas, and today the town reflects its former splendour. The **Kurpark**, a landscaped park established in 1854–67, was designed by Peter Joseph Lenné.

The **Spielbank** (1838), in Brunnenallee claims to be the oldest casino in the world. Built in 1887–90, the **Kaiser-Wilhelm-Bad** is still used as the main bath complex for therapeutic treatments. An Orthodox chapel, designed by Leonti Nikolayevich Benois for the Russian Orthodox nobility, was finished in 1899.

Environs
Saalburg, 7 km (4 miles) to the northwest, has a Roman fortress, which was completely reconstructed in 1898–1901. The fortress formed part of the *limes*, the fortified border that separated the Roman Empire from its Germanic neighbours in the 1st to 3rd century AD.

The grand edifice of the Kaiser-Wilhelm-Bad in the Kurpark, Bad Homburg

⑫ Eltville

Road map B5. 🚊 17,000. 🚌
ℹ️ Burgstrasse 1 (06123-90 98 0).
🎭 Biedermeier- und Sektfest (Jul).

In the 2nd century, the area that is now the old town was a Roman *latifundium*, a large agricultural estate. In 1332, Eltville was granted town status. Part of the Mainz diocese, it is today known for its excellent sparkling wine.

In 1337–45 the **Burg** (castle) was extended at the request of Archbishop Heinrich von Virneburg. The east wing of the castle was added in 1682–3 by Giovanni Angelo Barell. The only part of it remaining today is the five-storey residential tower; the rest of the building is a picturesque ruin. In the tower are original 14th-century wall paintings and friezes.

The twin-naved **Pfarrkirche St Peter und St Paul** (parish church) was built in 1350–1430. The vestibule has well-preserved wall paintings (1405) showing scenes from the Last Judgement. The town boasts several attractive mansions, including Hof Langenwerth von Simmern (1773), Stockheimer Hof (1550) and Gräflich-Eltzscher Hof (16th–17th century).

Crest of the Hessische Staatsweingüter-Vinothek, in Eltville

⑬ Wiesbaden

Road map C5. 🚊 280,000. 🚌
ℹ️ Marktplatz 1 (0611-17 29 930).
🎭 Internationale Maifestspiele (May), Theatrium (Jun), Rheingau Wine Festival (Aug), Christmas Market (Nov–Dec). 🌐 **wiesbaden.de**

Wiesbaden is the modern capital of Hesse. Highly valued as a spa by the Romans, who exploited the healing properties of its waters, the town grew from a small settlement known as *aquae mattiacorum* after the Germanic tribe of the Mattiacs. In 1774 the Nassau-Usingen family chose Wiesbaden as their residence. This, as well as the

The Baroque Biebrich Palace, south of Wiesbaden

subsequent rapid growth of the town as a spa resort in the 19th century, laid the foundations for its lasting prosperity. Today, the town is still dominated by large-scale developments carried out in the spirit and style of Classicism and Historicism.

The **Stadtschloss** (municipal castle), today the seat of the state parliament, was built in 1835–41. In Schlossplatz the Neo-Renaissance **Marktkirche**, built in 1853–62, soars above the town's other buildings. In front of the church stands a statue of Wilhelm I the Great von Nassau-Oranien. The oldest building in the town is the **Altes Rathaus** (old town hall), dating from 1610. In Wilhelmstrasse is the imposing Neo-Renaissance and Neo-Baroque **Hessisches Staatstheater** (state theatre). It was built in 1892–4 for Kaiser

Wilhelm II to the designs of the theatre architects Fellner and Helmer. Adjacent to the Marktkirche is the attractive Kurhauskolonnade (spa house colonnade). It was erected in 1825 and is the longest colonnade in Europe. The early 20th-century **Kurhaus** (spa house) itself, with its grand façade and portico, is the work of Friedrich Thiersch. Inside is the original **Spielbank** (casino), where Fyodor Dostoyevsky and Richard Wagner tried their luck at the tables.

To the south of the town centre stands **Schloss Biebrich**, where the counts von Nassau-Usingen resided until the early 19th century. The Schloss was built in stages during the 18th century. The north pavilion was built first, in 1700, followed nine years later by the south pavilion. The wings, which join the two pavilions, and the central rotunda were added during the first two decades of the 18th century. Finally, the two external wings were added in 1734–44, creating an overall horseshoe layout. The interior is richly furnished, predominantly in Baroque-Rococo style.

On the northern outskirts of the town is a large hill, the Neroberg, whose summit can be reached by funicular railway. At the top is the so-called **Griechische Kapelle** (Greek chapel). Built in 1847–55 by Philipp Hoffmann, it served as a mausoleum for Princess Elisabeth von Nassau, the niece of Alexander I Tsar of Russia, who died young.

The attractive façade of Hessisches Staatstheater in Wiesbaden

The ornate Gothic portal of Basilika St Valentin, in Kiedrich

⑭ Kiedrich

Road map B5. 🏔 3,400. 🚉
ℹ️ Markstr. 27 (06123-90 50 10).

The earliest recorded mention of Kiedrich was in the mid-10th century, in a document produced by the Archbishop Friedrich of Mainz. One of the town's main attractions is the **Basilika St Valentin**, a gem of Gothic architecture. The church was built in stages, beginning with the main hall (1380–90). The west tower was added in the early 15th century and the light, lofty choir in 1451–81. Some time later the central nave was raised to the level of the choir, creating a row of galleries above the aisles, and at the same time the magnificent star vaults were created. The whole project was financed from donations made by countless pilgrims who came to pray to the relics of St Valentine, kept here since 1454. A statue of the saint adorns the western portal. The early 15th-century tympanum depicts the *Annunciation* (on the left) and the *Coronation of the Virgin Mary* (on the right); above is an image of *God the Father giving His Blessing*, with two archangels

playing musical instruments. Inside, the church harbours an incredible wealth of ancient art treasures. The high altar and St Catherine's altar in the south aisle date from the late-Renaissance period. The magnificent Gothic stalls were created in 1510, while the church organ is one of the oldest in Germany, with pipes made in 1310. Next to the parish church stands a late-Gothic, two-storey funeral chapel built in 1445.

Kiedrich has several interesting old mansion houses, such as the Schwalbacher Hof (1732). The **Rathaus** (town hall) is evocative of the late-Gothic style, although it was built much later (1585–6).

Environs

Five km (3 miles) west of Kiedrich, in Oestrich, is **Kloster Eberbach**, a former Cistercian abbey. This vast complex, built between the 12th and 14th centuries, was once home to nearly 300 monks and is one of the best-preserved medieval monasteries in Germany. The church interior provided the setting for some of the scenes in the film *The Name of the Rose*, based on the novel by Umberto Eco. The Cistercians used to have their own vineyards here, and today the abbey buildings are used by the Hessian Wine Co-operative to press, ferment,

store and sell Eberbacher Steinberg, a famous white Rheingau wine.

A short way to the west, in **Winkel**, stands the Baroque castle of Reichardshausen, which in the 19th century was the home of Princess Luise von Nassau.

🏛️ Kloster Eberbach

Tel (06723) 91 78 100. **Open** Apr–Oct: 10am–6pm daily; Nov–Mar: 11am–5pm daily. **Closed** Carnival Mon, 24, 25, 31 Dec. 🚻 🗺️ **klostereberbach.de**

⑮ Rüdesheim

Road map B5. 🏔 10,000. 🚉
ℹ️ Rheinstrasse 29 (06722-906 150).
🎆 Fireworks (Jul), Weinfest (Aug).
🗺️ **ruedesheim.de**

Rüdesheim, enjoying a picturesque location on the banks of the Rhine, has a long history going back to Roman times. The town is famous for the **Drosselgasse**, a street lined with countless wine bars and shops. There are also the remains of two castles: the **Boosenburg** and the 12th-century **Brömserburg**, which also houses a wine museum.

Rüdesheim also has several historic mansions, including the half-timbered Brömserhof (1559) with a collection of musical instruments, and the early 16th-century Klunkhardshof. Above the town towers the **Niederwalddenkmal**, a statue of Germania, 10.5 m (34 ft) high, built to commemorate victory in the Franco-Prussian War of 1870–71, which resulted in German unification. The monument can be reached by a cable-car and affords views of Rüdesheim and the Rhine valley.

Gabled and half-timbered houses in Drosselgasse, in Rüdesheim

⑯ Frankfurt am Main

Frankfurt, nicknamed "Mainhattan" and "Chicago am Main" because of its skyscrapers, is one of the main economic and cultural centres of both Germany and Europe. The head-quarters of many major banks and newspaper publishers are based here, including those of the *Frankfurter Allgemeine Zeitung*, one of Europe's most influential newspapers. The city's International Book Fair is the world's largest event of its kind. Goethe was born in Frankfurt, and the Johann-Wolfgang-Goethe-Universität is one of Germany's most famous universities. The city also boasts magnificent art collections.

The Neo-Renaissance façade of the Alte Oper

🎭 Alte Oper
Opernplatz 1. **Tel** (069) 134 00.
The monumental old opera house stands near the Stock Exchange. Built in 1872–80, it was completely burned down during World War II. Subsequently rebuilt, it is today used as a conference centre. Its façade and decorations are a fine imitation of the Italian Renaissance style.

🏛 Eschenheimer Turm
Große Eschenheimer Strasse.
The Eschenheimer Turm, at the corner of Hochstrasse, presents a silhouette typical of old Frankfurt. A relic of the medieval town's fortifications, it was designed by Klaus Mengoz; construction began in 1400 and was completed in 1428 by Madern Gerthener. The façade of the tower features many attractive

Putti with model ship, at the front of the Börse

bay windows; it also has two reliefs depicting eagles, the symbol of the German empire and the city of Frankfurt.

🏛 Börse
Börsenplatz.
According to historical records, local merchants founded the town's first Stock Exchange in 1558. The new building, designed by Heinrich Burnitz and Oskar Sommer, was erected in 1864–79. It has been used again by stockbrokers since 1957, and is open to the public. Like the old opera house, the stock exchange is designed in Neo-Renaissance style.

🏛 Hauptwache
An der Hauptwache.
Built in 1730, the Hauptwache was originally a guardhouse. Later it was turned into a prison.

Dismantled stone by stone during the construction of the town's underground system, it was reassembled in its original form following the completion of the project. Since 1904 the Hauptwache has been a chic café and a popular meeting place.

🏛 Goethehaus
Großer Hirschgraben 23. **Tel** (069) 13 88 00. **Open** 10am–6pm Mon–Sat, 10am–5:30pm Sun. 🈯
Ⓦ **goethehaus-frankfurt.de**
Southwest of the Hauptwache is Johann Wolfgang Goethe's family home. The great German poet, novelist and dramatist was born here on 28 August 1749. The house, along with many other buildings in Frankfurt, was totally destroyed in World War II, but later lovingly restored. Its interior was reconstructed to represent the style typical of the mid- to late 18th century. Goethe lived in this house until 1775, when he moved to Weimar. The desk at which he wrote his early works, including the first versions of *Götz von Berlichingen* (1771) and *Egmont* (1774), has been preserved.
The adjacent building now houses the Goethemuseum. Opened in 1997, the museum recreates the atmosphere of the 1750–1830 period, and holds a collection of items related to the writer. There is an excellent library, which contains some of his writings.

The distinctive Neo-Classical rotunda of the Paulskirche

Portal of the Goethehaus, with the ancestral family crest

🏛 Paulskirche

Paulsplatz 11. **Tel** (069) 21 23 49 20.
Open 10am–5pm daily.

The distinctive Neo-Classical rotunda of the church was begun in 1786 but not completed until 1833, due to continuous hostilities with France. Today, however, this building is no longer thought of, or indeed used as, a church. After the first, albeit ill-fated, German National Assembly met here following the revolutionary upheavals of 1848–9, the church became a symbol of republican and liberal Germany. The Paulskirche now serves as a venue for many important events. Each year the awards ceremony for the prestigious German Publishers' Peace Prize takes place here.

🏛 Römerberg

Located in the centre of Frankfurt's old town, this square contains the Gerechtigkeits-brunnen (fountain of justice). Its highlight, however, is the **Römer** (literally the Roman). So-called after the remains of ancient settlements, it is a complex of 15th- to 18th-century houses, including the Altes Rathaus (old town hall), which were rebuilt after World War II. Opposite is a group of half-timbered houses, commonly referred to as Ostzeile. The Steinernes Haus (stone house) was originally built in

1464 for a Cologne silk merchant. It has been reconstructed and is now the home of the Frankfurter Kunstverein (artists' league).

The Ostzeile on the Römerberg, one of the symbols of Frankfurt

Frankfurt City Centre

1. Alte Oper
2. Eschenheimer Turm
3. Börse
4. Hauptwache
5. Goethehaus
6. Paulskirche
7. Römerberg
8. St Leonhardskirche
9. Historisches Museum
10. Nikolaikirche
11. Kunsthalle Schirn
12. Kaiserdom
13. Museum für Moderne Kunst
14. Ikonen-Museum
15. Museum für Angewandte Kunst
16. Deutsches Architekturmuseum
17. Jüdisches Museum
18. Städelsches Kunstinstitut

0 metres 400
0 yards 400

For additional map symbols *see back flap*

🏛 Jüdisches Museum

Untermainkai 14–15. **Tel** (069) 21 23 50
00. **Open** 10am–5pm Tue–Sun (to 8pm
Wed). 🐾 **w** juedischesmuseum.de

The Jewish community of
Frankfurt was the second largest
in Germany, after that of Berlin.
This museum, in the former
Rothschild Palace, documents
the rich cultural heritage of
Frankfurt's Jews.

🏛 St Leonhardskirche

Am Leonhardstr 25. **Tel** (069) 297 03
20. **Closed** for renovations until 2016.

Close to the banks of the
Main stands the church of
St Leonhard, a fine example
of Gothic and Romanesque
architecture. A five-naved hall-
church with an elongated choir,
it was built in stages in the 13th
and 15th centuries. Inside are
many treasures, including a
copy of Leonardo da Vinci's *Last
Supper* by Hans Holbein the
Elder, from 1501. Next to it is St
Mary's altar, created by master
craftsmen from Antwerp in
1515–20. On the north wall of
the choir visitors can see a fresco
depicting the *Tree of Life and the
Apostles* (1536) by Hans Dietz.

🏛 Historisches Museum

Fahrtor 2 (Römerberg). **Tel** (069) 21 23
55 99. **Open** 10am–5pm Tue, Thu–Sun,
10am–9pm Wed. 🐾 **w** historisches-
museum.frankfurt.de

The building housing the
history museum was finished in
1972. The museum has an interesting display of items relating
to Frankfurt's history, including
a fascinating model of the

The early-Gothic Alte Nikolaikirche, in
Frankfurt's Römerberg

medieval town, a collection of
local prehistoric finds and several
decorative architectural fragments from buildings that were
destroyed during World War II.

The adjacent building is
the Saalhof, which dates back
to the time of the Emperor
Friedrich I Barbarossa (1122–90).
New exhibition rooms are being
added to the museum, and are
planned to open in 2017.

🏛 Alte Nikolaikirche

Römerberg 11. **Tel** (069) 28 42 35.
Open Apr–Oct: 10am–8pm daily; Nov–
Mar: 10am–6pm daily.

This twin-naved church was
consecrated in 1290. Used as
a court church until the late
15th century, it now serves a
Lutheran congregation. Its
many statues of St Nicholas
(Santa Claus) are popular.

🏛 Kunsthalle Schirn

Römerberg 6. **Tel** (069) 299 88 20.
Open 10am–7pm Tue, Fri–Sun, 10am–
10pm Wed & Thu. 🐾 **w** schirn.de

One of Europe's most prestigious
exhibition buildings, the
Kunsthalle opened in 1986. It
hosts temporary art exhibitions
featuring archaeological themes
and the work of old masters and
contemporary artists.

🏛 Kaiserdom

Domplatz 14. **Tel** (069) 297 03 20.
Open 8am–8pm daily (from noon Fri;
from 9am Sat & Sun). Dommuseum:
Tel (069) 13 37 61 84. **Open** 10am–
5pm Tue–Fri, 11am–5pm Sat & Sun. 🐾
w dommuseum-frankfurt.de

Near the archaeological park,
where the ruins of a Carolingian
fortress have been unearthed,
stands the imperial cathedral,
used for the coronation of
German kings from 1356,
and of Holy Roman Emperors
from 1562. The cathedral,
dedicated to St Bartholomew
and Charlemagne, was built
between the 13th and 15th
centuries on the site of a
Carolingian chapel. It has several
priceless masterpieces of Gothic
art, including the magnificent
15th-century Maria-Schlaf-Altar
and a high altar dating from the
second half of the 15th century.
The choir has original 14th-
century stalls; above these
there is a fresco painted in 1427
which depicts scenes from
the life of St Bartholomew.

The Dom's huge tower affords
some magnificent views of
the town. While in the cloisters
is the Dommuseum which
has an interesting collection
of liturgical objects, sacred art
and precious artifacts.

🏛 Museum für Moderne Kunst (MMK)

Domstrasse 10. **Tel** (069) 21 23 04 47.
Open 10am–6pm Tue & Thu–Sun,
10am–8pm Wed. 🐾 **w** mmk-
frankfurt.de

The modern art museum
occupies a building that looks
like a slice of cake. It was
designed by Hans Hollein
in 1989–92. The museum's
collection represents all the
major artistic trends from the
1960s until the present day,

The magnificent late-Gothic high altar in the Kaiserdom

For hotels and restaurants in this area see pp499–500 and pp525–6

Hollein's modern design, housing the Museum für Moderne Kunst

and includes works by Roy Lichtenstein, Andy Warhol and Claes Oldenburg. Temporary exhibitions focus on multimedia shows, incorporating photography and video art.

Ikonen-Museum

Brückenstrasse 3–7. **Tel** (069) 21 23 62 62. **Open** 11am–5pm Tue–Sun, 11am–8pm Wed.

The museum of icons holds an extensive collection of Russian-Orthodox icons from the 16th–19th centuries. It is housed in the Deutschordenshaus, originally built in 1709–15 by Maximilian von Welsch for the Order of the Teutonic Knights. The present building is a faithful copy of the earlier Baroque three-wing structure destroyed in World War II. Inside is the 14th-century Teutonic Church of St Mary, with original altars and 14th- to 17th-century wall paintings.

Museum für Angewandte Kunst

Schaumainkai 17. **Tel** (069) 21 23 12 86. **Open** 10am–6pm Tue–Sun (to 8pm Wed). **museumangewandtekunst.de**

The Museum of Applied Arts was opened in 1983, in a building designed by Richard Meier. He used a Biedermeier house, the Villa Metzler, and added a modern wing. The museum has a collection of some 30,000 objects of applied art from Europe and Asia.

Nearby, in a villa in Schaumainkai, is the small but fascinating Museum der Weltkulturen (ethnography museum), which is worth a visit.

Deutsches Architekturmuseum

Schaumainkai 43. **Tel** (069) 21 23 88 44. **Open** 11am–6pm Tue–Sun (to 8pm Wed). **dam-online.de**

One of the most interesting museums in the Schaumainkai complex is undoubtedly the museum of architecture, opened in 1984 in an avant-garde building designed by Oswald Mathias Ungers. The museum has a permanent collection as well as temporary exhibitions concentrating mainly on developments in 20th-century architecture.

Nearby, at No 41 Schaumainkai, is the Deutsches Filmmuseum, which holds documents and objects relating to the art of filmmaking and the development of film technology. The museum has its own cinema, which shows old and often long-forgotten films.

Liebieghaus

Schaumainkai 71. **Tel** (069) 605 098 200. **Open** 10am–6pm Tue–Sun (to 9pm Thu). **liebieghaus.de**

Built for the Czech industrialist Baron Heinrich Liebieg in 1896, today this building houses a museum of sculpture, with works ranging from antiquity through to Mannerism, Baroque and Rococo. The museum also has superb examples of ancient Egyptian and Far Eastern art, as well as works from the Middle Ages and the Renaissance. Its highlights are the works of Neo-Classical masters such as Antonio Canova, Bertel Thorwaldsen and Johann Heinrich Dannecker.

The Liebieghaus, home of the museum of sculpture

Naturmuseum Senckenberg

Senckenberganlage 25. **Tel** (069) 754 20. **Open** 9am–5pm Mon, Tue, Thu & Fri, 9am–8pm Wed, 9am–6pm Sat & Sun. **senckenberg.de**

This museum, situated near the university, is one of the best natural history museums in Germany. Boasting a vast collection of plants and animals, including dinosaur skeletons, it contains human and animal mummies from Egypt.

Environs

Hanau, 30 km (19 miles) east of Frankfurt, is the birthplace of the Grimm brothers. An exhibition devoted to their lives and work is held at the local history museum, in Philippsruhe, a Baroque palace.

The Deutsches Architekturmuseum, in Schaumainkai

Frankfurt – Städelsches Kunstinstitut

The founder of this excellent museum, banker Johann Friedrich Städel, left his art collection to the town in 1815. Since then, the museum has grown through acquisitions and donations, and now contains many masterpieces from seven centuries of European art. It moved to a Neo-Renaissance building in 1878, on the picturesque "museum embankment" by the Main. In the 1920s it acquired the Hohenzollern collection from Sigmaringen. The museum has undergone renovation and new buildings have been constructed, including a subterranean exhibition hall for contemporary art.

★ The Geographer (1669)
Although the signature on the painting is not genuine, there is no doubt that this picture, depicting a scholar at work, is the work of Jan Vermeer van Delft.

Ecce Homo
Members of the family who commissioned this painting from Hieronymus Bosch also originally figured in it, but they were later painted over and now only a few figures are partially visible.

First floor

★ Blinding of Samson (1636)
Rembrandt's dramatic painting depicts the violent blinding of Samson by the Philistines after Delilah cut off his hair.

Gallery Guide

The ground floor is used for changing exhibitions of prints and drawings, as well as a book store and a museum shop. The first floor is devoted to 19th- and 20th-century art and the second floor to the Old Masters. An underground wing houses contemporary art.

Around 100,000 prints and drawings, dating from the 14th century to the present day and making up one of Germany's most valuable collections, are exhibited in this exhibition hall.

Main entrance

Library

★ Lucca Madonna
This small painting by Jan van Eyck, which evokes an intimate and intensely private atmosphere, takes its name from its former owner, Charles Ludwig de Bourbon, Duke of Lucca.

Second floor

Ground floor

Ideal Portrait of a Woman (c.1480)
Simonetta Vespucci, mistress of Giuliano Medici, is the subject of this painting by Sandro Botticelli. Her pendant belonged at the time to the Medici collection.

Pilgrimage to the Isle of Cythera (c.1710)
Jean-Antoine Watteau painted three pictures on this theme, inspired by Dancourt's play *The Three Sisters*. The museum holds the earliest of the three, which shows a Flemish influence.

Orchestra Players
(1870–74)
Edgar Degas, not completely satisfied with his painting, retrieved it from its owner. In 1874, he cropped it on three sides, added a bit at the top and repainted the entire painting.

Key

🟦 Old Master Paintings 1300–1800

⬜ Modern Art 1800–1945

⬛ Special Exhibitions

⬜ Department of Prints and Drawings

⑰ Darmstadt

Road map C5. 🗺 138,000. 🚉
ℹ️ Luisencenter, Luisenplatz 5 (06151-
134 513). 🎭 Days of Art Nouveau
(May), Schlossgrabenfest (May),
Heinerfest (early Jul), Herbstfest (Oct).
🌐 darmstadt-tourismus.de

The earliest historical records of
Darmstadt, which was probably
named after Darimund, a
Frankonian settler, date from the
12th century. Until 1479, the
castle and the town belonged to
the Counts von Katzenelnbogen,
and later to Hessian landgraves.
In 1567, the Landgraves von
Hessen-Darmstadt chose
Darmstadt as their residence,
and they lived here until 1918.

To the north of the old town
stands the **Residenzschloss**,
initially a ducal palace, and
from 1806 residence of the
Landgraves von Hessen-
Darmstadt. The Renaissance-
Baroque complex is centred
around three courtyards. The
earlier medieval castle, which
stood on the same site, burned
down in 1546. The present
palace was created in stages,
with its earliest parts, the
Renaissance wings, dating from
1567–97. The Glockenbau has a
35-bell carillon which can be
heard every half hour; it was
completed in 1663. Further
modifications, planned in 1715–
30, were never completed. Two
Baroque wings, the so-called
Neubau or Neuschloss (new
castle), surround older buildings

to the south and west. The
Schloss was bombed in World
War II and subsequently rebuilt.
Today it houses part of the
Technical University, while the
Glockenbau is home to the
fascinating **Schlossmuseum**
(castle museum). As well as
a splendid collection of coaches
and furniture, it contains the
famous *Darmstädter
Madonna* (1526), by Holbein.

Also worth seeing is
the late-Renaissance
Rathaus (town hall), built
in 1588–90, survived
World War II. The
15th-century choir of
the **Stadtkirche**
has an enormous
monument (1587) to
Magdalena zur Lippe,
first wife of Landgrave
Georg I the Pious. To the
southwest of the
Stadtkirche stands the
Altes Pädagog, built in
1629 as an educational
establishment.

To the north of the
Schloss is the
**Hessisches Landes-
museum** (regional museum of
Hesse), erected in 1892–1905.
Its collection includes artifacts
dating from the Roman era to
the 20th century. The museum
also has an excellent natural
history section, whose exhibits
include the impressive skeleton
of a mammoth as well as birds
of every species native to
southern Hesse. Set in the park

behind the museum is the
Baroque Prinz-Georg-Palais
(1710), which houses the
**Großherzoglich-Hessische
Porzellansammlung**, an
extensive porcelain collection.
The last Grand Duke of Hesse,
Ernst Ludwig, was an important
patron of the Jugendstil, the
German Art Nouveau
movement. He initiated the
building of an exhibition
and residential complex,
the **Mathildenhöhe**,
which was established
in 1901 in the grounds
of the former ducal
park, to serve the
existing artists' colony
led by Joseph Maria
Olbrich. Olbrich
designed the Ernst-
Ludwig-Haus, which
now houses the
**Museum Künstler-
kolonie**, an exhibition
space for the colony's
artists, as well as
the famous
Hochzeitsturm
(wedding tower),
erected in 1907–8 to
celebrate the Grand Duke's
wedding. The **Behrens-Haus**,
designed by the Hamburg
architect Peter Behrens, is sober
in contrast. The Orthodox
church of **St Mary Magdalene**
was built in 1897–9 by the
Russian architect Leonti
Nikolayevich Benois, in honour
of Alix, wife of the last tsar of
Russia and sister of Ernst Ludwig.

Statue on the door
of the Behrens-Haus
in Darmstadt

🏛 **Schlossmuseum**
Residenzschloss, Marktplatz 15.
Tel (06151) 240 35. **Open** 10am–5pm
Fri–Sun. 📷 obligatory.
🌐 schlossmuseum-darmstadt.de

🏛 **Hessisches Landesmuseum**
Friedensplatz 1. **Tel** (06151) 16 57 000.
Open 10am–6pm Tue, Thu & Fri,
10am–8pm Wed, 11am–5pm Sat
& Sun. 📷

🏛 **Museum Künstlerkolonie**
Olbrichweg 15/Mathildenhöhe.
Tel (06151) 13 33 85.
Open 11am–6pm Tue–Sun. 📷
🌐 mathildenhoehe.eu

🏛 **Großherzoglich-Hessische
Porzellansammlung**
Schlossgartenstr. 10. **Tel** (06151) 71 32
33. **Open** Apr–Oct: 10am–5pm Fri–Sun.

Hochzeitsturm and Orthodox Church in Mathildenhöhe, Darmstadt

For hotels and restaurants in this area see pp499–500 and pp525–6

The Carolingian Torhalle (gate-house) of the Kloster (abbey) in Lorsch

⑱ Lorsch

Road map C5. 🗺 10,700.
ℹ Marktplatz 1 (06251-175 26 0).
🖥 lorsch.de

This small town is mainly known for the **Kloster**, a Benedictine abbey first founded in 764 by Chrodegang of Metz and one of the most important cultural and intellectual centres in Europe in the Carolingian era. It reached the peak of its power in the 8th–13th centuries, before being sold to the Archbishop of Mainz in 1232. The Benedictines were forced to leave, and in their place the Cistercians arrived. The monastery was dissolved during the Reformation, and in 1621 the Spanish Army destroyed and plundered the greater part of the complex.

Fragments of the 13th-century nave, the towers and the gate-house, dating from c.790, are all that has survived. The original 8th-century church, a basilica without transept, burned down in 1090 and was rebuilt in the 12th century. The original crypt is the burial place of Ludwig II the German, the first ruler of the Eastern Franks. The **Torhalle** (gate-house) is one of the most important architectural remains of the Carolingian period, and it was listed as a UNESCO World Heritage site in 1991. Its lower section is made up of three arcades, modelled on Roman triumphal arches. The first-floor quarters above were probably used as a guest room

or courtroom, and from the 14th century they served as a chapel. Remains of the original wall paintings are still visible here. The façade is decorated with red and white stone mosaics inspired by Franco-Merovingian art. The vertical divides, created by pilasters and entablature, are copies of ancient designs – an architectural feature typical of the Carolingian Renaissance. The chapel's high roof and vaults date from the 14th century.

⑲ Michelstadt

Road map C5. 🗺 16,000.
ℹ Marktplatz 1 (06061-979 41 10).
🎪 Bienenmarkt (Whitsun), Christmas Market (Dec).

Michelstadt, set among the hills of the Odenwald, is first mentioned in historical records in 741. From the 13th century the town belonged to the von Erbach family (the future Counts von Erbach).

The town has preserved many historic half-timbered houses and presents a typical image of medieval Germany. The 16th-century **Kellerei** is built around the remains of an earlier castle dating from 970. It now houses a regional museum. The sight most popular with photographers is the half-timbered **Rathaus** (town hall), dating from 1484, with its three towers and an open ground-floor gallery.

Nearby stands the late-Gothic, 15th-century **Pfarrkirche St Michael** (parish church of St Michael). Inside are some interesting epitaphs including the double tombstone of Philipp I and Georg I, dating from the late 15th century. A true rarity is the 18th-century **synagogue**, which escaped being burned by the National Socialists in 1938.

In the Steinbach district of Michelstadt stands the **Einhardsbasilika**, a church dating from around 821. The first church built on this site, at the initiative of Einhard, a courtier of Charlemagne, was a small, pillared and vaulted basilica with a short choir ending with a rounded apse. Under the eastern section is a crypt. The parts which remain to this day include the main nave, the north aisle with an apse and the crypt which holds precious religious relics.

Environs
In **Fürstenau**, situated about 1 km (0.6 mile) northwest of Michelstadt, is a beautiful complex including the Altschloss (old palace), remodelled from a medieval castle, the Neuschloss (new palace), dating from 1810, the park and its garden pavilions.

Erbach, 3 km (2 miles) south of Michelstadt, became famous as a centre for the art of ivory carving. In No. 1 Otto-Glenz-Strasse is the Deutsches Elfenbeinmuseum (German ivory museum), which is devoted to this craft. Other attractions in this town include the Baroque Schloss (castle) and its interesting art collection.

The Carolingian Einhardsbasilika in Michelstadt-Steinbach

NORTH RHINE–WESTPHALIA

Originally consisting of two distinct provinces with somewhat diverging histories, the region of North Rhine-Westphalia today has its own strong identity. It encompasses the vast valley of the Ruhr river, rich in mineral deposits, where over the past 200 years huge conurbations have developed, comprising dozens of industrial cities that are gradually merging into one another.

As a province, the North Rhineland, situated along the lower Rhine valley, goes back to Roman times. In the Middle Ages most of this area was ruled by the Bishops of Cologne (Köln). The North Rhineland cities grew and prospered thanks to their trade links, and in the 19th century they became major centres of mining and heavy industry.

Westphalia forms the eastern part of the land. Once a Saxon territory, its history was often intertwined with that of the Rhineland. Only its western end has been heavily industrialized.

North Rhine-Westphalia is not the largest of the German regions, but with a population of nearly 18 million it is the most heavily populated one. It is often thought that the region, and in particular the heavily industrialized Ruhr valley, has little to offer to its visitors, but this is a mistaken belief. Its splendid past has left many priceless historic monuments and more recently, thanks to great investment, its industrial cities have transformed themselves into attractive cultural centres.

The history of towns such as Bonn, Aachen, Cologne (Köln) and Xanten goes back to Roman times, and they have preserved much of their ancient heritage to this day. Evidence of Romanesque art, which flourished in the Rhineland, is today apparent in numerous impressive abbeys dotted throughout the region and in the churches of Cologne, which also boasts the colossal Gothic Dom.

Much of North Rhine-Westphalia is rural, and the region offers thousands of kilometres of tracks for walking in the Teutoburg Forest and in the Northern Eifel mountains, as well as splendid conditions for watersports and fishing in the Sauerland. It also has surprisingly good ski slopes, such as in the Rothaar Mountains.

A typical lowland landscape near Xanten, in the Rhineland

◄ The historic town of Freudenberg, in the Siegerland region, is filled with half-timbered houses

Exploring North Rhine-Westphalia

Despite being heavily industrialized, the land of North Rhine-Westphalia has many attractions for visitors. At least two days should be set aside to admire the historic treasures in Cologne, while those who prefer museums – or shopping – might allocate more time for Düsseldorf. The towns of Bonn, Aachen and Münster should also feature on every visitor's schedule. The best areas for rest and relaxation are the mountain ranges of the Eifel and the Teutoburg Forest, ideally suited for walking and cycling holidays.

Burg Altena in the Sauerland

Sights at a Glance

Getting Around

There are international airports at Düsseldorf, Cologne–Bonn (Konrad-Adenauer-Flughafen), Niederrhein-Weeze and at Münster–Osnabrück. North Rhine-Westphalia has the highest density of motorways in Germany, making it easy to travel between cities, and providing links with other German regions, Belgium and the Netherlands.

Johanniskirche on the west side of the Münster, Essen

Roman amphitheatre in the Archäologischer Park in Xanten

Key

- ▭▭▭ Motorway
- ▬▬ Major road
- ∷∷∷ Minor road
- ▬ ▬ Under construction
- ⎯⎯ Main railway
- ⎯⎯ Minor railway
- ▬▬ International border
- ⎯⎯ Regional border

❶ Münster

Münster and its surroundings were already inhabited in Roman times, but its history proper started in the 9th century, with the establishment of a bishopric. Town status was granted in 1137, and in the 13th century Münster joined the Hanseatic League. In 1648 the Westphalian Peace Treaty was signed here, ending the Thirty Years' War. Münster's Westfälische Wilhelms-Universität (1773) is one of Germany's largest universities. World War II saw 90 per cent of the old town laid to ruins, but most of it has now been rebuilt.

🏠 Erbdrostenhof
Salzstrasse 38.
Closed to the public.

This beautiful mansion was skilfully positioned diagonally across a corner site. Designed by Johann Conrad Schlaun, it was built in 1753–7, and despite destruction in World War II it still enchants with its "wavy", late-Baroque façade.

🏠 Rathaus
Prinzipalmarkt. Friedenssaal: **Tel** (0251) 492 27 24. **Open** 10am–5pm Tue–Fri, 10am–4pm Sat & Sun. **Closed** 25 Dec. 📷

The imposing Gothic town hall, the pride of Münster, was almost completely destroyed during World War II. After its splendid reconstruction, it is again a major draw for visitors. The only parts that had escaped destruction were the furnishings of the main council chamber, which have been returned to their rightful place after the rebuilding work. It was here that

Houses on Prinzipalmarkt, reconstructed in the medieval style

on 15 May 1648 part of the Westphalian Treaty was signed, ending the Thirty Years' War.

⛪ Lambertikirche
Prinzipalmarkt.

St Lamberti is an excellent example of the hall-churches characteristic of Westphalia. It was built in 1375–1450, but the openwork finial of the tower dates from 1887. The cages hanging on the tower held the bodies of the leading Anabaptists, following the crushing of their commune in 1536. It is also worth taking a look at the relief depicting the *Tree of Jesse*, above the southwest entrance, and the figures of the apostles (c.1600) by Johann Koess.

🏠 Dom St Paulus
Domkammer: Domplatz. **Tel** (0251) 448 93. **Open** 6:30am–7pm daily (to 7:30pm Sun and hols). 📷

The most precious historic relic in Münster is undeniably its massive St Paulus' cathedral, built in

1225–65 and representing a transitional style between late Romanesque and early-Gothic. The vast basilica has two transepts, two choirs and two massive towers. The northern cloister was added in the 14th century, and in the 16th–17th centuries the passage that runs around the presbytery acquired a ring of chapels. In the vestibule stands a group of 13th-century sculptures. Especially worth seeing are the two altars by Gerhard Gröninger (1st half of the 17th century), the early 16th-century stained-glass windows brought here from Marienfeldand monuments of many bishops. The cathedral's best-known treasure is the astronomical clock (1540), with paintings by Ludger tom Ring the Elder and sculptures by Johann Brabender. At noon, figures show the Magi paying tribute to the infant Jesus to the sounds of the carillon.

🏛 LWL Museum für Kunst und Kultur
Domplatz 10. **Tel** (0251) 590 701. **Open** 10am–6pm Tue–Sun. 📷

Located in a sandstone building with increased exhibition space and facilities, the Westphalian regional museum specializes mainly in Gothic art, with a large collection of sculptures and altars rescued in World War II. Its most noteworthy exhibits include the works by Heinrich and Johann Brabender, Conrad von Soest and the Tom Ring family. Contemporary art is represented by, among others, August Macke's work.

Figure of a saint in Dom St Paulus

⛪ Überwasserkirche
Überwasserkirchplatz.

The Liebfrauenkirche (Church of Our Lady) is popularly named Überwasserkirche (church above the water), after the district on the banks of the tiny Aa river. This Gothic

The beautifully restored façade of the late-Gothic Rathaus

The Baroque-Classical Schloss, residence of Münster's prince-bishops

edifice was built in c.1340–46, on the site of a Romanesque Benedictine church. Inside are 16th-century votive paintings by Ludger and Hermann tom Ring

🏠 Residenzschloss
Schlossplatz 2.
This beautiful Baroque residence was built in 1767–87, by Prince-Bishop Maximilian Friedrich. It was designed by Johann Conrad Schlaun, a local master of Baroque architecture. Maximilian Friedrich started the redevelopment of Münster in the northern Baroque style. On his initiative the town acquired a large park, part of which was transformed into a botanical garden in 1803. After World War II, the castle was rebuilt and became the headquarters of Münster university.

🏛 Museum für Lackkunst
Windthorststrasse 26. **Tel** (0251) 41 85 10. **Open** noon–8pm Tue, noon–6pm Wed–Sun & public holidays. 🌐 (except free Tue). 📷 **W museum fuer-lackkunst.de**

This unique museum, set up by BASF Coatings and devoted to lacquer ware, has a good collection with beautiful items from different eras and from across Europe, as well as Iran, India, China and Japan.

Watermill in the open-air museum in Mühlenhof

🏠 Mühlenhof
Theo-Breider-Weg 1. **Tel** (0251) 98 12 00. **Open** Mar–Oct: 10am–6pm daily; Nov–Feb: 11am–4pm Mon–Fri & Sun.

This interesting open-air museum is situated on the banks of the Aasee, Münster's lake and recreation area. There are a number of rural dwellings with authentic furnishings and two mills (17th and 18th centuries).

🏠 Drostenhof
Wolbeck, Am Steintor 5.
Southeast of the town, in Wolbeck, is an original Renaissance mansion from the mid-16th century. Its exquisite gate-house leads into the courtyard of the mansion, which has original fireplaces and ceiling paintings.

Münster City Centre

① Erbdrostenhof
② Rathaus
③ Lambertikirche
④ Dom St Paulus
⑤ LWL Museum für Kunst und Kultur
⑥ Überwasserkirche
⑦ Museum für Lackkunst

0 metres 300
0 yards 300

➋ Münsterland

The region stretching in a narrow strip to the north of Münster is the land of horses and Wasserburgen (moated castles). The castles were surrounded by moats or built on islands to give their owners protection in the surrounding lowlands. Almost 50 Wasserburgen have survived, some converted into residences. Not all are open to visitors as most remain to this day in the hands of the family of the original owners. The best way to tour the flat Münsterland region is by car or bicycle.

② **Vischering** The magnificent Burg Vischering is one of the oldest and best-preserved castles in Westphalia. Founded in 1270, it was extended in the 16th and 17th centuries.

⑤ **Schloss Raesfeld**
The beautiful 17th century castle has some original 14th-century elements. Particularly worth seeing is the castle chapel with its Baroque altar.

① **Havixbeck** Two interesting castles are near this small town: the Renaissance Haus Havixbeck and the Renaissance-Baroque Burg Hülshoff, birthplace of and museum to the 19th-century writer Annette von Droste-Hülshoff.

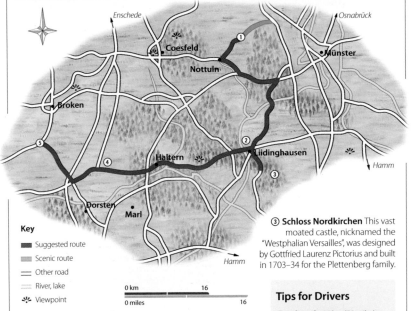

③ **Schloss Nordkirchen** This vast moated castle, nicknamed the "Westphalian Versailles", was designed by Gottfried Laurenz Pictorius and built in 1703–34 for the Plettenberg family.

Key

- ▬ Suggested route
- ▬ Scenic route
- ═ Other road
- ═ River, lake
- ☆ Viewpoint

0 km   16
0 miles   16

Tips for Drivers

Tour length: 97 km (58 miles).
Stopping-off points: Every town has inns, and there is a hotel in Schloss Lembeck.
Suggestions: All castles are open to visitors Tuesday to Sunday, with the exception of Nordkirchen, which opens only on Sundays and by reservation on other days.

④ **Schloss Lembeck**
In its present shape, the Lembeck castle complex is the result of Baroque remodelling, under the direction of Johann Conrad Schlaun. Nearby is a nature reserve.

❸ Kleve (Cleves)

Road map A3. 🚾 50,000. 🚗 🚌
ℹ️ Opschlag 11 13 (02821-89 50 90).

The town of Kleve is named after the high cliff, on which a castle was built in the 10th century. Around it, a settlement developed, which became a town in 1242. It was ruled by the dukes of Kleve, whose ambitions reached their peak in 1539, when Anne of Cleves married the English King Henry VIII.

During World War II Kleve lost most of its historic buildings. One that has survived is the imposing Gothic church of the Assumption of the Virgin Mary, **St Mariä Himmelfahrt** (1341–1426). It has remains of the high altar, dating from 1510–13, with reliefs by Henrik Douvermann and Jakob Dericks, as well as beautiful monuments to the von Kleve dukes. The former Franciscan **St Mariä Empfängnis**, a Gothic twin-nave hall-church from the first half of the 15th century, includes noteworthy features such as the Gothic stalls (1474) and a Baroque pulpit (1698). The well-preserved ducal castle of **Schwanenburg** was remodelled twice: in Gothic style in the late 15th century, and in Baroque style in 1636–66. Testifying to former splendour are the parks established in the mid 17th century by Johann Moritz von Nassau. The most beautiful of these is the **Neuer Tiergarten** (new animal garden). **Haus Koekkoek** once belonged to the Romantic painter Barend Cornalis Koekkoek, after whom it was named. The **Museum Kurhaus Kleve – Ewald Mataré-Sammlung** presents interesting and diverse art exhibitions.

🔲 Schwanenburg
Am Schlossberg. **Tel** (02821) 22 884.
Open Apr–Oct: 11am–5pm Mon–Fri, 10am–5pm Sat & Sun; Nov–Mar: 11am–5pm Sat & Sun. 🖼️

🏛️ Museum Kurhaus Kleve – Ewald Mataré-Sammlung
Tiergartenstrasse 41. **Tel** (02821) 750 10. **Open** 11am–5pm Tue–Sun. 🖼️

Environs
The suspension bridge across the Rhine – at 1,228 m (4,028 ft) the longest such structure in Germany – connects Kleve with **Emmerich**. Worth a visit here is the Martinskirche, with its exquisite, late-10th-century shrine of St Willibrod.

Twelve km (7 miles) to the southeast of Kleve lies the charming town of **Kalkar** which, in around 1500, was home to the famous Kalkar School specializing in woodcarving. The church of St Nicolai has superb furnishings dating from the same period.

Six km (4 miles) southeast is the moated castle of **Moyland**. It houses a modern art collection, which belongs to the brothers von der Grinten and includes over 4,000 works by the artist Joseph Beuys.

❹ Xanten

Road map A3. 🚾 21,500. 🚗 🚌
ℹ️ Kurfürstenstr. 9 (02801-772 200).

The history of Xanten goes back to the Romans, who founded the settlement of

The Hafentempel in the Archäologischer Park in Xanten

Colonia Ulpia Traiana near the local garrison. The present town, however, did not rise out of the ruins of the Roman town. It was established nearby, around the memorial church built on top of the grave of the martyr St Viktor. It was named *ad sanctos* (by the saints), later shortened to Xanten. A powerful town in the Middle Ages, Xanten also features in the Nibelung myth, and was said to be the birthplace of Siegfried.

The most important historic building in the town is the **Dom St Viktor**, which, according to legend, was built on the graves of St Viktor and members of the Thebian Legion. The surviving Gothic cathedral (1263–1517) holds the shrine of St Victor (1129), the early-Gothic stalls (1228) and, above all, the exquisite Marienaltar by Henrik Douvermann. There are also Gothic sculptures by the pillars of the main nave. Equally fascinating are the collegial buildings and the cloister holding the tombs of the canons.

Another sight worth visiting is the **Klever Tor**, a magnificent double town-gate, dating from the late 14th century, in the northwest of the town. The **Archäologischer Park**, on the site of the Roman town, and the **Römer Museum** display many reconstructed Roman public buildings including the impressive Hafentempel (harbour temple).

🔲 Archäologischer Park & Römer Museum
Wardter Str. **Tel** (02801) 29 99. **Open** 9am–6pm daily (Nov: 9am–5pm; Dec–Feb: 10am–4pm). 🖼️

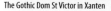

The Gothic Dom St Victor in Xanten

The picturesque exterior of Palace Haus Rodenberg in Dortmund-Aplerbeck

⑤ Dortmund

Road map: B4. 🚗 600,000. 🚉 🚌
ℹ Max-von-der-Grün-Platz 5–6
(0231-189 990). 📅 Dortmund à la
carte (Jun), Dortmund aller art (Aug),
Hansetage (Nov). 🆆 **dortmund-tourismus.de**

The large city of Dortmund is famous not only for its excellent beer and highly developed industry, but also for its more than 1,000 years of history. In the Middle Ages, the town grew rich through trade and joined the Hanseatic League; after a period of decline it flourished again in the 19th century.

A walk through the small old town will take visitors to the **Museum für Kunst-und Kulturgeschichte** (museum for art and cultural history) with displays of interiors from various periods, including Secessionist designs by Joseph Maria Olbrich. A short distance from here is the **Petrikirche**, a Gothic 14th-century hall-church, whose greatest attraction is its high altar (1521), the work of Gilles, a master from Antwerp. Also noteworthy is the former Dominican **Propsteikirche**, with its exquisite late-Gothic main altar. A shortcut across the market square and along Ostenhellweg takes the visitor to two more churches:

Statue on Alter Markt, in Dortmund

the **Reinoldikirche** and the **Marienkirche**. The former, dedicated to St Reinold, the patron saint of Dortmund, has an early-Gothic 13th-century main body and a late-Gothic, 15th-century presbytery. It includes many Gothic sculptures and furnishings. The second one, the church of St Mary, is a 12th-century Romanesque structure. It has a magnificent main altar, by Conrad von Soest (1415–20) and a statue of the Madonna (c.1230). Inside the impressive Dortmunder U tower, the **Museum am Ostwall** has an excellent modern art collection.

🏛 **Museum für Kunst-und Kulturgeschichte**
Hansastr. 3. **Tel** (0231) 502 55 22. **Open** 10am–5pm Tue–Sun (to 8pm Thu, from noon Sat). 📷

🏛 **Museum am Ostwall**
Leonie-Reygers-Terrasse 2. **Tel** (0231) 502 47 23. **Open** 11am–6pm Tue, Wed, Sat & Sun; 11am–8pm Thu, Fri.
🆆 **museumostwall.dortmund.de**

⑥ Essen

Road map B4. 🚗 600,000. 🚉 🚌 ℹ
Im Handelshof (am Hauptbahnhof 2)
(0201-194 33). 📅 Essen Original (Aug).
🆆 **essen.de**

It is hard to believe that this vast industrial metropolis has grown from a monastery, established in 852. The town owes its

growth and prominence to the Krupp family, who, over several generations from the mid-19th century, created the powerful German steel and arms industry.

The most important historic building in the town is the **Münster**, the former collegiate church of the canonesses. This unusual edifice consists of the 15th-century Gothic church of St John, an 11th-century atrium and the main church, which in turn has a Romanesque 11th-century frontage and a Gothic 14th-century main body. Without doubt the most precious object held by the church is the *Goldene Madonna*, a statue of the Virgin Mary with the Infant, made from sheet gold, probably c.980. The treasury has an outstanding collection of gold items from the Ottonian period.

Another important sight in Essen is the **Synagogue** built by Edmund Körner in 1911–13. The largest synagogue in Germany, it managed to outlast the Third Reich and is now a place of commemoration.

Visitors who are interested in 20th-century architecture should see the church of **St Engelbert** in Fischerstrasse, designed by Dominikus Metzendorf (1934–6), the town-garden in **Margarethenhöhe** built from 1909 to a design by Georg Metzendorf, and the opera house designed by the Finnish architect, Alvar Aalto.

Essen has much to offer to modern art enthusiasts. The **Museum Folkwang** boasts an excellent collection of 20th-century paintings, mainly German Expressionists. It also has a graphic arts section.

The **Grugapark** is a large green area with botanical gardens, zoo and the Grugahalle, where major concerts are held. To the south of the centre, on the banks of the Baldeneysee, stands **Villa Hügel**, which belonged to the Krupp family until 1945. Today interesting art exhibitions are frequently hosted here. Further south, in **Werden**, is the former Benedictine church of St Ludger, consisting of a 13th-century body preceded by a

The grand Villa Hügel, former home of the Krupp family in Essen

10th-century imperial frontage. The treasury holds many precious objects including a bronze crucifix from around 1060.

🏛 Museum Folkwang
Goethestr. 41. **Tel** (0201) 884 54 44. **Open** 10am–6pm Tue, Wed, Sat & Sun, 10am–8pm Thu, Fri. **Closed** 1 Jan, Easter, 1 May, 24 & 31 Dec.

Environs
Visitors interested in technology should visit **Bochum**, which is also the seat of the excellent Ruhr-Universität. There are two excellent museums: the **Deutsches Bergbau-Museum** devoted to mining, and the **Eisenbahnmuseum** (railway museum) in Dahlhausen. Both have world-class exhibits.

🕖 Duisburg

Road map B4. 🔺 540,000. 🚉 🚌
🛈 Königstr. 86 (0203-285 440).
🆆 ruhr-tourismus.de

Duisburg, on the edge of the Ruhr region, underwent a period of rapid development in the 19th and 20th centuries. Once a small town, it became the world's largest inland harbour thanks to its location at the spot where the Ruhr flows into the Rhine.

The small old town was almost totally destroyed in World War II, but the 15th-century Gothic **Salvatorkirche** (church of St Saviour) has been rebuilt. Some of the town's greatest attractions are its museums. The **Wilhelm-Lehmbruck-Museum** focuses on the work of the sculptor Lehmbruck, who was born in Duisburg. The museum has an interesting collection of

20th-century sculptures, including works by famous artists such as Salvador Dali, Henry Moore, Max Ernst, Emil Nolde and Joseph Beuys. Also worth visiting is the **Museum der Deutschen Binnenschifffahrt** with its collection of barges and inland waterway vessels. In the 16th century, Duisburg was the home of the famous geographer and cartographer Gerhard Mercator, whose collection of globes, maps and charts can now be seen in the **Kulture- und Stadthistorisches Museum**.

🏛 Wilhelm-Lehmbruck-Museum
Friedrich-Wilhelm-Str. 40. **Tel** (0203) 283 26 30. **Open** noon–6pm Wed, Fri, Sat; noon–9pm Thu; 11am–6pm Sun.

Environs
CentrO in **Oberhausen**, 14 km (9 miles) north of Duisburg, is the largest shopping and leisure complex in Europe.

Krefeld, 6 km (4 miles) south-west of Duisburg, has been a centre of silk fabric production from the 17th century, and the Deutsches Textilmuseum has over 20,000 exhibits, ranging from antiquity to the present day.

🕗 Wuppertal

Road map B4. 🔺 380,000. 🚉
🛈 Schlossbleiche 40 (0202-563 22 70); Elberfeld, Informationszentrum am Döppersberg (0202-194 33).
🆆 wuppertal.de

Wuppertal, capital of the Bergisches Land area, was created in 1929 by combining six towns strung along a 20-km (12-mile) stretch of the Wupper river. The towns are joined by the **Schwebebahn**, a monorail constructed in 1900. Carriages are suspended from a single rail, which rests on tall pillars.

The most interesting of the former towns is Elberfeld, with a museum of clocks, and the **Von-der-Heydt–Museum** of 19th- and 20th-century German art. The museum in the Friedrich-Engels-Haus in Barmen (Engelsstr. 10) is worth seeing, and Neviges has a Baroque pilgrimage church, with a much-visited miraculous picture of the Virgin Mary.

🏛 Von-der-Heydt-Museum
Elberfeld, Turmhof 8. **Tel** (0202) 563 62 31. **Open** 11am–6pm Tue, Wed, Fri–Sun, 11am–8pm Thu

The unusual monorail, linking Wuppertal's six constituent towns

⑨ Düsseldorf

Düsseldorf, the administrative capital of North Rhine-Westphalia, received its municipal rights in 1288. From the late 14th century it was the capital of the Duchy of Berg, and from 1614 that of the Palatine. The town owes much to Duke Johann Wilhelm, who lived here in 1690–1716. One of the most important industrial and cultural centres in the Rhine Valley, this European metropolis has a renowned university, superb museums and theatres and, as the German capital of fashion, many excellent shops.

🏛 Museum Kunst Palast

Ehrenhof 4–5. **Tel** (0211) 899 02 00.
Open 11am–6pm Tue–Sun (until 9pm Thu) 🅿 �️ 🛗 🚻 ☐ 🅦 smkp.de

This art museum is one of the most interesting in Germany, with a collection of paintings dating from the 16th to the 20th centuries, including works by Rubens, Cranach and Dutch masters of the 17th century. It also holds a large collection of paintings by the Düsseldorf Academy, active in the first half of the 19th century, whose best known artists were Peter von Cornelius and Friedrich Wilhelm Schadow.

🏛 Altstadt

The small old town area suffered severe damage during World War II. Among the surviving monuments it is worth seeing some of the beautiful town houses and the late-Gothic **Rathaus** (town hall), built in the years 1570–73. In front of it stands a famous equestrian

Interior of the Pfarrkirche St Andreas

statue of the Elector Jan Wellem, built in 1703–11 by Gabriel Grupello. The Düsseldorf castle, burned down in 1872, only has the **Schlossturm** (castle tower) remaining, which now houses a museum of navigation. Another building worth visiting is the Baroque, post-Jesuit **Pfarrkirche St Andreas** (parish church of St Andrew), from the years 1622–9. It has a central ducal mausoleum complex situated behind the presbytery, where the remains of Jan Wellem and others are kept. The **Lambertuskirche**, the former collegiate church of St Lambertus, is a Gothic hall-church with a tall front tower, built in 1288–1394. Some valuable furnishings have survived, including the Gothic sacramentarium and important Gothic ducal tombs, such as that of Duke Wilhelm V, from 1595–9.

Detail from the façade of the Lambertuskirche

🏛 Kunstsammlung Nordrhein-Westfalen

K20: Grabbeplatz 5.
Tel (0211) 838 12 04.
Open 10am–6pm Tue–Fri, 11am–6pm Sat & Sun. 10am–10pm 1st Wed of the month. K21: Ständehausstr. 1.
Tel (0211) 838 12 04.
Open As for K20. **Closed** 24, 25 & 31 Dec. 🅿 🏧 🛗 🚻

The art collection of the state of North Rhine-Westphalia is enormous, featuring mainly the work of 20th-century artists. Particularly

valuable are 88 paintings by Paul Klee, which were acquired in 1960. There are also works by Wassily Kandinsky, Marcel Duchamp, Piet Mondrian and Pablo Picasso. The gallery at Grabbeplatz is known as K20, and a second building at Ständehäusstr. 1, where contemporary art is exhibited, is known as K21. Temporary exhibitions are held nearby, at Kunsthalle Düsseldorf, which is at No. 4 Grabbeplatz.

🏛 Hetjens-Museum

Schulstrasse 4. **Tel** (0211) 899 42 10.
Open 11am–5pm Tue & Thu–Sun, 11am–9pm Wed. 🚻

This museum, in the Nesselrode Palace, is the oldest German museum devoted to ceramics. Visitors can learn about techniques for producing faience and porcelain, and see global exhibits from prehistory to the present day.

🏬 Königsallee

The "kings' avenue", often just referred to as Kö, was laid out at the beginning of the 19th century, along the edge of the old city moat. The Kö is lined with expensive shops. Luxurious galleries, exclusive boutiques, department stores, fashion houses and shopping malls are interspersed with bars and restaurants. Particularly noteworthy is the Art Nouveau Warenhaus Tietz (now housing the Kaufhof-Galleria department store), which was built in 1907–9, to a design by Joseph Maria Olbrich.

🌳 Hofgarten

Schloss Jägerhof. Goethemuseum: Jacobistrasse 2. **Tel** (0211) 899 62 62.
Open 11am–5pm Tue–Fri & Sun, 1–5pm Sat. 🚻

This charming park, originally laid out in 1769 for Elector Karl Theodor, was recreated in the English style at the beginning of the 19th century. The park is a marvellous setting for Schloss Jägerhof, a Baroque hunting lodge dating from the years 1752–63 and built according

The late-Baroque Schloss Benrath

to a design by Johann Josef Couven and Nicolas de Pigage. The castle was rebuilt after World War II. It now houses the Goethe-Museum, holding memorabilia and documents related to the writer's life, and a collection of 18th-century art, funded by Ernst Schneider.

Heinrich-Heine-Institut
Bilker Str. 12–14. **Tel** (0211) 899 29 02. **Open** 11am–5pm Tue–Fri & Sun; 1–5pm Sat.

The former city moat which runs alongside Königsallee

The celebrated German poet Heinrich Heine was born in Düsseldorf in 1797. This institute was established to preserve his legacy and to organize exhibitions. Düsseldorf's university and a number of streets have also been named after Heine.

Schloss Benrath
Benrather Schlossallee. **Tel** (0211) 892 19 03. **Open** Apr–Oct: 11am–5pm Tue–Fri, 11am–6pm Sat & Sun; Nov–Mar: 11am–5pm Tue–Sun.

Part of Düsseldorf since 1929, Benrath is home to this beautiful Neo-Classical hunting palace, built for the electors of the Palatine in 1755–73 by Nicolas de Pigage. Decor, beautiful furnishings and an extensive park and gardens have survived.

Kaiserswerth
Today a part of Düsseldorf, this area prides itself on a

history dating back to the 8th century. Its Pfarrkirche St Suitbertus, a Romanesque basilica from the 12th century, has the magnificent 13th-century golden relic of its patron saint. There are also the ruins of a palace, built in the 12th century for Friedrich I Barbarossa.

Environs
The "Neanderthal" part of the Düssel valley was originally named after the poet Joachim Neander. It became famous in 1856, when the remains of ape-like creatures were uncovered in a cave. A museum dedicated to these "Neanderthal Men" is located in Mettman, 17 km (11 miles) east of Düsseldorf.

VISITORS' CHECKLIST

Practical Information
Road map: B4. 600,000.
Immermannstrasse 65B (am Hauptbahnhof), Marktstrasse (0211 1720 2844).
Rosenmontagsumzug (Carnival Mon), Größte Kirmes am Rhein (end Jul).
w duesseldorf.de

Transport
Konrad-Adenauer-Platz.
north of the centre.

Düsseldorf City Centre
① Museum Kunst Palast
② Altstadt
③ Kunstsammlung Nordrhein-Westfalen
④ Hetjens-Museum
⑤ Königsallee
⑥ Hofgarten

For key to symbols *see back flap*

⑩ Neuss

Road map B4. 🚏 150,000. 🚉 🚌
ℹ️ Rathausarkaden, Büchel 6 (02131-403 77 95).

The history of Neuss goes back to Roman days. The town developed around a Bernhardine monastery, which became a girls' boarding school in the 12th century. The most famous building is the magnificent 13th-century Romanesque **Münster St Quirinus**. After a fire in 1741, a Baroque dome with a statue of St Quirin, the patron saint, was added to the eastern tower of the church. Also worth seeing is the Obertor (upper gate), built in 1200, one of the mightiest gates in the Rhineland.

⑪ Dormagen

Road map B4. 🚏 62,000. 🚉 🚌
ℹ️ Dormagen, Schlossstrasse 2–4 (02133-276 28 15). 🎭 Freilichtspiele in Zons (Jun–Sep).

This medium-sized town, which principally relies on its chemical industry, would not be found in a guide book were it not for two remarkable historic monuments within the city limits. On the banks of the Rhine lies the fortified customs town of **Zons**, established around 1373–1400 at the instigation of archbishop Friedrich von Saarwerden. This small regular, four-sided fortress has survived in excellent condition. The buildings in the settlement are mainly from a later time, but the walls and gates, as well as the ruined castle **Schloss Friedestrom** are among the most fascinating examples of medieval fortifications in the Rhine Valley.

Equally interesting is an excursion to **Knechtsteden**, west of Dormagen, where an amazing monastery was built for the Norbertines in the 12th century. Set amid woods and orchards, the vast twin-choired basilica has mighty towers in the eastern section. There are impressive murals, including a 12th-century mural of Christ in the western apsis, as well as attractive cloisters.

The Gothic post-Cistercian Bergischer Dom in Altenberg

⑫ Solingen

Road map B4. 🚏 165,000. 🚉 🚌 ℹ️
Clemens-Galerien Mummstr. 10 (0212-290 36 01). 🎭 Frühjahrskirmes (Mar).

Solingen is almost synonymous with its famous factory, where quality scissors and knives are produced. The main attraction in town is the **Klingenmuseum**, which shows cutting tools from the Stone Age to the present day.

Environs
Remscheid, 7 km (4 miles) east of Solingen has the Röntgen-Museum, dedicated to the German Nobel Prize winner Wilhelm Röntgen, who was born here and discovered

Baroque façade of the local Heimatmuseum in Remscheid

the X-ray. One of the most beautiful buildings is the Heimatmuseum with displays of typical regional interiors.

Schloss Burg, on the Wupper river, is the 12th-century fortress of the von Berg family. Many times rebuilt, it now houses a museum.

⑬ Altenberg

Road map B4. 🚏 5,745. 🚉 🚌
ℹ️ Eugen Heinen Platz 2, Odenthal (02174-41 99 50). 🌐 altenberg-info.de

Altenberg near Odenthal has preserved its **Bergischer Dom**, a former Cistercian cathedral and one of the most important destinations for pilgrims. Built in 1259–1379, it is also one of the most beautiful Gothic buildings in Germany. In accordance with their rules, the Cistercians built the church without a tower. The interior is furnished with Gothic works of art and has stunningly beautiful stained-glass windows, the altar of the *Coronation of the Blessed Virgin Mary* from the late 15th century, a beautiful 14th-century *Annunciation* and a sacrarium (1490). After the dissolution of the Order in 1803, the cathedral suffered a turbulent history. It now serves as a church for both Catholics and Protestants.

Children also enjoy a visit to Altenberg because of its **Märchenwald** (fairy-tale wood), an enchanted forest, with interactive scenes and statues representing popular fairy tales.

⑭ Köln (Cologne)

See pp402–9.

⑮ Aachen

Road map A4. 🏛 247,000. 🚉 🚌
ℹ Friedrich-Wilhelm-Platz (0241-180 29 60). 🏇 Frühjahrsbend (Apr), horse-riding competitions CHIO (Jul), Europamarkt der Kunsthandwerker (Sep).

Aachen owes its fame to its hot springs, whose healing powers were already highly rated by the Romans when they established baths here in the 1st–2nd centuries AD. The name of the town, *aquae grani* or Aquisgrani, also relates to the source.

The settlement grew mainly in the 8th century, when Charlemagne chose it as his principal residence in 768. He built a huge palace complex with chapel, cloistered courtyard and hall for himself.

When Charlemagne was crowned emperor in 800, Aachen became the capital of the Holy Roman Empire. Although the town soon lost this title, it remained an important destination for pilgrims because of the valuable relics brought here by Charlemagne. From the 10th to the 16th centuries, all German kings were crowned in the palace chapel.

In the 18th and 19th centuries, Aachen gained great importance as a spa. Many buildings from this era have long since vanished. Further destruction was inflicted

by World War II, yet some historic monuments have survived. The most important of these, in the centre of the old town, is the **Pfalz** (*see pp400–1*), a complex of buildings belonging to Charlemagne's former palace. They include a cathedral with a palace chapel and a hall which was rebuilt as the **Rathaus**.

In the old town, not far from the cathedral complex, is the church of St Folian, where a Gothic Madonna dating from 1411 has survived. A short distance south from here stands the Elisenbrunnen (fountain of Elizabeth), an exceptionally beautiful building where mineral water can be taken. It was built in 1822–7 according to designs by Johann Peter Cremer and Karl Friedrich Schinkel.

After admiring the attractive houses around the central market square visitors can enjoy the **Couven-Museum**. Based in an historic middle-class town house, it has an interesting collection dedicated to the life of the bourgeoisie in the 18th and 19th centuries. There is also a collection of ceramic tiles from the 16th–19th centuries.

The house where Israel Berr Josaphat Reuter established the first-ever news agency in 1850 (transferred to London a year later) now houses the

Statue of David Hansemann

Internationales Zeitungsmuseum, devoted to the history of the press, with over 200,000 newspapers from the 16th century to today. The building has undergone an extensive renovation to house a temporary exhibition space and lecture halls. It is also worth visiting the **Suermondt-Ludwig-Museum**, a short distance beyond the town centre, which has a great collection of art from the Middle Ages until the present day, including some sculptures and paintings from the 17th century. To the northeast of the old town extends the spa district of Aachen. Here, visitors can stroll through the spa park or spend an evening at the casino. Aachen also has much to offer lovers of modern art: the Ludwig-Forum für Internationale Kunst hosts interesting exhibitions.

🏛 **Internationales Zeitungsmuseum**
Pontstr. 13. **Tel** (0241) 432 49 10.
Open 10am–6pm Tue–Sun. 🌐 izm.de

🏛 **Suermondt-Ludwig-Museum**
Wilhelmstr. 18. **Tel** (0241) 47 98 00.
Open noon–6pm Tue–Fri (to 8pm Wed), 11am–6pm Sat & Sun. 🐾 🖥 📷 🏛

🏛 **Couven-Museum**
Hühnermarkt 17. **Tel** (0241) 432 44 21.
Open 10am–6pm Tue–Sun (1–6pm 1st Sat of month). **Closed** public hols. 🐾

Environs
Kornelimünster, 6 km (4 miles) southeast of the centre, is a beautiful place with a well-preserved old town and churches. The most important of these is the Propsteikirche St Kornelius, a former Benedictine monastery which dates from the early 9th century. The surviving building is a 14th-century Gothic basilica, extended by the early 16th century to an imposing five-nave structure. In the 18th century the octagonal chapel of St Kornelius was added at the axis of the presbytery.

The Neo-Classical building which houses the casino in Aachen's spa park

The Pfalz in Aachen

The original palace of Charlemagne in Aachen did not survive; of his vast construction only the Pfalzkapelle (palatine chapel) remains. Modelled on the church of San Vitale in Ravenna, Italy, it was built by Odo von Metz in 786–800. In the mid-14th century a front tower was added, and in the years 1355–1414 a new presbytery was built. Side chapels were added later, and in the 17th century the central section was covered by a dome.

Charlemagne's Throne
This modest throne, fashioned from marbled tiles, served as the coronation throne for successive German leaders.

Candelabra
This copper candelabra, a masterpiece of Romanesque craftsmanship, was a gift from Emperor Friedrich I Barbarossa.

KEY

① **Ungarnkapelle**

② **Antique Columns** The arcaded ambulatory is divided by beautiful columns, made from red marble and porphyry which had been brought from Ravenna and Rome.

③ **Hubertus- and Karls-kapelle**

④ **The Gothic presbytery** was modelled on Sainte-Chapelle in Paris.

⑤ **Matthiaskapelle**

⑥ **Annakapelle**

Main entrance

Bronze doors
The doors, dating from the time of Charlemagne, are the oldest historic monument of their kind in Germany.

★ Lotharkreuz
This magnificent cross (c 1000), decorated with a cameo showing a portrait of Emperor Augustus, is one of the most valuable exhibits in the Schatzkammer.

VISITORS' CHECKLIST

Practical Information
Cathedral: Münsterplatz.
Tel (0241) 47 70 90. **Open** 7am–7pm (6pm Jan & Feb). ◪ from 10am Mon–Fri, from 1pm Sat & Sun. Treasury: Klosterplatz 2.
Tel (0241) 47 70 91 27. **Open** 10am–1pm Mon, 10am–6pm Tue–Sun (5pm Jan–Mar), 10am–9pm first Thu of month.

★ The Shrine of Charlemagne
The Emperor Charlemagne was canonized as a saint in 1165 and in 1215 his remains were placed in this gold and silver casket by Friedrich II. It is on display in the presbytery.

★ Pala d'Oro
The front of the main altar is adorned with valuable gold sheets from c.1020, which were funded by Heinrich II.

Proserpina's Sarcophagus
This sarcophagus, in the Schatzkammer (treasury), is a beautiful example of early 3rd-century Roman sculpture. It is thought that the body of Charlemagne rested in this coffin until he was canonized.

Ambo
The ambo, a pulpit fashioned from gold-plated copper and inlaid with precious stones and ivories, was donated by Heinrich II in 1014.

⑭ Cologne (Köln)

Originally founded by the Romans, Cologne (Köln) is one of the oldest towns in Germany. The Franks ruled the town from the end of the 5th century, and Charlemagne raised its status to that of an archbishopric. Cologne has remained a powerful ecclesiastical centre – it boasts 12 Romanesque churches as well as the famous Gothic cathedral. In the Middle Ages the city also played a significant role in the Hanseatic League. Present-day Cologne is known for its trade fairs and as an important centre for art and culture, with excellent museums, historic buildings and art galleries. The highest number of visitors today come for the five days preceding Ash Wednesday, to watch the grand carnival processions.

🔼 St Andreas

Komödienstrasse 4–8.
This late-Romanesque basilica was founded c.1200, with a presbytery added in 1414–20. Particularly noteworthy are the beautiful capitals, which link the pillars between the naves, and the stalls (c.1420–30).

🔼 Pfarrkirche St Mariä Himmelfahrt

Marzellenstrasse 32–40.
The parish church of the Assumption of Mary is one of the few Baroque buildings in Cologne. It was built for the Jesuit Order in 1618–89. Its Romanesque and Gothic elements are not surviving parts of an earlier building, but a consciously created link with earlier styles.

🔼 Cologne Cathedral (Kölner Dom)

See pp406–7.

Picturesque houses on Fischmarkt

⊞ Römisch-Germanisches Museum

Roncalliplatz 4. **Tel** (0221) 244 38. **Open** 10am–5pm Tue–Sun (until 10pm first Thu of month).
This building houses a number of Roman and pre-Roman archaeological finds unearthed in Cologne and the Rhine Valley. On display are weapons, ornamental and artistic objects, the superb Dionysus mosaic and the monument to Poblicius.

⊞ Museum Ludwig

Heinrich-Böll-Platz. **Tel** (0221) 22 12 61 65. **Open** 10am–6pm Tue–Sun, 10am–10pm first Thu of month. 🖼
This museum has one of Europe's best collections of modern art. There are paintings by Picasso, German Expressionists, Surrealists, American Pop Artists and the Russian Avantgarde as well as many sculptures.

🔼 Groß St Martin

An Groß St Martin 9. **Tel** (0221) 27 79 47 47. **Open** 9am–7.30pm Tue–Fri, 10am–7.30pm Sat & Sun (Aug: 2–6pm daily).
This church, with its attractive triangular presbytery and vast tower dominating Fischmarkt, was founded for the Benedictine Order in the late 12th century. The Romans built a sports arena on this site with a swimming pool, remains of which have been uncovered under the crypt. The houses in the surrounding Martinsviertel are post-World War II, however they were built to historic designs with a medieval street layout.

⊞ Farina Haus

Obenmarspforten 21. **Tel** (0221) 399 89 94. **Open** 10am–7pm Mon–Sat, 11am–5pm Sun. 🖼 🔲 farina.org
Farina Haus traces the history of fragrance. Tours lead to the over 300-year-old cellar where the Italian perfumier Johann Maria Farina first began producing Eau de Cologne, now a generic brand recognized world-wide.

Panorama with the Rathaus, Groß St Martin and the Dom, with the Rhine in the foreground

For hotels and restaurants in this area see pp500–501 and pp526–9

A detail of the Gothic section of the Rathaus façade

🏛 Rathaus

Alter Markt. **i** (0221) 22 10. **Open** 9am–3pm Mon–Thu, 9am–noon Fri. Praetorium: Kleine Budengasse. **Tel** (0221) 223 94. **Open** 10am–5pm Tue–Sun. 🎨

The town hall is an irregular shape created by successive modifications. In the first phase, around 1330, a wing with a Hanseatic Hall was built, decorated with Gothic sculptures. In 1407–14 a vast Gothic tower was added, and in the 16th century the arcaded Renaissance Lions Courtyard and a magnificent front lodge were built. From Kleine Budengasse

an entrance leads to the *Praetorium*, the remains of a Roman town hall. A controversial "archaeology zone" and Jewish museum is under construction on Rathausplatz. It will showcase the excavated Roman walls and Jewish finds, including the remains of 12th-century ritual Jewish baths that were destroyed after the expulsion of the Jews in 1424.

🏛 Wallraf-Richartz-Museum – Fondation Corboud

See pp408–9.

🏛 Gürzenich

Gürzenichstrasse.
This Gothic building has a huge celebration hall (1437–44), which occupies the entire first floor. Next to it are the ruins of the Romanesque church Alt St Alban. It has a copy of the sculpture *Parents* by Käthe Kollwitz.

⛪ Minoritenkirche Mariä Empfängnis

Minoritenstrasse.
This modest Gothic Franciscan church was established in the 13th–14th centuries. It is an elegant three-naved basilica

without a tower, modelled on the Elisabethkirche in Marburg. There are historic furnishings and a 14th-century shrine with the remains of Johannes Duns Scotus, a Scottish Minorite.

Place of remembrance, in Alt St Alban, near the Gürzenich

Cologne City Centre

0 metres 400
0 yards 400

Exploring Cologne (Köln)

🏛 Kolumba Museum

Kolumbastrasse 4. **Tel** (0221) 933 19 30. **Open** noon–5pm Wed–Mon. 🖼

Designed by Swiss architect Peter Zumthor to much critical acclaim, this museum houses the archbishopric of Cologne's collection of religious art. The building, which opened in 2007, accommodates the ruins of the late Gothic church St Kolumba; a chapel built in the 1950s to house a statue of the Madonna which miraculously escaped bombing during World War II; and a unique archeological excavation that was made in the 1970s.

🏛 Schnütgen-Museum

Cäcilienstrasse 29. **Tel** (0221) 22 12 23 10. **Open** 10am–6pm Tue–Sun (to 8pm Thu). 🖼

The Romanesque church of St Cecilia, built in 1130–60 as a nunnery, was taken over in 1479 by the Augustinian Sisters; today it houses the Schnütgen-

The Romanesque church of St Gereon, with its vast dome

Museum. Destroyed during World War II and subsequently rebuilt, this museum specializes in religious art, mainly from the Middle Ages. Its collection includes magnificent sculptures, gold and ivory items and sacral objects.

🏛 St Peter

Leonhard-Tietz-Straße 6.

The late-Gothic church of St Peter is a galleried basilica, built in 1515–39. Following its destruction in World War II, the former vaulting was replaced by a ceiling. The church's greatest attractions include its Renaissance stained-glass windows (1528–30) and the magnificent *Crucifixion of St Peter*, painted after 1637 by Peter Paul Rubens, who spent his childhood here and whose father lies buried in the church.

Detail from Stadtmuseum

🏛 St Maria im Kapitol

Marienplatz 19. **Open** 10am–6pm Mon–Sat, 1–6pm Sun.

Originally built in the early part of the 11th century, as a convent, the church's extension and remodelling took until the early 13th century. Noteworthy are its extensive crypt and the mid-11th-century wooden door in the west closure, richly carved with reliefs depicting scenes from the life of Christ. It also has a superb Renaissance rood screen, and is the only church in Cologne with cloisters.

🏛 Overstolzenhaus

Rheingasse 8.

World War II deprived Cologne of many of its historic residential buildings, but this one has been lovingly restored. Built for a prosperous patrician family in the 13th century, it is regarded as one of the town's finest Gothic houses.

🏛 St Maria Lyskirchen

An Lyskirchen 12. **Open** 10am–6pm Mon–Sat, 10am–4pm Sun.

This, the smallest Romanesque church in Cologne, was built around 1220 and slightly remodelled in the 17th century. Its greatest attractions are magnificent frescoes depicting scenes from the Bible, which adorn the vaults (c.1250), as well as the *Schöne Madonna*, a statue of the Virgin with the Infant Christ (c.1420).

🏛 Imhoff-Stollwerck-Museum (Schokoladen Museum)

Rheinauhafen 1a. **Tel** (0221) 931 88 80. **Open** 10am–6pm Tue–Fri, 11am–7pm Sat & Sun. 🖼

This fantastic museum of chocolate explains the history of cocoa bean cultivation as well as the cultural significance, use and marketing of chocolate. It also shows the production process, and lets visitors sample the product.

🏛 St Georg

Georgsplatz 17. **Open** 9am–5pm daily.

This church was built around the middle of the 11th century,

Romanesque Churches

Cologne has 12 surviving Romanesque churches, bearing testimony to the importance of the Church in the town's development. Built on the graves of martyrs and early bishops of Cologne, the forms of the churches influenced the development of Romanesque architecture well beyond the Rhineland. Almost all the churches were damaged in World War II. Some, such as the church of St Kolumba, have not been restored, but most were returned to their former glory.

Towerless westwork

Tower at the junction of the naves

Front tower

Trefoil eastern closure

St Andreas

St Aposteln

For hotels and restaurants in this area see pp500–501 and pp526–9

The attractive Romanesque church of St Kunibert, seen from the Rhine

originally as a transept basilica with two choirs. In the mid-12th century the west choir was replaced by a massive frontage, but the towers were never added.

⬆ St Pantaleon

Am Pantaleonsberg 2. **Open** 9am–5pm Mon–Sat, noon–5pm Sun.

A little way from the centre is this exquisite church, a former Benedictine monastery founded c.950 by Archbishop Bruno, brother of Emperor Otto I. The archbishop and the Empress Theophanu, who completed the building, are both buried here. The church has a superb late-Gothic choir screen with richly carved ornamentation.

▦ Severinsviertel

The Severin Quarter, a district on the southern edge of the old town, owes its name to the 13th-century Romanesque church of St Severinus. The church, largely remodelled in the Gothic style in the 15th and 16th centuries, features rich original furnishings and has a mid-10th-century crypt.

⬆ St Aposteln

Neumarkt 30. **Open** 10am–1pm, 2–5pm daily.

The vast 12th-century church of the Apostles, which towers over Neumarkt, is one of the most interesting Romanesque churches in the Rhineland. The original basilica has a trefoil eastern closure, a low tower at the junction of the naves and a tall front tower. It was given two further slim turrets flanking the apse of the presbytery.

From Neumarkt, Hahnenstrasse leads to Rudolfplatz and the Hahnentor, perhaps the most beautiful of all surviving medieval gates.

⬆ St Gereon

Gereonsdriesch 2–4. **Open** 9am–5pm daily.

This church must be the most unusual edifice in all of Germany. Its oldest part, an oval building surrounded by small conchas, was built in the late 4th century on the graves of martyrs and – according to legend – founded by St Helen. The Romanesque presbytery is an 11th-century

addition and, in 1219–27, the oval was encircled with a ten-sided, four-storey structure in early-Gothic style. This is topped with a vast dome, 48 m (157 ft) in diameter, with ribbed vault.

⬆ St Ursula

Ursulaplatz 24. **Open** 10am–noon, 3–5pm Mon–Sat, 3–4.30pm Sun.

This church was built in the 12th century, on the site of an earlier church probably dating from c.400. In the late 13th century the presbytery was rebuilt in Gothic style. The Baroque golden chamber at the southern end, added in the 17th century, is lined with many shrines. According to legend, these hold the remains of St Ursula and 11,000 virgins, all of whom were reputedly killed at the hands of the Huns. The town insignia of Cologne also testify to the veneration of the virgins.

⬆ St Kunibert

Kunibertsklostergasse 2. **Open** 10am–1pm, 3–6pm Mon–Sat, 12.30–6pm Sun.

Bishop Kunibert was buried in a church on this site in 663. The present Romanesque church (1215–47) has precious Romanesque stained-glass windows (c.1220–30).

The medieval Hahnentor, exit from Cologne towards Aachen

Tower at the junction of the nave

Biforium

Trefoil eastern closure

Groß St Martin

Stairway towers flanking the westwork (frontage)

St Pantaleon

Pair of front towers

Semi-circular apse

St Kunibert

Cologne Cathedral (Kölner Dom)

The most famous Gothic structure in Germany, the Kölner Dom is also unusually complex, whether in terms of its splendour, its size or even simply the date of its construction. The foundation stone was laid on 15 August 1248, the presbytery consecrated in 1322. The cathedral was built gradually until c.1520. It then remained unfinished until the 19th century, when Romanticists revived interest in it. The building was finally completed in 1842–80, according to the rediscovered, original Gothic designs.

Pinnacles
Elaborately decorated pinnacles top the supporting pillars.

Cathedral Interior
The presbytery, the ambulatory and the chapels retain a large number of Gothic, mainly early-14th-century, stained-glass windows.

KEY

① **Petrusportal**, or the portal of St Peter, the only one built in the second half of the 14th century, has five Gothic figures.

② **Buttresses** support the entire bulk of the cathedral.

③ **Semicircular arches** transfer the thrust of the vaults onto the buttresses.

④ **The contemporary German artist** Gerhard Richter created an abstract stained-glass collage in 2007.

Main entrance

Engelbert Reliquary (c.1630)
The cathedral treasury is famous for its large collection of golden objects, vestments and the fine ornamentation of its liturgical books.

★ Gothic Stalls
The massive oak stalls, built in 1308–11, were the largest that have ever been made in Germany.

High Altar
The Gothic altar slab, which dates back to the consecration of the presbytery, depicts the Coronation of the Virgin Mary, flanked by the twelve apostles.

★ Shrine of the Three Kings
This huge Romanesque reliquary was made by Nikolaus von Verdun in 1190–1220, to hold the relics of the Three Kings, which were brought to Cologne in 1164 for Emperor Friedrich I Barbarossa. It is decorated with scenes from the Salvation History.

★ Altar of the Magi
This splendid altar (c.1442), the work of Stephan Lochner, is dedicated to the Three Kings, the patrons of Cologne.

Mailänder Madonna
This fine early-Gothic carving of the Milan Madonna and Child dates from around 1290. It is currently displayed in the Marienkapelle.

Wallraf-Richartz-Museum & Fondation Corboud

This museum was named after Ferdinand Franz Wallraf, who bequeathed his art collection to the city in 1824, and Johann Heinrich Richartz, who funded the first building. Medieval and early modern paintings (1250 to 1550) form the core of the collection. There are also works by Rubens and Rembrandt, as well as examples from Impressionism, Realism and Symbolism. In 2001 the Wallraf-Richartz-Museum moved to a new building, incorporting many new works from the collection of Gérard Corboud.

Bleaching the Linen (1882)
Max Liebermann created this painting in the early stages of his career, when his work was largely concerned with Realism.

★ **Stigmatization of St Francis** (c.1616)
This dark and mysterious painting, originally created by Peter Paul Rubens for the Capuchin church in Cologne, is untypical of the artist's work.

Second floor

Reclining Girl (1751)
This young nude, arranged on her bed in a provocative pose, is an example of the light-hearted works of so-called "boudoir art" that François Boucher specialized in.

Foyer

★ **Fifer and Drummer** (1502–4)
This subtle painting, the wing of an altarpiece, is the work of Albrecht Dürer, who included himself in the scene – the drummer is a self-portrait of Dürer himself.

Main entrance

Gallery Guide

Each floor in the museum displays paintings belonging to one era. On the first floor, the exhibition begins with a collection of art dating from the Middle Ages; the second floor holds 17th–18th century art, and on the third floor works of art from the 19th century are displayed, organized by the schools of art they represent.

Third floor

First floor

Girls on a Bridge (1905)
Edvard Munch covered the same subject several times *(see p441)*. The version held in Cologne is one of the earliest, and features an urbanized landscape.

Jacob accuses Laban of giving him Lai instead of Rachel as a wife (1628)
This biblical scene was painted by one of the most outstanding Dutch masters, Hendrick ter Brugghen.

Old Woman and Boy
(c.1650–60)
This scene was painted by Bartolome Esteban Murillo. This artist excelled not only as the master of charmingly sentimental depictions of the Madonna, but was also an excellent observer of everyday life in 17th-century Spain.

Key
- ☐ Medieval paintings
- ☐ 17th- and 18th-century paintings
- ☐ 19th- and 20th-century paintings
- ☐ Non-exhibition space

Madonna and Child (1325–30)
This central panel of a polyptych by Simone Martini is thought to have originated from the San Agostino church in San Giminiano.

One of the artificial reservoirs in the northern Eifel

⑯ Northern Eifel

Road map A4. ℹ Kalvarienbergstr. 1,
54595 Prüm (0180) 500 22 83 🎭 Bad
Münstereifel: Burg in Flammen (Jul).

Barely 20 per cent of the Eifel
mountain range is in North
Rhine-Westphalia. Low, forested
mountains line the valley of the
Rur river, which has been
dammed in several places. The
resulting artificial lakes provide a
perfect opportunity for relaxation
and sporting activities. There are
also many attractive towns and
fascinating monuments.

Blankenheim is famed for its
picturesque half-timbered
houses, the late-Gothic church
and the frequently modified
12th-century castle of the counts
von Manderscheid-Blankenheim,
which today is a youth hostel.
The source of the Ahr river can
also be seen here – a house was
built over the top of it in 1726.

In **Schleiden**, the castle,
built in the 12th century and
frequently rebuilt up until the
18th century, is worth visiting.
There is also a late-Gothic church
with valuable stained-glass
windows and an impressive
organ dating from 1770.

Probably the most beautiful
town in this region is **Monschau**,
which until 1919 was called
Montjoie. It is known also for the
Montjoier Düttchen (croissants)
and an excellent mustard. The
ruin of a 13th-century castle
towers on a hill. At its foot, the
Rur river runs through a narrow
valley, with attractive small
towns, narrow, steep streets
and timber-frame houses from
various eras. In Hasenfeld visitors
can see a dam dating from 1904,
and an amazing hydro-electric

building, decorated in a way that
reflects its purpose. One of the
most interesting monuments of
this region is the Steinfeld
monastery, with a history
dating from the 10th century. In
1121 the Augustinians settled
here, and in 1126 they accepted
the rule of St Norbert of Xanten,
and this became the first
monastery on German territory.
A beautiful Romanesque
basilica was built in the second
half of the 12th century. It has
retained wall paintings from the
12th and 14th centuries, and
vaulted ceilings from the 16th
century. The **Rheinisches
Freilichtmuseum
Kommern** is an
open-air museum
with examples of
the building styles
typical of the
Northern Eifel. It is
also worth visiting
the town of
Euskirchen, which
has an attractive Gothic church
with superb furnishings, and
the moated castle of Veynau
(14–15th centuries). The spa
town of **Bad Münstereifel** dates

Picturesque half-timbered houses
in Monschau

back to 830, when a Benedictine
monastery was established
here. The present church is a
12th-century Romanesque
basilica with impressive
11th-century frontage. Also
worth seeing are the Gothic
town hall and a Romanesque
house, now housing a museum.

🏛 **Rheinisches Freilichtmuseum
Kommern**
Auf dem Kahlenbusch. Mechernich-
Kommern. **Tel** (02443) 998 00.
Open Apr–Oct: 9am–6pm; Nov–Mar:
10am–4pm. 🎭

⑰ Brühl

Road map B4. 🏔 42,000. 🚊 🚌
ℹ Uhlstr. 1 (02232-793 45).
🎭 Hubertusmarkt (Oct).

The small town of Brühl has one
of the most beautiful residential
complexes, since 1984 a UNESCO
World Heritage Site. As early as
the 13th century, a palace was
established here for the archbishops of nearby Cologne, but
this was destroyed in 1689. A
Baroque palace, **Augustusburg**,
was built on its foundations in
1725–8, according
to a design by
Johann Conrad
Schlaun. It was
named after the
instigator of the
building, Elector
Klemens August.
The building
was almost
immediately refurbished, with a
new façade and furnishings, the
work of François de Cuvilliés,
and in the 1940s a new staircase
was completed to a design by
Balthasar Neumann. After
devastation in World War II, the
palace was carefully restored,
and the magnificently furnished
late-Baroque and Rococo
interior, especially a stunning
dining room designed by
Cuvilliés, can now be seen
again. A path leads from the
orangery to a Gothic church
built for the Franciscans in the
15th century. The *Annunciation*
on the high altar is the work
of Johann Wolfgang van der
Auwer, while the magnificent
canopy above was designed

Merry-go-round at the
Phantasialand in Brühl

Phantasialand, one of the largest theme parks in Germany, near Brühl

by Balthasar Neumann. The castle is surrounded by a Baroque park, designed by Dominique Girard.

About 2 km (1 mile) east of the main residence is another castle, **Falkenlust**, built in 1729–40, to a design by Cuvilliés. Its captivating interior includes a lacquered and a mirror cabinet. Nearby stands an octagonal chapel, its interior decoration modelled on a secluded grotto.

It is also worth visiting the small villa near Augustusburg where the great Surrealist artist Max Ernst was born. It now houses a small display commemorating his work.

Another attraction, which draws a large number of visitors is **Phantasialand**, Germany's largest theme park. Several days are needed to see all the attractions of this vast fairground with its rollercoaster, water-rides and merry-go-rounds.

🏰 **Augustusburg**
Tel (02232) 440 00. **Open** Feb–Nov: 9am–noon & 1:30–4pm Tue–Fri, 10am–5pm Sat & Sun.

🏰 **Falkenlust**
Tel (02232) 440 00. **Open** Feb–Nov: 9am–noon & 1:30–4pm Tue–Fri, 10am–5pm Sat & Sun.

🎡 **Phantasialand**
Berggeiststr. 31–41. **Tel** (02232) 362 00. **Open** Apr–Oct: 9am–6pm daily, later in summer. 🅿

Environs
Two moated houses await the visitor at **Kerpen**, 27 km (17 miles) to the north: the small 16th-century castle of Lörsfeld, and the Baroque palace of Türnich, built in 1756–66.

In **Pulheim-Brauweiler**, 30 km (19 miles) to the north, is an extremely beautiful Benedictine monastery, founded in 1024. Building began in 1048, funded by Rycheza, the wife of the Polish King Boleslav Chrobry.

From here it is worth travelling another 23 km (14 miles) west to **Bedburg**, where the moated castle is worth seeing. This is a vast brick structure with four wings, which was established in stages over 300 years, starting in around 1300.

⑱ Bonn

See p412.

⑲ Königswinter

Road map B4. 🚶 35,000. 🚌 🚍 🛈
Drachenfelsstr. 51 (02223-91 77 11).

Königswinter lies in the centre of the Siebengebirge, an attractive range of small, wooded mountains (the "seven mountains"), excellently suited for walking. The most popular mountain is the Drachenfels (dragon's rock). The oldest mountain railway in Germany, built in 1883, takes visitors to the top (321 m/1,053 ft). During the ascent visitors can see the Neo-Gothic Drachenburg, a palace dating from 1879–84, and on the top are the ruins of the Gothic Drachenburg, dating from the 12th century. The "dragon" in the name relates to the myth of the Nibelungs – the dragon slain by Siegfried was supposed to have lived here.

The little town of Königswinter, at the foot of the mountains, has picturesque 17th-century half-timbered houses, town houses and late 19th-century hotels.

Environs
Bad Honnef, 6 km (4 miles) to the south, is a charming spa town known as "Nice on the Rhine", where the former chancellor Konrad Adenauer lived until his death. A museum commemorates this great politician.

Situated 15 km (9 miles) to the north is **Siegburg**, home to a Benedictine monastery from 1064 (closed to the public). The present church is a 17th-century building, reconstructed after World War II. The Anno-Schrein is a magnificent Romanesque reliquary box dating from 1183.

The Baroque Schloss Augustusburg in Brühl

⑱ Bonn

Bonn was founded by the Romans in 11 BC, and flourished thanks to the archbishops of Cologne. It gained fame because of Ludwig van Beethoven, who was born here in 1770, and Robert Schumann, who spent the final years of his life here. The world heard of Bonn when, on 10 May 1949, it was elevated to the status of capital of the Federal Republic of Germany. When parliament decided in 1991 to make Berlin the capital of the newly unified country, Bonn was deprived of its role, although six ministries stayed on.

The Baroque portal of the Beethovenhaus in Bonn

🏛 Beethovenhaus

Bonngasse 18–26. **Tel** (0228) 981 75 25. **Open** Apr–Oct: 10am–6pm daily; Nov–Mar: 10am–5pm Mon–Sat, 11am–5pm Sun. 🕸 🆆 **beethoven-haus-bonn.de**

The museum is housed in the Baroque 18th-century house where the composer Ludwig van Beethoven was born and lived until the age of 22. There is a large and impressive collection of memorabilia from his life.

🏛 Markt

The central market square in Bonn, shaped like a triangle, owes its present appearance to a mixture of modern and Baroque architecture. Its most outstanding feature is the late-Baroque **Rathaus** (town hall), built in 1737–8, to a design by Michel Leveilly. The centre of the market square is decorated with the Marktbrunnen, a fountain in the shape of an obelisk, erected in 1777 in honour of the Elector Maximilian Friedrich.

Not far from the Markt are some churches worth seeing. The first is the Gothic **Remigiuskirche**, built for the Franciscans in the years 1274–1317, and the second is the Baroque **Namen-Jesu-Kirche** built for the Jesuits according to a design by Jacob de Candreal in the years 1686–1717.

🏛 Rheinufer

The Rhine embankment, which changes its name several times along its course, runs along the western bank of the Rhine. Many of Bonn's attractions are grouped along this street. To the north of Kennedybrücke (Kennedy bridge) lies the Beethovenhalle, a vast concert and congress hall, and to the south of the bridge is the Bonn opera house. Next to the opera is the Alter Zoll, the former customs house, based in one of the bastions that were part of the 17th-century city defences.

🏛 Universität

Am Hofgarten.
Founded in 1818, the university is based in what is probably the most beautiful home for an educational institution anywhere in Germany. The stunningly attractive Baroque castle was built for the Elector Joseph Klemens in 1607–1705, to a design by Enrico Zuccalli, and extended after 1715 by Robert de Cotte.

🏛 Münster St Martin

Münsterplatz.
Bonn's cathedral is a magnificent example of Romanesque architecture in the Rhine Valley. The church was built in around 1150–1230, on the site of an earlier 11th-century cathedral, of which a three-naved crypt has survived. South of it, the romantic 12th-century Romanesque cloister is also worth seeing.

Gold clasps in the Rheinisches Landesmuseum

🏛 Rheinisches Landesmuseum

Colmantstrasse 14–16.
Tel (0228) 20 700.
Open 11am–6pm Tue–Fri & Sun, 1–6pm Sun. 🕸
🆆 **landesmuseum-bonn.lvr.de**

This interesting regional museum has a vast collection of excavated items dating back to Roman times, as well as medieval and modern art. The skull of a Neanderthal Man is also exhibited here.

The Baroque Elector's palace, housing Bonn University

For hotels and restaurants in this area see pp500–501 and pp526–9

🖼 Regierungsviertel

Until 1999 this was the central authority of one of the most powerful countries in Europe. Now it creates a somewhat desolate impression. Some ministries and offices have remained in Bonn, and the transfer to Berlin is under discussion, but the town is definitely changing.

The former Bundestag building, in the Regierungsviertel

🖼 Haus der Geschichte der BR Deutschland

Willy-Brandt-Allee 14. **Tel** (0228) 916 50. **Open** 9am–7pm Tue–Fri, 10am–6pm Sat & Sun.

This excellent free museum details the history of Germany after World War II, with fascinating multi-media displays. It is one of the architecturally impressive buildings which form Bonn's "Museums Mile".

🖼 Kunstmuseum Bonn

Friedrich-Ebert-Allee 2. **Tel** (0228) 77 62 60. **Open** 11am–6pm Tue–Sun, 11am–9pm Wed. **Closed** 24, 25 & 31 Dec; Sat, Sun & Mon in carnival. 🖼

This superb museum of 20th-century art, in an interesting building designed by Axel Schultes, has a great collection of Expressionist paintings, including many works by August Macke. Next to the museum is the Kunst- und Ausstellungshalle, which opened in 1992 as a venue for temporary exhibitions.

🖼 Bad Godesberg

The small spa town of Bad Godesberg was incorporated into Bonn in 1969. An elegant neighbourhood, its villas line the spa park. On top of the hill is the Godesburg, a ruined 13th-century castle.

VISITORS' CHECKLIST

Practical Information
Road map B4. 🚹 310,000.
ℹ️ Windeckstrasse 1 (0228-77 50 00). 🎭 Rhein in Flammen (1st Sat in May), Museumsmeilenfest (Jun), Beethovenfest (Sep), Jahrmarkt "Pützchens Markt" (Sep). 🆆 bonn.de

Transport
🚉 Hauptbahnhof. 🚌 ZOB.
✈️ Cologne-Bonn Konrad-Adenauer Flughafen (02203-404 001).

🖼 Poppelsdorf

This leafy southwestern suburb is home to the Baroque Schloss Clemensruhe (1715–18). Both the castle and its extensive park with an attractive botanical garden belong to the university. The Baroque pilgrimage church on the Kreuzberg, a low hill, houses the chapel of the Holy Steps, attributed to Balthasar Neumann.

The Baroque Schloss Clemensruhe, in Poppelsdorf

Bonn City Centre

① Beethovenhaus
② Markt
③ Rheinufer
④ Universität
⑤ Münster St Martin

For keys to symbols *see back flap*

The medieval Oberes Schloss in Siegen

⑳ Siegen

Road map B4. 🏠 100,000. 🚂 🚌
i Markt 2 (0271-404 13 16).
🎭 Kultur Pur (May/Jun), Rubensfest
(Jun/Jul), Weihnachtsmarkt (Dec).

Beautifully located amid the hills
on the high banks of the Sieg
river, Siegen is the largest town
in the Siegerland region. For
centuries the city was the residence of the dukes of Nassau.
Religious divisions in the family
resulted in two castles being
built in Siegen. The **Oberes
Schloss** (upper castle) is a
medieval building, frequently
refurbished in the 16th, 17th
and 18th centuries. The museum,
which has been opened inside
the castle, has some paintings
by Peter Paul Rubens, who was
born in Siegen. The lower
Unteres Schloss is a Baroque
palace, which replaced an
earlier building. In the centre
of Siegen it is also worth visiting
the **Nikolaikirche**, a 13th-
century hexagonal church

with a presbytery and tower,
which served as the ducal
family mausoleum.

Environs
In **Freudenberg**, 10 km (6 miles)
northwest of Siegen, is the
small settlement of Alter
Flecken, which is reproduced
in virtually all German guidebooks. Founded in 1666 at
the instigation of Duke Johann
Moritz von Nassau, the village
consists of identical half-
timbered houses.

㉑ Hagen

Road map B4. 🏠 210,950. 🚂 🚌
i Rathausstr. 13 (02331-207 58 94).
🎭 Marktschreiertage (Jan).

Hagen would probably not
feature in the guidebooks, were
it not for Karl Ernst Osthaus,
who created an artists' colony
here at the beginning of the
20th century, inviting Art
Nouveau designers such as
Peter Behrens and Henry van
der Velde. The magnificent
Hohenhof, Osthaus' home, was
created by van der Velde. It
houses the **Karl-Ernst-Osthaus-
Museum**, with a collection of
modern art. Behrens designed
the crematorium in the suburb
of Delstern and the beautiful
villas **Haus Cuno** (Haßleyer Str.
35) and **Haus Goedeke**
(Amselgasse). In the south of
the town is the Westfälisches

Freilichtmuseum, a popular
open-air museum, which
displays many historic
workshops and factories with
reconstructed equipment.

㉒ Sauerland

Road map B4. *i* Sauerland-Touristik,
Johannes-Hummel-Weg 1, 57392
Schmallenberg (02974-20 21 90).

The Sauerland is the region to
the south and east of the Ruhr
coalfields, making an obvious
holiday destination for the
inhabitants of this large,
industrialized conurbation.
Embracing the northern part
of the Rhenish slate massif, its
densely wooded mountains are
not high – the highest peak is
Hegekopf at 843 m (2,766 ft).
Crossed by rivers teeming with
fish and full of artificial lakes,
the area is perfect for walking,
cycling and fishing.
    Enjoyable days can be had on
an excursion to one of the caves
such as **Attahöhle, Dechen-
höhle** and **Heinrichshöhle** near
Iserlohn. There are charming
towns, too, and in **Breckerfeld**,
the Gothic parish church has
preserved a superb altar, from
around 1520. The main attraction
in **Altena** is the superb, gigantic
Burg (castle), built in the 12th
century and restored in the
early 20th century. In 1910 the
world's first youth hostel for
tourists was created here. The

One of the charming villages, nestling in the hilly landscape of the Sauerland

For hotels and restaurants in this area see pp500–501 and pp526–9

Timber-frame house, typical of the Sauerland landscape

14th-century Schloss Wocklum in **Balve** was rebuilt in the 18th century. One of the greatest tourist draws in the Sauerland is the **Möhnesee**, a lake with a huge dam, built in 1908–12 and bombed by Allied "dambusters" in 1943 with catastrophic consequences. **Arnsberg** has a regional museum and the lovely Neo-Gothic moated castle Herdringen with assorted furnishings from other castles.

In the south extend the Rothaargebirge (red-haired mountains). Their most beautiful town is the spa resort of Bad Berleburg, while the Kahler Asten mountain and the town of Winterberg are popular winter sports areas.

㉓ Soest

Road map B4. 🚗 50,000. 🚉 🚌
ℹ️ Teichsmühlengasse 3 (02921-66 35 00 50). 🎭 Bördetag (May), Gauklertag (Sep), Jahrmarkt Allerheiligenkirmes (Nov). 🌐 **soest.de**

The Westphalian town of Soest made its mark in history when, in about 1100, the town's civic rights were formulated and subsequently adopted by 65 other towns. Today the town captivates visitors with its well-preserved old town, its historic churches, and the almost completely intact walls which surround the town. The focus of the old town is the Romanesque **Propsteikirche St Patrokli**, founded in 965 by Bruno, archbishop of Cologne, and built in stages until the 13th century. Further historic buildings are grouped around the church: the 18th-century, Baroque **Rathaus** (town hall), the 12th-century Romanesque

Petrikirche with its Gothic presbytery, and the 12th-century **Nicolaikapelle**, a chapel with 13th-century wall paintings and an altar painted by Konrad von Soest.

In the northern part of the old town, two churches are worth seeing: the **Hohnekirche** with beautiful Gothic and early Baroque furnishings, and the **Wiesenkirche** with a magnificent group of stained-glass windows from the 14th and 15th centuries. The window above the northern portal shows the so-called Westphalian Last Supper, depicting a table laden with plentiful Westphalian smoked ham and local pumpernickel bread.

A 'Three Hares' window, an emblem of Paderborn

Environ
In **Lippstadt**, 23 km (14 miles) east of Soest, it is worth visiting the Gothic Marienkirche. In the suburb of Bökenförde is the 18th-century Baroque moated palace Schwarzenraben, and there is an early-Baroque castle in Overhagen.

㉔ Paderborn

Road map C3. 🚗 140,000. 🚉 🚌
ℹ️ Marienplatz 2 (05251-88 29 80). 🎭 Puppenfestspiele (Feb), Schützenfest (Jul), Liborifest (Jul–Aug), Liborikirmes (Oct).

Paderborn has featured on the historical map for over 1,000 years. In the 8th century Charlemagne built a palace here, and in about AD 800, a bishopric was established. The town's most important monument is the beautiful **Dom St Maria, St Kilian und St Liborius**, a Romanesque-Gothic cathedral. This enormous hall-church with two transepts and tall front tower suffered greatly during World War II, but it continues to captivate visitors with its magnificent decor on the richly carved portal, the great Romanesque crypt, interesting plaques and richly

decorated bishops' tombs and epitaphs. The diocesan museum holds the Imad-Madonna, funded by Bishop Imad, an outstanding figure of the Madonna and Child dating from 1051–8. On the northern side of the cathedral a section of the foundations of the emperor's palace can be seen, together with the **Bartholomäuskapelle** (chapel of St Bartholomew), the oldest hall-church in Germany, completed in 1017. To the south of the cathedral complex, on Rathausplatz, is the exceptionally beautiful **Rathaus** (town hall) dating from 1613–20.

An example of the Weser-Renaissance style, it is crowned with richly ornamented gables. The **Heinz-Nixdorf-Museumsforum** provides a pleasant break from the past – this museum is dedicated to the history of computers.

Environs
Near **Stukenbrock**, 15 km (9 miles) north of Paderborn, is the theme park Hollywood-Park and the fascinating Safariland, where more than 500 African animals roam freely.

Tower of the Romanesque-Gothic Dom in Paderborn

a Gothic church built for the Franciscans in 1248–1320.

The city's greatest attraction, however, is the magnificent **Abtei Corvey**, a monastery founded in 822. It was originally built as the church of St Stephen and St Vitus, but only the grandiose two-storey frontage completed in 885 survived. It became the model for several other churches built in Westphalia, while the main body of the church was rebuilt in the 17th century.

Front of the early-Romanesque Abtei Corvey in Höxter

㉕ Höxter

Road map C3. 🚹 35,000. 🚌 🚆
ℹ Weserstrasse 11 (05271-194 33).
🎵 Corveyer Musikwochen (May–Jun), Huxorimarkt (Sep), Kirchenmusiktage (Nov–Dec).

In a picturesque spot on the Weser river, Höxter can pride itself on its beautiful old town with many timber-frame houses, fragments of the city walls, a Renaissance **Rathaus** (town hall) from 1610, and important churches. The history of **Kilianikirche**, in the centre of the old town, goes back to the late 8th century, although in its present form it is a Romanesque building from the 11th–12th centuries. Also in the centre of Höxter is

㉖ Lemgo

Road map C3. 🚹 42,000. 🚆 🚌
ℹ Kramerstr 1. (05261-988 70).

This exceptionally pretty town was founded in 1190 by Bernhard II von Lippe. It was a member of the Hanseatic League, and had its heyday during the witch hunts of the 17th century. Today, Lemgo has numerous Renaissance monuments – it was spared during World War II, and the Gothic Nicolaikirche and Marienkirche, with Gothic wall paintings and a Renaissance organ by Georg Slegel, have survived. The pearl of the city is the beautiful **Rathaus** (town hall), built in the 15th–17th centuries. It contains an original pharmacy that is still in use.

Many timber-frame houses have also survived, the best ones in Papen-, Mittel- and Echternstrasse. The most beautiful house in Lemgo

Façade of a Renaissance pharmacy inside the Rathaus in Lemgo

is the **Hexenbürgermeisterhaus**. This "witches' mayor's house" (1571), an excellent example of Weser Renaissance, belonged to the mayor, Hermann Cothmann, who started the witch hunt. It now houses a town museum. Also worth visiting are the **Junkerhaus** (1891), the architect's home, and **Schloss Brake** (13th-16th centuries), a castle which now houses the **Weserrenaissance-Museum**.

🏛 **Weserrenaissance-Museum**
Schloss Brake. **Tel** (05261) 945 00.
Open 10am–6pm Tue–Sun. ♿

㉗ Teutoburger Wald (Teutoburg Forest)

Road map C3. ℹ Detmold, Rathaus Am Markt 5 (05231-97 73 28).
🎵 Sommerbühne (Aug), Andreas-Messe in Detmold (Nov).

A range of low mountains extending from Osnabrück through Bielefeld right up to Paderborn, the Teutoburg Forest is one of the most attractive tourist regions in Westphalia. The best base for walking and cycling holidays is **Detmold**, which has a very attractive old town with well-preserved timber-frame buildings from various periods, and the elegant Residenzschloss, the castle of the zur Lippe family. Originally medieval, the palace was rebuilt in the 16th century in the Weser-Renaissance style. The interior is composed of 17th and 19th

The picturesque Renaissance Rathaus in Höxter

◀ The Beethoven Monument on the Münsterplatz, Bonn

century furnishings. The star feature is a set of eight gobelins crafted in a Brussels workshop around 1670, showing scenes of Alexander the Great's triumphs. Furnishings from the 19th century include designs by Charles Le Brun.

Three km (2 miles) south of Detmold is the spot where in the year AD 9 Cherusko Arminius, known as Hermann, leader of the Germanic tribes, triumphed against the Roman army led by Varus. At the top of the mountain, the **Hermannsdenkmal**, a huge monument designed by Ernst von Bandel, was erected in 1838–75. It was supposed to symbolize the German struggle for unification.

Two fascinating attractions near Detmold are the **Adlerwarte Berlebeck**, an ornithological research station, where eagles and many other birds of prey can be observed, and the **Vogelpark Heiligenkirchen**, a bird park with over 2,000 varieties of birds in all shapes and sizes from all around the world.

Hermannsdenkmal, near Detmold

❷❽ Bielefeld

Road map C3. ![icon] 325,000. ![icon] ![icon]
![i] Niederwall 23 (0521-51 69 99).
![icon] Hermannslauf (Apr), Leinenweber-Markt (May), Bielefelder Kultur-Sommer (May–Sep), Sparrenburgfest (Jul), Weinmarkt (Sep), Weihnachtsmarkt (Dec).

On the edge of the Teutoburg Forest, Bielefeld owes its evolution to the production of and trading in linen. The old town is dominated by the **Sparrenburg** castle, built in the 13th century for the von Ravensberg family. In the 1500s the castle was surrounded by new fortifications including new bastions, and in the 19th century the residential part of the city was greatly extended.

The central feature of the old town is Alter Markt (old market), on which stands the

Nicolaikirche. This Gothic church suffered heavily In World War II, although the marvellous Antwerp altar (c.1520) was preserved. Nearby, on Obernstrasse, stands the **Crüwell-Haus**, an interesting late-Gothic town house from the early 16th century. The street leads to **St Jodokus-Kirche**, a late-Gothic church, whose greatest treasure is the amazing figure of the Black Madonna (c.1220). Further south is the **Kunsthalle**, a modern building with a significant collection of 20th-century art. It is also worth visiting the **Marienkirche** In the new town. Built in 1280–1330, this Gothic church holds the tomb of one of the von Ravensberg dukes (c.1320) and a high altar (c.1400) with a central Gothic section.

Environs
Picturesque **Herford**, 17 km (11 miles) north of Bielefeld, has timber-frame houses, beautiful Gothic churches and **MARTa Herford**, an art and design museum by Frank O. Gehry. In **Enger**, 21 km (13 miles) to the north, in the former church of the canons, a tomb dating from 1100 holds the remains of the Saxon Duke Widukind, buried in 807.

The spa town of **Bad Salzuflen**, with its pretty old town and spa, is ideal for relaxation.

An observation tower in the Sparrenburg complex in Bielefeld

The Wasserstrassenkreuzung (waterway junction) in Minden

❷❾ Minden

Road map C3. ![icon] 85,000. ![icon] ![icon]
![i] Domstrasse 2 (0571-829 06 59).
![icon] Klassik Open-Air (Jul/Aug).

Charlemagne created a bishopric here as early as 798. The town evolved thanks to its strategic location on the Weser river. The city's most important monument is the cathedral, **Dompfarrkirche St Petrus und St Gorgonius**. It has a Romanesque presbytery, transept and monumental frontage built in the 11th–12th centuries, although the body of the church is an example of early-Gothic style from the 13th century. It is worth visiting the church treasury with its 11th-century crucifix.

The **Rathaus** (town hall), with 13th-century lower sections, is worth seeing, as are Minden's many charming houses around the market square. A great attraction is the **Wasserstrassenkreuz** (waterway junction), where a 375-m (1,230 ft) long bridge takes the Mittellandkanal across the Weser river.

Environs
On top of a hill in **Porta Westfalica**, 6 km (4 miles) south of Minden, is a giant monument to Kaiser Wilhelm (1892–6) by Bruno Schmitz.

The **Westfälische Mühlenstrasse**, (Westphalian mill route), signposted around Minden, takes visitors past 42 different mills and windmills.

NORTHERN GERMANY

RATS ∴ APOTHEKE

Northern Germany at a Glance

Northern Germany has very varied landscapes, ranging from the sandy beaches on the Baltic and North Sea coasts to the moraine hills of Schleswig-Holstein and the moorlands of the Lüneburger Heide. Nature-lovers are enchanted by the countless lakes in Mecklenburg and the Harz mountains, while those interested in history or architecture enjoy the Renaissance castles along the Weser River and the Gothic brick architecture in former Hanseatic towns. Historic buildings in Goslar and Hildesheim testify to the importance of these two towns.

Locator Map

Helgoland is a popular tourist destination. Red cliffs as high as skyscrapers, a picturesque town and the sea aquarium are the star attractions of this island.

Niebüll

Flens

Schleswig

SCHLESWIG-HOLSTEIN
(See pp458–69)

Cuxhaven

Itzehoe

Elmshorn

Wilhelmshaven

Bremerhaven

Emden

Leer

Oldenburg

Bremen

Solt

Cloppenburg

LOWER SAXONY HAMBURG AND BREMEN
(See pp428–57)

Meppen

Nienburg

Lingen

Bramsche

Osnabrück

Hanover

Oldenburg, symbolized by its heraldic shield, is famous for its large collection of paintings and interiors in its Kunstmuseum (art museum).

Bremen, a historic harbour town, draws visitors with its many historic buildings and monuments, including a Renaissance-Gothic town hall.

◀ Handsome period buildings in Neuer Markt, Rostock

Fehmarn, one of the largest of the German islands, is linked with the German mainland by a railway bridge constructed in 1963.

Rügen enchants visitors with its chalky white cliffs, which contrast starkly with the deep blues and greens of the surrounding Baltic Sea.

Kiel

Oldenburg

Stralsund

eumünster

Greifswald

Rostock

Wismar

MECKLENBURG-LOWER POMERANIA
(See pp470–85)

Lübeck

amburg

Schwerin

Neubrandenburg

Ludwigslust

Neustrelitz

Lüneburg

0 kilometres   50

0 miles   50

Uelzen

Lübeck suffered massive damage in World War II, but its Gothic town hall survived the attacks and the city's beautiful old town has been rebuilt.

Celle

Wolfsburg

Brunswick

ildesheim

Goslar

Hamburg not only has attractive museums and valuable monuments, but also such lively and bustling places as the Fischmarkt, a huge market held every Sunday morning where it is possible to purchase virtually anything.

Gothic Brick Architecture

Brick was used as a building material in many parts of medieval Europe, but in Northern Germany it gave rise to the distinctive style of *Backsteingotik* (brick Gothic). Brick technology was introduced in the mid-12th century by Norbertine monks arriving from Lombardy. The style is characterized by a rich variety of vaults, the use of buttresses instead of supporting arches, and colourful designs achieved by using glazed bricks. Through trade and the activities of religious orders these forms spread throughout the Baltic region.

The storeys are divided by friezes.

The eastern façade of many churches, such as the Marienkirche in Prenzlau *(above)* was often crowned by an elaborate, ornamental gable.

Marienkirche in Lübeck

Considered the crowning achievement of Backsteingotik, this church, built from around 1260, became the model for countless others, including the cathedral in Schwerin. It is a triple-naved basilica, with a twin-towered façade, braced with buttresses.

A pointed arched portal, decorated with ceramic borders, was a typical feature of many village churches.

Main portal

Gables with tiled decorations and intricate openwork, such as this gable of the south chapel of the Nikolaikirche in Wismar, are a feature of many Lower Pomeranian churches.

The vast twin-towered façade symbolizes the power of its founders – wealthy Lübeck patricians.

Terracotta tiles with raised decorative motifs were used in brick architecture in place of stone bas-reliefs.

Turret for smallest church bell

The arcades between the naves are tall and narrow, culminating in acutely pointed arches.

Complex star vaulting with intricate ribbing replaced the earlier cross-ribbed vaulting.

Flying buttresses are rare in brick-built churches.

Stepped walls were used to dress the façades of the church. They were an important element in the construction.

Beam openings indicate that a robust type of scaffolding was used in the course of construction. The ends of the beams are incorporated in the walls.

Secular Brick Architecture

Brick architecture was not confined to churches – this style was used in magnificent town halls, weigh-houses, gateways and houses, mostly on narrow plots, with elaborate gables decorated with glazed bricks and white plasterwork.

Gothic house on the market square in Greifswald

Friezes on the arcades, such as this interlaced motif made from brick, are frequently used as a decorative element, even in village churches.

The German Coastline

The waters of two seas – the North Sea and the Baltic Sea – lap on northern Germany's shores, linked by the Kiel Canal, which cuts across the base of the Jutland peninsula. The cool climate on the coast makes for short summers yet, on a sunny day, the beaches are packed with holidaymakers, and a holiday here can have alot to offer. Heiligendamm was the first seaside resort to be established in Germany, in 1783 by a duke of Mecklenburg. By the end of the 19th century, spas with elegant villas, promenades and piers were springing up everywhere. A popular attraction are the *Strandkörbe* – huge wickerwork beach chairs.

The sand dunes form part of a nature reserve in the northern part of Sylt, the largest of the North Frisian islands.

The Cliffs of Helgoland have a characteristic reddish hue indicating the red sandstone from which they are composed.

NORDFRIESISCHE INSELN

Sylt

NORDFRIESLAND

Flensburg

199

199 201

201

Schleswig

76 • Kiel

Rendsburg

203

20

Helgoland

205

23 77

Neumünster

NORDSEE (NORTH SEA)

5

Itzehoe

206

21

E234/27

73

Elmshorn •

E4517

OSTFRIESLAND

72

495

73

• Pinneberg

Wilhelmshaven •

• Bremerhaven

• Hamburg

210

72

436

437

71

71

• Reinbek

Emden •

31

74

E22/1

E22/28

29

E22/A7

70

Oldenburg •

72

Borkum, one of the East Frisian islands, was once inhabited by whalers. Garden fences were often constructed from whale bones, and some have survived to the present day.

The Kiel Canal, known in Germany as the Nord-Ostsee-Kanal, was constructed in 1887–95. Around 40,000 vessels pass through the canal every year.

Bremerhaven is a vast port at the mouth of the Weser river. It was constructed from 1827 to support the port of Bremen, which is located farther inland, away from the sea.

Stralsund, a Hanseatic harbour town with a medieval layout, has a large number of well-preserved historic monuments.

On the small, flat island of Hiddensee all car traffic is banned. The island was much loved by the writer Gerhart Hauptmann, who lies buried here in the local cemetery.

The Coastline

The hinterland of the Baltic region is generally flat and sandy, but in some areas it is steep and rocky. For visitors the greatest draw are the islands: Rügen with its steep chalky cliffs, Usedom with its wide, sandy beaches and Hiddensee. Off the lowlands and the marshy coastal region in the hinterland of the North Sea coast extends the chain of Frisian islands.

The beach at Ahlbeck and the pier with its restaurant are the greatest attractions on the island of Usedom, at the mouth of the Oder river.

OSTSEE (BALTIC SEA)

•Bergen
RÜGEN

Stralsund

ODERBUCHT

Ribnitz-
- Damgarten

LÜBECKER
BUCHT

•Rostock

•Greifswald

Wismar

Anklam•

Güstrow

Uckermünde•

Schwerin

Rügen, famous for its unusual chalky cliff formations, was immortalized by Caspar David Friedrich and continues to inspire artists.

0 km   60
0 miles   60

Cross-Section of Watt (North Sea)

The Watt is a flat, boggy stretch of coastline, up to several kilometres wide, that is covered by the sea as the tide comes in, and laid bare as it goes out again. The Watt landscape is fairly monotonous, but it is fascinating to observe the rich flora and fauna, which has adapted to cope with life both underwater and exposed to the air.

Winkles and other small snails live in the coastal zone by the sea.

Starfish   Lugworm and sand cast   Sand gaper (mussel)

LOWER SAXONY, HAMBURG AND BREMEN

Three federal states – Lower Saxony and the independent city states of Hamburg and Bremen – cover an enormous terrain, embracing the whole of northwestern Germany. For the visitor they provide a series of memorable snapshots: the mighty cosmopolitan port of Hamburg, enchanting towns and villages with half-timbered houses and the blooming heather of the Lüneburger Heide.

Lower Saxony was formed in the 19th century through the merging of the kingdom of Hanover with the duchy of Brunswick, Oldenburg and Schaumburg-Lippe and other parts of northern Germany. The second-largest German state after Bavaria, it only ranks fourth in terms of the number of its inhabitants, being less densely populated than other states.

Lower Saxony is characterized by lowlands that become hillier in the south, culminating in the Harz Mountains. The only large cities are Hanover, a modern centre renowned for its trade fairs and for hosting Expo 2000, and Brunswick (Braunschweig), a venerable town that cherishes its link with the Saxon king Heinrich der Löwe, its first important ruler. The

Romanesque splendour of Hildesheim is a magnet for visitors, as are the Renaissance centres along the Weser River including Hameln, the charming towns of Celle, Lüneburg and Einbeck, and Wolfenbüttel, Stadthagen and Bückeburg which contain some remarkable Mannerist works of art.

Nature lovers will enjoy excursions to the Lüneburger Heide or paddling in the endless expanses of mud-flats in the North Sea. Tourists are also attracted by the sandy beaches of the East Frisian islands, as well as the solitary rock of the island of Helgoland.

The "free and Hanseatic" towns of Hamburg and Bremen rejoice in a different atmosphere, urban and urbane, tolerant and multicultural, based on centuries of trade with the world.

The glorious moorlands of the Lüneburger Heide, with tall juniper bushes and flowering heathers

◀ Statue of Roland in front of the town hall in Bremen

Exploring Lower Saxony, Hamburg and Bremen

Hamburg and Bremen, the region's largest cities, are also the most convenient bases for tourists, offering accommodation in every price category. The most attractive area in this region is the southeastern section, extending to the foothills of the Harz Mountains with picturesque towns, such as the university town of Göttingen, Romanesque Hildesheim or the stunningly beautiful merchant town of Goslar. A visit to the seaside and an excursion to the islands are also enjoyable.

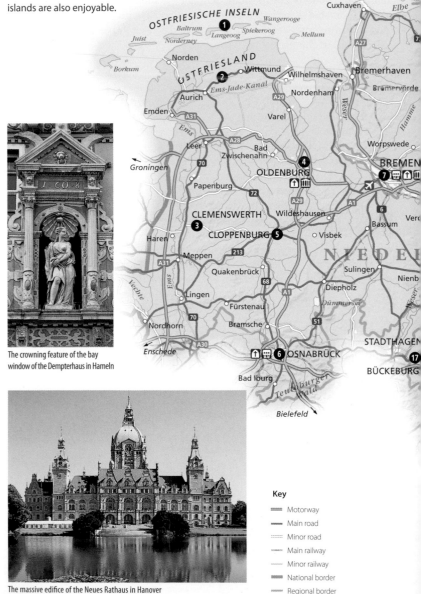

The crowning feature of the bay window of the Dempterhaus in Hameln

The massive edifice of the Neues Rathaus in Hanover

Key

≡ Motorway

— Main road

···· Minor road

— Main railway

— Minor railway

▪▪▪ National border

— Regional border

For additional map symbols *see back flap*

Getting Around

There are international airports in Hamburg, Bremen and Hanover. A network of motorways links Lower Saxony with Scandinavia (via Schleswig-Holstein), and with the rest of western Europe (via the Netherlands or southern Germany). An extensive rail network makes the entire state accessible, although bus connections are limited.

The Grosse Wallanlagen Park in Hamburg, laid out along the city's former fortifications

Sights at a Glance

1 Ostfriesische Inseln (East Frisian Islands)
2 Ostfriesland (Eastern Frisia)
3 Clemenswerth
4 Oldenburg
5 Cloppenburg
6 Osnabrück
7 *Bremen pp434–7*
8 *Hamburg pp438–43*
9 Altes Land
10 Stade
11 Lüneburg
12 Lüneburger Heide
13 Soltau
14 Celle
15 Wolfsburg
16 Stadthagen
17 Bückeburg
18 Brunswick (Braunschweig)
19 Wolfenbüttel
20 *Hannover (Hanover) pp448–9*
21 *Hildesheim pp452–3*
22 *Goslar pp454–5*
23 Einbeck
24 Göttingen
25 Duderstadt

Tours

26 The Weser Renaissance Trail

❶ Ostfriesische Inseln (East Frisian Islands)

Road map B2. 🚢 Emden-Borkum, Norden-Norddeich to Juist and Norderney, Nessmersiel-Baltrum, Bensersiel-Langeoog, Neuharlingersiel-Spiekeroog, Harlesiel-Wangerooge. 🚹 Leer, Ledastr. 10. (0491) 91 96 96 60. 🔲 **ostfriesland.de**

Moormuseum in Elisabethfehn, Ostfriesland

Along the North Sea Coast extends the belt of East Frisian Islands consisting of, from west to east: Borkum, Juist, Norderney, Baltrum, Langeoog, Spiekeroog and Wangerooge. All around them is the **Nationalpark Niedersächsisches Wattenmeer**, a large national park established to protect the unique ecosystem of the shallow seas. At low tide it turns into vast mud-flats, extending to the horizon. This is the time to tour the Watt, as it is known locally, either by horse-drawn carriage or barefoot – always making sure to return before the tide comes in!

The islands themselves, with their beautiful sandy beaches, sand dunes and healthy climate, are among the most popular holiday destinations in Germany.

The car-free island Juist, a 17-km (11-mile) strip of land less than 500 m (1,640 ft) wide, and Norderney with its main town of the same name are the most interesting islands. Neo-Classical villas recall the days when such figures as Heinrich Heine and Otto von Bismarck spent their holidays here. It is also worth

visiting Wangerooge, another island where cars are banned. Three lighthouses – Westturm, Alter Leuchtturm and Neuer Leuchtturm – indicate the island's role in the navigation of the Weser River estuary.

❷ Ostfriesland (East Frisia)

Road map B2. 🚆 Emden, Leer, Norden. 🚹 (0491) 91 96 96 60. 🎭 Kiewittmarkt (Jever, end Mar); Altstadtfest (Jever, Aug). 🔲 **ostfriesland.de**

East Frisia is a peninsula near the border with the Netherlands and the Jadebusen bay, at Wilhelmshaven. This is a land of flat meadows, grazing cows and windmills.

Emden, the region's capital, has an attractive town hall resembling that in Antwerp, and a town centre crossed by many canals. The **Kunsthalle Emden**, founded in the early 1990s by Henri Nannen, publisher of the magazine *Stern*, holds a remarkable collection of 19th-century paintings, including the works of many German Expressionists such as Emil Nolde, Max Beckmann and Oskar Kokoschka.

Another attraction is the **Moor- und Fehnmuseum** (moor and fen museum) in Elisabethfehn, which is dedicated to the extraction of peat. Its exhibits include the world's largest plough, as well as the story of Jever, the local beer. Also worth visiting are the Renaissance palace whose reception hall

has a ceiling with sunken panels, and next to the parish church the wood and stone tomb of the Frisian leader Edo Wiemken, made in 1561–4 by master craftsmen from Antwerp.

🏛 **Kunsthalle Emden**
Hinter dem Rahmen 13. **Tel** (04921) 975 00. **Open** 10am–5pm Tue–Fri, 11am–5pm Sat & Sun; 10am–9pm first Tue of month. 🅿

🏛 **Moor- und Fehnmuseum**
Oldenburger-Str. 1. **Tel** (04499) 22 22. **Open** Apr–Oct: 10am–5pm Tue–Sun.

❸ Clemenswerth

Road map B2. 🚆 Sögel or Lathen. 🚹 Papenburg, Rathausstr. 2 (04961-839 60). Schloss: **Tel** 05952-93 23 25. **Open** Apr–Oct: 10am–6pm Tue–Sun. **Closed** winter.

Emsland, to the south of East Frisia, extends along the Dutch border, a poor area since time immemorial, with moors and boglands. Only the discovery of oil in the 20th century engineered its progress. Sögel, 33 km (21 miles) south of Greater Papenburg, has the region's greatest attraction, the palatial hunting lodge or Schloss Clemenswerth, built from 1737–49. In search of solitude, the elector and archbishop of Cologne Clemens August commissioned the lodge from Johan Conrad Schlaun. The design was modelled on the pavilion-pagoda of Nymphenburg in Munich. Altogether it comprises seven pavilions with mansard roofs and a chapel. All the brick buildings were laid out on a green lawn, creating a star shape around the palace. Inside there is a museum of the region.

Nationalpark Niedersächsisches Wattenmeer in the Greefsiel area

❹ Oldenburg

Road map B2. 160,000.
Kleine Kirchenstr. 10 (0441 36 16 13 66). Hafenfest (7 days after Whitsun); Altstadtfest (end Aug); Kramermarkt (Sep/Oct).
oldenburg.de

A thousand years old, and once part of Denmark, this town remained the seat of a duchy until 1918.

The **Lambertikirche**, in the central market square, is a late-Gothic hall-church with a Neo-Classical rotunda added in 1797. The **Schloss**, the ducal residence, displays a similar marriage of styles, particularly Baroque and Neo-Classical. The **Landesmuseum für Kunst und Kulturgeschichte** (state museum of art and culture), based in the castle, is known mainly for its collection of paintings assembled by Wilhelm Tischbein, who lived here for 25 years. The affiliated **Augusteum**, a Neo-Renaissance building in a picturesque spot, holds the museum's modern collection.

▥ Landesmuseum für Kunst und Kulturgeschichte
Damm 1. **Tel** (0441) 220 73 00.
Open 10am–6pm Tue–Sun.
Closed 1 Jan, Good Friday, Easter, 1 May, 24, 25 & 31 Dec.

Environs
The town of **Bad Zwischenahn** is worth a visit. Its star attraction is the Gothic St Johanniskirche with frescoes from 1512.

A windmill in the open-air museum in Cloppenburg

❺ Cloppenburg

Road map B3. 29,000. Eschstr. 29 (04471-152 56). Mariä Geburtsmarkt (Sep).

The small market town of Cloppenburg boasts the **Museumsdorf**, the oldest open-air museum in Germany, established in 1934. On a vast site, 50 architectural monuments from all over Lower Saxony have been assembled. There are houses, including charming examples of the half-timbered style of Wehlburg, windmills and a small 17th-century church from Klein-Escherde near Hildesheim.

To the east of Cloppenburg lies Visbek. Here the visitor is taken back to the

Stone Age, with megalithic graves from 3,500 to 1,800 BC, including the 80-m (262-ft) long grave known as "Visbeker Bräutigam" (bridegroom) and the even larger, 100-m (321-ft) long "Visbeker Braut" (bride).

▥ Museumsdorf Cloppenburg
Bether Strasse 6. **Tel** (04471) 948 40.
Open Mar–Oct: 9am–6pm daily, Nov–Feb: 9am–4:30pm daily.

❻ Osnabrück

Road map B3. 157,000.
Bierstr. 22–23 (0541-32 32 202). Herbstjahrmarkt (early Nov).
osnabrueck.de

This Westphalian town has been a bishop's see since the time of Charlemagne. In 1648, negotiations took place here between representatives of Sweden and the Protestant duchies of the Reich. The signing of the Peace of Westphalia in 1648, which ended the Thirty Years' War, was announced from the town hall steps. It was also the birthplace of the writer Erich Maria Remarque in 1899.

Epitaph for Albert von Bevessen in the Dom in Osnabrück

Despite damage in World War II, **Dom St Peter**, Osnabrück's 13th-century cathedral, is worth visiting. It has a bronze baptismal font and enormous triumphal cross, and the late-Gothic Snetlage-Altar of the Crucifixion. From here a short walk takes the visitor to the market square, Marienkirche and the Gothic **Rathaus** (town hall), with a sculpture of Charlemagne.

Environs
South of Osnabrück is the western part of the Teutoburger Wald (Teutoburg Forest). The spa town of **Bad Iburg**, 12 km (8 miles) to the south of Osnabrück, has a monumental Benedictine monastery and bishop's palace. The Rittersaal (knights' hall) has a giant ceiling fresco depicting an architectural fantasy of fore-shortened perspectives.

The Schloss in Oldenburg, featuring Baroque and Neo-Classical styles

❼ Bremen

Bremen, together with its deep-water port Bremerhaven, constitutes a separate town state. Not so much a bustling modern metropolis as a peaceful country town, it is conscious of its historical origins dating back to Charlemagne. The townscape is not dominated by the port as in Hamburg, but by the old town with its magnificent cathedral and town hall. Bremen enjoyed prosperity from 1358 when it joined the Hanseatic League, its wealth based on the coffee and wool trade. Today, Bremen still benefits from its port, which ships around 700,000 cars a year.

Statue of the Bremen Town Musicians, by Gerhard Marcks

🏛 Rathaus

Marktplatz. **Tel** (0421) 30 80 00.
⏰ 11am, noon, 3pm, 4pm Mon–Sat, 11am–noon Sun. 🎫

The original Gothic building dating from 1405–10 was clad with a magnificent façade, one of the finest examples of Weser Renaissance architecture in northern Germany, designed by Lüder von Bentheim. He masterfully incorporated the Gothic figures of Charlemagne and seven Electors, as well as four prophets and four wise men. In the 40-m (131-ft) Große Halle (great hall) new laws were passed, as symbolized by the fresco (1932) of Solomon's court. Other Rathaus treasures include the Renaissance spiral staircase. On the western side of the town hall is the entrance to the "Ratskeller" where you can sample 600 different wines, and delight in the murals from 1927, by the Impressionist Max Slevogt.

Gabled houses and the statue of Roland in the Marktplatz

Exploring Bremen

Most of Bremen's tourist attractions are in the old town, on the east bank of the Weser River. The area is easy to pick out on a map as it is surrounded by a green belt, established when the town's fortifications were demolished. The Übersseemuseum (ethnography museum) is close to the old town, and trams run to Schwachhausen, where the Focke-Museum is based.

🏛 Marktplatz

On the main square of medieval Bremen stand the town hall and the cathedral, and, on the west side, several gabled houses. This lovely view is slightly marred by the unattractive 1960s Haus der Bürgerschaft, the state parliament building.

In front of the town hall stands a 10-m (32-ft) statue of Roland, dating from 1404. It is the largest of many similar statues in German towns, and the prototype for others. A nephew of Charlemagne, Roland symbolizes a town's independence. His gaze is

directed toward the cathedral, the residence of the bishop, who frequently sought to restrict Bremen's autonomy. Roland's sword of justice symbolizes the judiciary's independence, and the engraved motto confirms the emperor's edict, conferring town rights onto Bremen.

The second, more recent (1953) monument in the square is dedicated to the Bremen Town Musicians – a donkey, dog, cat and cockerel, who according to the Grimm fairy tale trekked to Bremen.

🏛 Schütting

Marktplatz.

On the southwestern side of Marktplatz stands this mansion used by the Merchants' Guild

The late-Renaissance façade of Bremen's Rathaus

For hotels and restaurants in this area see pp501–502 and pp529–31

for their conventions. It was built in 1537–9 by the Antwerp architect Johann der Buschener in Dutch Mannerist style. The eastern gable, more classically Renaissance, is the work of the local builder Carsten Husmann.

🏛 Dom

Tower and "Bleikeller": **Tel** (0421) 36 50 40. **Open** Apr–Oct: 10am–5pm (tower ascent to 4:30pm) Mon–Fri, 10am–2pm (tower ascent to 1:30pm) Sat, 2–5pm Sun.

This magnificent Romanesque cathedral, with its vast twin-towered façade, dates from the 11th century and has been extensively refurbished. At the end of the 19th century, while the southern tower was rebuilt, the façade was also reconstructed and a tower

The Mannerist Schütting, a meeting place for merchants

was added. Inside, it is worth looking at the sandstone bas-reliefs which divide the western choir stalls as well as fragments of Gothic stalls that were destroyed in the 19th century, with scenes of the Passion and the battle of Judas Machabeus. There is also a Baroque pulpit paid for by Christina the Queen of Sweden in 1638, and numerous

multi-coloured memorials, including one to Segebad Clüver by the entrance to the north tower (1457). The larger eastern crypt has interesting Romanesque capitals, while in the second eastern crypt visitors can admire the oldest Bremen sculpture of Christ the Omnipotent (1050) as well as the baptismal font. The latter has 38 bas-reliefs, and a bowl supported by four lions with riders. In the so-called "Bleikeller" (lead cellar) underneath the former church cloisters, eight perfectly preserved mummies are on show.

VISITORS' CHECKLIST

Practical Information
Road map: C2. 🚇 556,000. 🛈 Hauptbahnhof & Obernstrasse (01805 10 10 30). 🚢 Port tours (0421-33 89 89). Cruises: May–Sep: 10 & 11:30am, 1:30 & 3:15pm daily. 🎭 🛒 Sat & Sun. 🎪 6 Tage Rennen (Jan); Osterwiese (Apr); Vegesack Harbour Festival (Jun); Bremer Freimarkt (late Oct/early Nov); Christmas market (1–23 Dec). 🆆 **bremen-turismus.de**

Transport
🚇

Bas-reliefs on the western choir stalls in the Dom

Bremen Town Centre

① Marktplatz
② Rathaus
③ Dom
④ Schütting
⑤ Böttcherstrasse
⑥ Schnoorviertel
⑦ Kunsthalle
⑧ Überseemuseum

0 yards   500

🎫 Kunstsammlungen Böttcherstrasse Paula-Modersohn-Becker-Museum and Roseliushaus

Böttcherstr. 6–10. **Tel** (0421) 338 8222. **Open** 11am–6pm Tue–Sun. **w** pmbm.de

This once insignificant lane where coopers lived was transformed into Art Deco style in 1926–30 by Ludwig Roselius, a wealthy coffee merchant. The National Socialists preserved the street as an example of degenerate art. At the entrance to the street is a bas-relief by Bernhard Hoetger from 1920, of the Archangel Michael fighting a dragon.

The **Paula-Modersohn-Becker-Museum**, built in the Expressionist style, contains an art museum, while in the neighbouring 16th-century **Roseliushaus** the original period interiors can be admired. The street's other attraction is a carillon which chimes tuneful melodies every day at noon, 3pm and 6pm.

🎫 Schnoorviertel

Spielzeugmuseum: Schnoor 24. **Tel** (0421) 32 03 82. **Open** 10am–6pm daily.

This historic district of small houses dates from the 15th–18th centuries. One of Bremen's poorest areas before World War II, it miraculously escaped destruction. It has been restored gradually since 1958 and now

Archangel Michael fighting a dragon, on a bas-relief in Böttcherstrasse

teems with restaurants, cafés, souvenir shops and tourists. In the centre of the district is the Gothic **Johanniskirche**, which once belonged to the Franciscans. In accordance with the order's rules it has no tower, although this is compensated for by a decorative gable on the western façade, and three levels of arched alcoves and herringbone brickwork. The **Spielzeugmuseum** (toy museum) nearby is also worth visiting.

🎫 Kunsthalle

Am Wall 207. **Tel** (0421) 32 90 80. **Open** 10am–9pm Tue, 10am–5pm Wed–Sun. **w** kunsthalle-bremen.de

This art gallery on the edge of the old town lost most of its collection to Russia during World War II. The pieces that remained, as well as works subsequently acquired, make the collection of great importance. There are

works by Dürer, Altdorfer, Rubens, Jan Breughel, van Dyck and Rembrandt. There is also an excellent French section, with works by Delacroix, Denis, Monet and Manet, as well as 19th- and 20th-century German painters such as Beckmann and Kirchner. At the heart of the collection are about 40 paintings by Paula Modersohn-Becker.

🎫 Übersee-Museum

Bahnhofplatz 13. **Tel** (0421) 160 38 101. **Open** 9am–6pm Tue–Fri, 10am–6pm Sat & Sun.

This museum of overseas countries transports the visitor to faraway destinations. Founded in 1891, it was originally a museum of German colonialism and is now dedicated to the culture of non-European nations. Of special interest are exhibits on Pacific cultures, with life-sized models of houses and boats from the Solomon Islands.

🎫 Focke-Museum

Schwachhauser-Heerstr. 240. **Tel** (0421) 699 60 00. **Open** 10am–9pm Tue, 10am–5pm Wed–Sun.

The excellent collections of this museum compensate for its distant location. Founded in 1918, when the history museum was amalgamated with the decorative arts museum, it presents Bremen's art and culture from the Middle Ages to the present day. Exhibits from patrician houses and original sculptures from the façade of the town hall testify to the wealth of the Hanseatic town. Other sections are devoted to the archaeology of the region as well as to whaling and emigration to the US in the 19th and 20th centuries.

The nearby Rhododendronpark offers a pleasant respite from the museums. It includes 1,600 varieties of rhododendron which become a sea of flowers from late April to June.

Environs

Three places in the Bremen area are particularly worth a detour. About 50 km (31 miles) to the north lies Bremen's deep-sea harbour **Bremerhaven**, with the **Deutsches Schifffahrtsmuseum**.

Camille Pissarro, *Girl lying on a grassy slope*, Kunsthalle

Paula Modersohn-Becker (1876–1907)

A pupil of Fritz Mackensen and wife of Otto Modersohn, Paula Modersohn-Becker was the most significant artistic figure in Worpswede. She learned about the Impressionist use of colour

during visits to Paris, and her own unique sensibility made her a precursor of Expressionism. She became famous for her naturalistic paintings of poor, starving and even dying country folk. She died in childbirth, aged only 31, and this is how she was commemorated on her tombstone, in the peaceful village cemetery in Worpswede, by the sculptor Bernhard Hoetger.

Girl playing a flute in birch woods (1905)

Exhibits in the Große Kunstschau in Worpswede near Bremen

This wonderful marine museum, designed by the renowned architect Hans Scharoun, displays both originals and models of a wide range of ships, dating from the Roman Empire to the present day. A special hall displays the *Hanse Kogge*, a merchant ship dredged from the bottom of the Weser River in 1962. Displayed outside, in the open-air part of the museum, are the last great German sailing boat *Seute Deern*, the polar ship *Grönland* and *Wilhelm Bauer*, a U-boat from World War II.

The small village of **Worpswede**, northeast of Bremen, takes the visitor into the world of art. From 1889 until the end of World War II it was a famous artists' colony, situated in the middle of peat bogs. Apart from poets, such as Rainer Maria Rilke, and such architects as Bernhard Hoetger, the fame of this village rested principally on the painters: Fritz Mackensen, Otto Modersohn, Hans am Ende, Fritz Overbeck and Heinrich Vogeler. Unquestionably the greatest artist in Worpswede was Paula Modersohn-Becker, whose sad fairy-tale world of rustic subjects cannot be defined within one style. Work by the founding members is on display in the **Große Kunstschau and the Worpsweder Kunsthalle**.

Verden an der Aller, the picturesque bishops' residence and once a free town of the Reich, is known to sports enthusiasts thanks to its horse-racing tracks, training centres and stadiums, and the **Deutsches Pferdemuseum** (horse museum), with a large collection of equestrian artifacts. Seven horse auctions are held in the town each year, the main ones being in April and October.

Above the town rises the Dom with a large, steep roof. The hall of this cathedral, a modification of earlier basilicas, is architecturally interesting, with a multi-sided presbytery, a passageway dating from 1268–1311 and Romanesque cloisters and a tower. North of the cathedral is the Domherrenhaus, housing the Historisches Museum, with exhibits on regional history and archaeological and ethnographic departments.

The **Deutsches Auswandererhaus Bremerhaven** traces the history of more than 7 million Germans who emigrated via Bremerhaven, especially to the United States.

🏛 Deutsches Schifffahrtsmuseum
Bremerhaven, Hans-Scharoun-Platz 1. **Tel** (0471) 482 070. **Open** 10am–6pm daily (Nov–Feb: Tue–Sun only). 🅿

🏛 Große Kunstschau
Worpswede. Lindenallee 3 & 5. **Tel** (04792) 13 02. **Open** 10am–6pm daily (closed Mon in Nov–Mar) 🅿

🏛 Worpsweder Kunsthalle
Worpswede, Bergstr. 17. **Tel** (04792) 12 77. **Open** Apr–Oct: 10am–6pm daily; Nov–Mar: 11am–6pm daily. 🅿

🏛 Deutsches Pferdemuseum
Verden, Holzmarkt 9. **Tel** (04231) 80 71 40. **Open** 10am–5pm Tue–Sun.

🏛 Deutsches Auswandererhaus Bremerhaven
Columbusstr. 65. **Tel** (0471) 90220-0. **Open** Mar–Oct: 10am–6pm daily; Nov–Feb: 10am–5pm daily. Ⓦ **dah-bremerhaven.de**

The Dom in Verden an der Aller, with its unusually large roof

❽ Hamburg

Germany's second largest city, Hamburg has an openness to the world and a variety of architectural styles in its districts, making it a fascinating place to visit. For many years, Hamburg was a leading member of the Hanseatic League and an independent trading town, and in 1945 it became a city-state of the Federal Republic. Visitors are attracted by Hamburg's enormous port, situated right in the centre of the city, colourful entertainments in the red-light district St Pauli, many attractive parks and lakes as well as the warm welcome extended by the locals who, on first encounter, may seem a little cool.

A fountain in the Neo-Renaissance Rathausmarkt

Exploring Hamburg

The best way to get around Hamburg is by metro (U-Bahn and S-Bahn), using an all-day ticket (Tageskarte). The city centre can be explored on foot, including the area between the main railway station and the lake, along with the rest of the old town, the port and Hamburg's two largest museums.

🏛 Rathausmarkt

The symbol of Hamburg is the enormous Neo-Renaissance town hall, the fifth in the city's history. Previous town halls were destroyed by wars as well as a catastrophic fire in 1842. Little remains of the old town. The city's current appearance is characterized by 19th-century style as well as Modernism. The town hall itself, with its ornamental halls, is worth visiting.

The town hall square is enclosed on one side by Alsterfleet. Originally a small river, it is today one of numerous canals which have given Hamburg the name "Venice of the North". A monument in memory of the

Door knocker on St Petrikirche

victims of World War I is the work of the artist Ernst Barlach. Between Rathausmarkt and Gänsemarkt runs a network of elegantly roofed shopping arcades. These were built in the 19th century, and have since been continually extended.

🏛 Binnenalster

Elegant arcades lead from the Rathausmarkt to Binnenalster, a large lake in the middle of the city. Like the much larger Außenalster lake further north, it was created by damming the Alster River. On a sunny day, the Jungfernstieg, an elegant boulevard running the length of the Alster, is a pleasant place for a walk. Great views of the city can be had from the café in the Alsterpavilion. There is a small quay from which boats depart for the "Alsterrundfahrt", an excursion that takes the visitor all the way to the Außenalster and to smaller canals with views of the villas in the north of Hamburg and the cityscape of the centre with its five main towers.

🏛 St Petrikirche

Mönckebergstr. **Tel** (040) 325 74 00.
Open 10am–6:30pm Mon, Tue, Thu, Fri; 10am–7pm Wed; 10am–5pm Sat; 9am–9pm Sun.

The church of St Petri, originally Gothic, was extensively rebuilt in the Neo-Gothic style after the Great Fire of 1842. The Grabower Altar that once belonged to the church has been transferred to the Kunsthalle (see pp440–41). Tourists can still admire the Gothic sculpture of the Madonna, dating from 1470.

🏛 Jakobikirche

Jakobikirchhof 22. **Tel** (040) 303 73 70.
Open Oct–Mar: 11am–5pm Mon–Sat; Apr–Sep 10am–5pm Mon–Sat.

The church of St Jacobi, from 1340, was bombed during World War II, and subsequently rebuilt in its original style. Its captivating interior includes the largest Baroque organ in northern Germany, the work

The main altar in Jakobikirche

of Arp Schnitger. The triptych of St Luke in the presbytery of the southern nave, a magnificent example of late-Gothic art, was originally created in 1499 for Hamburg's cathedral, which was pulled down in 1804.

🏛 Kontorhausviertel

Deichtorhallen: Deichtorstr. 1–2. **Tel** (040) 32 10 30. **Open** 11am–6pm Tue–Sun (during exhibitions).
After World War I, a district of commercial offices known as Kontorhausviertel was built between Steinstrasse and Messberg. The **Chilehaus**, built by Fritz Höger in 1922–4, was an experiment in creating a traditional brick building with a Modernist design. This ten-storey building, with its pointed eastern façade resembling a ship's bow, became internationally famous as a symbol of Expressionist architecture.

Nearby are the enormous **Deichtorhallen**, market halls of the port built in 1911–12. Turned into dramatic exhibition halls in 1997, they are now used for major art exhibitions.

The Expressionist Chilehaus in Kontorhausviertel

🏛 Speicherstadt

Deutsches Zollmuseum: Alter Wandrahm 16a. **Tel** (040) 30 08 76 11. **Open** 10am–5pm Tue–Sun.
Located within the toll-free area of the port, this giant warehouse district is reached after crossing the customs post. It is the largest complex of warehouses in the world. The Neo-Gothic buildings, dating from the end of the 19th century, are separated by canals. They still serve as storerooms for coffee, tea and carpets. Listed as one of the city's historic monuments, Speicherstadt now houses the Speicherstadt Museum. The **Deutsches Zollmuseum**

(German customs museum) located by Kornhausbrücke tells the story of customs and excise from the Roman Empire to the present day. The **Internationales Maritimes Museum** covers 3,000 years of maritime history with displays of model ships, sea charts, compasses, sextants and a valuable copy of the first nautical atlas printed in 1657.

Hamburg City Centre

① Rathausmarkt
② Binnenalster
③ St Petrikirche
④ Jakobikirche
⑤ Kontorhausviertel
⑥ Speicherstadt
⑦ Kunsthalle
⑧ Altstadt (Old Town)

0 metres 250
0 yards 250

For keys to symbols *see back flap*

Kunsthalle

The most interesting art gallery in northern Germany, the Kunsthalle in Hamburg has a tradition dating back to 1817, when the Kunstverein (friends of the fine arts), proud of its middle-class, non-aristocratic background, was established. The museum opened to the public in 1869. The collection has a standard chronological review of European art movements, with an emphasis on 19th-century German Romantics, with works by Caspar David Friedrich and Philipp Otto Runge. A four-storey extension, the Galerie der Gegenwart (contemporary gallery), was built in 1996 to a design by the architect O M Ungers. Kunsthalle is undergoing a huge renovation until 2016 but remains open.

The Polar Sea (1823–4)
Caspar David Friedrich's dramatic seascape, with a sinking ship in the background behind the rising flow, is loaded with symbolism.

★ **Hannah and Simeon in the Temple** (c.1627) Thanks to his mastery of a sense of drama, Rembrandt succeeded in depicting the psychological make-up of his elderly subjects, who have recognized the Saviour in an unspoken message conveyed to the temple by Mary and Joseph.

High Altar of St Peter in Hamburg (1383)
This panelled painting, displaying a stunning wealth of detail, was produced by Master Bertram of Minden, the first artist in Germany to be identified by his name.

★ **Morning** (1808)
This painting by Philipp Otto Runge centres around Aurora, goddess of dawn, and was intended to be part of a series called "Times of the Day". The other works were never completed due to the artist's untimely death aged 33.

Main entrance

Ground floor

Self-Portrait with Model
(1910 and 1926) Sixteen years after first painting this picture, Ernst Ludwig Kirchner repainted areas, in order to emphasize the distance between model and artist.

VISITORS' CHECKLIST

Practical Information
Glockengießerwall.
Tel (040) 428 131 200. **Open**
10am–6pm Tue–Sun (to 9pm
Thu). Library: **Open** 11am–
5pm Tue–Fri (to 9pm Thu).
Café: **Open** 10am–11pm Tue–
Sun (to 9pm Thu).
w hamburger-kunsthalle.de

First floor

★ **Girls on the Pier** (1901) This painting is one of six variations on the same theme painted by Edvard Munch. The painter omitted the landscape, concentrating on the relationship and tensions between the girls.

Gallery Guide

On the ground floor, Rooms 2–10 and 16–19 contain works of art from the first half of the 20th century. On the first floor, Rooms 101–116 display the works of old masters. In Rooms 117–136 paintings from the 19th century are exhibited, and more works from the first half of the 20th century are shown in Rooms 137–148.

Stairs down to underground link to Galerie der Gegenwart

Stairs to basement and Hubertus-Wald-Forum with temporary exhibitions

Nana (1877) The subject of Édouard Manet's painting was the heroine of a Zola novel. Manet was not allowed to exhibit the painting in the Paris Salon because Nana was known as a Parisian courtesan.

Key
- Gallery of old masters
- 19th-century paintings
- 20th-century paintings (first half)
- Gallery of drawings
- Non-exhibition space

🏛 Altstadt (Old Town)

Hamburg's old town extends to the south of the Rathaus (town hall) but, following the Great Fire of 1842 and bombing during World War II, only a few original buildings remain. **Katharinenkirche** (St Catherine's), with its characteristic tower, was begun in the 13th century and completed in the 17th century. It has been restored after damage in World War II. Of the neighbouring Neo-Gothic **Nikolaikirche** only a single tower remained after 1945, the Nikolaiturm, which is the third tallest in Germany. It serves as a monument to the tragic consequences of war.

Deichstrasse is one of a few surviving streets in the old town, with the original façades still visible from both the road and the canal (the best view can be had from the Hohe Brücke bridge). One of the many famous local restaurants is "Zum Brandanfang", at No. 25. It is here that the Great Fire of 1842, which eventually destroyed most of the city, was said to have broken out.

Ornate Baroque pulpit in Hamburg's Michaeliskirche

🏛 Michaeliskirche

Observation tower: **Tel** (040) 37 67 80. **Open** May–Oct: 9am–7:30pm daily, Nov–Apr: 10am–5:30pm daily.

The massive Baroque church of St Michaelis, visible from afar with its 132-m (433-ft) tower (the "Michel"), is the main symbol of Hamburg.

The neon-lit Reeperbahn in St Pauli

The interior is preserved in a white, grey and gold colour scheme, and some of the fittings are made from tropical wood. The observation platform offers splendid views of the city and its extensive harbour.

🏛 Krameramtswohnungen

Krayenkamp 10. **Tel** (040) 37 50 19 88. **Open** 31 Mar–29 Nov: 10am–5pm Tue–Sun; 30 Nov–30 Mar: 10am–5pm Sat & Sun.

Near the Michaeliskirche, a section of the old town, the Krameramtswohnungen, has miraculously survived. These half-timbered houses were funded by the merchants' guild and built to house the widows of shopkeepers. Today they are occupied by tourist shops, cafés and restaurants.

🚢 The Port

Cap San Diego **Tel** (040) 36 42 09. **Open** 10am–6pm daily. Rickmer Rickmers **Tel** (040) 319 59 59. **Open** 10am–8pm daily.

Situated 104 km (62 miles) inland along the Elbe River, Hamburg is Europe's second largest port after Rotterdam, and the port dominates the panorama. Every year 12,000 ships dock here from 90 countries. From the U3 Baumwall metro station it is best to walk to **Landungsbrücken**, past the museum ships moored here: the freighter *Cap San Diego* and the sailing boat *Rickmer Rickmers* (1896). Landungsbrücken is a 200-m (656-ft) long building from where the passenger ferries depart. A tour of the harbour is highly recommended. Near Landungsbrücken, in a copperdomed building, is the entrance to Alter Elbtunnel (the old tunnel under the Elbe) where people and cars are lowered in a giant lift.

🏛 St Pauli

Infamous around the world, this area is also known as **Reeperbahn**, after the main street. It is a world of nightclubs and bars, pubs and theatres, sex clubs and brothels. It is here, in Hamburg's red-light district, that some teenage seasonal workers from Liverpool, the Beatles, started their careers. On Herbertstrasse, scantily clad women offer their services

Fischmarkt – A Market for Everything

This is an attraction for early risers or for those who never get to bed at all. From 5am (7am in winter) on Sundays the Auktionshalle (auction hall) and the nearby waterside turn into a colourful market place. Fishermen returning from the sea with their freshly caught fish compete with noisy greengrocers offering their wares and bric-à-brac merchants setting out stalls. Thousands of tourists mingle with sailors and ladies of the night relaxing with a cup of steaming mulled wine after a hard night's work in St Pauli. Here and there you can hear Plattdeutsch being spoken, the northern patois. Morning mass at 10am used to mark the end of this colourful spectacle, but today's public lingers on and then hurries off to bed instead of church.

Bric-à-brac on sale at a market stall in Fischmarkt

behind a metal barrier – women and those under 18 are forbidden entrance. St Pauli even has an Erotic-Museum, where next to the exhibits are reproductions of works by artists from Rembrandt to Picasso, which are said to "prove" that everything revolves around the female posterior.

Environs
The magnificent palace in **Ahrensburg** (1595), 23 km (14 miles) to the northeast, has Baroque and Rococo interiors open to visitors.

Façade of Schloss Ahrensburg, flanked by towers

❾ Altes Land

Road map C2.

On the flood plains stretching for more than 30 km (19 miles) between Hamburg and Stade, along the Lower Elbe River, is the Altes Land (old land). This area is fertile and has the largest number of orchards in Germany. Many visitors come here in May, when cherry and apple tree blossom turns everything into a sea of white and pink. In this riot of colour stand sturdy red-brick houses with white half-timbered panels, thatched roofs and carved gates. The most beautiful villages are **Neuenfelde**, **Jork**, **Borstel**, **Steinkirchen** and **Hollern**, with their richly furnished Baroque churches.

❿ Stade

Road map C2. 🔼 47,000.
🚇 U3 to Neugraben, then by train or catamaran from Landungsbrücken.
ℹ️ Hansestrasse 16 (04141-40 91 70).
🌐 **stade-tourismus.de**

This medieval Hanseatic town has retained most of its half-timbered buildings, with the most attractive in the **Alter Hafen** (old harbour). There is a also a quaint crane and the **Schwedenspeicher** (Swedish granary) dating from the Swedish occupation during the Thirty Years' War (1692–1705). It is now home to the **Schwedenspeicher-Museum**, a museum with exhibits on the town's history and defence system, including wheels from 700 BC, which were part of a Bronze-Age cart. Nearby, an interesting building at Am Wasser West 7 houses the **Kaufmann Collection**, with works by Worps-wede artists. The

The Baroque portal of the Dutch-influenced Rathaus in Stade

entire old town is surrounded by preserved modern fortifications. Other attractions are the **Bürgermeister-Hintze-Haus** at Am Wasser West 23, a house built for the mayor, Hintze, in 1617–46, and the exquisite Baroque **Rathaus** (town hall) from 1667, its design revealing Dutch influence.

The 14th-century Gothic church of **St Wilhadi** boasts an interesting Gothic hall and a leaning tower, while **St Cosmas and Damiani**, founded after the Great Fire of 1659, features marvellous Baroque furnishings.

🏛 **Schwedenspeicher-Museum**
Am Wasser West 39. **Tel** (04141) 79 77 30. **Open** 10am–5pm Tue–Fri, 10am–6pm Sat & Sun. 🈺

The half-timbered houses along the waterside of Alter Hafen in Stade

⓫ Lüneburg

Road map D2. 🏛 70,000. 🚉
ℹ️ Rathaus, Am Markt (04131-
207 66 20). 🌐 **lueneburg.de**

It is hard to believe
that this small, former
Hanseatic town was once
one of the wealthiest in
Germany. Its prosperity
was founded on salt
mines. Opened in 956,
they provided work for
more than 2,000 people by the
late Middle Ages and were the
largest industry in Europe.

Lüneburg's most important
monument is the **Rathaus** (town
hall). The interior is even more
intriguing than the frequently
rebuilt façade, in particular the
Großer Ratssaal (the main hall)
with its Gothic stained-glass
windows and 16th-century
frescoes of the Last Judgement,
as well as the Große Ratsstube
(council chamber) with
Renaissance woodwork by
Albert von Soest. A remarkable
collection of municipal
silverware can be found in the
Ostpreußisches Landesmuseum.

Johanniskirche, one of
Lüneburg's three Gothic churches, stands on Am Sande. It
has a 108-m (354-ft) west tower,
which leans more than 2 m (6 ft)
from the perpendicular. In one
of its five naves there is a
panelled painting dating from
1482–5, the masterful work of
the German painter Hinrik
Funhof. Also interesting is the
soaring basilica of **Michaeliskirche**, consecrated in 1409.

Not far from here is the old
port on the Ilmenau River.

A typical farmstead in Lüneburger Heide

On Lüner Strasse stands the **Altes
Kaufhaus**, a former herring
warehouse with a Baroque
façade. The 14th-century wooden
crane was rebuilt in the 1700s.
It was used to load salt onto
ships. The decorative wavy brick
lines *(Taustäbe)* on many of the
old buildings are characteristic
of the town.

🏛 **Rathaus**
Am Markt. **Tel** (04131) 30 92 30.
⏰ 11am, 12:30pm, 2:30pm, 4pm
Tue–Sat; 11am, 2pm Sun.

⓬ Lüneburger Heide

Road map C2. ℹ️ Wallstr. 4,
Lüneburg (04131-30 99 60).
🌐 **lueneburger-heide.de**

South of Hamburg, between
the rivers Elbe and Aller, is a
sprawling area of heathland,
grazed by heifers and sheep
and buzzing with bees in the
heathers and pine forests.
Until the Middle Ages, this area
was covered by dense mixed
forests, but these were felled
to satisfy demand for wood
in the saltworks of Lüneburg.
The half-stepped terrain

provides grazing land for
Heidschnucken, the local
breed of sheep. The heather
moors are best seen at the
**Naturschutzpark Lüneburger
Heide**, a large area of nature
reserve founded in 1921. From
the village of Undeloh it is best
to continue by foot, bike or
carriage to the traditional village
of Wilsede. From Wilsede it is
not far to Wilseder Berg, the
highest peak of this moraine
region. The view of the
surrounding countryside is
particularly beautiful at the end
of August, when the purple
heather is blooming.

⓭ Soltau

Road map C2. 🏛 23,000. ℹ️ Am
Alten Stadtgraben 3 (05191-82 82 82).
🌐 **soltau.de**

The main attraction of the
town of Soltau is **Heidepark
Soltau**, a vast funfair with
trains, water rides and a
genuine Mississippi steamboat.
For nature lovers, there is the
Vogelpark Walsrode, 20 km
(12 miles) southwest of Soltau.
It holds about 1,000 species of
birds, from penguins to birds
of paradise. Aviaries, some
12-m (40-ft) tall, simulate the
birds' natural environment.

🎠 **Heidepark Soltau**
Tel (01805) 92 91 01. **Open** Apr–Oct:
9am–6pm daily (admission till 4pm).

🎠 **Vogelpark Walsrode**
Tel (05161) 604 40. **Open** Apr–Oct:
9am–7pm daily, Nov–Mar 10am–4pm
daily. 🌐 **weltvogelpark.de**

Environs
In grim contrast to both
parks stands **Bergen-Belsen**,
a concentration camp
constructed in the moorland
of Osterheide, about 30 km
(19 miles) south of Soltau.
A monument and small
museum commemorate
the place where 50,000
people were murdered,
among them Anne Frank.

🏛 **Gedenkstätte Bergen-Belsen**
Lohheide. **Tel** (05051) 47 59 200.
Open Apr–Sep: 10am–6pm;
Oct–Mar: 10am–5pm daily.

Eighteenth-century wooden crane in Lüneburg

For hotels and restaurants in this area see pp501–502 and pp529–31

Vogelpark Walsrode – a paradise with 1,000 different bird species

⑭ Celle

Road map C3. 🚊 74,000. 🚉
Schlossplatz. 🛈 Markt 14–6 (05141-
12 12). 🎨 Kunsthandwerkermarkt
(Whitsun). 🖥 **celle-tourismus.de**

Between 1378 and 1705, Celle
was the seat of distant relations
of the Welf family, the reigning
dynasty in the Duchy of
Brunswick-Lüneburg. The
Schloss (castle), rebuilt in
Renaissance style after 1533, has
a façade with octagonal towers,
gables and bay windows. It is one
of the main early-Renaissance
buildings in Germany. The
Gothic chapel was rebuilt in
Mannerist style to a design by
Martin de Vos, who created 76
of its paintings, including the
famous *Crucifixion* (late 1500s).

Celle prides itself on 500 half-
timbered houses, with the most
interesting ones in picturesque
Kalandgasse and Zöllnerstrasse.
Hoppner Haus, at Poststrasse 8,
is richly decorated with reliefs
of mythological beasts. Equally
interesting is the painted
decoration of the **Rathaus** (town

hall), a great example of Weser
Renaissance (*see p457*) from 1579.
From the **Stadtkirche** church
tower great views unfold. The
Baroque **Synagoge**, beyond
the old town, is the only one
surviving in northern Germany.

🏰 Schloss
Tel (05141) 12 454. **Open** Apr–Oct:
11am, noon, 1, 2 & 3pm Tue–Sun;
Nov–Mar: 11am & 3pm Tue–Sun. 🅿

⛪ Stadtkirche
Tel (05141) 7735. **Open** 10am–6pm
Tue–Sat. Tower: Apr–Oct: 10–11:45am
2–4:45pm Tue–Sat.

✡ Synagoge
Im Kreise 24. **Tel** (05141) 12 12.
Open noon–5pm Mon–Thu, Sun;
10am–3pm Fri.

Environs
The town of **Wietze**, 11 km
(7 miles) west of Celle, has been
a centre of petroleum since
1858. The **Deutsches
Erdölmuseum Wietze** provides
a very interesting overview on
the history of oil extraction.

The neighbouring village of
Wienhausen has a Cistercian

Kloster (monastery) with a
beautiful 13th–14th century
church. Worth seeing are its
Gothic frescoes, the presbytery
vaults and the 14th- and
15th-century tapestries.

🏛 Deutsches Erdölmuseum
Schwarzer Weg 7–9. **Tel** (05146) 92
340. **Open** Mar–Nov: 10am–5pm
Tue–Sun; Jun–Aug: 10am–5pm
Tue–Sun. 🅿

🏛 Kloster Wienhausen
Tel (05149) 18 660. 🕐 Apr–Oct: 10 &
11am, 2–5pm Tue–Sat, noon–5pm
Sun. 🅿

⑮ Wolfsburg

Road map D3. 🚊 123,000. 🚉
🛈 Willy-Brandt-Platz 3 (05361-89
99 30). 🖥 **wolfsburg.de**

During the 1930s, this small
village began to develop into a
sizeable town, based around
the Volkswagen car works.
Production of the "people's car"
was conceived by Hitler – every
German was to be able to afford
this inexpensive car, designed
by Ferdinand Porsche. The
model reached its peak during
the post-war economic boom
years. The **Volkswagenwerk**
factory is open to visitors.

Wolfsburg also has some
outstanding examples of
modern architecture: a cultural
centre designed by Alvar Aalto,
a city theatre designed by Hans
Scharoun and a planetarium.

🚌 Volkswagenwerk Autostadt
Stadtbrücke. **Tel** (0800) 28 86 78 238.
Open 9am–6pm daily. 🚐 every 30
mins. 🖥 **autostadt.de**

The façade of the Schloss with octagonal towers at the corners, in Celle

The Renaissance Schloss in Stadthagen

⑯ Stadthagen

Road map C3. 🚊 23,800. 🚆 ℹ️ Am Markt 1 (05721 92 50 05).
🌐 stadthagen.de

The counts of Schaumburg-Lippe used the Renaissance **Schloss** (castle) as their private residence. Apart from this and the town hall, the main attraction is the church of **St Martini**, with an early Baroque mausoleum, and a masterful bronze monument by Adrian de Vries, court artist to Rudolf II in Prague.

🏛 St Martini
Schulstr.18. **Tel** (05721) 78 070.
Open 9am–noon, 2–4pm Mon–Thu, 9am–noon Fri.

Environs
A gem of Romanesque architecture can be found at **Idensen** near Wunsdorf, 22 km (14 miles) from Stadthagen. The church interior of Alte Kirche (1120) is entirely painted with scenes from the Old and New testaments, and there is a vast Byzantine-style image of Christ's Enthronement on a vaulted ceiling.

⑰ Bückeburg

Road map C3. 🚊 21,000. 🚆
ℹ️ Schlossplatz 5 (05722-89 31 81).

In the 16th century this town became the capital of the principality of Schaumburg-Lippe. The philosopher Johann Gottfried von Herder was the preacher here. The **Stadtkirche** (town church), one of the first Protestant churches in Germany, is a pinnacle of Mannerism with its fantasy façade. Another

attraction is the **Schloss** with its enchanting chapel. The Goldener Saal (golden hall), from 1605, has a Götterpforte (portal of the divinities) and a beautiful panelled ceiling.

🏛 Stadtkirche
Lange Str. **Tel** (05722) 957 70.
Open 15 Apr–14 Oct: 10:30am–noon Tue–Fri, 2:30–4:30pm Tue–Sun, 15 Oct–14 Apr: 2:30–4:30pm Fri–Sun.

🏛 Schloss
Tel (05722) 50 39. **Open** Apr–Sep: 9:30am–6pm; Oct–Mar: 9:30am–5pm.

The opulent Goldener Saal in Schloss Bückeburg

⑱ Braunschweig (Brunswick)

Road map D3. 🚊 240,000. 🚆
ℹ️ Vor der Burg 1 (0531-470 20 40).
🎭 Festival of Chamber Music (May); Medieval Fair (May/Jun).

An important commercial and political centre from the early Middle Ages, Brunswick (Braunschweig) was chosen as town of residence by Heinrich der Löwe (Henry the Lion), ruler of Saxony and Bavaria. A member of the Welf family, he eventually lost in his struggle against the German emperor.

Very different in character but equally famous was Till Eulenspiegel, an ordinary man who poked fun at dim-witted citizens, the aristocracy and the clergy. His exploits were fictionalized in the 16th century, and he was immortalized with a fountain on Bäckerklint Square.

Brunswick's continued decline culminated in the almost total destruction of the town in 1944. During reconstruction, the concept of the "Traditionsinsel" was developed: small islands of rebuilt historic monuments adrift in a sea of modernism.

A tour of the town is best started from Burgplatz (castle square). Here is the **Burglöwe**, the monument of a lion funded by Heinrich in 1166 (the original is in a museum). Symbolizing Heinrich's rule, it was the first such sculpture to be erected since Roman days. The **Dom** (cathedral) is well worth seeing. In the north nave, an extension, are unusual turned pillars, and in the transept and presbytery are 13th-century frescoes. Its marvellous treasures include a gigantic seven-armed bronze candlestick, the tomb of Heinrich and his wife Mathilde, the Crucifix of Imerward and a wooden cross with the figure of Christ modelled on the sculpture of *Voltosanto* in Lucca. Visitors can also see the column of the Passion with the figure of Christ, the work of Hans Witten.

To the west of the cathedral lies the **Altstadtmarkt** (old town market). Here are the L-shaped **Rathaus** (town hall), with a cloister, and the Gothic church of **St Martini**. The beautiful **Gewandhaus** (cloth hall) is also worth seeing.

The Burglöwe, Heinrich der Löwe's monument in Brunswick

East of the cathedral is the **Herzog-Anton-Ulrich-Museum**, the oldest in Germany. It was opened to the public as a gallery by Duke Anton Ulrich and holds a variety of gems such as Rembrandt's *Family Portrait*, a Giorgioni self-portrait and Vermeer van Delft's *Girl with a Glass of Wine*.

🏛 Dom
Burgplatz. **Tel** (0531) 24 33 50.
Open 10am–5pm daily.

🏛 St Martini
Altstadtmarkt. **Tel** (0531) 161 21.
Open Jan–Apr. 10am–1.30pm Tue–Sat, May–Dec: 10am–1pm, 3–5pm Tue–Fri, 10am–5pm Sat, 10am–noon, 3–5pm Sun.

🏛 Herzog-Anton-Ulrich-Museum
Museumsstr. 1. **Tel** (0531) 122 50.
Closed for renovation.

The richly decorated portal of the Gewandhaus in Brunswick

Environs
In **Königslutter**, 35 km (22 miles) east of Braunschweig, Emperor Lothar initiated the building of the Benedictine **Kaiserdom**, a monastery church and later his burial place. The portal with figures of lions, a frieze with figures of fishermen, and the cloisters reflect the taste of the times and the northern Italian origin of architects and sculptors; only the frescoes are late 19th-century additions.

Helmstedt, 45 km (28 miles) to the east, is unjustifiably only associated with the former border crossing between East and West Germany. In 1576,

The Marienbrunnen fountain on Altstadtmarkt in Brunswick

Duke Julius of Brunswick founded the Julius Academy, one of Germany's most popular Protestant universities, where the Italian philosopher Giordano Bruno taught. Juleum (1592–7), the main building, has a central tower and two decorative gables. It is now home to the **Kreis- und Universitätsmuseum**, a regional museum and library.

🏛 Kaiserdom
Königslutter. **Tel** (05353) 91 21 29.
Open 9am–6pm daily, in winter to 5pm.

🏛 Kreis- und Universitätsmuseum
Collegienplatz 1. **Tel** (05351) 121 11 32. **Open** 10am–noon, 3–5pm Tue–Fri, 3–5pm Sat & Sun.

⑲ Wolfenbüttel

Road map D3. 🚗 53,000. 🚆
ℹ Stadtmarkt 7 (05331-86 280).
🎭 Osterleiermark (Easter); Altstadtfest (Aug).

This small town has a turbulent past. From 1432 until 1753 the Welf dukes moved their seat here from Brunswick. In the 16th century, innovative town design introduced wide avenues and spacious squares. Largely unscathed by World War II, the town has 500 historic half-timbered houses, and a magnificent library. The **Herzog-August-Bibliothek** holds 130,000 volumes, including the

most valuable book in the world, Heinrich der Löwe's Gospel book. Associated with the town are the philosopher Gottfried Wilhelm Leibniz and writer Gotthold Ephraim Lessing. The **Lessinghaus** houses a literature museum.

The centre of the town is dominated by the **Schloss**, the largest castle in Lower Saxony, refurbished in the Baroque style in 1714–16. It houses the **Schlossmuseum** with regional items such as furniture and tapestries. The Venussaal (hall of Venus) has beautiful Baroque ceiling frescoes. Opposite the castle is the **Zeughaus** (armoury), built in 1613–19 to a design by Paul Francke.

Continuing eastwards the visitor will get to the **Hauptkirche**, the 16th-century church dedicated to *Beatae Mariae Virginis*, the ducal pantheon and the leading example of Protestant Mannerist architecture. Begun in 1608, the church's façade has delicate reliefs, while the interior has an unusual combination of styles.

🏛 Schloss and Schlossmuseum
Schlossplatz 13. **Tel** (05331) 924 60.
Open 10am–5pm Tue–Sun.

Lessinghaus, Museum & Zeughaus:
Tel (05331) 80 82 14. **Open** 11am–5pm Tue–Sun. Herzog-August-Bibliothek: **Open** 10am–5pm Tue–Sun.

🏛 Hauptkirche
Michael-Praetorius-Platz 9. **Tel** (05331) 72 055. **Open** 10am–noon, 2–4pm Tue–Sat.

Baroque façade of Schloss Wolfenbüttel

⑳ Hanover (Hannover)

The capital of Lower Saxony, Hanover does not at first glance seem particularly exciting, but appearances can be deceptive: the town boasts interesting architecture in the historic centre, magnificent Baroque gardens and one of Europe's most important museums of modern art. Hanover's past was marked by its dynastic links with England, sharing the same ruler during the years 1714–1837. Annual industrial trade fairs have earned the town an international reputation, and in 2000 Hanover hosted the international exhibition Expo 2000 which attracted 18 million visitors.

Exploring Hanover

After the near-total destruction of the old town in 1944, many historic monuments have been rebuilt, and large green spaces encourage the visitor to explore the town on foot. It is best to follow an extensive circuit, starting from and returning to the railway station. The Baroque gardens at Herrenhausen in the northwest of the town are reached by metro (U-Bahn 4, 5).

🎭 Opernhaus

Opernplatz 1. **Tel** (0511) 99 99 11 11. The opera house was built in 1845–57 by George Ludwig Friedrich Laves, Hanover's most important architect, to a fine Neo-Classical design. Particularly charming is the façade with portico columns.

🏛 Niedersächsisches Landesmuseum

Willy-Brandt-Allee 5. **Tel** (0511) 980 76 86. **Open** 10am–5pm Tue–Sun, 10am–7pm Thu. 🖼

The most interesting part of the state museum of Lower Saxony is the picture gallery, which holds excellent German medieval and Renaissance paintings (Dürer, Spranger, Cranach), a good section with Dutch and Flemish paintings (Rubens, Rembrandt, van Dyck) as well as German paintings of the 19th and 20th centuries, with fine examples of Romanticism and Impressionism (Friedrich, Corinth, Liebermann).

🏛 Sprengel Museum

Kurt-Schwitters-Platz 1. **Tel** (0511) 16 84 38 75. **Open** 10am–8pm Tue, 10am–6pm Wed–Sun. 🖼

One of Europe's finest museums of modern art, the Sprengel-Museum reflects the city's role as an artists' mecca in the 1920s, before the National Socialists destroyed works of art that they designated as "degenerate". Hanover's controversial artist Kurt Schwitters worked here, as did El Lissitzky, whose *Kabinett der Abstrakten* (school of abstraction, 1928, reconstructed) is worth seeing. Funded by Bernhard Sprengel, a chocolate magnate, the museum was built in 1979, and holds works by Munch, Chagall and Picasso, as well as many more recent artists, including Christo.

The museum is located by the Maschsee, a large artificial lake created in the centre of the city in 1936. During the summer it teems with motor and sailing boats, while Hanoverians stroll around its banks.

Mueller's *The Lovers* (1920), in the Sprengel-Museum

🏛 Neues Rathaus

Trammplatz 2. **Tel** (0511) 168 45 333. Dome **Open** 9:30am–6pm Mon–Fri; 10am–6pm Sat & Sun.

The gigantic town hall symbolizes the lofty ambitions of the wealthier citizens at the beginning of the 20th century. It was built from 1901–13, on more than 6,000 beech pillars, modelled on a Baroque palace with a central dome, and decorated with Neo-Gothic and Secessionist detail. The Swiss artist Ferdinand Hodler created a vast painting enitled *Einigkeit* (unity) for the Debating Hall, which depicts the arrival of Protestantism in the town in 1533. A unique oblique lift takes you up to the dome from where there are wonderful views.

🏰 Leineschloss

Hinrich-Wilhelm-Kopf-Platz. In the historic city centre by the Leine River stands the Leineschloss, a 17th-century palace completely rebuilt by the local architect Laves between 1817 and 1842. It had to be rebuilt again after destruction

Façade of the vast Neues Rathaus, with its central dome

Interior of the church of St Georg und St Jacobus, in Marktplatz

in World War II, and now serves as headquarters for the Niedersächsischer Landtag (Lower Saxony state parliament). The porticos on the façade were modelled on ancient Greek temples.

Marktplatz
Although the houses on this square had to be almost completely rebuilt after World War II, this is one of the best examples of 15th-century red-brick architecture, with amazing gables with projections as well as figurative friezes of glazed terracotta. Nearby, the

Marktkirche St Georg und St Jacobus (church of St George and St Jacob) features a 14th-century nave with a characteristic four-pinnacled tower. The most valuable object among its furnishings is the Gothic altar, with scenes of the Passion and copper engravings by the renowned artist Martin Schongauer.

Herrenhäuser Gärten
Despite having been razed to the ground during World War II, the gardens in Hanover's Herrenhausen district are among the most beautiful Baroque gardens in Germany. They were established by Duchess Sophie von der Pfalz, daughter of Elizabeth Stuart and mother of England's George I. The Großer

Garten, the most important of the four gardens, has a formal layout modelled on 17th- and 18th-century Dutch parks. It is a botanical garden with fountains, including the Große Fontäne, the tallest in Europe with a 82-m (269-ft) water spout. There are grottoes, mazes, sculptures and decorative urns, and the hedges are some 21 km (13 miles) long.

The stunningly beautiful Baroque gardens in Herrenhausen

Hanover City Centre
1. Opernhaus
2. Niedersächsisches Landesmuseum
3. Sprengel Museum
4. Neues Rathaus
5. Leineschloss
6. Marktplatz

For keys to symbols see back flap

㉑ Hildesheim

The undisputed capital of Romanesque culture, the old town of Hildesheim was transformed into a heap of rubble by heavy bombing on 22 March 1945. The most important monuments have now been recreated, with mixed results, surrounded by modern developments. Two churches, the Michaeliskirche and the Dom St Mariä, are UNESCO World Heritage sites, and the Roemer-Pelizaeus-Museum of Egyptian Culture also makes a visit to Hildesheim worthwhile.

Wedekindhaus, a beautiful half-timbered house on Marktplatz

Exploring Hildesheim

Contrary to received wisdom, the city is best visited on foot. Visitors can park in the centre, for example near the church of St Michael, and then explore the main sights from here. A round tour, including the museums, should not take longer than around 4–5 hours. It is also possible to follow the Rosenroute (rose trail) around town which is marked on the pavements by white roses.

🔲 Marktplatz

Since gaining civic rights in the 11th century, the heart of the bishopric town has been its market square. Every detail has now been faithfully reconstructed, and it is easy to forget that the square looked totally different only a few years ago. In 1987, the Knochenhaueramtshaus (butchers' guild hall) was rebuilt, the largest and most famous half-timbered house in Germany, dating from 1529. Opposite are the Gothic town hall and the Tempelhaus, an original 15th-century building with round turrets and a half-timbered annexe, added in 1591. Reliefs depict the story of the Prodigal Son.

🏛 Andreaskirche

Andreasplatz. **Open** Apr–Sep: 9am–6pm Mon–Fri, 9am–4pm Sat, 11:30am–4pm Sun; Oct–Mar: 10am–4pm Mon–Sat, 11:30–4pm Sun. Tower May–Oct: 11am–4 pm Mon–Sat, noon–4pm Sun. **Closed** Nov–Apr.

The reconstructed Gothic church of St Andrew is notable for the brightness and the quality of the light that passes through its vast windows, as well as its

The picturesque Presbytery of Michaeliskirche, Hildesheim

soaring proportions. The 115-m (377-ft) tower was added in the 19th century.

🏛 Michaeliskirche

Michaelisplatz. **Tel** (05121) 34 410. **Open** Apr–Oct: 8am–6pm daily; Nov–Mar: 9am–4pm daily.

Built on the instructions of Bishop Bernward, the church is a textbook example of what became known as the Ottonian style, the early Romanesque culture of the Otto dynasty. Its characteristic feature is the streamlined simplicity of interior and exterior, with square pillars intersecting with the naves. The sarcophagus of the founder, St Bernward, is in the crypt in the western part of the church.

Bas-relief on the façade of Andreaskirche

Luckily, a rare painted 12th-century ceiling was removed during World War II and thus largely survived. It depicts the story of Redemption, from Adam and Eve through to Mary and the Saviour.

🏛 Roemer-Pelizaeus Museum

Am Steine 1. **Tel** (05121) 93 690. **Open** 10am–6pm Tue–Sun.

The pride of this museum is the Ancient Egyptian collection, one of the best in Europe, which includes the burial figures of Hem Om and the writer Heti from the Old Kingdom (c.2600 BC). It also has fine collections of Chinese porcelain and Inca artifacts, and it is famed for its temporary exhibitions on ancient cultures.

🏛 Dom St Mariä

Domhof. **Tel** (05121) 179 17 60. **Open** 10am–6pm daily. 🇼 dom-hildesheim.de

During a hunting expedition in 815, Ludwig der Fromme (the devout), son of Charlemagne, allegedly hung relics of the Virgin Mary on a tree. When he tried to remove them they would not budge – which he took to be a heavenly sign that a church should be founded on this site and a town

◀ A church towers over a row of houses in Kramer Street, Hanover

The Bernwardsäule in the Dom St Mariä – a huge bronze column

alongside it. The Tausendjähriger Rosenstock (1,000-year-old rose) of this legend grows to this day in the cathedral's apse, and even survived bombing. The cathedral was reconstructed after World War II, using a model of the church's 11th-century appearance.

Original works of art bear witness to the cathedral's foundry which flourished under bishop Bernward. Bronze double doors depict the Old Testament version of the Creation on one side, and the life of Christ according to

the New Testament on the other. The Bernwardsäule, a huge bronze column from 1022, was once topped by a crucifix. The column, with scenes from the life of Christ arranged as a spiralling picture story, recalls the column of Emperor Trajan in Rome. Two further important works of art are a chandelier from 1060, with a diameter of 3 m (10 ft), and a baptismal font (c.1225) based on the personifications of the four rivers of the Garden of Eden.

Godehardkirche
Godehardsplatz. **Tel** (05121) 34578. **Open** 9am–6pm daily.

This church is dedicated to Bernward's successor, bishop Godehard, who like him has been included in the canon of saints. Built in 1133–72, it is typical of local architecture, and also recalls the earlier church of St Michaelis. It has interesting carved capitals as well as a northern doorway with the Blessed Jesus Christ accompanied by St Godehard and St Epiphany.

Mauritiuskirche
Moritzberg.

Another Romanesque church worth visiting is the church of St Maurice, west of the centre.

Founded by bishop Hezilo and built in the years 1058–68, the church has enchanting cloisters, dating from the 12th century, and the sarcophagus of the founder of the church.

Presbytery of the massive Godehardkirche, flanked by towers

Hildesheim City Centre

1. Marktplatz
2. Andreaskirche
3. Michaeliskirche
4. Roemer-Pelizaeus-Museum
5. Dom St Mariä
6. Godehardkirche

0 metres   300
0 yards   300

    For hotels and restaurants in this area see pp501–502 and pp529–31

② Street-by-Street: Goslar

Goslar, at the foot of the Harz mountains, is a captivating town with 1,500 charming, half-timbered houses, the largest number in Germany. For 300 years the Holy Roman Emperors of Germany resided in Goslar, a member of the Hanseatic League also known as "the treasure chest of the North". Goslar's main source of wealth was the nearby mine in Rammelsberg, where zinc, copper and especially silver were mined. The townscape has remained largely unchanged, making it a great tourist attraction as well as a UNESCO World Heritage Site.

Guildhouse
(Hotel Kaiserworth)

Jakobikirche †

MARKT

HOHER WEG

KAISERBLEEK

DOM PLATZ

★ Rathaus
On the western side of the market square stands the 15th-century town hall. Its beautiful Huldigungssaal (hall of homage) has a ceiling and walls with Gothic frescoes.

Siemens-haus

★ Marktkirche
The Gothic Church of Saints Cosmas and Damian has Romanesque stained-glass windows and a bronze Renaissance baptismal font.

Statue of the Emperor Barbarossa

Key

— Suggested route

The Kaiserpfalz
The Emperors' palace is a stone building (1005–15), largely rebuilt in the 19th century. The chapel and the Emperors' hall with its superb paintings are worth seeing.

For hotels and restaurants in this area see pp501–502 and pp529–31

★ **Historic Half-Timbered Houses**
Many charming half-timbered buildings from various periods have survived in Goslar, creating compact rows of houses in the streets of the city centre.

St Annen Stift

MASSTRASSE

0 metres   50
0 yards   50

🏠 Siemenshaus
Schreiberstrasse 12. **Tel** (05321) 780
620. **Closed** to the public; call for
a tour.

This half-timbered house, one of the most attractive, was once owned by the Siemens family who have their roots in Goslar. Hans Siemens built it in 1693.

🏛 St Peter and Paul
Frankenberger Platz.

Located in the Frankenberg neighbourhood, this was one of 47 churches which once stood in the town. It was built in the 12th century, and the tympanum of the south portal dates from this period. Extensively refurbished, the church prides itself on its magnificent Baroque furnishings.

🏛 St Jakobi
Jakobi-Kirchhof. **Tel** (05321) 303 672.
Open 9:30am–4pm daily.

The present appearance of this church, the only Catholic one in Goslar, is the result of Gothic additions, although the structure of the walls remains Romanesque. The famous work of art in the church is the *Pietà* by Hans von Witten, but it is also worth looking at the wall paintings, the organ and the baptismal font.

🏛 Neuwerkkirche
Rosentorstrasse 27a. **Tel** (05321) 228 39.
Open Mar–Oct. 10am–noon & 2:30–4:30pm Mon–Sat; 2:30–4:30pm Sun.

This impressive late-Romanesque church was built in the 12th–13th centuries for the Cistercian Order, although the surviving monastic buildings date from the early 18th century. Inside, the wall paintings and the choir partition are of interest. The church is surrounded by a peaceful garden.

The train in the Bergbaumuseum in Rammelsberg

🏛 Breites Tor
Breite Strasse.

Some parts of the defensive system, dating mainly from c.1500, are well preserved. This "wide gate", which can be seen on the eastern approach of the town, is the most imposing part.

🏛 St Annen-Stift
Glockengiesserstrasse 65. **Tel** (05321)
398 700. **Open** 10am–noon Mon,
Thu, Fri.

The hospice of St Anna for orphans, the elderly and infirm was founded in 1494 and is the oldest preserved half-timbered house in Germany. Behind its picturesque façade is a beautiful small chapel with superb paintings on a wooden ceiling.

🏛 Bergbaumuseum Rammelsberg
Bergtal 19. **Tel** (05321) 750 122.
Open 9am–6pm daily

Goslar's mining museum is based in the 10th-century silver mine. One of the oldest industrial structures in the world, it is a UNESCO World Heritage Site. On display are mining tools and utensils used in various periods. Visitors can take a train ride through the mine and learn about the history of mining.

The above-ground buildings of the silver mine in Rammelsberg

❷❸ Einbeck

Road map C3. 🔲 29,400. 🔲
ℹ️ Rathaus, Markt Str. 13 (05561-313
19 10). 🅦 einbeck.de

In the Middle Ages, this town
had 600 breweries – more than
houses – and today it is still
known for its beers; Bockbier,
the famous German strong
beer, was invented here. Burned
down in 1540 and 1549, the
town was subsequently rebuilt
in a uniformly Renaissance style.
The historic town centre is
enclosed by the city walls.
More than 100 half-timbered
houses have survived to this
day. **Eickesches Haus**
(Marktstrasse 13) is
particularly eye-catching,
with a sculpted façade
based on biblical and
Classical stories. Other
picturesque houses
can be found in
Tiedexer Strasse and
in **Marktplatz**. The
latter boasts the **Rathaus**
(town hall) and the
Ratswaage (muni-
cipal weigh house)
and **Ratsapotheke**
(chemist). The tower of the
neighbouring **Pfarrkirche St
Jakobi** (parish church) leans
1.5 m (5 ft) from the erpendicular.
In 1741, a Baroque façade was
added to hide this.

Environs
15 km (9 miles) from Einbeck
is the spa town of **Bad
Gandersheim**. It grew up
around a Benedictine
monastery established here in
852, which in the 10th century
was the home of Roswitha von
Gandersheim, the first known
German dramatist.

❷❹ Göttingen

Road map C4. 🔲 129,000. 🔲
ℹ️ Altes Rathaus, Markt 9 (0551-499
800). 🎭 Händel-Festspiele (Jun);
Literaturherbst (Oct), Jazzfestival
(Nov); student festivals, such as
Stiftungsfest. 🅦 goettingen.de

Along with Tübingen, Marburg
and Heidelberg, Göttingen is one
of the most renowned German
university towns. Established in
1737 by the English King
George II, who was also the
ruler of Hanover, the university
taught the sons of wealthy
German, English and Russian
aristocrats. Important cultural
figures worked here, including
the writer Heinrich Heine, the
brothers Grimm and the explorer
Alexander von Humboldt.
Göttingen's reputation as an
educational centre continues
today, partly due to the establishment of the Max Planck
Institute, named after the scientist
who was born in the city and
developed the quantum theory.

Göttingen is a lively town
thanks to its student population, with dozens of cafés,
cosmopolitan restaurants
and bars. University
buildings are scattered
all over town, and the
Aula, a Neo-Classical
Assembly Hall, is
worth a visit. On
the Marktplatz in
the town centre stands
the **Rathaus** (town
hall) with a Gothic
stone façade. The
**Gänseliesel-
brunnen**, the goose girl
fountain, in front dates from
1901. It is kissed by students
who have passed their exams,
and much loved by tourists.

From the southeastern end of
the market square, Göttingen's
four main churches can be seen:
St Michael to the south, St Jakobi
to the north, St Johannis to the
west and St Albani to the east.
The latter two boast late-Gothic
altars worth visiting. Together,
they testify to Göttingen's
early importance
in the
Middle Ages.

**Stone crest on
Göttingen's Rathaus**

The twin-towered Gothic façade of
St Cyriakus in Duderstadt

❷❺ Duderstadt

Road map C4. 🔲 24,500. 🔲
ℹ️ Marktstr. 66 (05527-84 12 00).

To the south of the Harz
mountains, not far from the
former border with East
Germany, lies this often
overlooked gem. A walk around
the medieval town is best
started on **Obermarkt** (upper
market). Here stands the half-
timbered **Rathaus** (town hall),
with an interesting façade and
spiky towers. Inside it has
exhibition halls and a cultural
centre. East of the town hall
rises the Catholic **Probsteikir-
che St Cyriakus** with its rich
interior of altars and 15 Baroque
statues. **St Servatius**, its
Protestant counterpart,
combines Gothic architecture
with a Secessionist interior.
Nearby is the **Westertorturm**,
the only surviving town gate.
Its strangely spiralling finial
is not a decorative feature,
but the consequence of a
weakness in its design.

The Gothic Rathaus on Marktplatz in Göttingen

㉖ The Weser Renaissance Trail

The Weser Renaissance is an architectural and decorative style of northern Germany, dating from the mid-16th to the mid-17th century. Its tall roofs and gables were inspired by Dutch architecture, although it has many original features: the *Zwerchhäuser* (bay windows, one or more storeys high), the *Utlucht* (protruding sections of the façade), lavish decorations and multi-wing castles, some with spiral staircases in their towers.

① **Hameln**
Rattenfängerhaus (rat catcher's house), Hochzeitshaus (wedding house) and Demptersches Haus (Dempsters' house) are good examples of the Weser Renaissance style. The Romanesque-Gothic Münster (collegiate church) is also worth seeing.

③ **Bevern**
Another gem of the Weser Renaissance style, the castle in Bevern, near Holzminden, was built from Prussian stone in the years 1602–12. It has four wings as well as two towers in the corners of its courtyard.

② **Hämelschenburg**
The castle, built in 1588–1612, is a three-winged building, surrounded by a moat. It has an impressive exterior with towers and decorative gables; its original interiors are also preserved.

WESERGEBIRGE

Emmer *Weser*

240

283

64

83

497

Weser

SOLLING

64

241

241

Diemel

80

83

Weser

7

E45

④ **Münden**
The principal buildings that exemplify the Weser Renaissance style are the town hall and the castle, now a regional museum with a collection of ceramics. Fragments of a Renaissance fresco of Duke Eryk II of Calenberg can also be admired here.

0 km   20

0 miles   20

Tips for Drivers

Starting point: Hameln.
Length: 112 km (70 miles).
Stopping-off places: good restaurants and bistros can be found in all the towns and villages along the route.

SCHLESWIG-HOLSTEIN

Schleswig-Holstein is the northernmost German state, situated between the Baltic and the North Sea and bordered by the Elbe River and Denmark. Weather-beaten by the unstable marine climate, the Gothic brick buildings of Lübeck, queen of the Baltic coast, testify equally to the turbulent history of this region. Today, tourists visit Schleswig-Holstein for its wide sandy beaches and impressive lakes.

Originally, this state comprised two territories: Schleswig in the north, which was inhabited by Germanic tribes (Angles, Saxons, Vikings and Danes) in the Middle Ages, and Holstein in the south, mainly populated by Slavs, who converted to Christianity as late as the 12th century. Its more recent history was characterized by struggles between the Hanseatic towns and the rulers of Denmark. In the 18th century, the entire region, from Altona in the south (now part of Hamburg) to Kolding in the north, belonged to Denmark, but in 1866 it was annexed to Bismarck's Prussia. In 1920, the political borders that exist today were established when Denmark regained the northern part of Schleswig after a plebiscite, leaving a significant Danish minority on the German side.

Schleswig-Holstein is principally an agricultural region, and less densely populated than any other state in Germany. Art lovers are mainly drawn to Lübeck, the most powerful Hanseatic town in the Baltic during the Middle Ages. Lübeck's old town, an architectural gem, has now been listed as a UNESCO World Heritage Site. Other places offer surprises aplenty – the visitor will be captivated by the Romanesque churches around Flensburg, while the magnificent countryside more than compensates for the lack of major cultural monuments. A walk through the national park of Schleswig-Holsteinisches Wattenmeer, the moving sand dunes of the elegant island of Sylt, or a romantic sunset on the lake shores in Plön will leave lasting impressions.

The moated Renaissance Wasserschloss in Glücksburg

◄ Aerial view of a mudflat on Süderoogsand, one of the North Frisian islands

Exploring Schleswig-Holstein

Undoubtedly the greatest attraction in this two-part state is Lübeck, and at least one day should be set aside to visit this town. Kiel is a popular destination during the annual Kieler Woche, the world's largest sailing festival. The sun-kissed island of Sylt invites the visitor to linger for a few days, while the stunning scenery of Helgoland is best explored in a one-day trip from Cuxhaven or Büsum. Hotels in the larger towns, such as Schleswig, Kiel or Flensburg, and many provincial boarding houses, provide a good base for excursions.

Traditional buildings in Plön, the main town in the Holstein Switzerland Nature Reserve

Getting Around

The nearest international airport is Hamburg. Two motorways bisect Schleswig-Holstein: leaving Hamburg and the long queues for the Elbe Tunnel behind, the E47 (No 7) takes the visitor to Kiel and via Flensburg on to the Danish peninsula of Jutland, while the E22 (turning off the E47) leads via Lübeck to the Danish capital, Copenhagen.

The lake at Westensee Nature Reserve, where visitors can experience the captivating nature and wildlife close up

For additional map symbols see back flap

Sights at a Glance

Key

— Motorway
— Main road
— Minor road
— Main railway
— Minor railway
— National border
— Regional border

Ferries departing for excursions from the harbour in Kiel

Glücksburg

5 FLENSBURG

Kappeln

Schlei

A7

201

6 SCHLESWIG

Eckernförde

Gettorf

Owschlag

Altenholz

201

Rendsburg

Nord-Ostee-Kanal

A210

A7

205

A215

Nortorf

404

7 KIEL

Preetz

Selenter See

76

Kieler Bucht

Heiligenhafen

Puttgarden

Fehmarn

Burg

207

202

Oldenburg

A1

Bordesholm

Plön

Eutin

8

Bosau

Grosser Plöner See

HOLSTEINISCHE SCHWEIZ

Neustadt

Lübecker Bucht

Neumünster

A21

SCHLESWIG-HOLSTEIN

Itzehoe

206

Bad Segeberg

Bad Schwartau

A20

10 LÜBECK

Kaltenkirchen

Bad Oldesloe

A21

A20

Ratzeburger See

2 GLÜCKSTADT

Elmshorn

A23

A7

Norderstedt

Ahrensburg

RATZEBURG 9

Schaalsee

Wedel

Hamburg

A1

Trittau

Reinbek

Schwarzenbek

A24

Berlin

Geesthacht

Bolzenburg

Lüneburg

Owschlag

Rendsburg

Nortorf

0 kilometres 20

0 miles 20

❶ Helgoland

For lovers of spices in Germany, it may have seemed a bad deal when in 1890 Germany received Helgoland from Britain in return for Zanzibar, but the island is nevertheless worth a visit. Farthest out in the open sea (50 km/31 miles from the mainland), the island always had great strategic importance, and after 1945, Britain used it as a bombing target before it was returned to Germany in 1952. Today its fresh air and spectacular red cliffs attract thousands of tourists.

VISITORS' CHECKLIST

Practical Information
Road map B1. 🚊 1,900.
ℹ Lung Wai 28 (04725-20 67 99).
🌐 **helgoland.de**

Transport
🚢 Hamburg and Büsum.

① **Port**
On the flat part of the island is Unterland, a small town with 1,300 inhabitants and a port. Fishermen store their nets in the colourful little houses, referred to as Hummerbuden (lobster huts).

③ **Lange Anna**
Tall Anna, measuring about 40 m (131ft) high, is the best known red sandstone cliff. Nearby is the Lummenfelsen, which is the smallest nature reserve in Germany.

② **Oberland**
In the upper part of the island stands the Nikolaikirche, dating from 1959. Close by, and worth a visit, are 16th-century tombs.

0 metres   100
0 yards   100

Key

— Suggested route

Tips for Tourists

Starting point: the port of Helgoland.
Length: 1.7 km (1.1 miles).
Stopping places: there are numerous restaurants, bars and cafés all over the island.

❷ Glückstadt

Road map C2. 🏛 12,000. 🚍 🛈
Große Nübelstrasse 31 (04124-93 75
85). 🌐 **glueckstadt-tourismus.de**

The Danish king, Christian IV,
founded this little town in 1617
and although less impressive
than Hamburg, the town is
worth a visit for its layout –
roads radiate out from the
hexagonal market square,
once surrounded by
fortifications. On the square
stands the reconstructed
17th-century town hall as well
as the Baroque Stadtkirche
(town church). In 1648, parts
of the duchy of Holstein were
transferred to Glückstadt. Most
of the palaces built to house the
dukes survived, for example the
Palais Werner with its amazing
ballroom. The regional **museum**
is now in Brockdorf-Palais,
another palace from 1632.

🏛 **Detlefsen-Museum**
Am Fleth 43. **Tel** (04124) 93 76 30.
Open 2–5pm Wed (to 6pm Jun–Aug),
2–6pm Thu–Sat, 2–5pm Sun.

❸ Meldorf

Road map C1. 🏛 7,500. 🚍
🛈 Nordermarkt 10 (04832-97 800).
🌐 **meldorf-nordsee.de**

Meldorf has successfully
preserved the **Dithmarscher
Dom**, its cathedral, a
13th-century basilica with an
exterior rebuilt in the 19th
century. The vaulting in the
transept is decorated with
Gothic frescoes, depicting the
legends of saints Catherine,
Christopher and Nicholas. There
is a richly decorated dividing
wall (1603) and a grand triptych
of the Crucifixion (c.1520).

The port and waterfront of Flensburg

❹ Sylt

Road map B1. 🏛 50,000. 🚍 in
Westerland. 🛈 Westerland, Stephan-
strasse 6 (04651-820 20). 🌐 **sylt.de**

The island of Sylt, the largest of
the North Frisian islands, has
long attracted wealthy German
visitors. The 50-km (31-mile)
long island offers a rich variety
of landscapes: white, sandy
beaches, shifting sand dunes
near List, towering up to 25 m
(82ft) high, steep shorelines,
the Rotes Kliff (red cliff) near
Kampen and the Watt, the
endless expanse of mudflats in
the national park, Schleswig-
Holsteinisches Wattenmeer.
Westerland is Sylt's main
town, and its promenade,
Friedrichstrasse, is "the" place
to be seen. There is also an
interesting casino in a former
Secessionist spa building.

❺ Flensburg

Road map C1. 🏛 84,500. 🚍
🛈 Rathausstrasse 1 (0461-909 09 20).
🚤 Rum-Regatta in Flensburger Förde
(May/Jun).

The most northerly town in
Germany, Flensburg was an
important trading centre in the
16th century with 200 ships,
although at times it belonged
to Denmark. The **Nordertor**
(northern gate), dating from
1595, is an emblem of the
city. The shipping museum is
fascinating while the
Marienkirche has a Renaissance
altar, sculptures and the
painting *The Last Supper* (1598).
Nearby is the **Heilig-Geist-
Kirche** (church of the Holy
Ghost), which has belonged to
the town's Danish community
since 1588. Other interesting
churches are **Nikolaikirche**
which boasts a magnificent
Renaissance organ, and
Johanniskirche with a vaulted
ceiling dating from around
1500. Its painted scenes show
people disguised as animals,
which was a covert way of
criticizing the church and the
system of indulgences.

Environs
Schloss Glücksburg, 9 km
(6 miles) northeast of Flensburg,
a square castle with massive
corner towers on a granite base,
was built from 1582–7. Visit its
captivating castle chapel, the
Roter Saal (red hall) with its
low vaulting, and the valuable
collection of 18th-century
tapestries from Brussels. The
artist Emil Nolde lived and
worked in **Seebüll**, west of
Flensburg, from the age of
20 until his death in 1956.

The sandy beaches of the North Frisian island of Sylt, extending far to the horizon

The inner courtyard of Schloss Gottorf in Schleswig

❻ Schleswig

Road map C1. 🅰 27,000. 🚆
ℹ Plessenstr. 7 (04621-85 00 56).
🎭 Schleswig-Holstein Musik Festival throughout the region (Jul/Aug); Wikinger-Tage (Aug every other year).
🌐 **schleswig.de**

The main seat of the Vikings, Schleswig became a bishop's see as early as 947, and from 1544 to 1713 it was the residence of the dukes of Schleswig-Holstein-Gottorf, once related to the rulers of Denmark and Russia. They resided in **Schloss Gottorf**, a castle, which now houses the **Schleswig-Holsteinisches Landesmuseum** (regional museum) as well as northern Germany's most famous archaeological museum, the **Archäologisches Landesmuseum**, exhibiting

the *Moorleichen*, prehistoric corpses preserved in peat. It is also worth seeing the two-storey chapel (1590).

The **Dom** (cathedral) was built in stages between the 12th and 15th centuries. Its largest treasure is the Bordesholmer Altar, a triptych altar carved by Hans Brüggemann in 1514–21. A masterpiece of Gothic carving, it is 12 m (39 ft) high and comprises 392 figures; the only one to look straight at the visitor is the sculptor himself, bearded and hat askew (in the house of Abraham and Melchisede).

Visitors can also walk around the historic fishermen's district of **Holm**, and visit the **Wikinger-Museum Haithabu**, about 4 km (2 miles) from the town centre. The fortifications have

survived in the grounds of this historic Viking settlement. The museum is housed in a modern building, which looks like an upturned boat. Exhibits include the depiction of Viking life, models of boats, jewellery and everyday items.

🏛 **Schloss Gottorf/ Schleswig-Holsteinisches Landesmuseum/ Archäologisches Landesmuseum**
Tel (04621) 81 30. **Open** Apr–Oct: 10am–6pm daily; Nov–Mar: 10am–4pm Tue–Fri (to 5pm Sat & Sun).

🏛 **Wikinger-Museum Haithabu**
Tel (04621) 81 32 22. **Open** Apr–Oct: 9am–5pm daily; Nov–Mar: 10am–4pm Tue–Sun.

❼ Kiel

Road map C1. 🅰 245,000. 🚆
ℹ Andreas-Gayk-Strasse 31 (0431-67 91 00). Town hall: **Open** 9am–6pm Mon–Fri, 9am–1pm Sat. 🚢 🚤
🎭 Kieler Woche (end Jun).

Located at the end of the Kieler Förde inlet, Kiel marks the beginning of the Nord-Ostsee-Kanal (Kiel Canal), in service since 1895, with two giant locks. Ferries depart from Kiel for Scandinavia, and in the summer the "Kieler Woche" turns the town into a mecca for yachtsmen from around the world.

A walk along the Schweden-Kai (embankment) and surroundings will take visitors to the vast **Rathaus** (town hall), dating from the beginning of the 20th century, and the **Nikolaikirche** (church of St Nicholas) which was rebuilt after the devastation of World War II, with its baptismal font and Gothic altar. Ernst Barlach

Romanesque Baptismal Fonts

There are few places in the world where visitors can see as many Romanesque baptismal fonts as in Angeln. Generally fashioned from granite, they have been preserved in enchanting 12th-century churches, which can be visited by following a 63-km (39-mile) route along the roads linking Flensburg and Schleswig, Munkbrarup, Sörup, Norderbrarup, Süderbrarup and finally Ulsnis.

Font in the church in Borbry

Font in the church in Munkbrarup

Font in the church in Sörup

A house in Kiel's Schleswig-Holsteinisches Freilichtmuseum

created *Geistkämpfer*, the sculpture outside the church, which symbolizes the triumph of mind over matter. Pieces of the sculpture, which had been cut up by the National Socialists, were found and reassembled after the war.

The most interesting of Kiel's many museums is the **Schleswig-Holsteinisches Freilichtmuseum**, an open-air museum in Molfsee, 6 km (4 miles) from the centre of Kiel, where German rural architecture from the 16th–19th centuries is on show. Pottery, basket-making and baking are demonstrated and the products are sold here.

🏛 **Schleswig-Holsteinisches Freilichtmuseum**
Hamburger Landstrasse 97. **Tel** (0431) 65 96 60. **Open** Apr–Oct: 9am–6pm daily; Nov–Mar: 11am–4pm Sun. 🅿

❽ Holsteinische Schweiz (Holstein's Switzerland)

Road map D1. 🚌 🚊 Bahnhofstr. 3, Malente (0800 20 20 080). 🎷 Jazz-Festival in Plön (May); open-air opera during Sommerspiele in Eutin.

The moraine hills, which reach a height of 164 m (538 ft), and 140 lakes are the reasons why this area is known as Holstein's Switzerland. The best means of transport here is the bicycle, allowing visitors to appreciate the beauty of nature and the wealth of the fauna – ornithologists have counted 200 species of birds. The main centre of this holiday area is

Emil Nolde (1867–1956)

Born Emil Hansen, this great artist later adopted the name of the town in which he was born. After studying art in Copenhagen, Munich and Paris, Nolde devoted himself to painting, and was also successful in the graphic arts. From 1906–7 he belonged to the Expressionist group *Die Brücke*. He is known particularly for his use of vivid colours and highly expressive features, embuing his subjects with great emotion. Rejected and forbidden to paint by the National Socialists as an exponent of "degenerate art", Nolde settled and continued to paint in Seebüll, where a house was built for him to his own designs.

Plön on the Großer Plöner See (large Plön lake). Nearby is **Preetz**, an old shoemakers' town, which has a towerless Gothic church that belonged to a former Benedictine monastery. Older still is the Romanesque church in **Bosau**, a small town in a picturesque location on the Großer Plöner See. It was the first bishopric in this area, and home to Vizelin – the apostle of the Slavs.

It is also worth visiting **Eutin**, a small town full of picturesque buildings, which is sometimes referred to as the "Weimar of the north". The original Schloss, a brick structure with four wings, was built in the Middle Ages as the residence of the Lübeck bishops, but it was substantially altered in the years 1716–27. Worth seeing inside are the palace chapel, the Blauer Salon (blue salon) with Rococo stucco work, as well as paintings by Johann Heinrich Wilhelm Tischbein, which were inspired by the *Iliad* and the *Odyssey*, epic poems written by Homer.

The Dom in Ratzeburg

❾ Ratzeburg

Road map D2. 🏔 12,500. 🚌 ℹ Unter den Linden 1 (04541-80 00 886). 🎷 Drachenbootfest (Jun).

Ratzeburg, situated on an island in the Großer Ratzeburger See, is linked with the mainland by three causeways. The town was named after Ratibor, the duke of the Elbe River area. Henry the Lion established a missionary bishopric here in 1154, and later it became the residence of the Lauenburg dukes.

The **Dom** (cathedral) is one of the earliest examples of brick architecture, a style that was imported from Lombardy. The southern vestibule of the Romanesque basilica is particularly impressive – with herringbone-pattern brickwork and lines of black tiles as interior decoration. The Romanesque stalls, a 13th-century crucifix in a rainbow arch, the ducal gallery above the nave and the Baroque altar in the southern transept are some of its treasures.

The 17th-century Schloss in Plön, in Holstein's Switzerland

⑩ Street-by-Street: Lübeck

This "specific nest", as Lübeck was described by its most famous resident, Thomas Mann, is well worth a visit. The most important town in the Baltic basin by the end of the Middle Ages, it is now a magnet for fans of Backsteingotik, Gothic brick architecture which has been elevated to a national style. In Lübeck it is easy to see why: church interiors, the façades of buildings, the city gates, the unique town hall and even the medieval hospital resemble pictures from an illustrated history of architecture brought to life. Despite a few blunders, the city has been beautifully rebuilt after World War II and enjoys a positive revival.

Rathaus
Germany's most famous brick town hall, dating from 1226, has unusual walls and turrets.

Buddenbrookhaus
This beautiful Gothic building was once the home of Nobel prize-winning author Thomas Mann's grandparents. It is now a museum dedicated to the Mann family.

BREITE STRASSE

SCHLÜSSELBUDEN

HOLSTENSTRASSE

Heiligen-Geist-Hospital

★ Marienkirche
St Mary's Church, larger than the cathedral and situated behind the town hall, holds great art treasures.

Key

— Suggested route

Holstentor
This gate, once the only entrance into Lübeck, was built by Hinrich Helmstede in the years 1466–78, based on Flemish designs. It has become the emblem of the town.

Petrikirche
The church of St Peter, from the first half of the 14th century, is Lübeck's only five-naved church.

View of the Town
Lübeck and its seven towers can be seen from afar. Virtually all the tourist attractions are in the old town, which is enclosed by the river Trave and its channels.

St Anne's Museum
This museum, housed inside an Augustinian convent, portrays life and culture in 13th–18th-century Lübeck.

Freilichtbühne

ST ANNEN-STRASSE

MÜHLENSTRASSE

SANDSTRASSE

PFERDEMARKT

PARADE

MARLESGRUBE

DANKWARTS GRUBE

0 metres   150
0 yards   150

Herz-Jesu-Kirche
This 19th-century Catholic church houses a memorial to four clergymen who were executed during the Third Reich for their opposition to the war.

★ Dom
The cathedral, begun in 1173 at the time of Henry the Lion and completed in 1230, is 130 m (426 ft) long.

Marzipan From Lübeck

A favourite present from Lübeck is marzipan, which has been popular throughout Europe since the 19th century. The sweets are made from two-thirds sweet almonds imported from Venice and one-third sugar and aromatic oils. The Persians referred to it as *marsaban*, and in 1530 its name was recorded for the first time in Lübeck as *Martzapaen*. From 1806, the Niederegger patisserie perfected the recipe; they established a patisserie on Breite Strasse which operates to this day.

Exploring Lübeck

All the most important monuments, with the exception of the Holstentor, are situated within the old town, which is best explored on foot.

⬆ Marienkirche

Schüsselbuden 13. **Tel** (0451) 88 99 700. **Open** 9am–5pm daily, in winter to 4pm.

St Mary's church was constructed by the Lübeckers as a monument to themselves. The twin-towered basilica with transept and a passage-way around the polygon-shaped presbytery is the brick modification of a Neo-Classical French cathedral.

Its vast interior boasts the highest vaulted brick ceiling in the world (40 m/131 ft) which dominates the other interior features. These include a 10 m (32 ft) bronze Holy Sacrament (1476–9); a baptismal font in the main nave dating from 1337; the altar dedicated to the Virgin Mary in the Sängerkapelle (singers' chapel) made in Antwerp in 1518; and the main, late-Gothic Swarte-Altar

with the Madonna. The Briefkapelle, the southwestern side chapel built around 1310, is one of the earliest examples of star vaulting in Europe.

In one of the towers, the shattered fragments of the church bells have been left embedded in the floor where they fell during the bombing in 1942; the present bells are from St Catherine's in Gdansk.

⊞ Buddenbrookhaus

Heinrich- und Thomas-Mann-Zentrum, Mengstr. 4. **Tel** (0451) 122 42 43. **Open** Jan–Mar: 11am–5pm daily; Apr–Dec: 10am–6pm daily. **Closed** 24, 25, 31 Dec. 🎦

Literature lovers will wish to visit the Buddenbrook house. Behind its Rococo façade from 1758 is a museum devoted to the Mann family, the great writers who lived here in 1841–91. It is here that Thomas Mann wrote the family saga of the Buddenbrooks, after whom the house is named, and for which he was awarded the

Nobel Prize in 1929. The centre exhibits documents relating to this famous family, in particular to Thomas and Heinrich Mann, concentrating on their time in Lübeck and their emigration and exile after 1933.

⊞ Schabbelhaus

Mengstrasse 48 & 52.

Originally the western, wealthier half of Lübeck had many patrician houses, facing the streets with their ornate brick gables. Many of these were damaged in the bombing raids of March 1942, but after World War II they were carefully restored. The most interesting buildings survived in Mengstrasse, in particular the famous Schabbelhaus at No. 48. Built in 1558, this house gained a magnificent Baroque hall in the 18th century. Today it is an attraction in its own right as well as a restaurant.

Stepped gables of the Haus der Schiffergesellschaft

⊞ Haus der Schiffergesellschaft

Breite Strasse 2.

The house of the Marine Guild, which dates from 1535, has a splendid interior and now houses one of the city's most elegant restaurants. The façade has stepped gables and terraces/forecourts, typical of Lübeck.

⊞ Füchtingshof

Glockengießerstr. 23.

The eastern part of the town is of an entirely different character: narrow streets link charming

The multi-storey Burgtor, crowned by a Baroque cupola

The façade of the Gothic Heiliger-Geist-Hospital, with its spiky towers

Höfe (courtyards) and small, modest houses. The most interesting Höfe can be found at numbers 23 and 39. The Baroque portal of the Füchtingshof, at No. 23, leads to houses which, from 1639, were built for the widows of merchants and captains.

🏛 Günter-Grass-Haus
Glockengießerstr. 21. **Tel** (0451) 122 42 30. **Open** Apr–Dec: 10am–5pm daily; Jan–Mar: 11am–5pm Tue–Sun.

More than 1,100 exhibits (including drawings and manuscripts) here give an insight into the life and work of Nobel Prize-winning author and artist Günter Grass.

🏛 Burgtor
On the northern limits of the old town stands the castle gate, a second surviving gate of the historic fortifications. A Baroque finial was added to the gate in 1685. The tower's five storeys are decorated with uniform rows of windows and windbreaks.

✚ Heiligen-Geist-Hospital
Grosse Burgstr. **Tel** (0451) 79 07-841. **Open** Apr–Sep: 10am–5pm Tue–Sun; Oct–Mar: 10am–4pm Tue–Sun.

The Holy Ghost hospital is the best preserved medieval building of its type in central Europe. Built in the shape of the letter T, it has a shorter western section with a twin-aisled hall-church (c.1286), containing frescoes of *Christ and the Madonna on Solomon's Throne* and *Majestas Domini*. The second section contains the actual hospice. In 1820, small cubicles were created for the elderly, who lived here until 1970.

✝ Jakobikirche
This 15th-century church, which suffered only insignificant damage during World War II, has preserved its original, mainly Baroque features. Of particular note are the main altar as well as the side altar in the south chapel. The latter was established around 1500 by the mayor, Heinrich Brömbse, and depicts a scene of the Crucifixion carved in sandstone. Both the small and the large organ originate from the 15th century.

⛪ Katharinenkirche
Königstrasse. Museumskirche St Katharinen **Tel** (0451) 122 41 37. **Open** 15 Apr–30 Sep: 10am–5pm Fri–Sun.

St Catherine's, the only surviving monastic church, was built by the Franciscans, as is apparent from the absence of a tower and its monastic gallery in the presbytery of the main nave. The western façade, with its glazed

The bright interior of the Gothic Dom

brickwork, is of a high artistic quality. In the 20th century, sculptures carved by Ernst Barlach were added (*Woman in the Wind, Beggar on Crutches* and *The Singing Novitiate*). On the western side hangs the painting of *The Resurrection of Lazarus* by Jacopo Tintoretto, bought by a wealthy patrician; the sculpture of St George and the dragon is a copy of the famous original by the Lübeck artist Bernt Notke, which is now in Stockholm.

🏛 St Annen-Museum
St Annen Str. 15. **Tel** (0451) 122 41 37. **Open** Jan–May: 11am–5pm Tue–Sun, Apr–Dec: 10am–5pm Tue–Sun. **Closed** Easter, 24, 25, 31 Dec.

The Augustinian convent houses unusual Lübeck art treasures. There is an impressive number of wooden Gothic altars, commissioned by wealthy families for their private chapels in one of the five churches. The altars were supposed to bring them eternal salvation after death, and to symbolize the wealth and prestige of the family during their lifetime. Gems of the collection are the Hans Memling altar with Christ's Passion, and the external side wings of the Schonenfahrer Altar by Bernt Notke.

⛪ Dom
Tel (0451) 747 04. **Open** Apr–Oct: 10am–6pm daily; Nov–Mar: 10am–4pm daily.

The cathedral, completed in 1341, takes the form of a Gothic hall-church. Its most precious possession is the Triumphal Cross sculpted from a 17-m (55-ft) oak tree by Bernt Notke, a celebrated local artist. The giant figures, resplendent with emotion, include Adam and Eve, as well as the founder, bishop Albert Krummedick. Among numerous memorials, that dedicated to bishop Heinrich Bocholt, made from bronze, stands out. Additionally, two valuable sculptures can be seen; *Holy Mary Mother of God* with a crown composed of stars, as well as the *Beautiful Madonna* in the southern nave (1509). Note the bronze baptismal font by Lorenz Grove from 1455, with its three kneeling angels.

MECKLENBURG-LOWER POMERANIA

The medieval towns of Schwerin, Wismar, Rostock and Stralsund, as well as several magnificent architectural monuments, provide reason enough to visit this part of Germany, yet it also offers a largely untouched landscape of forests and lakes. Along the Baltic coastline, tourists delight in the beautiful sandy beaches of Darß or Usedom, but above all they head for the island of Rügen, with its famous white cliffs.

Mecklenburg-Vorpommern (Lower Pomerania), a mosaic of regions, can look back on an eventful history. In the 12th century, indigenous Slav tribes were colonized and converted to Christianity. The region became part of the Holy Roman Empire and German colonialism resulted in the Slavs' rapid assimilation. In the Middle Ages, several towns became rich trading centres and joined the Hanseatic League. From the 18th century, the Swedish Empire was the most powerful political force in this part of Europe. It ruled Wismar, Rügen and Stralsund until 1803 and 1815 respectively, when the territories became part of Prussia, and later the German Reich. During World War II the Baltic towns suffered terrible destruction and then from neglect under the German Democratic Republic: in 1953 all the hotels were nationalized and the unique buildings in the Hanseatic towns were left to decay or were destroyed.

After reunification, although still one of the poorest states in Germany, Mecklenburg-Lower Pomerania today has become an idyllic holiday destination. Improvements in the infrastructure, new hotels and restaurants have brought positive change, and it has much to offer. Nature lovers, walkers and cyclists, for example, can enjoy the Mecklenburg lake district and the island of Rügen. Fans of architecture will find a wealth of interest in the palace in Ludwigslust and the castle of Güstrow, as well as the Gothic brick architecture in town halls, churches and smaller buildings.

The beautiful white chalk cliffs on the island of Rügen sweep down to the blue Baltic Sea

◀ The superb Schloss of Schwerin, on an island in the middle of Schwerin lake

Exploring Mecklenburg-Lower Pomerania

This is a large region with mostly minor roads so visitors are well advised to allow extra time to explore it. The area can be divided into three: the west, stopping off in pretty Wismar or charming Schwerin with its fairy-tale castle; the centre, with the major port of Rostock as a base, and the east, which can be explored from Stralsund or Greifswald. In the central Mecklenburger Seenplatte is Müritz National Park, a vast area of lakes and forests that is ideal for camping, walking and sailing. It is also a good plan to set aside a few days for relaxation on the sandy beaches of Darß, Zingst, Usedom or Rügen.

Mecklenburg's glorious beaches

Sights at a Glance

Neuer Markt, surrounded by charming gabled buildings, Rostock

Key

═══ Motorway

── Main road

⋯⋯ Minor road

┄┄ Main railway

── Minor railway

▬▬ National border

▬▬ Regional border

For additional map symbols see back flap

Getting Around

International flights land at Hamburg and Berlin, domestic flights at Rostock and Heringsdorf on Usedom. Ferries go from Denmark, Sweden and Lithuania to Sassnitz and Rostock, and the E55/A19 motorway runs from the south to Schwerin and Rostock.

Rügen, lit by dawn sunlight

Kap Arkona

Hiddensee

Sassnitz

RÜGEN

Prerow

Zingst

Waase **11**

Bergen

Darss

Ahrenshoop   Barth

10 STRALSUND

Putbus

105

Ribnitz-Damgarten

194

96

Greifswalder Bodden

Grimmen

Wieck

16 PEENEMÜNDE

110

Recknitz

A20

GREIFSWALD **12**

13 WOLGAST

Gnoien

MECKLENBURG-VORPOMMERN

Demmin

111

109

111

USEDOM

Heringsdorf

Ahlbeck

Peene

110

15

Teterow

Kummerower See

ANKLAM **14**

Usedom

Oderhaff

Malchin

Reuterstadt

Zarow

Uckermünde

Malchiner See

Basedow

96

197

104

Friedland

9

108

NATIONALPARK MÜRITZ

NEUBRANDENBURG

7

Lecker

Randau

Waren

192

Tollensesee

A20

109

Pasewalk

8

Malchow

Müritzsee

Stargard

104

Mecklenburgische Seenplatte

198

Neustrelitz

198

198

Szczecin

A11

Mirow

96

Berlin

Wittstock

Berlin

0 kilometres   30

0 miles   30

The attractive cloisters of Schloss Güstrow

● Schwerin

Despite protests from Rostock, the smaller town of Schwerin was chosen as the capital of the newly united state of Mecklenburg-Lower Pomerania. This was an inspired choice as the town is picturesquely situated amid several lakes, with a fairy-tale castle on an island, and an enchanting old town with many Neo-Classical and historic buildings that survived World War II largely unscathed. Apart from a brief spell, the Mecklenburg dukes resided in Schwerin from 1318–1918. Intellectual life flourished here in the 16th century and so the city is known as "Florence of the North".

The Neo-Renaissance Schloss on an island in Schweriner See

Exploring Schwerin

The old town of Schwerin is situated between Pfaffenteich railway station and Schweriner See, a vast 65-sq km (25-sq mile) lake. All its major attractions can easily be visited on foot. Close by to the north is Schelf, which was once a separate town.

🏠 Schloss

Schlossinsel. **Tel** (0385) 52 52 920.
Open 15 Apr–14 Oct: 10am–6pm daily; 15 Oct–14 Apr: 10am–5pm Tue–Sun.

Situated on Burg Island, this castle is often referred to as the "Neuschwanstein of Mecklenburg", after the famous Bavarian castle. It was, in fact, largely built earlier (1843–57) to an eclectic design by Georg Adolph Demmler and Friedrich August Stüler, who were inspired by the turrets of Château Chambord in France. Major refurbishment tried to re-create some of the castle's original Renaissance features, of which only the ceramic decorations have remained. Inside, the castle

chapel built by Johan Batista Parra in 1560–63 has survived. The elegant rooms in the castle – Thronsaal (throne chamber), Ahnengalerie (ancestral gallery), Rote Audienz (red auditorium), Speisesaal (dining chamber) – are decorated with gilded stucco work. Despite the proliferation of their styles these rooms delight visitors, transporting them back to the 19th century.

🏠 Burg- und Schlossgarten

The remaining part of the island is occupied by the Burggarten (fortress garden), which has an orangery and an artificial grotto, built from granite around 1850. A bridge leads to the larger Schlossgarten (castle garden), a favourite place for the town's inhabitants to relax. The Kreuzkanal, a canal built in 1748–56, one of the garden's axes, is lined with copies of Baroque statues including the *Four Seasons*, created by the renowned sculptor of the Dresden Zwinger, Balthasar Permoser.

🏛 Staatliches Museum

Am Alten Garten 3. **Tel** (0385) 595 80.
Open Apr–Oct: 10am–8pm Tue, 10am–6pm Wed–Sun; Oct–Apr: 10am–5pm Tue–Sun. 🖼

The state art museum stands in Alter Garten, one of the most attractive squares in Germany, where the waters reflect the castle and Neo-Renaissance theatre. The museum, which features lions on its façade and a portico with Ionic columns, houses an art collection based on that of Duke Christian Ludwig II, a testimony to his taste and erudition. As well as works by German artists such as Cranach, Liebermann and Corinth, and the Dutch painters Hals and Fabritius, it holds works by many French artists. This includes 34 paintings by Jean-Baptiste Oudry, who was court painter to Ludwig XIV, as well as paintings by Dadaist artist Marcel Duchamp and sculptures by expressionist artist Ernst Barlach.

🏛 Rathausplatz

The town hall square is surrounded by the homes of wealthy citizens, often with 19th-century façades concealing older walls. This is true of the Gothic town hall, which is hidden under an English mock-Tudor-style façade. Demmler was the architect who was responsible for numerous Neo-Renaissance and Neo-Gothic buildings, the showpieces of Schwerin. One of the outstanding buildings in the market square is Neues

Venus and Amor (1527) by Lucas Cranach in the Staatliches Museum

The Dom and houses in Schwerin

Gebäude on the north side. This "new building" is a covered market from 1783–5, with a showpiece façade comprising 12 Doric columns.

🏛 Dom St Maria und St Johannes

Am Dom 4. **Tel** (0385) 56 50 14. Tower **Open** Apr–Oct: 10am–5pm Mon–Sat, noon–5pm Sun; Nov–Mar: 11am–2pm Mon–Fri, 11am–4pm Sat, noon–3pm Sun. 🎫

This cathedral is regarded as the most important work of Gothic brick architecture in the Baltic region, in spite of its Neo-Gothic tower, which affords a marvellous view of the entire town. The basilica, dating from 1240–1416, with its wide transept and passageway around the presbytery and its wreath of chapels, is reminiscent of the design of French cathedrals.

A number of outstanding original features compare well with the finest works from Antwerp during this time. They include the wooden late-Gothic multi-panelled Crucifixion worked in sandstone, the 14th-century baptismal font, a memorial to Duchess Helen of Mecklenburg created by the Vischer workshop in Nuremberg and the tombstones of Duke Christopher and his wife (1595).

🏛 Freilichtmuseum Schwerin-Muess

Alte Crivitzer Landstrasse 13. **Tel** (0385) 208 41-0. **Open** late Apr–late Sep: 10am–6pm Tue–Sun; late Sep–Oct: 10am–5pm Tue–Sun. 🎫

VISITORS' CHECKLIST

Practical Information
Road map D2. 🏛 110,000.
ℹ Am Markt 14 (Rathaus) (0385-59 252 12). 🎭 Schlossfestspiele (Jun–Jul), Drachenboot (Aug), Altstadtfest (Sep).
🌐 schwerin.com

Transport
🚉 Am Bahnhof.

The museum contains a collection of Mecklenburg folk architecture, including 17 houses of the 17th–19th centuries, which strive to recreate the look of an original village. Combine a visit with a leisurely day on the beach in Zippendorf.

Houses of an earlier era in open-air Freilichtmuseum in Schwerin-Mueß

Schwerin City Centre

① Schloss
② Burg- und Schlossgarten
③ Staatliches Museum
④ Rathausplatz
⑤ Dom St Maria und St Johannes

0 metres   300
0 yards   300

One of 24 waterfalls in Ludwigslust Park

❷ Ludwigslust

Road map D2. 🚉 12,600. 🚍 north of centre, 15 min. walk. ❖ Schlossstr. 36 (03874-52 62 51).
🌐 **stadtludwigslust.de**

At the beginning of the 18th century, the small village of Klenow was founded here; from 1765 it grew into a town. The town was laid out around the **Schloss**, residence of the dukes of Mecklenburg-Schwerin until 1837. The "Versailles of Mecklenburg" is quite different from its French namesake. The Baroque palace was built entirely in brick, concealed beneath sandstone from the Ruda hills. The ornate interior, particularly the elegant Goldener Saal (gold hall), was decorated in Ludwigsluster Carton, a type of papier-mâché, in order to cut costs.

In the mid-19th century, the vast **Schlosspark** was redesigned by Peter Joseph Lenné as an English-style landscaped garden. On a scenic walk round the garden, the visitor can discover some 24 waterfalls, a canal, artificial ruins, a stone bridge and the mausoleum of Helena Pavlovna, daughter of Tsar Peter I, who died tragically young. In the town you will find the Protestant **Stadtkirche**, built in 1765–70 to look like an antique temple. In the presbytery is a giant mural, *The Adoration of the Shepherds*.

🏰 **Schloss**
Tel (03874) 57 19 0. **Open** 15 Apr–14 Oct: 10am–6pm daily; 15 Oct–14 Apr: 10am– 5pm Tue–Sun. **Closed** 24, 31 Dec. 🎟

⛪ **Stadtkirche**
Tel (03874) 21 968. **Open** varies, call ahead.

❸ Gadebusch

Road map D2. 🚉 6,600. 🚍
❖ Mühlenstr. 19 (03886-21 21 10).
🌐 **gadebusch.de**

This small town, next to the former East–West border, has two interesting historic monuments. The **Stadtkirche**, which dates from 1220, is the oldest brick church in Mecklenburg. Its cross vaulting, chunky pillars and goblet-shaped capitals are Romanesque in style. One of its most precious pieces is the bronze baptismal font (1450). Angels hold the bowl, on which 22 scenes of the Passion were sculpted by an unknown artist.

In the 16th and 17th centuries, the **Schloss** was the residence of distant relations of the dukes of Mecklenburg. Resembling the castle in Wismar, it is decorated with glazed reliefs and pilasters. It is not open to visitors.

Baptismal font in the Stadtkirche in Gadebusch

❹ Wismar

Road map D2. 🚉 55,000. 🚍
❖ Am Markt 11 (03841-19 433).

Wismar is undoubtedly one of the most attractive towns in Mecklenburg. During the Middle Ages, it was an important Hanseatic centre, as evidenced by the monumental brick church, which is completely out of proportion with the provincial town of today. After the Thirty Years' War, in 1648, the Swedes were established in the town, and rebuilt it as the strongest fortress in Europe. In 1803 they leased Wismar to Mecklenburg, but never claimed it back.

The town centre has a grand market square measuring 100 x 100 m (328 x 328 ft), with **Wasserspiele** (well-house), a Dutch-Renaissance pavilion from 1602 in the centre. Water was piped here from a source 4 km (2 miles) away, until 1897, to supply 220 private and

The Baroque residence of the dukes of Mecklenburg-Schwerin in Ludwigslust

Alter Schwede and Wasserspiele in the market square in Wismar

16 public buildings. The most beautiful house on the square is the **Alter Schwede** (old Swede), built about 1380, with a protruding Gothic brick gable. To the west of the market there are two churches, which act as sad examples of the GDR's neglect of its historical legacy. The reconstruction of the **Georgenkirche**, badly damaged in World War II, was begun in 1989, and it will soon be returned to its former glory. The **Marienkirche** has only one surviving tower – the ruined nave was blown up in 1960. Nearby lies the **Fürstenhof**, residence of the dukes of Wismar. The north wing is the most interesting – its Mannerist style was inspired by the Italian town of Ferrari and northern European ceramic traditions (such as Lübeck workshop). The magnificent sandstone portal is flanked by pairs of intertwined fauns. **Nikolaikirche** is a gem of Wismar architecture. Spared in World War II, the façade of this late-Gothic basilica from the 14th and 15th centuries is decorated with glazed friezes of mythological creatures, saints and, at the peak of the transept,

A relic of fauns from the portal of Fürstenhof in Wismar

a huge rose window. The proportions of the interior and the height of the vaulted main nave measuring 37 m (121 ft) are captivating. Some of the interior fixtures and fittings came from other churches in the city, which were either ruined or no longer exist, including the so-called Krämeraltar with a sculpture of the *Beautiful Madonna and Child* (c.1420). The room by the tower has the most complete cycle of frescoes in the region (c.1450).

❺ Bad Doberan

Road map D1. 🚊 11,900. 🚌
ℹ️ Severinstr 6 (038203-621 54).

When Duke Henry Borwin was hunting deer, a passing swan reportedly shouted "*Dobr Dobr*" (a good location) as the deer fell. Borwin duly founded the most important Cistercian monastery of the Baltic region here. The **Münster** was built in 1295–1368, with a severe interior and a small bell, in accordance with the order's rules which stipulate that no tower should be built. The interior is fascinating, its walls surfaced in red, with white plasterwork and colourful ribbing. Most of the original fixtures and fittings have survived almost intact. Among the treasures are a vast, gilded panelled painting, produced in Lübeck in 1310, a 12-m (39-ft) Holy Sacrament made from oak, a small cupboard holding the chalice and relics from an earlier

Romanesque building, as well as a statue of the Virgin Mary. Beautiful tombs mark the resting places of the rulers of Mecklenburg, of the Danish Queen Margaret, and Albrecht, King of Sweden, who died in 1412. Visitors can walk around the outside of the church which has a pleasant lawn. Beyond you can find a small octagonal building, beautifully decorated with glazed brickwork – this lovely piece of 13th-century architecture is the morgue.

A stroll around the health spa is also recommended. Right in its centre it has two early 19th-century pavilions with Chinese features – an ideal place for a coffee break.

Environs

Another adventure the visitor could try is a trip on the "Molli", a narrow-gauge railway that links Bad Doberan with Heiligendamm and Kühlungsborn, where there is a 4-km (2-mile) long beach. On the way, a little gem of 13th-century country architecture, the church in **Stefenshagen**, calls for a visit. On its south portal, see the terracotta figures of the apostles. Across the presbytery runs a brickwork relief with mythological creatures.

🏛 **Doberaner Münster**
Klosterstrasse 2. **Tel** (038203) 627 16.
Open May–Sep: 9am–6pm daily (from 11am Sun); Mar, Apr, Oct: 10am–5pm daily (from 11am Sun); Nov–Feb: 10am–4pm daily (from 11am Sun). 🗓 daily.

The monumental Cistercian Münster in Bad Doberan

The imposing Schloss, dominating the skyline of Güstrow

❻ Güstrow

Road map D2. 🚉 32,500. 🚋
ℹ️ Franz-Parr-Platz 10 (03843-68 10 23). 🌐 **guestrow.de**

Güstrow is one of the most harmonious towns of the former German Democratic Republic, with an attractive old town, unmarred by pre-fabricated tower blocks. All the most important monuments are within easy reach. The town is dominated by the **Schloss**, built from 1558 by Franz Parr, a member of a renowned family of sculptors and architects from northern Italy. German, Italian and Dutch elements come together here, including fantas-tical chimneys and two-storey arcades in the courtyards. The architect's brother decorated the Festsaal (ballroom) with a hunting frieze – the stucco heads of the deer have real antlers.

In the nearby **Dom**, a brick cathedral of the 13th and 14th centuries, there is a fascinating Gothic altar (c.1500). Look for the vast figures of the apostles on the pillars of the nave and the 16th-century tomb of Duke Ulrich and his two wives, with a large genealogical family tree of all three of them. In the north nave hangs the burly *Schwebende* (Hovering Angel), a remarkable work by Ernst Barlach, who lived here from 1910 until his death in 1938. He described his works to Bertolt Brecht as: "beautiful without beautifying, sizeable without

enlarging, harmonious without smoothness, and full of vitality without brutality". Barlach's work bore the brunt of National Socialist condemnation – the original *Schwebende* was melted down and made into cannons but the copy that replaced it was made from the original plaster cast. Other works by Barlach can be seen in the museum dedicated to him.

It is worth concluding a visit to this town in the market, near which rises the **Pfarrkirche St Marien**. This church has a magnificent high altar, a panelled work of art with painted wings by Belgian artists (c.1522).

Environs
The open-air museum in **Groß-Raden**, near Sternberg, is popular with tourists as well as archaeology students. A village has been re-created with houses, workshops and a system of fortifications.

🏛️ **Archäologisches Freilichtmuseum**
Groß-Raden. **Tel** (03847) 22 52.
Open Apr–Oct: 10am–5:30pm daily; Nov–Mar: 10am–4:30pm Tue–Sun.
Closed 24 Dec, 31 Dec.

❼ Neubrandenburg

Road map E2. 🚉 75 000. 🚋
ℹ️ Stargader Str. 17 (0395-19 433).
🌐 **neubrandenburg-touristinfo.de**

Founded in 1248 as a sister town to Brandenburg on the Havel, the town was laid out in the form of a regular oval. It prospered as a trading centre until the Thirty Years' War, after which it fell into disrepair. As a result it now has what is probably the only example of post-World War II concrete tower blocks surrounded by medieval town walls, which have survived virtually intact. The walls extend for 2.3 km (2515 yds), originally with a keep open to the interior, and subsequently interspersed with half-timbered houses, known as **Wiekhäuser** (there were once 58, of which 24 survive). Of the four city gates the most interesting are **Friedländer Tor** (begun in 1300), with inner and outer gateways and a tower, as well as Neues and Stargarder Tor, decorated on the town side with mysterious terracotta figures of women with raised hands (c.1350).

In the town centre stands the medieval **Marienkirche**, which was damaged during World War II and is now restored as a concert hall.

Environs
The castle in **Stargard**, some 10 km (6 miles) to the south, is the oldest secular building in Mecklenburg. Its 4 m (13 ft) walls were begun in 1200; the residence in 1236. Today it houses a youth hostel.

A typical half-timbered Wiekhaus in the town wall in Neubrandenburg

⑧ Nationalpark Müritz

There are about a thousand lakes between Schwerin and Neubrandenburg; the largest of these is Müritzsee, to the east of which a national park was established in 1990. A particularly attractive part of the lake district is the so-called Mecklenburgische Schweiz (Swiss Mecklenburg), with its hilly moraines, such as Ostberg, 115 m (377 ft) above sea level. Tourists are attracted by the breathtaking scenery, perfect conditions for water sports and fascinating castles and palaces.

VISITORS' CHECKLIST

Practical Information
Road map: E2. *i* Waren, Neuer Markt 21. (03991-66 61 83); Neustrelitz, Strelitzerstr. 1 (03981-25 31 19).

① **Basedow**
For 600 years Basedow was in the hands of the von Hahn family, who built this irregular three-winged palace.

Malchiner See

② **Schlitz**
This palace is the most important Neo-Classical monument in Mecklenburg (1800–1823). In its beautiful landscaped park stands the Nymphenbrunnen, the famous fountain of nymphs. Cast in 1903 in Secessionist style for the Berlin department store Wertheim, it was transferred to this site in 1930.

Kölpinsee

Müritz

Woterfitzsee

Jäthensee

Zierrker See

Grosse Labussee

Woblitz-See

④ **Müritz**
Müritz (meaning 'small sea') is, at 115 sq km (44 sq miles), the second largest lake in Germany after Lake Constance.

⑤ **Neustrelitz**
The palace (1712) was the seat of distant relations of the Mecklenburg-Strelitz dukes who established the town and its church, and after 1733 resided here.

③ **Waren**
Waren, an ideal base for tourists, is close to Binnenmüritz with its beaches and shops with watersports equipment for sale or hire.

Key

■ Tour route

▨ Scenic route

═ Minor road

≈ River, lake

ᗸ Viewpoint

0 km 15

0 miles 15

❼ Rostock

The history of the most important German port in the Baltic has been turbulent. This prosperous Hanseatic town had established trade links with distant ports such as Bergen (Norway), Riga (Latvia) and Bruges (Belgium) as early as the 15th century. In 1419 the first university in northern Europe was founded here, and it flourished again in the 19th century. After it suffered heavy damage in the Allied air raids of 1942, Rostock was rebuilt on a grand scale as the GDR's showpiece.

VISITORS' CHECKLIST

Practical Information
Road map D1. 🚆 200,000. 🛈
Neuer Markt 3. (0381-381 22 22).
🌐 rostock.de 🎭 Warnemünder
Woche (Jul), Hansesail (Aug).

Transport
🚉

Kröpelinerstrasse – a promenade with 17th century houses

Exploring Rostock

A visit to the town is best started from the Neuer Markt (new market), from where the most important monuments can easily be reached on foot.

🏛 Rathaus

The town hall, on Neuer Markt, has a Baroque façade (added in 1727–9), from which seven Gothic towers of the original building emerge. At the rear of the building, in Große Wasserstrasse, it is worth seeking out Kerkoffhaus, the best preserved Gothic house in Rostock with a splendidly ornate façade featuring glazed brickwork, dating from 1470.

🏛 Steintor

A few minutes south of Neuer Markt is the Steintor, the best known of the gates in the old city wall. One of only three surviving gates of the original fortifications (at one time with 22 gates), it received its characteristic crowning feature during the Renaissance.

⛪ Marienkirche

Am Ziegenmarkt 4. **Tel** (0381) 492 33 96. **Open** phone to check times. 📷
This church, meant to exceed the height of its Lübeck counterpart, was completed in the mid-15th century, after almost 250 years of construction. The nave, built after the original roof had collapsed, has an untypical, short body, while the massive western tower is as wide as three naves. Interconnected swathes of glazing decorate the exterior of the church, while much of the white-washed interior features star vaulting. The main attraction is the astronomical clock, built in 1472 by maestro Düringer of Nuremberg. Its mechanism will show the correct

Baptismal font in the Marienkirche

time and date until 2017. Every afternoon its clockwork apostles parade before the tourists.

🏛 Kröpelinerstrasse

The most popular street in the city is lined by houses from the 17th to the 19th centuries. In summer students congregate around the "Brunnen der Lebensfreude" (fountain of happiness) on the Universitätsplatz (university square). The main university building was built in the years 1867–70 in Neo-Renaissance style. The southern part of the square is occupied by a palace with a beautiful Baroque hall where concerts are performed. A Neo-Classical annexe with a Doric colonnade (1823) stands nearby. A statue on the square commemorates the town's most famous resident, Field Marshal Blücher, who helped defeat Napoleon at Waterloo.

Environs

Between Rostock and Stralsund lies a delightful coastal area. The peninsula, with the three former islands of **Fischland**, **Darß** and **Zingst**, attracts visitors to its quiet, beautiful beaches and splendid natural scenery. Particularly attractive are the villages of **Ahrenshoop**, which was originally an artists' colony, **Prerow**, which has traditional fishermen's houses and churches, and **Wieck**, with its charming thatched houses. A national park has been established here, and includes Darß and its magnificent forest, Zingst, the west coast of Rügen and the island of Hiddensee.

The richly decorated pulpit in the Marienkirche

⑩ Stralsund

After Lubeck, Stralsund is the most interesting Hanseatic town in northern Germany. During its history, it has had to defend its independence against Lübeck, Denmark, Holland and Sweden. In the Thirty Years' War, General Wallenstein vowed that he would take the town even if it was chained to heaven – but he failed. Subsequently, Lower Pomerania stayed under Swedish rule for 200 years until 1815, when it became Prussian. Despite its turbulent history, 811 protected buildings survived in the old town, among them some truly remarkable examples of architecture.

The Rathaus with its small turrets

Exploring Stralsund

The town centre of Stralsund is surrounded by water on all sides – in the north by the Strelasund bay, and on the other sides by lakes formed in the moats of the former bastions, Knieperteich and Frankenteich. All the most interesting historic monuments are easily accessible on foot from here.

🏛 Alter Markt

The old market square affords the best view of the filigree façade of the town hall, beyond which stands the vast edifice of St Michael's church. It is surrounded by houses from various eras, of which the two most important are the Gothic Wulflamhaus, and the Commandantenhaus, Baroque headquarters of the town's former Swedish commandant. The Rathaus dates from the 13th century with a 14th-century façade and ground-floor arcades, and resembles the one in Lübeck. In 1370 the Hanseatic League and the defeated

Portal of the Nikolaikirche

Danish king signed a peace treaty here.

The Nikolaikirche, built from 1270–1360, was inspired by French Gothic cathedrals as well as the Marienkirche in Lübeck. It has rare free-standing flying buttresses in brick, which are much more unusual than in stone. Inside there are several intriguing furnishings, for example, the statue of St Anna (c.1290), an astronomical clock (1394), as well as fragments of the Novgorod stall with various fascinating scenes including one of hunting for sables. The Baroque main altar was designed in 1798 by renowned Berlin architect and sculptor Andreas Schlüter.

🏛 Kulturhistorisches Museum

Mönchstr. 25/27.
Tel (0381) 12 87 90.
Open Feb–Nov: 10am–5pm daily.

The Katharinenkloster, a former 15th-century Dominican abbey, now houses two museums. Its abbey rooms provide an appropriate setting for historic exhibitions – the refectory has vaults supported by stylish columns – including copies of the famous Viking treasure from Hiddensee and a collection of 18th- and 19th-century toys and dolls' houses. A branch of the Museum, in Böttcherstrasse, has a collection devoted to village life, folklore and costumes of the Baltic region.

VISITORS' CHECKLIST

Road map E1. 🚗 62,000.
ℹ Alter Markt 9 (03831-246 90).
ⓦ **stralsund.de**
🎉 Sundschwimmen (Jul);
Wallenstein-Tage (Jul); Stralsunder
Segelwoche (Jun).

Transport
🚉

🏛 Deutsches Meeresmuseum

Katharinenberg 14. **Tel** (03831) 265 0210. **Open** 10am–5pm daily (Jun–Sep: to 6pm). **Closed** 24, 31 Dec.

Highlights of this museum of the sea, based in a former Dominican convent and the Ozeanum building, include almost 100 aquariums stocked with sharks, seahorses, coral fish and giant turtles, and a 16-m (52-ft) long skeleton of a fin whale. It is also a scientific establishment research-ing the life of sea organisms.

🏠 Marienkirche

Tower **Open** 10am–noon, 2–4pm Mon–Fri, 10am–noon Sat. Organ concerts: summer: 11am Mon–Wed, Fri–Sun.

Dominating the Neuer Mark is the town's largest church, St Mary's, built in 1383–1473, with an octagonal tower (with good views of Stralsund). Star vaulting lightens the impact of the monumental 99-m (325-ft) high interior. Main attractions are Gothic frescoes, carved wooden figures of saints and a late-Gothic baptismal font. The huge Baroque organ is used for concerts in summer.

Marienkirche with its dominant, octagonal tower

⓫ Rügen

The largest of Germany's islands at 926 sq km (357 sq miles), Rügen is also the most beautiful and diverse, boasting steep cliffs next to sandy beaches and a hilly hinterland with forests and peat bogs. The island is only 50 km (31 miles) across, yet its rugged coastline extends for hundreds of miles. The Huns once ruled here, and their tombs can still be seen. It was fortified by the Slavs, then ruled by Danes and Swedes. In 1815 Rügen came under Prussian rule, and in 1936 it was linked to the mainland by the 1 km- (0.6 mile-) long Rügendamm.

Kap Arkona
There are two lighthouses on Kap Arkona. The smaller was built in 1827 and is now a museum. The larger was built in 1902 and is still in use.

Key

- ▬ Motorway
- ═ Main road
- 🚢 Ferry crossing
- ✸ Viewpoint

★ Waase
At this typical fishing village on the island of Ummanz, an unusual work of art has survived: an altarpiece from Antwerp, from around 1520.

0 km — 5
0 miles — 5

KEY

① **Hiddensee** is a small island and is accessible by ferry from Stralsund or Schaprode on Rügen. Horse-drawn carts and bikes replace cars in this oasis of tranquillity.

Jasmund Peninsula
The northeast of the peninsula is occupied by the Stubnitz forest of beech trees, which continues down to the sea, interrupted by dazzling white chalk cliffs. The symbol of Rügen, they inspired artists like Caspar David Friedrich.

VISITORS' CHECKLIST

Practical Information
Road map E1. 🛈 Bergen, Markt 23 (03838-811 206). Binz, Heinrich-Heine-Str. 7 (038393-148 148); Hiddensee, Norderende 162, Vitte (038300-642 26); Putbus, Alleestr. 35 (038301-4 31).
🎭 In Ralswiek (near Bergen) open-air performances take place under the title of "Festival of Klaus Störtebeker" (Jun–Sep).
W **ruegen.de**

Transport
🚌

★ Nationalpark Jasmund
An attractive walk starts at the viewpoint of Königsstuhl (king's seat; 119 m/390 ft), continues along the Hochuferweg (cliff-top walk), past Victoriasicht and Wissower Klinken viewpoints, to end at Sassnitz.

Ostseebad Binz
Rügen's largest and most popular seaside resort, Binz has a beautiful white beach, grand early 20th-century villas and a pier.

★ Putbus
This elegant late Neo-Classical town was planned after 1807 on the model of Bad Doberan. Its centrepiece is the theatre, which was built in 1819 to a design by Wilhelm Steinbach.

Tromper Wiek

Lohme

Glowe

NATIONAL PARK JASMUND

Großer smunder Bodden

Sagard

Sassnitz

J A S M U N D

Kleiner Jasmunder Bodden

Prorer Wiek

rgen

Ostseebad Binz

Ostseebad Sellin

Ostseebad Baabe

Putbus

Ostseebad Göhren

Rügischer Bodden

Greifswalder Bodden

For hotels and restaurants in this area see pp503 and pp532–3

⑫ Greifswald

Road map E1. 🚏 54,000. 🚆
ℹ️ Rathaus Am Markt (03834-853 61
380). 🎵 Musical concerts
"Greifswalder Bachwochen" (Jun); Jazz
Evenings in Eldena (Jul); Fischerfest
(Jul). 🌐 **greifswald.info**

This former Hanseatic town is
situated 5 km (3 miles) from the
Bay of Greifswald. From afar the
picturesque silhouette of the
town with its three church
towers, nicknamed Fat Mary,
Little Jakob and Long Michael,
appears like a painting by
Caspar David Friedrich – the
town's most famous resident –
come to life. Charm pervades
the old town, its architectural
mix resulting from 40 years of
East German rule. Greifswald, an
important academic centre and
market town, has geared up
more for tourism since 1989. It is
certainly worth a visit – a short
walk from east to west enables
visitors to see all the most
important monuments in town.

The 14th-century **Marienkirche** has a vast square
tower, giving it a rather squat
appearance and its nickname,
Fat Mary. Inside, the church
contains the remains of frescoes
and an amazing Renaissance
pulpit depicting the Reformation figures of Luther, Bugenhagen and Melanchthon. The
Gemäldegalerie has a collection
of paintings by Caspar David

Friedrich, including his famous
landscapes of the ruined
monastery of Eldena, *Ruined
Eldena in the Riesengebirge*,
which he transposed to the
mountains of present-day
Poland and Czech Republic.

The market square with
its Baroque town hall is
surrounded by patrician
houses, with exemplary rich
brickwork façades (particularly
numbers 11 and 13). Nearby
rises the vast **Dom St Nikolai**.
The cathedral's octagonal
tower, topped with a Baroque
helm, affords extensive views
of the town. The Rubenow-Bild
(1460), one of the paintings
inside, depicts the founding
professor of Greifswald's
university in front of Mary,
Mother of God.

Environs

Wieck, an attractive working
fishing village, is now
incorporated into Greifswald.
It has a drawbridge dating from
1887, reminiscent of typical
Dutch bridges. The Cistercian
monastery of **Eldena**, just
1 km (0.6 mile) south of Wieck
district, was made famous by
the Romantic paintings of
Caspar David Friedrich. The
monastery was founded in
1199 and plundered by the
Swedes in 1637. Its ruined red
walls amid the green grass and
trees look wildly romantic.

Alter Speicher – the half-timbered
granary in Wolgast

⑬ Wolgast

Road map E1. 🚏 15,000. 🚆 ℹ️
Rathausplatz 10 (03836-60 01 18). 🎵
Hafenfest (Jul). 🌐 **stadt-wolgast.de**

From 1295 the seat of the
Pomeranian-Wolgast dukes,
Wolgast castle was destroyed in
1713, when Peter the Great
ordered the town to be burned.
A notable surviving building is
the 12-sided cemetery chapel
with star vaulting, supported
by a single column. The most
valuable work of art can now
be seen in **Pfarrkirche St Petri**,
a 14th-century parish church.
Dating from the turn of the
17th to the 18th century, the
Totentanz frieze is an imitation

Renovated houses around the Fischmarkt in Greifswald

For hotels and restaurants in this area see p503 and pp532–3

of the famous *Dance of Death* by Hans Holbein in Basle. Another notable artifact is the epitaph of Duke Philip I, crafted in 1560 by the Saxon artist Wolf Hilinger.

Other attractions in the town are the **Alter Speicher**, an 80 m- (262 ft-) long half-timbered granary (Burgstrasse, 1836), and the family home of Philipp Otto Runge, famous romantic painter and adopted son of Hamburg.

🏛 **Philipp-Otto-Runge-Gedenkstätte**
Kronwieckstrasse 45. **Tel** (03836) 20 30 41. **Open** May–Oct: 11am–6pm Tue–Fri, 11am–4pm Sat & Sun.

One of the models in the Otto Lilienthal-Museum in Anklam

⑭ Anklam

Road map E2. 🏔 16,400. 🚋
ℹ Markt 3, Rathaus (03971-835 154).
🌐 **anklam.de**

A former Hanseatic town, Anklam's erstwhile importance is revealed by its vast defensive walls, in which is set the mid-15th-century city gate, **Steintor**. It is worth visiting the Gothic **Marienkirche**. Inside, the church's octagonal pillars and the arches of its arcades are painted with graceful figures which reveal a Lübeck influence. A museum recalls the life and inventions of Otto Lilienthal, born here in 1848. After observing storks, he built a flying machine and completed his first flight in 1891. In total he created 2000 machines, none of which flew further than 350 m (1148 ft).

🏛 **Otto-Lilienthal-Museum**
Ellbogenstrasse 1. **Tel** (03971) 24 55 00. **Open** Jun–Sep: 10am–5pm

Fishing boat on the beach at Usedom

daily; Oct & May: 10am–5pm Tue–Fri, 1pm–5pm Sat & Sun; Nov–Apr: 11am–3:30pm Wed–Fri, 1pm–3:30pm Sun.

⑮ Usedom

Road map E2. 🚋 ℹ Heringsdorf, Kurverwaltung, Waldstr. 1 (038378-477 10); Ahlbeck, Kurverwaltung, Dünenstr. 45 (038378-244 14).

The island, named after the village of Usedom and separated from the mainland by the Peenestrom, is the second largest in Germany at 445 sq km (172 sq miles). A small corner in the east was incorporated into Poland after 1945. Usedom is almost as attractive as Rügen, possessing white beaches, forests, peat bogs and bays overgrown with rushes in the south. It is linked with the mainland by two drawbridges (near Anklam and Wolgast). The resorts follow one another like pearls on a string: Bansin, Heringsdorf and Ahlbeck, known as the "three sisters", are connected by a wide beach. At the beginning of the 20th century they evolved into elegant holiday resorts, with white villas, hotels and boarding houses, as typical of seaside resorts. Worth a visit is the industrialist Oechler's house in Heringsdorf (Delbrückstr. 5), which has an antique appearance with mosaics on its

façade. During the past few years, the early 20th-century piers in all three spas have been rebuilt and restored. The longest, in Heringsdorf, is also the second largest in Europe, after one in Poland. The Marienkirche, one of the island's main attractions, was erected in the 19th century.

⑯ Peenemünde

Road map E1. 🏔 650.

Historically, the most interesting spot on the island of Usedom is the **museum** at Peenemünde, which is located on military territory. It demonstrates the evolution of space travel, pioneered at this research station since 1936. During World War II, long-distance rockets, powered by liquid fuel and known as V-2 (*Vergeltungswaffe*; retaliatory weapon), were produced here, which inflicted heavy damage on the cities of London and Antwerp in 1944. After the war the Luft engineer, Wernher von Braun, worked for NASA and helped develop the Apollo rockets.

🏛 **Historisch-technisches Museum**
Im Kraftwerk. **Tel** (038371) 50 50. **Open** Apr–Sep: 10am–6pm; Oct–Mar: 10am–4pm. **Closed** Mon (Nov–Mar).
🌐 **peenemuende.de**

V-2 rocket in Peenemünde

TRAVELLERS' NEEDS

WHERE TO STAY

It is relatively easy to find a room in a hotel or a pension in Germany, even in small towns or large villages. The range of prices for a night's accommodation is wide, depending on the standard of services offered and the location of the establishment. In smaller towns located in attractive tourist areas, it is also possible to find rooms to rent at a reasonable rate in private homes. In large towns and cities it is harder to find inexpensive accommodation. If cost is a consideration, it may be necessary to take a room in a hotel that is some distance from the city centre. Within the list of hotels provided on pages 492–503 there is a large range of hotels and pensions, which represent various price categories and a high standard of services. Tourist offices supply lists of accommodation options and may be able to find a room for you. Information on types of accommodation can be found on pages 490–91.

The lounge area of the fun budget hotel Circus, Berlin *(see p492)*

The Range of Hotels

German hotels are rated according to a star system that is also used in many other countries. The number of stars awarded to an establishment depends on the facilities offered rather than the standard of service. As a result, it may be possible to enjoy a more pleasant stay in a small hotel that has only one star than in a three-star hotel that offers lifts, a restaurant, swimming pool and business centre, but where refurbishment is long overdue.

The word *"Garni"* in the name of the hotel indicates that there is not a restaurant on the premises, but only a dining room where breakfast is served. *"Apartmenthotel"* means that the establishment is comprised of suites that include equipped kitchens or a kitchen annexe. The price of suites is such that it is not worth booking them for just one night, although a booking of several days for a family or group of friends can turn out to be very economical.

Standards vary enormously between hotels. In large cities visitors will have no difficulty in finding a deluxe (and, of course, expensive) hotel, which will typically be part of an international chain. The choice of less expensive accommodation usually, though not necessarily always, entails accepting a lower standard of service or a less convenient location.

Away from the larger cities, high prices generally apply to rooms in comfortable hotels in particularly peaceful and beautiful locations, or to those located within historic palaces or villas. Smaller hotels in such areas usually offer good accommodation at affordable prices, and visitors can enjoy their stay in small, but cosy and comfortable, rooms.

How to Book

As with many European destinations, hotel accommodation in Germany can be booked directly by telephone, email or through the hotel's website. Reservations can also be made through a local tourist office or a third party provider, such as Expedia.de or Hotels.com.

Hotels may request written confirmation of the booking and will almost certainly ask for a credit card number to guarantee the reservation. Give an indication of expected time of arrival especially if it's likely to be late at night. This will ensure that the room is held for you.

For those who have not pre-booked, the local tourist office can usually find a hotel room or provide information about rooms in private homes.

Luxurious bar at Adlon Kempinski, Berlin *(see p492)*

◀ The shopping centre Quartier 206, on Berlin's Friedrichstrasse

The deluxe Fairmont Hotel Vier Jahreszeiten in Hamburg *(see p502)*

International and German Chain Hotels

Virtually all the well-known international hotel chains are present in Germany, and there are also hotels belonging to German chains. Many towns in Germany have an Ibis, which can be relied on to provide inexpensive, usually two-star accommodation.

Somewhat more expensive, and of a higher standard, are the hotels belonging to the Best Western chain. Their excellent standard of service, combined with an affordable price, ensures their popularity with visitors. Hotels belonging to the Sorat group have a similar standard to Best Western establishments and are also recommended. They can be two-, three- or even four-star, and their premises always have interesting interiors, often designed by renowned architects. Many hotels belonging to chains are, in fact, four- or deluxe five-star. Among the finest are the Kempinski and Vier Jahreszeiten hotels. In addition to these, there is no shortage of hotels belonging to chains such as Hilton, Holiday Inn, InterContinental, Mercure, Ramada and Hyatt Regency.

Hotels in Historic Buildings

Germany has numerous palaces, castles and other historic buildings that have been converted into hotels. Often the name *Schlosshotel* is used to indicate that an establishment is a hotel within a palace. Many of these hotels are members of international organizations, such as **European Castle Hotels and Restaurants** or **Romantik Hotels & Restaurants**, which can provide further information

Hotel Prices

A complicated hotel categorization system operates in Germany, with a diverse range of prices depending on the season, as well as on various events that are taking place. In resort areas, hotels are obviously most expensive during the summer, while in large cities visited frequently for business the most expensive seasons are spring and autumn. In cities where commercial fairs are held, prices may double during the most popular fairs – for example, in Berlin during the tourist fair ITB, in Hanover during the information-computer fair CeBIT and in Frankfurt during the car and publishing fairs. The same is true in Munich during the October beer festival.

Many hotels offer significant reductions at weekends, and sometimes there is the opportunity of a discount for those who turn up without a reservation. Booking early may also secure a discounted rate. Prices can sometimes be negotiated for longer bookings, especially during periods when business is slack.

Additional Costs

Tax is included in the basic price of a hotel room, but tips should be given for additional services such as having your baggage taken to your room or having theatre tickets reserved for you. Additional costs can come as a surprise when you settle your bill. In the most expensive hotels, for example, breakfast is not included in the cost of the room. Most hotels have their own parking facilities, but the cost may be unacceptably high. Check in advance the cost of making direct-dialled telephone calls from your room, as well as the commission charged by the hotel for cashing travellers' cheques and the rate offered when exchanging currency. Using the mini-bar and pay-to-view TV channels in your room can also prove to be expensive.

The elegant spa in the Hotel de Rome, Berlin *(see p492)*

Minimalist decor at the Motel One München *(see p495)*, a budget option in Munich

Gasthof and Pensionen

A *Gasthof* is a traditional inn with a restaurant on the ground floor and rooms to rent on the upper floor. Be aware, however, that this simple description covers a wide range of establishments – from small, inexpensive, family-run hotels with modestly equipped rooms, to luxurious and elegant accommodation in an exquisitely restored country inn.

Pensionen are less formal establishments than hotels and are typically run by a family. They usually provide modest sleeping quarters, breakfast and a pleasant family atmosphere. They are always comfortable and very clean, at affordable prices.

Inexpensive Accommodation

Germany has a well-established and widely developed chain of youth hostels *(Jugendherberge)*, and these provide the most affordable option for an overnight stay. A youth hostel can be found in every large town, as well as in small holiday centres. The most attractive are those that are located in old castles, beautiful villas or other historic buildings. Most hostels are of a high standard. Accommodation may be provided in double and triple rooms, as well as in dormitories.

In order to be eligible to use youth hostels, you must be in possession of a valid membership card issued by the Youth Hostels Association (YHA). This can be obtained from the YHA in your own country. Although overnight accommodation is open to anyone in possession of a valid membership card, things are slightly different in Bavaria. In this region, young people are given priority, but older people can stay, too (although for an additional charge), as can families with young children.

The cost for a one-night stay with breakfast is around €13.50–25. Unless you have a sheet sleeping bag, you must hire one at the hostel, for which an additional charge will be made. The hostels are usually closed during the day, so you must ensure that all arrangements connected with your stay are in place before 9am or after 4–4:30pm. In large cities during the high season, when demand for beds is particularly heavy, your stay may be limited to 2–3 nights.

Guesthouse near Neuschwanstein

Private accommodation provides another inexpensive option. In attractive tourist areas, it is quite common for owners of large villas and private houses to rent rooms to tourists, often offering breakfast as well. Houses with rooms available to rent are indicated by the sign *Fremdenzimmer* or *Zimmer frei*. Details of such accommodation can be obtained and booked in tourist information offices.

During the summer months in university towns, students may also benefit from accommodation in hotels that house university students during term times. Again, information about such accommodation may be found at tourist offices.

Agrotourism

Agrotourism, a type of farm holiday, is very popular in Germany as an attractive, low-cost and eco-friendly accommodation choice. The rooms are of a perfectly acceptable standard, and meals are often also provided.

For younger children, it is a great thrill to observe the daily work on a farm. There may also be the possibility of horse-riding, or of hiring bicycles, a boat or fishing tackle. Agrotourist holidays can be booked through **LV digital GmbH** and **AG Urlaub & Freizeit auf dem Lande**. For more information on eco-friendly stays, *see p545*.

Mountain Accommodation

Mountainous regions of Germany are generally well prepared to accommodate walkers and can offer truly idyllic retreats. Shelters, hostels and mountain hotels can be found not only along Alpine trails, but also in the Thuringian Forest, the Black Forest and the Harz Mountains. Details about such accommodation can be obtained from local tourist information offices.

Camping and Caravanning

Travelling with a camping trailer, camper van or just a tent is very popular in Germany, which has a highly developed network of more than 2,000 camping sites. Of a generally high standard, sites have washrooms and kitchens. There is usually a shop and café, and some even have swimming pools.

Disabled Travellers

Virtually all hotels of a higher standard are equipped to accommodate disabled guests. At least one entrance will have ramp access, and a few rooms will have bathrooms adapted to the needs of those who are confined to a wheelchair. In lower-category hotels, though, specially adapted fixtures and fittings tend to be rarer. In such hotels, you may have to negotiate steep stairs to reach rooms on the upper floors.

In order to receive additional help and advice during their trip, disabled travellers can contact the **Bundesarbeitsgemeinschaft Selbsthilfe e.V.**, or the **Bundesverband Selbsthilfe Körperbehinderter e.V.**

Travelling with Children

In most hotels, cots and high chairs can be obtained, and there is often no additional accommodation charge for a young child. In better hotels, a few hours of babysitting can usually be booked. For older children, expect to pay for an extra bed.

Recommended Hotels

The hotels recommended in the following listings have been chosen because they represent the best that German accommodation has to offer in hospitality, location and value.

Budget hotels offer good value accommodation, ideal for shorter stays, while mid-range hotels include some facilities. So-called business hotels offer Wi-Fi connectivity and the use of meeting rooms.

Boutique hotels tend to be small and usually feature high design elements, while luxury hotels encompass the finest of Germany's upscale hotels.

A mountain shelter in Oybin, Saxony

Pensionen offer a personable experience, with breakfast, while *Gasthöfe* are traditional inns with a restaurant. Historic options may be an old hotel or a hotel in an old building.

Entries highlighted as DK Choice are those that stand out. They may have an enviable location, offer an incredible service or be particularly charming. Whatever the reason, they guarantee a memorable stay.

DIRECTORY

Information on Accommodation & Reservations

European Castle Hotels and Restaurants
W european-castle.com

Hotel Reservation Service (HRS)
Blaubach 32, 50676 Cologne.
Tel (0221) 207 76 00.
W hrs.com

Romantik Hotels & Restaurants
W romantikhotels.com

Trivago GmbH
Bennigsen-Platz 1, 40474 Düsseldorf.
Tel (0211) 54 06 50.
W trivago.de

Youth Hostels

Deutsches Jugendherbergswerk DJH Service GmbH
Im Gildepark,
Leonardo da-Vinci-Weg 1, 32760 Detmold.
Tel (05231) 993 60.
W jugendherberge.de

Agrotourism

AG Urlaub & Freizeit auf dem Lande
Lindhooper Str. 63, 27283 Verden. Tel (04231) 966 50.
W bauernhofferien.de

LV digital GmbH
Hülsebrookstr. 2–8, 48165 Münster.
Tel (02501) 801 1195.
W landreise.de

Mountain Accommodation

DAV Summit Club
Am Perlacher Forst 186, 81545 Munich.
Tel (089) 64 24 00.
W dav-summit-club.de

Verband Deutscher Gebirgs- und Wandervereine
Wilhelmshöher Allee 157–159, 34121 Kassel.
Tel (0561) 93 87 30.
W wanderverband.de

Camping and Caravanning

Deutscher Camping-Club
Mandlstr. 28, 80802 Munich. Tel (089) 380 14 20. W camping-club.de

Disabled Travellers

Bundesarbeitsgemeinschaft Selbsthilfe
Kirchfeldstr. 149, 40215 Düsseldorf.
Tel (0211) 31 00 60.
W bag-selbsthilfe.de

Bundesverband Selbsthilfe Körperbehinderter (BSK)
Altkrautheimerstr. 20, 74238 Krautheim.
Tel (06 294) 428 10.
W bsk-ev.org

Club Behinderter und ihrer Freunde (CBF)
Pallaswiesenstr. 123a, 64293 Darmstadt.
Tel (06151) 812 20.
W cbf-da.de

Where to Stay

Berlin

Eastern Centre

City Hostel Berlin €
Budget **Map** 4 B3
Glinkastrasse 5, 10117
Tel *238 866 850*
W cityhostel-berlin.com
Simple, modern rooms with en
suite bathrooms. A great terrace
bar for evening drinks. Free
breakfast and Wi-Fi.

Three Little Pigs Hostel Berlin €
Budget **Map** 4 B4
Stresemannstrasse 66, 10963
Tel *263 958 80*
W three-little-pigs.de
Set in an old convent building in
a vibrant, multicultural area with
great night-life. Free parking.

Maritim proArte Hotel €€
Mid-Range Hotel **Map** 1 F4
Friedrichstrasse 151, 10117
Tel *30 20 335*
W maritim.de
Large, contemporary hotel with
clean and generous-sized rooms.
Good location, within walking
distance of the Brandenburg
Gate and Museum Island.

DK Choice

Adlon Kempinski €€€
Luxury **Map** 1 F4
Unter den Linden 77, 10117
Tel *226 115 55*
W kempinski.com
The Adlon has won numerous
plaudits, both for its impeccable
standards of service and for
being the final word in opulence.
The hotel has exquisite
bedrooms, and facilities such
as Michelin-starred gourmet
dining and an enormous spa.

Luxurious suite at the acclaimed Adlon Kempinski

Cosmo €€€
Boutique
Spittelmarkt 13, 10117
Tel *585 822 22* **Map** 5 D3
W designhotels.com
A haven of tranquility amid the
bustle of the Mitte. Elegant
rooms have high-end furnishings.

Hotel de Rome €€€
Luxury **Map** 4 C2
Behrenstrasse 37, 10117
Tel *460 60 90*
W hotelderome.com
Classy furnishings and alfresco
dining on a rooftop terrace at
this lavish hotel.

Western Centre

Hotel am Schloss Bellevue €
Budget **Map** 3 E1
Paulstrasse 3, 10557
Tel *391 12 27*
W hotelamschlossbellevue.de
Small, intimate hotel with
innovative rooms decorated by
a young local grafitti artist.

Altberlin €€
Historic **Map** 3 F4
Potsdamer Strasse 67, 10785
Tel *26 06 70*
W altberlin-hotel.de
Converted from a town house,
the well-located Altberlin is fur-
nished in authentic period style.

Grand Hotel Esplanade €€
Luxury **Map** 3 E4
Lützowufer 15, 10785
Tel *25 47 80*
W esplanade.de
Excellent amenities at this plush
hotel. Convenient location.

Q Hotel €€
Boutique **Map** 2 A4
Knesebeckstrasse 67, 10623
Tel *810 06 60*
W hotel-q.com

Price Guide

Prices are based on one night's stay in
high season for a standard double room,
inclusive of service charges and taxes.

€	up to €75
€€	€75 to €125
€€€	over €125

Surprisingly affordable designer
hotel aimed mainly at corporate
travellers. Futuristic decor.

Savoy €€
Luxury **Map** 2 A4
Fasanenstrasse 9–10, 10623
Tel *31 10 30*
W hotel-savoy.com
Historic hotel famous for its
refined decor and attentive
service. Excellent restaurant and
well-stocked bar.

Further Afield

DK Choice

Circus €
Budget **Road Map** E3
Rosenthaler Strasse 1, 10119
Tel *200 039 39*
W circus-berlin.de
This fun hotel, located close to
the city's night-life, has high
standards of service and great
value. Numerous extras on offer,
from bike rentals to rickshaw
tours and baby-sitting. Enjoy
the elaborate breakfast spread,
or a coffee at the Circus Café.

Andel's €€
Business **Road Map** E3
Landsberger Allee 106, 10369
Tel *453 05 30*
W vi-hotels.com
Award-winning hotel with
brilliant city views and regular
tram and train links. Rooms are
smart and spacious, and there's
an extensive breakfast buffet.

Riehmers Hofgarten €€
Historic **Road Map** E3
Yorckstrasse 83, 10965
Tel *780 988 00*
W riehmers-hofgarten.de
A grand mansion with elegant
decor set in a 19th-century
courtyard. All modern amenities.

Villa Kastania €€
Boutique **Road Map** E3
Kastanienallee 20, 14052
Tel *300 00 20*
W villakastania.com
Rooms are decorated with great
attention to detail. Spa facilities
available. Impeccable service.

The decadent Hotel Schloss Lübbenau is set in Schloss Park

Ackselhaus €€€
Boutique **Road Map** E3
Belforter Strasse 21, 10405
Tel *443 376 33*
ⓦ ackselhaus.de
A restored 19th-century property with a lovely garden and individually designed rooms.

Brandenburg

**BRANDENBURG/HAVEL:
Sorat Hotel Brandenburg** €€
Mid-Range Hotel **Road Map** E3
Altstädtische Markt 1, 14770
Tel *(03381) 5970*
ⓦ sorat-hotels.com
Good for leisure and business travellers alike as facilities include free Wi-Fi and a fitness centre.

CHORIN: Waldsee Hotel €
Gasthof **Road Map** E2
Neue Klosterallee 12, 16230
Tel *(03336) 653111*
ⓦ waldseehotel-frenz.de
Family-run hotel in beautiful woods by an old monastery. Simple rooms with floral decor.

**FRANKFURT AN DER ODER:
Palais am Kleistpark** €
Boutique **Road Map** F3
Fürstenwalder St 47, 15234
Tel *(0335) 56150*
ⓦ hotel-gallus.de
Calm lodgings with Art Nouveau rooms oozing timeless elegance.

**LÜBBENAU: Hotel
Schloss Lübbenau** €€€
Historic **Road Map** E3
Schlossbezirk 6, 03222
Tel *(03542) 8730*
ⓦ schloss-luebbenau.de
Former palace with elegant *fin-de-siècle* rooms and a spa with pretty mosaics and vaulted ceilings.

POTSDAM: Froschkasten €
Pensionen **Road Map** E3
Kiezstr 4, 14467
Tel *(0331) 291315*
ⓦ froschkasten.de
Simple pine-furnished rooms above one of Potsdam's oldest and most authentic inns.

**POTSDAM: Hotel am
Luisenplatz** €€€
Gasthof **Road Map** E3
Luisenplatz 5, 14471
Tel *(0331) 971900*
ⓦ hotel-luisenplatz.de
Early 18th-century town house with antique furnishings. Rates include a superb breakfast.

**POTSDAM: Hotel Villa
Monte Vino** €€€
Historic **Road Map** E3
Gregor-Mendel-Strasse 27, 14469
Tel *(0331) 2013339*
ⓦ hotelvillamontevino.de
Located on a former vineyard, this is perfect for a peaceful getaway.

DK Choice

**RHEINSBERG: Pension
Holländermühle** €
Historic **Road Map** E2
Holländer Mühle 01, 16831
Tel *(033931) 2332*
ⓦ hollaender-muehle.de
This family-run pension has a novel setting in a windmill built in 1894. The bright and simple rooms are all individually decorated. There is also a good restaurant serving regional food.

RHEINSBERG: Der Seehof €€
Gasthof **Road Map** E2
Seestrasse 18, 16831
Tel *(033931) 4030*
ⓦ seehof-rheinsberg.de
Mid-18th-century farmhouse. The bright and cheerful rooms have balconies and lake views.

Saxony-Anhalt

DESSAU: Prellerhaus €
Boutique **Road Map** E3
Gropiusallee 38, 06846
Tel *(0340) 6508250*
ⓦ bauhaus-dessau.de
Stay in the minimalist former Bauhaus student rooms within an iconic school building. Communal bathrooms, and a gorgeous dining room.

DESSAU: An den 7 Säulen €€
Pensionen **Road Map** E3
Ebertallee 66, 06846
Tel *(0340) 61 96 20*
ⓦ pension7saeulen.de

Friendly family-run place in the Bauhaus district. Bright, modern rooms and sauna facilities.

EISLEBEN: Graf von Mansfeld €€
Historic **Road Map** D4
Markt 56, 06295
Tel *(03475) 66300*
ⓦ hotel-eisleben.de
Venerable hotel in the bustling main square. Good rooms, some with four-poster beds. Excellent restaurant.

HALLE: Apart-Hotel Halle €€€
Boutique **Road Map** D4
Kohlschütterstrasse 5–6, 06114
Tel *(0345) 52590*
ⓦ apart-halle.de
Art Nouveau place with themed rooms based on German cultural figures. Sauna and whirlpool tubs.

**MAGDEBURG: Arthotel
Magdeburg** €€
Boutique **Road Map** D3
Breiter Weg 9, 39104
Tel *(0391) 620780*
ⓦ arthotel-magdeburg.de
Designed by the Austrian artist Hundertwasser, the exterior is fantastical while the rooms are furnished with colourful decor.

**MAGDEBURG: Ratswaage Hotel
Magdeburg** €€
Mid-Range Hotel **Road Map** D3
Ratswaageplatz 1, 39104
Tel *(0391) 59260*
ⓦ ratswaage.de
Centrally located hotel with a sauna and fabulous breakfast buffet. Good weekend discounts.

**NAUMBURG: Hotel Stadt
Aachen** €€
Historic **Road Map** D4
Markt 11, 06618
Tel *(03445) 261060*
ⓦ hotel-stadt-aachen.de
Vine-covered lodgings on the market square with dark-wood antiques and floral touches.

**QUEDLINBURG: Hotel Garni
am Dippeplatz** €
Historic **Road Map** D4
Breite Strasse 16, 06104
Tel *(03946) 77140*
ⓦ hotel-propstei-vorwerk.de
Located in a 1680 half-timbered building, this welcoming hotel features tasteful rooms.

QUEDLINBURG: Theophano €€€
Historic **Road Map** D4
Markt 13–14, 06484
Tel *(03946) 96300*
ⓦ hoteltheophano.de
Traditional, half-timbered rustic hotel in an unbeatable central location. Many rooms have canopied beds.

For more information on types of hotels *see page 491*

TANGERMÜNDE:
Schloss Tangermünde €€€
Historic   Road Map D3
Amt 1, 39590
Tel *(0393) 22 7373*
W schloss-tangermuende.de
Prestigious hotel with attentive
service, dark-beamed rooms,
sauna and fantastic restaurant.

LUTHERSTADT WITTENBERG:
Pension am Schwanenteich €€
Pensionen   Road Map E3
Töpferstr 1, 06886
Tel *(03491) 402807*
W wittenberg-schwanenteich.de
Small, centrally located pension
with bright and airy en suite
rooms and great half-board deals
in its traditional restaurant.

Saxony

BAUTZEN: Schloss Schaenke €€
Pensionen   Road Map F4
Burgplatz 5, 02625
Tel *(03591) 304990*
W schloss-schaenke.net
This family-run hotel opposite
the Schloss Ortenburg castle
has simple, elegant rooms and
a fantastic breakfast buffet.

BAUTZEN: Villa Antonia €€
Historic   Road Map F4
Lessingstrasse 1, 02625
Tel *(03591) 501020*
W hotel-villa-antonia.de
Late-1890s villa in a quiet part of
town. Elegantly renovated, with
big, comfortable rooms.

CHEMNITZ: Schlosshotel
Klaffenbach
Historic   Road Map E4
Wasserschlossweg 6, 09123
Tel *(0371) 26110*
W schlosshotel-chemnitz.de
A spectacular moated castle in
the centre of Chemnitz. The
rooms are large and simply
furnished. Great value for money.

CHEMNITZ: Hotel an der
Oper €€€
Business   Road Map E4
Strasse der Nationen 56, 09111
Tel *(0371) 6810*
W hoteloper-chemnitz.de
Elegant hotel close to the opera
house. The rooms are modern,
with impressive bathrooms.

DRESDEN: Schloss Eckberg €€
Historic   Road Map E4
Bautzner Strasse 134, 01099
Tel *(0351) 80990*
W schloss-eckberg.de
A 19th-century castle with stylish
furnishings, elegant grounds and
a superb restaurant.

The imposing façade of the Steigenberger Grandhotel Handelshof, Leipzig

DRESDEN: Taschenbergpalais
Kempinski €€
Luxury   Road Map E4
Taschenberg 3, 01067
Tel *(0351) 49120*
W kempinski.com
Renowned hotel, right next to
the Royal Palace. Most rooms
have views of the river or Altmarkt.

DRESDEN:
Innside by Melia €€€
Business   Road Map E4
Salzgasse 4, 01067
Tel *(0351) 795150*
W innside.com
At this hotel in a central location
rooms have avant-garde decor
and there is a rooftop bar.

FREIBERG: Alekto €€
Historic   Road Map E4
Am Bahnhof 3, 09599
Tel *(03731) 79 40*
W alekto.de
An elegant Art Nouveau
building. Some rooms are a
little old-fashioned, but all offer
great value.

GÖRLITZ: Romantik Hotel
Tuchmacher €€
Historic   Road Map F4
Peterstrasse 8, 02826
Tel *(03581) 4731*
W tuchmacher.de
Dating back to the 16th century,
the Romantik offers individually
decorated rooms.

DK Choice

LEIPZIG: Steigenberger
Grandhotel Handelshof €€€
Luxury   Road Map E4
Salzgässchen 6, 04109
Tel *(0341) 3505810*
W steigenberger.com
A modern, elegant hotel on
Leipzig's historic Naschmarkt.
The huge rooms are decorated
in an avant-garde style and
there are two superb
restaurants plus a brasserie to
choose from. Unusual for
Germany's five-star hotels, Wi-Fi
here is free.

MORITZBURG:
Landhaus Moritzburg €€
Gasthof   Road Map E4
Schlossallee 37, 01468
Tel *(035207) 89690*
W landhaus-moritzburg.de
An excellent choice for a country
escape close to Moritzburg. Cosy
rooms and a restaurant with a
lovely terrace.

ZITTAU: Schwarzer Bär €
Pensionen   Road Map F4
Ottokarplatz 12, 02763
Tel *(03583) 5510*
W hotel-schwarzer-baer.de
Simple hotel, just outside of
the city centre, offering large,
good value rooms perfect for
families. Traditional if slightly
dated decor.

Thuringia

ALTENBURG: Engel €€
Pensionen   Road Map E4
Johannisstrasse 27, 04600
Tel *(03447) 56510*
W hotel-engel-altenburg.de
Family-run pension in the heart
of old Altenburg with individually
decorated rooms and a charming
cellar bar.

EISENACH: Steigenberger
Hotel Thuringer Hof €€
Mid-Range Hotel   Road Map C4
Karlsplatz 11, 99817
Tel *(03691) 280*
W steigenberger.com
Excellent value hotel with an
extravagant lobby. Comfortable,
low-key rooms, a fine restaurant
and spa facilities.

ERFURT: Pullman Erfurt
am Dom €€€
Luxury   Road Map D4
Theaterplatz 2, 99084
Tel *(0361) 64450*
W pullmanhotels.com
Centrally located accommo-
dation with spacious rooms
and extravagant bathrooms.
Opulence at a relatively
affordable price.

**ERFURT: Zumnorde am
Anger** €€€
Historic Road Map D4
Anger 50–51, 99084
Tel *(0361) 568 00*
W hotel-zumnorde.de
Historic building offering refined
rooms with period furniture.
Good beer garden.

GOTHA: Augustinerkloster €
Historic Road Map D4
Jüdenstrasse 27, 99867
Tel *(03621) 302910*
W augustinerkloster-gotha.de
This former monastery has a
historic façade, but features
contemporary interiors.

**JENA: Steigenberger
Esplanade Jena** €€
Modern Road Map D4
Carl-Zeiss-Platz 4, 07743
Tel *(03641) 800*
W steigenberger.com
Situated next to Jena University,
this hotel boasts imaginative
design and big, bright rooms.

OBERHOF: Hotel Haus Saarland €
Gasthof Road Map D4
Zeller Strasse 13, 98559
Tel *(036842) 52117*
W haus-saarland.de
Lovely family-owned and run
inn. Simple but comfortable
rooms. Great buffet breakfast.

DK Choice

WEIMAR: Villa Hentzel €€
Boutique Road Map D4
Bauhausstrasse 12, 99423
Tel *(03643) 86580*
W hotel-villa-hentzel.de
This elegant 19th-century hotel
has welcomed numerous writers
and also guests of note. The
beautifully renovated rooms are
individually furnished and have
historic features. The hotel offers
wonderful value for money.

**WEIMAR: Best Western
Premier Grand Hotel
Russischer Hof** €€€
Historic Road Map D4
Goetheplatz 2, 99423
Tel *(03643) 7740*
W russischerhof-weimar.de
The over 200-year-old Russischer
Hof is a luxurious, elegant
hotel with modern amenities.

**WEIMAR: Romantik Hotel
Dorotheenhof Weimar** €€€
Luxury Road Map D4
Dorotheenhof 1, 99427
Tel *(03643) 4590*
W dorotheenhof.com
Reasonably priced luxury in
superb surroundings. Choose
from a range of spacious rooms.

Munich

Ibis München City West €
Budget Road Map D7
Westendstrasse 181, 80686
Tel *(089) 5794970*
W ibis.com
International chain hotel for
those who want simple and
functional lodgings at low prices.

Carat Hotel €€
Budget Map 1 F5
Lindwurmstrasse 13, 80337
Tel *(089) 230380*
W carat-hotel-muenchen.de
Centrally located hotel with
simple, bright rooms and a large
breakfast buffet, including
various healthy options.

**Holiday Inn Munich
City Centre** €€
Budget Map 3 F5
Hochstrasse 3, 81669
Tel *(089) 48034444*
W holidayinn.com
A popular and central choice,
respected for its well-equipped
rooms and excellent restaurant.

Hotel Laimer Hof €€
Historic Road Map D7
Laimer Strasse 40, 80639
Tel *(089) 1780380*
W laimerhof.de
Neo-Renaissance villa with
classically furnished rooms.
Free bikes to explore surroundings.

Hotel Seibel €€
Historic Road Map D7
Theresienhöhe 9, 80339
Tel *(089) 5401420*
W seibel-hotels-munich.de
Good-value rooms in a 19th-
century Art Deco building near
the Oktoberfest area.

DK Choice

**Motel One München
Sendlinger Tor** €
Budget Map 1 F5
*Herzog-Wilhelm-Strasse 28,
80331*
Tel *(089) 51777250*
W motel-one.com
This reliable budget chain has
really gone from strength to
strength, and for good reason.
Motel One offers excellent
value rooms with bright
turquoise features that lend a
certain minimalist elegance.
There is also a great café-bar
and lounge on site.

Charles Hotel €€€
Luxury Map 1 F3
Sophienstrasse 28, 80333
Tel *(089) 5445550*
W charleshotel.de
This fantastic hotel has huge
rooms with good views over the
nearby botanical gardens.

Cortiina €€€
Boutique Map 2 C4
Ledererstrasse 8, 80331
Tel *(089) 2422490*
W cortiina.com
Elegant hotel whose individually
decorated rooms and cocktail bar
ooze boutique opulence.

Hotel Bavaria €€€
Boutique Road Map D7
Gollierstrasse 9, 80339
Tel *(089) 5080790*
W hotel-bavaria.com
Long-standing family-run hotel.
Bright rooms with charming
touches. Good breakfast buffet.

Louis Hotel €€€
Modern Map 2 B5
Viktualienmarkt 6, 80331
Tel *(089) 41119080*
W louis-hotel.com
Lovely, airy rooms with natural
stone tiles and wooden floors,
complemented by Italian fabrics.

The spacious lounge at Motel One München Sendlinger Tor, Munich

For more information on types of hotels *see page 491*

Spa facilities at the Kempinski Hotel Berchtesgaden Bavarian Alps, Berchtesgaden

Platzl €€€
Business **Map** 2 B4
Sparkassenstrasse 10, 80331
Tel *(089) 237030*
🅦 platzl.de
Warm and modern accommodation, a stylish spa and a fantastic 16th-century restaurant and pub, Platzl promises an enjoyable stay.

Vier Jahreszeithen Kempinski
Luxury **Map** 2 C4
Maximilianstrasse 17, 80539
Tel *(089) 21252799*
🅦 kempinski.com
Prestigious hotel with boutique-style rooms and a variety of five-star facilities, including a steam bath and sauna.

Bavaria

AUGSBURG: Steigenberger Drei Mohren €€€
Historic **Road Map** D6
Maximilianstrasse 40, 86150
Tel *(0821) 50360*
🅦 steigenberger.com
In the heart of the old town, timeless elegance combines here with modern amenities and a spa.

BAMBERG: Barockhotel am Dom €€
Historic **Road Map** D5
Vorderer Bach 4, 96049
Tel *(0951) 54031*
🅦 barockhotel.de
Baroque details feature throughout this smart hotel, which dates back to the sixteenth century. Lovely breakfast buffet.

BAMBERG: Hotel National €€
Historic **Road Map** D5
Luitpoldstrasse 37, 96052
Tel *(0951) 509980*
🅦 hotel-national-bamberg.de
Grand 19th-century building with modern, brightly decorated rooms and a bar.

BAMBERG: Hotel Nepomuk €€€
Historic **Road Map** D5
Obere Mülbrücke 9, 96049
Tel *(0951) 98420*
🅦 hotel-nepomuk.de
Old timber-framed hotel with an exceptional location next to the river. Rooms have modern facilities.

BAYREUTH: Ramada Residenzschloss Bayreuth €€€
Business **Road Map** D5
Erlanger Strasse 37, 95444
Tel *(0921) 75850*
🅦 wyndhamhotelgroup.de
Standard chain hotel with comfortable modern rooms, a sauna and a good restaurant.

BERCHTESGADEN: Laroshäusel €
Pensionen **Road Map** E7
Am Larosbach 11, 81417
Tel *(08652) 3736*
🅦 berchtesgaden-ferien.de
A small establishment in a beautiful location at the foot of the Watzmann. Laroshäusel makes a very good base for hiking tours.

BERCHTESGADEN: Vier Jahreszeiten €€
Budget **Road Map** E7
Maximilianstrasse 20, 83471
Tel *(08652) 9520*
🅦 hotel-vierjahreszeiten-berchtesgaden.de
Family-run hotel with traditional Bavarian decor throughout and alpine views from many rooms.

DK Choice

BERCHTESGADEN: Kempinski Hotel Berchtesgaden Bavarian Alps €€€
Luxury **Road Map** E7
Hintereck 1, 83471
Tel *(08652) 97550*
🅦 intercontinental.com
This exclusive five-star establishment has exceptional views of the Alps from almost every part of the hotel, including the minimalist bedrooms and the luxurious spa and pools. The gourmet restaurants on site specialize in various cuisines.

FÜSSEN: Hotel Hirsch €€€
Boutique **Road Map** D7
Kaiser-Maximilian-Ptaz 7, 87629
Tel *(0049) 8362 93980*
🅦 hotelfuessen.de
Bavarian antiques meet modern amenities in one of many successful combinations of new and old at this boutique hotel.

DK Choice

GARMISCH-PARTENKIRCHEN: Gasthof Fraundorfer €
Gasthof **Road Map** D7
Ludwigstrasse 24, 82467
Tel *(08821) 9270*
🅦 gasthof-fraundorfer.de
As much a celebration of Bavarian culture as a guesthouse, Gasthof Fraundorfer has beautiful murals, individually decorated rooms with regional themes and nightly dancing and yodeling performances in the restaurant and bar.

GARMISCH-PARTENKIRCHEN: Hotel Edelweiss €€€
Pensionen **Road Map** D7
Martinswinkelstrasse 15–17, 82467
Tel *(08821) 2454*
🅦 hoteledelweiss.de
Romantic family-run guesthouse with spotless and spacious country-style rooms.

INGOLSTADT: Altstadthotel Guesthouse Die Galerie €€€
Boutique **Road Map** D6
Gymnasiumstrasse 9, 85049
Tel *(0841) 88690*
🅦 altstadthotel-ingolstadt.de
Angular design dominates in this spotless mid-range hotel with a café, sauna and rock garden.

INGOLSTADT: Hotel Ammerland Garni €€€
Boutique **Road Map** D6
Hermann-Paul-Müller-Strasse 15, 85055
Tel *(0841) 953450*
🅦 hotel-ammerland.de
Great choice away from the town centre, with creatively-styled rooms, two saunas and a bar.

LINDAU: Hotel-Spiegel-Garni €€
Pensionen **Road Map** C7
In der Grub 1, 88131
Tel *(08382) 94930*
🅦 hotel-spiegel-garni.de
Rooms here range from simple to extravagantly alpine, with wood-clad interiors and floral drapes.

LINDAU: Bayerischer Hof €€€
Luxury **Road Map** C7
Bahnhofplatz 2, 88131
Tel *(08382) 9150*
🅦 bayerischerhof-lindau.de

Neo-Classical building in a prime lakefront location with views of the lion, lighthouse and the alps. Spacious rooms with 19th century furnishings.

LINDAU: Reutemann €€€
Mid-Range Hotel   Road Map C7
Ludwigstrasse 23, 88131
Tel *(08382) 9150*
W reutemann-lindau.de
Stylish hotel with an extraordinary harbourside location, airy rooms, a spa and an excellent restaurant.

NUREMBERG: Dürer Hotel €€
Modern   Road Map D6
Neutormauer 32, 90403
Tel *(0911) 2146650*
W duerer-hotel.de
Located next to the Albrecht-Dürer-Haus, the Dürer features spacious rooms decorated in rich colours. For relaxation, guests have access to a sauna, steam room and Mediterranean garden.

NUREMBERG: Elch €€
Historic   Road Map D6
Irrerstrasse 11, 90403
Tel *(0911) 2492980*
W hotel-elch.de
Clean and simple family-run lodging in a historic 14th-century house with exposed beams.

NUREMBERG: Hotel Victoria €€
Boutique   Road Map D6
Königstrasse 80, 90402
Tel *(0911) 24050*
W hotelvictoria.de
Lovely and clean four-star hotel in a listed building located opposite the train station. There's an extensive breakfast buffet and a café serving delicious cakes.

NUREMBERG: Hotel Drei Raben €€€
Boutique   Road Map D6
Königstrasse 63, 90402
Tel *(0911) 274380*
W hoteldreiraben.de
Modern trendy accommodation with bold colour schemes, a bar and tasty breakfast buffet.

NUREMBERG: Le Méridien Grand €€€
Boutique   Map D6
Bahnhofstrasse 1–3, 90402
Tel *(0911) 23220*
W lemeridiennuernberg.com
Elegant hotel with sleek Art Deco and Art Nouveau furnishings. Excellent regional brasserie.

DK Choice

OBERAMMERGAU: Hotel Maximilian €€€
Gasthof   Road Map D7
Ettaler Strasse 5, 82487
Tel *(08822) 948740*
W maximilian-oberammergau.de
This alpine hotel features a striking array of boutique rooms, along with a luxurious spa. There is also a fantastic Mediterranean restaurant and a beer garden to sample the hotel's own brews.

OBERSTDORF: Saschas Kachelofen €
Gasthof   Road Map C7
Kirchstrasse 3, 87561
Tel *(08322) 97750*
W saschas-kachelofen.de
Traditional, family-run inn set above a rustic restaurant.

PASSAU: Wilder Mann €€
Historic   Road Map E6
Rathausplatz, 94032
Tel *(0851) 35071*
W wilder-mann.com
Central hotel that sports heavy traditional furniture including one royal wedding bed.

PASSAU: Hotel Schloss Ort €€€
Modern   Road Map E6
Im Ort 11, 94032
Tel *(0851) 34072*
W hotel-schloss-ort.de
Pleasant rooms, but the picturesque location is the highlight.

REGENSBURG: Goldenes Kreuz €€€
Boutique   Road Map D6
Haidplatz 7, 93047

Tel *(0941) 55812*
W hotel-goldeneskreuz.de
Lovely collection of small suites in a centrally located historic building. Wonderful café.

REGENSBURG: Goliath €€€
Boutique   Road Map D6
Goliathstrasse 10, 93047
Tel *(0941) 2000900*
W hotel-goliath.de
Goliath promises bold colours and modern design along with great views from the rooftop terrace.

ROTHENBURG: Gerberhaus €€
Historic   Road Map C6
Spitalgasse 25, 91541
Tel *(09861) 94900*
W hotel-gerberhaus.de
Country-style rooms in a beautiful converted 16th-century tannery.

ROTHENBURG: Burg-Hotel €€€
Historic   Road Map C6
Klostergasse 1–3, 91541
Tel *(09861) 94890*
W burghotel.eu
Hotel combining a 12th-century structure with trendy designs. Sauna and spa facilities.

WÜRZBURG: Central Hotel Garni €€
Budget   Road Map C5
Koellikerstrasse 1, 97070
Tel *(0931) 4608840*
W centralhotel-wuerzburg.de
Centrally located good-value hotel with basic but good rooms and buffet breakfasts.

WÜRZBURG: Hotel Grüner Baum €€
Pensionen   Road Map C5
Zeller Strasse 35, 97082
Tel *(0931) 450680*
W gruener-baum-wuerzburg.de
Small rooms in a traditional Franconian inn. Breakfast buffet.

WÜRZBURG: Hotel Würzburger Hof €€€
Modern   Road Map C5
Barbarossaplatz 2, 97070
Tel *(0931) 53814*
W hotel-wuerzburgerhof.de
Würzburger Hof features richly decorated rooms in wide variety of styles and price ranges.

Baden-Württemberg

BADEN-BADEN: Am Markt €€
Pensionen   Road Map B6
Marktplatz 18, 76530
Tel *(07221) 27040*
W hotel-am-markt-baden.de
Friendly, family-run pension with basic rooms and views over the charming marketplace.

Stylishly designed room at Le Méridien Grand, Nuremberg

For more information on types of hotels *see page 491*

Traditionally-styled room at Graf Zeppelin, Stuttgart

**BADEN-BADEN: Bad-Hotel
Zum Hirsch** €€€
Historic **Road Map** D6
Hirschstrasse 1, 76530
Tel *(07221) 9390*
W heliopark-hirsch.de
Thermal spring water flows
from the taps in this charming
Old Town hotel. Also boasts a
splendid ballroom.

**BADEN-BADEN: Brenner's
Park Hotel** €€€
Luxury **Road Map** B6
Schillerstrasse 4–6, 76530
Tel *(07221) 9000*
W brenners.com
An effortlessly elegant hotel
with extravagant antique
furnishings across its rooms
and lounges.

**FREIBURG IM BREISGAU:
Schemmer** €€
Budget **Road Map** B7
Eschholzstrasse 63, 79106
Tel *(0761) 207490*
W hotel-schemmer.de
Tidy little town house with modest
accommodation, some rooms
have shared baths.

DK Choice

**FREIBURG IM BREISGAU:
Zum Roten Bären** €€€
Historic **Road Map** B7
Oberlinden 12, 79098
Tel *(0761) 387870*
W roter-baeren.de
Germany's oldest hotel, Zum
Roten Bären opened in 1120
and became part of the city
gate in 1250. The contemporary
rooms have the occasional
antique providing a sense of
history. First-class breakfasts.

**HEIDELBERG: Der
Europäische Hof** €€€
Luxury **Road Map** C6
Friedrich-Ebert-Anlage 1, 69117
Tel *(06221) 5150*

W europaeischerhof.com
One of Heidelberg's premier
hotels with individually
decorated rooms, several great
restaurants and a bar.

HEIDELBERG: Hirschgasse €€€
Luxury **Road Map** C6
Hirschgasse 3, 69120
Tel *(06221) 4540*
W hirschgasse.de
The former lodgings of Mark Twain
and Otto von Bismarck is a gem
with museum-worthy antiques.

**KARLSRUHE: Hotelwelt
Kübler** €€
Boutique **Road Map** B6
Bismarckstrasse 39–43, 76133
Tel *(0721) 1440*
W 4a-hotelwelt.de
Variety of rooms from standard
mid-range to themed suites.
On-site microbrewery.

KONSTANZ: Barbarossa €€
Historic **Road Map** C7
Obermarkt 8–12, 78462
Tel *(07531) 128990*
W barbarossa-hotel.com
Mid-range hotel with a
frescoes covering the walls.
This building played host to
Friedrich I in 1183.

**KONSTANZ: Steigenberger
Inselhotel** €€€
Luxury **Road Map** C7
Auf der Insel 1, 78462
Tel *(07531) 1250*
W steigenberger.com
Prestigious establishment in a
medieval Dominican monastery.
Located on its own island.

**LUDWIGSBURG:
Hotel Favorit** €€
Mid-Range Hotel **Road Map** C6
Gartenstrasse 18, 71638
Tel *(07141) 976770*
W hotel-favorit.de
Great hotel with cheerful pine-
furnished pastel rooms. Sauna
and an extensive breakfast buffet.

**MAULBRONN:
Hotel Klosterpost** €€
Historic **Road Map** C6
Klosterstrasse 2, 75433
Tel *(07043) 1080*
W hotel-klosterpost.de
Traditional half-timbered 13th-
century inn with bright rooms
and a good regional restaurant.

MEERSBURG: Hotel Löwen €€
Historic **Road Map** C7
Marktplatz 2, 88709
Tel *(07532) 43040*
W hotel-loewen-meersburg.de
Romantic medieval building with
beautiful geranium-filled
windows and snug rooms.

STUTTGART: Hotel Espenlaub €€
Mid-Range **Road Map** C6
Charlottenstrasse 27, 70182
Tel *(0711) 210910*
W stadthotels-erkurt.de
Basic hotel with small, bright
and simple rooms and a modest
complimentary breakfast buffet.

STUTTGART: Graf Zeppelin €€€
Luxury **Road Map** C6
Arnulf-Klett-Platz 7, 70173
Tel *(0711) 20480*
W steigenberger.com
This five-star hotel promises 19th-
century elegance. Classical as
well as avant-garde rooms.

**STUTTGART: Der
Zauberlehrling** €€€
Boutique **Road Map** C6
Rosenstrasse 38, 70182
Tel *(0711) 2377770*
W zauberlehrling.de
Located in the hip Bohnenviertel
district. Tasteful themed rooms,
from Japanese to faded *fin de siècle*.

TÜBINGEN: Hotel am Schloss €€
Historic **Road Map** C6
Burgsteige 18, 72070
Tel *(07071) 92940*
W hotelamschloss.de
Half-timbered place with colour-
ful window boxes and fine town
views from below the castle.

TÜBINGEN: Hotel Krone €€€
Luxury **Road Map** C6
Uhlandstrasse 1, 72072
Tel *(07071) 13310*
W krone-tuebingen.de
Prestigious riverside hotel with
bright rooms, a sophisticated
gourmet restaurant and chic bar.

ULM: Hotel Bäumle €€
Pensionen **Road Map** C6
Kohlgasse 6, 89073
Tel *(0731) 62287*
W hotel-baeumle.de
Housed in a renovated over
500-year-old building with
good-value standard rooms.

DK Choice

ULM: Hotel Schiefes Haus €€€
Historic   Road Map C6
Schwörhausgasse 6, 89073
Tel *(0731) 967930*
W hotelschiefeshausulm.de
This famous half-timbered
establishment built in 1443 has
wood-beam ceilings and floors
so crooked that the bed legs
are of different lengths. The
property's rustic nature has been
well-preserved, with plush
additions such as bathrooms
with spacious tubs.

Rhineland-Palatinate and Saarland

DK Choice

**BACHARACH:
Rhein Hotel**   €€
Historic   Road Map B5
Langstrasse 50, 55422
Tel *(06743) 1243*
W rhein-hotel-bacharach.de
Rhein is an excellent family-
run, half-timbered hotel in an
atmospheric location
between the town ramparts
and the Rhine. On offer are
spotless rooms, a superb
regional restaurant with
excellent Riesling wines, an
extensive breakfast buffet and
free bike rental.

**BOPPARD: Bellevue
Rheinhotel**   €€
Historic   Road Map B5
Rheinallee 41, 56154
Tel *(06742) 1020*
W bellevue-boppard.de

The picturesque exterior of Hotel Schiefes
Haus, Ulm

Grand 19th-century waterfront
hotel with antique-decorated
rooms overlooking the Rhine.
There's an atmospheric wine-
cellar bar and a choice of
restaurants. Buffet breakfast.

MAINZ: Hof Ehrenfels   €€
Historic   Road Map B5
Grebenstrasse 5–7, 55116
Tel *(06131) 9712340*
W hof-ehrenfels.de
Smart hotel in a 15th-century
convent overlooking the Dom.

**MAINZ: Hyatt
Regency Mainz**   €€€
Luxury   Road Map B5
Malakoff-Terrasse 1, 55116
Tel *(06131) 731234*
W mainz.regency.hyatt.com
Sophisticated five-star hotel
in a striking modern building that
integrates a 19th-century fort
and overlooks the Rhine.

**OBERWESEL: Hotel
Römerkrug**   €€
Historic   Road Map B5
Marktplatz 1, 55430
Tel *(06744) 9499106*
W hotel-roemerkrug.rhine
castles.com
This dignified half-timbered
guesthouse has old-fashioned
rooms with modern amenities.

**OBERWESEL: Burghotel Auf
Schönburg**   €€€
Historic   Road Map B5
Auf Schönburg, 55430
Tel *(06744) 939 30*
W burghotel-schoenburg.de
A castle restored in 1914 with
10th-century foundations. Lovely
interiors and terrace restaurant.

**SAARBRÜCKEN: Hotel
Madeleine**   €€
Budget   Road Map B6
Cecilienstrasse 5, 66111
Tel *(0681) 857780*
W hotel-madeleine.de
A family-run hotel with small
and bright rooms, free bike rental
and bargain mid-week rates.

SPEYER: Hotel Domhof   €€
Historic   Road Map B6
Bauhof 3, 67346
Tel *(06232) 13290*
W domhof.de
Stay in this ivy-clad hotel with
spacious antique-furnished
rooms overlooking a cobbled
courtyard. There is also a superb
breakfast buffet.

ST MARTIN: St Martiner Castell €€
Historic   Road Map B6
Maikammerer Strasse 2, 67487
Tel *(06323) 9510*
W hotelcastell.de

St Martiner is an attractive
castle-hotel with well priced
rooms. Its restaurant serves
German and French staples. Set
in an exceptionally pretty village.

TRIER: Becker's   €€
Boutique   Road Map A5
Olewiger Strasse 206, 54295
Tel *(0651) 938080*
W weinhaus-becker.de
Stylish vineyard guesthouse in a
wine-producing suburb of Trier.
Room decor reminiscent of
Japanese minimalism.

TRIER: Casa Chiara   €€
Pensionen   Road Map A5
Engelstrasse 8, 54292
Tel *(0651) 270730*
W casa-chiara.de
Friendly hotel with good
breakfasts and spotless rooms,
some with views of a Roman
city gate.

TRIER: Villa Hügel   €€€
Luxury   Road Map A5
Bernhardstrasse 14, 54295
Tel *(0651) 937100*
W hotel-villa-huegel.de
Upmarket Art Nouveau villa
sporting cheerful rooms and a
terrace with lovely valley views.

**WORMS: Parkhotel
Prinz Carl**   €€€
Historic   Road Map B5
Prinz-Carl-Anlage 10–14, 67547
Tel *(06241) 3080*
W parkhotel-prinzcarl.de
Located in a 19th-century
barracks with large, cheerful
rooms. On site bar and restaurant.

Hesse

**ALSFELD: Zum
Schwalbennest**   €€
Gasthof   Road Map C4
Pfarrwiesenweg 12–14, 36304
Tel *(06631) 911440*
W hotel-schwalbennest.de
Serene and cheerful Zum
Schwalbennest offers
comfortable rooms, a rustic
restaurant and a beer garden.

**BAD HOMBURG:
Maritim Hotel**   €€€
Mid-Range Hotel   Road Map C5
Ludwigstrasse 3, 61348
Tel *(06172) 6600*
W maritim.de
Impeccably decorated rooms
with balconies overlooking a
park. Guests have use of the
pool, sauna, fitness centre,
and an elegant shopping
arcade that can be accessed
from the hotel.

For more information on types of hotels *see page 491*

**DARMSTADT: Jagdschloss
Kranichstein** €€€
Historic **Road Map** C5
Kranichsteiner Strasse 261, 64289
Tel *(06151) 130670*
Ⓦ hotel-jagdschloss-kranichstein.de
Fabulous luxury accommodation
in a beautiful Renaissance castle.

**ELTVILLE AM RHEIN:
Kronenschlösschen** €€€
Luxury **Road Map** B5
Rheinallee, 65347
Tel *(06723) 640*
Ⓦ kronenschloesschen.de
Stylish rooms with individual
furnishings and lovely bathrooms.
Fine-dining restaurant on site.

**FRANKFURT AM MAIN:
Hamburger Hof** €€
Modern **Road Map** C5
Poststrasse 10-12, 60329
Tel *(069) 271 396 90*
Ⓦ hamburgerhof.com
Stylish hotel with sleek design
and a breakfast buffet.

**FRANKFURT AM MAIN:
Grandhotel Hessischer Hof** €€€
Luxury **Road Map** C5
Friedrich-Ebert-Anlage 40, 60325
Tel *(069) 754 00*
Ⓦ hessischer-hof.de
Exquisitely styled building with
well-equipped classic rooms,
some furnished with antiques.

**FULDA: Maritim Hotel
am Schlossgarten** €€
Mid-Range Hotel **Road Map** C5
Pauluspromenade 2, 36037
Tel *(0661) 28 20*
Ⓦ maritim.de
Ostentatious yet elegant lodgings
with a pool and spacious rooms,
some with balconies.

DK Choice

**KASSEL: Schlosshotel Bad
Wilhelmshöhe** €€€
Luxury **Road Map** C4
Schlosspark 8, 34131
Tel *(0561) 308 80*
Ⓦ schlosshotel-kassel.de
A refined hotel in the
magnificent Wilhelmshöhe
Bergpark. Rooms are large and
stylish; ask for the superior
rooms or suites for the best
views over Kassel. Good
wellness and spa facilities.

**LIMBURG: Hotel
Zimmermann** €€
Pensionen **Road Map** B5
Blumenröder Strasse 1, 65549
Tel *(06431) 46 11*
Ⓦ hotelzimmermann.de
Relaxed vibe, with ornate rooms
and marble-clad bathrooms.

MARBURG: Vila Vita Rosenpark
€€€
Luxury **Road Map** C4
Anneliese-Pohl-Allee 7-17, 35037
Tel *(06421) 600 50*
Ⓦ rosenpark.com
Elegant hotel with a glass-domed
lobby, impeccable service, several
apartments, two restaurants, a
café and a wine cellar with tastings.

**MICHELSTADT: Zum
Grünen Baum** €€
Gasthof **Road Map** C5
Grosse Gasse 17, 64720
Tel *(06061) 24 09*
Ⓦ gruenerbaum-michelstadt.com
A charming half-timbered inn
with inviting rooms and an
award-winning restaurant.

**RÜDESHEIM AM RHEIN:
Jagdschloss Niederwald** €€€
Historic **Road Map** B5
Niederwald 1, 65385
Tel *(06722) 710 60*
Ⓦ niederwald.de
Historic hunting castle with a
tennis court, swimming pool and
a restaurant with panoramic views.

WEILBURG: Schlosshotel €€
Historic **Road Map** B5
Langgasse 25, 35781
Tel *(06471) 509 00*
Ⓦ schlosshotel-weilburg.de
Set in a luxurious Renaissance
castle with tastefully decorated
rooms and a good restaurant.

**WETZLAR: Landhotel
Naunheimer Mühle** €€
Gasthof **Road Map** B5
Mühle 2, 35584
Tel *(06441) 935 30*
Ⓦ naunheimer-muehle.de
Traditional to modern rooms and
a rustic restaurant located right
next to the Lahn River.

WIESBADEN: Nassauer Hof €€€
Luxury **Road Map** B5
Kaiser-Friedrich-Platz 3–4, 65183
Tel *(0611) 13 30*
Ⓦ nassauer-hof.de
Exclusive, opulent hotel with
superb rooms, an acclaimed
restaurant and a wellness area.

North Rhine-
Westphalia

**AACHEN: Best Western
Hotel Royal** €€
Mid-Range Hotel **Road Map** A4
Jülicher Strasse 1, 52070
Tel *(0241) 182 280*
Ⓦ royal.bestwestern.de
This city-centre hotel has
gorgeous minimalist rooms done

in beautiful soft colours. The
suites are equipped with private
terraces and kitchenettes.

**AACHEN: Pullmann
Aachen Quellenhof** €€€
Luxury **Road Map** A4
Monheimsallee 52, 52062
Tel *(0241) 913 20*
Ⓦ pullmannhotels.com
A grand establishment with
elegant rooms and suites, a
wellness area and a fantastic
on-site brasserie.

BIELEFELD: Brenner Hotel €€
Mid Range Hotel **Road Map** C3
Otto-Brenner-Strasse 135, 33607
Tel *(0521) 299 90*
Ⓦ brenner-hotel-bielefeld.de
Small bowling alley, a restaurant
and a quirky bar at this quaint
little hotel.

**BONN: Apartmenthotel
Kaiser Karl** €€
Mid-Range Hotel **Road Map** B4
Vorgebirgsstrasse 56, 53119
Tel *(0228) 981 41 999*
Ⓦ kaiser-karl-hotel-bonn.de
Choose from nicely decorated
rooms or serviced apartments
with well-equipped kitchenettes.

**BONN: Schlosshotel
Kommende Ramersdorf** €€
Historic **Road Map** B4
Oberkasseler Strasse 10, 53227
Tel *(0228) 440 734*
Ⓦ apartment-hotel-bonn.de
This beautiful castle has antique-
filled hallways, individually styled
rooms and a superb restaurant.

COLOGNE: NH Köln City €€
Business **Road Map** B4
Holzmarkt 47, 50676
Tel *(0221) 272 28 80*
Ⓦ nh-hotels.com
This centrally located hotel
houses comfortable rooms and a
good Mediterranean restaurant.

A glimpse of a luxurious suite at the Vila Vita
Rosenpark, Marburg

DK Choice

COLOGNE: Excelsior Hotel Ernst €€€
Luxury   Road Map B4
Trankgasse 1–5, 50667
Tel *(0221) 27 01*
W excelsiorhotelernst.com
A historic and truly grand hotel beside Cologne's magnificent cathedral, with rooms and suites that are contemporary but retain classical features. Restaurants here include the world-renowned, Michelin-starred Taku.

The magnificentl lake-front façade of the Dorint Park Hotel, Bremen

COLOGNE: Hotel im Wasserturm €€€
Boutique   Road Map B4
Kaygasse 2, 50676
Tel *(0221) 200 80*
W hotel-im-wasserturm.de
Stay in an interestingly-shaped room fitted with all the amenities in this former water tower.

DORTMUND: Cityhotel Dortmund €€
Mid-Range Hotel   Road Map B4
Grafenhof 6, 44137
Tel *(0231) 477 96 60*
W cityhotel-dortmund.de
Efficient hotel with comfortable rooms. Terrific breakfast buffet.

DÜSSELDORF: Novum Business Hotel Madison Düsseldorf Hauptbahnhof €€
Mid-Range Hotel   Road Map B4
Graf-Adolf-Strasse 94, 40210
Tel *(0211) 168 50*
W novum-hotels.de
Range of tasteful, inviting rooms in a convenient central location.

DÜSSELDORF: Steigenberger Parkhotel €€€
Luxury   Road Map B4
Königsallee 1a, 40212
Tel *(0211) 138 10*
W steigenberger.com
Well-styled rooms and a fantastic restaurant with a diverse menu.

ESSEN: Welcome Hotel €€
Mid-Range Hotel   Road Map B4
Schützenbahn 58, 45127
Tel *(0201) 177 90*
W welcome-essen.de
Colourful place with a well-equipped rooms and a great garden restaurant.

HÖXTER: Ringhotel Niedersachsen €€€
Mid-Range Hotel   Road Map C3
Grubestrasse 3–7, 37671
Tel *(05271) 68 80*
W hotelniedersachsen.de
Airy rooms, some with large wooden beams. Four restaurants, a wellness spa and a pool.

LEMGO: Im Borke €€
Gasthof   Road Map C3
Salzufler Strasse 132, 32657
Tel *(05266) 16 91*
W hotel-im-borke.de
Peaceful, family-friendly hotel with a popular restaurant.

MÜNSTER: Romantik Hotel Hof zur Linde €€€
Gasthof   Road Map B3
Handorfer Werseufer 1, 48157
Tel *(0251) 327 50*
W hof-zur-linde.de
A lovely farm cottage hotel with magnificent river views and fireplaces in the suites and cottages.

MÜNSTER: Schloss Wilkinghege €€€
Historic   Road Map B3
Steinfurter Strasse 374, 48159
Tel *(0251) 144 270*
W schloss-wilkinghege.de
Castle with modern comfort and historic charm, as well as a refined on-site restaurant.

SIEGEN: Best Western Parkhotel Siegen €€€
Mid-Range Hotel   Road Map B4
Koblenzer Strasse 135, 57072
Tel *(0271) 338 10*
W parkhotel-siegen.bestwestern.de
Stylishly furnished rooms and a sauna in a serene location.

WUPPERTAL: Art Fabrik & Hotel €
Boutique   Road Map B4
Bockmühle 16–24, 42289
Tel *(0202) 283 70*
W art-fabrik-hotel-wuppertal.de
A former property of Friedrich Engels with spacious rooms, saunas and an artistic touch.

XANTEN: Fürstenberger Hof €€
Pensionen   Road Map A3
Fürstenberg 11, 46509
Tel *(02801) 16 13*
W fuerstenbergerhof-xanten.de
A castle-like building in a nature reserve. Rooms furnished with chandeliers and antiques.

Lower Saxony, Hamburg and Bremen

BREMEN: Heldt €€
Pensionen   Road Map C2
Friedhofstrasse 41, 28213
Tel *(0421) 4360 300*
W hotel-heldt.de
Small establishment with tastefully furnished rooms and apartments. Free bike rental.

BREMEN: Dorint Park Hotel €€€
Luxury   Road Map C2
Im Bürgerpark, 28209
Tel *(0421) 340 80*
W hotel-bremen.dorint.com
Stay in this opulent hotel located in a lovely area in Bremen. Comfortable rooms and several good bars and restaurants.

BREMEN: Landhaus Höpken's Ruh €€€
Gasthof   Road Map C2
Oberneulander Landstrasse 69, 28355
Tel *(0421) 205 8540*
W hoepkens-ruh.de
Stylish, small hotel set in parkland, with individually furnished rooms and a commendable restaurant.

CELLE: Hotel am Braunen Hirsch €€
Mid-Range Hotel   Road Map C3
Münzstrasse 9c, 29223
Tel *(05141) 939 30*
W hotelambraunenhirsch.de
Bright and comfortable rooms with modern design. There is also a historic restaurant next door.

CELLE: Fürstenhof Celle €€€
Luxury   Road Map C3
Hannoversche Strasse 55–56, 29221
Tel *(05141) 20 10*
W fuerstenhof-celle.de
Fürstenhof Celle offers fabulous accommodation, with English country-style rooms, an impressive fitness area and a gourmet restaurant.

For more information on types of hotels *see page 491*

CLOPPENBURG: Park Hotel €€
Gasthof   Road Map B3
Burgstrasse 8, 49661
Tel *(04471) 661416*
W parkhotel-cloppenburg.de
Lovely, quiet hotel by the Soeste
river. Stylish rooms, sauna, golf
and tennis facilities.

DUDERSTADT: Zum Löwen €€
Modern   Road Map C4
Marktstrasse 30, 37115
Tel *(05527) 849000*
W hotel-zum-loewen.de
Zum Löwen features sleek rooms,
a beautiful pool and a famous
regional restaurant.

GOSLAR: Brusttuch €
Historic   Road Map D3
Hoher Weg 1, 38640
Tel *(05321) 346 00*
W brusttuch.de
Located in a medieval Old Town
building with quaint rooms and
all modern amenities.

GOSLAR: Der Achtermann €€€
Boutique   Road Map D3
Rosentorstrasse 20, 38640
Tel *(05321) 700 00*
W der-achtermann.de
This Art-Deco-style hotel has
a large pool and sauna area as
well as a good restaurant.

GÖTTINGEN: Gebhards €€€
Luxury   Road Map C4
Goetheallee 22–23, 37073
Tel *(0551) 496 80*
W gebhardshotel.de
Beautifully furnished rooms,
sauna and whirlpool facilities and
a traditional German restaurant.

**HAMBURG: Gastwerk
Hotel Hamburg** €€
Historic   Road Map C2
Beim Alten Gaswerk 3, 22761
Tel *(040) 890 624 24*
W gastwerk.com
An impressive renovated gas-
works plant. Industrial-styled

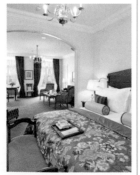

Spacious, elegant suite at Fairmont Hotel
Vier Jahreszeiten, Hamburg

Key to Price Guide *see page 492*

rooms and lofts fitted with all
modern amenities, along with
an exceptional spa.

DK Choice

**HAMBURG: Fairmont Hotel
Vier Jahreszeiten** €€€
Historic   Road Map C2
Neuer Jungfernstieg 9–14, 20354
Tel *(040) 349*
W fairmont-hvj.com
A large, elegant hotel with great
views of the Alster from most
rooms. With its subdued design,
excellent service, an award-
winning restaurant and a great
spa and fitness club, Fairmont
never ceases to impress. Come
here for the subtle luxury.

**HAMBURG:
The George Hotel** €€€
Gasthof   Road Map C2
Barcastrasse 3, 220 87
Tel *(040) 2800300*
W thegeorge-hotel.de
British-style inspired hotel with
dark wood in the traditional rooms
and a fantastic Italian restaurant.

**HAMBURG: Le Royal
Meridien** €€€
Luxury   Road Map C2
An Der Alster 52–56, 200 99
Tel *(040) 210 00*
W lemeridienhamburg.com
Minimalist rooms, an excellent
spa and great views of Hamburg
along the banks of the Alster.

**HANOVER: Central-Hotel
Kaiserhof** €€€
Historic   Road Map C3
Ernst-August-Platz 4, 301 59
Tel *(0511) 36830*
W centralhotel.de
Classically furnished rooms in a
historic building. The acclaimed
restaurant serves trout sourced
from the courtyard fountain.

**HANOVER: Kastens Hotel
Luisenhof** €€€
Gasthof   Road Map C3
Luisenstrasse 1-3, 30159
Tel *(0511) 304 40*
W kastens-luisenhof.de
An elegant mansion with large,
quiet rooms, and good spa and
fitness facilities. Great views.

**HILDESHEIM: Parkhotel
Berghölzchen** €€
Historic   Road Map C3
Am Berghölzchen 1, 31139
Tel *(05121) 97 90*
W berghoelzchen.de
An old hotel with comfortable
rooms. Do not forget to try the
delicious regional food that has
been served here since 1770.

**KÖNIGSLUTTER: Avalon
Hotelpark Königshof** €€
Modern   Road Map D3
Braunschweigerstrasse 21a, 38154
Tel *(05353) 50 30*
W hotelpark-koenigshof.de
Large hotel with cheerful rooms,
various sports amenities and a
good restaurant.

LÜNEBURG: Bremer Hof €€
Gasthof   Road Map D2
Lüner Strasse 12, 21335
Tel *(04131) 22 40*
W bremer-hof.de
Comfortable rooms, some with
old wooden beams, in a family-
run hotel dating to 1889. The
restaurant serves local cuisine.

**OLDENBURG: Best Western
Hotel Heide** €€
Mid-Range Hotel   Road Map B2
Melkbrink 49–51, 26121
Tel *(0441) 80 40*
W hotel-heide-oldenburg.de
Conveniently located, this chain
hotel has large rooms and an
elegant restaurant.

**OSNABRÜCK: Romantik
Hotel Walhalla** €€€
Historic   Road Map B3
Bierstrasse 24, 49074
Tel *(0541) 349 10*
W hotel-walhalla.de
This museum-like hotel, dating
back to 1690, has spacious rooms
and suites. Beer garden, lounge
bar and restaurant too.

**WOLFENBÜTTEL: Parkhotel
Altes Kaffeehaus** €€€
Gasthof   Road Map D3
Harztorwall 18, 38300
Tel *(05331) 88 80*
W parkhotel-wolfenbuettel.de
Comfortable, quiet, parkside
hotel with good-sized rooms
and a great French restaurant.

**WOLFSBURG: Brackstedter
Mühle** €€
Gasthof   Road Map D3
Zum Kühlen Grunde 2, 38448
Tel *(05366) 900*
W brackstedter-muehle.de
Peaceful hotel in an old millhouse
with simple rooms, a restaurant
and a beautiful winter garden.

Schleswig-Holstein

KIEL: Kieler Kaufman €€€
Luxury   Road Map C1
Niemannsweg 102, 24105
Tel *(0431) 881 10*
W kieler-kaufmann.de
Kieler Kaufman is a stylish old
villa with richly decorated rooms
befitting an English country house.

Comfortable room with splashes of colour at the Dorint Hotel Söl'ring Hof, Sylt

LÜBECK: Kaiserhof
Historic   Road Map D2   €
Kronsforder Allee 11–13, 23560
Tel *(040) 244440*
w kaiserhof-luebeck.de
A grand hotel with impressive rooms and a fish restaurant.

RATZEBURG: Der Seehof
Pensionen   Road Map D2   €€€
Lüneburger Damm 1–3, 23909
Tel *(04541) 860 100*
w derseehof.de
Set between two lakes, this hotel's rooms have lovely balcony views. Good seafood restaurant.

SCHLESWIG: Waldschlösschen
          €€€
Luxury   Road Map C1
Kolonnenweg 152, 24837
Tel *(04621) 38 30*
w hotel-waldschloesschen.de
Well-located, with bright rooms, great food and a swimming pool.

SYLT: Aarnhoog
Luxury   Road Map C1   €€€
Gaat 13, Keitum, 25980
Tel *(04651) 39 90*
w faehrhaus-hotel-collection.de
Excellent traditional hotel amid the dunes and forests. Rooms feature antique furniture.

DK Choice

SYLT: Dorint Hotel Söl'ring Hof
Luxury   Road Map C1   €€€
Am Sandwall 1, 25980
Tel *(04651) 83 62 00*
w soelring-hof.de
Peeking out over the dunes to a wide view of the sea, this wonderful thatch-roofed building is a destination in itself. The rooms are first-class and often booked weeks in advance. Enjoy the outstanding spa facilities and world-class cuisine.

Mecklenburg-Lower Pomerania

BAD DOBERAN: Grand Hotel Heiligendamm
Luxury   Road Map D1   €€€
Prof-Dr-Vogel-Strasse 16–18, 18209
Tel *(038203) 74 00*
w grandhotel-heiligendamm.com
A stately seaside hotel in a castle with classy rooms, several quality restaurants and a spa.

GREIFSWALD: Kronprinz
Gasthof   Road Map E1   €€
22 Lange Strasse, 17489
Tel *(03834) 79 00*
w hotelkronprinz.de
Kronprinz features lovely, uncluttered rooms and a rustic German brasserie downstairs.

GÜSTROW: Kurhaus am Inselsee
Gasthof   Road Map D2   €€
Heidburg 1, 18273
Tel *(03843) 85 00*
w kurhaus-guestrow.de
Peaceful accommodation by a lake with comfortable rooms with all the amenities.

NEUBRANDENBURG: Landhotel Broda
Gasthof   Road Map E2   €€€
Oelmühlenstrasse 29, 17033
Tel *(0395) 56 91 70*
w landhotel-broda.de
Located in a forest near a lake, this small hotel has quiet rooms and a wellness centre.

ROSTOCK: GreifenNest
Pensionen   Road Map D1   €
August-Bebel-Strasse 49b, 18055
Tel *(0381) 877 56 18*
w greifennest.de
Affordable, basic lodging in rooms with clean private facilities and a communal lounge.

Suite with sea views at Dorint Strandhotel Binz, Rügen

ROSTOCK: Neptun Hotel
Luxury   Road Map D1   €€€
Seestrasse 19, 18119
Tel *(0381) 777 7777*
w hotel-neptun.de
This luxury resort on the beach promises guests fantastic panoramic seaviews.

RÜGEN: Herrenhaus Bohlendorf
Pensionen   Road Map E1   €€
Bohlendorf bei Wiek, 18556
Tel *(038391) 770*
w bohlendorf.de
Pretty villa with bright rooms, a terrace café and a reading room.

DK Choice

RÜGEN: Dorint Strandhotel Binz
Luxury   Road Map E1   €€€
Strandpromenade 58, 18609
Tel *(038393) 430*
w hotel-ruegen.dorint.com
Dorint is a fabulous seaside resort where the rooms have a nautical theme, crisp linen and big windows that overlook the sea. Choose between two fantastic restaurants, one serving gourmet Mediterranean and the other regional seafood.

RÜGEN: Hotel Vier Jahreszeiten Binz
Luxury   Road Map E1   €€€
Zeppelinstrasse 8, 18609
Tel *(038393) 500*
w vier-jahreszeiten.de
A classy spa hotel near the town and beach. Modern, bright rooms.

SCHWERIN: Schloss Basthorst
Historic   Road Map D2   €€
Schlossstrasse 18, 19089
Tel *(03863) 52 50*
w schloss-basthorst.de
Stay in a beautiful 18th-century manor house with renovated rooms and a wellness centre.

STRALSUND: Radisson Blu Stralsund
Mid-Range Hotel   Road Map E1   €
Grünhufer Bogen 18–20, 18437
Tel *(03831) 377 30*
w radissonblu.com
Scandinavian-style hotel with an attached spa and water park.

WARNEMÜNDE: KurPark Hotel
Luxury   Road Map E1   €€€
Kurhausstrasse 4, 18119
Tel *(0381) 440 29 90*
w kurparkhotel-warnemuende.de
This lovely old resort has airy rooms, some with balconies, and an impressive restaurant.

WHERE TO EAT AND DRINK

While German cuisine may not enjoy the same reputation as that of, say, France, visitors can nevertheless eat very well here. A large number of establishments specialize in regional cuisine, which, although often heavy, is always very appetizing. It is also fairly easy to find good restaurants serving ethnic cuisine such as Italian, Greek, Indian, Chinese, Thai or Turkish. In past years, many fine eateries, owned and run by renowned master chefs, have opened in Germany. Not surprisingly, the cuisine served here is of the highest European standards.

From the many thousands of restaurants in Germany, we have listed the finest on pages 510–33. These have been chosen across a range of price categories for their variety, service and good value.

Types of Restaurants

The term restaurant in Germany includes both eateries offering exquisite cuisine and excellent service, at steep prices, as well as popular local establishments with affordable prices. A *Gasthaus* is a traditional inn specializing in straight-forward regional cuisine. Similar food is served in a *Ratskeller* located in the town hall cellar. These usually have atmospheric, stylized interiors that are well adapted to the vaulted, dark spaces of the historic cellars. A *Weinstube* is a wine bar on the lines of an old-fashioned tavern. Here, good, usually local, wine is served along with a limited menu of quality food. A *Bierstube* is similar, except that the beverage is beer.

While the term café has a variety of connotations in Germany, it is usually a good choice for breakfast and lunch. However, guests are welcome to stop in at any time of day for a cup of coffee, ice cream, a slice of cake, a beer or wine. There is often music in the evenings.

A *Kneipe*, which has a similar atmosphere to an English pub, is a great place to spend an evening. Patrons generally come here to drink, but there are usually a few hot dishes on offer too. Self-service venues offering snacks are known as *Imbiss*. These can have a very varied character, from a stall serving baked sausages and cans of drink to elegant kiosks offering a large choice of salads and fast food. These kiosks are often run by Germans with immigrant backgrounds, so Greek, Arabic, Turkish and Thai food tends to be well repre-sented. Many larger shops, particularly department stores, will also have a cafeteria for weary shoppers.

What and When to Eat

Breakfast is usually a hearty affair and involves several types of bread, cheeses, sausages and jam. On Sundays, brunch buffets are offered in many places until 2pm. Otherwise lunch is generally

Al fresco dining at Guglhof, a French restaurant in Berlin *(see p511)*

served between noon and 2pm, when most establishments offer an excellent salad or a bowl of filling soup. Many restaurants serve a special fixed-price menu for lunch that is significantly cheaper than in the evening. Restaurants start to fill up after 6pm, although dinner is most usually eaten after 8pm.

Opening Hours

Cafés generally open from 9am, while restaurants are open from noon, sometimes with a break from 3 to 6pm. The most expensive places only open for dinner and are frequently closed one day in the week.

Menu

In all restaurants and cafés, a menu with prices should be displayed at the door. Some of the better establish-ments will have a menu in English as well as in German, and where they do not, staff

The cheerful interior of Der Butt in Rostock *(see p533)*

Elegant dining room of the highly acclaimed Fährhaus in Sylt *(see p532)*

should be able to help with a translation. In several less expensive places, there is an additional daily menu with attractive seasonal dishes – often written on a blackboard.

Reservations

Making an advance reservation is essential in the best restaurants and advisable in many good and popular standard restaurants as well, particularly on weekend nights. Those who have not made any reservations can try one of the popular restaurant complexes for a table.

Prices and Tips

The cost of a restaurant -meal in Germany depends massively on the location. A three-course meal without alcohol might typically cost €20, but in the centre of larger cities a minimum of €30 would be more usual. In a luxury restaurant, the bill for a six-course meal, without drinks, can cost in excess of €80. The price of alcoholic drinks are varies, but beer is usually cheapest.

Prices include service and tax, but it is usual to leave a tip – around 10 per cent of the total bill. Credit cards are not as widely accepted in Germany, but restaurants and cafés that accept credit cards usually display the logos of acceptable cards near the entrance.

Visitors with Disabilities

If a table with wheelchair access is required, it is best to specify this when making the reservation. It is also a good idea to check if toilets are disabled-friendly at the time of making bookings.

Dress Code

Germans usually dress casually, comfortably and practically, preferring a sporty style to a more formal attire. When going out in the evenings, many women – regardless of their age – wear trousers and comfortable low-heeled shoes, though some prefer elegant dresses. Men generally wear jackets and ties only during office hours. Going to a restaurant does not require dressing up. However, guests will not look or feel out of place in formal clothes in the more expensive, gourmet restaurants.

Children

Restaurants usually provide high chairs for toddlers and, particularly during lunch, offer light dishes for children. In places that do not have such arrangements, it is always possible to order small portions for kids.

Vegetarians

Vegetarianism is increasingly popular in Germany, but the number of vegetarian restaurants is still very limited. Restaurants serving only German food will have the most limited selection, though there should be at least one or two vegetarian dishes. Italian restaurants – very common

Pasternak Russian restaurant, a long-time favourite in Berlin*(see p511)*

and usually very good – are a better choice for vegetarians, as are Indian or Thai establishments.

Recommended Restaurants

The restaurants recommended on the following pages have been chosen for their quality food, good value and decent service, and include a broad range of cuisines from Persian to Mediterranean, and North African to Chinese.

In a restaurant offering traditional German food expect to see a lot of hearty dishes, stews and breads on the menu. Regional German restaurants will specialize in dishes of the region, usually with locally sourced ingredients. Modern German food tends to take its influences from the traditional menu but add innovative twists and more delicate flavours.

Entries highlighted as DK Choice are those that offer something extra special. This may be their superb location, romantic atmosphere, particularly creative dishes, sensational cuisine or impeccable service. Book in advance and expect to enjoy a memorable meal.

Dine with splendid fjord views at Hotel Bellevue's seafood restaurant in Kiel *(see p531)*

The Flavours of Germany

Germany is famous for its hearty sausages, meats, breads, beer and wine. But German cuisine is much more regionally varied than many visitors might imagine. In addition to standard high-calorie plates, young chefs are coming up with creative new versions of German classics and old regional recipes. The key to this new trend is the fresh German produce found at colourful farmers' markets and old-world stores in quaint little towns around the country. Locally grown vegetables, pork, poultry and game, as well as freshwater and ocean fish, freshly made breads, cakes and dumplings are usually of a very high standard.

Harzer Roller and Emmentaler cheeses

Coffee and cakes at a typical city *Konditorei* (café)

Northern and Eastern Germany

The frugality and hardships of life in the northern and East German lowlands and coast are reflected in the hearty fish- and game-based dishes found in this region. Ocean fish like halibut, sea bass, cod, herring or plaice feature in local dishes like Hamburg's *Finkenwerder*

Scholle (plaice fried with North Sea shrimps and bacon), as do freshwater fish such as pike-perch (a Berlin-Brandenburg favourite) or trout, served as *Grüne Forelle* or *Forelle Müllerin Art*, two herb-oriented recipes for roasted trout. Warming winter soups and stews such as lentil or potato soup or *Pichelsteiner Eintopf* (a one-pot dish with meat, potatoes and

vegetables cooked in broth) are omnipresent – as is the famous potato salad, which is served in numerous ways. In East Germany, Thuringian and Saxonian cuisines have made a stunning comeback with *Thüringer Bratwurst* (spicy, roasted sausage served with hot mustard), *Sauerbraten* (roast beef marinated in vinegar) and some of

Mehrkornbrötchen (mixed grain roll)

Laugenbrötchen (salty sourdough rolls)

Berliner Landbrot (mild rye bread)

Grau-oder Mischbrot (wholewheat)

Semmel (milk-dough roll)

Selection of typical German loaves and bread rolls

Classic German Food

Many of the classic German dishes revolve around meat, particularly pork and poultry. Berliners and North Germans love *Kasseler Nacken*, a salted and dried slice of pork, served with mashed potatoes and *Sauerkraut*, while Bavarians prefer roast pork knuckle. There are delicious fish recipes, too, with Hamburg and Northern Germany leading the way. Ocean fish dishes like *Matjes* (salted herring with onions and cream served with baked potatoes) are now enjoyed throughout the country, as are freshwater fish and even sweet river crabs. German pasta and dumplings, along with soups, and a great selection of desserts and cakes round up any classic German menu.

Maultaschen, large pasta parcels, are stuffed with a meat or vegetable filling and served in soup or with butter.

Pork salamis

Display of traditional German sausages in a Berlin butcher's shop

Germany's best cakes, such as *Dresdner Christstollen* (Christmas cake with raisins, nuts and marzipan) or *Baumkuchen* (a very sweet, multi-layered pyramid cake covered in chocolate glaze).

Western and Southern Germany

This part of Germany, and in particular the German wine regions around the rivers Rhine, Mosel and Neckar, has always had a love of superb, often French-influenced, gourmet feasts. Alsace-Lorraine is a fascinating hotch potch of French and German cooking. Regions such as the Pfalz, Schwaben, Franken, the Black Forest and many others, have also developed their own, very distinctive, delicious and often

very hearty cuisines. The Pfalz, for example, is famous for its *Pfälzer Saumagen*, a sow's stomach filled with sausage, herbs and potatoes; the Schwaben are known for their *Maultaschen* and an endless varieties of *Spätzle*

A selection of fresh vegetables from the Brandenburg region

(curly pasta); and the Franken for their *Nürnberger Rostbrat-würstchen* (little spicy roast sausages), various fish dishes, using rare types such as sheatfish, and perhaps the best gingerbread found anywhere in the country. In the far southeast, Austrian and Eastern European influences are evident in great goulash and dumpling dishes. But pride of place possibly goes to the Bavarians, whose hearty, no-nonsense dishes are what the world considers to be German cuisine. Here, *Weißwürste* (white sausages with a beer pretzel) are enjoyed in the morning, often with a beer, while dinner might be soup with liver dumplings, roast pork, *Sauerkraut* and a pile of potato dumplings.

NEW GERMAN CUISINE

In the early 1970s, chefs like Eckart Witzigmann broke free of the high-carb diet of postwar times, and cooked light, delicate "nouvelle" German dishes with superb ingredients in innovative combinations. Witzigmann, still Germany's most popular chef, won the first three German Michelin stars in 1979. A new generation of chefs calling themselves "Junge Wilde" (young wild) are still enjoying the shock waves today: healthy, international cooking is the norm in restaurants and homes, and almost no traditional recipe is sacrosanct.

Zanderfilet, or Havel-Zander, is delicious pan-fried pike-perch served with a vegetable sauce, onions and potatoes.

Schweinshaxe is roast pork knuckle, best accompanied by Sauerkraut, potato dumplings and a good, strong beer.

Rote Grütze mixes summer berries with spices and red wine, which is set into a jelly and topped with cream.

What to Drink

Throughout Germany, beer is undoubtedly the most popular drink, and each region has its own beer-brewing traditions. However, the country is also renowned for excellent wines, which are produced in the south. The most well known are Mosel and Rhine wines, although these are not necessarily better than Franconian wines. Stronger spirits and liqueurs are also available, as are some very pleasant non-alcoholic cold drinks.

Shop in Eberbach stocked with wine from the adjoining monastery

Hot Drinks

In German establishments there is no difficulty in getting a cup of tea (*Tee*), but don't be surprised if the waiter asks whether you mean mint tea (*Pfefferminztee*) or camomile (*Kamillentee*), since herbal infusions are popular in Germany. To be sure of being served Indian tea, it is advisable to specify *Schwarztee* when placing the order. Coffee is another popular drink. In general, filter coffee, which is fairly mild, is served. For customers who prefer a stronger coffee, it is best to order an espresso.

Herbal infusions include mint and camomile tea

Non-Alcoholic Cold Drinks

Various types of carbonated drinks and fruit juices – ubiquitous throughout Europe and the US – are popular, and an extensive choice is available in every café and restaurant in Germany. A refreshing non-alcoholic drink is *Apfelschorle*, which is apple juice mixed with equal proportions of sparkling mineral water. (The alcoholic version is *Weinschorle*, which is wine mixed with mineral water.) Another popular non-alcoholic drink is *Spezi*, which is a mixture of cola and Fanta.

Although tap water is generally safe to drink, it is not usually served with restaurant meals. To order a bottle of mineral water, ask for *Mineralwasser*, adding the phrase "*stilles Wasser*" if still water is preferred.

Mineralwasser (Mineral water)

Limonade (Lemonade)

Apfelschorle

Spirits and Liqueurs

Strong spirits are often drunk after heavy meals, particularly pork dishes. It is best to order one of the popular drinks distilled from rye or wheat, such as *Doppelkorn*. Brandy (known as *Weinbrand*) is also produced in Germany. Liqueurs are also popular, as is a spirit flavoured with herbs and roots (known as bitters). Among the most popular are *Kümmerling* and *Jägermeister* while, in Berlin, *Kaulsdorfer Kräuterlikör* is served. In many restaurants various kinds of whisky can be ordered, including well-known Scottish and Irish brands and popular American bourbons, but connoisseurs may miss their personal favourites. Italian restaurants often serve grappa, a grape spirit, after a meal, while in Greek restaurants ouzo – an aniseed spirit – may be offered.

Bitter-sweet spirit, Jägermeister

Herbal/root-flavour spirit, Kümmerling

Weizen Doppelkorn (rye spirit)

Wines

Germany is renowned for its excellent white wines, particularly those made from the Riesling grape. Among the most highly prized wines are those from the Rheingau region. Lovers of red wine might like to try Assmannshausen Spätburgunder wine, which is produced from the Pinot Noir grape.

Germany has a system of classifying wines into three groups according to their quality: the lowest quality is *Tafelwein*, then *Qualitätswein* and the highest quality *Qualitätswein mit Prädikat*. The latter includes wines produced from appropriately selected grapes, which is always confirmed on the bottle label. The term *Trocken* indicates a dry style, *Halbtrocken*, semi-dry and *Süß* means sweet. Very good sparkling wines, known as *Sekt*, are also produced in Germany.

Riesling Schloss Vollrads

Mainstockheimer Hofstück Spätburgunder

Spätburgunder from the Rheingau region

Beers

Beermat with brewery logo

Each region of Germany has its own beer-brewing tradition: the most popular breweries in the north are Jever in Freesia and Beck's in Bremen, along with Bitburger, Warsteiner and Karlsberg. In the Rhine region, the biggest producers are DAB from Dortmund and König in Duisburg. In Berlin, Schultheiss, Berliner Kindl and Engelhardt compete for the primary position, while in Dresden the main beers are produced by a brewery in Radeberg. Bavaria is by far the major brewing centre – the names of the breweries Löwenbräu, Hofbräu and Paulaner are known to beer lovers around the world. The oldest brewery in the world, Weihenstephan, is also in Bavaria. The most commonly drunk beer is Pils, a bottom-fermented lager of the pilsner type. Brown ales are also popular, particularly in the south. Schwarzbier, a bottom-fermented brown ale of over 4 per cent alcohol, is increasingly popular. Weizenbier, a bitter top-fermented beer, also has many fans, as has Bock, which is strong, at around 6 per cent alcohol.

Löwenbräu beer

König Ludwig Dunkel beer

Schultheiss beer

Wheat beer mixed with fruit juice, Berliner Weiße mit Schuss – speciality of Berlin

Franziskaner Hefe Weissbier beer

A tankard of beer with the essential head of foam

Where to Eat and Drink

Berlin

Eastern Centre

12 Apostel   €
Italian   **Map** 4 C1
Georgenstrasse 2, 10117
Tel *(030) 201 02 22*
Located under the railway arches
near Friedrichstrasse station, this
eatery serves 12 types of pizza,
named after the apostles, cooked
to perfection in a stone oven.

Hasir Ocakbasi   €
Turkish   **Map** 5 F5
Adalbertstrasse 12, 10999
Tel *(030) 614 23 73*
Berlin's love affair with the *döner
kebab* began here in 1971. Large
selection of chargrilled meat and
fish dishes, delicious *mezes* and
home-made desserts.

Max und Moritz   €
Traditional German   **Map** 5 F5
Oranienstrasse 162, 10969
Tel *(030) 695 159 11*
A bustling over 100-year-old
eatery serving generous helpings
of traditional German fare, such
as *Schnitzel* and meatballs. Large
selection of beers, too.

Nante Eck   €
Traditional German   **Map** 4 C2
Unter den Linden 35, 10117
Tel *(030) 22 48 72 57*
Berlin-style cheap eats are on
offer at this casual pub. Fill up
on calf's liver with port sauce or
meatballs with mustard, washed
down with good local beer.

Zum Nussbaum   €
Traditional German   **Map** 5 E2
Am Nussbaum 3, 10178
Tel *(030) 242 30 95*
This reconstructed country inn
serves traditional Berlin cuisine –
rollmops, vegetable and fish
pancakes, *Bouletten* (spicy meatballs) – along with local beers.

**Augustiner am
Gendarmenmarkt**   €€
Regional German   **Map** 4 C2
Charlottenstrasse 55, 10117
Tel *(030) 204 540 20*
Decorated with oak barrels and
wooden panelling, this Bavarian
pub serves hearty German fare,
including baked *Eisbein* (knuckle
of pork) with *Sauerkraut* and beef
goulash in a beer sauce.

Facil   €€
Modern Fusion   **Map** 4 A3
Potsdamer Strasse 3, 10785
Tel *(030) 590 051 234*
A glass-roofed pavilion is the
backdrop for Berlin master chef
Michael Kempf's inspired cuisine,
which uses the freshest market
produce and subtly exotic spices.

Gambrinus   €€
Traditional German   **Map** 4 C1
Krausnickstrasse 1, 10115
Tel *(030) 282 60 43*
A traditional *Kneipe* (pub) with
dark-wood furnishings, old-
fashioned tiles and framed posters
of Old Berlin. Massive portions of
dishes such as *Eisbein* (knuckle of
pork) and homemade stews.

Zur Letzten Instanz   €€
Traditional German   **Map** 5 F2
Waisenstrasse 14–16, 10179
Tel *(030) 242 55 28*   **Closed** *Sun*
Berlin's oldest pub, dating from
1621, serves classic German fare,
including *Eisbein* (pork knuckle)
and *Rinderroulade* (beef olive),
in a wood-panelled room with
a majolica-tiled stove.

Käfers Dachgarten   €€
Modern German   **Map** 1 E4
Platz der Republik, 11011
Tel *(030) 226 29 90*
A roof-garden restaurant with
spectacular views. Sample sophisticated German dishes, made with
fresh regional produce, and
choice wines. Book in advance.

Vau   €€
French   **Map** 4 C2
Jägerstrasse 54–55, 10117
Tel *(030) 202 97 30*   **Closed** *Sun*
Celebrity TV chef Kolja Kleeberg
won this classy restaurant a
Michelin star with his inspired
take on French cooking. The
striking interior is best described
as modern meets Art Nouveau.

Borchardt   €€€
French/German   **Map** 4 C2
Französische Strasse 47,10117
Tel *(030) 81 88 62 62*
Politicians and celebrities flock to
this restaurant with retro decor
from early 1900s. *Schnitzel* is the
mainstay of an ever-changing
menu. Reserve ahead.

DK Choice

Fischers Fritz   €€€
French   **Map** 4 C3
Charlottenstrasse 49, 10117
Tel *(030) 203 363 63*
The creative flair of the chef has
turned Fischers Fritz into an
award-winning restaurant. The
meat dishes are tempting, but it
is the seafood dishes that get
most accolades. Try the Breton
lobster roasted with salt, chilli
and coriander, or the fillet of
Mediterranean red mullet with
mashed potatoes, Nyons olives
and tomatoes. The two-course
lunch menu is good value.

Western Centre

Café am Neuen See   €
German/Italian   **Map** 2 C3
Lichtensteinallee 2, 10787
Tel *(030) 254 49 30*   **Closed** *Sun*
This café, with its charming
lakeside terrace, offers Bavarian
snacks and draught beers, as
well as Italian mains such as
pizzas. There are boats to rent
and a sandpit for kids. Warm
seating in winter.

**Café-Restaurant Wintergarten
im Literaturhaus**   €
German/International   **Map** 2 A5
Fasanenstrasse 23, 10719
Tel *(030) 882 54 14*
Take a break from shopping
on Ku'damm and visit this

Al fresco dining at Zum Nussbaum, a traditional inn

café-restaurant favoured by artists and intellectuals. Breakfast and international dishes are served in Art Nouveau interiors.

Dicke Wirtin €
Traditional German Map 2 A4
Carmerstrasse 9, 10623
Tel *(030) 312 49 52*
This authentic Berlin *Kneipe* (pub) serves a menu of hearty food. Select the *Eintopf* (a steaming hot pot), and the Berliner Kindl, one of the nine draught beers available.

Florian €
Traditional German Map 2 A4
Grolmanstrasse 52, 10623
Tel *(030) 313 91 84*
A small restaurant with an understated charm that attracts celebrities. Excellent south-western German cuisine with a modern twist is prepared with organic produce.

Gaststätte Ambrosius €
Traditional German Map 3 D4
Einemstrasse 14, 10785
Tel *(030) 264 05 26*
Nourishing home cooking, with specialities such as tasty potato soup and Berlin-style liver served with onions and apple sauce.

Belmondo €€
French Map 2 A3
Knesebeckstrasse 93, 10623
Tel *(030) 362 872 61*
Red leather banquettes and photos of the actor Jean-Paul Belmondo lend a touch of French elegance to this bistro. Excellent fish and seafood dishes, including a sensational *bouillabaisse*.

Grüne Lampe €€
Russian Map 2 A5
Uhlandstrasse 51, 10719
Tel *(030) 887 193 93*
Popular with Russian expats, who love the authentic food on offer. Large selection of

The homely dining room at Pasternak

zakuski (starters) and *blini* (buckwheat pancakes). Vegetarian options available, too.

La Mano Verde €€
Vegan Map 2 A4
Kempinski Plaza, Uhlandstrasse 181–183, 10623
Tel *(030) 827 031 20*
A treat for non meat-eaters: this strictly vegan restaurant uses only plant-based ingredients and has several gluten-free dishes on its menu. Choose one of the inspired daily specials.

Die Quadriga €€€
European Map 2 B5
Eislebener Strasse 14, 10789
Tel *(030) 214 050*
French and other European creations are served at this restaurant located inside the Hotel Brandenburger Hof.

Further Afield

Baraka €
North African Road Map E3
Lausitzer Platz 6, 10997
Tel *(030) 612 63 30*
Baraka serves an appetizing range of Moroccan and Egyptian specialities, including tagines, couscous and vegetarian dishes.

Horváth €
Modern German Road Map E3
Paul Lincke Ufer 44, 10999
Tel *(030) 612 899 92* **Closed** Mon
This award-winning restaurant offers creatively constructed, sophisticated cuisine. The desserts are also a highlight.

Ming Dynastie €
Chinese Map 5 F2
Brückenstrasse 6, 10179
Tel *(030) 308 756 80*
This excellent Chinese restaurant serves an extensive menu that includes regional dishes, dim sum and Peking duck.

Gugelhof €€
French Road Map E3
Knaackstrasse 37, 10435
Tel *(030) 442 92 29*
Lively restaurant offering Alsatian specialities such as *tarte flambé* and lamb cassoulet.

E.T.A. Hoffmann €€
Modern Austrian/German
Road Map E3
Yorckstrasse 83, 10965
Tel *(030) 780 988 09*
A creative spin on traditional Austrian and German recipes. The cushion of Brandenburg venison with Gatow radish and potato noodles is a definite highlight.

For more information on types of restaurants *see page 504*

Brandenburg

BRANDENBURG:
Bismarck Terrassen €
Regional German   Road Map E3
Bergstrasse 20, 14770
Tel *(03381) 30 09 39*
Huge helpings of dishes such
as duck with red cabbage and
dumplings can be enjoyed at this
earthy local pub cluttered with
kitsch 19th-century memorabilia.

BUCKOW: Fischerkehle €€
Modern German   Road Map E4
Fischerberg 7, 15377
Tel *(033433) 374*
Enjoy lovely lakeside dining at
this fish and game specialist.
Delicacies include rosefish with
boiled potatoes, and game
ragout with *Spätzle* (regional
noodles) and cranberries.

CHORIN: Alte Klosterschänke €
Regional German   Road Map E2
Am Amt 9, 16230
Tel *(033366) 53 01 00*
Traditional restaurant located
in an exquisite 18th century
half-timbered building. Fresh,
seasonal, organic food.

CHORIN: Immenstube
at Hotel Haus Chorin
Regional German   Road Map E2
Neue Klosterallee 10, 16230
Tel *(033366) 500*   **Closed** *Wed*
Honey makes an appearance in
every dish at this largely organic
restaurant that relies on local
produce. The delicious honey-
marinated pork roast is a must.

COTTBUS: Mosquito €
South American   Road Map F3
Altmarkt 22, 3046
Tel *(0355) 288 904 44*
This cocktail bar pulls in droves
of locals for both its great Cajun
jerk chicken and the delightful
Sunday brunch buffet.

Tastefully decorated restaurant at
Hotel Schloss Lübbenau, Lübbenau

Key to Price Guide *see page 510*

FRANKFURT AN DER
ODER: Nirwana €
Indian   Road Map F3
Marktplatz 3, 15230
Tel *(0335) 53 45 21*
Delicious North Indian food
comes with quick and friendly
service here. Well-priced lunch-
time specials are on offer as well.

LEHNIN: Markgraf €€
Austrian/German   Road Map E3
Friedenstrasse 13, 14797
Tel *(03382) 76 50*
A small menu of tasty Austrian
and German dishes is available
at this smart hotel restaurant.

LEHNIN: Rittergut Krahne €€
Traditional German   Road Map E3
Krahner Hauptstrasse 6A, 14797
Tel *(033835) 60 88 91* **Closed** *Tue–Thu*
This eatery in a converted barn
serves traditional food based on
seasonal ingredients – expect
asparagus in spring, mushrooms
in summer and goose in winter.

LÜBBEN: Schlossrestaurant
Lübben €
Modern German   Road Map E3
Ernst-von-Houwald-Damm 14, 15907
Tel *(03546) 40 78*
Contemporary versions of
regional dishes are on offer at this
elegant local palace. The business
lunch is a genuine bargain.

LÜBBENAU: Hotel Schloss
Lübbenau €€
International   Road Map E3
Schlossbezirk 6, 3222
Tel *(03542) 87 30*
This high-end hotel restaurant
relies on fresh local ingredients to
create a variety of contemporary
fish and meat dishes.

LÜBBENAU: Steakhaus
Santa Fe €€
Steakhouse   Road Map E3
Robert Koch Strasse 45, 03222
Tel *(03542) 88 87 70*
Steaks, burgers and Tex-Mex fare
are served in mock-Western
surroundings here. There is even
a table in a covered wagon.

ORANIENBURG:
Schlossrestaurant
Oranienburg €€€
Regional German   Road Map E3
Am Schlossplatz, 16515
Tel *(03301) 702547*
Housed inside the city castle, the
menu of fine cuisine in a Baroque
setting includes wild game.

POTSDAM: Drachenhaus €
Regional German   Road Map E3
Maulbeerallee 4a, 14469
Tel *(0331) 505 38 08*   **Closed** *Nov–
Feb: Mon*

Inviting café atmosphere at
Drachenhaus, Potsdam

This elegant little café in a
pagoda-style building serves
hearty Brandenburg specialities.

POTSDAM: Froschkasten €
Regional German   Map E3
Kiezstrasse 3–4, 14467
Tel *(0331) 291315*
An old Prussian eatery in a
traditional inn serving basic
regional cuisine, including
several scrumptious fish dishes.

POTSDAM: Hafthorn €
Modern German   Road Map E3
Friedrich Ebert Strasse 90, 14467
Tel *(0331) 280 08 20*
This hip pub is often packed with
a fashionable crowd. Simple but
good snacks – superb burgers
and *Rösti* (potato pancakes).

POTSDAM: Indian Garden €
Indian   Road Map E3
Kurfürstenstrasse 35, 14467
Tel *(0331) 585 71 85*
Enjoy excellent home-made
Indian food in smart
surroundings at this fantastic
restaurant. Attentive service.

POTSDAM: La Madeleine €
Crêperie   Road Map E3
Lindenstrasse 9, 14467
Tel *(0331) 270 54 00*
Small crêperie serving more than
30 variations of crêpes, ranging
from delicious buckwheat with
goat's cheese salad to the more
unusual chicken curry.

POTSDAM: Arlecchin €€
Mediterranean   Road Map E3
Hebbelstrasse 54, 14467
Tel *(0331) 243 77 20*
From pasta filled with duck to
fish fillet with bell peppers and
walnut sauce, this restaurant
serves delicious Mediterranean
fusion dishes with an emphasis
on Italy in a very friendly setting.

POTSDAM: Café Heider €€
Classic German **Road Map** E3
Friedrich-Ebert-Strasse 29, 14467
Tel *(0331) 270 55 96*
Open from morning to late
evening, Café Haider has been
serving great German food since
1878. Pay a visit in the afternoon
for a sumptuous slice of cake.

**POTSDAM: Friedrich Wilhelm
at Hotel Bayrisches Haus** €€
Modern German **Road Map** E3
Elisenweg 2, 14471
Tel *(0331) 550 50* **Closed** *Sun & Mon*
The premier address for German
nouvelle cuisine, this charming
hotel restaurant features
inventive gourmet delights.

DK Choice

POTSDAM: Juliette €€
French **Road Map** E3
Jägerstrasse 39, 14467
Tel *(0331) 270 17 91* **Closed** *Tue*
A classy, romantic place with
candles, white tablecloths and
a crackling fire. The changing
menu oozes French flair and
may include dishes such as
loach with couscous and
avocado, or steak with truffles
and *foie gras*. Come here for the
superb *crème brûlée* and the
exemplary wine list. Vegetarians
are well catered for, too.

**POTSDAM: Speckers
Landhaus** €€
French **Road Map** E3
Jägerallee 13, 14469
Tel *(0331) 280 43 11* **Closed** *Sun
& Mon*
This modern, family-run
restaurant is as unpretentious
as it is high-class. Fresh local
produce dominates the creative
menu. Good-value set lunch.

**RHEINSBERG: Steakhaus at
Schloss Hotel Rheinsberg** €
Traditional German **Road Map** C2
Seestrasse 13, 16831
Tel *(033931) 390 59* **Closed** *Nov–Feb*
Diners build their own dishes
using South American cuts of
meat and a selection of sides
at this great steakhouse.

Saxony-Anhalt

DESSAU: Goa €
Indian **Road Map** E3
Albrechtstrasse 26, 06844
Tel *(0340) 870 56 26*
Relish authentic Indian food at
this restaurant as well as the
comprehensive cocktail menu.

DESSAU: Kornhaus €
International **Road Map** E3
Kornhausstrasse 146, 06846
Tel *(0340) 650 199 63*
A genuine Bauhaus restaurant,
with a graceful riverside balcony
and contemporary cuisine. The
fish dishes are a cornerstone of
the well-priced daily menu.

DESSAU: Mensa €
German **Road Map** E3
Kleiststrasse 2/Seminarplatz, 06846
Tel *(03496) 67 64 02* **Closed** *Sat
& Sun*
Mensa offers a basic cafeteria
experience, with fresh daily
dishes served in a stylishly
minimalist Bauhaus interior.

EISLEBEN: Lutherschenke €
Traditional German **Road Map** D4
Lutherstrasse 19, 06295
Tel *(03475) 61 47 75*
This traditional-style inn cooks
hearty dishes dating back to
medieval times. Expect lots of
deer, pork liver and turkey.

The modern-styled exterior of
Kornhaus, Dessau

HALLE: Hallesches Brauhaus €
Traditional German **Road Map** D4
Grosse Nikolaistrasse 2, 06108
Tel *(0345) 212 570*
An Old Town microbrewery with
good beers and hearty regional
favourites, such as goulash with
dumplings and dark beer sauce.

HALLE: La Fontana €
Italian **Road Map** D4
Augustwiebel Platz 8, 06108
Tel *(0345) 682 53 50*
This Italian joint with a cheerful
atmosphere and an open kitchen
serves generous portions and
delicious pizza. Reserve ahead.

HALLE: Ökoase €
Vegetarian **Road Map** D4
Kleine Ulrichstrasse 2, 06108
Tel *(0345) 290 16 04* **Closed** *Sun*
Vegetarian cuisine with bargain
canteen lunches and table
service in the evenings, when
dishes such as *Rosti* with pears
and Roquefort are served.

**LUTHERSTADT WITTENBERG:
Brauhaus Wittenberg** €
Regional German **Road Map** E3
Markt 6, 06886
Tel *(03491) 43 31 30*
A lively pub with an attractive
courtyard serving portions of
hearty staples, including ribs and
Bratwurst, plus a variety of beers.

**LUTHERSTADT WITTENBERG:
Zum Schwarzen Baer** €
Traditional German **Road Map** E3
Schlossstrasse 2, 06886
Tel *(03491) 41 12 00*
The menu at this old-fashioned
dark-wood pub is a homage to
the humble potato, which even
features in the desserts.

The beautifully-styled dining room of Friedrich Wilhelm at Hotel Bayrisches Haus, Potsdam

For more information on types of restaurants *see page 504*

LUTHERSTADT WITTENBERG:
Alte Canzley   €€
International   Road Map E3
Schlossplatz 3, 06886
Tel *(03491) 42*
An excellent organic restaurant in
a 14th-century building. The
experimental menu features inno-
vative choices, like beef in black
beer and asparagus ice cream.

LUTHERSTADT WITTENBERG:
Tante Emmas   €€
Traditional German   Road Map E3
Markt 9, 06886
Tel *(03491) 41 97 57*   **Closed** *Mon*
This quirky, traditional
establishment furnished with
curios, whips up refined German
standards such as *Schnitzel.*

MAGDEBURG: Le Frog   €
International   Road Map D3
Heinrich Heine Platz 1, 39114
Tel *(0391) 531 35 56*
Highlights of Le Frog's extensive
menu include local game and
wild mushrooms. There is also a
great weekend brunch. Regular
live music in the beer garden.

MAGDEBURG: Wenzel
Prager Bierstuben   €
Czech   Road Map D3
Leiterstrasse 3C, 39104
Tel *(0391) 544 66 16*
This relaxed, informal restaurant
is part of a chain of rustic Czech
pubs that specializes in good
beers and hearty meat dishes.

MAGDEBURG: Liebig   €€
International   Road Map D3
Liebigstrasse 3, 39104
Tel *(0391) 555 67 54*
Trendy bar, café and restaurant
with appetizing international
food, ranging from curries to
steaks and Mediterranean dishes.

MAGDEBURG: Petriförder   €€
International   Road Map D3
Petriförder 1, 39104
Tel *(0391) 597 96 00*
The eclectic menu at this large
riverside restaurant features
many Italian dishes, as well as
Schnitzel and Argentinian steaks.

NAUMBURG: Mohrencafé
am Dom   €
German   Road Map D4
Steinweg 16, 06618
Tel *(03445) 20 45 65*
A little café with a small but
delicious lunch menu. The rabbit
or duck served with red cabbage
and dumplings is a must-trys.

NAUMBURG: Toscana   €
Regional German   Road Map D4
Topfmarkt 16, 06618
Tel *(03445) 28 92 14*

The picturesque setting of Schloss Tangermünde, Tangermünde

Look out for scrumptious
traditional local dishes here, such
as *Naumburger Rahmtöpfchen* (a
pork chop smothered in a
creamy onion sauce).

QUEDLINBURG: Brauerei Lüdde €
Traditional German   Road Map D4
Blasiistrasse 14, 06484
Tel *(03946) 70 52 06*
A barn-sized microbrewery with
a beautiful, bustling beer garden.
On offer are solid, traditional
meals and a wide range of beers.

QUEDLINBURG: Theopano   €€
Modern German   Road Map D4
Markt 13, 06484
Tel *(03946) 96 300*
Contemporary regional cuisine
in an old half-timbered house.
Highlights on the menu include
cod and veal, and the handmade
truffles make for a great finale.

TANGERMÜNDE: Exempel   €
Regional German   Road Map D3
Kirchstrasse 40, 39590
Tel *(039322) 44899*
Situated in a former schoolhouse
and featuring original furnishings,
Exempel serves old-fashioned
dishes along with the local beer.

DK Choice

TANGERMÜNDE: Schloss
Tangermünde   €€
Traditional German
                      Road Map D3
Amt 1, 39590
Tel *(039322) 73 73*
This elegant restaurant, set in an
atmospheric 17th-century castle,
offers wonderful river views. The
menu lists high-end versions of
rustic dishes, such as wild boar,
Eisbein (pickled ham) and
zander plus gourmet set meals.

WÖRLITZ: Gastwirtschaft
im Küchengebäude   €€€
Regional German   Road Map E3
Schlossstrasse, 06786
Tel *(034905) 223 38*
A beer garden and restaurant
in the old palace kitchens.
Sample such fare ranging
from goose, deer, gnocchi to
steaks. There's also a buffet of
various salads.

Saxony

AUGUSTUSBURG: Café
Friedrich   €
Bistro   Road Map E4
Hans-Planer-Strasse 1, 09573
Tel *(037291) 66 66*
This lovely bistro is located in a
picturesque part of the town
relies on more than 100 years of
family tradition and is good for
light meals as well as dinners.
The cakes are a must-try.
Amazing castle views.

BAD MUSKAU:
Am Schlossbrunnen   €€
Regional German   Road Map F4
Köbelner Strasse 68, 02953
Tel *(035771) 52 30*
A delightful family-run restaurant
offering typical dishes based on
local produce, including fish from
the nearby lakes. Do not miss the
home-made ice creams.

BAUTZEN: Bautzener
Brauhaus   €
Traditional German   Road Map F4
Thomas-Mann-Strasse 7, 02625
Tel *(03591) 49 14 56*
Choose from several beers,
including Schwarzbier and the
original Pilsner, at this brewery.
The menu offers scrumptious
German fare at affordable prices.

**CHEMNITZ: Gasthaus an
der Schlossmuhle** €
Traditional German   **Road Map** E4
Schlossberg 3, 09113
Tel *(0371) 335 25 33*
Historic hotel restaurant in a
splendid location above the lake,
with superb views. The simple
yet delicious food has made it a
popular neighbourhood haunt.

CHEMNITZ: Korfu €
Greek   **Road Map** E4
Zschopauer Strasse 169A, 09126
Tel *(0371) 401 10 92*   **Closed** *lunch
Mon & Tue*
With a beer garden and a large
interior inspired by the Greek
islands, this popular venue
can get quite lively at peak times.
The menu features Greek classics
and tasty desserts.

CHEMNITZ: Villa Esche €€
European   **Road Map** E4
Parkstrasse 58, 09120
Tel *(0371) 236 13 63*   **Closed** *Mon*
Set in gorgeous surroundings,
this wonderful restaurant serves
modern European dishes – with
a focus on German fare. Good-
value set lunches and cookery
courses on offer. Lovely garden.

DK Choice

DRESDEN: Schillergarten €
Regional German
Road Map E4
Schillerplatz 9, 01309
Tel *(0351) 81 19 90*
Located in a historic building
next to the Blaus Wunder bridge,
this fine restaurant and pub is
the perfect place to eat well and
at a reasonable price in the city
centre. Sample great local food,
including first-class *Bratwurst*,
as well as an extensive range of
beers. There is also a wonderful,
lovely summer terrace on the
embankment of the Elbe River.
Reserve ahead.

DRESDEN: Cuchi €€
Asian   **Road Map** E4
Wallgässchen 5, 01097
Tel *(0351) 862 75 80*
Chinese, Japanese and
Vietnamese cuisines are fused
together to create outstanding,
inventive dishes here. For the
purists, there is sushi.

DRESDEN: Ogura €€€
Japanese   **Road Map** E4
An der Frauenkirche 5, 01067
Tel *(0351) 864 29 75*
One of Germany's best sushi
restaurants, Ogura also serves
soups, *tempura* and Kirin beer.
Good-value set menus.

Bright and modern dining area of Café
Restaurant, Meissen

**DRESDEN: Sternerestaurant
Caroussel** €€€
Fine dining   **Road Map** E4
Königstrasse 14, 01097
Tel *(0351) 800 30*
Expect only the finest food in the
luxurious surroundings of this
proud award-winning restaurant.

KAMENZ: Goldner Hirsch €
Italian/German   **Road Map** F4
Markt 10, 01917
Tel *(035787) 8350*
This stylish restaurant offers
mainly Italian food, while the
rustic Ratskeller downstairs
serves classic German fare.

LEIPZIG: Diego €
South American   **Road Map** E4
Waldstrasse 64, 04105
Tel *(0341) 308 64 77*
Specializing in Mexican, Colum-
bian and Brazilian food, this
popular restaurant has a varied
menu and hosts a lively clientele.

LEIPZIG: Pho Viet €
Vietnamese   **Road Map** E4
Katharinastrasse 15, 04109
Tel *(0341) 99391747*
A minimalist interior makes the
perfect ambiance for a fresh
Vietnamese meal. Try the *Banh
Mi*, a baguette filled with meat,
vegetables and a tasty sauce.

LEIPZIG: Zest €
Fusion   **Road Map** E4
Bornaische Strasse 54, 04277
Tel *(0341) 231 91 26*
A fresh and creative take on
modern European cuisine, with
plenty of vegetarian dishes on the
menu. The great-value fare and an
extensive wine list make Zest
worth the trip from the city centre.

LEIPZIG: Auerbachs Keller €€
Regional German   **Road Map** E4
Grimmaische Strasse 2–4, 04109
Tel *(0341) 21 61 00*
One of the town's oldest eateries,
Auerbachs Keller serves first-class
German cuisine, including a variety
of game dishes. There is also a great
selection of beer to help wash it all
down. Reserve in advance.

LEIPZIG: Michaelis €€
International   **Road Map** E4
Paul-Gruner-Strasse 44, 04107
Tel *(0341) 267 80*   **Closed** *Sun*
Set in a building that dates back
more than 100 years, Michaelis
offers imaginative food in an
intimate atmosphere. There is a
nice terrace, too.

MEISSEN: Domkeller €€
Traditional German   **Road Map** E4
Domplatz 9, 01662
Tel *(03521) 45 76 76*
Founded in 1470, Domkeller is
the oldest restaurant in town.
Savour generous portions of
German food and great beer
in a warm, friendly atmosphere.

One of Leipzig's oldest restaurants, the Auerbachs Keller is dramatically decorated

For more information on types of restaurants *see page 504*

**MORITZBURG: Churfürstliche
Waldschaenke** €
Regional German   **Road Map** E4
Grosse Fasanenstrasse, 01468
Tel *(035207) 86 00*
Serving mainly food from the
Saxony region, this place boasts
an enviable location, surrounded
as it is by woods on all sides. It
also has one of the best wine
cellars in the region.

PIRNA: Deutsches Haus €
Modern German   **Road Map** F4
Niedere Burgstrasse 1, 01796
Tel *(03501) 468 80*   **Closed** *Mon*
Popular with locals, this place
specializes in modern cuisine
from around the region. Superb
selection of beers and wine.

PIRNA: Escobar €
South American   **Road Map** F4
Obere Burgstrasse 1, 01796
Tel *(03501) 58 27 73*
A treat for those looking for a
break from German cuisine,
this café, bar and restaurant
has decor reminiscent of 1950s
Latin America. Friendly staff.

TORGAU: Central Hotel €
Regional German   **Road Map** E4
Friedrichplatz 8, 04860
Tel *(03421) 73 28*
A simple yet elegant restaurant
inside a gorgeous 1908 building.
The food is great value and just
about the best in town.

ZWICKAU: Brauhaus Zwickau €
Regional German   **Road Map** E4
Peter-Breuer-Strasse 12–20, 08056
Tel *(0375) 303 20 32*
Housed in a historic building, the
Brauhaus serves its own beer and
delicious local dishes, from
Currywurst to *Schnitzel*, hearty
soups and a selection of
vegetarian options.

Thuringia

ALTENBURG: Altenburger Hof €
International   **Road Map** E4
Schmöllnsche Landstrasse 8, 04600
Tel *(03447) 584*
Altenburger Hof's restaurant
offers good food at decent prices.
There are both a casual café and
a smart restaurant on site.

EISENACH: Trattoria La Grappa €
Italian   **Road Map** C4
Frauenberg 8–10, 99817
Tel *(03691) 73 38 60*
The Neapolitan owners have
turned this locale into an authentic
slice of southern Italy, where the
menu features all the staples of
Italian cuisine.

EISENACH: Lutherstuben €€
Traditional German   **Road Map** C4
Katharinenstrasse 13, 99817
Tel *(03691) 293 90*
This historic restaurant in the
Eisenacher Hof Hotel specializes
in the favourite dishes of Martin
Luther. The bar has an excellent
selection of beers and wine.

ERFURT: Feuerkugel €
Regional German   **Road Map** D4
Michaelisstrasse 3–4, 99084
Tel *(0361) 789 12 56*
In the heart of Erfurt, this
restaurant offers an authentic
Thuringian experience. Divine
food is served in huge portions
and there is plenty of top-quality
beer, both best enjoyed in the
pretty courtyard.

**ERFURT: Haus zum
Naumburgischen Keller** €
Regional German   **Road Map** D4
Michaelisstrasse 49, 99084
Tel *(0361) 540 24 50*
Located in a 19th-century half-
timbered building, this restaurant
serves excellent food and beer.
Try the *Rostbratel* (roasted meat
with braised onions).

ERFURT: Zum alten Schwan €
Bistro   **Road Map** D4
Gotthardtstrasse 27, 99084
Tel *(0361) 67 400*
A simple and good-value bistro
with a wide range of light salads
and soups, as well as more filling
main courses.

**ERFURT: Clara Alboth's
Restaurant im Kaisersaal** €€
International   **Road Map** D4
Futterstrasse 15/16, 99084
Tel *(0361) 568 82 07*   **Closed** *Mon*
One of the best restaurants in
the city, Clara Alboth offers

inventive, contemporary cusine
and celebrates high-quality, fresh,
local ingredients.

**ERFURT: Köstritzer Zum
güldenen Rade** €€
International   **Road Map** D4
Marktstrasse 50, 99084
Tel *(0361) 561 35 06*
There is something here for
everyone: from typical and
reliable local staples to more
innovative modern Italian
and French creations, not
excluding a wide range of
vegetarian dishes.

GERA: Goldener Drachen €
Chinese   **Road Map** D4
Altenburger Strasse 4, 07546
Tel *(0365) 269 51*
In a part of Germany not greatly
known for exotic cuisine, this
excellent Chinese restaurant is
well worth a visit. Includes a
pleasant covered courtyard.

**GOTHA: Hotel am
Schlosspark** €€
Regional German   **Road Map** D4
Lindenauallee 20, 99867
Tel *(03621) 442*
The indoor plants and sunny
outdoor surroundings add to
the casual and comfortable
atmosphere at this hotel
restaurant, with a fantastic menu
and selection of beers.

JENA: Schwarzer Bär €
Regional German   **Road Map** D4
Lutherplatz 2, 07743
Tel *(03641) 4060*
Schwarzer Bär is housed in a
historic building, close to the
university. Sample culinary
delights such as the Goethe
set menu (potato soup, lamb
and sausages).

The colourful Clara Alboth's Restaurant im Kaisersaal, Erfurt

The elegantly decorated Ratskeller set in Munich's old town hall

JENA: Scala €€€
International   Road Map D4
Leutragraben 1, 07743
Tel *(03641) 35 66 66*
Scala is a wonderful restaurant on the 27th floor of the former Carl Zeiss Jena tower. Delight in fantastic food while enjoying panoramic city views.

MÜHLHAUSEN: Brauhaus zum Löwen €
Traditional German   Road Map D4
Felchtaer Strasse 3, 99974
Tel *(036014) 710*
This local brewery serves its own beer in the pub and restaurant. Most of the food is traditional German staples, but the sausages, in particular, are worth a try.

SCHMÖLLN: Bellevue €
Fine Dining   Road Map E4
Am Pfefferberg 7, 04626
Tel *(034491) 70 00*
Inventive food is complemented by a terrific wine list at this refined hotel restaurant. There is also a beautiful garden terrace.

WEIMAR: Café und Restaurant Frauentor €
Bistro   Road Map D4
Schillerstrasse 2, 99423
Tel *(03643) 511322*
A charming bistro with an adjoining bakery that makes some of the best cakes in town. Excellent-value food and a fine *simple coffee* too.

WEIMAR: Zum Schwarzen Bären €
Regional German   Road Map D4
Markt 20, 99423
Tel *(03643) 85 38 47*
One of Weimar's oldest restaurants, Zum Schwarzen Bären offers a Thuringian gastropub experience right in the centre of town. Simple, tasty food includes delicious *Bratwurst*, and zander with *Sauerkraut*.

DK Choice

WEIMAR: Anna Amalia €€
Fine dining   Road Map D4
Markt 19, 99423
Tel *(03643) 8020*
Located in Hotel Elephant, this award-winning, Michelin-starred gourmet restaurant offers contemporary dining in a historic 17th-century building. The tasting menu is an eight-course extravaganza featuring outstanding Mediterranean food as well as a range of fine wines.

WEIMAR: Scharfe Ecke Weimar €€
Traditional German   Road Map D4
Eisfeld 2, 99423
Tel *(03643) 20 24 30*
Great-value local food – large portions of Thuringian sausages and potato dumplings with a choice of sauces – is served inside an old guesthouse. There is delicious beer, too.

Munich

Augustiner Bräustuben €
Regional German   Road Map D7
Landsberger Strasse 19, 80339
Tel *(089) 50 70 47*
Jolly *Bierstube* (beer hall) with long benches to sit on. Dumplings are served with duck, pork knuckle or simply smothered in mushroom sauce. Food from 10am to 11pm.

Augustinerbräu €
Regional German   Map 2 A4
Neuhauser Strasse 27, 80331
Tel *(089) 231 83 257*
The walls of this historic beer hall are adorned with frescoes. Solid traditional food is served with excellent beer from one of Bavaria's best-known breweries. Fast and friendly service.

Café Glockenspiel €
International   Map 2 B4
Marienplatz 28, 80331
Tel *(089) 26 42 56*
Café-restaurant with magnificent rooftop views from its terrace. Highlights on the menu include seafood with glass noodles and saffron seafood risotto.

Fisch Poseidon €
Seafood   Map 2 C5
Westenriederstrasse 13, 80331
Tel *(089) 29 92 96*   **Closed** *Sun*
Diners come to this basic, no-frills restaurant specializing in fresh fish dishes for the brilliant *bouillabaisse* and the superb seafood spaghetti. Self-service.

Fraunhofer €
Regional German   Road Map D7
Fraunhoferstrasse 9, 80469
Tel *(089) 26 64 60*
This traditional inn serving Bavarian food began as a bakery in the 18th century and it still exudes historical charm.

Hofer – Der Stadtwirt €
Regional German   Map 2 C4
Burgstrasse 5, 80331
Tel *(089) 242 10 444*   **Closed** *Sun*
Bavarian and Austrian dishes are served in a wonderful historical setting in one of Munich's oldest bourgeois houses.

Goa €
Indian   Map 3 D5
Thierschstrasse 8, 80538
Tel *(089) 211 117 89*
A small and friendly restaurant with a wide variety of Indian food – from chicken and lamb curries to *biryani* and *tandoori*.

Refettorio €
Italian   Road Map 2 C3
Marstallplatz 3, 80539
Tel *(089) 228 01 680*
Stylish, modern restaurant serving innovative variations on classical Italian dishes.

For more information on types of restaurants *see page 504*

The lively bar at seafood restaurant Bar München, Munich

Kulisse €
International   Map 2 C4
Maximilianstrasse 26, 80539
Tel *(089) 29 47 28*
The Kammerspiele theatre's restaurant offers a wide choice of dishes ranging from Asian to Bavarian. The outside tables are good for people-watching.

Der Pschorr €
Regional German   Map 2 B5
Viktualienmarkt 15, 80331
Tel *(089) 442 383 940*
This bustling inn celebrates Bavarian culture with excellent beer and traditional fare made with mainly local ingredients.

Riva Tal €
Italian   Map 2 C5
Im Tal 44, 80331
Tel *(089) 22 22 40*
This pizzeria and espresso bar is a popular spot for after-work drinks, but serves standard Italian dishes all day. Cheerful service.

Sushi Sano €
Japanese   Map 1 F5
Josephspitalstrasse 4, 80331
Tel *(089) 26 74 90*   **Closed** *Sun*
Dine on authentic sushi and noodle dishes at this popular restaurant. Takeaway boxes are available for picnics.

Tavernetta €
Italian   Map 2 C4
Hildegardstrasse 9, 80539
Tel *(089) 212 694 24*   **Closed** *Sun*
Quality fare includes fine seafood pasta dishes and satisfying *antipasti* such as courgette and wild mushroom *carpaccio*. Leave some room for the tiramisu.

The Victorian House €
British   Map 2 B5
Frauenstrasse 14, 80469
Tel *(089) 255 469 47*
One of a chain of English-themed cafés. Good for breakfast and sandwich lunches. For afternoon tea, try the Earl Grey with scones.

Weisses Bräuhaus €
Traditional German   Map 2 C5
Im Tal 7, 80331
Tel *(089) 290 13 80*
A well-established *Bierstube* (beer hall) with a touristy yet authentic feel. Try the appetizing liver dumplings or sausages served with *Sauerkraut*.

DK Choice

Wirtshaus in der Au €
Regional German   Road Map D7
Lilienstrasse 51, 81669
Tel *(089) 448 14 00*
Waitresses at this lovely Bavarian inn sport traditional *Dirndl* dresses. The special experimental dumplings on offer include spinach and beetroot versions. They have also published a cookbook, and run a dumpling restaurant, Münchner Knödelei, on the Oktoberfest grounds during the festival.

Traditional English-inspired decor at and at The Victorian House, Munich

Pageou €€
International   Map 2 B3
Kardinal-Faulhaber-Strasse 10, 80333
Tel *(089) 242 31 310*   **Closed** *Sun*
Michelin-starred chef Ali Güngörmüş' creations are based on simple, fresh produce and reflect influences from Asia to the Mediterranean.

Ratskeller €€
Regional German   Map 2 B4
Marienplatz 8, 80331
Tel *(089) 219 98 90*
Set in the charming old town-hall cellars, this large and touristy restaurant serves good-quality local specialities.

Le Stollberg €€
French   Map 2 C4
Stollbergstrasse 2, 80539
Tel *(089) 242 434 50*   **Closed** *Sun*
Excellent, carefully prepared French-inspired food is made with high-quality ingredients at this bright and airy restaurant.

Bar München €€€
International   Map 2 C4
Maximilianstrasse 36, 80539
Tel *(089) 22 90 90*
A chic and upmarket place with mouthwatering seafood on an oft-changing menu. Good-value set business lunches and amazing cocktails.

Restaurant Pfistermühle €€€
Regional German   Map 2 C4
Pfisterstrasse 4, 80331
Tel *(089) 237 038 65*   **Closed** *Sun*
A small, seasonal and regionally inspired menu is served under elegant 16th-century arches here. Impeccable service. Reserve in advance.

DK Choice

Trader Vic's €€€
Polynesian   Map 2 A3
Promenade platz 2–6, 80333
Tel *(089) 212 200*
Creative Polynesian food and exotic cocktails are served in the relaxed, colourful cellar-bar of the plush Hotel Bayerischer Hof. Popular with locals and visitors alike, not to mention celebrities such as Tina Turner.

Weinhaus Neuner €€€
International/
Regional German   Map 1 F4
Herzogspitalstrasse 8, 80331
Tel *(089) 260 39 54*   **Closed** *Sun*
The menu at this smart wine bar presents strong Mediterranean influences. There are piquant Bavarian mustard sauces as well.

Bavaria

ANSBACH: Madame Thu Trang €
Japanese/Indochina **Road Map** D6
Platenstrasse 2, 91522
Tel *(0981) 972 33 99* **Closed** *Tue*
Hidden in a little passage in the
shopping district, this incongruous
little eatery's menu includes
sushi, Indonesian curries and
traditional Vietnamese dishes
worth going out of the way for.

AUGSBURG: Berghof €
Regional German **Road Map** D6
Bergstrasse 12, 86199
Tel *(0821) 998 43 22*
Bright, country-style inn taking a
fresh, approach on typical Bavarian
dishes – cooked to perfection.

AUGSBURG: Drei Königinnen €€
Regional German/
Mediterranean **Road Map** D6
Meister-Veits-Gässchen 32, 86152
Tel *(0821) 15 84 05*
Highly regarded for its bustling
upmarket beer garden, this
restaurant also serves pleasing
Spätzle (egg noodles) and other
pasta dishes.

AUGSBURG: Manyo €€
Japanese **Road Map** D6
Schertlinstrasse 12a, 86159
Tel *(0821) 57 11 19* **Closed** *Mon, Tue*
Watch teppanyaki being
prepared on an iron griddle at
this restaurant with a convivial
ambience. Book ahead.

BAMBERG: Hofbräu €
Traditional German **Road Map** D5
Karolinenstrasse 7, 96049
Tel *(0951) 533 21*
A classy restaurant with good
Schnitzel, warm and friendly

The minimalist and authentic interior of
Japanese restaurant Manyo, Augsburg

Spectacular views from the terrace at
Restaurant 360°, Berchtesgaden

service, and live piano music on
Mondays. Reservations advised
for this popular spot.

BAMBERG: Poseidon €
Greek **Road Map** D5
Habergasse 11, 96047
Tel *(0951) 254 22* **Closed** *Tue*
A cheerful, family-run Greek
restaurant featuring dark wooden
beams. On the menu are
traditional dishes such as octopus
salad, baked feta and *gyros*
(shavings of roasted meat, served
with rice, tzaziki and Greek salad).

**BAMBERG: Hoffmanns Steak
& Fish** €€
International **Road Map** D5
Schillerplatz 7, 96047
Tel *(0951) 700 08 85* **Closed** *Sun*
Renowned for its incredible
steaks, Hoffmanns is also widely
credited with intoducing
nouvelle cuisine to Bamberg.
Choose from a range of
innovative dishes served in an
elegant environment.

BAMBERG: Fellini €€€
Italian **Road Map** D5
Urbanstrasse 6, 96047
Tel *(0951) 208 61 03* **Closed** *Sun*
Fresh, simple and beautifully
presented Italian cuisine is
served by enthusiastic waiters
here. Fine drinks menu too.
Book ahead on weekend nights.

**BAYREUTH: Hansl's
Holzofen Pizzeria** €
Italian **Road Map** D5
Friedrichstrasse 15, 95444
Tel *(0921) 543 44*
The thin and crunchy pizzas
topped with fresh produce,
served straight from the wood-
fired oven, are as delicious as
they are misshapen. This tiny
eatery has only three tables;
however, takeaway is available.

**BERCHTESGADEN:
L'Osteria al Parco** €
Italian **Map** E7
Kälbersteinstrasse 2, 83471
Tel *(08652) 96 45 55* **Closed** *Tue*
This authentic Italian *osteria*
offers a small menu featuring
delicious pizzas and pasta. The
restaurant's interior design is
rustic and cosy.

DK Choice

**BERCHTESGADEN:
Restaurant 360°** €€€
International **Road Map** E7
Hintereck 1, 834/1
Tel *(08652) 975 50*
The premier dining spot in
the InterContinental Resort,
Restaurant 360° is named after
the spectacular mountain views
from its panoramic windows.
Watch delicious local ingredients
being transformed into exquisite
regional and international
dishes in the open kitchen.
Many of the choices on the
menu are rich and meaty, but
there are also several nutritious
and health-conscious options.

BURGHAUSEN: Chilli's €
International **Road Map** E7
Maktler Strasse 5, 84489
Tel *(08677) 87 75 50*
Come here for an extensive
range of Mexican and Indian
dishes, as well as steaks and fresh
fish. The house speciality is baked
potatoes. Good-value set lunches.

**CHIEMSEE: Fritzi's
Biergarten** €
Regional German **Road Map** E7
Frauenchiemsee 39, 83256
Tel *(08054) 90 29 36*
This lakeside beer garden
is a great place to watch the
sunset while sampling fresh
Chiemsee fish and other
regional specialities.

FÜSSEN: Michelangelo €
Italian **Road Map** D7
Reichenstrasse 33, 87629
Tel *(08362) 92 49 24* **Closed** *Mon*
Giant pizzas and home-made
pasta dishes are served up in
wonderfully decorated interiors
and a small garden.

**GARMISCH-PARTENKIRCHEN:
Colosseo** €
Italian **Road Map** D7
Klammstrasse 7, 82467
Tel *(08821) 528 09*
Large, crispy pizzas and delicious
pasta dishes ensure that this
Italian restaurant is always
packed, despite its discreet
location above a supermarket.

For more information on types of restaurants *see page 504*

GARMISCH-PARTENKIRCHEN:
Vaun €€
Modern German **Road Map** D7
Zugspitzstrasse 2, 82467
Tel *(08821) 730 81 87* **Closed** *Sun*
Striking modern interiors with
flavours to match. Delicacies
include tomato and gin soup and
poached trout with radish.
Booking recommended.

INGOLSTADT: Daniel €
Regional German **Road Map** D6
Roseneckstrasse 1, 85049
Tel *(0841) 352 72* **Closed** *Mon*
Located in a 500-year-old building,
this inn serves excellent quality
traditional food. Lovely garden.

INGOLSTADT: Taj Mahal €
Indian **Road Map** D6
Beckerstrasse 11, 85049
Tel *(0841) 981 46 18*
Decorated with wooden carvings
and colourful fabrics, this
restaurant offers good-quality
North Indian food and popular
bargain lunch buffets.

KEMPTEN: Rendez-vous
à Quiberon €
French **Road Map** C7
Rathausstrasse 2, 87435
Tel *(0831) 520 81 16*
Rendez-vous à Quiberon serves
unusually well-priced French
cuisine. Go for the smoked salmon
and radish *galette* (pancake) for a
perfect summer meal.

LANDSHUT: Taverna Delphi €
Greek **Road Map** E6
Isargestade 742, 84028
Tel *(0871) 211 59* **Closed** *Mon*
Black-and-white photographs
adorn the walls of this modern
bistro. Unpretentious food with
crisp, fresh flavours includes feta
salads, meat skewers and fish.

LINDAU: Alte Post €€
Regional German **Road Map** C7
Fischergasse 3, 88131
Tel *(08382) 934 60*
Dark-wood decor at this inn
serving *Schnitzel*, boiled beef
and home-made *Maultaschen*
(giant Swabian ravioli). The
cobbled terrace makes for lovely
summer dining.

LINDAU: Zum Sünfzen €€
Regional German **Road Map** C7
Maximilianstrasse 1, 88131
Tel *(08382) 58 65*
An atmospheric and traditional
restaurant in a 14th-century
building. The speciality is fresh
Bodensee fish, though the
venison is also fantastic. Booking
ahead is recommended.

LINDAU: Villino €€€
Asian/Italian **Road Map** C7
Hoyerberg 34, 88131
Tel *(08382) 934 50*
Savour amazing gourmet food
inspired by Asian and Italian
flavours at this exquisite family-
run hotel restaurant with an
idyllic garden and terrace.

DK Choice

NUREMBERG:
Bratwurstherzle €
Regional German **Road Map** D6
Brunnengasse 11, 90402
Tel *(0911) 22 68 10* **Closed** *Sun*
This unpretentious place in the
Old Town has been serving
grilled Nürnberg mini-sausages
and *Sauerkraut* since 1526. Sit
at the shared tables in the half-
timbered interior or outside on
the street. Good selection of
beers and Franconian wines.
Reservations recommended.

NUREMBERG:
Bratwurstglöcklein €
Regional German **Road Map** D6
Waffenhof 5, 90402
Tel *(0911) 22 76 25*
This historical inn dating back
to 1313 serves Franconian set
meals consisting of dumpling
soup, pork knuckle and sausages
simmered in onions and vinegar.

NUREMBERG: Padelle d'Italia €
Italian **Road Map** D6
Theatergasse 17, 90402
Tel *(09112) 74 21 30* **Closed** *Sun*
This smart, family-run *trattoria*
serves home-made pasta dishes,
thin-crust pizzas, scrumptious
antipasti platters and delicious
seafood. Superb wine list.

NUREMBERG: Red Curry House €
Indian/Thai **Road Map** D6
Lorenzer Strasse 29, 90402
Tel *(0911) 621 74 17* **Closed** *Sun*
Choose from a variety of mouth-
watering Asian curries at this
informal restaurant. Vegetarian
options and takeaway available.

NUREMBERG: Schanzenbräu
Schankwirtschaft €
Regional German **Road Map** D6
Adam-Klein-Strasse 27, 90429
Tel *(0911) 937 767 90*
A tavern with a great beer garden.
The small menu includes German
classics, such as *Bratwurst*, and
vegetarian choices.

NUREMBERG: Herr Lenz €€
Organic **Road Map** D6
Kernstrasse 29, 90429
Tel *(0911) 598 53 85* **Closed** *Sun*
A colourful neighbourhood
bistro featuring first-rate daily
specials comprising soups,
beef *bourguignon* and a
glorious chocolate cake.

Dine al fresco at Bratwurstherzle, Nuremberg

Homely and welcoming dining area of Vinothek Tiepolo, Würzburg

NUREMBERG: Nassauer Keller €€
Regional German   **Road Map** D6
Karolinenstrasse 2–4, 90402
Tel *(0911) 225 967*   **Closed** *Sun*
Housed in an atmospheric, vaulted medieval cellar, this is the place for a unique dining experience. The sausages are exemplary.

NUREMBERG: Wittmanns €€
Organic   **Road Map** D6
Beckschlagergasse 8, 90403
Tel *(0911) 33 10 88*   **Closed** *Sun & Mon*
Bright, modern restaurant serving nouvelle cuisine. Dishes include soups, meats and vegetarian options with produce mainly sourced from the region.

NUREMBERG: Essigbrätlein €€€
Modern German   **Road Map** D6
Weinmarkt 3, 90403
Tel *(0911) 225 131*   **Closed** *Sun & Mon*
An intimate little restaurant with remarkable food, wines and service. The daily menu often features fish and exquisite desserts. Reserve in advance.

NUREMBERG: Wonka €€€
International   **Road Map** D6
Johannisstrasse 38, 90419
Tel *(0911) 39 62 15*   **Closed** *Sun & Mon*
Relatively unpretentious gourmet gem. The changing menu offers a range of tasty dishes with exotic flair – from soups to seafood and desserts. Great wine pairings.

NUREMBERG: Würzhaus €€€
Modern German   **Road Map** D6
Kirchenweg 3A, 90419
Tel *(0911) 937 34 55*   **Closed** *Sun*
The trendy decor at Würzhaus perfectly complements the small portions of imaginative gourmet food accompanied by fine wine pairings.

OBERAMMERGAU: Zauberstub'n €
Traditional German   **Road Map** D7
Ettaler Strasse 58, 82487
Tel *(08822) 46 83*   **Closed** *Mon*
Wood-clad inn with a solid, traditional menu. The owner entertains his diners with magic tricks, making this place a must for those travelling with kids.

PASSAU: Pizzeria Gallo Nero €
Italian   **Road Map** E6
Schmiedgasse 5, 94032
Tel *(0851) 363 15*   **Closed** *Tue*
Smart bistro offering an extensive menu of pizzas, pasta dishes and grilled fish. The mussels in white wine are recommended.

PASSAU: Heilig Geist €€
Regional German   **Road Map** E6
Heilig-Geist-Gasse 4, 94032
Tel *(0851) 26 07*   **Closed** *Wed*
A rustic, wood-panelled *Weinstube* with tiled stoves, specializing in Bavarian food – mostly local fish, pork and beef. Reserve a table in the courtyard for a romantic meal.

REGENSBURG: Steidle Wirt €
Regional German   **Road Map** D6
Am Ölberg 13, 93047
Tel *(0941) 56 08 20*
This is a traditional family-run inn with a small seasonal menu and lovingly prepared daily specials. Warm, friendly owners. Reservations recommended.

REGENSBURG: Zur geflickten Trommel €
Traditional German   **Road Map** D6
Gesandtenstrasse 2, 93047
Tel *(0941) 569 964 89*
This medieval-themed tavern with candles, fur-covered benches and costumed staff is just the place to try *Flammkuchen* (Alsatian pizza).

REGENSBURG: Papageno €€
Italian   **Road Map** D6
Keplerstrasse 14, 93047
Tel *(0941) 630 81 65*   **Closed** *lunch Mon–Fri*
Choose from an authentic Italian menu, including a first-class *osso buco* (veal and tomato stew), and enjoy your food beneath a whitewashed vaulted ceiling.

ROTHENBURG: Gasthof Goldener Greifen €
Traditional German   **Road Map** C6
Obere Schmiedgasse 5, 91541
Tel *(09861) 22 81*
Classic German food is served in the historic setting of a 15th-century house. Specialities include spicy goulash soup, *Schnitzel* and Swabian pot roast.

ROTHENBURG: Hotel-Restaurant Kloster-Stüble €
Regional German   **Road Map** C6
Herrngasse 21, 91541
Tel *(09861) 93 88 90*
A popular inn housed in a 1534 farmhouse with town views from the terrace. Relish traditional delicacies such as pork roast with crackling, mushrooms and bread dumplings.

ROTHENBURG: Eisenhut €€€
International   **Road Map** C6
Herrngasse 3–5/7, 91541
Tel *(09861) 70 50*
The antique furnishings in the dining room of this premier hotel are reminiscent of an aristocratic country manor. The varied menu features gourmet seasonal and international dishes.

STRAUBING: Unterm Rain €
Regional German   **Road Map** E6
Unterm Rain 15, 94315
Tel *(09421) 227 72*
Basic and cheerful, this traditional restaurant and beer garden serves big portions of pan-German specialities, including *Schnitzel* and sausages.

WÜRZBURG: Auflauf €
International   **Road Map** C5
Peterplatz 5, 97070
Tel *(0931) 4 04 48*
A charming bistro specializing in casseroles and noodle gratins. Guests choose from the menu or assemble their own creations.

WÜRZBURG: Bella Napoli da Luigi €
Italian   **Road Map** C5
Neubaustrasse 16, 97070
Tel *(0931) 517 06*
A dependable Italian menu and a cheerful vibe ensure that this restaurant is always bustling with regulars. Interesting daily specials.

For more information on types of restaurants *see page 504*

Fabulous views from Steinburgs Restaurant, Würzburg

WÜRZBURG: Vinothek Tiepolo €
Regional German   Road Map C5
Innerer Graben 22, 97070
Tel *(0931) 561 63*
Elegant *Weinstube* with lots of fish on the seasonal menu and some 130 different wines to wash it all down with.

WÜRZBURG: Ratskeller €€
Regional German   Road Map C5
Langgasse 1, 97070
Tel *(0931) 130 21*
Reliable regional food is served in the impressive cellars of the city's town hall. The cinnamon and *Silvaner* white wine soup, if available, is a must-try.

WÜRZBURG: Steinburgs Restaurant €€€
International   Road Map C5
Mittlerer Steinbergweg 100, 97080
Tel *(0931) 97 020*
Surrounded by vineyards and overlooking the city, this romantic riverside castle is a gourmet's delight. The wonderful selection of Franconian wines is unparalleled. Reserve in advance.

Baden-Württemberg

BADEN-BADEN: Le Jardin de France €€€
International   Road Map B6
Lichtentaler Strasse 13, 76530
Tel *(07221) 300 78 60*   **Closed** *Sun & Mon; Tue (Jan & Feb)*
An elegant gourmet restaurant under a vaulted glass ceiling. Ingredients that heavily feature are truffles, *foie gras*, turbot (flatfish) and Alsatian pigeon.

BADEN-BADEN: Medici €€€
International   Road Map B6
Augustaplatz 8, 76530
Tel *(07221) 20 06*
Former guests at this *belle époque*-style restaurant include

Bill Clinton and Nelson Mandela. Savour culinary delights with the town's most fashionable crowd.

FREIBURG IM BREISGAU: Englers Weinkrügle €
Regional German   Road Map B7
Konviktstrasse 12, 79098
Tel *(0761) 38 31 15*
Enjoy scrumptious German cuisine at this wood-panelled *Weinstube* (wine bar). The amazing Black Forest dessert (cherries in hot liqueur with vanilla ice cream) is unmissable.

FREIBURG IM BREISGAU: Hausbrauerei Feierling €
Traditional German   Road Map B7
Gerberau 46, 79098
Tel *(0761) 24 34 80*
First-class pub food, including giant *Schnitzel*, can be had at this cheerful microbrewery with a fantastic beer garden.

FREIBURG IM BREISGAU: Pizzeria Taormina €
Italian   Road Map B7
Schwabentorring 4, 79098
Tel *(0761) 341 60*   **Closed** *Tue*
This modest eatery arguably serves the best pizzas in town – and at reasonable prices. Takeaway, too.

FREIBURG IM BREISGAU: Oberkirchs Weinstuben €€
Regional German   Road Map B7
Münsterplatz 22, 79098
Tel *(0761) 202 68 69*
This excellent traditional hotel restaurant offers large portions of regional delicacies, including pheasant and ox.

FRIEDRICHSHAFEN: Weinstube Glückler €€
German/French   Road Map C7
Olgastrasse 23, 88045
Tel *(07541) 221 64* **Closed** *Sat (May–Aug)*
Small wine tavern with a delightful range of local fish dishes and many

varieties of Breton *galette* (crusty cake) the in-house speciality.

FRIEDRICHSHAFEN: Felders €
International   Road Map C7
Karlstrasse 42, 88045
Tel *(07541) 391 955*
Hearty breakfasts and creative lunches are served at hip Felders, while dinner menus are strong on fish. There's also a bar and a waterfront terrace.

FRIEDRICHSHAFEN: Restaurant im Zeppelin Museum €€
Regional German/Seafood
Road Map C7
Seestrasse 22, 88045
Tel *(07541) 953 00 88*   **Closed** *Mon (Nov–Apr)*
A popular harbourside restaurant with an eclectic menu ranging from well-priced Swabian specials to Norwegian salmon.

HEIDELBERG: Alte Münz Schnitzelhaus €
German/Austrian   Road Map C6
Neckarmünzgasse 10, 69117
Tel *(06221) 43 46 43*
This traditional place offers 100 varieties of *Schnitzel* dishes, from the classic Viennese to more exotic versions, such as a serving with a spicy chocolate sauce.

HEIDELBERG: Zum Roten Ochsen €
Traditional German   Road Map C6
Hauptstrasse 217, 69117
Tel *(06221) 209 77*
The collectables and sepia photos on the walls at this atmospheric student haunt bear witness to its popularity since the early 19th century.

HEIDELBERG: Simplicissimus €€€
French   Road Map C6
Ingrimstrasse 16, 69117
Tel *(06221) 673 25 88*   **Closed** *Sun*
Superb French cuisine, including imaginative beef, veal and seafood concoctions. Sit in the

intimate dining room or in the pretty, flower-filled courtyard.

KARLSRUHE: Casa Aposto €
Italian   Road Map B6
Waldstrasse 57, 76133
Tel *(0721) 160 77 73*
Delight in quality Italian cuisine and outstanding ice cream. In good weather, there is outdoor seating in a bustling square.

**KONSTANZ: Brauhaus
Johann Albrecht**   €
Regional German   Road Map C7
Inselgasse 17, 78462
Tel *(07531) 250 45*
A charming microbrewery with a good array of beers and well-priced pub food, such as *Schnitzel* and *Flammkuchen* (thin bread base topped with onion, lardons and crème fraîche). Good-value buffet menu.

KONSTANZ: Hafenhalle €€
Regional German   Road Map C7
Hafenstrasse 10, 78462
Tel *(07531) 211 26*
Large, smart restaurant in an old harbourside warehouse. Simple canteen food is served in the beer garden. Great for breakfast.

KONSTANZ: Staader Fährhaus €€
Regional German/
Mediterranean   Road Map C7
Fischerstrasse 30, 78464
Tel *(07531) 361 67 63*   **Closed** *Wed*
Off the beaten path, but worth the trek for fresh, creative fish dishes accompanied by organic, local ingredients.

LUDWIGSBURG: Alte Sonne €€
French   Road Map C6
Bei der Katholischen Kirche 3, 71634
Tel *(07141) 643 64 80*   **Closed** *Mon & Tue*
Innovative cuisine ranging from *bouillabaisse* to Breton-style lamb goulash. There is a relaxed, informal brasserie as well.

MAINAU: Schwedenschenke €€€
Regional German/
Swedish   Road Map C7
Insel Mainau, 78465
Tel *(07531) 303 156*
Romantic island restaurant serving great Swedish meatballs for lunch and *haute cuisine* for dinner, including fresh local fish.

MANNHEIM: C-Five €€€
French/Italian   Road Map B5
Zeughaus, 68155
Tel *(0621) 122 95 50*
A stylish spot serving high-end French and Italian fare in a con-verted premises dating back to the 18th century, and more basic pasta dishes and salads at the bar.

MAULBRONN: Klosterkatz €€
Italian   Map C6
Klosterhof 21, 75433
Tel *(07043) 80 89*
Good, everyday Italian food is served in an atmospheric monastery courtyard.

MEERSBURG: Zum Becher €€
Regional German   Road Map C7
Höllgasse 4, 88709
Tel *(07532) 90 09*
This rustic, cluttered *Weinstube* serves fine traditional food and local fish. Extensive wine list.

DK Choice

REICHENAU: Riebel €
Seafood   Road Map C7
Seestrasse 13, 78479
Tel *(07534) 76 63*   **Closed** *Sat & Mon dinner; Sun*
Owned and run by fishermen, this basic restaurant does a brisk trade in superbly simple grilled fish served with fresh side salads. The seafood soup is another highlight. Share a long, communal table with the locals who gather here for lunch. Takeaway available.

**ST BLASIEN: Hotelrestaurant
Klostermeisterhaus** €€
European   Road Map B7
Im Süssen Winkel 2, 79837
Tel *(07672) 848*
Sample slick modern European cuisine – grilled zander with sauerkraut mousse, beef tenderloin or saddle of venison – in an early 19th-century villa.

**STUTTGART: Brauhaus
Calwer-Eck**   €€
Regional German   Road Map C6
Calwer Strasse 31, 70173
Tel *(0711) 222 49 440*
Stuttgart's oldest micro-brewery features organically produced, seasonal beers. Typical local food includes *Maultaschen*.

STUTTGART: Nirvan €€
Persian   Road Map C6
Eberhardstrasse 73, 70173
Tel *(0711) 24 05 61*
Authentic Middle-Eastern decor and excellent grilled lamb, poultry and veal dishes at this basement restaurant.

**STUTTGART:
Tauberquelle**   €€
Regional German   Road Map C6
Torstrasse 19, 70173
Tel *(0711) 553 29 33*   **Closed** *Sun*
Good-value Swabian favourites, cooked to perfection, include *Gaisburger Marsch* (beef stew), *Käsespätzle* (noodle with cheese and fried onions) and *Rostbraten* (beef steak).

STUTTGART: Délice €€€
International   Road Map C6
Hauptstätter Strasse 61, 70178
Tel *(0711) 640 32 22*   **Closed** *Sat & Sun*
This intimate, six-table restaurant offers inventive high-quality gourmet food and an award-winning, first-class wine list.

The bright and stylish dining room at Schwedenschenke, Mainau

For more information on types of restaurants *see page 504*

**TÜBINGEN: Restaurant
Mauganeschtle** €
Regional German **Road Map** C6
Burgsteige 18, 72070
Tel *(07071) 929 40*
The speciality at this half-timbered
establishment, in Hotel am
Schloss, is *Maultaschen*. Fine
views over the town.

TÜBINGEN: Weinstube Forelle €€
Regional German **Road Map** C6
Kronenstrasse 8, 72070
Tel *(07071) 240 94*
The walls in this traditional wine
bar are painted with vines, cherubs
and heraldic crests. The trout in
almond butter and the game
dishes are excellent.

**ULM: Zunfthaus
der Schiffleute** €€
Regional German **Road Map** C6
Fischergasse 31, 89073
Tel *(0731) 644 11* **Closed** *Sun*
Set in a 15th-century fishermen's
guild house, the menu consists
of only seasonal ingredients. Do
not miss the exceptional *Spätzle*.

ULM: Zur Forelle €€
Regional German **Road Map** C6
Fischergasse 25, 89073
Tel *(0731) 639 24*
In a snug 1626 house with an
original Napoleonic cannonball
in one wall, Zur Forelle serves
high-end versions of regional
dishes such as beef stew.

Rhineland-Palatinate
and Saarland

BACHARACH: Altes Haus €
Regional German **Road Map** B5
Oberstrasse 61, 55422
Tel *(06743) 12 09* **Closed** *Wed*
There are plenty of options at this
archetypal old Rhine inn: trout
makes an ideal light meal, while

The elaborate sign to Altes Haus,
Bacharach

wild boar in wine sauce is an
appealing, substantial main.

**BACHARACH: Posthof
Bacharach** €
Regional German **Road Map** B5
Oberstrasse 45–49, 55422
Tel *(06743) 947 18 30*
In a beautiful half-timbered
building traditional fare is served.
Try the *Flammkuchen* (thin bread
base topped with onion, lardons
and crème fraîche).

DK Choice

**BACHARACH: Stübers
Restaurant** €€
Traditional German
Road Map B5
Langstrasse 50, 55422
Tel *(06743) 12 43*
This family-run restaurant is set
in a half-timbered building with
an elegant dining room and a
delightful terrace. The highlight
is the pot roast. Impeccable
service. Book ahead.

BOPPARD: Severus Stube €
Regional German **Road Map** B5
Untere Marktstrasse 7, 56154
Tel *(06742) 32 18* **Closed** *Wed
lunch; Thu*
This welcoming, wood-beamed
inn offers hearty lamb and pork
dishes at reasonable prices.

**BOPPARD: Weinhaus
Heilig Grab** €
Regional German **Road Map** B5
Zelkesgasse 12, 56154
Tel *(06742) 23 71*
An over 200-year-old wine tavern
with a pretty shaded garden. Try
the superb *Flammkuchen* (thin
bread base topped with onion,
lardons and crème fraîche).

KOBLENZ: Los Gauchos €€
South American **Road Map** B5
Am Plan 7, 56068
Tel *(0261) 140 06*
Many dishes are *flambéed* (covered
in alcohol and set alight) at your
table at this excellent steakhouse.

KOBLENZ: Weinhaus Hubertus €€
Regional German **Road Map** B5
Florinsmarkt 6, 56068
Tel *(0261) 311 77*
Dating from 1696, this *Weinstube*
(wine bar) serves local fish and
wine, as well as seasonal treats.

MAINZ: Geberts Weinstuben €€
Regional German/
Mediterranean **Road Map** B5
Frauenlobstrasse 94, 55118
Tel *(06131) 61 16 19* **Closed** *Mon*
This elegantly decorated wine
tavern is a cut above the rest for

The tastefully decorated dining room
at Stübers Restaurant, Bacharach

its fish and game dishes and fine
choice of wines.

**MAINZ: Haus des
Deutschen Weines** €€
Regional German **Road Map** B5
Gutenbergplatz 3–5, 55116
Tel *(06131) 22 13 00*
Good-quality and inexpensive
regional food such as marinated
salmon and venison are comple-
mented by an extensive wine list
from all over Germany.

SAARBRÜCKEN: Zum Stiefel €
Regional German **Road Map** B6
Am Stiefel 2, 66111
Tel *(0681) 93 64 50* **Closed** *Sun*
Hearty portions of provincial
food – potato rissoles, and leek,
meat and potato casserole – are
served in this *Bierstube*.

DK Choice

SPEYER: Zum Alten Engel €
Regional German **Road Map** B6
Mühlturmstrasse 7, 67346
Tel *(06232) 709 14*
Set in a brick-vaulted cellar,
this atmospheric restaurant is
furnished with paintings and
antiques. On the menu are
meaty, substantial regional
classics such as liver dumplings
and pig's stomach. Good wine
list. Reserve ahead.

SPEYER: Backmulde €€€
Regional German/French
Road Map B6
Karmeliterstrasse 11–13, 67346
Tel *(06232) 715 77* **Closed** *Sun
dinner; Mon*
This high-end gourmet restaurant
delivers imaginative culinary
treats such as quail stuffed with
lamb and oysters in champagne.

Refined interiors of Restaurant Villa Rothschild, Frankfurt am Main

ST GOAR: Silcher Stuben, Hotel zum Goldenen Löwen €€
Regional German   Road Map B5
Heerstrasse 82, 56329
Tel *06741 16 74*
Top-notch traditional fare in an 18th-century Baroque building. Delicacies include *Pfälzer Saumagen* (cabbage in pig's stomach) and *Spanferkal Braten* (roasted suckling pig).

ST GOAR: Hotel Schloss Rheinfels €€€
Regional German/Mediterranean
Road Map B5
Schlossberg 47, 56329
Tel *(06741) 80 20*   **Closed** *Mon*
This stunning restaurant is part of a historic castle in a picturesque location. It specializes in local game; try the smoked venison with celery and mango.

ST GOARSHAUSEN: Rheingold €
Regional German   Road Map B5
Professor-Müller-Strasse 2, 56346
Tel *(06771) 450*
This riverside restaurant serves great meatball and vegetable stews. There are splendid castle views from the upstairs terrace.

TRIER: Bagatelle €€
French   Road Map A5
Zurlauber Ufer 78, 54292
Tel *(0651) 995 69 90*
Fine French food is cooked to perfection at this restaurant in a prime location directly on the River Mosel.

TRIER: Zum Domstein €€
Regional German   Road Map A5
Hauptmarkt 5, 54290
Tel *(0651) 744 90*
Choose from the recipes of Emperor Tiberius's cook and dine like a Roman. The sauces are delightfully rich.

WORMS: Ambiente €€
Italian   Road Map B5
Weckerlingplatz 6, 67547
Tel *(06241) 304 98 88*   **Closed** *Mon*
This quality restaurant with modern decor serves tasty pizzas and impeccable meat dishes such as *scaloppina* or *piccata alla milanese*. For dessert, have tiramisu or ice cream.

Hesse

ALSFELD: Kartoffelsack €
Traditional German   Road Map C4
Kirchplatz 16, 36304
Tel *(06631) 20 57*   **Closed** *Wed*
Kartoffeln (potatoes) are the main ingredient of all the dishes here – whether in soups or in casseroles, whether chipped or fried.

BAD HOMBURG: Hölderlins €
Traditional German   Road Map C5
Louisenstrasse 15, 61348
Tel *(06172) 680 47 11*
A bright and comfortable café offering satisfying breakfasts and Sunday brunches to kick off the day. Tasty national and local dishes are served in the evening.

BAD WILDUNGEN: Ratswinkelkeller €
Regional German   Road Map C4
Billsteinstrasse 67, 34537
Tel *(05621) 51 90*   **Closed** *Mon*
Over 100 varieties of waffles, along with many local dishes, served in generous proportions. Nice terrace and beer garden.

DARMSTADT: Café Habibi €
Vegan   Road Map C5
Landwehrstrasse 13, 64293
Tel *(06151) 660 27 60*   **Closed** *Mon*
The vegan and vegetarian creations in this old-fashioned

café are magical. Excellent food is made with organic ingredients and packed with flavour. Order the *gyro* (filled pita) wraps, and finish with the tiramisu.

EGELSBACH: Schuhbeck's Check Inn €€
International   Road Map C5
Am Flugplatz, 63329
Tel *(06103) 485 93 80*
Situated in an atmospheric old hangar overlooking the regional airfield, this restaurant serves great local food with Mediterranean and Asian influences. There is also a microbrewery and beer garden.

ELTVILLE: Gourmet Restaurant Schwarzenstein €€€
Gourmet   Road Map B5
Rosengasse 32, 65366
Tel *(06722) 995 00*   **Closed** *Mon & Tue*
This wonderful restaurant is housed in a modern pavilion with views of the vineyards on the banks of the Rhine. The ingredients are carefully chosen and meticulously prepared, and accompanied by award-winning wines.

FRANKFURT AM MAIN: Zum Schwarzen Stern €€
International   Road Map C5
Römerberg 6, 60311
Tel *(069) 29 19 79*
Well-prepared seasonal and international dishes are served in a medieval building. Try the *Tafelspitz* (boiled beef).

DK Choice

FRANKFURT AM MAIN: Restaurant Villa Rothschild €€€
French   Road Map C5
Im Rothschildpark 1, 61462
Tel *(06174) 290 80*   **Closed** *Sun & Mon*
Situated in a mansion resembling a castle, this award-winning restaurant is one of the best in Germany and a must-visit for gourmets. The chef and his team specializes in imaginative relations of French haute cuisine, perfectly complemented by the excellent and extensive selection of wines and champagnes. Reservations recommended.

FULDA: Dachsbau €€
Traditional German   Road Map C5
Pfandhausstrasse 8, 36037
Tel *(0661) 741 12*   **Closed** *Mon & Tue*
An intimate and friendly restaurant serving creatively presented German cuisine. Reserve ahead.

The warm and artistic-styled dining room in Käfers Bistro, Wiesbaden

GIESSEN: Schlosskeller €€
Traditional German   Road Map C4
Brandplatz 2, 35390
Tel *(0641) 383 06* **Closed** *Sat lunch &
Sun dinner*
Excellent food and the lovely
ambience in the vaulted cellar of
this medieval building promise
an exquisite dining experience.

KASSEL: Restaurant Santé €€€
Gourmet   Road Map C4
Konrad-Adenauer-Strasse 117, 34132
Tel *(0561) 94 04 80*   **Closed** *Sun
dinner*
Located near the magnificent
Wilhelmshöhe, with nice views
over Kassel, this restaurant at Zum
Steinernen Schweinchen offers
fine culinary delights. À la carte
and set menus and superb wines.

KIEDRICH: Klostermühle €€
Traditional German   Road Map B5
An der Klostermühle 3, 65399
Tel *(06123) 40 21*   **Closed** *Mon*
Enjoy traditional recipes and fruity
Rheingau wines at this romantic
former monastery. Try the *Tafelspitz*
(boiled beef served with horse-
radish) with a glass of Riesling.

KLOSTER EBERBACH:
Klosterschänke €€
Regional German   Road Map B5
Pfortenhaus, 65346
Tel *(06723) 99 299*
Specialities at this atmospheric
12th-century former monastery
include regional Rheingau dishes
and wines made from grapes
harvested on the property.

LIMBURG: Wirsthaus
Obermühle €€
Modern German   Road Map B5
Am Huttig 3, 65549
Tel *(06431) 584 00 84*   **Closed** *Mon*
Charming restaurant next
to a 12th-century water mill.
The amazing *Schnitzel*, steaks
and other regional delicacies
reflect the ongoing evolution
of German cuisine.

LORSCH: Gaststätte Schillereck €
International   Road Map C5
Schillerstrasse 27, 64653
Tel *(06251) 570 10 27*   **Closed** *Fri*
An unexpected find for
gastronomes on a budget.
Outstanding food and wines,
combined with great service,
create a memorable dining
experience.

MARBURG: Das Kleine
Restaurant €€
French   Road Map C4
Barfüssertor 25, 35037
Tel *(06421) 222 93*   **Closed** *Mon*
Small restaurant, big on flavour
and style. Four-course set menus
blend French and German techniques with eclectic ingredients
and artistic presentation. Superb
wine list with over 400 options.

MICHELSTADT: Drei Hasen €€
Regional German   Road Map C5
Braunstrasse 5, 64720
Tel *(06061) 710 17*
The "Three Hares" is renowned
for its traditional ambience, as
well as its delectable cuisine,
especially the fish dishes. The
interior has a strong rustic charm,
and there is a large beer garden.

OFFENBACH: Markthaus
am Wilhelmsplatz €
Traditional German   Road Map C5
Bieberer Strasse 9b, 63065
Tel *(069) 801 018 83*
Warm restaurant with an outside
terrace overlooking the town
market. Authentic dishes on the
menu include *Handkäse* (sour
milk cheese), home-made *Wurst*
(sausage) and roast pork.

RÜDESHEIM AM RHEIN:
Kronenstube €€
German/Mediterranean
    Road Map B5
Rheinuferstrasse 10, 65685
Tel *(06722) 40 30*
Classic French and contemporary
German cuisine is served with a

variety of regional wines in a
rustic setting. In summer, the
flower-clad terrace offers lovely,
scenic views over the Rhine.

WEILBURG: Alte Reitschule €€
Traditional German   Road Map B5
Langgasse 25, 35781
Tel *(06471) 509 00*
This picturesque restaurant
serves a small range of seasonal
dishes. The terrace offers
wonderful views of the Schloss
and the surrounding area.

WETZLAR: Der Postreiter €€
Traditional German   Road Map B5
*Konrad-Adenauer-Promenade 20,
35578*
Tel *(06441) 90 30*
This restaurant in the Bürgerhof
Hotel prepares fresh, seasonal
local cuisine – trout is the
speciality. Ask the staff to help you
select from the extensive wine list.

WIESBADEN: Käfers Bistro €€
French   Road Map B5
Kurhausplatz 1, 65189
Tel *(0611) 53 62 00*
A spacious and busy bistro
combining German portions
and produce with French
subtlety. There is a good
variety of wines from the
region, and a large terrace
for outside dining.

North Rhine-
Westphalia

AACHEN: Sankt Benedikt €€€
International   Road Map A4
Benediktusplatz 12, 52076
Tel *(02408) 28 88* **Closed** *Sat lunch &
Sun*
Choose from a creative award-
winning menu featuring French
and international fare. Impressive
wine selection and friendly
service. Book ahead as there are
only a handful of tables.

AACHEN: Schloss Schönau €€€
International **Road Map** A4
Schönauer Allee 20, 52072
Tel *(0241) 1 / 35 77* **Closed** *Sat lunch
& Sun*
Gourmet food in an opulent
11th-century castle with breath-
taking views of the countryside.
The set menus include a seafood
option, and there is a vast array
of wines and champagnes.

**BIELEFELD: Westfälische
Hofstube** €€
Regional German **Road Map** C3
Niedernholz 2, 33699
Tel *(0521) 209 00*
The Oldentruper Hof Hotel's
restaurant prepares traditional
delicacies from the Westphalia
area and a few international
dishes too. In autumn, ask for the
venison specialities.

BONN: Altes Treppchen €€
International **Road Map** B4
Endenicher Strasse 308, 53173
Tel *(0228) 62 50 04* **Closed** *Sat lunch
& Sun*
A snug restaurant that uses organic
ingredients in a menu of excellent
meat and fish dishes – including
ox, venison, black sole and char.

**BONN: Zur Lindenwirtin
Aennchen** €€
International **Road Map** B4
Aennchenplatz 2, 53173
Tel *(0228) 31 20 51* **Closed** *Sun*
A romantic restaurant with
impeccable service, international
dishes and a carefully chosen
wine list. Lovely garden.

BONN: Halbedel's Gasthaus €€€
French **Road Map** B4
Rheinallee 47, 53173
Tel *(0228) 35 42 53* **Closed** *Mon*
First-rate service, innovative
cuisine and an impressive list of
700 wines, just a stone's throw
from the Rhine.

COLOGNE: Alcazar €
French/German **Road Map** B4
Bismarckstrasse 39A, 50672
Tel *(0221) 51 57 33*
An institution in Köln's humming
nightlife quarter, this appealing
little bar/restaurant fuses French
and German cuisine. Lunch is
the best bet for a table, since
evenings are often packed solid.

COLOGNE: Engelbät €
Crêperie **Road Map** B4
Engelbertstrasse 7, 50674
Tel *(0221) 24 69 14*
Enjoy delicious crêpes filled with
cheese, spinach, fresh garlic and
other ingredients (savoury or
sweet) at this trendy crêperie
in the trendy Belgian quarter.

COLOGNE: Pöttgen €
Traditional German **Road Map** B4
Landmannstrasse 19, 50825
Tel *(0221) 55 52 46* **Closed** *Mon*
This cheerful restaurant has been
in the Pöttgen family for four
generations, and several recipes
can be traced back to the family's
ancestors. Great value.

COLOGNE: Il Carpaccio €€
Italian **Road Map** B4
Lindenstrasse 5, 50674
Tel *(0221) 23 64 87* **Closed** *Sun*
Relish fantastic home-made
pasta and other classic Italian
dishes made with top quality
ingredients in a stylish setting.
Remarkable wine selection and
live music at weekends.

COLOGNE: L'Escalier €€€
French **Road Map** B4
Brüsseler Strasse 11, 50674
Tel *(0221) 205 39 98* **Closed** *Sun
& Mon*
A restaurant with a passion for
innovative French cuisine with
German influences. The elegant
modern dining area is a great
place for lunch or dinner.

COLOGNE: Maitre €€€
French **Road Map** B4
Olympiaweg 2, 50933
Tel *(0221) 48 53 60* **Closed** *Mon
& Tue*
The restaurant of the Landhaus
Kuckuck hotel has a reputation
for its fine cuisine and well-
stocked wine cellar. The changing
menu uses seasonal produce.

COLOGNE: Le Moissonier €€€
French **Road Map** B4
Krefelder Strasse 25, 50670
Tel *(0221) 72 94 79* **Closed** *Sun
& Mon*
Fabulous French food made with
the finest ingredients and served
in a warm interior. Expect dishes
such as Icelandic cod, braised
rabbit and Australian beef fillet.

DETMOLD: Strate's Brauhaus €
Traditional German **Road Map** C3
Lange Strasse 35, 32756
Tel *(05231) 99 99 45*
Set in a historic house filled with
brewing paraphernalia. Enjoy
specialities such as *Pickert* (crispy
fried potato pancakes with raisins)
with Strate's home-brewed
Pilsner and cloudy wheat beers.

DK Choice

DORTMUND: The View €
Regional German **Road Map** B4
Leonie-Reygers-Terasse, 44137
Tel *(0231) 476 47 80* **Closed** *Sun–
Thu*
Unique "club kitchen" on the top
floor of the monumental former
Dortmunder U brewery tower.
Open only on Friday and
Saturday nights, The View serves
tasty, affordable food. The whole
place converts into a lively club
attracting a trendy crowd. Ask
for a table by the window and
visit the terrace for superb views.

DUISBURG: Walsumer Hof €
Seafood **Road Map** B4
Rheinstrasse 16, 47179
Tel *(0203) 49 14 54* **Closed** *Mon*
The distinctive nautical decor
in this restaurant is the perfect
match for the superb seafood. Try
the catch of the day – grilled,
steamed or fried to order.

**DÜSSELDORF: Brauerei Uerige
in der Altstadt** €
Traditional German **Road Map** B4
Berger Strasse 1, 40213
Tel *(0211) 86 69 90*
The highlight at this legendary
brewpub is the renowned *Altbier*
(an amber bitter served in little
glasses). Savour solid German fare
in the unforgettable atmosphere
of several dimly lit rooms.

The vibrant interior of The View, Dortmund

The attractive façade of Im Schiffchen, Düsseldorf

DÜSSELDORF: Libanon   €€
Lebanese   Road Map B4
Berger Strasse 19–21, 40213
Tel *(0211) 13 49 17*
Typical Middle-Eastern fare is
served in generous portions
at Libanon. Occasional belly-
dancing shows in the evening.

DÜSSELDORF: Im Schiffchen €€€
French   Road Map B4
Kaiserswerther Markt 9, 40489
Tel *(0211) 40 10 50* **Closed** *Sun & Mon*
Reserve well in advance at this
popular restaurant. Well-informed
staff advise on the extensive menu
and the 900-strong wine list.

ESSEN: Tio Pepe   €
Spanish   Road Map B4
Witteringstrasse 92, 45130
Tel *(0201) 878 984 15* **Closed** *Sun*
Enjoy tasty, fresh Spanish dishes
in stylish interiors. There is no real
menu – the chef comes up with
proposals based on guests' tastes.
For dessert, try the delectable
crema catalana flambeada
(similiar to *crème brûlée*).

ESSEN: Casino Zollverein   €€
International   Road Map B4
Gelsenkirchener Strasse 181, 45309
Tel *(0201) 83 02 40*   **Closed** *Mon*
Located in an old mine, the
dining hall alone, with its
industrial look, is worth the trip.
The New World cuisine served is
seasonal and original, and retains
hints of traditional miners' food.

ESSEN: Résidence   €€€
International   Road Map B4
Auf der Forst 1, 45219
Tel *(02054) 95590* **Closed** *Sun & Mon*
The highly acclaimed Résidence
attracts patrons from afar. The
chef produces irresistible cuisine
– particularly seafood dishes –
that never fails to impress.

**HAGEN: Altes Pfingsten
Brauhaus**   €
Traditional German   Road Map B4
Voerder Strasse 52, 58135
Tel *(02331) 418 53*
Wood panelling and stained
glass characterize the interior of
this restaurant, which serves
good-value regional specialities
and pan-German classics.

**HÖXTER: Bauernstube
Schenkenküche**   €
Traditional German   Road Map C3
Kapenberg 6, 37671
Tel *(05278) 889*   **Closed** *Mon–Fri*
Set in a farmhouse; kids can
play among haystacks as parents
savour delicious offerings such
as baked ham *flambé* (cooked
in flaming alcohol) with wild
berry sauce.

LEMGO: Im Borke   €
Regional German   Road Map C3
Salzufler Strasse 132, 32657
Tel *(05266) 16 91* **Closed** *Wed & Thu
lunch*
A little restaurant with lots of
rustic charm. The menu features
regional food, as well as a few
international dishes.

MONSCHAU: Wiesenthal   €
Modern German   Road Map A4
Laufenstrasse 82, 52156
Tel *(02472) 860*
The menu at this refined
restaurant in the Carat Hotel
offers creative food made with
seasonal produce from the region.

MÜNSTER: Alter Pulverturm   €
Traditional German   Road Map B3
Breul 9, 8143
Tel *(0251) 458 30*
This quiet and peaceful spot
located along Münster's promenade features a pleasant beer
garden. The extensive menu
offers a variety of German dishes.

MÜNSTER: Landhaus Eggert €€
International   Road Map B3
Zur Haskenau 81, 48157
Tel *(0251) 32 80 40*   **Closed** *Mon
& Tue*
The varied menu at this fine-dining
restaurant in a family-owned
country-house hotel explore
international cuisine while show-
casing the region's best dishes.

MÜNSTER: Villa Medici   €€
Italian   Road Map B3
Prozessionsweg 402, 48145
Tel *(0251) 342 18* **Closed** *Sun & Mon*
Dine on well-balanced and
wonderfully presented, imaginative food in one of Germany's
best Italian restaurants. A multi-
course set menu is also on offer.

PADERBORN: Balthasar   €€€
International   Road Map C3
Warburger Strasse 28, 33098
Tel *(05251) 244 48* **Closed** *lunch Tue
& Wed; Sun & Mon*
An attractive restaurant that
enthusiastically mixes art with
food. The chef creates inventive
dishes using a variety of interesting ingredients and suggests
wines to complement the food.

**SIEGBURG: Gaststätte
zur Talsperre**   €
Modern German   Road Map B4
Barschosser Strasse 55, 53721
Tel *(02241) 38 39 88*
Modern takes on classic dishes
such as chanterelle mushrooms
in cream sauce and pangasius
(cat fish) fillet at this charming
restaurant. Wash down with a
freshly tapped Bitburger (pilsner).

**TROISDORF: Forsthaus
Telegraph**   €€
International   Road Map B4
Mauspfad 3, 53842
Tel *(02241) 766 49*   **Closed** *Mon &
Tue; Wed lunch*

The grand and stylish interior of Casino Zollverein, Essen

Hidden in a forest, this restaurant serves international dishes in a sophisticated setting, combining the best of all styles and cuisines. Book ahead.

WUPPERTAL: Scarpati €€€
Italian **Road Map** B4
Scheffelstrasse 41, 42327
Tel *(0202) 78 40 74* **Closed** *Mon*
A classic Italian restaurant serving fresh and flavourful pasta dishes that are worth the calories. The dining area has a pleasant view over the garden.

XANTEN: Restaurant Neumeier €
Regional German **Road Map** A4
Orkstrasse 19–21, 46509
Tel *(02801) 715 70*
The dishes served here are rich in variety and the beer garden is judged to be the most attractive in town. In summer, a grill buffet attracts many visitors.

Lower Saxony, Hamburg and Bremen

BRUNSWICK: OX US Steakhouse €€
International **Road Map** D3
Güldenstrasse 7, 38100
Tel *(0531) 24 39 00*
Enjoy delicious steaks cooked to perfection in American style and in a modern setting. The extensive choice of special dishes includes the Wagyu beef fillet in Kobe style and half grilled Canadian lobster.

BREMEN: Ratskeller €
Traditional German **Road Map** C2
Am Markt, 28195
Tel *(0421) 305 98 88*
Housed in Germany's oldest wine cellar, established over 600 years ago, Ratskeller has an extensive wine selection to suit all budgets and serves tasty food in a magnificent setting.

BREMEN: Das Kleine Lokal €€
International **Road Map** C2
Besselstrasse 40, 28203
Tel *(0421) 794 90 84* **Closed** *Sun & Mon*
An intimate restaurant offering everything from regional recipes to international fare. Small portions of delicious dishes are served on beautifully designed crockery. Friendly service.

BREMEN: Meierei Bürgerpark €€
Mediterranean **Road Map** C2
Bürgerpark 1, 28209
Tel *(0421) 340 86 19* **Closed** *Mon & Tue*
This Art Nouveau Swiss chalet

in the middle of a park has been serving great food since 1881. The menu features dishes with Mediterranean flavours, as well as some seasonal local choices.

BREMEN: Schröter's Leib und Seele €€
International **Road Map** C2
Schnoor 13, 28195
Tel *(0421) 32 66 //*
Stylish yet welcoming, this is one of the best places to sample typical Bremen fare and international cuisine. There is also a bistro for less upmarket dining.

BÜCKEBURG: Ambiente €€
German/Italian **Road Map** C3
Herminenstrasse 11, 31675
Tel *(05722) 96 70*
With high-glass ceilings, lots of house plants and a little summer garden, this serene restaurant offers mainly German and Italian cuisine, served in generous portions.

CELLE: Bier-Akademie €€
German **Road Map** C3
Weisser Wall 6, 29221
Tel *(05141) 234 50*
The raw beef roulade is what keeps attracting guests at this all-German restaurant, along with the beef and pork dishes, not forgetting the great selection of beers.

CELLE: Endtenfang €€
French **Road Map** C3
Hannoversche Strasse 55–56, 29221
Tel *(05141) 20 10* **Closed** *Mon & Tue*
Highly acclaimed restaurant Endtenfang offers fantastic French cuisine, as well as a few Mediterranean-inspired dishes. The sommelier helps select the perfect accompaniment from more than 800 wines.

CLOPPENBURG: Margaux €€
International **Road Map** B3
Lange Strasse 66, 49661
Tel *(04471) 24 84* **Closed** *Mon & Tue*
The enthusiastic young chef at friendly restaurant Margaux expertly combines different styles and ingredients to create an enjoyable menu. Highlights include lobster and scallops. Excellent wine list.

GÖTTINGEN: Gaudi €€
Mediterranean **Road Map** C4
Rote Strasse 16, 37073
Tel *(0551) 531 30 01* **Closed** *Sun*
Colourful and unorthodox, this restaurant is naturally named after the Catalan architect Antoni Gaudí. The extensive tapas selection is perfect for a light lunch. For dinner, be sure to choose one of the fish dishes.

HAMBURG: Café Paris €
French **Road Map** C2
Rathausstrasse 4, 20095
Tel *(040) 325 277 77*
Enjoy delicious French food, as well as delightful cakes and coffee, at this gorgeous former butchery with Art Nouveau tiled walls and ceiling. The bistro menu includes highlights such as oysters, steak tartare and a host of cheeses.

HAMBURG: Fischmarkt €
Seafood **Road Map** C2
Ditmar-Koel-Strasse 1, 20459
Tel *(040) 36 38 09* **Closed** *Sun*
A bustling and friendly restaurant found, as the name implies, inside the city's popular fish market hall. The ambience is warm and informal, and the helpful staff provide useful suggestions on specific dishes and wine selection. Non-fish options are also available.

The grand former wine cellars that house the dining room at Ratskeller, Bremen

For more information on types of restaurants *see page 504*

The well-stocked bar at Die Bank, Hamburg

HAMBURG: Von der Motte €
Bistro   Road Map C2
Mottenburger Twiete 14, 22765
Tel *(040) 57 24 09 62*   **Closed** *Mon*
A lovely place for a rich breakfast,
an informal lunch of salads,
sandwiches or great soups, or
afternoon cake and coffee.

HAMBURG: Au Quai €€
Mediterranean   Road Map C2
Grosse Elbstrasse 145, 22767
Tel *(040) 380 377 30*   **Closed** *Sun*
An old cold-storage depot has
been transformed into a chic,
contemporary restaurant serving
excellent fresh seafood, sushi and
sashimi, as well as meat dishes.
Book a table on the terrace for
great views across the harbour.

DK Choice

HAMBURG: Die Bank €€
Modern German Road Map C2
Hohe Bleichen 17, 20354
Tel *(040) 238 00 30*   **Closed** *Sun*
Inside a magnificent historic
former bank, this elegant dining
hall is always buzzing. The
acclaimed chef creates
unexpected variations of well-
known local dishes with an
emphasis on fresh fish and
vegetables. The wine list is
equally impressive. Expect a
business clientele for lunch
and an arty crowd for dinner.

HAMBURG: Fardi €€
Syrian   Road Map C2
Hofweg 72, 22085
Tel *(040) 36027440*
From *falafel* and lamb sausages
to *couscous* and fish dishes, Fardi
serves delicious specialities from

Syria, always keeping an eye on
quality and good service.

HAMBURG: Fischereihafen €€
Seafood   Road Map C2
Grosse Elbstrasse 143, 22767
Tel *(040) 38 18 16*
Gourmets flock to this charming
restaurant with harbour views for
the delicious seafood. The menu
includes sushi and sashimi as well
as traditional fare, such as smoked
eel fillet on scrambled eggs.

**HAMBURG: Henssler
& Henssler** €€
Fusion   Road Map C2
Grosse Elbstrasse 160, 22767
Tel *(040) 386 990 00*   **Closed** *Sun*
Run by renowned German
celebrity chef Steffen Henssler
and his father, this stylish and
well-liked restaurant serves a
fusion of Californian and
Japanese cuisine.

HAMBURG: Rach & Ritchy €€
International   Road Map C2
Holstenkamp 71, 22525
Tel *(040) 89726170*   **Closed** *Sun*
This colourful *Grillhaus* (grill
house) serves fantastic meat and
seafood dishes. The emphasis is
on grilled steaks from both the
local area and afar, prepared in a
special infrared grill oven.

HAMBURG: Tassajara €€
Vegetarian   Road Map C2
Eppendorfer Landstrasse 4, 20249
Tel *(040) 483801*   **Closed** *Sun*
Specializing in all the shades of the
vegetarian diet, from vegan to
ovo-lacto, the chef prepares meat-
free variations of European and
Asian dishes. Pleasant outdoor
patio for warmer days.

HAMBURG: Jacobs €€€
International   Road Map C2
Elbchaussee 401–403, 22609
Tel *(040) 82 25 405*   **Closed** *Mon
& Tue*
Housed in the beautiful Louis
C Jacob Hotel, this restaurant
is one of the best in the city.
International cuisine with French
influences is accompanied by a
remarkable wine selection.
Terrace dining in warm weather.

HANOVER: Clichy €€
French   Road Map C3
Weissekreuzstrasse 31, 30161
Tel *(0511) 31 24 47*   **Closed** *Sun*
A beautiful, classy restaurant
serving modern interpretations
of French cuisine, with some
German and Italian influences.
Try one of their fish specialities.

HANOVER: Die Insel €€
French/Mediterranean
                          Road Map C3
Rudolf-von-Bennigsen-Ufer 81, 30519
Tel *(0511) 83 12 14*
Enjoy picturesque views of Lake
Masch from the elegant dining
room and fantastic terrace. The
menu is full of beautifully
presented dishes with subtle
flavours and spices.

HANOVER: Gallo Nero €€
Italian   Road Map C3
*Gross-Buchholzer-Kirchweg
72B, 30655*
Tel *(0511) 546 34 34*   **Closed** *Tue;
Sat lunch*
Set in a homely barn with
exposed beams, Gallo Nero
serves top-quality Northern
Italian cuisine, made using simple
ingredients with refined sauces
and spices.

HANOVER: Hindenburg Klassik €€
German/Mediterranean
Road Map C3
Gneisenaustrasse 55, 30175
Tel *(0511) 85 85 88* **Closed** *Sun*
This relaxed, modern restaurant
is renowned for its home-made
pasta, truffles and seafood dishes.
There is a bar serving amazing
cocktails and outside seating.

HANOVER: Pier 51 €€
International **Road Map** C3
Rudolf-von-Bennigsen-Ufer 51, 30173
Tel *(0511) 807 1800*
Built on a pier jutting over Lake
Masch, Pier 51 is a stylish, award-
winning restaurant offering light
and scrumptious fish, meat and
pasta dishes. Enjoy a cocktail on
the elegant terrace afterwards.

HANOVER: Titus €€
International **Road Map** C3
Wiehbergstrasse 98, 30519
Tel *(0511) 83 55 24* **Closed** *Sun
& Mon*
Both the lunch and the dinner
menus at this welcoming living
room style restaurant list fabulous
creations such as octopus with
quail and wild garlic crumble.

KÖNIGSLUTTER: Merlin €€
International **Road Map** D3
Braunschweiger Strasse 21A, 38154
Tel *(05353) 50 30*
Fantastic seasonal cuisine –
including good meat and fish
dishes – is on offer in the bright
dining room of the Königshof
Hotel's restaurant. Friendly staff.

OLDENBURG: Kiebitzstube €€
Traditional German **Road Map** B2
Europaplatz 4–6, 26123
Tel *(0441) 80 80*
Located in the City Club
Hotel, Kiebitzstube is a formal,

classic-looking place with well-
composed set menus and a
good wine list.

OSNABRÜCK: VIla Real €€
Mediterranean **Road Map** B3
Natruper-Tor-Wall 1, 49076
Tel *(0541) 609 60* **Closed** *Sun*
An upmarket restaurant
combining fresh ingredients
with great imagination. Enjoy
country-themed dishes – lobster,
scallops or one of the other
delicious seafood choices.

STADTHAGEN: Blanke €€
Seafood **Road Map** C3
Rathauspassage 5, 31655
Tel *(05721) 817 86* **Closed** *Mon*
Blanke has been serving
wonderfully fresh seafood
since 1924. There is a vast
array of fish and shellfish
dishes on offer. The ambience
is rustic and relaxed.

**WOLFENBÜTTEL: Altes
Kaffeehaus** €€
International **Road Map** D3
Harztorwall 18, 38300
Tel *(05331) 88 80*
This elegant restaurant in the
Park Hotel offers large portions
of good-value regional fare. In
winter, sit downstairs in the
attractive wine grotto with vaulted
ceilings. There is a terrace for
dining in the summer months.

WOLFSBURG: La Fontaine €€
International **Road Map** D3
Gifhorner Strasse 25, 38442
Tel *(05362) 94 00* **Closed** *Sun
& Mon*
A charming award-winning
restaurant with a lovely terrace.
The chefs combine regional and
international produce to create
innovative dishes.

The informal terrace with superb views at Hotel Bellevue, Kiel

Schleswig-Holstein

AHRENSBURG: Berlin Milljöh €
International/
Regional German **Road Map** C2
Grosse Strasse 15, 22926
Tel *(04102) 529 19*
This friendly little tavern is a great
place to savour international and
local dishes – steak, roast beef,
herring – at affordable prices.

AHRENSBURG: Le Marron €€
International **Road Map** C2
Lübecker Strasse 10A, 22926
Tel *(04102) 23 04 00*
Situated in the Park hotel, Le
Marron is highly regarded for its
diverse cuisine and impeccable
service. The Ahrensburg fish
platter and the home-made
Lobscouse (beef or lamb stew)
are not to be missed.

BAD MALENTE: Weisser Hof €
Regional German **Road Map** D1
Vossstrasse 45, 23714
Tel *(04523) 992 50*
Sample Holstein food accompanied by German and Austrian
wines at this welcoming
restaurant. In spring, the menu
features asparagus specialities.

**FLENSBURG: Im Alten
Speicher** €€
International **Road Map** C1
Speicherlinie 44, 24937
Tel *(0461) 120 18*
This tastefully decorated restau-
rant with several dining rooms is
located in a former grain ware-
house. Enjoy generous portions
of delicious seafood and steak.

DK Choice

HUSUM: Eucken €€
International **Road Map** C1
Süderstrasse 2–10, 25813
Tel *(04841) 83 30* **Closed** *Mon
& Tue*
An intimate hideaway in the
romantic, red-brick Altes
Gymnasium hotel. This gourmet
restaurant is named after Rudolf
Eucken, a former teacher who
won the 1908 Nobel Prize for
Literature. Enjoy imaginative
international dishes with
regional influences. The
set menus combine exotic fish
dishes with veal, calf and lamb.

KIEL: Hotel Bellevue €€
Seafood **Road Map** C1
Bismarckallee 2, 24105
Tel *(0431) 389 40*
Watch ships sail by on Kiel fjord
while enjoying consistently
delicious seafood. Superb staff.

For more information on types of restaurants *see page 504*

LÜBECK: Historischer Weinkeller €
International   Road Map D2
Koberg 6–8, 23552
Tel *(0451) 762 34*
Located in the wine cellar of a
13th century hospital, this grand
restaurant has retained its historic
ambience. The extensive menu
has meat and regional fish dishes.

LÜBECK: Wullenwever   €€
Regional German   Road Map D2
Beckergrube 71, 23552
Tel *(0451) 70 43 33*   **Closed** *Sun
& Mon*
Innovative regional cuisine is
served in this elegant restaurant
with a number of communal and
private dining rooms. The chef
happily gives out his recipes.

**RATZEBURG: Hansa Kleine
Restaurant**   €€
International   Road Map D2
Schrangenstrasse 25, 23909
Tel *(04541) 864100*
The Hansa hotel's restaurant
bases its menu around seasonal
vegetables and fish. Small dining
area with a mellow atmosphere.

**SCHLESWIG: Schleswig
Strandhalle**   €€
International/German
          Road Map C1
Strandweg 2, 24837
Tel *(04621) 90 90*
A cheerful restaurant with a family
friendly atmosphere, welcoming
staff and a great range of dishes.
The dining room overlooks the
Schlei river.

SIEK: Alte Schule   €€
Modern German   Road Map D2
Hauptstrasse 44, 22962
Tel *(04107) 87 73 10*   **Closed** *Mon*
Set in an old schoolhouse, Alte
Schule serves excellent regional

dishes with French influences.
The set menus are themed
"Earth" and "Sea" to reflect the
origin of the ingredients.

SYLT: Sansibar   €€
Regional German   Road Map C1
Hörnumer Strasse 80, 25980
Tel *(04651) 96 46 46*
A boisterous hangout for
Germany's high society, this
restaurant has a rustic setting
and warm service. Fresh fish
and meat dishes attract many
visitors each day.

SYLT: Fährhaus   €€€
International   Road Map C1
Heefwai 1, 25980
Tel *(04651) 939 70*   **Closed** *Mon;
Oct–May: Sun*
This highly regarded and
award-winning restaurant
boasts incredible sea views.
The chef uses contrasting
ingredients and flavours to
create delicious dishes.

SYLT: Restaurant Jörg Müller €€€
International   Road Map C1
Süderstrasse 8, 25980
Tel *(04651) 277 88*   **Closed** *Tue*
An acclaimed restaurant
attracting guests from all
over Europe. The chef
blends regional produce in
imaginative dishes. Great
wine list, too.

UETERSEN: La Cuisine   €€
French   Road Map C2
Marktstrasse 23, 25436
Tel *(04122) 40 21 32*   **Closed** *Tue*
Gourmet cuisine from southern
France and the Mediterranean.
The fish dishes – depending on
availability – are particularly
good, and there is an excellent
selection of French wines.

Mecklenburg-
Lower Pomerania

AHLBECK: Das Ahlbeck   €€
International/Regional German
          Road Map E2
Dünenstrasse 48, 17419
Tel *(038378) 499 49 21*
With a grand classical interior and
a terrace overlooking the beach,
this hotel restaurant is a great
choice, especially in summer. On
the menu is a mix of regional
and international fare.

**BAD DOBERAN: Friedrich
Franz**   €€
International   Road Map D1
*Prof-Dr-Vogel-Strasse 16–18,
Heiligendamm, 18209*
Tel *(038203) 74 00* **Closed** *Mon & Tue*
There are just 10 tables at
this cosy gourmet restaurant in
the Grand Hotel Heiligendamm.
Dine on regional and French-
inspired cuisine with fantastic
sea views.

**DASSOW: Schlossrestaurant
1745**   €€
Mediterranean   Road Map D2
Am Park 1, 23942
Tel *(038827) 884 80*
This romantic fine-dining
restaurant in Schwansee castle
has vaulted ceilings and serves
divine food. The terrace offers
sea views, while the snug bar has
a fireplace.

**GREIFSWALD:
Fischer-Hütte**   €
Regional German   Road Map E1
An der Muhle 8, 17493
Tel *(03834) 83 96 54*
Situated on the fishing harbour,
this restaurant is *the* place to go

The homely yet elegant interior of Fährhaus, Sylt

The atmospheric interior of Scheel's, Stralsund

to enjoy freshly caught fish from the region, prepared in the northern German way. You can choose between matjes, herring, and a large variety of cod and shellfish dishes.

GÜSTROW: Kurhaus am Inselsee €
Regional German   **Road Map** D2
Heidberg 1, 18273
Tel *(03843) 85 00*
With lovely views of the lake and a very pleasant terrace, this hotel restaurant offers a local menu served to the sound of the tinkling piano.

NEUBRANDENBURG: Gasthaus Zur Lohmühle €
Traditional German   **Road Map** E2
Am Stargarder Tor, 17033
Tel *(0395) 544 28 43*
Set in a lovely half-timbered water mill dating back to the 14th century, this restaurant offers home-cooked German cuisine, including game, fish and Mecklenburg specialities.

NEUBRANDENBURG: Zur Alten Münze €€
Regional   **Road Map** E2
Burg 2–3, Burg Stargard, 17094
Tel *(039603) 274 00*   **Closed** *Mon*
The restaurant/*Weinstube* at this beautiful castle estate serves flavourful, uncomplicated regional dishes and crisp *Flammkuchen* (thin bread base topped with onions, lardons and crème fraîche). Everyone dresses up on the occasional medieval-themed nights.

ROSTOCK: Rosmarin'o Steakhouse €€
International   **Road Map** D1
Am Strande 3A, 18055
Tel *(0381) 252 30 90*
In addition to its entrecotes steaks, beef fillets, and juicy burgers, this family friendly restaurant also provides a good selection of kids' dishes.

DK Choice

ROSTOCK: Der Butt €€€
French   **Road Map** D1
Am Yachthafen 1, 18119
Tel *(0381) 504 00*   **Closed** *some Sun*
In the Hohe Düne hotel's restaurant, the award-winning chef uses regional, organic ingredients to create superb French-influenced *haute cuisine*. The two set menus offer an amazing range of delicious dishes. The walk through the glass wine cellar is a particular treat for wine connoisseurs. Reservations recommended.

RÜGEN: Brasserie Loev €€
French   **Road Map** E1
Hauptstrasse 20–22, 18609
Tel *(038393) 390*
The Loev Hotel's classic French style brasserie is enviably located on the town's main boulevard. Hearty meat and fish dishes and several mouthwatering steak choices feature on the menu.

RÜGEN: Freustil €€
Regional German   **Road Map** E1
Zeppelinstrasse 8, Ostseebad Binz,18609
Tel *(038393) 50444*   **Closed** *Mon & Tue (in winter)*
Creative cuisine inspired by the Baltic islands and their natural environment. There are lots of vegetarian options available, too.

RÜGEN: Schlossrestaurant Ralswiek €€
International   **Road Map** E1
Parkstrasse 35, 18528
Tel *(03838) 203 20*
Enjoy dishes such as *Rügener* (creamy fish soup) and roast Baltic flounder at this restaurant with an emphasis on regional and seasonal ingredients. There are also candlelit dinners and barbecue evenings.

SCHWERIN: Alt Schweriner Schankstuben €
Regional German   **Road Map** D2
Schlachterstrasse 9–13, 19055
Tel *(0385) 592 53 13*
Waitresses in traditional attire serve filling regional fish and meat dishes at this welcoming restaurant. There is a summer terrace beneath the linden trees.

SCHWERIN: Altstadtbrauhaus Zum Stadtkrug €
Regional   **Road Map** D2
Wismarsche Strasse 126, 19053
Tel *(0385) 593 66 93*
This atmospheric brewery/restaurant dating back to 1936 still brews excellent beer in huge copper tanks. There are plenty of meat-based dishes, *Schnitzel* and other regional spcialities.

SCHWERIN: Weinhaus Wöhler €
German/Italian   **Road Map** D2
Puschkinstrasse 26, 19055
Tel *(0385) 55 58 30*
This historic *Weinstube* (wine bar) built in 1819 features wood-panelled walls, stained-glass windows and an inner courtyard. The tasty food is a combination of regional and Italian fare.

STRALSUND: Brasserie Grand Café Stralsund €
French   **Map** E1
Neuer Markt 2, 18439
Tel *(03831) 703514*
A very pleasant spot for any time of the day. Large breakfast buffet in the morning, French bistro-style lunch with omelettes, baguettes, and salads, and many consistent dishes for hungrier diners.

STRALSUND: Scheel's €€
International   **Road Map** E1
Fährstrasse 23–25, 18439
Tel *(03831) 2833112*
Sophisticated restaurant in the cellar of the Scheelehof hotel. Exquisite regional meat and fish dishes are served by an enthusiastic young team of chefs.

For more information on types of restaurants *see page 504*

SHOPPING IN GERMANY

Germany is known for its regional handicrafts, high quality manufacturing, good wines and beers, as well as wonderful bread, cakes and fresh produce. Make sure you sample some of the various cakes from the *Konditorei*. Organic food and produce is also big in Germany, more so than elsewhere in Europe. All towns have the usual international brands of clothing and accessories, as do German department stores. The food markets are a real treat for seasonal local produce and are a meeting place for locals once or twice a week. The pedestrian precinct is also common in German town centres where there is usually a department store, a post office, boutiques and a weekly market, as well as cosy cafés and ice-cream parlours. Often it is considered the social hub of the town.

Opening Hours

Shops are allowed to remain open until 8pm on weekdays and Saturdays. As a general rule, they open between 9 and 10am and close at 8pm. Department stores are also open until 8pm. However, in smaller towns, shops will often close at lunchtime from 12:30 to 2:30pm and in the evening at 6:30pm.

On the last four Sundays before Christmas, shops stay open until 6pm. The only other shops opening on Sundays are those in railway stations and some of the bakeries and cake shops (though these only open for a few hours in the morning). Everything shuts on public holidays. Outside these hours the only places open are petrol stations or railway kiosks.

Dispensing chemists work on a rota so that there is always one open 24 hours in each town. Each chemist displays a sign in the window saying which one is on duty.

Methods of Payment and VAT Refunds

Cash is widely used for small items and at markets. Large department stores take credit cards, as do international chains of boutiques. Smaller shops will not accept cheques, so visitors are advised to use cash where credit cards are not taken. Cash machines are widely available, though some are located inside the bank and only accessible during opening hours.

Visitors from countries outside the EU can claim a VAT refund *(Mehrwertsteuer)* in shops displaying the Tax-Free sign. Ask for a special form to be completed and, on leaving the country, all forms have to be stamped for a refund at the border, which may be given on the spot or sent to your address at a later date. Goods bought tax-free must remain unopened in the original packaging for a valid refund at the border.

Sales

End of season goods are sold off at a discounted price during the twice-yearly sales *(Schlussverkauf)* – in summer at the end of July and in winter at the end of January. Depending on trading, discounts of 30 to 70 per cent may be given.

Food market in Munich selling fresh local farmers' produce

Green Shopping

Germans are very ecologically aware when it comes to shopping and recycling. They buy locally when it comes to basics and fresh fruit and vegetables, supporting local farmers and small businesses. Shoppers can be seen all over the country with their wicker shopping baskets at markets and local stores, and any additional bags are reusable cotton totes, rather than plastic bags. Cotton bags are also available to buy at cash desks in every supermarket or department store, and you are always asked if you need a plastic bag or whether you can do without. Organic shopping has boomed. Organic super-markets have opened up in

One of Germany's very popular organic supermarkets

every city, selling fresh and packaged food, cosmetics, clothing and household goods.

Fashion

What Germany does best in the way of clothing and accessories is casualwear, jeanswear, sportswear and outerwear. Typical brands originating in Germany are Esprit, S. Oliver, Hugo Boss, Bogner, Adidas and Puma. German fashion design is classic, purist and discreet.

Although it is not on a par with Italy or France, well-known names on the international scene include Jil Sander, Strenesse, Wolfgang Joop, Escada and the famous couturier Karl Lagerfeld. Classic department store chains are Karstadt and Galeria Kaufhof; there are also independent department stores such as Ludwig Beck in Munich. Speciality stores (Fachhandel) are still common in German towns, especially for leather goods and homeware. International chains have a high presence, though mixed brand boutiques are still thriving.

Factory outlets are another way of getting hold of German design, albeit for seconds or reduced goods. Metzingen has a high concentration – Hugo Boss was the first outlet, followed by Bogner, Jil Sander and Escada. Other stores worth trying here are Villeroy & Boch in Mettlach and Puma in Herzogenaurach.

High fashion in the KaDeWe department store in Berlin

Regional Products

There are many high quality regional products on sale throughout Germany which make ideal souvenirs. The most common are glass from Saxony and Bavaria, porcelain and ceramics from Meissen in Saxony, and gourmet products and intricate carved wooden objects, such as cuckoo clocks from the Black Forest. Traditional toys, dolls and dolls houses are common around the Nuremberg area with its long standing reputation of toy manufacturing and traditional Christmas markets. In terms of food, marzipan is a speciality of Lübeck, gingerbread comes from Nuremberg, jams from the Black Forest, cheese from Allgäu, ham from Westphalia, and each region has its own special sausages.

Traditional beer tankard

Markets

Once or twice a week, local farmers set up their stalls in town centres in the market square or a car park. They sell farm produce from the region,

Gingerbread (Lebkuchen) on sale at a market stall

as well as imported goods, such as exotic fruits. It is a colourful, lively sight full of local flavour. Flea markets are also popular all over Germany.

Food and Drink

Wine and beer are readily available at supermarkets. Specialist wine stores are also common in most towns. Germans drink a lot of sparkling water at home, often mixed with sparkling apple juice (Apfelsaftschorle), as well as beer, wine and other soft drinks. All these are bought at the wholesaler (Getränkemarkt) with a deposit on bottles and crates. Local food is best sought in the markets, though supermarkets and specialist delicatessen offer a good choice as well.

Size Chart

Women's dresses, coats and skirts

European	36	38	40	42	44	46	48
British	10	12	14	16	18	20	22
American	8	10	12	14	16	18	20

Women's shoes

European	36	37	38	39	40	41
British	3	4	5	6	7	8
American	5	6	7	8	9	10

Men's suits

European	44	46	48	50	52	54	56	58 (size)
British	34	36	38	40	42	44	46	48 (inches)
American	34	36	38	40	42	44	46	48 (inches)

Men's shirts (collar size)

European	36	38	39	41	42	43	44	45 (cm)
British	14	15	15½	16	16½	17	17½	18 (inches)
American	14	15	15½	16	16½	17	17½	18 (inches)

Men's shoes

European	39	40	41	42	43	44	45	46
British	6	7	7½	8	9	10	11	12
American	7	7½	8	8½	9½	10½	11	11½

OUTDOOR ACTIVITIES AND SPECIALIST HOLIDAYS

Germany is home to some of the most active holiday-makers in the world, so it is certainly fitting that there is an abundance of leisure activities available throughout the country. Outdoor pursuits of every kind are readily accessible, from mountain sports, such as climbing, skiing and hiking, to water sports, such as sailing, water-skiing and diving. Numerous other, slightly less adventurous activities such as golf, tennis, biking and spas are available and all are thoroughly organized and regulated. Any regional tourist office can provide you with detailed information and advice about planning your outdoor activities.

Walking in the Trettachtal valley in the Bavarian Alps

General Sporting Information

The **Deutscher Sportbund** can provide a great deal of general information about sport in Germany.

Walking and Hiking

Walking trails are everywhere in Germany, from the most demanding of Alpine trails to gentler excursions in the Erzgebirge of Saxony *(see p170)* and over the hills and mountains of the picturesque Thuringian Forest *(see pp194–5)* and Black Forest *(see pp330–31)*.

Before setting off on an expedition you should get maps showing the walking trails in your chosen region. Detailed information can be obtained from the **Deutscher Volkssportverband** (German Sports Federation) or the **Deutscher Wanderverband** (German Hiking Club). Guided walking excursions can also be organized through the local tourist offices or by contacting the **Deutscher Wanderverband**.

The **DAV Summit Club** is also a very useful source of information.

Cycling

Cycling is a great way of enjoying the German countryside. In most towns and tourist areas, bicycles can be hired for just a few days or for a week or more. A bike can easily be transported on trains and on the urban U-Bahn or S-Bahn trains for a minimal fee. You will find that most towns and cities are bike-friendly with cycle lanes and plenty of bike stands. For those interested in mountain biking and more adventurous cycling there are many great places to visit, and the **ADFC (Allgemeiner Deutscher Fahrrad-Club)** (German Cycling Federation) can supply maps, guidebooks and advice.

Water Sports

Germans enjoy all kinds of water sports. Water-skiing and wake-boarding are extremely popular, especially at lakes equipped with static towing lines, where upon payment of an hourly fee you can take as many trips skiing around the lake as you want. The **Deutscher Wasserski- und Wakeboard Verband** can provide detailed advice on locations and prices.

There are excellent sailing opportunities in the lakeland areas of Mecklenburg *(see pp472–3)*, the coastal regions and on Lake Constance *(see pp324–5)*. As is the case in most countries, you must demonstrate sailing knowledge before being allowed to hire a full-sized boat or small catamaran by showing a valid sailing licence. To find out more about sailing locations, boat hires and regulations, contact the **Deutscher Segler-Verband**. There are also plenty of opportunities for scuba diving. These are mostly centred on the lakes

Cyclists outside a traditional tavern in Rhineland-Palatinate

or the protected coastal regions. The **Verband Deutscher Sporttaucher (VDST)** (German Divers' Association) can provide up-to-date advice.

Canoe trips can be taken on many of the country's rivers – from calm and picturesque stretches of water and the canals of the Spreewald *(see p145)*, to exhilarating adventures in rapidly flowing Alpine streams that demand professional skill.

Canoeing on a stretch of the River Main in Miltenberg

Golfing on the Castle Hotel course in Kronberg, Hesse

Golf and Tennis

Over the last decade or so, golf has become hugely popular in Germany and the number of courses has increased. Golf is usually played at a club, however. You usually need to prove a certain level of golfing proficiency before you are allowed onto the course. This can be achieved by showing a membership card from a course or club back home. Alternatively, look for one of the "Pay & Play" courses, which can be found throughout the country and usually have only six holes. For further information contact the **Deutscher Golf Verband**.

Most large German towns have tennis courts that can be hired for a few hours and there is almost always a private tennis club in all the sizeable towns and cities. For more information on how to make a booking, contact the **Deutscher Tennis Bund**.

Skiing and Mountain Sports

The most renowned centre for skiing is still Garmisch-Partenkirchen *(see p284)*. Other regions such as the Black Forest *(see pp330–31)* and the Erzgebirge *(see p170)* also offer skiing. Some of the larger cities have indoor skiing halls, though they are a poor substitute for the Alps *(see pp208–9)*. Cross-country skiing is also popular, and there are many well-prepared routes. Information can be obtained from local tourist information offices or contact the **Haus des Ski, Deutscher Skiverband DSV** (German Ski Association).

The Alps are the centre of German climbing. Here you can find sport climbers mixing with Alpinists. The Allgäu region is probably the most well-known place for climbers but challenges can also be found in the Ries basin. The **Verband Deutscher Berg- und Skiführer (VDBS)** (Association of German Mountain and Ski Guides) can help you with hiring a guide.

Interesting rock formations that provide memorable challenges are not only to be found in the Alps, but throughout Germany. Places such as the Harz Mountains *(see p151)*, Fichtelgebirge and the Schwäbische Alb *(see pp318–19)* are all outstanding places for sport climbing. Also, you can find indoor climbing gyms in most cities. The **Deutscher Alpenverein (DAV) Bundes-geschäftsstelle** (German Alpine Association) can help with all your climbing requirements.

National Parks

Germany has a richly varied landscape, from mountains to coasts, and has many nature reserves, biosphere reserves and national parks. From the swamp-like Spreewald *(see p145)* to the lush forests and mountain peaks of the Bavarian Forest *(see p275)*, each park has its own spectacular natural characteristics and offers a range of different visitor services and facilities.

All parks have sign-posted trails and most have special maps for walking, biking or jogging tours. These are also excellent locations for observing and enjoying the flora and fauna of Germany's various regions. Many parks have notices posted to inform visitors about the animals and plants indigenous to the area. To find out more about the various locations and holidays available in Germany's national parks and nature reserves contact the **Verband Deutscher Naturparke** or **Europarc Deutschland**.

Mountain sports in the Schildenstein Mangfall mountains

Camping and Caravanning

During the months of July, August and September there are a great many foreign holiday-makers on Germany's autobahns heading for the camping parks. The word "camping" in Germany means primarily caravanning, not pitching a tent. Most sites are privately owned and offer a lot of extras. The majority have wash facilities, snack stands or restaurants as well as small shops and play-grounds. The more upscale parks will offer electricity as well as group activities, caravans and bungalows for hire. To find out more contact the **Deutscher Camping-Club**. Tent-pitching holidays are also possible and this is strongly regulated in order to avoid misuse of national parks. Tents are often allowed in the camping parks mentioned above and many national parks have places set aside for pitching tents and lighting campfires. **Backpacker Network Germany**. is a good resource for information about camping.

Burgenstrasse (Castle Road) scenic route following the Rhine

Spiegelau, the well-known hiking spot in the Bavarian Forest

Historic and Scenic Routes

Germany has over 50 official driving routes. These routes highlight the best features of an individual region. The following are just a few of many excellent drives. The **Burgenstrasse** (Castle Road) is over 1,000 km (620 miles) long, from Mannheim *(see p298)* through Bavaria to Prague. It offers plenty of romantic castles

and historical sites. The **Deutsche Märchenstrasse** (Fairytale Route) covers more than 600 km (370 miles) from Bremen *(see pp434–7)* to Hanau *(see p381)*, linking more than 70 towns and villages associated with the Brothers Grimm and the realm of fairytales, sagas, myths and legends. The **Deutsche Weinstrasse**. (Wine Route) *(see p351)* is 85 km (52 miles) and runs from Bad Dürkheim to Bad Berzabern. The **Touristik Arbeitsgemeinschaft Romantische Strasse** (Romantic Road) is Germany's most famous and popular tourist route. It runs for 350 km (217 miles) through a rich and varied landscape along the River Main to the Alps. The **Tourismusverband Ruppiner Land "Deutsche Tonstrasse"** (Ceramics Route) is a circular route running 215 km (134 miles) through the Ruppiner Land area of northern Brandenburg *(see pp134–5)*.

Specialist Holidays

Language tours offer you the chance to immerse yourself in German culture. Living arrangements range from homes to hotels and hostels, depending upon budget. The **Goethe Institut** is the best place for information on this type of holiday.

Wine holidays are becoming more commonplace because German wines are coming back into popularity. Most winemakers offer tastings and small meals,

but some also offer packaged holidays. To find out more about wine holidays contact **Deutsches Weininstitut GmbH** or **Viniversität – Die Weinschule GmbH**.

There are equestrian centres in many parts of Germany where visitors can ride under supervision or head off on their own. Specialized weekends or week-long riding vacations are available throughout Germany. More information can be obtained from the **Deutsche Reiterliche Vereinigung**.

Spa Vacations

Germany has more than 350 health and spa resorts, as well as numerous hotels and holiday centres, where your wellbeing is the top priority. Cultural delights, culinary experiences, sights of historical importance and physical activites all form part of the German philosophy of looking after yourself, known as "Das Wellness". Health and fitness breaks are available all year round and facilities vary from the minimalist ultra-modern to marble and gold imperial luxury, with everything in between. Each region has something special to offer, though some of the most well-known spas are in the Black Forest *(see pp330–31)*, on the East Frisian Islands *(see p432)* and in Schleswig-Holstein *(see pp459–69)*. The **Deutscher Heilbäder-verband** can help you find the right spa and holiday package.

Wine from the Mosel

DIRECTORY

General Sporting Information

Deutscher Sportbund
Siemensstrasse 14,
63263 Neu-Isenburg.
Tel (069) 67 000.
W dosb.de

Walking and Hiking

DAV Summit Club
Am Perlacher Forst 186,
81545 München.
Tel (089) 64 24 01 94.
W dav-summit-club.de

Deutscher Volks-sportverband
Fabrikstrasse 8,
84503 Altötting.
Tel (08671) 963 10.
W dvv-wandern.de

Deutscher Wanderverband
Wilhelmshöher Allee 157–159, 34121 Kassel.
Tel (0561) 938 730.
W wanderverband.de

Cycling

ADFC (Allgemeiner Deutscher Fahrrad-Club)
Grünenstrasse 120,
28199 Bremen.
Tel (0421) 34 62 90.
W adfc.de

Water Sports

Deutscher Segler-Verband
Gründgensstrasse 10,
22309 Hamburg.
Tel (040) 632 00 90.
W dsv.org

Deutscher Wasserski-und Wakeboard Verband
Am Campingpark 10,
49597 Rieste.
Tel (5464) 969 11 66.
W wasserski-online.de

Verband Deutscher Sporttaucher (VDST)
Bundesgeschäftsstelle,
Berliner Str. 312,
63067 Offenbach.
Tel (069) 981 90 20.
W vdst.de

Inline Skating

Experts in Speed
Thalkirchner Str. 101,
81371 München.
Tel (089) 720 15 150.
W experts-in-speed.de

Golf and Tennis

Deutscher Golf Verband
Postfach 21 06,
65189 Wiesbaden.
Tel (0611) 99 02 00
W golf.de/dgv

Deutscher Tennis Bund
Hallerstrasse 89,
20149 Hamburg.
Tel (040) 41 17 80.
W dtb-tennis.de

Skiing and Mountain Sports

Deutscher Alpenverein (DAV) Bundesgeschäfts-stelle
Von-Kahr-Strasse 2–4,
80997 München.
Tel (089) 14 00 30.
W alpenverein.de

Haus des Ski, Deutscher Skiverband DSV
Am Erwin-Himmelseher-Platz Hubertusstrasse 1,
82152 Planegg.
Tel (089) 85 79 00.
W deutscherskiverband.de

Verband Deutscher Berg- und Skiführer (VDBS)
Fraunhoferstrasse 4,
82377 Penzberg.
Tel (08856) 936 09 13.
W bergfuehrer-verband.de

National Parks

Europarc Deutschland
Pfalzburger Strasse 43/44,
10717 Berlin.
Tel (030) 288 788 20.
W europarc-deutschland.de

Verband Deutscher Naturparke
Holbeinstrasse 12,
53175 Bonn.
Tel (0228) 921 28 60
W naturparke.de

Camping and Caravanning

Backpacker Network Germany
Senefelder Strasse 8,
10437 Berlin.
Tel (0177) 362 82 41.
W german-hostels.de

Deutscher Camping-Club
Mandlstrasse 28,
80802 München.
Tel (089) 380 14 20.
W camping-club.de

Historic and Scenic Routes

Burgenstrasse
(Castle Road) Allee 28,
74072 Heilbronn.
Tel (07131) 973 50 10.
W burgenstrasse.de

Deutsche Märchenstrasse
(Fairytale Route)
Kurfürstenstrasse 9,
34117 Kassel.
Tel (0561) 920 479 10
W deutsche-maerchenstrasse.de

Deutsche Weinstrasse (Wine Route)
Martin-Luther-Strasse 69,
67433 Neustadt an der Weinstraße.
Tel (06321) 91 23 33.
W deutsche-weinstrasse.de

Tourismusverband Ruppiner Land "Deutsche Tonstrasse" (Ceramics Route)
Fischbänkenstr. 8,
16816 Neuruppin.
Tel (03391) 65 96 30.
W deutscheton strasse.de

Touristik Arbeitsgemeinschaft Romantische Strasse (Romantic Road)
Segringer Strasse 19,
91550 Dinkelsbühl.
Tel (09851) 55 13 87.
W romantische strasse.de

Specialist Holidays

Deutsche Reiterliche Vereinigung
Freiherr von Langen-Strasse 13, 48231 Warendorf.
Tel (025 81) 636 20.
W pferd-aktuell.de

Deutsches Weininstitut GmbH
Gutenbergplatz 3–5,
55116 Mainz.
Tel (06131) 282 90.
W deutscheweine.de

Goethe Institut
Dachauer Strasse 122,
80637 München.
(Postal address: P.O. Box 19 04 19, 80604 München).
Tel (089) 15 92 10.
W goethe.de
50 Princes Gate, Exhibition Road, London SW7 2PH.
Tel (020) 7596 4000
or (020) 7594 0240.

Viniversität – Die Weinschule GmbH
Bilker Allee 49,
40219 Düsseldorf.
Tel (0211) 390 020.
W viniversitaet.de

Spa Vacations

Deutscher Heilbäderverband
Charlottenstrasse 13,
10969 Berlin.
Tel (030) 24 63 69 20.

SURVIVAL GUIDE

Bus

PRACTICAL INFORMATION

Germany is a country that is particularly well prepared to receive visitors. Every town, large or small, has a helpful tourist information centre that can assist with finding accommodation and provide information about local restaurants, attractions and activities. Virtually all the larger cities have websites with up-to-date information on hotels, restaurants, museums and historic monuments. The country is served by an excellent public transport system and a first-rate network of roads and motorways, which makes getting around quick and easy. There is a plentiful supply of comfortable, affordable tourist accommodation in Germany, but it is worth bearing in mind that hotels can become booked up quickly during the festivals and fairs that occur throughout the year in different parts of the country.

When to Go

In Germany, a pleasant vacation can be enjoyed at any time of the year. If you are planning to visit cities and historic monuments, however, it is best to come in the spring or early autumn. July and August are ideal for a restful holiday by the sea, in the lake districts or in the mountains. Arriving in Bavaria in the last half of September offers the chance to take part in Oktoberfest. In December, Christmas markets all over the country enchant shoppers with their old-world charm, while later in the winter, skiing is a popular pursuit in the Black Forest, the Alps, and the Harz Mountains.

Road traffic increases during school holidays, the dates of which may vary between states. Roads can also be quite busy at the start of the "long weekends" that occur at Easter, Whitsun, and around other national holidays.

Visas and Passports

Citizens of EU countries can enter Germany with a national identity card. Visitors from the UK, Ireland, the US, Canada, Australia and New Zealand will need a full passport. Non-EU citizens may visit Germany for up to 3 months without a visa; after that a residence permit (Aufenthaltserlaubnis) is required. For more information and to check the visa requirements visitors should consult the website of their German embassy. Visitors from South Africa need to obtain a valid visa before entering Germany for any length of stay.

Germany is one of the 25 European countries that are part of the Schengen Agreement for shared border control. Once you enter a Schengen country, you may travel continuously between the member countries for up to 90 days. Non-EU visitors require a passport when entering the Schengen Zone and a Schengen visa is required for visitors from most Asian and African states.

Customs Regulations

German regulations prohibit importation of drugs, animals and exotic plants that are under special protection. Importation of cigarettes is also regulated. An adult may bring in 200 cigarettes or 50 cigars, and 250g (9oz) of tobacco, as well as one litre of spirits and two litres of wine. You can also import up to 5 kg (11 lb) of food, but restrictions apply to meat and dairy products. Beyond these limits, goods must be cleared by Customs when entering the country.

Tourist Information

Tourist information centres can be found in all German cities, as well as most of the larger towns. They provide information on accommodation, addresses and opening hours of historic monuments and museums, cruises, organized excursions and city tours, as well as brochures covering the most important tourist information. They sell useful guidebooks, maps and postcards and may be able to find and book hotel rooms.

The embassies of most countries, including the UK and US, are located in Berlin. Consulates are also based in other major German cities.

Oktoberfest celebrations at the Theresienwiese, Munich

◄ A modern train station in Germany

Tourist information centre in Berlin

Admission Prices

Admission to museums and monuments can be expensive and prices vary. Entry to a small regional museum, for example, may cost as little as €2–5, a large state-run museum around €5–12, while a private venue may charge up to €14. Admission to smaller churches is usually free, but a fee may be charged in some cathedrals, monastic churches and church treasuries.

In many cases, discounted tickets are available for students, seniors and families. Combination tickets, offering entry to multiple sites, are often good value (see p544).

Opening Hours

Opening hours of shops, offices, and other businesses depend on the size of the town. In larger cities, typical opening hours are from 9am–6pm, while large stores are open until 8pm. Banks have shorter hours in smaller towns (see p548). Trading is limited on Saturdays, especially in rural areas and on Sundays and public holidays; only airport and train station shops are open (see pp534–5).

Museums in Germany are generally open from 9am–6pm, in smaller towns from 10am to 4 or 5pm. Some museums open later, on Wednesdays or Thursdays, while on Mondays most museums tend to be closed. Larger churches in major cities are accessible to tourists throughout the day. In smaller places, visits may require prior arrangements.

Language

Although German is spoken nationwide, many areas have dialects that are virtually incomprehensible, even to those from neighbouring regions. Travellers can usually be understood in Germany by speaking English, particularly in larger cities and in places that are frequented by tourists.

Social Customs and Etiquette

Although generally friendly, Germans tend to be very honest and direct, sometimes to the point of seeming rude. However, most people, particularly the older generation, attach great importance to courteous behaviour. You constantly hear *"Guten Tag"* when entering a shop, and *"Auf Wiedersehen"* – or the more youthful *"Tschüss"* – when leaving. Germans are also very punctual and consider even a small delay to be impolite. Arriving slightly early for an engagement is regarded as courteous.

Among younger Germans, however, ideas of politeness are changing. Older people and women are shown less respect and are no longer automatically offered seats on public transport. Another change is the tolerance shown towards unruly children by parents and other adults.

The German dress code, except in a work environment and among the older generation, is rather casual. Formal dress is required in only the most upmarket restaurants. Nudity in parks and at beaches may shock some visitors.

Most traffic rules are strictly observed. Crossing the street on a red light, even if the road is deserted, is considered an offence and can result in an official reprimand.

Accessibility of Public Conveniences

Public toilets (often automatic cubicles) can usually be found without much difficulty in large cities. Instructions on how to use these facilities are given in several languages on the doors. Public toilets can also be found in museums, cafés, restaurants and department stores. Men's toilets are marked *Herren* and ladies' *Damen* or *Frauen*.

Taxes and Tipping

There are no standard rates for tipping in Germany, but taxi drivers are usually tipped €1–2. Service and tax is generally included on restaurant bills, but it is usual to leave a tip of about 10 per cent of the bill.

Exterior of Museum Brandhorst in Munich *(see p224)*

Kids' Kingdom at the Deutsches Museum in Munich *(see pp232–3)*

Travellers with Special Needs

Germany is relatively well prepared to receive disabled travellers. Large museums and important historic monuments have ramps or lifts for wheelchair access and public toilet facilities are designed to accomodate disabled travellers. The majority of hotels are well equipped for disabled travellers *(see p491)*. A large proportion of public transport vehicles have been adapted for wheelchair users. Public transport companies are also making efforts to accommodate visually impaired people.

A disabled person may, however, still have problems in gaining access to some places, such as the smaller museums, certain historic monuments, and toilets in restaurants, which are often located in the cellar.

Contact **NatKo** for detailed information on travelling with special needs in Germany. Companies such as **Directions Unlimited** (in the US) and **Holiday Care** (in the UK) also offer useful information and advice for disabled travellers.

Travelling with Children

Families travelling in Germany benefit from a range of cost-cutting discounts. The majority of hotels and guesthouses offer discounts for children *(see p491)*. Discounts or even free travel for the youngest children are available on various forms of transport and there are

similar concessions in most museums. In many German cities it is possible to purchase family tickets that provide substantial discounts on fares and admission fees.

Restaurants can usually provide a high chair for toddlers and offer a special *Kindermenu* (children's menu) with smaller portions. Public toilets in railway stations, airports and motorway service stations, as well as in many museums and stores, usually offer a separate facility for mothers and babies.

An ISIC card (international student identity card)

Gay and Lesbian Travellers

Germans have a very relaxed and welcoming attitude toward gay travellers, especially in Berlin, Cologne, Hamburg, Munich, and Frankfurt, where

there is a lively gay scene with a variety of hotels, clubs and bars. Gay pride is celebrated nationwide with Christopher Street Day parades and festivals throughout June and July. The **National Tourist Office** offers detailed information on gay cultural events nationwide.

Travelling on a Budget

You can save on airfares by travelling to Germany off-season and flying with a low-cost carrier *(see p552)*. Cheap hostels can be found in most German cities, providing an option that is increasingly popular with families *(see p490)*. For eating out, try one of the many cheap eateries *(Imbiss),* for German *Wurst* or ethnic food. Some of the larger German cities sell city cards that double as public transport passes and discount cards at museums and events. City cards can be purchased at tourist offices, many hotels, and public transport ticket counters. For several cities, the cards can also be bought online before travel.

For students, an **International Student Identity Card** (ISIC) entitles the holder to a 50 per cent discount to many museums and reductions on some theatre and cinema tickets. It also allows students to get discounts on hostel prices, air tickets, rental cars and bicycles.

Christopher Street Day celebrations, Berlin

Time

Germany uses Central European Time (GMT plus one hour). Clocks move forward one hour on the last Sunday in March and back on the last Sunday in October.

Electricity

UK 220V appliances can be used with an adaptor; US 110V appliances will also need a transformer.

Responsible Tourism

Germany is one of the most environmentally aware countries in Europe, with 17 per cent of the energy used coming from renewable sources. Agrotourism is gaining popularity as a cost effective holiday option (see p490), and bicycle tours and walking holidays are increasingly common (see p559). An eco-friendly alternative to staying in a hotel is camping; there are over 2,000 camping sites throughout Germany (see p491).

Hostels and hotels are becoming increasingly aware of environmental issues and encourage the responsible use of resources. German eco-tour operator **Viabono** offers a search engine for eco-hotels and lodges across Germany. The **Blaue Schwalbe** ("Blue Swallow") is an eco-award given to hotels meeting certain sustainability standards and offering organic local food. The **Verträglich Reisen** website provides a full list of accredited

hotels. In Bavaria, environmentally friendly hotels are awarded the *Umweltsiegel* (eco-label).

Organic and locally grown produce is clearly labelled and widely available at most shops and supermarkets. Many towns hold regular markets selling organic and traditional produce, allowing visitors to give back to the local community.

Information on local green tourism activities and initiatives can be found in tourist offices.

Stall at Oktomarkt, an organic market in Kollwitzplatz, Berlin

DIRECTORY

Embassies

Australia
Wallstrasse 76–79,
10179 Berlin.
Tel (030) 880 08 80.
Fax (030) 880 08 8-210.
w germany.embassy.gov.au

Canada
Leipziger Platz 17,
10117 Berlin.
Tel (030) 20 31 20.
Fax (030) 20 31 25 90.
w kanada-info.de

Republic of Ireland
Jägerstr. 51,
10117 Berlin.
Tel (030) 22 07 20.
Fax (030) 22 07 22 99.
w embassyofireland.de

New Zealand
Friedrichstrasse 60,
10117 Berlin.
Tel (030) 20 62 10.
Fax (030) 20 62 11 14.
w nzembassy.com

South Africa
Tiergartenstrasse 18,
10785 Berlin.
Tel (030) 22 07 30.
Fax (030) 22 07 31 90
w suedafrika.org

United Kingdom
Embassy: Wilhelmstrasse
70, 10117 Berlin.
Tel (030) 20 45 70.
Fax (030) 20 45 75 49.
w britische botschaft.de
Consulate: Möhlstrasse 5,
81675 München.
Tel (089) 21 10 90.

United States of America
Embassy: Pariser Platz 2,
10117 Berlin.
Tel (030) 8 30 50.
Fax (030) 83 05 10 50.
w usembassy.de
Consulates:
Clayallee 170,
40191 Berlin.
Tel (030) 8 30 50.

Königinstrasse 5,
80539 Munich.
Tel (089) 288 80.
Giessener Str. 30,
60435 Frankfurt am Main.
Tel (069) 7535-0.

Tourist Offices

National Tourist Office
PO Box 2695, London,
W1A 3TN, UK.
Tel (020) 7317 0908.
w germany-tourism.de

Berlin Tourist Information
Tel (030) 25 00 23 33.
w visitberlin.de/en

Travellers with Special Needs

Directions Unlimited
123 Green Lane, Bedford
Hills, NY 10507, USA.
Tel (800) 533 53 43.

Holiday Care
Tel 0845 124 9971.
w tourismforall.org.uk

NatKo e.V. (Nationale Koordinationsstelle Tourismus für Alle)
Düsseldorf. **Tel** (0211) 336
80 01. w natko.de

Gay and Lesbian Travellers

w gay-web.de
w gay.de/

Travelling on a Budget

ISIC Card
w isic.org

Responsible Tourism

Blaue Schwalbe/ Verträglich Reisen
w vertraeglich-reisen.de

Viabono
Tel (02205) 919 83 50.
w viabono.de

Security and Health

Germany is a safe place for visitors, but it is always a good idea to take sensible precautions especially in larger towns and cities. Extra caution should be taken against pickpockets – particularly on public transport or in busy tourist areas. It is worth using a money belt or other means of hiding your money and documents. Taking out medical insurance cover is always advisable when travelling abroad, but for minor health problems that do not require the services of a doctor, pharmacists are a good and easily accessible source of assistance.

Policeman and policewoman

Police

German police can be easily identified by their blue uniforms, except in Bavaria and the Saarland where the traditional green uniforms are still worn. Investigators of criminal offences, *Kriminalpolizei*, are generally dressed in plain clothes. They will produce their identification and badge as necessary.

Municiple officers and traffic wardens also wear the navy-blue uniforms. They are in charge of minor offences such as illegal parking, crossing at a red light, littering or riding a bicycle on the sidewalk and are entitled to check documents and issue fines.

To report a crime, it is necessary to go to a local police station (*Polizeiabschnitt*) and, in event of theft, get a *Bericht*, the report required by insurance. In the case of a traffic accident or an emergency, call 110 or 112.

What to Be Aware of

Violent crime is very rare in Germany and the law is enforced energetically. The most serious threat for a tourist is always the pickpocket. These thieves tend to prowl in crowded places, such as railway platforms, train carriages and buses. They also frequent popular tourist sights and any events where large groups of people are likely to gather. It is best to leave your valuable items and documents in the hotel safe. Park your car in the hotel car park whenever possible and never leave valuable items in the vehicle, especially if it has to be left in the street overnight. Should you become the victim of a crime, the **Crime Victim Hotline** offers a counselling service.

Buying counterfeit items like cigarettes from street vendors is an offence and should be avoided.

Although alcohol is sold at every fuel station, drinking and driving is not a good idea and it is against the law to drive with a blood alcohol level over 50mg/dl, the equivalent of one beer.

It is illegal to use your mobile phone while driving or even sitting in a car with the engine running; doing so can result in a fine of €40.

Be aware of cyclists. They tend to be everywhere but the autobahn, and have right of way in dedicated bike lanes.

A woman travelling on her own will not surprise anyone in Germany and only the usual safety precautions need be taken. However, it is best to avoid certain areas in towns where there is a lively nightlife, particularly in large cities – for example, the Reeperbahn in Hamburg. Hitchhiking is quite popular in Germany, but a better option for single women may be to use the services of *Mitfahr-zentrale (see p557)*.

In an Emergency

The national emergency number for medical assistance and the fire brigade is 112. In a medical emergency, call an ambulance, which will take you to the nearest emergency room (*Rettungsstelle*). In large hotels, medical care for minor ailments can often be provided on the premises.

If a road accident or breakdown occurs call for help on your mobile phone (110 or 112 for police and ambulance). Several break-down companies offer roadside assistance *(see p557)*. If your car breaks down in the middle of nowhere, you can call 0800 6 683 663 on your mobile phone. This automobile emergency service is equipped to track you down. If you witness a crime on the platform of an under-ground or commuter railway, a designated emergency alarm button can be used to summon assistance. Special alarm buttons, within small red boxes, also provide a direct connection with the fire brigade (*Feuerwehr*). These alarm buttons are easy to find, usually located in prominent positions on the streets and in large department stores.

In an emergency, consulate officials can help travellers with legal or other advice, locate a translator, or contact family members. In some circumstances they may be able to lend money for a ticket home *(see p545)*.

Alarm button for the fire brigade

Fire engine from the Berlin fire brigade

Ambulance of the paramedic
rescue services

Traditionally coloured white and blue
police car

Lost and Stolen Property

Before leaving home it is
advisable to take out an insurance policy to cover property
against loss or theft. Theft
and burglaries must be
reported to the police
immediately and a certificate
obtained to confirm that the
loss has been reported; this is
needed if an insurance claim
is submitted.

If property has been lost,
it is worth checking at a lost
property office (Fundbüro).
These exist in every German
city. The **Deutsche Bahn** has
its own lost property offices,
as do transport systems in
individual towns.

In the event of a lost or stolen
mobile phone, inform the
service provider immediately to
have the account locked and
avoid unwanted charges on
your bill. They may also be able
to trace the phone. You should
also report a theft to the
nearest police station. The
police will need the phone's

identification number
(IMEI). To replace lost or
stolen passports, visit your
local consulate who can
issue a replacement. Keep
a photocopy of your pass-
port/ID in your luggage to
reduce hassle if it gets lost
or stolen.

Hospitals and Pharmacies

For a serious illness or
injury, visit a hospital
(Krankenhaus) or call an
ambulance. All emergency
rooms are part of the
public health system, so
your EHIC or supplemen-
tary insurance will cover
you. The symbol for
hospitals is a red cross on
white background.

Pharmacies in Germany
are indicated by a red
stylized letter "A" for
Apotheke and are usually
open 8am–6pm; in small
towns they may close
1–3pm. In larger towns
there is always a rota and
this is clearly displayed in the
window of each pharmacy
with a note of addresses.
Information on rota pharmacies
may also be obtained from
tourist offices, local newspapers
or the internet.

Minor Hazards

Germany poses few serious
health hazards for travellers.
Tap water is safe to drink
throughout the country,
there are no prevalent
diseases, and the country is

Entrance to a pharmacy in Heidelberg

DIRECTORY

Emergency Services

Crime Victim Hotline
Tel 01803 343434.
Tel 0800 1 11 01 11
(Telephone counselling).

Fire Brigade and Medical Emergency
Tel 112.

Police
Tel 110 or 112.

Automobile Rescue Services

Notruf des Bundesverbands der Autoversicherer
Tel 0800 6 683 663.

Lost Property

Deutsche Bahn (Rail)
Lost and Found Office
Tel 0180 699 66 33.

Hospitals and Pharmacies

🆆 med-kolleg.de
🆆 apotheken.de (for nearest after-hours pharmacy)
🆆 zahnnotdienst.de (after-hours dentist search)

well served with hospitals
and pharmacies. No vaccin-
ations are required when
entering Germany.
However, ticks are prevalent
in forests and rural areas,
especially during summer, and
visitors should seek medical
advice if bitten.

Health Insurance

Citizens of countries within
the European Union with a
European Health Insurance
Card (EHIC) are entitled to free
medical care in Germany. It is
also advisable to take out some
form of supplementary health
insurance, as some services,
such as repatriation costs, are
not covered.

If plans include sporting
activities, particularly dangerous
sports, make sure the policy
covers rescue services (for
example, mountain rescue).
This type of insurance is usually
much more expensive.

Banking and Local Currency

Debit and credit cards are widely accepted in Germany, but it is still advisable to travel with some cash. Many of the smaller shops, cafés, and bars, do not accept credit cards. Cash can be easily obtained from automatic cash points (ATMs), and bank branches are easy to find. Bureaux de change are located at airports and larger railway stations.

Banks and Bureaux de Change

There are no limits on the amount of foreign currency that can be brought into the country and credit and debit cards are accepted in most of the larger hotels, restaurants and shops. Foreign currency can be exchanged in a bank or exchange bureau (*Wechselstube*). Both offer a similar rate, but usually charge a commission. Be sure to check commission rates and confirm how much you will have to pay before beginning a transaction. Money can also be changed at special ATMs. Some hotel reception desks will change cash, but the exchange rate may be poor.

Most banks are open Monday–Friday 9am–5pm, with a break for lunch, and once a week they are open until 6pm. Opening hours may be a little longer in larger cities and some of the larger branches open until 1pm on Saturdays. It is often more convenient to take advantage of the services offered by branches located in airports and larger railway stations as soon as you arrive.

Cash point machine (*Geldautomat*)

Travellers' cheques are best purchased in euro denominations and can be used to pay for goods and services or hotel bills, but they are not always accepted. It is often better to pay by cash or card.

For wiring money, contact a Western Union branch in a major city. If you hold a bank-issued **Visa** or **MasterCard** credit card, you can transfer money through the **Western Union Bank** website.

For all financial transactions in Germany, decimals are indicated by a comma and thousands by a point.

ATMs

The most convenient way to get cash is at an ATM (*Geldautomat*), found on main streets and in shopping centres, airports and railway stations. Most have multilingual instructions or are self-explanatory and carry logos showing which cards are accepted.

Costs for cash withdrawals vary, so contact your bank for advice before traveling, to avoid any high fees.

Debit and Credit Cards

In Germany, the most popular cards are **Maestro** debit cards. **Visa**, **MasterCard** and **American Express** are widely accepted; **Diner's Club** a little less so. Always check that credit or debit cards are an acceptable method of payment before making a purchase, and watch for minimum charges in restaurants and cafés.

Lost credit cards or travellers' cheques should be reported immediately to the issuing bank or company.

DIRECTORY

Lost Credit Cards/ Travellers' Cheques

All Cards
Tel 116 116
(nationwide free number).

American Express
Tel (069) 97 97 20 00.

Barclaycard
Tel (040) 89 09 98 77.

Diner's Club
Tel (069) 90 01 50 14.

EC/Maestro and Bank Cards
Tel 01805 021021.

MasterCard
Tel 0800 819 10 40.

VISA
Tel 0800 811 8440.

Wiring Money

Western Union Bank
Tel 0800 181 1797
(free hotline).
Tel (069) 85 09 83 73 (English).
w westernunionbank.com

A branch of Sparkasse branch, Berlin

Currency

The euro (€) is the common currency of the European Union. It went into general circulation on 1 January 2002. Germany was one of the 12 original countries taking the euro; the Deutschmark was phased out by mid-2002. EU members using the euro as sole official currency are known as the Eurozone.

Euro notes are identical throughout the Eurozone countries, each one including designs of fictional architectural structures and monuments. The coins, however, have one side identical (the value side), and one side with an image unique to each country. Both notes and coins are accepted in all of the participating EU countries (not all European nations belong to the Eurozone).

Euro Bank Notes

Euro bank notes have seven denominations. The €5 note (grey in colour) is the smallest, followed by the €10 note (red), €20 note (blue), €50 note (orange), €100 note (green), €200 note (yellow) and €500 note (purple). All notes show the stars of the European Union.

5 euros

10 euros

20 euros

50 euros

100 euros

200 euros

500 euros

2 euros

1 euro

50 cents

20 cents

10 cents

Coins

The euro has eight coin denominations: €2 and €1; 50 cents, 20 cents, 10 cents, 5 cents, 2 cents and 1 cent. The €2 and €1 coins are both silver and gold in colour. The 50-, 20- and 10-cent coins are gold. The 5-, 2- and 1-cent coins are bronze.

5 cents

2 cents

1 cent

Communications and Media

Postal and telecommunications services in Germany work very efficiently. Though it may be necessary to queue for a few minutes for service, letters and postcards are usually delivered within the country in 24 hours. Public phones are simple to use, many with foreign language instructions, but they are becoming rarer due to the popularity of mobile phones. The distinctive yellow mail-boxes are a common sight.

Telekom phones at Frankfurt Hauptbahnhof

International and Local Telephone Calls

Public telephones are serviced by **Deutsche Telekom** and can still be found in busy places like railway stations and malls. Most phones will only accept telephone cards, which can be purchased at Telekom shops, fuel stations and newsstands. Some older telephones however, are coin-operated and require a minimum deposit, which is the cost of a single local call. Travellers can also purchase an international phone card, which is valid in several countries and can be used when calling from a public telephone, a mobile or a hotel phone. The cards offer low rates on calls abroad and have a prepaid balance – ask to see call rates before purchase.

Call shops are common in all major German cities and provide an economical way to make international calls. They usually charge a small initial fee, and then offer a low rate per minute, which is paid at the end of the call. These shops also sell international phone cards and often double as internet cafés.

Depending on the time and day, different tariffs apply to local, intercity and international calls. The most expensive period to make a call is between 7am and 6pm. Calls cost less between 6pm and 9pm, and later in the evening they are even cheaper. Likewise, calls are cheaper on weekends than on weekdays.

Mobile Phones

Mobile phone coverage is generally good throughout the country, although the signal may be weaker in more remote areas. German mobile phones use standard European frequencies, so UK phones will work provided they have a roaming facility enabled. North American phones will only operate in Germany if they are tri- or quad-band.

Making and receiving calls outside your home country can be very expensive and travellers should check roaming charges before travel. If you are planning to use your phone frequently, it may be economical to buy a local SIM card with a German telephone number from a local provider such as **Base**. Aldi and Lidl supermarkets across Germany offer various budget prepaid SIM-card packages that are cheap to buy and easy to recharge with vouchers from these shops. Check with your service provider to ensure your phone is SIM-unlocked and compatible with local technology. Anti-terrorism laws have made it more complicated for non-residents to buy a SIM card, as travellers will need a valid ID and a German address (a hotel address should work).

If your phone is Wi-Fi capable, you can save on roaming costs by locating a free Wi-Fi (wireless internet) network and making calls with **Skype**. Bear in mind that as useful as a smartphone can be overseas, all data use will be charged at a higher rate.

It is wise to carry your mobile provider's contact details so you can deactivate your card if your phone is lost or stolen.

Internet and Email

Many hotels include internet access in their room rates, but this varies, so be sure to check in advance. Some hotels have internet terminals allowing guests to check emails and go online for free.

Useful Telephone Numbers

- Directory enquiries, national numbers: 11 833 or 11 837 (English service).
- National telephone directory (White Pages): www.dastelefonbuch.de
- Directory enquiries, international numbers: 11 834.
- International calls: Dial 00, wait for dialling tone, then dial country code, area code + number, omitting first 0.
- Country codes: UK 44; Eire 353; Canada and US 1; Australia 61; South Africa 27; New Zealand 64.

Internet cafés, where online access can be obtained for a small fee (typically €1–2 per hour), can be found in most towns and cities.

Wi-Fi access is increasingly available in Germany. Expect to find Wi-Fi at many cafés, libraries, hostels and hotels. Most networks are password-protected and an access code is required, although it is often provided free of charge to the customer. Free Wi-Fi hotspots are located in public areas around most larger towns and cities. It is best to refrain from doing any torrent downloads in Germany that may be legal in your home country, as you may be held liable for high fines.

A kiosk selling newspapers and cigarettes

Postal Services

Dedicated Deutsche Post offices have virtually disappeared and postal services are instead offered by **Postbank Finanzcenter**, newsstands and some other shops, including selected supermarkets. These retailers also sell phone cards, postcards and mailing supplies.

Stamps are sometimes sold with postcards, or can be bought from vending machines. It costs €0.80 to send a postcard or small letter anywhere abroad. When posting a letter in a mail-box, be aware that some boxes have two slots – one for

Postbank logo

Information plaque indicating the collection times

Opening for local letters

Opening for long-distance mail

The distinctive yellow mail-box of Germany's official postal service

local post only, the other for all other destinations.

For quick delivery of a package, look for one of the courier services. **DHL** is the national parcel delivery service. Packages can be sent via DHL from post offices or DHL-affiliated retailers. **Federal Express** or **UPS** are also available, but they are more business-oriented.

Newspapers and Magazines

Every city or state has its own newspapers and listings magazines. In Berlin the most widely read newspapers are *Berliner Zeitung*, *Der Tagesspiegel* and *Berliner Morgenpost*. In southern Germany it is *Süddeutsche Zeitung*. Popular national newspapers include *Frankfurter Allgemeine Zeitung* and *Bild*. *Der Spiegel*, Germany's leading news magazine, has an English-language version online. Major German cities have a listings magazine called *PRINZ* – where *PRINZ* is not available, ask for the *Stadtmagazin*.

Foreign language publications, such as the *International New York Times*, the *Guardian*, *Le Monde*, *El País*, and *Corriere della Sera*, are available at kiosks, railway stations and airports.

Television and Radio

German television is exclusively in German – all foreign movies are dubbed rather than subtitled. Non-German broadcasts are hard to find, but hotels usually provide some English-language

channels, such as *BBC World*, *CNN* and *NBC Super Channel*.

German sports channels often show soccer highlights, and major sporting events can be watched at most sports bars. Very little English-language radio is available terrestrially, although *BBC World* and *NPR* can be picked up in most parts of Germany.

DIRECTORY

International and Local Calls

Deutsche Telekom
W telekom.com

Mobile Phones

BASE
W base.de

Skype
W skype.com

Internet and Email

Internet cafés
W online-cafes.net

Wi-Fi hotspots
W hotspot-locations.de

Postal Services

DHL Express
Tel (0)1805 34 53 001 (national).
Tel (0)1805 34 53 003 (international).
W dhl.de

FedEx
Tel (01806) 111 800.
W fedex.de

Postbank Finanzcenter
W post.de

UPS
Tel (0)1805 882 663. W ups.com

TRAVEL INFORMATION

Travelling in Germany is very efficient and easy. All of the big cities have airports, most of which offer international connections. The entire country is linked by a dense network of motorways with convenient facilities for travellers, while main roads are also of a high standard and are well signposted. Rail travel throughout the country is comfortable and reliable; for longer journeys it is worth taking advantage of the fast connections offered by InterCity Express (ICE). Buses are also comfortable and efficient and are particularly useful in rural areas not served by rail. In German cities, trams, buses and sometimes underground rail systems provide reliable services.

The arrival hall of Dusseldorf airport

Arriving by Air

Germany's most important airports are Frankfurt am Main, Munich, Cologne-Bonn and Düsseldorf, from where connecting flights can be made to other German cities. Airport expansion in Berlin will create a major air hub on completion in 2017/18.

The country's national carrier, **Lufthansa**, operates regular, scheduled flights to most of the world's major destinations. **British Airways** also offers regular flights to Germany from London (Heathrow and Gatwick) as well as from several regional airports in the United Kingdom.

The US is well served, with flights to German cities, particularly to Frankfurt, which is Germany's largest airport and one of the busiest in Europe. Direct flights are usually available from major US cities, including New York (JFK), Washington, DC, Boston, Chicago, San Francisco and Los Angeles. Although Canada does not have many direct flights to Germany, **AirCanada** operates a regular flight from Toronto to Frankfurt.

Among the busiest airports are Düsseldorf, Munich, and Cologne-Bonn. In 2017 or 2018, Tegal airport in Berlin will close to make way for the Berlin Brandenburg International Airport (BER) at Schönefeld, a major new airport, which will serve the whole of the capital. Frankfurt am Main is the largest German airport and comprises of two huge terminals, which are connected by a fast over-ground railway. The modern

Control tower at Munich's international airport

Munich airport is somewhat smaller but still very busy. When changing planes, transfers may take longer due to the long walk between two terminals. Düsseldorf is smaller than Frankfurt and Munich Airports and easier to navigate, with a central building connecting the three terminals. Cologne-Bonn, a smaller airport, is usually hassle-free. Leipzig-Halle is an important air-traffic hub in the east of Germany due to its train station that connects to the long-distance network.

Tickets and Fares

The cost of scheduled airfares can vary considerably, so early reservation and online price comparison is a good idea. Cheap Apex tickets work for those who are unlikely to change their travel plans. They are not available for one-way journeys. All Apex airfares must be booked well in advance (usually at least 14 days); some require a 28-day advance booking to qualify for the lowest airline ticket prices.

When buying a ticket it is worth finding out about any price reductions for children, young people and elderly passengers. Students and passengers under the age of 26 are often eligible for discounts. If the journey is going to be undertaken by a large group, it is worth checking whether a group discount on the fare or a free ticket for the group leader is available.

Once booked, it is extremely difficult if not impossible to reschedule discount tickets, so it is wise to take out insurance to cover the loss if travel plans have to be changed.

The exterior of Cologne Bonn airport

The cheapest airfares are often those offered by low-cost airlines such as **EasyJet** and **Ryanair**, or by discount agents. The latter offer discounted seats on charter or scheduled flights.

Domestic Flights

In addition to Lufthansa, there are a number of smaller carriers in Germany including **Air Berlin** and **Germanwings**. These carriers offer good quality air links with airports across Germany, including smaller cities. They also often offer cheaper fares than Lufthansa on internal and international routes.

On Arrival

Prior to departure, you should check with authorities or online which items cannot be brought to Germany and what the import regulations are *(see p542)*. Normally, clearing customs and immigration is fast and painless in German airports.

All major German airports are served by public transportation. Information on transport into the city centre, tickets and fares can be found in the arrival hall or the lobby. Tickets should be purchased from vending machines before boarding trains or buses. On most forms of public transport, one or two pieces of luggage may be carried at no extra cost.

Taxis are available from all of the main city airports. It is best to pre-book a taxi or confirm the cost of the journey before travelling.

DIRECTORY

Airlines

Air Berlin
Tel (030) 34 34 34 34.
W airberlin.com

Air Canada
W aircanada.com

British Airways
Tel (0421) 5575 758.
W britishairways.com

Delta Air Lines
Tel (069) 29 99 37 71.
W delta.com

EasyJet
W easyjet.com

Germanwings
Tel (0180) 6320 320.
W germanwings.com

Lufthansa
Tel (069) 86 799 799.
W lufthansa.com

Qantas
Tel (069) 299 57 14 21.
W qantas.com

Ryanair
W ryanair.com

United Airlines
Tel (069) 50 98 50 51.
W united.com

Airport	Information	Distance from Centre	Journey Time to Centre by Taxi	Journey Time to Centre by Public Transport
Berlin Tegel	(030) 60 91 77 50	9 km (5 miles)	20 min	Bus: 25 min
Berlin Schönefeld	(0180) 500 01 86	20 km (12 miles)	45 min	S-Bahn: 35 min
Cologne-Bonn	(02203) 40 400 1	Bonn: 28 km (17.5 miles); Cologne: 17 km (10.5 miles)	Bonn: 15 min Cologne: 10 min	Bus to Bonn: 35 min Bus to Cologne: 45 min
Dresden	(0351) 881 33 60	9 km (5.5 miles)	25 min	Bus: 30 min
Düsseldorf	(0211) 12 10	8 km (5 miles)	25 min	S-Bahn: 13 min
Frankfurt am Main	(01805) 372 46 36	10 km (6 miles)	20 min	Tram: 11 min S-Bahn: 10 min
Hamburg	(040) 50750	13 km (8 miles)	30 min	Bus: 30 min
Hanover	(0511) 97 70	12 km (7.5 miles)	20 min	S-Bahn: 13 min
Leipzig-Halle	(0341) 224 11 55	Leipzig: 20 km (12 miles); Halle: 24 km (15 miles)	Leipzig: 30 min Halle: 40 min	S-Bahn to Leipzig: 15 min S-Bahn to Halle: 12 min
Munich	(089) 97500	40 km (25 miles)	45 min	S-Bahn: 40 min Bus: 45 min
Nuremberg	(0911) 937 00	6 km (4 miles)	20 min	Bus: 45 min U-Bahn: 12 min

Travelling by Train and Ferry

Travelling around Germany by train is not the cheapest form of transport, but it is undoubtedly one of the most comfortable. German trains are renowned for their punctuality, safety and cleanliness, though in peak travel season, visitors may feel that these are a little overrated. Germany is also well served by ports to which ferries and passenger ships operate.

InterCity Express train

Arriving by Train

There are regular rail services into Germany from most European cities. Travelling by train from the UK usually costs more than flying. The most common routes into Germany are to travel to Brussels by **Eurostar** or take the **Eurotunnel** shuttle to France and continue your journey by road or rail.

Travelling by Train

Germany's fastest trains, InterCity Express (ICE), can travel at more than 200 km/h (125 mph), which means that a journey from Hamburg to Munich takes only 6 hours. *ICE* and *ICE Sprinter* trains (even faster) operate on routes linking the largest cities.

Somewhat slower and less expensive are the *InterCity (IC)* trains, which stop only at larger towns and cities. When travelling over shorter distances it is often quicker to take the *Regional Express (RE)* trains. Alternative service providers like **Metronom** often have lower fares than **Deutsche Bahn** but run less frequently.

Train aficionados can enjoy a trip on one of the steam-engine trains travelling along the Baltic coast (**Rasender Roland**) or a mountain route (**Brockenbahn**).

Logo of German railways
(Deutsche Bahn)

Railway Stations

In large towns and cities, railway stations are generally located in the centre. They include several shops (often open on Sundays), car rental firms, hotel reservation bureaux, and other services, such as cash points, left luggage provision and public toilets with shower facilities.

Tickets and Fares

Train fares are expensive in Germany and express trains have a surcharge (*Zuschlag*). For multiple train trips, buy a BahnCard, which gives a 25 or 50 per cent discount. Otherwise, discounts are available only if tickets are bought 3 or 7 days ahead and low-price seats have not sold out.

When planning a lengthy stay in Germany and travelling around the country, it is worth acquiring an InterRail card, which is available to every European citizen, regardless of age. Regional tickets, offering unlimited travel within a state for a set period of time, are also available. Each year the variety of discounted fares to which this card entitles the bearer is extended, so it is worth checking out the full range. Schoolchildren and students

DIRECTORY

Travelling by Train

Brockenbahn/Harzer Schmalspurbahn
Tel (03943) 55 80.
W hsb-wr.de

Deutsche Bahn
Tel 0180 699 66 33.
Tel (08718) 80 80 66 (UK).
W bahn.de
W bahn.co.uk

Eurostar
Tel 08432 186 186.
Tel 03432 186 186 (UK).
W eurostar.com

Eurotunnel
Tel 08443 35 35 35.
W eurotunnel.com

Metronom (Bremen-Hamburg-Hanover-Göttingen)
Tel (0581) 164 164.
W der-metronom.de

Brockenbahn
Tel (03943) 55 80.
W hsb-wr.de

Rasender Roland
Tel (038301) 88 40 12.
W ruegensche-baederbahn.de

Tickets and Fares

InterRail
W interrail.eu

Eurail
W eurail.com

Ferries

Color Line
Tel (040) 38 10 96 9113 (calling from outside of Germany).
W colorline.com

Scandlines
Tel (0381) 77 88 77 66 (calling from outside of Germany).
W scandlines.de

Train Routes and Ferry Ports in Germany

0 km 75

0 miles 75

Århus, Fredericia

Westerland (Sylt)

Flensburg

Copenhagen

Ostseebad Binz

Niebüll

Puttgarden

Stralsund

Neumünster

Kiel

Warnemünde

Rostock

Seebad Heringsdorf

Lübeck

Norddeich Mole

Hamburg

Schwerin

Pasewalk

Emden

Ludwigslust

Neustrelitz

Szczecin

Emden Außenhafen

Oldenburg

Bremen

Wittenberge

Uelzen

Stendal

Berlin

Frankfurt (Oder)

Amsterdam Schipol

Bad Bentheim

Osnabrück

Hanover

Wolfsburg

Potsdam

Magdeburg

Warsaw, Poznán

Amsterdam

Rheine

Brunswick

Lutherstadt Wittenberg

Krakow

Recklinghausen

Münster

Bielefeld

Hildesheim

Halle (Saale)

Leipzig

Riesa

Görlitz

Cottbus

Gelsenkirchen

Hamm

Paderborn

Göttingen

Nordhausen

Dresden

Wroclaw

Oberhausen

Dortmund

Bochum

Kassel

Weimar

Duisburg

Essen

Hagen

Eisenach

Erfurt

Jena

Düsseldorf Flughafen

Wuppertal

Bebra

Düsseldorf

Solingen

Prague, Brno, Vienna, Budapest

Cologne

Aachen

Montabaur

Bonn

Limburg

Giessen

Fulda

Saalfeld

Brussels, Paris

Koblenz

Lichtenfels

Frankfurt am Main

Wiesbaden

Aschaffenburg

Bamberg

Mainz

Würzburg

Erlangen

Luxembourg

Ffm Flughafen

Darmstadt

Nuremberg

Trier

Mannheim

Heidelberg

Ansbach

Regensburg

Kaiserslautern

Saarbrücken

Karlsruhe

Treuchtlingen

Plattling

Vienna, Linz

Paris

Baden-Baden

Aalen

Ingolstadt

Passau

Stuttgart

Offenburg

Augsburg

Paris, Strasbourg

Tübingen

Ulm

Munich

Vienna, Graz, Budapest, Klagenfurt, Zagreb, Ljubljana

Freiburg

Memmingen

Friedrichshafen

Kempten

Kufstein

Salzburg

Berchtesgaden

Singen

Lindau

Konstanz

Oberstdorf

Garmisch-Partenkirchen

Innsbruck, Verona, Milan, Venice

Basel

Zürich, Interlaken, Brig, Chur

Zürich

Bregenz, Zürich, Innsbruck

Key

— Main railway lines

⛴ Ferry port

are entitled to a reduced-rate card. Non-European residents can buy a Eurail global, regional or country pass.

Train tickets can be bought and reservations made online, at travel agents or at the *Reise-zentrum* (travel centre) at railway stations. It is simple to plan your journey yourself using this facility. Seat reservations cost €5 per person for a return trip if paid online with a ticket purchase, or €9 at a ticket counter.

Advance booking is necessary for ICE Sprinter and Thalys trains (between Cologne and Aachen). The sleeper CityNightLine trains also require reservations. On all other trains, reservations are advisable when travelling at peak times or in a group.

Arriving by Ferry

Visitors travelling to Germany by car from the UK will have to decide which crossing to use (unless using the Channel Tunnel). The crossings from Dover to Ostend, in Belgium, or to Calais, in France, are the shortest, while the Harwich to Hook of Holland route is useful for those travelling from further

north. There are many links between German ports and other countries. The main ferry terminals are Kiel, Lübeck and Rostock on the Baltic Sea coast. Color Line runs a service from Oslo (Norway) to Kiel and Scandlines operate between Rostock and Puttgarden to Denmark. Ferry lines also run ferries from Denmark.

Ship taking passengers to Helgoland

Travelling by Car and Coach

A fast and comfortable way of travelling around Germany is to use the motorways. The excellent network of toll-free routes guarantees fast progress over longer distances, while a well-maintained system of main roads enables you to reach interesting places throughout the country. Motorways have the advantage of regularly sited service stations, where travellers can stop for fuel and something to eat. On lesser roads and in remote areas, petrol stations may be few and far between.

A selection of traffic signs one might encounter on German roads

Arriving by Car

With the addition of Poland and the Czech Republic to the Schengen Area, border check-points are now largely non-existent. Border stations do occasionally check cars, and trucks. Trains and tourist buses are sometimes stopped for passport checks.

Those wishing to drive to Germany from the UK will need to travel to France, Belgium or the Netherlands with their vehicle either by ferry or on the Eurotunnel shuttle *(see p554)*.

Motorway telephone

and have regularly spaced petrol stations as well as service areas with parking areas, toilets, restaurants and motels. On the hard shoulder there are yellow poles with emergency buttons, which can be used to call for help in case of breakdown or accident. An *Autobahn* (motorway) is indicated by the letter "A" and a number – some also have a letter "E" and a number, denoting that the road crosses the German border. A *Bundesstrasse* (main road) is indicated by the letter "B" and a number.

What You Need

Drivers must carry a valid driving licence as well as their vehicle's registration document and a valid insurance policy. Cars must carry a plate indicating country of origin, a first-aid kit and a red warning triangle in case of breakdown.

If you plan to drive in large cities, you will need an environmental badge (*Umweltplakette, see p558*).

Roads and Tolls

The German motorway network is extensive. Roads are toll-free

Additional Road Signs

In addition to internationally understood road signs on German roads, there are a few other signs. On motorways, for example, a yellow triangular warning sign with a row of cars is a warning about the possibility of traffic jams, which may be accompanied by the word *Stau*. On mountain roads, a warning sign showing a car tyre wrapped in a chain, accompanied by the word *Schnee*, warns against

driving without chains when there is snow.

A diversion is indicated by the colour yellow and the word *Umleitung*, while the diversion route is indicated by the letter "U" followed by the number of the road. A sign with the word *Baustelle* always precedes a stretch that is being renovated.

A sign showing a horizontal blue arrow with the word *Einbahnstrasse* indicates a one-way street.

Rules of the Road

Germans on the whole drive in accordance with the regulations. They are generally courteous but can be a little aggressive, particularly on motorways. German drivers hurtle along the outside lane at great speed and get annoyed if they have to slow down because of other drivers. Visitors should be very careful if they are not used to driving on the right.

Seatbelts are compulsory and children under 12 must sit in the back, with babies and toddlers in child seats.

In the event of an accident on the motorway, or if a traffic jam necessitates an abrupt reduction in speed, drivers should turn on their flashing emergency lights to warn drivers behind of the impending danger.

Driving after drinking a glass of beer or wine (50mg/dl) is allowed, but if an accident occurs, the consequences will be more severe if alcohol is found in your blood.

In built-up areas the speed limit is 50 km/h (31 mph); beyond this it is 100 km/h (62 mph), and on motorways there is no limit. When travelling

Fuel station at a motorway service area

Cars in heavy traffic on the Autobahn A3 near Ratingen

with a caravan or trailer outside built-up areas, do not exceed 70 km/h (44 mph), and on motorways 100 km/h (62 mph). Drivers will be fined for speeding, tailgating and parking offences. Note that parking meters may be quite far away from where you park.

Breakdown Services

In the event of a breakdown, turn on your flashing emergency lights and position a warning triangle 100 m (100 yd) behind your vehicle. Roadside assistance is offered by **ADAC** and **AVD** automobile associations – although they may insist you become a member. If you breakdown when lost, use one of the telephones set at intervals along the hard shoulder (see p556). If a road accident occurs, contact the police immediately.

Car Hire

Car-hire firms such as **Avis**, **Hertz** and **Sixt Rent-a-Car** can be found at airports and railway stations. They need to produce their passport and driving licence. Most rental agencies require drivers to be over the age of 21 and to have an international licence.

Hitchhiking

Hitchhiking is popular among young people, but a safer method of finding a lift or a travelling companion is through ride-share agencies such as **Mitfahrzentrale** or **Blablacar**, where drivers offer spare seats on a journey for an agreed fee. You can even catch a ride from or to other EU countries, (including the UK).

Arriving by Coach

Travelling to Germany by coach from the UK is not a very attractive option, as the journey times are very long. Routes are operated by **Eurolines**, depart at Victoria Coach Station and arrive at Berlin's central coach station at the Funkturm (ZOB). Other routes, also departing from Victoria Station, terminate in Frankfurt, Düsseldorf, Cologne, Dortmund or Munich.

Travelling by Coach

There is a good network of inter-city coach services in Germany, and journeys tend to be cheaper than by express train. Most towns have a central station (Zentraler Omnibus Bahnhof) near the train station. It is here that most bus services originate and where timetables can be obtained and tickets purchased. **MeinFernbus** is a leading long-distance coach provider. All national bus companies have websites, making ticket purchases easy. Many local coach services also operate from the central bus station, so it is easy to make a connection on arrival. **Reisebus 24** offers a search and reservation portal for bus tours of Germany.

DIRECTORY

Breakdown Services

ADAC
Tel (0180) 222 22 22.

AVD
Tel (0800) 990 99 09.

Car Hire

Avis
Tel (061) 71 680.
W avis.com

Hertz
Tel (01806) 33 35 35.
W hertz.com

Sixt Rent-a-Car
Tel (01805) 25 25 25.
W sixt.com

Hitchhiking

Mitfahrzentrale
W mitfahrzentrale.de

Coach Companies

Berlin Linien Bus
Tel (030) 860 96 211.
W bex.de

Eurolines
W touring.com

Meinfernbus
Tel (01805) 15 99 15.
W meinfernbus.de

Reisebus 24
(bus tours across Germany)
Tel (030) 2000 7747.
W reisebus24.de

Comfortable, long-distance, Meinfernbus coaches

Travelling within Cities

Driving around Germany's huge cities is not easy, and the historic centres are best visited on foot. Large towns often suffer from traffic congestion and parking can be hard to find. It is advisable to leave your car in a car park on the outskirts and use the city/suburban railway (S-Bahn), underground (U-Bahn), trams or city buses. The latter operate frequent services and can usually avoid traffic jams as they run in dedicated traffic lanes. All modes of public transport run less frequently on weekends.

Electric car charging station in Berlin

Green Travel

Public transportation in Germany is extensive and reliable within urban areas and there are fast train connections between cities. There is not much need for a car unless you wish to explore the countryside extensively. Some car rental companies offer hybrid or electric cars, and many taxis run on bio fuel.

There is an emphasis on public and alternative transport in Germany. Many cities have introduced low-emission zones, which only allow vehicles with an **Umwelt Permit** (*Umwelt-plakette*). Tourists need to obtain this permit prior to travelling to Germany in their own car (*see p559*). It can be bought online or from any participating garage in Germany.

Bike rentals are everywhere, and with a good network of bike lanes and paths, Germany is a safe country to ride a bicycle. Drivers are very aware of bikes. Many tour operators offer guided bicycle tours – a good way to start and gather confidence on two wheels. **German Cycling Tours** offers guided bike tours of Germany and **Fahrradreisen** runs a portal with search engines for bicycle tours and accommodation, arranged by region, price and date. **Bike & Bus** is an interesting concept that works like a shuttle for cyclists. You tour Europe by bus while your bike is transported in a trailer and available for use where the shuttle stops.

U-Bahn and S-Bahn

Most big German cities have a network of fast connections by underground railway (U-Bahn) and commuter rail (S-Bahn). The U-Bahn offers frequent services – in peak hours, every 3–5 minutes – and individual stations are quite close to each other. The S-Bahn offers less frequent services, every 10–20 minutes, and connects city centres with the suburbs.

Generally, S- and U-Bahn, buses and trams within a city use the same tickets. Tickets can be bought from machines at the entrance to stations or on platforms; the tickets often need to be validated in timestamp machines nearby. Railway stations have no ticket-operated barriers, but tickets are frequently checked and €40 fines are imposed on the spot for those not holding a valid ticket.

U-Bahn stations are indicated by square signs with a white "U" on a dark blue background, while S-Bahn stations have round signs with a white "S" on a green background. On maps of the network, each line of the U- and S-Bahn is marked in a different colour and has its own number. The direction of the route is indicated by the name of the terminus station. On every platform a display shows the destination of the next incoming train. A white circle or oval on the map indicates an interchange station.

Carriage doors on U- and S-Bahn trains are sometimes opened manually, but they close automatically. Passengers are not allowed to board the train after an operator's call of "*Zurückbleiben!*" (stay back!).

Buses

Bus operating hours vary from city to city and are much shorter in rural areas. Timetables can be found online or in ticket or tourist offices. Bus tickets can be purchased from the driver.

During the journey, the driver generally announces the name of the bus stop that the bus is approaching. In the centre of town, this is not so important, as in heavy traffic the bus stops at every bus stop. However, further away from the city centre or when traffic is lighter, you will need to listen for these announcements. At many bus stops, the driver will pull in only on request, so passengers must press the "Halt" button in plenty of time.

A city bus in Munich

A modern type of tram found in Munich

Trams

Trams are comfortable and do not get stuck in traffic jams. They run as frequently as buses and have similar operating hours – check with local tourist offices or online for more details.

Tickets

Large cities are generally divided into public transport zones, with the cost of a ticket depending on which zones are travelled through.

In addition to standard tickets (*Normaltarif*), there are also cheaper tickets (*Kurzstrecke*) that limit you to short distances. In many cities you can buy tickets in the form of a strip, which is punched according to the length of your journey.

Children under 14 travel at a reduced rate, while those under the age of six go free. Other types of tickets include a one-day ticket (*Tageskarte*), a one-day group ticket (*Gruppen-tageskarte*), and a weekly ticket (*7-Tage-Karte*). Some towns issue a WelcomeCard that includes travel, plus discounts at local attractions.

Most U-Bahn and S-Bahn trains permit transportation of bicycles in designated cars with a separate ticket.

Driving

Many cities, including Berlin, Munich and Cologne, have introduced a low-emissions zone, indicated by the word *Umwelt* in a red circle. All vehicles must carry a permit in these zones or incur a fine. Permits can be bought online (*see Directory*). Alternatively, use "Park and Ride" (P+R) facilities near S-Bahn stations.

Watch out for bus lanes marked by round blue signs, which can only be used by taxis and cyclists.

Parking in towns can be difficult, the best option is to find a car park (*Parkhaus*). Cars left in a controlled parking zone must display a ticket bought from a machine nearby. Illegally parked cars can be towed; retrieving them is expensive and difficult.

Cream coloured taxis that operate throughout German cities

Taxis

Taxis are a comfortable though expensive way of getting around. If several people share a cab however, it can be cheaper than using the bus or train. All taxis are cream coloured and have a "TAXI" sign on the roof; this is illuminated if the taxi is free. Taxis can be hailed on the street or booked by telephone. They can also be picked up at taxi ranks.

Cycling

Germany has numerous cycle lanes, making it safe, and many junctions have special lights for cyclists. Bikes can be hired from hostels or at various hire places (*Fahrradverleih*). In some major cities, you can use the **Call-A-Bike** hire system. You can rent a bike using a credit card, paying €0.08 per minute (up to a maximum of €15 for 24 hours).

DIRECTORY

Green Travel

Bike and Bus
W bike-and-bus.de

Fahrradreisen
W fahrradreisen.de

German Cycling Tours
W germancyclingtours.com

Umwelt Permits
W umwelt-plakette.de

Public Transportation Networks

BVG Berlin
W bvg.de

HVV Hamburg
W hvv.de

MVV Munich
W mvv-muenchen.de

VGF Frankfurt/M
W vgf-ffm.de

Taxis

Berlin
Berlin Taxi
Tel (030) 21 01 01.

Frankfurt
Taxis Frankfurt
Tel (069) 25 20 25.

Hamburg
Taxi Hamburg
Tel (040) 666 666.

Munich
Taxi Central
Tel (089) 21 610.

Cycling

Call-A-Bike
Tel (069) 42 72 77 22.
W callabike-interaktiv.de

Bicycles for public hire near the Hofgarten in Berlin

General Index

Acknowledgments

Dorling Kindersley and Wiedza i Życie would like to thank the following people for their help in preparing this guide:

Additional Text Michał Jaranowski, Barbara Sudnik-Wójcicka, Grażyna Winiarska, Konrad Gruda, Bożena Steinborn

Additional Photographs Amin Akhtar, Francesca Bondy, Maciej Bronarski, Demetrio Carrasco, Witold Danilkiewicz, Dorota Jarymowicz and Mariusz Jarymowicz, Claire Jones, Grzegorz Kłosowski, Renata and Marek Kosińscy, Sergiusz Michalski, Nils Meyer, Ian O'Leary, Jürgen Rough Guides / Diana Jarvis, Rough Guides / Roger d'Olivere, Scheunemann, Andrzej Zygmuntowicz and Ireneusz Winnicki, Władysław Wisławski

Publishing Manager Helen Townsend

Managing Art Editor Kate Poole

Consultant Gerhard Bruschke

Factcheckers Joel Dullroy, Claudia Himmelreich, Barbara Sobeck, Jürgen Scheunemann

Director of Publishing Gillian Allan

Revisions Team Emma Anacootee, Sam Atkinson, Claire Baranowski, Sonal Bhatt, Arwen Burnett, Susi Cheshire, Sherry Collins, Lucinda Cooke, Jo Cowen, Surya Deogun, Joel Dullroy, Conrad Van Dyk, Petra Falkenberg, Jeremy Gray, Marcus Hardy, Lucinda Hawksley, Kaberi Hazarika, Christine Heilman, Jacky Jackson, Claire Jones, Sumita Khatwani, Rahul Kumar, Leena Lane, Maite Lantaron, Jude Ledger, Carly Madden, Hayley Maher, Nicola Malone, Jeroen van Marle, Claire Marsden, Ferdie McDonald, Sam Merrell, Rebecca Milner, Kate Molan, Casper Morris, Sangita Patel, Helen Peters, Marianne Petrou, Dave Pugh, Marisa Renzullo, Lucy Richards, Simon Ryder, Sands Publishing Solutions, Sadie Smith, Solveig Steinhardt, James Stewart, Andrew Szudek, Rebecca Taylor, Leah Tether, Craig Turp, Jeroen van Marle, Karen Villabona, Birgit Walter, Stewart J. Wild, Christian Williams

Additional Picture Research Rachel Barber, Marta Bescos, Rhiannon Furbear, Ellen Root, Nikhil Verma

The publisher would also like to thank all the people and institutions who allowed photographs belonging to them to be reproduced, as well as granting permission to use photographs from their archives:

Archäologische Staatssammlung in Munich; Arthothek (Jürgen Hinrichsowi); Bavaria Filmstadt; Bayerisches Nationalmuseum in Munich; Bildarchiv Preussischer Kulturbesitz in Berlin (Heidrun Klein); Bildvorlagen Römerschatz – Gäubodenmuseum Straubing (Dr Prammer); Bischöfliches Dom- und Diözesanmuseum Mainz (Dr Hansowi-Jurgenowi Kotzurowi); Brecht-Weigel-Gedenkstätte in Berlin (Elke Pfeil); Bridgeman Art Library; Bröhan-Museum in Berlin (Ingrid Jagr and Frau Betzker); Brücke-Museum in Berlin; Brüder-Grimm-Museum in Kassel; Corbis; Das Domkapitel (Gertraut Mockel, Büro Dr Georg Minkenberg); Deutsches Apothekenmuseum in Heidelberg; Deutsches Historisches Museum in Berlin (Kathi Rumlow); Deutsche Presse Agentur (dpa) in Berlin (Tanija Teichmann); Deutsches Museum in Munich (Sigrid Schneider and Marlene Schwarz); Deutsches Schifffahrtsmuseum in Bremerhaven (Hansowi-Walterowi Kewelohowi); Deutsches Tapetenmuseum Kassel (Sabine Thümmler); Deutsches Technikmuseum Berlin (Renate Förster); Diözesanmuseum in Bamberg (Birgit Kandora); Dombauverwaltung des Metropolitankapitels Köln (Birgit Lambert); Dresden Museum für Geschichte der Stadt Dresden (Dr Christel Wünsch); Flash Press Media (Sylwii Wilgockiej); Forschungs- und Gedenkstätte Normannenstraße (Stasi-Museum) in Berlin (Andrei Holland-Moritz); Fürstlich Hohenzollernsche Schlossverwaltung in Sigmaringen (Heldze Boban); Gemäldegalerie Alte Meister (Steffi Reh); Gemäldegalerie Neue Meister (Gisela Mehnert); Germanisches Nationalmuseum in Nuremberg (Hermanowi Maué); Hamburger Bahnhof in Berlin; Hamburger Kunsthalle; Hessisches Landesmuseum Kassel; Käthe-Kollwitz-Museum in Berlin (A. Ingrid Findell); Komische Oper Berlin (Gaby Hofmann); Kunstmuseum Düsseldorf (Anne-Marie Katins); Kunstsammlungen Paula Modersohn in Bremen (Hubertusowi Morgenthalowi); Kunst-

sammlungen zu Weimar (Angelice Goder); Kunstverlag Maria Laach (Helmutowi Keipowi); Kurdirektion des Berchtesgadener Landes (Vroni Aigner, Birgit Tica); Landesmuseum Trier (Margot Redwanz); LBB Photo Archives (Dyrektorowi Christophowi Kalischowi); Linden-Museum Stuttgart, Staatliches Museum für Völkerkunde (Dr Doris Kurelli); Lutherstube in Wittenberg (Jutcie Strehle); Markgräfliches Opernhaus in Bayreuth; Mercedes-Benz-Museum in Stuttgart; Museum am Ostwall in Dortmund; Museum der Bildenden Künste in Leipzig (Roswitha Engel); Museum Folkwang in Essen, Stadt Essen (Mr Hildebrandowi); Museum of the City of Berlin; Porzellansammlung (Ulrike Maltschew); Rheinisches Landesmuseum Bonn (Dr Gerhard Bauchhenß); Rüstkammer (Yvonne Brandt); Schlösserverwaltung in Munich (Frau Gerum); Seebul Ada und Emil Nolde (Dr Andreasowi Fluckowi); Staatliche Graphische Sammlung in Munich (Wiebke Tomaschek); Staatliche Kunstsammlungen Dresden, Albertinum, Grünes Gewölbe; Staatliche Porzellan-Manufaktur Meißen GMBH (Christine Mangold); Staatliche Schlösser und Gärten, Pforzheim (Herr Braunowi); Staatsarchiv Hamburg (Kathrin Berger); Staatsgalerie Stuttgart (Frau Fönnauer); Städelsches Kunstinstitut in Frankfurt am Main (Elisabeth Heinemann); Stadt Köln, Wallraf-Richartz-Museum in Cologne (Dr Hoswitha Neu-Kock and Dr Mai); Stadtmuseum in Munich; Stiftung Luthergedenkstätten in Sachsen-Anhalt; Stiftung Preussische Schlösser und Gärten Berlin (Carli Kamarze); Superstock Polska Sp. z.o.o. (Elżbiecie Gajewskiej); Von der Heydt-Museum Wuppertal (Margarecie Janz); Wartburg-Stiftung in Eisenach (Petrze Wilke); Zefa (Ewie Kozłowskiej)

The publisher would also like to thank the following for their assistance on the guide: Joanna Minz for coordinating information, Tamara and Jacek Draber for their help with correspondence and telephone contacts, Jürgen Christoffer of Deutscher Wetterdienst for meteorological information.

Picture Credits
a-above; b-below/bottom; c-centre; f-far; l-left; r-right; t-top.

Works of art have been reproduced with the permission of the following copyright holders: DACS, London 2011: 31c, 35c, 63clb, 91cl, 93tl, © Munch Museum/Munch - Ellingsen Group, BONO, Oslo/DACS, London 2011 92cra, 409cra, 441cra; © Succession Picasso/DACS, 2011 100tl, 317crb.

Aachener Dom: (Copyright: Domkapitel Aachen – photo. Ann München) 400cla, 400cb, 401t (Skarbiec), 401cra, 401crb, 401br, 401bl; **Hotel Adlon Kempinski:** 492bl; **Alamy Images:** alwaysstock, LLC/Michael Hill 538tr; David Angel 70; archivberlin Fotoagentur GmbH/J. Henkelmann 111tl; Arco Images GmbH 528b, 534cr; Jon Arnold Images/Walter Bibikow 26tr; Michael bennett 428; Bildagentur-online / Schoening 557bl, BL Images Ltd 10tc, 235cr; Caro/Waechter 559c; FAN travelstock/Sabine Lubenow 536br, 537cl; FocusEurope 93tl, Iconotexc/Ettore Venturini 535tr; imagebroker 202-3, 386, 458, 470; imagebroker/Manfred Bail 235tl, 556bl; imagebroker/Michael Fischer 537br; INTERFOTO 8-9; Andre Jenny 234cra; Kolvenbach 528tl; Yadid Levy 234bl, 506cla; Muhs 86; John Norman 132; PjrTravel 326-7, 499br; Gillian Price 536cl; Robert Stainforth 552cla; **Albertinum:** (Dresden) 176tr; **Clara Alboth's Restaurant:** 516br; **Allianz Arena München Stadion GmbH:** 237tl; **Altes Haus:** 524bl; **Amt für Stadtmarketing und Touristik, Limburg:** 366cla; **Archäologische Staatssammlung:** (Munich) 223br; **Arthothek:** 34tr, 34bc, 35cra, 35bc, 58tl, 180cla, 180bc, 181tl, 181ca, 181ca, 181bc, 181br, 226cla, 440cla, 440clb, 440bl, 441cra, 441bc, 448t; Joachim Blauel 35crb, 54tr, 226tr, 226bc, 227crb, 298cr; 226cla, 227tl, 227cra, 263tr; Bayer d'Mitko 227br; Sophie-R. Gnamm 230cr; Alexander Koch 35cra; Christoph Sandig 474br; G. Westermann 436bl, 441tc; **Auerbachs Keller Restaurant:** 515br. **Basic AG** 534bl; **Bavaria Filmstadt:** 231tl; **Hotel Bayrisches Haus:** 513bl; **Bayerische Staatsoper:** Wilfried Hösl 236bl; **Hotel Bellevue:** 505br, 531bl; **Berlin Tourismus Marketing GmbH:** www.berlin-tourist-information.de 101br, 543tl, 545cra; **BerlinerFestspiele:** Bianka Gobel 113tr; **Berliner Sparkasse:** 548bl; **Brecht-Weigel-Gedenkstätte:** (Berlin) 105bc; **Bridgeman Art Library:** 38bl, 107tl, 502crb; **Bronarski Maciej:** 354tr, 354cla, 354clb, 355tc, 355cra, 355crb, 355bc; **Bröhan-Museum:** (Berlin) 100tl; **Brüder-Grimm-Museum:** (Kassel) 368cra, 372tr (© Staatliche Museum Kassel). **City of Munich – Fire Department:** 547tl; **Congress-und Tourismus-Zentrale Nürnberg:** 261tl; **Corbis:** 33tr, 33clb, 33bl, Annebicque Bernard/ Sygma 507tl; Massimo Borchi 340; Wolfgang Deuter/zefa 215cr;

Werner Dieterich 162, 450-1;
Jack Fields 176c, ivoivanov 364; Sylvain Sonnet 486-7; Herbert Spichtinger/zefa 236cra; Michael S.Yamashita 507c; Danilkiewicz Witold: 429b, 470, 478tl; Deutsches Museum, Munich: 544tl; Deutsches Postbank: 551clb; Deutsches Apothekenmuseum: (Heidelberg) 302tr; Deutsches Technikmuseum Berlin: 85br; Deutsches Historisches Museum Berlin: (Zeughaus) 30bc, 32c, 38ca, 38cla, 38clb, 38br, 39cla, 39tl, 39tc, 39clb, 39cb, 39crb, 39cbr (Holz & Kunststoff), 40cla, 50, 56tl (R. Bemke), 56cra (Jurgen Liepe), 56cb, 56b (A.C. Theil), 57tl (R. Boemke), 58br, 59tr, 59cla, 60clb, 64bc, 64br, 130tr, 130bl; Deutsches Schifffahrtsmuseum Bremerhaven: 54cla; Die Bank Brasserie: 530t; dpa: 30ca, 31tl, 31cra, 31crb, 31br, 31bl, 32tr, 39cla, 39cra, 39bl, 40tr, 43br, 44cla, 47cr, 64ca, 143cra, 209tl, 465tr; Claus Felix 47bl; Matthias Hiekel 44bc; Wulf Hirschberger 45tr; Wolfgang Kluge 32bl; Wolfgang Kumm 65clb; Kay Nietfeld 43tr; Frank Mächler 45tc; Carsten Rehder 42ca; Wulf Pfeiffer 45cl; Martin Schutt 46tc, 185br; Roland Scheidemann 47tl; Ingo Wagner 65tl; Heinz Wieseler 46bl; DK Images: Hotel Adlon Kempinski, Berlin / Britta Jaschinski 488br; Posteritati/Judith Miller 116cl; Dorint Hotels & Resorts: 501tr; Drachenhaus Restaurant: 512tr; Dreamstime.com: Adoggster 15t; Francesco Carucci 65br; Editor77 547clb; Eixeneize 75tl; Europhotos 394tl, Mitchell Gunn 42tl, Ictclgollos 10tl, Platnilkov 14bl; Ivan Kravtsov 338tr; Dmitry Rozhdestvenskiy 13tr; Rumifaz 72cl; Tanyae 172cl; Anibal Trejo 17tr; Wam 1975 14tr; Yew Fai Wong 220br; Dresden Museum für Geschichte der Stadt Dresden: 59crb. Eisenach-Wartburg Stiftung: 190cla, 190clb, 190bc, 191ca; L'Escalier Restaurant: 528tl. Hotel Fährhaus Sylt: 505tl; Fairmont Hotels & Resorts: 502bl, 503bc; Foto-Thueringen: Barbara Neumann 126cb; Fotolia: draghicih 146; Foto 540-1; Jörg Hackemann 416-7; take 11tr. Gäubodenmuseum Straubing: 51bl; Germanisches Nationalmuseum: (Nuremberg) 264-5 (all images); Getty Images: AFP 547cla, 559br; Richard l'Anson 292; Danita Delimont 242, 356-7; Sean Gallup 558cla; Oliver Gerhard 186; Dennis Grombkowski 43cl; Tina & Horst Herzig 537tr; LatitudeStock - TTL 420-2; Hans-Peter Merten 22; narvikk 66-7; Richard Nebesky 126tr; Popperfoto 31tr; Andreas Rentz 544br; Patrik Stollarz 42bl, 557tl; Grünes Gewölbe: (Dresden) 176t. Hamburger Bahnhof: (Berlin) 97bl; Hamburger Kunsthalle: (Hamburg) 34cla, 440tr; Hessisches Landesmuseum Kassel: 368cla, 368bl (© Staatliche Museum Kassel Deutsches Tapetenmuseum); Hohe Duene Hotel: 504bl; Hyatt Regency Mainz: 499bl. Ihr Herzle-Team: 520b; Intercontinental Berchtesgaden Resort: 496tl, 519tc; KaDeWe store, Berlin: Quelle 535bl; Käfers Bistro: 526t; Käthe-Kollwitz-Museum: (Berlin) 91cl; Kłosowski Grzegorz: 28cra; Kloster Maulbronn: 306bc, 306clb, 307tl, 307ca, 307cra, 307br; Köln-Bonn Airport: 553tl; Kölner Dom: 406cl, 406br, 407tl, 407cra, 407cb, 407bl, 407br (© Dombauarchiv Köln, Matz und Schenk); Komische Oper: (Berlin) Monika Ritterhaus 112br; Kosińscy, Renata and Marek: 28clb, 28bla, 28blb, 29cla, 29tlb, 29blb, 209ca, 209tr, 209cl, 209cr, 209crb; Kunstmuseum Düsseldorf: 34clb; Kunstsammlungen Paula Modersohn: 437tl; Motel One: 490tl; Kunstverlag Maria Laach: 338br, 362tr, 362rla, 363tl, 363cra, 363crb, 363bl; Kurdirektion der Berchtesgadener Landes: Storto, Leonberg 280bl. Landesmuseum Trier: Thomas Zühmer 346c; Linden Museum für Völkerkunde: (Stuttgart) 314cla; Lübeck and Travemuende Tourist-Service GmbH: HLTS 466cla; Ludwigsburg – Schloss: 310ca, 310clb, 310bl, 311tc; Lutherstube: (Wittenberg) 131tl. Mainz – Dom: 339bl (© M. Hankel-Studio); Manyo Restaurant: 519bl; Café Restaurant Meissen: 515tc; Mercedes-Benz-Museum: (Stuttgart) 314tr; Le Méridien Grand Hotel Nürnberg: 497bl; Meyer Nils: 64crb; Michalski Sergiusz: 24t; Mittelalterliches Museum: (Rothenburg ob der Tauber) 266br; mosellandtouristik: RFMFT 349cb; Motel One: 495bl; Munich Police: 540cla; Museum der Bildenden Künste:

(Leipzig) 55tl (MdbK, Gerstenberger 1994); Museum Brandhorst: 543br; Museum Folkwang: (Essen) 35tc; Museum für Naturkunde: (Berlin) 97br; Musikinstrumenten-Museum: (Berlin) 89cra. Nationalmuseum: (Munich) 223clb. Opernhaus: (Bayreuth) 256cla. Panorama: 527bl; Pasternak Restaurant: 511tr; Philharmonie: (Berlin) 89tl; Photolibrary: imagebroker. net/Martin Moxter 550cla; Popkomm GmbH: 113bl; Presse-und Informationsamt des Landes Berlin BTM/Drewes 96bl; BTM/Koch 96cla; G. Schneider 47tl. Ratskeller Bremen: 529br; Ratskeller Munich: 517t; Restaurant Bar München: 518tl; Rhein Hotel Bacharach: 524tr; Rheinisches Landesmuseum Bonn: 412cr; Ringhotel Schloss Tangermünde: 514tr; Rocco Forte Hotel de Rome: 489br; Rosas Dance Company, Belgium: Herman Sorgeloos 113cr. Schauspielhaus (Konzerthaus Berlin): 76bc; Scheel's Restaurant: 533t; Hotel Schloss Lübbenau: 493tl, 512bl; Schloss Sigmaringen: 319br; Karsten Schirmer: 112cla; Schlösserverwaltung (Munich): 250cla, 251tl, 251cra, 251cr, 251br, 286tr, 286cla, 286clb, 286br; Schlosshotel Steinburg: 522t; Schwedenschenke Restaurant: 523b; Sea Life München: 237cr; STA Travel: 544cra; Staatsarchiv Hamburg: 54-5; Staatliche Museen Preußischer Kulturbesitz: (Berlin) 52c, 59br, 60–61, 61tl, 61br, 62tc, 62cra, 62bl, 63tr, 63bl, 63clb, 63br, 64tl, 69br, 69cra, 80cla, 81cra, 94rlh, 95rb, 108tl, 129cb; Hans-Joachim Bartsch 53crb, 53br, 59bl; Jorg P. Anders 88ca, 88clb, 92cra, 94tr, 94cla, 94b, 95tl, 95cra, 95d; Grammes 52br; Klaus Göken 60br, 80bl, 81d; Erich Lessing 80tr, 81crb; Jurgen Liepe 79c, 80clb; Georg Niedermeister 81tc; Arne Psille 51br, 52tr, 52bl; Steinkopf 88tc; Staatliche Porzellan-Manufaktur Meißen GMBH: 38cra, 128tr, 128cra, 128clb, 128br, 129tc, 129c, Klaus Tänzer 129cra; Staatsgalerie Stuttgart: 316tr, 316cla, 316clb, 316br, 317tl, 317cra, 317tc, 317cr, 317br; Städelsches Kunstinstitut: (Frankfurt am Main) 382tr, 382cla, 382clb, 383tc, 383cra, 383crb, 383bc; Stadtmuseum Berlin: Hans-Joachim Bartsch 57bl; Stadtmuseum: (Munich) 218tl; Hans-Joachim Bartsch 5cl; Sudnik 29crb; Stasi-Museum: 106bc; Steigenberger Graf Zeppelin: 498tl; Steinberger Hotel Group: 494tr; Stiftung Preussische Schlösser & Gärten Berlin: Roland Handrick 103 ca; Roland Handrick 103crb; 58c, 102cl, 102cb, 103br, 139cr, 140b, 142tl, 142cb, 143bl; Stiftung Topographie des Terrors: 85tr; Superstock: imagebroker.net 174-5, 332-3; MIVA Stock 98, 124-5; Alexander Schnurer/ imagebroker.net (© Steve Vidler/Prisma 210; Westend61 2-3; Tourismuszentrale Rügen GmbH: Dieter Lindemann 482tr; The Victorian House Restaurant: 518bc; Vila Vita Rosenpark: 500br; Villa Rothschild Kempinski: 525tl; Vinothek Tiepolo: 521tl; Wallraf-Richartz-Museum: (Cologne) 408tr, 408cla, 408clb, 408bl, 409tl, 409tc, 409cr, 409cb, 409bl (© Rheinisches Bildarchiv); www.dresden.de: Christoph Münch 172tr; Zefa: 29cl, 206–7c, 391c, 426bra, 426tr, 427cb, 454cla, 455tr, 455b, 457bl; Bloemendal 5t; Damm 25b, 402b, 292, 398bc, 471b; Fickstein 27br, 427tl, 427tr; Freytag 23b, 208tr, 331tc; 37ca, 460bl, 473tr; Kehrer 29cr, Kinne 410tl, 410bc; Kohlhas 413tc; Rossenbach 402c, 414b, 415tl, 463b, 474cla; Rose 415ca; Steeger 427t; Streichan 367tr, 387b; Svenja-Foto 398tr, 407cra; M. Winkel 406tr; Zwinger: (Dresden) 178tc, 178br, 179bc; Gemäldegalerie Alte Meister 179crb.

Jacket Front and Spine – AWL Images: Gavin Hellier

Front Endpaper – Alamy Images: Michael Bennett Ltl; imagebroker Ltr, Rtr, Lcr; John Norman Rcra; Corbis: Massimo Borchi Lbl; Werner Dieterich Rcrb; ivoivanov Lcl; Getty Images: Richard l'Anson Lbr; Danita Delimont Rbr; Oliver Gerhard Rclb; Superstock: Vidler Steve/Prisma Rbl.

All other images © Dorling Kindersley.

Special Editions of DK Travel Guides

DK Travel Guides can be purchased in bulk quantities at discounted prices for use in promotions or as premiums. We are also able to offer special editions and personalized jackets, corporate imprints, and excerpts from all of our books, tailored specifically to meet your own needs.

To find out more, please contact:
in the United States **specialsales@dk.com**
in the UK **travelguides@uk.dk.com**
in Canada DK Special Sales at
specialmarkets@dk.com
in Australia **penguincorporatesales@
penguinrandomhouse.com.au**

Phrasebook

In an Emergency

Where is the telephone?	**Wo ist das Telefon?**	*voh ist duss tel-e-fone?*
Help!	**Hilfe!**	*hilf-uh*
Please call a doctor	**Bitte rufen Sie einen Arzt**	**bitt**-uh **roof**'n zee ine-en artst
Please call the police	**Bitte rufen Sie die Polizei**	**bitt**-uh **roof**'n zee dee poli-tsy
Please call the fire brigade	**Bitte rufen Sie die Feuerwehr**	**bitt**-uh roof'n zee dee **foyer**-vayr
Stop!	**Halt!**	*hult*

Communication Essentials

Yes	**Ja**	*yah*
No	**Nein**	*nine*
Please	**Bitte**	*bitt-uh*
Thank you	**Danke**	*dunk-uh*
Excuse me	**Verzeihung**	*fair-**tsy**-hoong*
Hello (good day)	**Guten Tag**	**goot**-en tahk
Goodbye	**Auf Wiedersehen**	*owf-**veed**-er-zay-ern*
Good evening	**Guten Abend**	*goot'n **ahb**'nt*
Good night	**Gute Nacht**	*goot-uh **nukht***
Until tomorrow	**Bis morgen**	*biss **morg**'n*
See you	**Tschüss**	*chooss*
What is that?	**Was ist das?**	*voss ist duss*
Why?	**Warum?**	*var-**room***
Where?	**Wo?**	*voh*
When?	**Wann?**	*vunn*
today	**heute**	*hoyt-uh*
tomorrow	**morgen**	*morg'n*
month	**Monat**	*mohn-aht*
night	**Nacht**	*nukht*
afternoon	**Nachmittag**	*nahkh-mit-tahk*
morning	**Morgen**	*morg'n*
year	**Jahr**	*yar*
there	**dort**	*dort*
here	**hier**	*hear*
week	**Woche**	*vokh-uh*
yesterday	**gestern**	*gest'n*
evening	**Abend**	*ahb'nt*

Useful Phrases

How are you? (informal)	**Wie geht's?**	*vee gayts*
Fine, thanks	**Danke, es geht mir gut**	*dunk-uh, es gayt meer goot*
Until later	**Bis später**	*biss **shpay**-ter*
Where is/are?	**Wo ist/sind…?**	*voh ist/sind*
How far is it to…?	**Wie weit ist es…?**	*vee **vite** ist ess*
Do you speak English?	**Sprechen Sie Englisch?**	*shpresh'n zee **eng**-glish*
I don't understand	**Ich verstehe nicht**	*ish fair-**shtay**-uh nisht*
Could you speak more slowly?	**Könnten Sie langsamer sprechen?**	*kurnt-en zee lung-zam-er shpresh'n*

Useful Words

large	**gross**	*grohss*
small	**klein**	*kline*
hot	**heiss**	*hyce*
cold	**kalt**	*kult*
good	**gut**	*goot*
bad	**schlecht**	*shlesht*
open	**geöffnet**	*g'**urff**-nett*
closed	**geschlossen**	*g'**shloss**'n*
left	**links**	*links*
right	**rechts**	*reshts*
straight ahead	**geradeaus**	*g'**rah**-der-**owss***

Making a Telephone Call

I would like to make a phone call	**Ich möchte telefonieren**	*ish mer-shtuh tel-e-fon-**eer**'n*
I'll try again later	**Ich versuche es später noch einmal**	*ish fair-zookh-uh es **shpay**-ter nokh ine-mull*
Can I leave a message?	**Kann ich eine Nachricht hinterlassen?**	*kan ish **ine**-uh nakh-risht hint-er-**lahss**-en*
answer phone	**Anrufbeantworter**	*an-roof-be-**ahnt**-vort-er*
telephone card	**Telefonkarte**	*tel-e-**fohn**-kart-uh*
receiver	**Hörer**	*hur-er*
mobile	**Handy**	*han-dee*
engaged (busy)	**besetzt**	*b'zetst*
wrong number	**falsche Verbindung**	*falsh-uh fair-**bin**-doong*

Sightseeing

library	**Bibliothek**	*bib-leo-**tek***
entrance ticket	**Eintrittskarte**	*ine-tritz-**kart**-uh*
cemetery	**Friedhof**	*freed-hofe*
train station	**Bahnhof**	*barn-hofe*
gallery	**Galerie**	*gall-er-ree*
information	**Auskunft**	*owss-koonft*
church	**Kirche**	*keersh-uh*
garden	**Garten**	*gart'n*
palace/castle	**Palast/Schloss**	*pallast/shloss*
place (square)	**Platz**	*plats*
bus stop	**Haltestelle**	*hal-te-shtel-uh*
national holiday	**Nationalfeiertag**	*nats-yon-**ahl**-fire-tahk*
theatre	**Theater**	*tay-**aht**-er*
free admission	**Eintritt frei**	*ine-tritt fry*

Shopping

Do you have/ Is there…?	**Gibt es…?**	*geept ess*
How much does it cost?	**Was kostet das?**	*voss **kost**'t duss*
When do you open/ close?	**Wann öffnen Sie? schließen Sie?**	*vunn **off**'n zee shlees'n zee*
this	**das**	*duss*
expensive	**teuer**	*toy-er*
cheap	**preiswert**	*price-vurt*
size	**Größe**	*gruhs-uh*
number	**Nummer**	*noom-er*
colour	**Farbe**	*farb-uh*
brown	**braun**	*brown*
black	**schwarz**	*shvarts*
red	**rot**	*roht*
blue	**blau**	*blau*
green	**grün**	*groon*
yellow	**gelb**	*gelp*

Types of Shop

antique shop	**Antiquariat**	*antik-**var**-yat*
chemist (pharmacy)	**Apotheke**	*appo-**tay**-kuh*
bank	**Bank**	*bunk*
market	**Markt**	*markt*
travel agency	**Reisebüro**	*rye-**ze**r-boo-roe*
department store	**Warenhaus**	*vahr'n-hows*
chemist's, drugstore	**Drogerie**	*droog-er-**ree***
hairdresser	**Friseur**	*freezz-**er***
newspaper kiosk	**Zeitungskiosk**	*tsytoongs-kee-osk*

bookshop	**Buchhandlung**	*bookh-hant-loong*
bakery	**Bäckerei**	*beck-er-eye*
post office	**Post**	*posst*
shop/store	**Geschäft/Laden**	*gush-eft/lard'n*
film processing shop	**Photogeschäft**	*fo-to-gush-eft*
self-service shop	**Selbstbedienungs- laden**	*selpst-bed-ee-nungs-lard'n*
shoe shop	**Schuhladen**	*shoo-lard'n*
clothes shop	**Kleiderladen, Boutique**	*klyder-lard'n boo-teek-uh*
food shop	**Lebensmittel- geschäft**	*lay-bens-mittel-gush-eft*
glass, porcelain	**Glas, Porzellan**	*glars, Port-sellahn*

Staying in a Hotel

Do you have any vacancies?	**Haben Sie noch Zimmer frei?**	*harb'n zee nokh tsimm-er-fry*
with twin beds?	**mit zwei Betten?**	*mitt tsvy bett'n*
with a double bed?	**mit einem Doppelbett?**	*mitt ine'm dopp'l-bet*
with a bath?	**mit Bad?**	*mitt bart*
with a shower?	**mit Dusche?**	*mitt doosh-uh*
I have a reservation	**Ich habe eine Reservierung**	*ish harb-uh ine-uh rez-er-veer-oong*
key	**Schlüssel**	*shlooss'l*
porter	**Pförtner**	*pfert-ner*

Eating Out

Do you have a table for…?	**Haben Sie einen Tisch für…?**	*harb'n zee tish foor*
I would like to reserve a table	**Ich möchte eine Reservierung machen**	*ish mer-shtuh ine-uh rezer-veer-oong makh'n*
I'm a vegetarian	**Ich bin Vegetarier**	*ish bin vegg-er-tah-ree-er*
Waiter!	**Herr Ober!**	*hair oh-bare!*
The bill (check), please	**Die Rechnung, bitte**	*dee resh-noong bitt-uh*
breakfast	**Frühstück**	*froo-shtock*
lunch	**Mittagessen**	*mit-targ-ess'n*
dinner	**Abendessen**	*arb'nt-ess'n*
bottle	**Flasche**	*flush'uh*
dish of the day	**Tagesgericht**	*tahg-es-gur-isht*
main dish	**Hauptgericht**	*howpt'gur isht*
dessert	**Nachtisch**	*nahkh-tish*
cup	**Tasse**	*tass-uh*
wine list	**Weinkarte**	*vine-kart-uh*
tankard	**Krug**	*khroog*
glass	**Glas**	*glars*
spoon	**Löffel**	*lerff'l*
teaspoon	**Teelöffel**	*tay-lerff'l*
tip	**Trinkgeld**	*trink-gelt*
knife	**Messer**	*mess-er*
starter (appetizer)	**Vorspeise**	*for-shpize-uh*
the bill	**Rechnung**	*resh-noong*
plate	**Teller**	*tell-er*
fork	**Gabel**	*gahb'l*

Menu Decoder

Aal	*arl*	eel
Apfel	*upf'l*	apple
Apfelschorle	*upf'l-shoorl-uh*	apple juice with sparkling mineral water
Apfelsine	*upf'l-seen-uh*	orange
Aprikose	*upri-kawz-uh*	apricot
Artischocke	*arti-shokh-uh*	artichoke
Aubergine	*or-ber-jeen-uh*	aubergine (eggplant)
Banane	*bar-narn-uh*	banana
Beefsteak	*beef-stayk*	steak
Bier	*beer*	beer
Bockwurst	*bokh-voorst*	a type of sausage
Bohnensuppe	*burn-en-zoop-uh*	bean soup
Branntwein	*brant-vine*	spirits
Bratkartoffeln	*brat-kar-toff'ln*	fried potatoes
Bratwurst	*brat-voorst*	fried sausage
Brötchen	*bret-tchen*	bread roll
Brot	*brot*	bread
Brühe	*bruh-uh*	broth
Butter	*boot-ter*	butter
Champignon	*shum-pin-yong*	mushroom
Currywurst	*kha-ree-voorst*	sausage with curry sauce
Dill	*dill*	dill
Ei	*eye*	egg
Eis	*ice*	ice/ ice cream
Ente	*ent-uh*	duck
Erdbeeren	*ayrt-beer'n*	strawberries
Fisch	*fish*	fish
Forelle	*for-ell-uh*	trout
Frikadelle	*Frika-dayl-uh*	rissole/hamburger
Gans	*ganns*	goose
Garnele	*gar-nayl-uh*	prawn/shrimp
gebraten	*g'braat'n*	fried
gegrillt	*g'grilt*	grilled
gekocht	*g'kokht*	boiled
geräuchert	*g'rowk-ert*	smoked
Geflügel	*g'floog'l*	poultry
Gemüse	*g'mooz-uh*	vegetables
Grütze	*grurt-ser*	groats, gruel
Gulasch	*goo-lush*	goulash
Gurke	*goork-uh*	gherkin
Hammelbraten	*hamm'l-braat'n*	roast mutton
Hähnchen	*haynsh'n*	chicken
Hering	*hair-ing*	herring
Himbeeren	*him-beer'n*	raspberries
Honig	*hoe-nikh*	honey
Kaffee	*kaf-fay*	coffee
Kalbfleisch	*kalp-flysh*	veal
Kaninchen	*ka-neensh'n*	rabbit
Karpfen	*karpf'n*	carp
Kartoffelpüree	*kar-toff'l-poor-ay*	mashed potatoes
Käse	*kayz-uh*	cheese
Kaviar	*kar-vee-ar*	caviar
Knoblauch	*k'nob-lowkh*	garlic
Knödel	*k'nerd'l*	noodle
Kohl	*koal*	cabbage
Kopfsalat	*kopf-zal-aat*	lettuce
Krebs	*krayps*	crab
Kuchen	*kookh'n*	cake
Lachs	*lahkhs*	salmon
Leber	*lay-ber*	liver
mariniert	*mari-neert*	marinated
Marmelade	*marmer-lard-uh*	marmalade, jam
Meerrettich	*may-re-tish*	horseradish
Milch	*milsh*	milk
Mineralwasser	*minn-er-arl-vuss-er*	mineral water
Möhre	*mer-uh*	carrot
Nuss	*nooss*	nut
Öl	*erl*	oil
Olive	*o-leev-uh*	olive
Petersilie	*payt-er-zee-li-uh*	parsley
Pfeffer	*pfeff-er*	pepper
Pfirsich	*pfir-zih*	peach
Pflaumen	*pflow-men*	plum
Pommes frites	*pomm-fritt*	chips/ French fries
Quark	*kvark*	soft cheese
Radieschen	*ra-deesh'n*	radish
Rinderbraten	*rind-er-brat'n*	joint of beef
Rinderroulade	*rind-er-roo-lard-uh*	beef olive
Rindfleisch	*rint-flysh*	beef
Rippchen	*rip-sh'n*	cured pork rib
Rotkohl	*roht-koal*	red cabbage
Rüben	*rhoob'n*	turnip
Rührei	*rhoo-er-eye*	scrambled eggs
Saft	*zuft*	juice
Salat	*zal-aat*	salad

Salz	*zults*	salt
Salzkartoffeln	*zults-kar-toff'l*	boiled potatoes
Sauerkirschen	*zow-er-keersh'n*	cherries
Sauerkraut	*zow-er-krowt*	sauerkraut
Sekt	*zekt*	sparkling wine
Senf	*zenf*	mustard
scharf	*sharf*	spicy
Schaschlik	*shash-lik*	kebab
Schlagsahne	*shlahgg-zarn-uh*	whipped cream
Schnittlauch	*shnit-lowhkh*	chives
Schnitzel	*shnitz'l*	veal or pork cutlet
Schweine- fleisch	*shvine-flysh*	pork
Spargel	*shparg'l*	asparagus
Spiegelei	*shpeeg'l-eye*	fried egg
Spinat	*shpin-art*	spinach
Tee	*tay*	tea
Tomate	*tom-art-uh*	tomato
Wassermelone	*vuss-er-me-lohn-uh*	watermelon
Wein	*vine*	wine
Weintrauben	*vine-trowb'n*	grapes
Wiener Würstchen	*veen-er voorst-sh'n*	frankfurter
Zander	*tsan-der*	pike-perch
Zitrone	*tsi-trohn-uh*	lemon
Zucker	*tsook-er*	sugar
Zwieback	*tsvee-bak*	rusk
Zwiebel	*tsveeb'l*	onion

Numbers

0	null	*nool*
1	eins	*eye'ns*
2	zwei	*tsvy*
3	drei	*dry*
4	vier	*feer*
5	fünf	*foonf*
6	sechs	*zex*
7	sieben	*zeeb'n*
8	acht	*uhkht*
9	neun	*noyn*
10	zehn	*tsayn*
11	elf	*elf*
12	zwölf	*tserlf*
13	dreizehn	*dry-tsayn*
14	vierzehn	*feer-tsayn*
15	fünfzehn	*foonf-tsayn*
16	sechzehn	*zex-tsayn*
17	siebzehn	*zeep-tsayn*
18	achtzehn	*uhkht-tsayn*
19	neunzehn	*noyn-tsayn*
20	zwanzig	*tsvunn-tsig*
21	einundzwanzig	*ine-oont- tsvunn-tsig*
30	dreißig	*dry-sig*
40	vierzig	*feer-sig*
50	fünfzig	*foonf-tsig*
60	sechzig	*zex-tsig*
70	siebzig	*zeep-tsig*
80	achtzig	*uhkht-tsig*
90	neunzig	*noyn-tsig*
100	hundert	*hoond't*
1000	tausend	*towz'nt*
1 000 000	eine Million	*ine-uh mill-yon*

Time

one minute	eine Minute	*ine-uh min-oot-uh*
one hour	eine Stunde	*ine-uh shtoond- uh*
half an hour	eine halbe Stunde	*ine-uh hullb-uh shtoond-uh*
Monday	Montag	*mohn-targ*
Tuesday	Dienstag	*deens-targ*
Wednesday	Mittwoch	*mitt-vokh*
Thursday	Donnerstag	*donn-ers-targ*
Friday	Freitag	*fry-targ*
Saturday	Samstag/ Sonnabend	*zums-targ zonn-ah-bent*
Sunday	Sonntag	*zon-targ*
January	Januar	*yan-ooar*
February	Februar	*fay-brooar*
March	März	*mairts*
April	April	*april*
May	Mai	*my*
June	Juni	*yoo-ni*
July	Juli	*yoo-lee*
August	August	*ow-goost*
September	September	*zep-tem-ber*
October	Oktober	*ok-toh-ber*
November	November	*no-vem-ber*
December	Dezember	*day-tsem-ber*
spring	Frühling	*froo-ling*
summer	Sommer	*zomm-er*
autumn (fall)	Herbst	*hairpst*
winter	Winter	*vint-er*

Road Map of Germany